Making Americans Healthier

Making Americans Healthier

Social and Economic Policy as Health Policy

Robert F. Schoeni, James S. House, George A. Kaplan,
and Harold Pollack, Editors

The National Poverty Center Series on Poverty and Public Policy

Russell Sage Foundation ◆ New York

The Russell Sage Foundation

The Russell Sage Foundation, one of the oldest of America's general purpose foundations, was established in 1907 by Mrs. Margaret Olivia Sage for "the improvement of social and living conditions in the United States." The Foundation seeks to fulfill this mandate by fostering the development and dissemination of knowledge about the country's political, social, and economic problems. While the Foundation endeavors to assure the accuracy and objectivity of each book it publishes, the conclusions and interpretations in Russell Sage Foundation publications are those of the authors and not of the Foundation, its Trustees, or its staff. Publication by Russell Sage, therefore, does not imply Foundation endorsement.

Library of Congress Cataloging-in-Publication Data

Making Americans healthier : social and economic policy as health policy / [edited by] Robert F. Schoeni . . . [et al.].
    p. ; cm.
    Includes bibliographical references.
    ISBN-13: 978-0-87154-747-7 (alk. paper) 1. Medical policy—United States. 2. Social policy—Health aspects—United States. 3. Economic policy—Health aspects—United States. 4. Public health—Social aspects—United States. 5. Public health—Economic aspects—United States. I. Schoeni, Robert F. II. Russell Sage Foundation.
    [DNLM: 1. Health Policy—United States. 2. Health Status—United States. 3. Public Health—United States. 4. Public Policy—United States. 5. Socioeconomic Factors—United States. WA 540 AA1 S62 2007]
    RA395.A3S694 2007
    362.10973—dc22   2007031269

The paper used in this publication meets the minimum requirements of American National Standard for Information Sciences—Permanence of Paper for Printed Library Materials. ANSI Z39.48-1992.

Text design by Suzanne Nichols.

RUSSELL SAGE FOUNDATION
112 East 64th Street, New York, New York 10021
10 9 8 7 6 5 4 3 2 1

Contents

PREFACE   xi

PART I   INTRODUCTION   1

Chapter 1   THE HEALTH EFFECTS OF SOCIAL AND ECONOMIC POLICY:
THE PROMISE AND CHALLENGE FOR RESEARCH AND POLICY
James S. House, Robert F. Schoeni, George A. Kaplan,
and Harold Pollack   3

PART II   EDUCATION POLICY   27

Chapter 2   EDUCATION AND HEALTH: EVALUATING THEORIES
AND EVIDENCE
David M. Cutler and Adriana Lleras-Muney   29

Chapter 3   HEALTH EFFECTS OF HUMAN
DEVELOPMENT POLICIES
Daniel P. Keating and Sharon Z. Simonton   61

PART III   INCOME TRANSFER POLICY   95

Chapter 4   INCOME SUPPORT POLICIES AND HEALTH AMONG
THE ELDERLY
Pamela Herd, James S. House, and Robert F. Schoeni   97

Chapter 5   DID THE INTRODUCTION OF FOOD STAMPS AFFECT BIRTH
OUTCOMES IN CALIFORNIA?
Janet Currie and Enrico Moretti   122

PART IV   CIVIL RIGHTS   143

Chapter 6   LIFTING GATES, LENGTHENING LIVES: DID CIVIL RIGHTS
POLICIES IMPROVE THE HEALTH OF AFRICAN AMERICAN
WOMEN IN THE 1960S AND 1970S?
George A. Kaplan, Nalini Ranjit, and Sarah A. Burgard   145

PART V	MACROECONOMIC AND EMPLOYMENT POLICY	171
Chapter 7	MACROECONOMIC CONDITIONS, HEALTH, AND GOVERNMENT POLICY Christopher J. Ruhm	173
Chapter 8	THE NEW EMPLOYMENT CONTRACT AND WORKER HEALTH IN THE UNITED STATES Richard H. Price and Sarah A. Burgard	201
PART VI	WELFARE POLICY	229
Chapter 9	WELFARE REFORM AND INDIRECT IMPACTS ON HEALTH Marianne P. Bitler and Hilary W. Hoynes	231
Chapter 10	THE EFFECTS OF WELFARE AND CHILD SUPPORT POLICIES ON MATERNAL HEALTH AND WELL-BEING Jean Knab, Irv Garfinkel, and Sara McLanahan	281
PART VII	HOUSING AND NEIGHBORHOOD POLICY	307
Chapter 11	RESIDENTIAL ENVIRONMENTS AND OBESITY: WHAT CAN WE LEARN ABOUT POLICY INTERVENTIONS FROM OBSERVATIONAL STUDIES? Jeffrey D. Morenoff, Ana V. Diez Roux, Ben B. Hansen, and Theresa L. Osypuk	309
Chapter 12	ARE SOME NEIGHBORHOODS BETTER FOR CHILD HEALTH THAN OTHERS? Rebecca C. Fauth and Jeanne Brooks-Gunn	344
PART VIII	CONCLUSION	377
Chapter 13	SOCIAL AND ECONOMIC POLICIES AS HEALTH POLICY: MOVING TOWARD A NEW APPROACH TO IMPROVING HEALTH IN AMERICA Harold Pollack, George A. Kaplan, James S. House, and Robert F. Schoeni	379
	INDEX	391

About the Authors

ROBERT F. SCHOENI is professor of public policy and economics, and research professor at the Institute for Social Research, the University of Michigan.

JAMES S. HOUSE is Angus Campbell Collegiate Professor of Sociology and Survey Research, professor of public policy, research professor in the Survey Research Center of the Institute for Social Research at the University of Michigan, and an elected member of the American Academy of Arts and Sciences, the Institute of Medicine, and the National Academy of Sciences.

GEORGE A. KAPLAN is the Thomas Francis Collegiate Professor of Public Health, director of the Center for Social Epidemiology and Population Health, a research professor at the Survey Research Center at the University of Michigan, and an elected member of the Institute of Medicine, the Academy of Behavioral Medicine Research, and the National Academy of Social Insurance.

HAROLD POLLACK is associate professor of social service administration and faculty chair of the Center for Health Administration Studies, University of Chicago.

MARIANNE P. BITLER is assistant professor of economics at the University of California, Irvine, and a faculty research fellow of the National Bureau of Economic Research.

JEANNE BROOKS-GUNN is Virginia and Leonard Marx Professor of Child Development at Teachers College and the College of Physicians and Surgeons at Columbia University.

SARAH A. BURGARD is assistant professor of sociology and epidemiology and assistant research professor, Population Studies Center, at the University of Michigan.

JANET CURRIE is professor of economics and chair of the Department of Economics at Columbia University.

DAVID M. CUTLER is Otto Eckstein Professor of Applied Economics at Harvard University and Research Associate at the National Bureau of Economic Research.

REBECCA C. FAUTH is senior researcher at The Work Foundation in London and a research affiliate at the National Center for Children and Families, Columbia University.

IRV GARFINKEL is Mitchell I. Ginsberg Professor of Contemporary Urban Problems at the School of Social Work and the co-director of the Center for Research on Population, Health, and Society, Columbia University.

BEN B. HANSEN is assistant professor of statistics and faculty associate, Survey Research Center, University of Michigan.

PAMELA HERD is assistant professor of public affairs and sociology, and research associate at the Institute for Research on Poverty at the University of Wisconsin, Madison.

HILARY W. HOYNES is professor of economics at the University of California, Davis, and a co-editor of *American Economic Journal: Economic Policy*.

DANIEL P. KEATING is research professor and director of the Center for Human Growth and Development, professor of psychology, psychiatry, and pediatrics and faculty associate of the Survey Research Center, Institute for Social Research at the University of Michigan, and fellow at the Canadian Institute for Advanced Research.

JEAN KNAB is the director of the Fragile Families and Child Wellbeing Study and a research associate at the Center for Research on Child Wellbeing at Princeton University.

ADRIANA LLERAS-MUNEY is assistant professor of economics and public affairs at the Woodrow Wilson School of Princeton University.

SARA McLANAHAN is William S. Tod Professor of Sociology and Public Affairs at Princeton University, and directs the Center for Research on Child Wellbeing.

JEFFREY D. MORENOFF is associate professor of sociology and research associate professor at the Survey Research Center and Population Studies Center in the Institute for Social Research at the University of Michigan.

ENRICO MORETTI is associate professor of economics at the University of California, Berkeley, where he holds the Michael Peevey and Donald Vial Chair in Labor Economics.

THERESA L. OSYPUK is assistant professor of epidemiology at Northeastern University Bouve College of Health Sciences.

RICHARD H. PRICE is Barger Family Professor of Organizational Studies and research professor in the Survey Research Center at the University of Michigan.

NALINI RANJIT is a research investigator at the Center for Social Epidemiology and Population Health at the University of Michigan, Ann Arbor.

ANA V. DIEZ ROUX is professor of epidemiology and associate director of the Center for Social Epidemiology and Population Health at the University of Michigan.

CHRISTOPHER J. RUHM is Jefferson-Pilot Excellence Professor of Economics at the University of North Carolina at Greensboro and research associate at the National Bureau of Economic Research.

SHARON Z. SIMONTON is a research fellow at the Institute for Social Research at the University of Michigan.

Preface

Three observations motivated the writing of this book:

- First, gaps in health between social and economic groups—by education, income, wealth, neighborhood, and race, for example—are massive. These gaps have persisted for decades. They are not narrowing, despite growing awareness at all levels of government and throughout the clinical and research communities that health disparities pose central challenges to American society.

- Second, our nation spends billions of dollars each year on policies and programs that seek to improve social and economic outcomes. However, the policy communities influential in these domains have largely adopted programs without considering the potential substantial effects these may have on individual and population health. Substantial benefits—or perhaps costs, in the case of policies that worsen health status—are therefore not considered.

- Third, our nation continues to grapple with rising health care costs which are unparalleled across the globe. At the same time, by most indicators American population health has declined relative to that of many other nations.

Taken together, we believed that these three observations justified a concerted effort to assess the effects of social and economic policies on health, and this book is the product of our efforts.

The chapters include research in six policy domains: education policy, income transfer policy, civil rights, macroeconomic and employment policy, welfare policy, and housing and neighborhood policy. While policies in other domains were considered, these six domains were chosen because they represent especially promising areas for investigation based on existing evidence and data.

We believe that the project, and the broader agenda it seeks to advance, requires the involvement of scientists from a diverse set of disciplines, all of which have contributed to prior research in this area. Therefore, five of the six policy domains are represented by two papers each, typically one paper authored by economists or policy researchers, and the other by social epidemiologists. For some individual chapters, the team of authors includes scholars from these and other backgrounds. Moreover, we ourselves come from diverse disciplines which have played central roles in this emerging research area, including economics, epidemiology, public health, public policy, and sociology. Disciplines represented by other chapter authors and discussants include child and human development, medicine, psychology, social work, and statistics.

The project team first met in Ann Arbor in October 2004, where initial outlines of chapters were shared among all authors. David Mechanic, Chris Paxson, and Len Syme each provided a broad critical perspective on the project as well as detailed comments on the individual chapter outlines. Based on discussions at the first meeting, the editors agreed on the set of papers that would be presented at the final conference, "Health Effects of Non-health Policies," which was held in February 2006 in Washington, D.C. The versions of the chapters presented at the final conference are available at the National Poverty Center website.

At the conference, each chapter was discussed by two experts in the field: one representing the policy and economic perspective, and one representing the social epidemiologic perspective. The authors and editors benefited greatly from the insights of the chapter discussants: Lisa Berkman, Rebecca Blank, Ray Catalano, Doug Elmendorf, Harry Holzer, Christopher Jencks, Thomas Kane, Kim Lochner, Doug Miller, Katherine Newman, Narayan Sastry, and David Williams. During the last session of the conference, David Mechanic, Harold Pollack, and Len Syme provided a broad perspective on the research effort which heavily influenced the introduction and the conclusion to the book. Two anonymous reviewers of the initial book manuscript provided valuable feedback that improved every chapter, as did the editorial work of Suzanne Nichols of the Russell Sage Foundation.

For most of the project, Laura Lee provided very able and energetic administrative support, as did Sarah Marsh at the end; and Cathy Doherty and Patricia Rayl assisted at several important points.

The entire project, including the conferences and the book production, was supported by the Assistant Secretary for Planning and Evaluation of the U.S. Department of Health and Human Services through the National Poverty Center at the University of Michigan, the Russell Sage Foundation, the Robert Wood Johnson Foundation, and the Annie E. Casey Foundation. James Knickman and Michael McGinnis of the Robert Wood Johnson Foundation, Mike Laracy of the Annie E. Casey Foundation, and Eric Wanner of the Russell Sage Foundation each lent important support at critical points.

Finally, Becky Blank and Sheldon Danziger initially proposed that the National Poverty Center sponsor our enterprise, and they both, but especially Sheldon, provided constant support and input throughout the project which benefited the conference and book in many ways. Without their unswerving efforts, for which we are very grateful, none of this would have come to pass.

While this is the first book devoted to the role of social and economic policy in determining health in the United States, it will clearly not provide the last word. Much work is yet to be done. But even if the only benefit of this book is that social and economic policy communities begin to take into consideration the potential effects of such policies on health when formulating and evaluating options, or conversely, the health policy community begins to think beyond traditional health care and public health to incorporate social and economic policy, it will have been well worth the effort.

Robert F. Schoeni
James S. House
George A. Kaplan
Harold A. Pollack

Part I

Introduction

Chapter 1

The Health Effects of Social and Economic Policy: The Promise and Challenge for Research and Policy

James S. House, Robert F. Schoeni, George A. Kaplan, and Harold Pollack

The United States faces a growing paradox between its declining levels of population health relative to other wealthy nations—and even to some developing ones—and its burgeoning spending on health insurance and medical care. By an increasing margin each year, the United States spends a larger percentage of its gross domestic product (GDP) on health care than any other nation, with health care expenditures now totaling $1.9 trillion per year and large increases projected over coming decades (Chernew, Hirth, and Cutler 2003).

Scholars, policy makers, and citizens debate the marginal value and cost-effectiveness of these expenditures. Specific advances—for example, neonatal intensive care, highly active antiretroviral therapy (HAART), improved cardiac care, and new outpatient pharmaceuticals—bring gains in longevity and well-being which meet standard benchmarks for cost-effectiveness (Cutler 2004). Yet other care is of uncertain effectiveness or low quality (Institute of Medicine 2001a, 2001b). Moreover, increasing medical expenditures create serious challenges for individuals, employers, and all levels of government. Expenditure growth threatens the continued availability and affordability of health insurance and medical services, and creates fiscal strains at the federal, state, and local levels which reduce nonmedical assistance to needy people and spending in other non-health areas such as education and infrastructure (Baicker 2001).

Paradoxically, despite marked growth in medical-care spending, the United States's standing on major indicators of population health such as life expectancy at birth and infant mortality has declined relative to other wealthy nations, as well as relative to some much less affluent ones (Organization for Economic Co-Operation and Development [OECD] 2005; United Nations Development Programme 2005). As shown in table 1.1, while rising in rank over the past half century in per-

TABLE 1.1 / U.S. Rank Among Thirty OECD Developed Nations on Indicators of Population Health and Percent GDP Spent on Health

			Percentage of GDP Spent on Health		
Year	U.S. Rank on Life Expectancy at Birth	U.S. Rank on Infant Mortality	United States Rank	United States Spending	Average Spending Among All Other OECD Countries
1960	15.5	12	2	5.1%	3.7%
1970	19	14	3, tied	7.0	5.0
1980	14	18	1	8.8	6.7
1990	18	21	1	11.9	6.8
2000	22	25	1	13.3	7.6
2003	23	27	1	15.2	8.6

Source: Authors' compilation from OECD Health Statistics (2006).

cent of GDP spent on health, the United States has fallen during this time period from being among the top nations in life expectancy and infant mortality to a ranking near the bottom among the thirty nations of the Organization for Economic Co-operation and Development or OECD. Only Mexico, Turkey, and three relatively new OECD members from the former Soviet bloc (Hungary, the Czech Republic, and the Slovak Republic) consistently rank below the United States on such indicators.

Most current political and policy analysis related to health in the United States focuses on medical-care and insurance expenditures, incentives, and prices. Much less attention is paid to levels of population health beyond the worry that controls and reductions necessary to constrain spending growth may adversely affect overall health or health within specific vulnerable groups. Much can be done to enhance the quality and cost-effectiveness of American health care, and many contributors to this volume have actively addressed these challenges in other venues.

However, this chapter and the research presented throughout this book pursue a different agenda: to address neglected opportunities for improving population health via social and economic policy outside of the traditional domains of preventive and curative health care. The concentration in so many health policy discussions on medical services as the sine qua non for improving population health neglects historical knowledge about the causes of major changes in the health of populations. It also neglects real opportunities outside the domain of medical care to improve population health.

It may seem paradoxical and impossible that a society could achieve better population health without explicitly increasing health care expenditures, but this is only if we assume that health care is the major determinant of health. As dramatic and consequential as medical care is for individual cases and for specific conditions, much evidence suggests that such care is not, and probably never has been, the major determinant of levels or changes in population health. This evidence is consistent with data suggesting a low to near-zero correlation between health care expenditures and levels of population health across wealthier OECD nations, as well as with data that show declining rates of return to health from growing health care expenditures over time in the United States (Cutler, Rosen, and Vijan 2006). Rather, economic, social, psychological, behavioral, and environmental factors are increasingly recognized as the major determinants of population health (McGinnis and Foege 1993; McKeown 1979; McKinlay and McKinlay 1977; Preston 1977; Bunker, Frazier, and Mosteller 1994; Bengtsson 2001; Kaplan, Everson, and Lynch 2000; McGinnis, Williams-Russo, and Knickman 2002). If health care, whether therapeutic or preventive, is not the major determinant of health, then health policy must move beyond a single-minded focus on the delivery and financing of health care. We must understand through research and practice the health effects of the wide range of social and economic policies that are, arguably, major determinants of the level and distribution of health in populations.

UNDERSTANDING NONMEDICAL DETERMINANTS OF HEALTH

A brief historical perspective is necessary to understand why and how social and economic policies may be equally or more important than health policies in maintaining and improving population health. Within the United States and many developed and developing nations, the scientific success of the germ theory of disease between the mid-nineteenth and mid-twentieth centuries fostered hegemony of a solely biomedical perspective on the health of individuals and populations. The general decline, and in some cases eradication, of feared infectious diseases suggested that understanding microbiological bases of life and disease provided a golden pathway to improved population health. Bacteriology, virology, genetics, and basic molecular, cellular, and developmental biology—together with their translation into the practice of health care—allowed continual advances and improvements in health. Many scientists and most policy makers and citizens continue to share this biomedical perspective, which shone brightly in the mid-twentieth century, epitomized by the discovery of polio vaccines and their use to virtually eradicate the disease.

However, the rise of modern "epidemics" of chronic disease—particularly heart disease and cancer—within an aging population began to cloud this picture by the late 1950s. The dramatic increase in these diseases in the mid-twentieth century virtually arrested the long-term rise in life expectancy from the late 1950s to the late 1960s, and revitalized several strands of medical and public health research which recognize the important, and sometimes dominant, role of socioeconomic, psychosocial, and behavioral determinants of health.

One scientific strand was derived from the early research of Walter Cannon (1932), Hans Selye (1956), and others showing that perturbations in the relation between organisms and their psychosocial as well as their physical-chemical-biological environments (created by physical, social, or psychological challenges or stressors) led to adaptive arousal of biological and physiological systems in the form of heightened heart rate, blood pressure, hormonal secretions, and depressed immune response. These are perhaps best known collectively under Selye's rubric of stress. These physiological changes could, if prolonged, lead to long-term dis-regulation of homeostatic and adaptive systems, physical diseases (including hypertension, infection, and autoimmune disorders), and even death. This work led to burgeoning new fields of psychoneuroendocrinology and psychoneuroimmunology (Ader, Felten, and Cohen 1991) and showed how a broad range of socioeconomic and psychosocial factors could "get under the skin" and produce physical illness (Taylor, Repetti, and Seeman 1997).

Between the mid-eighteenth and mid-nineteenth centuries, and accelerating in the first half of the twentieth century, human life expectancy in Europe and North America grew more than in all of prior human history (Coale 1974; Fogel 2004). Although this dramatic improvement in human health roughly coincided in time and space with the development of modern biomedical science and its translation into health care practice, and hence might be presumed to have been caused by these developments, taking off from the work of McKeown (1979, 1988), historical demography and economics showed that most of the improvement for many diseases occurred prior to and independently of the discovery of the causative bacterial or viral agents or the application of this knowledge via preventive (for example, vaccination) or therapeutic (for example, pharmacologic treatment) medical practice (McKinlay and McKinlay 1977; Preston 1977).

John Bunker, Howard Frazier, and Frederick Mosteller (1994) have estimated that only about five years of the almost thirty-year increase in United States life expectancy over the twentieth century were due to preventive or therapeutic medical practice. This is consistent with more recent estimates that medical care likely accounts for 10 to 20 percent of the variation in population health in the United States and other developed countries (McGinnis, Williams-Russo, and Knickman 2002; McGinnis and Foege 1993).

The exact nonmedical factors responsible for the great historical rise in life expectancy are impossible to identify retrospectively in a definitive way, but general socioeconomic development and benefits facilitated by it—most notably improvements in nutrition, public and household sanitation, housing, clothing, and general conditions of life—played a central role. Some of these developments were also influenced by biomedical science (for example, sanitation) or were not always entirely salutary (for example, urbanization) (Bengtsson 2001). Their spread and effectiveness also varied as a function of different political and cultural contexts, being, for example, greater in nations with strong central governments (Kunitz and Pesis-Katz 2005; Kunitz 2006).

Concurrently, the rise of chronic diseases produced a major shift in the epidemiologic conception of and search for their causes—a shift from identifying a single necessary, proximate causal agent to identifying multiple contingent causal forces or risk factors. None of these risk factors are necessary to produce disease, but each interacts with others, increasing the likelihood of developing major chronic diseases and the pathogenic physiology underlying them (Kannel 1971; Aronowitz

1998). Epidemiology initially focused on biological risk factors such as blood pressure, blood lipids (especially cholesterol), respiratory flow and volume, and electrocardiographic abnormalities.

However, research leading to the first Surgeon General's Report on Smoking and Health (Advisory Committee to the Surgeon General 1964) showed that behaviors were also key risk factors for chronic diseases, with tobacco use being the leading cause of the twentieth century epidemic of lung and respiratory cancers, and a major contributor to rising rates of other cancers and cardiovascular disease. Other behaviors such as immoderate eating, alcohol use, and a sedentary lifestyle were similarly identified as major disease risk factors (Berkman and Breslow 1983). Health research and policy targeted smoking, and now obesity as well (with its key determinants of diet and nutrition, and of calorie expenditure and physical activity), as key—and still growing in the case of obesity—threats to adult and child health (McGinnis and Foege 1993).

For both smoking and obesity, much effort has been focused on understanding the pathophysiological mechanisms producing adverse health effects, as well as the individual-level factors that influence initiation, maintenance, and cessation of these behaviors. Intensive research on tobacco-related health hazards and on smoking cessation has entered its sixth decade. Despite basic scientific advances in these areas, it is now widely recognized that trends in smoking and other health risk behaviors are driven primarily by economic and social developments, and by policies that once fostered and now limit individuals' opportunity and motivation to buy and smoke tobacco products (Warner 2001; Levy, Bauer, and Lee 2006).

Using epidemiological methods similar to those that identified blood pressure, cholesterol, cardiovascular and respiratory function, smoking, diet and nutrition, alcohol consumption, and physical inactivity as major risk factors for the newly epidemic chronic diseases, social epidemiology has over the last several decades identified a growing range of economic, social, environmental, and psychological variables that are comparably potent risk factors for health. These include social relationships and supports, chronic and acute stress, psychological and personality dispositions, engagement with productive social roles and organizations, and the social as well as physical-chemical-biological environments in which people live and work (House 2002; House and Kaplan 2004; Kaplan 1985, 1992; Berkman and Kawachi 2000).

Perhaps the most striking and important development in social epidemiology over the last quarter century has been the discovery (or rediscovery) of large, persistent, and even increasing disparities in health by socioeconomic position and race-ethnicity (Marmot, Kogevinas, and Elston 1987; Pappas et al. 1993; Wilkinson 1996; Kaplan and Lynch 1997; House and Williams 2000; Kaplan et al. 1987). These disparities are dramatic and important in several ways. First, the sheer size of the disparities is striking: there are many years, and even decades, of difference in life expectancy and the ages at which people come to develop major health problems and associated limitations or disability (House and Williams 2000). Second, the disparities are pervasive across almost all specific causes and indicators of morbidity, limitations and disability, and mortality (U.S. Department of Health and

Human Services 2000), and across vast expanses of historical time and geographical space, even as the specific causes of morbidity, limitations and disability, and mortality vary and change over time and space (Link and Phelan 1995, 2000). Finally, as might be expected from the foregoing patterns, socioeconomic position and race-ethnicity (or actually the way that race and ethnicity came to be socially defined and enacted) shape people's experience of and exposure to almost all risk factors for health—psychosocial, biomedical, and environmental (Marmot, Bobak, and Smith 1995; Lynch et al. 1996; House and Williams 2000).

MOVING UPSTREAM AND DOWNSTREAM IN UNDERSTANDING PSYCHOSOCIAL, ENVIRONMENTAL AND BIOMEDICAL DETERMINANTS OF HEALTH

Current research on psychosocial, biomedical, and environmental determinants of health has moved in two directions. The more common direction has been "downstream," understanding the psychophysiological mechanisms and processes by which psychosocial risk factors "get under the skin" to affect physical as well as mental health (Taylor, Repetti, and Seeman 1997; Steptoe and Marmot 2002). This downstream approach explicitly or implicitly leads in the direction of identifying biomedical approaches to mitigate the health impact of social and economic risk factors for health (for example, finding pharmacological or other treatments to mitigate the impact of social deprivations, stress, isolation, and other factors on health).

An "upstream" approach is most pertinent to the work collected in this book. This approach seeks to understand broader aspects of social life, and planned and unplanned changes therein, that shape exposure to and experience of psychosocial and environmental risk factors for health (House and Williams 2000; Kaplan 1995). Figure 1.1 provides an integrative schematic framework for considering the full range of determinants of health. Our focus here will be on the social, political, and economic conditions—and particularly public policies—that may importantly affect health by shaping exposure to and experience of major risk factors. Many public policies strongly impact health because they strongly impact the socioeconomic, psychosocial, and environmental determinants of health. We consider primarily domestic social and economic policies, but this approach could be extended to other policy areas such as environmental protection and aspects of international policy.

Socioeconomic position is central to figure 1.1 and to more basic theories of human capital and status attainment (Blau and Duncan 1967; Becker 1964). Socioeconomic position provides a rubric for a series of interconnected human capital resources, including education, occupation, income, and wealth (House and Williams 2000; Lynch and Kaplan 2000). All of these resources have been shown to be important correlates of health.

Socioeconomic position is determined by characteristics of individuals, their biological and family background, and the educational, occupational, social, and

FIGURE 1.1   /   A Conceptual Framework for Understanding Determinants of Social
Inequalities in Health and Aging

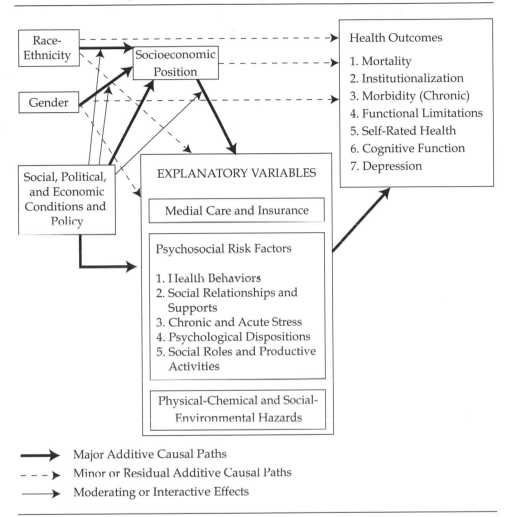

Source: House (2002).
Note: As indicated in the text, health outcomes can affect socioeconomic position and explanatory
variables. For the sake of graphic simplicity and clarity, such effects are not explicitly indicated
above.

economic contexts in which they live and work. Although not depicted on the sim-
plified schematic of figure 1.1, health status also feeds back to socioeconomic position, with health shocks causing interruptions in human capital accumulation and
reducing labor market earnings.

Enhancing the social and economic factors that are components of socioeconomic position is the putative object of public (and private) policies under the

purview at the federal level of the Departments of Education, Labor, Commerce, Treasury, Housing and Urban Development, and the human services side of the Department of Health and Human Services, along with analogous agencies in state and local government. These factors also are influenced by the policies pursued by private educational, work, economic, and voluntary organizations, as a function both of their own objectives and of public policies which may stimulate or inhibit private sector activities such as affirmative action, education and training, growth and development of occupations and professions, the nature and level of wages, salaries and fringe benefits, and patterns of savings and investment (Hacker 2002). To date, very few of these public and private socioeconomic policies have considered health in either formulating or justifying policies or evaluating their impacts. This volume seeks to change this state of affairs.

THE PROMISE AND CHALLENGES IN RESEARCH AND PRACTICE ON HEALTH EFFECTS OF SOCIAL AND ECONOMIC POLICY

In essence, we believe that health research and policy in the United States must move toward models recently advocated and adopted in Canada (Health Canada 1998), Sweden (Swedish National Institute of Public Health 2003; Stahl et al. 2006), and the broader European Union (Stahl et al. 2006) that consistently consider evaluating the health impact of *all* policy—not just health policy (Raphael and Bryant 2006; Navarro 2007). This is similar to the way that we have come to think about and evaluate the environmental impact of policy beyond explicitly environmental policy (Irwin and Scali 2005).

The Promise

A greater and more explicit focus on the actual and potential health effects of social and economic policy could strengthen scientific understanding of the social and economic determinants of health and their amenability to change via public (and private) policy. It could also help to extricate health policy and more general public policy from America's growing paradox of unparalleled levels and growth of health care spending, yet declining standing in population health relative to other developed countries.

Much evidence strongly suggests that social and economic factors and policy may powerfully influence individual and population health. However, policy makers—who are often from backgrounds in economics, political science, law, or public policy—reasonably ask whether and how epidemiologic evidence that a given social or economic variable (such as education) is associated with and even predicts health translates into a conclusion that policies which increase individual or population education will necessarily improve individual or population health. Crucial evidence on this issue can come from evaluating the health consequences or impacts of education or income policies. Thus we need greater attention to health in all aspects of the policy planning and evaluation process. Such attention will provide crucial scientific evidence as to whether, how, and to what extent education, income, and other social and economic factors and policies affect health.

Existing research suggests that a wide range of social and economic policy should significantly and substantially affect health. To the extent that such policy-based research confirms this pattern, we can consider a broad range of public and private policies beyond the realm of health care as mechanisms for promoting health and preventing or alleviating disease. These social and economic policies may have additional beneficial consequences for health that are equally or more important than the consequences they were formulated to produce. In addition, social and economic policies may be more cost-effective for maintaining and improving health than increased spending on health care, and hence even constitute alternatives to some current health care spending (Lleras-Muney and Cutler, chapter 2, this volume).

Considering their health impact can also benefit the development and implementation of policies which target dimensions of individual well-being and social performance other than health. For example, an education intervention may have larger than expected effects on labor market outcomes because the increase in education has the unintended effect of improving health status, which in turn makes workers more productive or able to provide additional work hours, and hence to receive higher pay. In the public or private sector, deciding whether, when, and how to implement new policies is often influenced by cost-benefit calculation. Given the potential range and size of both positive and negative health outcomes that flow from policy changes, even if totally unintended, health effects can be central factors in decisions about the nature of contemplated changes in public or private policy seemingly unrelated to health. It is therefore increasingly hard to justify not considering potential health impacts in the design, implementation, and evaluation of any contemplated policy change, even in areas which may superficially seem far removed from issues of health and health policy.

The Challenges

However, realizing this promise of increased research and policy on the health effects of social and economic policy requires confronting a number of challenges, which have shaped the organization of this book and the conference from which it derives. We characterize these challenges as the three Cs: causality, cost-effectiveness, and can we do it?

Causality Concern about causality in the relationship between social and economic factors and health has increased markedly in recent years in the statistical, biostatistical, social, and policy sciences. The essence of the concern is the belief that the only way to establish a causal connection or relationship is via a randomized experiment or the closest possible nonexperimental analog to it (Heckman 1992, 2000;

Heckman and Vytlacil 2005; Rubin 1974; Pearl 2000; for a somewhat different perspective, see Marini and Singer 1988). According to this view, the value and validity of any given piece or body of empirical evidence depends on how closely it approximates the ideal of the randomized experimental trial. Thus, for example, where randomized social policy experiments are not available or possible, as is typically the case, economics and public policy have often utilized naturally occurring variations or changes (also known as *shocks*) that are essentially random because they are accidental (such as the social security "notch," an accidental variation of benefits for people born at different times), arbitrary (such as cutoff dates for age at school enrollment), random (such as lottery winnings), or otherwise exogenous to the variables of interest (such as the demise of the Communist Soviet regime of Eastern Europe from 1989 to 1991). However, too often this search for the closest approximation to an experiment neglects or deemphasizes consideration of the fidelity in either the nature or magnitude of the exogenous shock to the broader phenomenon of interest, such as the normal processes that generate income or education or variations therein and their putative effects on health.

A different tradition and conception of causality characterizes broader and more substantively focused social and epidemiological science. Here causal inferences and models derive their validity and power less from adherence to specific research designs and statistical methods, but rather from the accretion and consistency of a broad range of research and evidence, drawn from diverse methods and sources. Thus, epidemiological scientists (Broadhead et al. 1983; Lilienfeld and Lilienfeld 1980) have traditionally drawn inferences about the causal or risk-factor status of a given variable relative to a given health outcome from the accumulating body of evidence showing strength and consistency of statistical associations across a wide range of studies, temporal ordering or prediction from cause to effect, a gradient of response (which may be nonlinear), experimental data on animals and humans consistent with nonexperimental human data, and a plausible theory of biological mechanisms explaining observed associations.

Both of these traditions or perspectives have value, and ideally they will come to convergent conclusions. In the language of research design, the former approach focuses more on maximizing the internal validity of research and evidence for causal inference; the latter focuses more on maximizing the external validity of the causal inferences, or their generalizability to the real world and phenomena of ultimate interest.

We see increased engagement and interchange between these different approaches to causality as critical to future progress in research and policy regarding the health effects of social and economic policy. Thus, we have tried to represent a balance of researchers and research from the social epidemiologic perspective and from the perspectives of economics and public policy for each of the six policy areas in this book. This has produced, both within and across chapters and disciplinary boundaries, constructive engagement and interchange around issues of causal inference that we hope will serve as a model for future work on the health impacts of social and economic policy.

In the end, both scientific inferences and policy decisions must be drawn based on the full range of available evidence, even if, as is often the case, it cannot in some ways be considered definitive. For example, we illustrate how, in the area of cigarette smoking and health, social and health research and policy have grappled, generally successfully, with scientific issues of causality and the formulation of public policy on the basis of available evidence, even if imperfect.

Cost-Effectiveness Even if the impact of a social or economic factor on health passes the causal test, one could contend that it would be too costly in monetary or other ways relative to its putative effects, and hence is not cost-effective. Precise cost-benefit analysis is made more difficult in an area such as health, which is not easily measured in terms of a dollar metric. However, estimates of economic or other costs in relation to increases in the length or quality of life are possible and increasingly used (Drummond et al. 1997; Cutler 2004). Large scale changes or interventions in terms of social research and policy are complicated, difficult, and expensive, but so are the development, implementation, and utilization of major innovations and new procedures and technologies in medical care.

The cost-effectiveness of potential innovations in social and economic policy needs to be evaluated not only absolutely, but also relative to the cost-effectiveness of not implementing them, or of implementing them half-heartedly. They also must be evaluated relative to alternative changes and increases in health care, many of which may show real impacts in a clinical trial but only limited impacts, or even countervailing adverse impacts, from the perspective of overall population health, and some of which lack a strong evidentiary foundation (Institute of Medicine 2001a, 2001b, 2005).

Can We Do It? Even if a non-health policy, intervention, or practice is recognized as causal and potentially cost-effective with respect to health, the objection will be raised that we simply cannot do it because it is politically, ethically, organizationally, or technically unfeasible in some way. Obviously any economic or social policy must be feasible to be successful in achieving its goals, but it is important to carefully scrutinize and evaluate both a priori and *ex ante* assertions of infeasibility and to reevaluate them as social, economic, and political conditions change. Health-directed social and economic policy may in the long run prove as feasible and as cost-effective as more traditional health policy.

Cigarette Smoking and Health as an Illustration of Overcoming the Three Challenging Cs The case of cigarette smoking and health provides an apt and salient example of how a behavior and related policies outside the area of health came, over time, to avoid or transcend the challenges and potential pitfalls of the three Cs and substantially affect population health, although the process took more than a century. Tobacco has a long and complex history in American and other societies (Kluger 1997; Warner 2001; Brandt 2007). The original development, marketing, social taxation, and regulation of cigarettes as a consumer good had little or nothing to do with health or health policy; it had a great deal to do with economics, agriculture, commerce, and related areas of policy. Yet even as cigarette consumption rapidly increased in the United States and parts of Europe in the first half of the twentieth century, evidence began to accumulate in medical practice and science that the growth of cigarette production and consumption might be a major cause of rising epidemics of chronic disease—initially and most notably respiratory cancer, but then also cardiovascular disease and a broader range of cancers.

It took, however, several decades to achieve some scientific and policy consensus that cigarette smoking was causally deleterious to health, initially crystallized in the first Surgeon General's Report on Smoking and Health (Advisory Committee to the Surgeon General 1964). Substantive disagreements with this conclusion continued to be expressed over subsequent decades by skeptics ranging from distinguished scientists (for example, Ronald A. Fisher (1958)) to cigarette producers, marketers, and users. These views were fueled by the absence of definitive randomized trials on human subjects, which were ethically impossible in this context, yet remained the scientific gold standard of proponents of stricter causal inference.

Even as causality was increasingly accepted, many doubted that it was technically, economically, politically, ethically, or legally possible to limit or reduce the consumption of cigarettes, at least in cost-effective ways. Nevertheless, shifting coalitions of public health, political, economic, and policy actors worked toward policies to restrict or eliminate the marketing, sale, or consumption of tobacco and cigarettes. Biomedical and health research and policy focused on trying to understand, and hence interdict, the harmful aspects of cigarette smoke and smoking as well as the psychophysiological and behavioral processes involved in initiation, management, and ultimate cessation of smoking.

In the end, the efforts outside of the traditional health research and health care sector, ranging from taxation to restrictions on when and where people could buy or smoke tobacco products, proved far more feasible and cost-effective in reducing smoking than efforts via the health care system, much less efforts to somehow block the adverse health effects of tobacco smoke. The consequent declines in smoking-related disease and death provided further evidence consistent with the causal impact of smoking and health, without any definitive approximation of a randomized experiment or clinical trial on humans. Although advances have been made in understanding how and why cigarette smoking is so harmful to health, these advances have not produced corresponding clinical advances to reduce mortality and morbidity among continued smokers. Survival curves for smokers diagnosed with lung cancer have remained quite stable since the 1970s. Virtually the entire observed decline in lung cancer mortality is therefore attributable to smoking cessation. There is no reason that science and policy regarding a variety of other social and economic determinants of health cannot mirror developments in the science and policy of smoking and health.

IMPROVING THE INTERFACE BETWEEN THE SCIENCE AND POLICY OF SOCIAL AND ECONOMIC DETERMINANTS OF HEALTH

Overcoming the challenges of the three Cs and realizing the promise of social and economic determinants of health requires some adjustments to existing strategies of both research on social determinants of or disparities in population health, and of translating research into policy or practice. There is now a well-established paradigm and a supportive institutional structure for basic biomedical science and its translation into health policy and practice. Prototypically, the process begins with publicly and privately supported basic research on the determinants and processes of health and disease. It then moves to development of clinical or public health interventions via pharmacologic, surgical, or other methods. Then, it proceeds to randomized clinical trials of these methods. Where trials show a favorable balance of efficacy and potential benefit to safety and potential risk, the process proceeds to application in clinical and public health practice.

We realize that we present an idealized process. Proponents (and critics) of evidence-based medicine note that too few medical practices and procedures have been validated through randomized clinical trials (Timmermans and Mauck 2005; Cutler 2004). Medical care and public health face many serious challenges in the design and implementation of such trials, as well as to the application of the resulting insights within clinical care. Nevertheless, nothing approaching this paradigmatic process exists for social and economic determinants of health, with deleterious consequences for both scientific understanding and their potential value for policies that improve health.

Two issues seem most problematic here. First, even where basic research from animals and humans provides strong evidence of the health impact of socioeconomic and psychosocial factors, there is no publicly or privately supported infrastructure for systematically translating this research into policy and practice. The professions of public policy, business administration, public health, social work, education, law, and related organizations in the public and private sectors provide some similar infrastructure for the translation of more basic research from the social and behavioral sciences into policy and practice. However, compared with the biomedical sphere, the foundations of these professions are less strongly and less explicitly grounded in basic science, deriving more heavily and inductively from clinical intuition and practice. Most of these fields also have little focus on physical health as a major object of their practice, except, of course for public health, which nevertheless remains more focused on biological and biomedical pathways than on the socioeconomic and psychosocial factors that influence these pathways. Thus, a more explicit focus by these professions in research, training, and practice on the relevance and consequences for health of their central substantive concerns could foster development of new interventions, policies, and practices relevant to health, and could also broaden development of these professional fields.

An equal or greater need is to foster social and economic analogs of clinical trials—a climate and technology for experimental introduction and testing of potential new polices and practice in terms of their health effects. Experimental introduction and evaluation of policy interventions (on the model of the Negative Income Tax Experiments of the 1970s (Pechman and Timpane 1975), the numerous social experiments led by the MDRC over the past three decades (accessed at http://www.mdrc.org), or the field experiments conducted by scholars at the Abdul Latif Jameel Poverty Action Lab at MIT (accessed at http://www.poverty actionlab.org)) provides the best and closest analog to the randomized clinical trial for economic and social determinants of health, and hence can provide important new information for basic science as well as an empirical basis for further policy decisions and action.

When such economic and social policy experiments have been done, they have been implemented with a dominant focus on specific outcomes important in the income-support and welfare-reform debate (for example, welfare program participation, employment, wages, and marital dissolution). These experiments were therefore less valuable than they might have been in exploring other outcomes of equal moment, including health, (Munnell 1986). Despite such limitations, the chapters included in this volume highlight cases where some attempt has been made to evaluate the health effects of experimental or actual interventions in social and economic areas of public policy. Because the evaluation of health effects of these policies is most often not included at the onset in the design of evaluation of these policies, only rudimentary health measures are typically available, or the health measures are only collected on follow-up surveys.

Randomized evaluations are often informative and sometimes contradict widely accepted causal accounts from nonexperimental data. The recent experience of the Women's Health Initiative (Writing Group for the Women's Health Initiative Investigators 2002) randomized trial of postmenopausal estrogen therapy illustrated how such a clinical trial can contradict plausible accepted inferences from purely observational and other nonexperimental studies. However, Ross Prentice and colleagues (2005) also suggest, in line with discussion above, that the differing samples and follow-up periods in the randomized trials versus observational studies may account for many of the differing results. Thus, as stressed by Morenoff and colleagues (chapter 11, this volume) there is also a continuing need for and a value of nonexperimental research. Increased inclusion of health measures in major social and economic studies (such as the Current Population Survey, the National Longitudinal Surveys, and the Panel Study of Income Dynamics) and of social and economic data in major health studies (such as the National Health Interview Survey and the National Health and Nutrition Examination Survey) would also greatly accelerate progress in understanding social and economic determinants of health and the potential role of social and economic policy in health.

In sum, advancing research and policy regarding the health effects of social and economic factors and policies requires the same kind of investment in basic research and in the translations of this research into policy and practice that have been so successfully made in terms of the biomedical determinants of health over the past half century. The payoff in terms of improved health could be great and could help to achieve a more cost-effective health policy, even helping to restrain the current, apparently inexorable, and increasingly problematic rise in expenditures for health care.

GOALS AND MEANS OF THIS BOOK

This book seeks to stimulate increased research and practice on the health impacts of social and economic policy. We have chosen to focus on six policy domains for which there is an epidemiologically well-supported linkage to health, though as might be expected the nature and extent of such linkages varies somewhat across areas. There is also completed and ongoing research in each area that provides some tentative assessment of the health impact of major policies usually undertaken for reasons having little or nothing to do with health. In each area, we brought together two sets of authors, one more grounded in the social epidemiology or demography of health, and one more heavily grounded in policy analysis or basic social science fields (for example, economics or psychology). Constructively engaged communication and collaborations across these domains of research and practice will encourage a broader and less health care focused science and policy of health. In sum, our work has three overall goals:

1. To stimulate greater research on the health impact of social and economic policies, including greater efforts to incorporate health measures into the evaluation of a broad range of policy in areas other than health and with motivating objectives other than health

2. To encourage more explicit efforts to formulate social and economic policy, interventions, and practices with health impacts as one of their primary objectives

3. To stimulate the development of a model of health policy formulation and evaluation that includes not only the traditional biomedical players, but also representatives of major social and economic policy areas that influence health

We seek to advance these general objectives by focusing on six key areas of social and economic policy with potentially sizable effects on health: education policy, income-support policy, civil-rights policy, macroeconomic and employment policy, welfare policy, and housing and neighborhood policy. These domains capture only a portion of the full array of policies affecting the socioeconomic position of individuals over the life course. However, each of the six areas affects the socioeconomic position of key populations of medical and public health concern. In each area, we commissioned leading social scientists and public health researchers to examine the linkage of these ostensibly "non-health" policy areas and interventions to population health.

Education

The impact of education on health and health disparities remains one of the most widely researched topics in social epidemiology and public health. Epidemiologists have long documented that educated men and women are healthier than their fellow citizens. Many potential explanations have been proposed to explain how, whether, and why education strongly matters for health, and thus how, whether, and why public educational policies might improve population health.

Adriana Lleras-Muney and David Cutler (chapter 2, this volume) document large education-health relationships from both observational studies and natural experiments, and trace out several of the key causal pathways. The better jobs and higher income of the more highly educated partially account for these differences (Lantz et al. 1998, 2001). However, other evidence and new analyses indicate that educated people are more likely than others to wear seat belts, to exercise, to eat low-fat diets, to utilize preventive care, and to avoid smoking. Educational attainment is also associated with future-oriented behaviors, which increases individuals' motivation to invest in personal health and acquire skills that lower the costs of learning pertinent health information. Overall, there is a considerable potential impact of education on health, with such effects greatly enhancing the cost-effectiveness of policy investments in education.

From a policy perspective, Daniel Keating and Sharon Simonton (chapter 3, this volume) consider human development and educational policies focused on children. A wide array of such policies, ranging from Head Start to paid job-protected maternal leave, have beneficial effects for health and human capital and well-being more generally. The expansion of human development policies has the potential to improve child health outcomes while reducing racial and socioeconomic health disparities in the United States.

Income-Support Policies

The positive cross-sectional and predictive relationship of income to health is widely recognized. However, the health impact of economic transfer programs remains controversial. Pamela Herd, James House, and Robert Schoeni (chapter 4, this volume) examine income-support policies and health among the elderly, particularly the impact of the Supplemental Security Income (SSI) program. Using cross-state, cross-time benefit changes to estimate the effect of SSI generosity on disability, they produce a striking finding: increased generosity of state SSI benefit policies is associated with significantly reduced probability of experiencing mobility limitations. This association was strongest within the bottom quartile of the income distribution—those most likely to take up SSI coverage and for whom increases in income are likely to be most consequential for health.

Examining a different type of income-support policy, Janet Currie and Enrico Moretti (chapter 5, this volume) use detailed California natality data from the 1960s to examine the incidence of adverse birth outcomes before and after implementation of the Federal Food Stamp Program. Their most striking finding was negative: introduction of the program did not bring about any large, obvious reduction in the incidence of low birth weight (which was their key measure of adverse birth outcomes), perhaps due to other countervailing influences on individual and population health during the period of introduction of the Food Stamp Program. At the same time, the authors do not preclude the possibility that the Food Stamp Program had more subtle positive effects for infants or improved other health outcomes.

Civil Rights

Given the known strong disparities in health between racial-ethnic groups, most importantly through socioeconomic position, but also independent of it (House and Williams 2000), public policies directed at reducing de facto or de jure racial discrimination and racial disadvantage provide a social policy arena that has potentially large implications for individual and population health. Such policies, and accompanying social practices, construct categories of race-ethnicity and, more importantly, their implications for socioeconomic attainment, places of residence and work, and access to health care (Anderson, Bulatao, and Cohen 2004; Bulatao and Anderson 2004).

One of the most profound and far-reaching transformations of public policy and social life in America during this century has occurred via legislation, judicial decisions, and administrative actions in the area of civil rights, especially since the 1960s. Such large social, political, and economic changes deserve study in their own right, but also for the implications they have for the nature and quality of life and health among minority populations.

George Kaplan, Nalini Ranjit, and Sarah Burgard (chapter 6, this volume) explore the consequences of postwar civil rights gains for a broad range of health outcomes and causal pathways. They document striking improvements in cardiovascular health among African American women between 1964 and 1974, particularly in the South. The strongest of these improvements in health status coincided in space and time with the most dramatic social, legal, and economic changes brought about through civil rights policies, consistent with a recent line of economic research (Almond, Chay, and Greenstone 2006).

Macroeconomic and Employment Policy

The relationship between macroeconomic conditions and health is another key area of research and scholarly debate. Researchers and policymakers have long noted that economic recession heightens specific health risks (depression and suicide risk, physical health problems, and even perhaps mortality) among those who become unemployed. Researchers have also known that long-term increases in national wealth are correlated with improved population health, not least because such wealth provides resources for key public health investments. They have traditionally assumed that cyclical economic fluctuations would display a similar correlation with population health.

Christopher Ruhm (chapter 7, this volume) challenges these assumptions and shows that economic booms bring their own characteristic health risks, perhaps because good times increase demand for cigarettes, alcohol, and (other) intoxicating substances, thus increasing risk of traumatic injury. Economic booms also foster other potential health risks, such as those associated with increased overtime work. Ruhm underscores that both recessions and economic booms bring distinctive threats to population health which may be susceptible to policy influence through sin taxes, unemployment benefit policies, and other interventions. Intriguingly, Ruhm finds weaker correlations between cyclical economic conditions and health within societies that feature strong economic safety nets, hence perhaps mitigating the impact of macroeconomic cycles on personal disposable income and consumption.

Richard Price and Sarah Burgard (chapter 8, this volume) consider the potential adverse health implications of changing economic and organizational policies in the American and global economies that increase job losses or transitions, reduce job security, or increase "nonstandard" work that is temporary, contractual, part-time, or without fringe benefits. Existing research suggests adverse health effects on individuals experiencing either unemployment or job insecurity, and they provided initial suggestive evidence on the relationships between nonstandard work and health and well-being. They also describe a long-term program of randomized trials that shows the positive health and labor force effects of a training program for unemployed people.

Welfare Policy

The 1990s witnessed fundamental changes in American income supports for low-income families beginning with authorization of state waivers from federal guidelines and culminating in the 1996 welfare reform that abolished Aid to Families with Dependent Children (AFDC)—arguably the most substantial and significant change in social welfare policy for decades. The sixty-year-old AFDC cash entitlement for low-income mothers and their children was replaced with Temporary Assistance for Needy Families (TANF), a program that provides only transitional support. The decade also witnessed major increases in in-kind transfers, such as the Earned Income Tax Credit, and in expanded health insurance coverage for poor and near-poor children. It is a difficult task to evaluate the health impact of these major and manifold changes in state and national social welfare policy.

Marianne Bitler and Hilary Hoynes (chapter 9, this volume) explore the impact of welfare programs, focusing on policies adopted in selected states—Connecticut, Florida, Iowa, Minnesota, and Vermont—during the early and mid-1990s. These data are derived from experimental designs that allow the authors to estimate unbiased causal effects of reform on health insurance coverage, health care utilization, employment, and health status. Drawing from a survey of the literature as well as the new analyses of the experimental data, they suggest that welfare reform had modest and mixed impacts on health outcomes. While the results from the early 1990s waiver period may not generalize to TANF, they suggest that welfare-to-work programs need not have large negative health effects.

Jean Knab, Sara McLanahan, and Irv Garfinkel (chapter 10, this volume) choose a different focus and explore the impact of welfare reform and child support policies on maternal health. Unique data from the Fragile Families study following the 1996 reforms shows that increases in welfare generosity are associated with improved maternal mental health status. However, the impact is not linear: marginal increases in welfare generosity are associated with *reduced* mental health among women who are already in settings with relatively generous benefits. Additionally, increases in the stringency of child support enforcement are associated with decreases in mental health. These findings are in many ways surprising and worrisome, and justify the need for additional investigation using alternative data and methods.

Housing and Neighborhood Policy

The likely important, but causally complex, issue of neighborhood effects highlights a fundamental empirical challenge in linking public policies and health. Where one lives, with whom one lives, the physical and social properties of one's local environment, including proximity to economic resources or to specific sources of risk are all associated with one's health. At the same time, people are not randomly assigned across space. People sort or are sorted into neighborhoods and communities based on personal preferences, opportunities, and constraints, and community features develop around particular individuals because of their demands and characteristics. Differences in health status and well-being across these neighborhoods and communities may therefore reflect the sorting process rather than the causal impact of these locations themselves.

Jeffrey Morenoff and colleagues (chapter 11, this volume) explore whether policy initiatives aimed at changing features of the residential environment can measurably improve health, focusing on residential environments and obesity using recent detailed data from the Chicago Community Adult Health Study. Controlling for individual-level factors, they find notable variation across neighborhoods in body mass index and in obesity-related risk factors. They provide "suggestive, though far from conclusive evidence" that the physical and social environment of neighborhoods influences levels of physical activity, especially among women. These authors make a particular contribution by reviewing both the strengths and limitations of observational and randomized study designs in exploring neighborhood effects

Jeanne Brooks-Gunn and Rebecca Fauth (chapter 12, this volume) review data on neighborhood effects on adult and child health, especially from two mobility experiments: Moving to Opportunity (MTO) and the Yonkers Project in Yonkers, New York. They note striking gender patterns in outcomes from MTO. Girls appeared to derive more favorable long-term gains than boys did from movements to low-poverty areas. These authors also note favorable impacts for adult mental health and emotional well-being (though not on adult substance-use patterns) from such MTO moves. In the Yonkers Project, these authors find that movement to low-poverty areas improved some simple indicators of adult physical health. They find little benefit for indicators of child health associated with movement to low-poverty areas.

CONCLUSION

A growing body of evidence suggests that upstream social and economic determinants of health are of major health importance, and hence that social and economic policy and practice may be the major route to improving population health. The present volume seeks to assess where we are and where we might most fruitfully go next to understand whether, how, and why six major policy arenas impact health; and whether, how, and to what extent public and private policies in these areas can be modified in ways that will improve health. The work reviewed and presented in this volume provides a foundation for a more comprehensive health policy intimately connected with the broad social and economic factors that affect population health (Kaplan 2001). It also promises to help our nation escape the dubious distinction of having the highest health care expenditures in the world coupled with the worst public health outcomes of any major industrial democracy.

REFERENCES

Ader, Robert, David L. Felten, and Nicholas Cohen, editors. 1991. *Psychoneuroimmunology*, 2nd edition. San Diego, Calif.: Academic Press.

Advisory Committee to the Surgeon General. 1964. "Smoking and Health." Washington: U.S. Department of Health, Education and Welfare.

Almond, Douglas, Kenneth Y. Chay, and Michael Greenstone. 2006. "Civil Rights, the War on Poverty, and Black-White Convergence in Infant Mortality in the Rural South and Mississippi." MIT Working Paper N. 07-04. Boston, Mass.: Massachusetts Institute of Technology.

Anderson, Norman B., Rodolfo A. Bulatao, and Barney Cohen. 2004. *Critical Perspectives on Racial and Ethnic Differences in Health in Late Life*. Washington: The National Academies Press.

Aronowitz, Robert A. 1998. *Making Sense of Illness: Science, Society, and Disease*. New York: Cambridge University Press.

Baicker, Kate. 2001. "Government Decision-Making and the Incidence of Federal Mandates." *Journal of Public Economics* 82(2): 147–94.

Becker, Gary. 1964. *Human Capital*. Chicago, Ill.: University of Chicago Press.

Bengtsson, Tommy. 2001. "Mortality: The Great Historical Decline." In *International Encyclopedia of the Social and Behavioral Sciences*, edited by Neil J. Smelser and Paul B. Baltes. Oxford: Elsevier.

Berkman, Lisa F., and Lester Breslow. 1983. *Health and Ways of Living: The Alameda County Study*. London: Oxford University Press.

Berkman, Lisa F., and Ichiro Kawachi. 2000. *Social Epidemiology*. New York: Oxford University Press.

Blau, Peter, and Otis Dudley Duncan. 1967. *The American Occupational Structure*. New York: John Wiley and Sons.

Brandt, Allan M. 2007. *The Cigarette Century: The Rise, Fall, and Deadly Persistence of the Product That Defined America*. New York: Basic Books.

Broadhead, W. Eugene, Berton H. Kaplan, Sherman A. James, Edward H. Wagner, Victor J. Schoenbach, Roger Grimson, Siegfried Heyden, Gösta Tibblin, and Stephen H. Gehlbach. 1983. "The Epidemiological Evidence for a Relationship Between Social Support and Health." *American Journal of Epidemiology* 117(5): 521–37.

Bulatao, Rodolfo A., and Norman B. Anderson. 2004. *Understanding Racial and Ethnic Differences in Health in Late Life: A Research Agenda*. Washington: The National Academies Press.

Bunker, John P., Howard S. Frazier, and Frederick Mosteller. 1994. "Improving Health: Measuring Effects of Medical Care." *The Milbank Quarterly* 72(2): 225–58.

Cannon, Walter B. 1932. *The Wisdom of the Body*. New York: W. W. Norton and Company, Inc.

Chernew, Michael E., Richard A. Hirth, and David M. Cutler. 2003. "Increased Spending on Health Care: How Much Can the United States Afford?" *Health Affairs* 22(4): 15–25.

Coale, Ansley. 1974. "The History of the Human Population." *Scientific American* 231(3): 41–51.

Cutler, David M. 2004. *Your Money or Your Life: Strong Medicine for America's Health Care System*. New York: Oxford University Press.

Cutler, David M., Allison B. Rosen, and Sandeep Vijan. 2006. "The Value of Medical Spending in the United States, 1960–2000." *New England Journal of Medicine* 355(9): 920–7.

Drummond, Michael F., Bernard O'Brien, Greg L. Stoddart, and George W. Torrance. 1997. *Methods for the Economic Evaluation of Health Care Programmes*. 2nd edition. New York: Oxford University Press.

Fisher, Ronald A. 1958. "Cancer and Smoking." *Nature* 182(4635): 596–7.

Fogel, Robert William. 2004. *The Escape from Hunger and Premature Death*. Cambridge: Cambridge University Press.

Hacker, Jacob S. 2002. *The Divided Welfare State: The Battle over Public and Private Social Benefits in the United States*. Cambridge: Cambridge University Press.

Health Canada. 1998. *Taking Action on Population Health*. Ottawa, Ont.: Health and Welfare Canada.

Heckman, James J. 1992. "Randomization and Social Policy Evaluation." In *Evaluating Welfare and Training Programs*, edited by Charles Manski and Irwin Garfinkel. Cambridge, Mass.: Harvard University Press.

———. 2000. "Causal Parameters and Policy Analysis in Economics: A Twentieth Century Retrospective." *Quarterly Journal of Economics* 115(1): 45–97.

Heckman, James J., and Edward J. Vytlacil. 2005. "Econometric Evaluation of Social Programs." In *Handbook of Econometrics*, edited by James J. Heckman and Edward Leamer. Amsterdam: Elsevier.

House, James S. 2002. "Understanding Social Factors and Inequalities in Health: 20th Century Progress and 21st Century Prospects." *Journal of Health and Social Behavior* 43(2): 125–42.

House, James S., and George A. Kaplan. 2004. "The Psychosocial Nature of Physical Health." In *A Telescope on Society: Survey Research and Social Science at the University of Michigan and Beyond*, edited by James S. House, F. Thomas Juster, Robert L. Kahn, Howard Schuman, and Eleanor Singer. Ann Arbor, Mich.: University of Michigan Press.

House, James S., and David R. Williams. 2000. "Understanding and Reducing Socioeconomic and Racial/Ethnic Disparities in Health." In *Promoting Health: Intervention Strate-*

gies from Social and Behavioral Research, edited by Brian D. Smedley and S. Leonard Syme. Washington: National Academies Press.

Institute of Medicine. 2001a. *Crossing the Quality Chasm.* Washington: National Academies Press.

———. 2001b. *To Err is Human: Building a Safer Health System.* Washington: National Academies Press.

———. 2005. *Informing the Future.* Washington: National Academies Press.

Irwin, Alec, and Elena Scali. 2005. "Action on the Social Determinants of Health: Learning from Previous Experiences, A Background Paper Prepared for the WHO Commission on Social Determinants of Health." Geneva: Commission on Social Determinants of Health, World Health Organization.

Kannel, William B. 1971. "Habits and Heart Disease Mortality." In *Prediction of Lifespan,* edited by Erdman Palmore and Frances C. Jeffers. Lexington, Mass.: Heath.

Kaplan, George A. 1985. "Psychosocial Aspects of Chronic Illness: Direct and Indirect Associations with Ischemic Heart Disease Mortality." In *Behavioral Epidemiology and Disease Prevention,* edited by Robert M. Kaplan and Michael H. Criqui. New York: Plenum Publishing Corporation.

———. 1992. "Health and Aging in the Alameda County Study." In *Aging, Health Behaviors and Health Outcomes,* edited by K. Warner Schaie, Dan Blazer, and James S. House. Mahwah, N.J.: Lawrence Erlbaum Associates.

———. 1995. "Where Do Shared Pathways Lead? Some Reflections on a Research Agenda." *Psychosomatic Medicine* 57(3): 208–12.

———. 2001. "Economic Policy is Healthy Policy: Findings from the Study of Income, Socioeconomic Status, and Health." In *Income, Socioeconomic Status, and Health: Exploring the Relationships,* edited by James A. Auerbach and Barbara K. Krimgold. Washington: National Policy Association.

Kaplan, George A., and John W. Lynch. 1997. "Whither Studies on the Socioeconomic Foundations of Population Health (Editorial)." *American Journal of Public Health* 87(9): 1409–11.

Kaplan, George A., Susan A. Everson, and John W. Lynch. 2000. "The Contribution of Social and Behavioral Research to an Understanding of the Distribution of Disease: A Multilevel Approach." In *Promoting Health: Intervention Strategies from Social and Behavioral Research,* edited by Brian D. Smedley and S. Leonard Syme. Washington: National Academies Press.

Kaplan, George A., Mary N. Haan, S. Leonard Syme, M. Minkler, and M. Winkleby. 1987. "Socioeconomic Status and Health." In *Closing the Gap: The Burden of Unnecessary Illness,* edited by Robert W. Amler and H. Bruce Dull. New York: Oxford University Press.

Kluger, Richard. 1997. *Ashes to Ashes: America's Hundred-Year Cigarette War, the Public Health, and the Unabashed Triumph of Philip Morris.* New York: Vintage Books.

Kunitz, Stephen J. 2006. *The Health of Populations: General Theories and Particular Realities.* New York: Oxford University Press.

Kunitz, Stephen J., and Irena Pesis-Katz. 2005. "Mortality of White Americans, African Americans, and Canadians: The Causes and Consequences for Health of Welfare State Institutions and Policies." *The Milbank Quarterly* 83(1): 5–39.

Lantz, Paula M., James S. House, James M. Lepkowski, David R. Williams, Richard P. Mero, and Jieming Chen. 1998. "Socioeconomic Factors, Health Behaviors, and Mortality: Results from a Nationally Representative Prospective Study of U.S. Adults." *Journal of the American Medical Association* 279(21): 1703–8.

Lantz, Paula M., John W. Lynch, James S. House, James M. Lepkowski, Richard P. Mero,

Marc Musick, and David R. Williams. 2001. "Socioeconomic Disparities in Health Change in a Longitudinal Study of U.S. Adults: The Role of Health Risk Behaviors." *Social Science and Medicine* 53(1): 29–40.

Levy, David T., Joseph E. Bauer, and Hye-ryeon Lee. 2006. "Simulation Modeling and Tobacco Control: Creating More Robust Public Health Policies." *American Journal of Public Health* 96(3): 494–8.

Lilienfeld, Abraham M., and David E. Lilienfeld. 1980. *Foundations of Epidemiology*. New York: Oxford University Press.

Link, Bruce G., and Jo C. Phelan. 1995. "Social Conditions as Fundamental Causes of Disease." *Journal of Health and Social Behavior* 35(Extra Issue): 80–94.

———. 2000. "Evaluating the Fundamental Cause Explanation for Social Disparities in Health." In *Handbook of Medical Sociology*, 5th edition, edited by Chloe E. Bird, Peter Conrad, and Allen Fremont. Upper Saddle River, N.J.: Prentice Hall.

Lynch, John W., and George A. Kaplan. 2000. "Socioeconomic Position." In *Social Epidemiology*, edited by Lisa F. Berkman and Ichiro Kawachi. New York: Oxford University Press.

Lynch, John W., George A. Kaplan, Richard D. Cohen, Jaakko Tuomilehto, and Jukka T. Salonen. 1996. "Do Cardiovascular Risk Factors Explain the Relation Between Socioeconomic Status, Risk of All-Cause Mortality, Cardiovascular Mortality, and Acute Myocardial Infarction?" *American Journal of Epidemiology* 144(10): 934–42.

Manpower Demonstration Research Corporation (MDRC). No Date. Web site. Accessed September 11, 2007, at http://www.mdrc.org.

Marini, Margaret M., and Burton Singer. 1988. "Causality in the Social Sciences." In *Sociological Methodology* 18: 347–409.

Marmot, Michael G., Martin Bobak, and George Davey Smith. 1995. "Explanations for Social Inequalities in Health." In *Society and Health*, edited by Benjamin C. Amick III, Sol Levine, Alvin R. Tarlov, and Diana C. Walsh. New York: Oxford University Press.

Marmot, Michael G., Manolis Kogevinas, and Mary Alan Elston. 1987. "Social/Economic Status and Disease." *Annual Review of Public Health* 8: 111–35.

Massachusetts Institute of Technology, Abdul Latif Jameel Poverty Action Lab. No date. Web site. Accessed September 11, 2007, at http://www.povertyactionlab.com.

McGinnis, J. Michael, and William H. Foege. 1993. "Actual Causes of Death in the United States: Dying." *Journal of the American Medical Association* 270(18): 2225–43.

McGinnis, J. Michael, Pamela Williams-Russo, and James R. Knickman. 2002. "The Case for More Active Policy Attention to Health Promotion." *Health Affairs* 21(2): 78–93.

McKeown, Thomas. 1979. *The Role of Medicine: Dream, Mirage or Nemesis*. Princeton, N.J.: Princeton University Press.

———. 1988. *The Origins of Human Disease*. London: Blackwell Publishing.

McKinlay, John B., and Sonja J. McKinlay. 1977. "The Questionable Contribution of Medical Measures to the Decline of Mortality in the United States in the Twentieth Century." *Milbank Memorial Fund Quarterly* 55(3): 405–28.

Munnell, Alice H., editor. 1986. *Lessons from the Income Maintenance Experiments*. Boston, Mass.: Federal Reserve Bank of Boston.

Navarro, Vicente. 2007. "What Is a National Health Policy?" *International Journal of Health Services* 37(1): 1–14.

Organization for Economic Co-Operation and Development (OECD). 2005. *Health at a Glance: OECD Indicators 2005*. Paris: OECD.

Pappas, Gregory, Susan Queen, William Hadden, and Gail Fisher. 1993. "The Increasing Disparity in Mortality Between Socioeconomic Groups in the United States, 1960 and 1986." *New England Journal of Medicine* 329(2): 103–9.

Pearl, Judea. 2000. *Causality: Models, Reasoning and Inference.* Cambridge: Cambridge University Press.

Pechman, Joseph A., and P. Michael Timpane, editors. 1975. *Work Incentives and Income Guarantees: The New Jersey Negative Income Tax Experiment.* Washington: Brookings Institute.

Prentice, Ross L., Robert Langer, Marcia L. Stefanick, Barbara V. Howard, Mary Pettinger, Garnet Anderson, David Barad, J. David Curb, Jane Kotchen, Lewis Kuller, Marian Limacher, and Jean Wactawski-Wende. 2005. "Combined Postmenopausal Hormone Therapy and Cardiovascular Disease: Toward Resolving the Discrepancy between Observational Studies and the Women's Health Initiative Clinical Trial." *American Journal of Epidemiology* 162(5): 404–14.

Preston, Samuel H. 1977. "Mortality Trends." *Annual Review of Sociology* 3: 163–78.

Raphael, Dennis, and Toba Bryant. 2006. "The State's Role in Promoting Population Health: Public Health Concerns in Canada, USA, UK, and Sweden." *Health Policy* 78(1): 39–55.

Rubin, Donald B. 1974. "Estimating Causal Effects of Treatments in Randomized and Nonrandomized Studies." *Journal of Educational Psychology* 66(5): 688–701.

Selye, Hans. 1956. *The Stress of Life.* New York: McGraw-Hill.

Stahl, Timo, Matthias Wismar, Eeva Ollila, Eero Lahtinen, and Kimmo Leppo, editors. 2006. *Health in All Policies: Prospects and Potentials.* Helsinki, Finland: Ministry of Public Health and Affairs.

Steptoe, Andrew, and Michael Marmot. 2002. "The Role of Psychobiological Pathways in Socioeconomic Inequalities in Cardiovascular Disease Risk." *European Heart Journal* 23(1): 13–25.

Swedish National Institute of Public Health. 2003. *Sweden's New Public Health Policy: National Public Health Objectives for Sweden.* Stockholm: National Institute of Public Health.

Taylor, Shelley E., Rena L. Repetti, and Teresa Seeman. 1997. "Health Psychology: What Is an Unhealthy Environment and How Does It Get Under the Skin?" *Annual Review of Psychology* 48: 411–47.

Timmermans, Stefan, and Aaron Mauck. 2005. "The Promises and Pitfalls of Evidence-Based Medicine." *Health Affairs* 24(1): 18–28.

United Nations Development Programme. 2005. *Human Development Report 2005: International Cooperation at a Crossroads.* New York: United Nations Development Programme.

U.S. Department of Health and Human Services. 2000. *Healthy People 2010.* Washington: United States Department of Health and Human Services.

Warner, Kenneth E. 2001. "Smoking and Health." In *International Encyclopedia of Social and Behavioral Sciences,* edited by N. J. Smelser and P. B. Baltes. New York: Elsevier.

Wilkinson, Richard G. 1996. *Unhealthy Societies: The Afflictions of Inequality.* New York: Routledge.

Writing Group for the Women's Health Initiative Investigators. 2002. "Risks and Benefits of Estrogen Plus Progestin in Healthy Post-Menopausal Women, Principal Results from the Women's Health Initiative Randomized Controlled Trial." *Journal of the American Medical Association* 288(3): 321–33.

Part II

Education Policy

Chapter 2

Education and Health:
Evaluating Theories and Evidence

David M. Cutler and Adriana Lleras-Muney

There is a well-known large and persistent association between education and health. This relationship has been observed in many countries and time periods, and for a wide variety of health measures.[1] The differences between the more and the less-educated are significant: in 1999, the age-adjusted mortality rate of high school dropouts ages twenty-eight to sixty-four was more than twice as large as the mortality rate of those with some college (Lyert et al. 2001, table 26).

Substantial attention has been paid to these "health inequalities." Gradients in health by education are now systematically monitored in many countries (the United States includes them as part of its Healthy People 2010 goals). Countries such as the United Kingdom have target goals of reducing health disparities specifically through education or factors correlated with education.[2] Through understanding the possible causal relationships between education and health and the mechanisms behind them, we can assess the extent to which education policies can or should be thought of as health policies.

We note at the outset that this is a controversial topic. A number of authors have written about education-related health inequalities, and the conclusions frequently differ. To some extent, this is a result of data limitations. Many of the data sets that we and others employ use health measures that are self-reported. In addition to true differences in health, there are also some differences related to knowledge of existing conditions, which may itself be related to education. It is also very important, however, that work on the mechanisms underlying the link between health and education has not been conclusive. Not all relevant theories have been tested, and, when they have, studies often conflict with each other. We highlight the discrepancies as best we can. We do not resolve the differences here—that is an enormous task, and is not doable with current information. Noting the points of disagreement is important in its own right, however. Along the way, we indicate where more research would be particularly valuable.

THE RELATIONSHIP BETWEEN HEALTH AND EDUCATION

To document the basic correlations between education and health, we estimate the following regression:

$$H_i = c + \beta E_i + X_i \delta + \varepsilon_i \qquad (2.1)$$

where H_i is a measure of individual i's health or health behavior, E_i stands for i's years of completed education, X_i is a vector of individual characteristics that includes race, gender, and single year of age dummies, c is a constant term, and ε is the error term. The coefficient on education β (also referred to as the education gradient) is the object of interest, and it measures the effect of one more year of education on the particular measure of health. We focus on individuals who are twenty-five and older because they have most likely already completed their education. Education is included either in years (as in the labor literature), or using dummies for each year of education, to be as flexible as possible. We first report results for the entire sample, and then for different demographic groups. We estimate linear models for continuous variables. For dichotomous variables we estimate logit probability models and report the marginal effects.

The data we employ are from various years of the National Health Interview Survey (NHIS) in the United States.[3] We use the NHIS because it has a large number of health outcomes and behaviors. Generally, results from the NHIS match other surveys with self-reports (Cutler and Glaeser 2005) and even physical assessments, though clearly there are exceptions such as weight and height. We note possible reporting issues as we present the results.

Table 2.1 reports the coefficient on years of schooling in explaining various measures of health. The first outcome we look at is whether an individual died within five years of the interview. In the NHIS this is determined by matching individual information to death certificates through the National Death Index (see appendix for more details). Then we look at gradients in the self-report of a past acute or chronic disease diagnosis. Most of these diseases are very serious (cancer or heart disease, for example), and people would certainly know if they had been diagnosed with them. (Although it is possible that conditional on having the disease, the more educated are more likely to know about it. If that is the case, then the gradients we report for these diseases could partially reflect differential diagnosis and knowledge; however, this is not the case for mortality.) Of course, since the sample is of people who are alive, differential mortality between better educated and less educated is an issue. But this would tend to *reduce* reported gradients if less educated people are more likely to die when they have any disease and thus are not alive to report the disease.

The first column includes a very basic set of controls: a full set of age dummies, race, and gender. The results (column 1) show that individuals with higher levels of education are less likely to die within five years. The second block of the table

TABLE 2.1 / Effect of Education on Health, Adults Twenty-Five and Over

Dependent Variable	With Limited Controls		With Broader Controls		With Occupation and Industry		Obs	Mean
	Years of Education	SE	Years of Education	SE	Years of Education	SE		
Five-year mortality	−0.0017**	[0.0002]	−0.0011**	[0.0002]	−0.0010**	[0.0002]	35394	0.05
Self-Report of disease diagnosis								
Heart condition	−0.0054**	[0.0011]	−0.0035**	[0.0013]	−0.0033*	[0.0014]	28343	0.31
Cancer	0.0018**	[0.0004]	0.0011*	[0.0005]	0.0009	[0.0005]	28180	0.07
Stroke	−0.0010**	[0.0002]	−0.0004*	[0.0002]	−0.0003*	[0.0001]	22480	0.03
Ulcer	−0.0032**	[0.0005]	−0.0012*	[0.0006]	−0.0006	[0.0006]	28255	0.08
Hepatitis	0.0008	[0.0004]	0.0013**	[0.0005]	0.0013**	[0.0005]	27821	0.04
Chickenpox	0.0096**	[0.0008]	0.0058**	[0.0009]	0.0048**	[0.0009]	26410	0.85
Hay fever or sinusitis, past twelve months	0.0075**	[0.0010]	0.0064**	[0.0012]	0.0046**	[0.0013]	28307	0.22
Pain, past twelve months	−0.0060**	[0.0012]	−0.0053**	[0.0015]	−0.0037*	[0.0015]	28345	0.49
Sickness, past two weeks	−0.0037**	[0.0008]	−0.0025**	[0.0009]	−0.0032**	[0.0010]	28334	0.15
Asthma episode, past twelve months	−0.0007	[0.0004]	−0.0002	[0.0004]	−0.0007	[0.0004]	28156	0.03
Ulcer past twelve months	−0.0024**	[0.0002]	−0.0009**	[0.0003]	−0.0006**	[0.0002]	27584	0.02
Hypertension	−0.0066**	[0.0009]	−0.0048**	[0.0011]	−0.0046**	[0.0011]	28321	0.25
High cholesterol °	−0.0059**	[0.0014]	−0.0045**	[0.0016]	−0.0036*	[0.0017]	20110	0.32
Emphysema	−0.0011**	[0.0002]	−0.0006**	[0.0001]	−0.0004**	[0.0001]	23997	0.02
Asthma	0.0002	[0.0007]	0.0008	[0.0008]	−0.0003	[0.0008]	28258	0.09
Diabetes	−0.0032**	[0.0004]	−0.0015**	[0.0004]	−0.0016**	[0.0004]	28151	0.07
Functioning								
In fair or poor health °	−0.0152**	[0.0006]	−0.0082**	[0.0005]	−0.0073**	[0.0005]	35774	0.12
Anxiety (scale from 0 to 8)	−0.0483**	[0.0041]	−0.0286**	[0.0046]	−0.0316**	[0.0050]	28350	1.05
Depression (scale from 0 to 16)	−0.1268**	[0.0068]	−0.0748**	[0.0077]	−0.0711**	[0.0084]	28350	1.2
Effect of health								
Number of work loss days, past twelve months	−0.5768**	[0.0857]	−0.4680**	[0.0933]	−0.4082**	[0.1086]	19112	5.15
Number of bed days, past twelve months	−0.5623**	[0.0663]	−0.3442**	[0.0776]	−0.3767**	[0.0875]	27935	4.75
Depression hindered life, past month[a]	−0.0165**	[0.0024]	−0.0061*	[0.0027]	−0.0063*	[0.0028]	7722	0.62
Any functional limitations	−0.0160**	[0.0011]	−0.0104**	[0.0013]	−0.0104**	[0.0014]	28263	0.33

Source: Authors' compilation.
Note: The first column (limited controls) includes a full set of age dummies, race, and gender.
The second column (broader controls) adds Hispanic origin, family income, family size, major activity, region, MSA, marital status, and whether covered by health insurance.
Outcomes marked with ° came from waves of the NHIS that did not collect health-insurance data, so health insurance is not included in these regressions.
The third column adds occupation and industry dummies to the limited and broader controls.
[a] Question was asked only of individuals who reported experiencing at least one negative affective state, most or all of the time.
* significant at 10 percent; ** significant at 5 percent.

shows that the more educated also report having lower morbidity from the most common acute and chronic diseases (that is, heart condition, stroke hypertension, cholesterol, emphysema, diabetes, asthma attacks, and ulcer). The only exceptions are cancer, chicken pox, and hay fever. Differential reporting of hay fever could possibly be related to differential knowledge of disease (better educated people will be more likely to go to specialists for testing). This might be the explanation for cancer as well; skin cancer is the most common cancer and could be subject to reporting bias. But this might not be the whole explanation. Some evidence suggests that some cancer risk factors are adverse for the better educated (as with late childbearing age and breast cancer). It may also be that better educated people are more likely to survive with cancer, or that better care for competing risks keeps the better educated alive long enough to die of cancer.

Differences in chronic disease prevalence are similar. Better educated people are less likely to be hypertensive, or to suffer from emphysema or diabetes. The third set of rows shows that physical and mental functioning is better for the better educated. The better educated are substantially less likely to report themselves in poor health and less likely to report anxiety or depression. Finally, the last block shows that better educated people report spending fewer days in bed or not at work due to disease and have fewer functional limitations.

The magnitude of the relationship between education and health varies across conditions, but it is generally large. An additional four years of education lowers five year mortality by 0.6 percentage points (relative to a base of 5 percent); it also reduces the risk of heart disease by 2.16 percentage points (relative to a base of 31 percent) and the risk of diabetes by 1.3 percentage points (relative to a base of 7 percent). Four more years of schooling lowers the probability of reporting in fair or poor health by 6 percentage points (the mean is 12 percent) and reduces lost days of work to sickness by 2.3 each year (relative to 5.15 on average). Although the effects of gender and race are not shown, the magnitude of four years of schooling is roughly comparable in size to being female or being African American. These are not trivial effects.

The reasons for these associations are multi-factorial, although it is likely that these health differences are in part the result of differences in behavior across education groups. Table 2.2 shows the relation between education and various health risk factors: smoking, drinking, diet and exercise, use of illegal drugs, household safety, use of preventive medical care, and care for hypertension and diabetes. Overall, the results suggest very strong gradients where the better educated have healthier behaviors along virtually every margin (although some of these behaviors may also reflect differential access to care). Those with more years of schooling (we report the effects of four more years) are less likely to smoke (11 percentage points relative to a mean of 23 percent), to drink a lot (seven fewer days of five or more drinks in a year, among those who drink, of a base of eleven days), to be overweight or obese (5 percentage points lower obesity, compared to an average of 23 percent), or to use illegal drugs (0.6 percentage points less likely to use illegal drugs, relative to an average of 5 percent). Interestingly, the better educated report having tried illegal drugs more frequently, but they gave them up more readily.

TABLE 2.2 / Effect of Education on Health Behaviors, Adults Twenty-Five and Over

| Dependent Variable | With Limited Controls | | With Broader Controls | | With Occupation and Industry | | | |
	Years of Education	SE	Years of Education	SE	Years of Education	SE	Obs	Mean
Smoking								
Current smoker	−0.0218**	[0.0009]	−0.0186**	[0.0011]	−0.0141**	[0.0012]	28154	0.23
Number of cigarettes a day (smokers)	−0.3780**	[0.0672]	−0.4129**	[0.0703]	−0.2926**	[0.0736]	6276	16.65
Made serious attempt to quit °	0.0133**	[0.0025]	0.0105**	[0.0027]	0.0084**	[0.0028]	9211	0.62
Alcohol								
Had twelve or more drinks in entire life	0.0187**	[0.0009]	0.0097**	[0.0011]	0.0098**	[0.0011]	28042	0.78
Drink at least once per month	0.0319**	[0.0014]	0.0183**	[0.0016]	0.0183**	[0.0017]	27711	0.45
Number of days had five or more drinks past year	−1.7572**	[0.1711]	−1.5787**	[0.1858]	−1.2149**	[0.2094]	16311	11.1
Average number of drinks on days drank	−0.1720**	[0.0138]	−0.1410**	[0.0136]	−0.1131**	[0.0157]	16491	2.38
Diet or exercise								
Body mass index (BMI)	−0.1996**	[0.0127]	−0.1270**	[0.0150]	−0.1269**	[0.0157]	27253	26.88
Overweight (BMI greater or equal to 25)	−0.0172**	[0.0013]	−0.0122**	[0.0015]	−0.0113**	[0.0016]	27253	0.60
Obese (BMI greater or equal to 30)	−0.0129**	[0.0009]	−0.0087**	[0.0011]	−0.0088**	[0.0012]	27237	0.23
How often eat fruit or vegetables per day	0.0658**	[0.0033]	0.0585**	[0.0039]	0.0515**	[0.0040]	28350	1.88
Ever do vigorous activity	0.0489**	[0.0015]	0.0359**	[0.0017]	0.0322**	[0.0018]	28000	0.38
Ever do moderate activity	0.0418**	[0.0014]	0.0306**	[0.0016]	0.0286**	[0.0017]	27724	0.51
Illegal drugs (ages twenty-five to forty-four)								
Ever used marijuana °	0.0189**	[0.0018]	0.0085**	[0.0021]	0.0092**	[0.0024]	16220	0.46
Used marijuana, past twelve months °	−0.0009	[0.0007]	−0.0021*	[0.0008]	−0.001	[0.0009]	16212	0.08

TABLE 2.2 / (*Continued*)

Dependent Variable	With Limited Controls		With Broader Controls		With Occupation and Industry			
	Years of Education	SE	Years of Education	SE	Years of Education	SE	Obs	Mean
Ever used cocaine °	0.0055**	[0.0011]	0.0003	[0.0013]	0.0009	[0.0014]	15929	0.15
Used cocaine, past twelve months °	−0.0003	[0.0003]	−0.0004	[0.0003]	−0.0001	[0.0003]	15247	0.02
Ever used any other illegal drug °	0.0047**	[0.0013]	0.0005	[0.0015]	0.0023	[0.0018]	16175	0.20
Used other illegal drug, past twelve months °	−0.0015*	[0.0006]	−0.0012	[0.0007]	−0.0007	[0.0007]	15726	0.05
Household safety								
Know poison control number °	0.0466**	[0.0025]	0.0337**	[0.0029]	0.0301**	[0.0032]	8517	0.60
One or more working smoke detectors °	0.0207**	[0.0009]	0.0113**	[0.0009]	0.0101**	[0.0010]	34455	0.79
House tested for radon °	0.0066**	[0.0004]	0.0038**	[0.0003]	0.0032**	[0.0004]	33478	0.04
Home paint ever tested for lead °	−0.0001	[0.0007]	0.0001	[0.0006]	−0.0007	[0.0006]	11519	0.05
Automobile safety								
Always wear seat belt °	0.0295**	[0.0011]	0.0236**	[0.0012]	0.0185**	[0.0013]	35585	0.68
Never wear seat belt °	−0.0097**	[0.0005]	−0.0078**	[0.0006]	−0.0057**	[0.0006]	35567	0.09
Recommended preventive care								
Ever had mammogram (age forty or older)	0.0149**	[0.0011]	0.0081**	[0.0013]	0.0072**	[0.0013]	10126	0.86
Had mammogram, past two years (age forty or older)	0.0270**	[0.0021]	0.0153**	[0.0025]	0.0155**	[0.0026]	10061	0.55
Ever had pap smear test	0.0045**	[0.0004]	0.0028**	[0.0004]	0.0022**	[0.0003]	15064	0.96
Had pap smear, past year	0.0258**	[0.0017]	0.0143**	[0.0019]	0.0121**	[0.0020]	15129	0.62
Ever had colorectal screening (age forty or older)	0.0217**	[0.0014]	0.0169**	[0.0016]	0.0153**	[0.0016]	17586	0.29

TABLE 2.2 / (Continued)

Dependent Variable	With Limited Controls		With Broader Controls		With Occupation and Industry		Obs	Mean
	Years of Education	SE	Years of Education	SE	Years of Education	SE		
Had colonoscopy, past year (age forty or older)	0.0060**	[0.0008]	0.0045**	[0.0008]	0.0034**	[0.0008]	17490	0.09
Ever been tested for HIV	0.0126**	[0.0013]	0.0132**	[0.0015]	0.0113**	[0.0016]	26456	0.32
Had an STD other than HIV/ AIDS, past five years	0.0003	[0.0004]	0.0000	[0.0004]	0.0001	[0.0004]	14659	0.02
Had flu shot, past twelve months	0.0172**	[0.0012]	0.0123**	[0.0014]	0.0091**	[0.0014]	28013	0.31
Ever had pneumonia vaccination	0.0052**	[0.0007]	0.0045**	[0.0008]	0.0046**	[0.0008]	27554	0.16
Ever had hepatitis B vaccine	0.0185**	[0.0011]	0.0178**	[0.0013]	0.0126**	[0.0014]	26826	0.20
Received all three hepatitis B shots	0.0154**	[0.0009]	0.0147**	[0.0011]	0.0097**	[0.0011]	26453	0.15
Among diabetics								
Are you now taking insulin	−0.0008	[0.0038]	−0.0039	[0.0046]	−0.0031	[0.0048]	2006	0.33
Are you now taking diabetic pills	−0.0059	[0.0040]	0.0023	[0.0048]	−0.0011	[0.0049]	1997	0.66
Blood pressure high at last reading °	−0.0043**	[0.0005]	−0.0033**	[0.0005]	−0.0029**	[0.0005]	33569	0.08
Among hypertensives								
Still have high bp °	−0.0104**	[0.0022]	−0.0079**	[0.0024]	−0.0077**	[0.0026]	8591	0.49
High bp is cured (versus controlled) °	0.0006	[0.0027]	−0.0022	[0.0031]	−0.0023	[0.0033]	4185	0.26

Source: Authors' compilation.
Note: The first column (limited controls) includes a full set of age dummies, race, and gender.
The second column (broader controls) adds Hispanic origin, family income, family size, major activity, region, MSA, marital status, and whether covered by health insurance.
Outcomes marked with ° came from waves of the NHIS that did not collect health-insurance data, so health insurance is not included in these regressions.
The third column adds occupation and industry dummies to the limited and broader controls.
* significant at 10 percent; ** significant at 5 percent.

Similarly, the better educated are more likely to exercise and to obtain preventive care such as flu shots (7 percentage points relative to an average of 31 percent), vaccines (7 percentage points relative to an average of 20 percent for hepatitis B vaccination), mammograms (10 percentage points relative to an average of 54 percent), pap smears (10 percentage points relative to an average of 60 percent), and colonoscopies (2.4 percentage points relative to an average of 9 percent). Among those with chronic conditions such as diabetes and hypertension, the more educated are more likely to have their condition under control. Furthermore, they are more likely to use seat belts (12 percentage points more likely to always use a seat belt, compared to the average of 68 percent), to have a house with a smoke detector (10.8 percentage points relative to an average of 79 percent), and to have had their house tested for radon (2.6 percentage points relative to a base of 4 percent). All of these behavioral effects are very large.

It is worth noting that these health behaviors explain some, but not all, of the differences in health. For example, in the famous Whitehall Study of British civil servants (Marmot 1994), smoking, drinking, and other health behaviors explain only one-third of the difference in mortality between those of higher rank and those of lower rank. Although the Whitehall Study did not focus on educational differences, we find similar results. In the NHIS, the effect of education on mortality is reduced by 30 percent when controlling for exercise, smoking, drinking, seatbelt use, and use of preventive care (results available upon request). This is perhaps an underestimate—one cares also about the length of time smoked, the specific cigarettes smoked, the number of puffs taken, and the like. But absent measurement error in behaviors, the result implies that there must be unobserved health behaviors that also contribute to health differences, or alternatively, that the more educated might be healthier due to reasons or behaviors that are not known to improve health. Equally important, we do not understand why the more educated make larger investments in their health.

The relationship between education and health shows up across countries as well. Figure 2.1 shows the simple correlation between average education (using the well-known Barro-Lee international data) and life expectancy (without any additional controls). As average education increases, life expectancy improves, although the returns appear to be larger for poorer countries.

The same is true within countries as well. The more educated are more likely to live longer not only in the United States, but also in Canada (Mustard et al. 1997), Israel (Manor et al. 1999), and both Western and Eastern Europe,[4] including Russia (Shkolnikov et al. 1998). This relationship has also been documented in developing countries, such as Bangladesh (Hurt, Rossmands, and Saha 2004), Korea (Khang, Lynch, and Kaplan 2004), and China (Liang et al. 2000). In most cases, however, education is not associated with lower cancer mortality.

Heterogeneous Effects

The basic correlations we just described do not fully describe important aspects of the relationship between education and health. For example, it is important to

FIGURE 2.1 / The Relationship Between Education and Life Expectancy
Across Countries

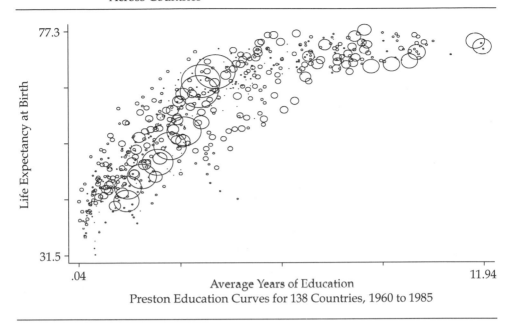

Preston Education Curves for 138 Countries, 1960 to 1985

Source: Authors' calculation using the Barro-Lee international data.
Note: Circle size is proportional to country population.

know whether the returns to schooling are constant for every additional year of
school, regardless of the initial level of schooling, or, for example, whether the benefits from primary schooling might exceed those from higher education. To better
understand the shape of the relationship between education and health, we esti
mate non-parametric models that include a dummy variable for each year of
schooling as explanatory variables (rather than years of education as a continuous
variable as in tables 1 and 2), and we include the same basic demographic controls
we included previously.

Figure 2.2 plots the estimated effects for a number of measures of health and
health behaviors. We chose four representative health measures (mortality, self-reported health status [SRHS], depression, and functional limitations) and four measures of behaviors that cover a range of different areas: smoking is an addictive behavior that is known to adversely affect health and potentially has an important
social component; colorectal screening is preventive but may be related to access
to health care; wearing a seat belt is also preventive but not monetarily costly; and
lastly smoke detectors at home, which relates to general safety. Although the estimates are noisy (some education categories have very few observations), they
show that for many outcomes, there are returns beyond high school completion
(twelve years of schooling). Education matters for health not just because of basic
reading and writing skills.

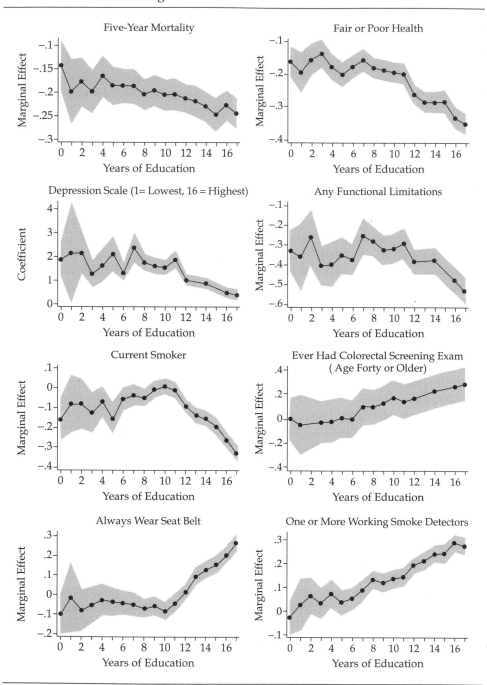

Source: Authors' compilation.
Note: Marginal effects from logit regressions on education, controlling for race and gender. The shaded areas are 95 percent confidence intervals for each coefficient.

For some outcomes, the relationship between years of schooling and health appears to be linear (see mortality, colorectal screenings, and smoke detectors). For other outcomes, such as functional limitations, smoking, and obesity, the relationship is nonlinear, with an increased effect of an additional year of school only for people who are better educated. In all cases, however, the relationship between education and health is roughly linear after ten years of school; we do not see large evidence of sheepskin effects in health—that is, there does not appear to be an additional health benefit associated with the completion of a degree beyond what would be expected given the number of years of schooling (although for some outcomes, such as SHRS and functional limitations, there may be a small effect of high school graduation). In contrast, there are clear sheepskin effects on wages (Tyler, Murnane, and Willett 2000). Subject to the possibility of small effects that we cannot measure accurately (for example, the product of the sheepskin effect in wages and the impact of income on health may be small), this allows us to reject the idea that the health returns to education (the health benefit associated with one more year of schooling) are driven by the labor-market returns to education. This also implies that there may be substantial health returns to education policies that promote college attendance.

The effects of education on health and health behaviors also differ along other dimensions. These effects vary significantly for individuals of different ages. Figure 2.3 shows the coefficients of education estimated by single year of age. Some of these education gradients (mostly those related to behaviors) fall continuously with age (for example, smoking, seat-belt use, and owning a smoke detector); whereas others increase with age until middle age, and then start to fall (for example, functional limitations, depression, and colorectal screening). In all cases, however, we find that the effect of education starts to fall sometime between ages fifty and sixty. Other studies have also documented smaller effects of education on mortality for older individuals (Elo and Preston 1996). Interestingly, some studies also find that the health differences associated with income also diminish after middle age (Smith 2005), though this is not true in all studies (Wolfson et al. 1993).

Some of the decline in the education gradient after age fifty must certainly be due to the selective survival of the more educated (Lynch 2003). There may also be additional cohort effects—education may have become more important for younger cohorts. Or education may simply matter less after retirement, when individuals have stable incomes and universal insurance coverage. It is difficult to separate these effects.

There are important differences by gender as well. Table 2.3 shows the impact of education for men and women (the second and third columns), blacks and whites (the fourth and fifth columns), and rich and poor (the sixth and seventh columns). The table reports whether the marginal effect of education is significantly different for the two groups, as well as the effect of one more year of education as a percentage of the mean level for the group (to account for the fact that different groups may have different baselines). In more than half the cases, education has a statistically indistinguishable effect for men and women. In some cases, education has a greater impact for women (for example, depression and obesity). In other cases, the effect is greater for men (for example, mortality and heavy drinking). It is not known whether these differences result from biology or behavior.

FIGURE 2.3 / Effect of Education on Various Health Measures, By Single Year of Age

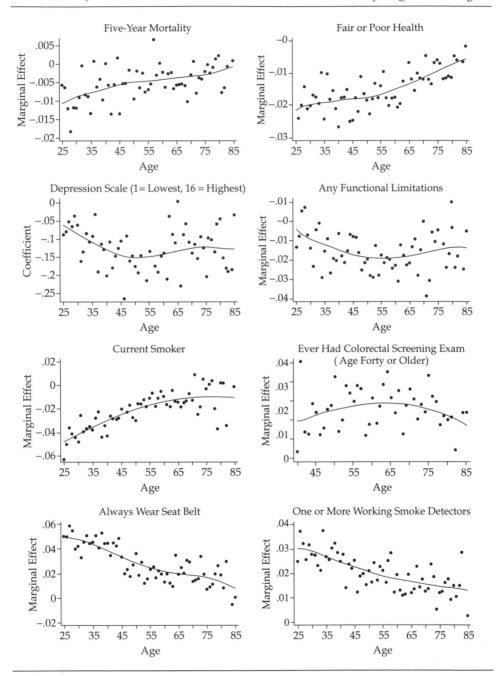

Source: Authors' compilation.
Note: Marginal effects from age-specific logit regressions on education, controlling for race and gender. Curve fitted using a locally weighted regression smoother, with a bandwidth of 0.8.

In the next two columns we compare gradients for whites and blacks. Again, the coefficients are similar most of the time. Where they differ, education gradients are larger for whites than for blacks (with the exception of smoke detectors), although the effects are closer when they are rescaled as a percentage of the mean. One possible explanation is that the quality of education is lower for blacks than for whites, though we have no direct evidence on this. These findings are also consistent with lower returns to education on wages among blacks (see Barrow and Rouse 2005 for discussion).

Lastly, we examine whether education matters more for those with low family incomes (incomes below twenty thousand dollars). However, we note here that because education affects income, and health may determine income, it is more difficult to interpret these results. In most cases that we examine, education matters more among the nonpoor than among the poor. This suggests that income and education are complementary in the production of health. This would be the case if, for example, education allows people to know about specific new treatments and income allows them to purchase the treatment. The results by race and income together suggest that socioeconomic status (SES) advantages are complementary (or cumulative). They also suggest that interactions between education and other variables may be important.

The Education Gradient Over Time

Education gradients in mortality appear to be increasing both in the United States (Pappas et al. 1993)[5] and Europe (Mackenbach et al. 2003; Kunst et al. 2002). As a result, even though life expectancy is improving for all, the differences in life expectancy have become larger between those who are college educated and those who are not. Other measures of health confirm these findings. For example, Brian Goesling (2005) finds that there has been an increase in the effect of education on self-reported health since 1982. Looking at the same period, Robert Schoeni, Vicki Freedman, and Linda Martin (2005) find that although disability rates in the United States have fallen, they have fallen more among the educated. The gradient in some health behaviors is also increasing: there were very small differences in smoking rates between education groups prior to the Surgeon General's Report in 1964, but these differences are substantial today (Pamuk et al. 1998, figure 35). Although compositional changes could be driving the observed differences—educational attainment has increased enormously over time—the results suggest that health inequalities could continue rising.

Spillovers Across People

It is well known that maternal education is strongly associated with infant and child health, both in the United States (Meara 2001; Currie and Moretti 2003) and in developing countries (Strauss and Thomas 1995). More educated mothers are

TABLE 2.3 / Effect of Education by Gender, Income, and Age for Selected Outcomes

	All	Male	Female	White	Black	Income at Least 20,000	Income Less than 20,000
Five-year mortality							
	−0.002	−0.002	−0.001**	−0.001	−0.002	−0.001	−0.002
	(0.0002)	(0.0003)	(0.0002)	(0.0002)	(0.0006)	(0.0002)	(0.0005)
	[−3.92%]	[−3.17%]	[−1.78%]	[−2.33%]	[−2.11%]	[−2.44%]	[−1.53%]
Any functional limitations							
	−0.016	−0.014	−0.018	−0.018	−0.012	−0.013	−0.003**
	(0.001)	(0.001)	(0.002)	(0.001)	(0.003)	(0.001)	(0.002)
	[−4.94%]	[−4.95%]	[−4.93%]	[−5.21%]	[−5.81%]	[−4.68%]	[−0.62%]
In fair or poor health							
	−0.015	−0.013	−0.017	−0.015	−0.022**	−0.008	−0.021**
	(0.001)	(0.001)	(0.001)	(0.001)	(0.002)	(0.001)	(0.001)
	[−12.21%]	[−11.63%]	[−12.61%]	[−12.93%]	[−7.44%]	[−11.28%]	[−8.85%]
Depression scale (0 = lowest, 16 = highest)							
	−0.127	−0.093	−0.161**	−0.132	−0.138	−0.101	−0.074
	(0.007)	(0.009)	(0.010)	(0.008)	(0.019)	(0.008)	(0.014)
	[−10.5%]	[−9.0%]	[−11.9%]	[−13.2%]	[−10.5%]	[−10.1%]	[−3.6%]
Obese (BMI greater or equal to 30)							
	−0.013	−0.009	−0.017**	−0.013	−0.012	−0.014	−0.005**
	(0.001)	(0.001)	(0.001)	(0.001)	(0.003)	(0.001)	(0.002)
	[−5.69%]	[−4.00%]	[−7.52%]	[−5.98%]	[−4.11%]	[−6.63%]	[−2.04%]
Moderate activity							
	0.042	0.043	0.04	0.045	0.035	0.041	0.027**
	(0.001)	(0.002)	(0.002)	(0.002)	(0.004)	(0.002)	(0.002)
	[8.14%]	[8.36%]	[7.95%]	[8.43%]	[11.23%]	[7.47%]	[7.46%]
Current smoker							
	−0.024	−0.03	−0.018**	−0.024	−0.019**	−0.028	−0.008**
	(0.001)	(0.002)	(0.001)	(0.001)	(0.003)	(0.001)	(0.002)
	[−9.25%]	[−10.4%]	[−7.78%]	[−9.54%]	[−8.49%]	[−11.71%]	[−2.70%]
Number of days had five or more drinks past year							
	−1.744	−2.556	−0.450**	−1.888	−2.478	1.571	−1.257
	(0.170)	(0.275)	(0.095)	(0.197))	(0.553)	(0.178)	(0.335)
	[−15.8%]	[−14.1%]	[−13.4%]	[−17.6%]	[−18.6%]	[−15.4%]	[−6.9%]
Ever had colorectal screening (age forty or older)							
	0.022	0.027	0.017	0.024	0.014	0.024	0.014**
	(0.001)	(0.002)	(0.002)	(0.002)	(0.003)	(0.002)	(0.002)
	[7.39%]	[8.83%]	[5.96%]	[7.86%]	[10.77%]	[8.16%]	[4.73%]
Always wear seat belt							
	0.03	0.031	0.029	0.032	0.019**	0.032	0.017**
	(0.001)	(0.002)	(0.001)	(0.001)	(0.003)	(0.002)	(0.002)
	[4.32%]	[4.83%]	[3.97%]	[4.62%]	[5.40%]	[4.51%]	[2.84%]
Has smoke detector							
	0.021	0.021	0.02	0.019	0.034**	0.014	0.02**
	(0.001)	(0.001)	(0.001)	(0.001)	(0.003)	(0.001)	(0.002)
	[2.60%]	[2.70%]	[2.50%]	[2.39%]	[2.69%]	[1.63%]	[2.92%]

Source: Authors' compilation.
Note: OLS coefficients or marginal effects with standard errors in parentheses. Brackets express the coefficient as a percentage of the variable mean. Asterisks are for tests of equality between coefficients: ** 5 percent.

less likely to have low- or very low-birthweight babies, and their babies are less likely to die within their first year of life. These effects persist well into adulthood: Anne Case, Angela Fertig, and Christina Paxson (2005) find that mother's education predicts self-reported health at age forty-two.

Recent research further suggests that more educated children have an effect on the health of their parents: Erica Field (2005) finds that parents of individuals who obtained more schooling were subsequently more likely to stop smoking.

It is also possible that having an educated spouse positively affects health. For example, Grace Egeland and colleagues (2002), as well as H. Bosma and colleagues (1995), find that even controlling for an individual's own education, those who are married to more educated spouses have lower mortality rates (although this finding is not universal; for example, see Suarez and Barrett-Connor 1984). Having a more educated spouse is also associated with better health and health behaviors such as smoking and excessive drinking (Monden et al. 2003). Of course it is difficult to know whether this relationship is driven by assortative mating or whether it reflects a causal effect.

IS THE EFFECT OF EDUCATION ON HEALTH CAUSAL?

In a very broad sense, there are three possible reasons for the link between health and education: One possibility is that poor health leads to low levels of schooling. Another possibility is that increasing education improves health. Lastly, there may be external factors that increase both schooling and health. It is important for policy to understand how much of the observed correlation between education and health can be explained by each of these explanations. Subsidies for schooling would only be effective in improving the health of the population if in fact education causes health.

A causal relationship from health to education could result from experiences during childhood if children in poor health obtain less schooling and they are also more likely to be unhealthy adults. For example, children that are born with low or very low birthweight (a health marker at birth) obtain less schooling that those born with greater weights (Black, Devereux, and Salvanes 2005) (this is even true among twins; Behrman and Rosenzweig 2004). Low birthweight is also predictive of poor health later in adulthood (Barker 1995; Roseboom et al. 2001). Similarly, older children who are sick or malnourished during childhood are more likely to miss school, less likely to learn while in school, and ultimately obtain fewer years of schooling (Case, Fertig, and Paxson 2005). Sick children are also more likely to become sick adults (Case, Lubotsky, and Paxson 2002). Edward Miguel and Michael Kremer (2004) and Hoyt Bleakley (2002) show that provision of deworming drugs significantly increased years of schooling in contemporary Kenya and the prewar American South, respectively.

What is not clear is the extent to which the observed correlation between education and health in the current United States is driven by the effects of disease on children's development. We doubt this can be the entire explanation. If this was important, one would expect the education gradient to be diminishing over time: very few children in the United States today are unable to attend school because of their health. On the contrary, the education gradient is rising.

Unobserved factors such as family background, genetic traits, or other individual differences such as the ability to delay gratification could also explain why the more educated are healthier. For example, richer parents are more likely to invest more in their children's health and in their education. Smarter individuals may be more likely to obtain more schooling and also to take better care of themselves. Another often-cited possibility is that individuals with lower discount rates (that is, those who are more patient) are more likely to invest more heavily in both education and health (Fuchs 1982).

Although in principle any of these external factors could account for the entirety of the correlation, there are reasons to be skeptical. Previous attempts to control for these factors have generally found that they cannot explain the entire effect of education on health. To look at this further, we added measures of family background and individual characteristics to our NHIS results. Column 2 of tables 1 and 2 adds controls for Hispanic ethnicity, family income, family size, major activity, region, metropolitan statistical area (MSA), marital status, and health insurance coverage. Adding these measures lowers the effect of education—on average the effect of education declines by about 38 percent for health measures and about 28 percent for health behaviors[6]—but it generally remains large and significant (similar to findings in Elo and Preston 1996).

The final possibility is that more or better education leads to improved health. Some recent evidence from quasi-natural experiments suggests that at least part of the correlation between education and health is indeed causal.

One set of studies focused on the correlation between education and health measures in adulthood. To obtain a causal estimate of education, these studies looked to see if individuals who were forced to go to school through various policies were subsequently healthier than those who were not. Adriana Lleras-Muney (2005) considers the case of the United States in the first half of the twentieth century, when many states increased the number of years children were required to attend school. This study shows that individuals born in states which require more years of school obtained more education and, conditional on surviving to adulthood, they also had substantially lower mortality rates much later in life. Similarly, Philip Oreopolous (2003), Jacob Nielsen Arendt (2005), and Jelena Spasojevic (2003) find that increases in minimum schooling laws in England and Ireland (Oreopolous), Denmark (Arendt), and Sweden (Spasojevic) respectively improved the health of the population. Other studies provide additional quasi-experimental evidence that education improves health (Grossman, forthcoming), but only for primary and secondary schooling.

There is also evidence of a causal effect of maternal education on infant health. Janet Currie and Enrico Moretti (2003) look at the effect of increases in the number of colleges (which lowers the cost of attending school) on women's educational attainment and their infants' health. They find that women in counties where colleges opened were more likely to attend college and had healthier babies. These health improvements resulted in part because these women engaged in healthier practices during pregnancy (they were less likely to smoke and drink and obtained more prenatal care). Also, education altered their reproductive behavior: more educated women were more likely to be married at the time of birth and have fewer children.

The evidence from natural experiments supports the theory that there is a causal effect of education on health. It is important to note that all of these papers look at quantity of schooling—there is no evidence that we know of on the quality of education.[7] There is also no causal evidence on whether the content of education matters for health (for example, whether the returns to vocational versus academic curricula are different, or whether it matters whether individuals major in science or humanities). Moreover these papers do not entirely explain why education improves health, although several theories have been proposed about how more education can result in better health.

We also note another drawback of these natural experiments: they rely on manipulations that affect individuals whose return to schooling is likely to be different from the average returns of the population. For example, compulsory schooling laws were intended to increase the education of those at the lower end of the distribution of education; they most likely had no impact on those who were planning to go to college. This makes it difficult to predict the effect of programs that affect everyone in the population or that are directed toward different populations. Using the results from these studies, it is therefore not possible either to quantify how much of the observed correlation between education and health in the population can be accounted for by reverse causality or by external factors.

POSSIBLE MECHANISMS FOR THE RELATIONSHIP BETWEEN EDUCATION AND HEALTH

The central question raised by these results is *why* education affects health. Without a clear understanding of this, it is difficult to identify which interventions will be most effective.

Income and Access to Health Care

Education may improve health simply because it results in greater resources in general, which include access to health care. This is perhaps the most obvious economic explanation. The fact that the health returns to education increased in the 1980s and 1990s at the same time that the labor returns to education rose (Autor, Katz, and Kearney 2005) is consistent with this theory. However, this theory is not the whole of the explanation for several reasons. First, as documented in tables 1 and 2, controlling for income and health insurance (and other basic predictors of labor market success such as marital status and ethnicity) does not seem to explain away the effect of education; rather, these variables, particularly income, account for about a third of the effect.[8] But because income is measured with substantial error, and because measures of permanent income are generally not available, it is possible that a larger fraction of the effect of education may be due to income.

However, it is unlikely that income and health care can *entirely* account for the association between education and health. Differences in health across education groups often emerge before the health care system becomes involved: evidence shows there are significant education differences in the incidence of disease and in the risk factors associated with disease, such as smoking. Also, as we showed in table 2.2, there are education gradients in seat-belt use, exercise, reading food labels, and other behaviors for which neither income nor health insurance is important. Finally, smoking, illegal drug use, and excessive drinking are more prevalent among the less educated, even though these behaviors are financially costly.

Labor Market

More highly educated individuals may have "better" jobs that, in addition to paying higher incomes and providing health insurance, offer safer work environments. But this too cannot be the entire explanation. Previous studies (Lahelma et al. 2004) find that controlling for job characteristics such as occupation is not sufficient to explain education health gradients. We reproduce these findings here. In both tables 1 and 2, we add controls for occupation and industry dummies (column 3). For the majority of health measures that we examine (table 2.1), adding these controls has very little effect on the coefficient of education, and in some cases the effect of education actually becomes stronger. The effect of education on health behaviors (table 2.2) is generally either reduced by adding these controls (for example, in the cases of smoking and days drinking), or it remains stable. But in all cases, the effect of education remains significant (except for marijuana use). Because there are significant health gradients for women as well as for men, and since gradients can be observed early in life, it is unlikely that current or past characteristics of the labor environment are at the root of education gradients, unless they operate, for example, through intergenerational transmission. Thus, although education changes an individual's labor-market experience, this does not appear to be the main mechanism by which education improves health.

These results also suggest that environmental exposure is not an important contributor to education gradients in health since occupation and industry do not affect our estimated coefficients much, and we obtain similar results when controlling for residential location. However we only observe job characteristics and geographic location at one point in time, and the effects of hazardous exposures may be cumulative and operate with long lags.

David Snowdon, in his famous series of studies (2001), finds that "the sisters [of Notre Dame] with a college degree has a much better chance of surviving to old age . . . [the sisters] had similar lifestyles whether or not they graduated from college: Income was not a factor, they did not smoke, and they shared virtually the same health care, housing and diet" (41). Interestingly, language ability upon entrance to the convent (for example, the complexity of sentences) predicted the onset of Alzheimer's disease, suggesting instead a role for cognition and information.

Value of the Future

Though income, health insurance, and other resource factors may not affect health per se, they may change an individual's incentives to invest in health. If education provides individuals with a better future along several dimensions—it gives access to more income, it makes one happier, and generally improves one's outlook on the future (in economic terms, it increases the present discounted value of future lifetime utility)—people may be more likely to invest in protecting that future. Similarly, in their theoretical model, Kevin Murphy and Robert Topel (2005) find that as incomes rise, willingness to pay for health improvements increases as well. This theory would also explain why the less educated are more likely to engage in riskier behaviors (the value of living to advanced ages is lower), and it is also consistent with smaller gradients for women and for blacks. This theory is difficult to test, so we do not have a sense about its quantitative importance.

Information and Cognitive Skills

Education can also provide individuals with better access to information and improved critical thinking skills (although note of course that those with higher skills may also be more likely to get more education). The more educated do appear to be better informed and to make use of new health-related information before others. For example, the educated were more likely to quit smoking after the 1964 Surgeon General's Report first publicized the dangers of smoking (de Walque 2004) Similarly, Damien de Walque (2005) finds that educated women in Uganda were more likely to use condoms and less likely to have AIDS (this relationship emerged only in 2000, after a decade of information campaigns; in 1990, education did not predict incidence of AIDS).

However, differences in information can explain only a small part of the differences across education groups (Meara 2001; Kenkel 1991). Today, most individuals are well aware of the dangers associated with smoking, and yet smoking is still more prevalent among the uneducated. The same is true of obesity, which is inversely related to education in women.

These results do not imply that health education should not be undertaken; reducing education gradients is only one of many possible objectives of policy interventions. Rather, it suggests that health education programs will not diminish education gradients in health; indeed, they may increase gradients, at least for several decades.

How information is used and the manner in which it is received matters. The more educated are more likely to trust science: according to a 1999 National Science Foundation survey (National Science Foundation 2000), 71 percent of those with a college degree or higher thought that the benefits of new technologies strongly outweigh the harmful results, whereas only 25 percent of those with less than a high school degree thought so. This may be due in part to the fact that more educated individuals are more likely to understand the nature of scientific inquiry.[9]

Education might matter for health not just because of the specific knowledge one obtains in school, but rather because education improves general skills, including critical thinking skills and decision-making abilities. Reading is one of those skills. Small studies find that patients with poor reading skills are less likely to understand discharge instructions after an emergency room visit (Spandorfer et al. 1995), and are less likely to know about their asthma condition or utilize their inhalers correctly (Williams et al. 1998). Education may improve decision making by teaching individuals how to avoid common errors in cognition, such as small sample biases, or by lowering deliberation time and costs.

More generally, the more educated could be better at learning. There is some suggestive evidence consistent with this hypothesis. Adriana Lleras-Muney and Frank Lichtenberg (2002) find that, controlling for income and insurance, the more educated are more likely to use drugs more recently approved by the Federal Drug Administration (FDA); this is only true for individuals who repeatedly purchase drugs for a given condition and thus have an opportunity to learn. Similarly, Darius Lakdawalla and Dana Goldman (2001), as well as Case, Fertig, and Paxson (2005), find that the health gradient is larger for chronic diseases, where learning over time is possible, than for acute diseases.

Alternatively, the more educated could have an advantage in using complex technologies. Mark Rosenzweig and T. Paul Schultz (1989) show that contraceptive success rates are identical for all women for "easy" contraception methods such as the pill, but the rhythm method is much more effective for educated women. Dana Goldman and James Smith (2002) report that more educated individuals are more likely to comply with AIDS and diabetes treatments, both of which are notoriously demanding. This may be true for some behaviors, where regular self-monitoring or therapy is required, but is unlikely to be the only mechanism. Many noncomplex health behaviors, such as seat-belt use, also have strong education gradients.

It seems that part of the gradient between education and health is a result of the cognitive skills that come with education (although no causal evidence is available). There are no estimates of the share of the education effect attributable to this channel however.

Preferences

Education may alter other important individual characteristics that affect health investments and ultimately health. Gary Becker and Casey Mulligan (1997) suggest that higher schooling causes lower discount rates. One possible mechanism is that education raises future income, thus encouraging individuals to invest in lowering their discount rate. Going to school is in itself an exercise in delaying gratification, so it may contribute to lower discount rates in that way. Data on discount rates by education are difficult to come by. The more educated appear to have lower discount rates, although the relationship is weak (Fuchs 1982). There is no evidence we know of that education lowers discount rates.

Alternatively, education could affect health through risk aversion. People who have more schooling could learn to dislike risk more. However, the empirical relationship between education and risk aversion appears to be U-shaped and thus inconsistent with health gradients: very high and very low education levels are associated with more risk taking, whereas individuals with moderate amounts of schooling are the most risk averse (Barsky, Juster, and Kimball 1997).

Moreover, the available evidence suggests that changes in preferences are not the main reason why education affects health. The few studies that we know of which have investigated this question by directly including measures of risk aversion (Fuchs 1982) and discount rates (Leigh 1990; Fuchs 1982) in models explaining health behaviors find that only a small portion of the education gradient is explained by differences in these preference parameters.[10] Of course it is worth keeping in mind that these parameters are difficult to measure. Also, economic analyses consider only single measures of risk aversion and time preferences, which are generally related to individual preferences over monetary outcomes. Risk preferences with respect to health and life may differ from risk preferences over money; the same may be true for discounting.

Rank

Education might matter for health because it changes one's relative position or rank in society, and rank by itself might affect health. Health in animals (Sapolsky 1993, 1998; Petticrew and Davey-Smith 2003) and perhaps in humans (Marmot 2002) depends on the relative position one has in the social distribution. It is hypothesized that this relationship emerges because individuals at the lower end of the hierarchy have less control over their lives and are constantly subjected to arbitrary demands by others, causing increases in stress and subsequently resulting in stress-related diseases. More educated individuals are indeed less likely to report negative emotions, including depressive symptoms, anxiety, and hostility, which are associated with worse health later in life (Adler et al. 1994; Gallo and Matthews 2003). When faced with negative life events, the more educated are less emotionally responsive as well (McLeod and Kessler 1990). They also report higher sense of control and higher self-esteem, which are associated with better health (Ross and Mirowsky 1999). In studies that document these correlations, it is not clear whether education leads to changes in rank, which in turn affects self-control, or whether self-control affects education and rank.

While the evidence for these theories is intriguing, it cannot be the entire explanation.[11] Life expectancy in the United States and other western countries has increased in the last thirty years, even though the levels of various likely stressors (such as income inequality, crime, and other measures of low social capital) have increased. Also, Bruce Link and Jo Phelan (1996) suggest that cardiovascular disease (which is argued to be correlated with stress) was more prevalent in high SES groups sixty years ago. More generally, they argue that there are gradients in diseases that are not known to be related to stress.

Social Networks

A different theory stresses social support systems: the more educated have larger social networks which provide financial, physical, and emotional support, and may in turn have a causal effect on health (Berkman 1995). The available evidence suggests that even though the more educated are more socially connected overall (for example, they have more friends and are more likely to be married), social networks do not appear to explain the association between health and measures of SES (Berkman and Syme 1979). A clinical trial conducted in the late 1990s found that initiation of cognitive behavioral therapy and antidepressant medication after people had a heart attack did not improve event-free survival (Berkman et al. 2003).

Beyond support, friends and family provide peer recognition or disapproval. Through this mechanism, peers can also have a large influence on negative behaviors, such as drinking and smoking. A large literature shows that individuals with friends who smoke, drink, do drugs, or commit suicide are more likely to engage in the same activities. Use of natural experiments suggests that at least part of this relationship is causal (Sacerdote 2001). If more educated people have more educated friends, who are more likely to behave healthily and value health, the peer effects of networks exacerbate the effects of an individual's own education. Although this does not explain why the more educated behave differently to begin with, it is important for policy to know whether there are indeed multiplier effects.

Other Theories

Inspired by Link and Phelan (1995), David Cutler, Angus Deaton, and Adriana Lleras-Muney (2006) propose that gradients in health arise or increase when there is knowledge and technology available to prevent or treat disease (a similar theory is tested in Glied and Lleras-Muney 2003),[12] because there is a universal demand for better health; those with more education (or more income or power) are likely to use new knowledge and new techniques more rapidly and more effectively. This idea is consistent with the hypothesis of the fundamental causes of disease (Link and Phelan 1995), which suggests that education gives an individual "a wide range of serviceable resources, including money, knowledge, prestige, power and beneficial social conditions, that can be used to one's health advantage" (Link and Phelan 2005, 73). In the absence of knowledge and technology, gradients may exist for other reasons (such as stress) or may even be reversed (as is the case with cancers of the reproductive system among women). However, this suggests that, in the absence of policies that specifically address health inequalities, increases in medical innovation will result in larger, not smaller, gradients (van Doorslaer et al. 1997). This theory is consistent with the evidence that health is improving for all education groups but more so for the more educated. However, this theory does not explain why there are gradients in diseases with no treatment, nor does it explain why differences in smoking and seat-belt use have persisted so long.

Summary

Several mechanisms are likely to be involved in better health to some degree and for at least some outcomes, though the relative magnitude of different explanations is unknown. Some hypotheses seem unlikely to be very important: presence of health insurance, preferences over time, and risk do not appear to account for a good part of the association between education and health. Differences in information and cognition, especially in the presence of medical innovations may matter quite a bit, though we are not completely certain about the magnitude of the effect. The role of stress is uncertain.

POLICY IMPLICATIONS

People value health highly. As a result, the health returns to education can outweigh even the financial returns. Many estimates suggest that a year of education increases earnings by about 10 percent (or perhaps eighty thousand dollars in present value over the course of a lifetime). We calculate rough estimates of the monetary returns of one more year of schooling in terms of increased life expectancy. These numbers are only suggestive, as they are based on multiple assumptions (most importantly, we use OLS estimates of the effect of education on mortality and interpret them as causal effects). Using data from the National Longitudinal Mortality Study (NLMS) we find that one more year of education increases life expectancy by 0.18 years if we use a 3 percent discounting rate; or by 0.6 years without any discounting (it is not clear that one would want to discount health improvements in the same manner one discounts income streams over time). Assuming that a year of health is worth $75,000—a relatively conservative value (Cutler 2004)—the increased life expectancy translates into approximately $13,500 to $44,000 in present value. These rough calculations suggest that the health returns to education increase the total returns to education by at least 15 percent, and perhaps by as much as 55 percent. The actual returns are possibly higher since our calculations do not take into account the possibility that education improves the quality (not just the quantity) of life. Such returns suggest public policy should do more to promote education.

Even if we accept that a large part of the association between education and health is causal, and that increasing educational attainment improves health, some important questions remain before we can have an appropriate policy response. Causal effects of education on health would call for education subsidies only to the extent that there is a market failure and individuals are investing at suboptimal levels; otherwise, individuals would base their education decisions on the health benefits along with the financial benefits. Possible rationales for education subsidies include the idea that individuals may be unaware of the health benefits of education when they make their education decisions, that they are constrained by credit, that some groups do not know about or are excluded from higher education, or that there are externalities to education and health beyond the individual affected.[13] Although there are known externalities in the case of infectious diseases, these are a relatively small share of the health profile in the United States today, where most of the health benefits to education are in reduced rates of chronic disease. There is substantial evidence for the effects of mother's education on children's health; whether one considers these externalities or not is somewhat subject to debate. There may be other externalities across individuals, but causal estimates of these are not available. Whether the other market failures exist or not is empirically less clear. The results in Adriana Lleras-Muney's study (2005) do suggest individuals are not fully aware of the health returns to education, since compulsory schooling yielded such large returns in terms of mortality. Oreopoulos (2003) also finds evidence that individuals' education investments are suboptimal given the rate of return. It is not known whether this is due to lack of information or to credit constraints.

The issue of causality is also important. Although there is evidence of causal effects of education on health at lower levels of schooling, it is not known if the education returns observed after that level are causal. Nor is it known if there are returns to higher quality education. Better understanding of the heterogeneity of the returns to education is also needed. In order to improve health, it may prove more cost effective to target populations with the largest returns to health, even though this may exacerbate inequities.

In addition, understanding the mechanism by which education affects health is important for policy. It may be more cost effective to tap the mechanism than to increase educational attainment. For example if the entire education effect operated through income, and income improved health, then it would possibly be cheaper to transfer income directly, rather than to subsidize schooling. But increasing educational attainment may prove to be the correct policy response if, for example, there is no alternative (or no cheaper alternative) method to acquire the skills that ultimately affect health.

Finally, understanding the general equilibrium effects is important as well. If the effect of education operates mainly through income, increasing the education level of those with the least education may lower the income returns to schooling, and thus ultimately may decrease the corresponding health benefits. On the other hand, if the effect operates mainly through the acquisition of information in school, this would not be the case. Spillovers would also increase the returns to education.

In spite of these caveats, education policies have the potential to have a substantial effect on health. Assuming that the observed correlations between education and health are long-term causal effects from education to health, and that the relationship is linear and identical across gender, race, and other groups, we can roughly calculate the health returns of education policies. Susan Dynarski (2003) finds that offering one thousand dollars (in 1998 dollars) of grant aid results in an increase in education of 0.16 years, which translates into 0.03 to 0.10 years of additional life (depending on discounting). This is roughly $2,250 to $7,200 in present value. This is a very large rate of return. If there is any uncertainty about whether education truly improves health, it is far better to err on the side of more subsidies as opposed to less.

NOTES

1. These relationships have been extensively documented elsewhere. A few references follow: For mortality in the United States, see Evelyn Kitagawa and Philip Hauser (1973), Bruce Christenson and Nan Johnson (1995), Angus Deaton and Christina Paxson (2001), and Irma Elo and Samuel Preston (1996); for risk factors, see Mark Berger and J. Paul Leigh (1989), Jeffrey Sobel and Albert J. Stunkard (1989), Nancy Adler et al. (1994); for diseases and morbidity, see Theodore Pincus, Leigh F. Callahan, and Richard V. Burkhauser (1987); for health behaviors, see William Sander (1995), Donald Kenkel (1991), Ellen Meara (2001), and J. Paul Leigh and Rachna Dhir (1997). Several review papers also report these associations; for example, see Michael Grossman (forthcoming).

2. For a discussion of initiatives in the UK, see http://www.dh.gov.uk/PolicyAndGuidance/HealthAndSocialCareTopics/HealthInequalities/fs/en.

3. We draw on data from the 1990, 1991, and 2000 waves of the National Health Interview Survey (NHIS). Whenever possible, we use data from the 2000 survey, which allow us to control for health insurance coverage. (The 1990 and 1991 surveys did not collect health insurance data.) From 1990, we use the Health Promotion and Disease Prevention Supplement to analyze self-reports of high cholesterol, fair or poor health, and attempted smoking cessation, in addition to all outcomes related to household safety, automobile safety, and control of hypertension. All data on illegal drug use are drawn from the Drug and Alcohol Use Supplement to the 1991 NHIS. The remaining outcome variables are from the Person and Adult Sample of the 2000 NHIS. We analyze data on individuals at least twenty-five years old, dropping observations with missing data for any of the covariates. For our mortality analyses, we also link the 1990 data to the National Death Index (NDI), a centralized, nationwide database of information from death certificates. Individuals from the NHIS missing key identification data were deemed ineligible by the NDI, so we omit them from our analyses. Our mortality measure is a binary indicator of death from any cause before the start of 1996.

   Most of our other outcomes are self-explanatory, but a few require a bit more clarification on details. Self-reports of acute or chronic disease diagnoses came from questions of the form, "Has a doctor ever told you that you have . . . ?" The heart condition variable reflects whether the respondent has ever been diagnosed with hypertension, coronary heart disease, angina, a heart attack, or any other heart condition or disease. The pain variable reflects whether the respondent had joint aches in the past twelve months or neck pain, lower back pain, jaw pain, or severe headaches in the past three months. The sickness variable reflects whether the respondent had a cold or stomach problems over the past two weeks. Mental health outcomes were constructed by summing the respondent's subjective assessments of feelings of nervousness, restlessness, sadness, hopelessness, effort, and worthlessness. The respondent estimated how often he or she had experienced each of these affective states over the past thirty days: none of the time, a little of the time, some of the time, most of the time, or all of the time. These responses were coded on a scale from zero to four, respectively, and then summed to produce scales of anxiety (the sum of nervousness and restlessness) and depression (the sum of sadness, hopelessness, effort, and worthlessness). With regard to depression interfering with the respondent's life, the relevant question was asked only of individuals who reported experiencing at least one negative affective state, most or all of the time.

4. For Europe the relationship has been documented in various papers by the Mackenbach group. For example, for Finland, Norway, Italy, the Czech Republic, Hungary, and Estonia, see Johan Mackenbach et al. (1999); for Netherlands, Sweden, Denmark, Norway, France, Italy, Finland, and the United Kingdom, see Anton Kunst and Johan Mackenbach (1994). For Switzerland, see Matthias Bopp and Christoph Minder (2003).

5. Samuel Preston and Irma Elo (1995) find increasing education gradients in the United States for males but not for females.

6. We calculated the average reduction in the coefficient of education only among measures for which the coefficient of education was significant and for which education improved the outcome (for health outcomes, we excluded cancer, hepatitis, chicken pox, hay fever, and asthma self reports; among behaviors, we excluded recent use of marijuana and cocaine, lead test in home, had an STD in past five years, behaviors among diabetics, and high blood pressure cured).

7. However, Catherine Ross and John Mirowsky (1999) find that college selectivity, in addition to years of schooling, is predictive of health.

8. Clearly, it may not be legitimate to include these as controls since both income and insurance could be endogenous, determined by health and health behaviors.

9. According to the same survey, 53 percent of those with more than a college degree understand the nature of scientific inquiry (measured by individuals' understanding of the value of randomized experiments and of probabilities), whereas only 4 percent of those with less than a high school degree do.

10. Paul Leigh (1990) finds that controlling for time and risk preferences reduces the effect of education on seat-belt use by 25 to 35 percent. He uses several proxies for both time preferences and risk aversion; it is not clear that they are only measuring the parameters of interest. And he only looks at seat-belt use. Victor Fuchs (1982) finds almost no reduction of the effect of education on composite measures of self-reported health.

11. It is worth noting that this theory is difficult to test. For example, it is not clear whether ordering alone within the hierarchy matters, or whether distance would matter as well. Also, although in social animals rank may be easily defined (groups tend to be small and hierarchies uniquely defined), it is much less clear how to measure rank in modern industrial societies. There are a variety of reference groups that individuals may fit into, defined by their workplace, educational status, or geographic location, and individuals may have different ranks within each of these groups simultaneously (Deaton and Paxson 1999).

12. Sherry Glied and Adriana Lleras-Muney (2003) provide suggestive evidence that education gradients are larger for diseases with more medical progress, although a substantial part of the gradient remains even after accounting for medical progress and its interaction with education.

13. Some believe that disparities by themselves are externalities if people do not enjoy living in an unequal society. Others have argued that inequality leads to worse health outcomes. Both of these arguments are controversial, so we do not push these factors greatly.

REFERENCES

Adler, Nancy E., Thomas Boyce, Margaret A. Chesney, Sheldon Cohen, Susan Folkman; Robert L. Kahn; S. Leonard Syme. 1994. "Socioeconomic Status and Health, the Challenge of the Gradient." *American Psychologist* 49(1): 15–24.

Arendt, Jacob Nielsen. 2005. "Does Education Cause Better Health? A Panel Data Analysis Using School Reform for Identification." *Economics of Education Review* 24(2): 149–60.

Autor, David, Lawrence F. Katz, and Melissa S. Kearney. 2005. "Trends in U.S. Wage Inequality: Re-Assessing the Revisionists." National Bureau of Economic Research working paper No. 11627. National Bureau of Economic Research, Cambridge, Mass.

Barker, David J. P. 1995. "Fetal Origins of Coronary Disease." *British Medical Journal* 311(6998): 171–4.

Barrow, Lisa, and Cecilia Elena Rouse. 2005. "Do Returns to Schooling Differ by Race and Ethnicity?" *American Economic Review* 95(2): 83–87.

Barsky, Robert B., F. Thomas Juster, and Miles S. Kimball. 1997. "Preference Parameters and Behavioral Heterogeneity: An Experimental Approach in the Health and Retirement Study." *Quarterly Journal of Economics* 112(2): 537–79.

Becker, Gary S., and Casey B. Mulligan. 1997. "The Endogenous Determination of Time Preference." *Quarterly Journal of Economics* 112(3): 729–58.

Behrman, Jere R., and Mark R. Rosenzweig. 2004. "Returns to Birthweight." *Review of Economics and Statistics* 86(2): 586–601.

Berger, Mark C., and J. Paul Leigh. 1989. "Schooling, Self Selection and Health." *Journal of Human Resources* 24(3) 433–55.

Berkman, Lisa F. 1995. "The Role of Social Relations in Health Promotion" *Psychosomatic Medicine* 57(3): 245–54.

Berkman, Lisa F., and S. Leonard Syme. 1979. "Social Networks, Host Resistance and Mortality: A Nine Year Follow-up Study of Alameda County Residents." *American Journal of Epidemiology* 109(2): 186–204.

Berkman, Lisa F., James Blumenthal, Matthew Burg, Robert M. Carney, Diane Catellier, Marie J. Cowan, Susan M. Czajkowski, Robert DeBusk, James Hosking, Allan Jaffee, Peter G. Kaufmann, Pamela Mitchell, James Norman, Lynda H. Powell, James M. Raczynski, and Neil Schneiderman. 2003. "Effects of Treating Depression and Low Perceived Social Support on Clinical Events After Myocardial Infarction: The Enhancing Recovery in Coronary Heart Disease Patients (ENRICHD) Randomized Trial." *Journal of the American Medical Association* 289(23): 3106–16.

Black, Sandra E., Paul J. Devereux, and Kjell Salvanes. 2005. "From the Cradle to the Labor Market? The Effect of Birth Weight on Adult Outcomes." National Bureau of Economic Research Working Paper No. 11796. National Bureau of Economic Research, Cambridge, Mass.

Bleakley, Hoyt. 2002. "Disease and Development: Evidence from Hookworm Eradication in the American South." Mimeo. Population Research Center, NORC, University of Chicago.

Bopp, Matthias, and Christoph E. Minder. 2003. "Mortality by Education in German Speaking Switzerland, 1990–1997: Results from the Swiss National Cohort." *International Journal of Epidemiology* 32(3): 346–54.

Bosma, H., A. Appels, F. Sturmans, V. Grabauskas, and A. Gostautas. 1995. "Educational Level of Spouses and Risk of Mortality." *International Journal of Epidemiology* 24(1): 119–26.

Case, Anne, Angela Fertig, and Christina Paxson. 2005. "The Lasting Impact of Childhood Health and Circumstance." *Journal of Health Economics* 24(2): 365–89.

Case, Anne, Darren Lubotsky, and Christina Paxson. 2002. "Economic Status and Health in Childhood: The Origins of the Gradient." *American Economic Review* 92(5): 1308–34.

Christenson, Bruce, and Nan E. Johnson. 1995. "Educational Inequality in Adult Mortality: An Assessment with Death Certificate Data from Michigan." *Demography* 32(2): 215–29.

Currie, Janet, and Enrico Moretti. 2003. "Mother's Education and the Intergenerational Transmission of Human Capital: Evidence from College Openings." *Quarterly Journal of Economics* 123(4): 1495–1532.

Cutler, David. 2004. *Your Money or Your Life: Strong Medicine for America's Health Care System.* New York: Oxford University Press.

Cutler, David M., and Edward Glaeser. 2005. "What Explains Differences in Smoking, Drinking, and Other Health Related Behaviors?" 95(2): 238–42.

Cutler, David, Angus Deaton, and Adriana Lleras-Muney. 2006. "The Determinants of Mortality." *Journal of Economic Perspectives* 20(3): 97–120.

de Walque, Damien. 2004. "Education, Information and Smoking Decisions: Evidence from Smoking Histories, 1940–2000." World Bank Working Paper No. 3362. Washington: World Bank.

———. 2005. "How Does the Impact of an HIV/AIDS Information Campaign Vary with Educational Attainment? Evidence from Rural Uganda." World Bank Working Paper No. 3289. Washington: World Bank.

Deaton, Angus, and Christina Paxson. 1999. "Mortality, Education, Income, and Inequality Among America Cohorts." In *The Economics of Aging*, Volume 8, edited by David Wise. Chicago, Ill.: University of Chicago Press.

———. 2001. "Mortality, Education, Income and Inequality Among American Cohorts." In *Themes in the Economics of Aging*, edited by David Wise. Chicago, Ill.: Chicago University Press, for NBER.

Dynarski, Susan M. 2003. "Does Aid Matter? Measuring the Effect of Student Aid on College Attendance and Completion." *American Economic Review* 93(1): 279–88.

Egeland, Grace M., Aage Tverdal, Haakon E. Meyer, and Randi Selmer. 2002. "A Man's Heart and a Wife's Education: 12 Year Coronary Heart Disease Mortality Follow-up in Norwegian Men." *International Journal of Epidemiology* 31(4): 799–805.

Elo, Irma T., and Samuel H. Preston. 1996. "Educational Differentials in Mortality: United States, 1979–85." *Social Science and Medicine* 42(1): 47–57.

Field, Erica. 2005. "Are There Upward Intergenerational Education Spillovers on Health? The Impact of Children's Education on Parents' Smoking Cessation." Mimeo. Harvard University.

Fuchs, Victor R. 1982. "Time Preference and Health: An Exploratory Study." In *Economic Aspects of Health*, edited by Victor R. Fuchs. Chicago, Ill.: University of Chicago Press.

Gallo, Linda C., and Karen A. Matthews. 2003. "Understanding the Association Between Socioeconomic Status and Physical Health: Do Negative Emotions Play a Role?" *Psychological Bulletin* 129(1): 10–51

Glied, Sherry, and Adriana Lleras-Muney. 2003. "Health Inequality, Education and Medical Innovation." National Bureau of Economic Research Working Paper No. 9738. National Bureau of Economic Research, Cambridge, Mass.

Goesling, Brian. 2005. "The Rising Significance of Education for Health?" *Social Forces* 85(4): 1621–44.

Goldman, Dana P., and James P. Smith. 2002. "Can Patient Self-Management Explain the SES Health Gradient." *Proceedings of the National Academy of Science* 99(16): 10929–34.

Grossman, Michael. Forthcoming. "Education and Nonmarket Outcomes." In *Handbook of the Economics of Education*, edited by Eric Hanushek and Finis Welch. Amsterdam: Elsevier.

Hurt, Lisa S., Carine Rossmands, and Somnath Saha. 2004. "Effects of Education and Other Socioeconomic Factors in Middle Age Mortality in Rural Bangladesh." *Journal of Epidemiology and Community Health* 58(4): 315–20.

Kenkel, Donald. 1991. "Health Behavior, Health Knowledge and Schooling." *Journal of Political Economy* 99(2): 287–305.

Khang, Young-Ho, John W. Lynch, and George A. Kaplan. 2004. "Health Inequalities in Korea: Age- and Sex-Specific Educational Differences in the 10 Leading Causes of Death." *International Journal of Epidemiology* 33(2): 299–308.

Kitagawa, Evelyn M., and Philip M. Hauser. 1973. *Differential Mortality in the United States: A Study in Socioeconomic Epidemiology*. Cambridge, Mass.: Harvard University Press.

Kunst, Anton E., and Johan P. Mackenbach. 1994. "The Size of Mortality Differences Associated with Educational Level in Nine Industrialized Countries." *American Journal of Public Health* 84(6): 932–7.

Kunst, Anton E., Vivan Bos, Otto Andersen, Mario Cardano, Giuseppe Costa, Seeromanie Harding, Örjan Hemström, Richard Layte, Enrique Regidor, Alison Reid, Paula Santana, Tapani Valkonen, and Johan P. Mackenbach. 2002. "Monitoring of Trends in Socioeconomic Inequalities in Mortality: Experiences from a European Project." Paper presented to the IUSSP, Seminar on Determinants of Diverging Trends in Mortality. Rostock, Germany, June 19–21, 2002.

Lahelma, Eero, Pekka Martikainen, Elina Laaksonen, and Akseli Aittomaki. 2004. "Pathways Between Socioeconomic Determinants of Health." *Journal of Epidemiology and Community Health* 58(4): 327–32.

Lakdawalla, Darius, and Dana Goldman. 2001. "Understanding Health Disparities Across Education Groups." National Bureau of Economic Research Working Paper No. 8328. National Bureau of Economic Research, Cambridge, Mass.

Leigh, J. Paul. 1990. "Schooling and Seat-belt Use." *Southern Economics Journal* 57(1): 195–207.

Leigh, J. Paul, and Rachna Dhir. 1997. "Schooling and Frailty Among Seniors."*Economics of Education Review* 16(1): 45–57.

Liang, Jersey, John F. McCarthy, Arvind Jain, Neal Krause, Joan M. Bennett, and Shengzu Gu. 2000. "Socioeconomic Gradient in Old Age Mortality in Wuhan, China." *Journals of Gerontology Series B: Psychological Sciences and Social Sciences* 55(4): S222–33

Link, Bruce G., and Jo Phelan. 1995. "Social Conditions as the Fundamental Causes of Disease." *Journal of Health and Social Behavior* 35(Extra Issue): 80–94.

———. 1996. "Understanding Sociodemographic Differences in Health: The Role of Fundamental Social Causes." *American Journal of Public Health* 86(4): 471–3.

———. 2005. "Fundamental Sources of Health Inequalities." In *Policy Challenges in Modern Health Care*, edited by David Mechanic, Lynn B. Rotgut, David C. Colby, and James R. Knickman. New Brunswick, N.J.: Rutgers University Press.

Lleras-Muney, Adriana. 2005. "The Relationship Between Education and Adult Mortality in the United States." *Review of Economic Studies* 72(1): 189–221

Lleras-Muney, Adriana, and Frank R. Lichtenberg. 2002. "The Effect of Education on Medical Technology Adoption: Are the More Educated More Likely to Use New Drugs?" National Bureau of Economic Research Working Paper No. 9185. National Bureau of Economic Research, Cambridge, Mass.

Lyert, Donna L., Elizabeth Arias, Betty L. Smith, Sherry L. Murphy, Kenneth D. Kochanek. 2001. "Deaths: Final Data for 1999." Washington: Centers for Disease Control and Prevention.

Lynch, Scott M. 2003. "Cohort and Life Course Patterns in the Relationship Between Education and Health: A Hierarchical Approach." *Demography* 40(2): 309–31.

Mackenbach, Johan P., Anton E. Kunst, Feikje Groenhof, Jens-Kristian Borgan, Giuseppe Costa, Fabrizio Gaffiano, Peter Jozan, Mall Leinsalu, Pekka Martikainen, Jitka Rychtarikova, and Tapani Valkonen. 1999. "Socioeconomic Inequalities in Mortality Among Women and Among Men: An International Study." *American Journal of Public Health* 189(23): 1800–6

Mackenbach, Johan P., Vivan Bos, Otto Anderson, Mario Cardano, Giuseppe Costa, Seeromanie Harding, Alison Reid, Orjan Hemstrom, Tapani Valkonen, and Anton E. Kunst. 2003. "Widening Socioeconomic Inequalities in Mortality in Six Western European Countries." *International Journal of Epidemiology* 32(5): 830–7.

Manor, Orly, Avi Eisenbach, Eric Paritz, and Yechiel Friedlander. 1999. "Mortality Differentials Among Israeli Men." *American Journal of Public Health* 89(12): 1807–13.

Marmot, Michael G. 1994. "Social Differences in Health Within and Between Populations." *Daedalus* (Fall): 61–74.

———. 2002. "The Influence of Income on Health: Views of an Epidemiologist." *Health Affairs* 21(2): 31–46.

McLeod, Jane, and Ronald Kessler. 1990. "Socioeconomic Status Differences in Vulnerability to Undesirable Life Events." *Journal of Health and Social Behavior* 31(2): 162–72.

Meara, Ellen. 2001. "Why Is Health Related to Socio-Economic Status? The Case of Pregnancy and Low Birth Weight." National Bureau of Economic Research Working Paper No. 8321. National Bureau of Economic Research, Cambridge, Mass.

Miguel, Edward, and Michael Kremer. 2004. "Worms: Identifying Impacts on Education and Health the Presence of Treatment Externalities." *Econometrica* 72(1): 159–217.

Monden, Christian W.S., Frank van Lenthe, Nan Dirk De Graaf, and Gerbert Kraaykamp. 2003. "Partner's Own Education: Does Who You Live with Matter for Self-Assessed Health, Smoking and Excessive Alcohol Consumption?" *Social Science and Medicine* 57(10): 1901–12.

Murphy, Kevin M., and Robert H. Topel. "The Value of Health and Longevity." *Journal of Political Economy* 114(5): 871–904.

Mustard, Cameron A., Shelley Derksen, Jean-Marie Berthelot, Michael Wolfson, and Leslie L. Roos. 1997. "Age Specific Education and Income Gradient in Morbidity and Mortality in a Canadian Province." *Social Science and Medicine* 45(3): 383–97.

National Science Foundation. 2000. *Science and Engineering Indicators, 2000.* Washington: National Science Foundation, NSB 00–87.

Oreopoulos, Philip. 2003. "Do Dropouts Drop Out Too Soon? Wealth, Health, and Happiness from Compulsory Schooling." Mimeo, University of Toronto.

Pamuk, Elsie, D. Makus, K. Heck, C. Reuben, K. Lochner. 1998. *Socioeconomic Status and Health Chartbook. Health, United States, 1998.* Hyattsville, Md.: National Center for Health Statistics.

Pappas, Gregory, Susan Queen, Wolber Hadden, and Grail Fisher. 1993. "The Increasing Disparity in Mortality Between Socioeconomic Groups in the United States, 1960 and 1986." *New England Journal of Medicine* 329(2): 103–9.

Petticrew, Mark, and George Davey-Smith. 2003. "Monkey Business: What Do Primate Studies of Social Hierarchies, Stress, and the Development of CHD Tell Us About Humans?" *Journal of Epidemiological Community Health* 57(Supplment 1): A1–21.

Pincus, Theodore, Leigh F. Callahan, and Richard V. Burkhauser. 1987. "Most Chronic Diseases Are Reported More Frequently by Individuals with Fewer than 12 Years of Formal Education in the Age 18–64 U.S. Population." *Journal of Chronic Diseases* 40(9): 865–74.

Preston, Samuel H., and Irma T. Elo. 1995. "Are Educational Differentials in Adult Mortality Increasing in the United States." *Journal of Aging and Health* 74(4): 476–96.

Roseboom, Tessa J., Jan H. P. van der Meulen, Anita C. Ravelli, Clive Osmond, David J. Barker, and Otto P. Bleker. 2001. "Effects of Prenatal Exposure to the Dutch Famine on Adult Disease in Later Life: An Overview." *Twin Research* 4(5): 293–8.

Rosenzweig, Mark R., and T. Paul Schultz. 1989. "Schooling, Information and Nonmarket Productivity: Contraceptive Use and Its Effectiveness." *International Economic Review* 30(2): 457–77.

Ross, Catherine E., and John Mirowsky. 1999. "Refining the Association Between Education and Health: The Effects of Quantity, Credential and Selectivity." *Demography* 36(4): 445–60.

Sacerdote, Bruce. 2001. "Peer Effects with Random Assignment: Results for Dartmouth Roommates." *Quarterly Journal of Economics* 116(2) 681–704.

Sander, William. 1995. "Schooling and Quitting Smoking." *Review of Economics and Statistics* 77(1): 191–9.

Sapolsky, Robert M. 1993. "Endocrinology Alfresco: Psychoendocrine Studies of Wild Baboons." *Recent Progress in Hormone Research* 48: 437–68.

———. 1998. *Why Zebras Don't Get Ulcers. An Updated Guide to Stress, Stress-Related Diseases, and Coping.* New York: W. H. Freeman.

Schoeni, Robert F., Vicki A. Freedman, and Linda G. Martin 2005. "Socioeconomic and Demographic Disparities in Trends in Old-Age Disability." TRENDS Working Paper No. 05-1, June 2005, University of Michigan.

Shkolnikov, Vladimir M., David A. Leon, Sergey Adamets, Eugeniy Andreev, and Alexander Deev. 1998. "Educational Level and Adult Mortality in Russia: An Analysis of Routine Data 1979 to 1994." *Social Science and Medicine* 47(3): 357–69.

Smith, James P. 2005. "Unravelling the SES Health Connection." *Population and Development Review* 30(Supplement: Aging, Health, and Public Policy): 108–32.

Snowdon, David. 2001. *Aging with Grace*. New York: Bantam Books.

Sobel, Jeffrey, and Albert J. Stunkard. 1989. "Socioeconomic Status and Obesity: A Review of the Literature." *Psychological Bulletin* 105(2): 260–75.

Spandorfer, John M., David J. Karras, Lynn A. Hughes, and Craig Caputo. 1995. "Comprehension of Discharge Instructions by Patients: A Preliminary Study." *Annals of Emergency Medicine* 25(1): 71–74.

Spasojevic, Jelena. 2003. "Effects of Education on Adult Health in Sweden: Results from a Natural Experiment." Ph.D. dissertation, City University of New York Graduate Center.

Strauss, John, and Duncan Thomas. 1995. "Human Resources: Empirical Modeling of Household and Family Decisions." In *Handbook of Development Economics*, Volume 3, edited by J. Behrman and T. N. Srinivasan. Amsterdam: Elsevier.

Suarez, Lucina, and Elizabeth Barrett-Connor. 1984. "Is an Educated Wife Hazardous to Your Health?" *American Journal of Epidemiology* 119(2): 244–9.

Tyler, John H., Richard J. Murnane, and John B. Willett. 2000. "Estimating the Labor Market Signaling Value of the GED." *Quarterly Journal of Economics* 115(2): 431–68.

U.S. Surgeon General's Advisory Committee on Smoking and Health. 1964. "Smoking and Health: Report of the Advisory Committee of the Surgeon General of the Public Health Service." Office of the Surgeon General, Public Health Service Publication No. 1103.

van Doorslaer, Eddy, Adam Wagstaff, Han Bleichrodt, Samuel Calonge, Ulf-G Gerdtham, Michael Gerfin, Jose Geurts, Lorna Goss, Unto Hakkinen, and Robert Leu. 1997. "Income-Related Inequalities in Health: Some International Comparisons." *Journal of Health Economics* 16(1): 93–112.

Williams, Mark V., David W. Baker, Eric G. Honig, Theodore M. Lee, and Adam Nowlan. 1998. "Inadequate Literacy Is a Barrier to Asthma Knowledge and Self-Care." *Chest* 114(4): 1008–15.

Wolfson, Michael C., Geoff Rowe, Jane F. Gentleman, and Monica Tomiak. 1993. "Career Earnings and Death: A Longitudinal Analysis of Older Canadian Men." *Journal of Gerontology* 48(4): S167–79.

Chapter 3

Health Effects of Human Development Policies

Daniel P. Keating and Sharon Z. Simonton

A growing body of evidence documents the substantial effects on health of social policies whose focus is not on health per se, such as those that explicitly target social policy arenas such as human development. Here we focus specifically on the health effects of early-childhood development policies. Because human development policies have typically played a minor role in policy discussions about health, it is important to define their scope and outline a general conceptual framework to support their relevance before reviewing evidence to illustrate their connection with health.

Human development policies include leave policies; labor laws that determine work conditions, hours, benefits, and flexibility of workplaces; policies determining the availability, cost, and quality of child care and early-childhood education programs; funding for and access to all levels of public education; the social composition, quality, and content of public education; eligibility for, levels, and types of public assistance programs provided; state and local expenditures on other public services such as police and corrections, housing and community development, and community recreational facilities and resources; and others. Human development policies shape the most proximal social structures, institutions, and material conditions of daily life that may determine individual health across multiple domains through the life course and which may, in the aggregate, determine population-level distributions of health outcomes. Although we do not explore the health effects of all of these human development policies, they indicate the range of policy decisions whose impact on health needs to be better understood.

Socioeconomic gradients—the differential distribution of health outcomes across subgroups of a population having differing levels of SES—have long been observed across multiple domains for population well-being: morbidity and mortality outcomes (Kunst and Mackenbach 1994; Kaplan and Keil 1993; Kunst and Mackenbach 1992; Antonovsky 1967); health behaviors (Lantz et al. 2001; Lynch,

Kaplan, and Salonen 1997); psychosocial well-being (Muntaner et al. 2004; Tremblay 1999); and cognitive performance, literacy, and academic achievement (Willms 1999b; Brooks-Gunn, Duncan, and Rebello Britto 1999). We have argued that this full range of health outcomes—physical, mental, socioemotional, literacy, and academic competence—may be fruitfully combined within a multidimensional omnibus indicator termed *developmental health* (Keating and Hertzman 1999) in order to fully capture the multiple dimensions of individual and population health.

Recent reviews of contemporary research support the claim that health throughout the life course is strongly influenced by social and developmental determinants, and that many such determinants are not disease specific, in that they may be associated with multiple health outcomes through the life course. The contribution of developmental determinants to health is increasingly recognized in epidemiologic, developmental, and economic analyses (Galobardes, Lynch, and Smith 2004; Kuh and Ben-Shlomo 2004; Smith 2004; Case, Lubotsky, and Paxson 2002; Harper et al. 2002; Kaplan et al. 2001). The evidence for this link is increasingly substantial, even if the underlying mechanisms remain unclear.

W. Thomas Boyce and Daniel P. Keating (2004) described a set of linked questions that articulate the connections from observations of SES gradients in developmental health to the mechanisms underlying these observed gradients to the policy implications of this integrated understanding:

> Is there evidence that experiences in early development have life course consequences for health? If so, are these consequences substantial enough (that is, account for enough variance in subsequent health outcomes) to warrant significant investment? If so, is there evidence that changes in childhood circumstances show positive life course benefits to health, to test whether observed associations are more than merely correlational? If so, is there theory and evidence that affords an understanding of the underlying developmental mechanisms, such that interventions can be properly guided and unintended harm avoided? Finally, are the identified interventions feasible in current policy contexts, and what arguments can be made to make them more viable?(428)

It is necessary to examine associations between human development policies and developmental health outcomes to begin to formulate systematic answers to these questions. We explore the extent to which human development policies may influence individual developmental health outcomes, socioeconomic gradients, and overall population health. Additionally, there are also specific biodevelopmental mechanisms that may underlie social disparities in developmental health. Two general levels of educational and human development policies are relevant: early-childhood intervention programs as well as national educational and human development policies that form the context and background for early-childhood intervention programs implemented in the United States. While much of the data in this area focuses primarily on the United States, we draw upon international research whenever possible.

SOCIOECONOMIC GRADIENTS

A socioeconomic gradient describes the relationship between a health outcome and a measure of SES for individuals residing in a specific community during a specific time period (Willms 2003b). Gradients are evident across all measures for SES, which are indicators for an individual or family's relative location within an encompassing social structure: education, income, wealth, and occupational status. Socioeconomic gradients are also notably evident across the full range for each measure of SES; they are not concentrated below a discrete poverty or deprivation threshold demarcating increased risk (Marmot et al. 1991). Socioeconomic gradients offer a summary measure of the average level and distribution of a developmental health outcome across a specified measure of SES for a particular population.

A growing body of research has documented variation among socioeconomic gradients in developmental health outcomes within and between countries (Willms 2004; Cavelaars et al. 2000; Mackenbach et al. 2000; Willms 1999b; Cavelaars et al. 1998). While epidemiologic research has generally focused upon describing socioeconomic gradients and identifying the social determinants of disease, much less attention has been paid to the underlying social processes that may differentially distribute these social determinants within and between populations and their constituent subgroups (Graham 2004). Indeed, it has been argued that such distributional processes have in recent history supplanted absolute material deprivation and sanitation as primary determinants of population health and social disparities in many countries (Fogel 2003).

The field of education offers a rich body of methodological and empirical literature examining intra- and intercountry variation in socioeconomic gradients for measures of literacy and academic performance. Several consistent themes arise from a review of the literature. First, international evidence from the Organisation for Economic Co-operation and Development (OECD) countries indicates a high level of intra- and intercountry variation for levels and slopes of socioeconomic gradients for quantitative skills, reading, and overall literacy (Willms 2004; Willms 1999b). Second, countries that have higher levels of academic performance typically have flatter slopes and relatively higher levels of achievement and literacy among adults and children from lower socioeconomic backgrounds. Third, intercountry differences for academic performance and literacy outcomes among students from higher SES households tend to be much smaller than those observed for children having parents with lower levels of socioeconomic status.

This pattern of decreasing variation, or convergence, across countries or jurisdictions for outcomes observed among individuals having higher levels of SES has been described as the "hypothesis of converging gradients" (Willms 2003b). While youth and adults from higher SES backgrounds consistently exhibited high and comparable levels of literacy and academic performance across countries and smaller constituent jurisdictions, literacy and achievement outcomes for students from more disadvantaged backgrounds varied considerably across countries, states, and provinces (Willms 2004; Willms 1999a; Willms 2003a). Figure 3.1, which shows relationships between literacy scores and parental education for youths ages sixteen to twenty-five in seven OECD countries, illustrates this pattern of converging socioeconomic gradients. Average levels of achievement and literacy exhibit inverse associations with the slope of the gradient: countries and jurisdictions having the highest average levels of achievement exhibited shallower gradients and consequently lower levels of inequality of outcomes across measures of SES.

Epidemiologic studies of population-level health outcomes across OECD countries have also noted lower average levels of mortality and less inequality across levels of SES among countries having more egalitarian educational and human development policies (Vagero and Erikson 1997; Kunst and Mackenbach 1994; Vagero and Lundberg 1989). Countries having higher average levels of literacy and lower inequality across socioeconomic groups for literacy and educational outcomes also have lower levels of inequality for adult mortality (Vagero and Erikson 1997; Vagero and Lundberg 1989) and lower infant mortality rates (Navarro and Shi 2001). Societies with the highest average levels of population health and flatter socioeconomic gradients tend to be those that have been most successful in ensuring the well-being of the most disadvantaged subgroups of the population.

These findings suggest that the adverse effects of low SES on developmental health outcomes are neither uniform across societies nor necessarily inevitable. While groups having lower levels of SES do consistently exhibit higher risk for adverse developmental health outcomes across all known societies, the extent of inequality across levels of SES differs substantially across social contexts. Inequalities for developmental health outcomes are socially produced. The differing socioeconomic gradients observed in developmental health outcomes across countries and jurisdictions may reflect the influence of differing human development policies that underlie and shape the social distributions of risk factors and determinants of developmental health outcomes across populations and their constituent subgroups.

Human development policies may be potential points of leverage for addressing health inequalities and improving overall population health. Adult educational attainment is prior to and predictive of employment status, occupational opportunities, working conditions, and income; these are in turn associated with many adult health behaviors and outcomes. Parental education is also significantly associated with many child developmental health outcomes (Chen, Matthews, and Boyce 2002; Brooks-Gunn, Duncan, and Rebello Britto 1999; Tremblay 1999; Willms 1999b). Childhood SES also has significant effects on a number of adult developmental health outcomes including cognitive function (Kaplan et al. 2001); psychosocial functioning (Harper et al. 2002); and physical health outcomes such as cardiovascular disease, hemorrhagic stroke, and stomach cancer (Galobardes, Smith, and Lynch 2006; Galobardes, Lynch, and Smith 2004; Hayward and Gorman 2004).

FIGURE 3.1 / Quantitative Literacy Scores for Youth Ages Sixteen to Twenty-Five, International Adult Literacy Study, 1994

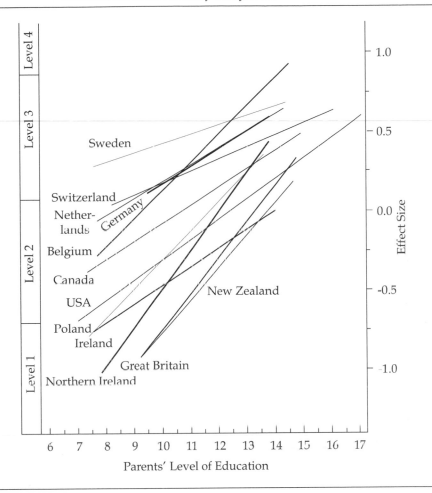

Source: Adapted and updated from Willms (1999a, Figure 5.1).

Human development policies, which may determine distributions of educational attainment and other measures of SES across populations, may concomitantly shape underlying distributions of the social determinants of health and disease across the life course through a variety of potential pathways. Such policies may differentially distribute access to physical, material, educational, financial, social, educational, and informational resources needed for optimal development. They may also determine social topologies: who interacts with whom. Social interactions may influence developmental health outcomes through role-model effects, local norms of behavior, social and informational networks, and peer-group influences (Durlauf 2001). One must consider the mechanisms that may be molded and calibrated by the social processes which are shaped by human development policies. This is essential in order to understand how these social forces "get under the skin" to be expressed in a wide range of developmental health outcomes across the life course (Boyce and Keating 2004; Worthman and Kuzara 2005).

FROM CHILD DEVELOPMENT TO HEALTH: GETTING UNDER THE SKIN

Identifying the precise links connecting social disparities to differences in actual social transactions, to the shaping of biodevelopmental processes, and to the ongoing effects of resulting biodevelopmental variability on developmental health outcomes across the life course constitutes a major interdisciplinary program of research. The goal of such a research program would be to satisfy the constraints arising from the nature of empirically observed social gradients in health (particularly the pervasiveness of the social gradients across many types of health outcomes and their life-course durability) and from our understanding of potential biodevelopmental mechanisms that could generate these patterns. We define candidate biodevelopmental systems as those which are responsive to differences in early life experience, exhibit the long-term effects of these differential early life experiences, and influence developmental health outcomes. We briefly note three candidate biodevelopmental systems that show promise of satisfying these criteria.

Candidate Biodevelopmental Systems

The first of these candidate systems focuses on the notion of psychosocial control that figures prominently in some contemporary theories of social disparities and health (Marmot 2004). The functioning of the stress-response system (which is biologically based in the limbic hypothalamic-pituitary-adrenal [L-HPA] system) is a prime candidate for understanding the biodevelopmental origins and effects of this psychosocial factor. Our understanding of how the L-HPA system develops and functions is increasing rapidly (Gunnar and Donzella 2002). There is good evidence that L-HPA function is shaped by early social experience in both animal and human models, both by normative variations in parental warmth and sensitivity as well as by more extreme variations such as neglect and abuse. There is also strong evidence from animal models (and increasingly from human studies) that such early patterning has long-term effects on the functioning of the L-HPA system, and that normative variations in the experience of uncertainty (that is, perceived lack of control) and social evaluation (that is, status and dominance relationships) during adulthood evoke strong cortisol responses (Dickerson and Kemeny 2004). The final link is the increasingly established link between excess or dysregulated cortisol response and deleterious effects on numerous organs, with consequences for both morbidity and mortality (McEwen 2005; Sapolsky 2005; Worthman and Kuzara 2005).

A second candidate system focuses on the notion of social participation, belonging, and connection. The psychosocial aspects of this have been implicated in the literature on social disparities and health; the biodevelopmental aspects seem to play out most prominently in disruptions to the functioning of the serotonergic system (Suomi 2000). Evidence from animal and human studies both point toward disruptions in the attachment relationship between (typically) mother and infant as a primary source of social disruptions in the serotonergic system. It is also important to note that there is genetic variation in the serotonergic system (in the serotonin transporter gene, 5-HTTLPR), and that this is expressed in both animal and human studies as a *gene-environment interaction* such that genetic risk is activated *only* in circumstances of disrupted parent-child relationships. This is seen in studies of peer rearing in rhesus macaques (Suomi 2000) and through a developmental history of abuse and neglect in humans (Caspi et al. 2003). The observed consequences of a disrupted serotonergic system are manifold, including elevated risk for depression, aggression, and substance abuse. Evidence suggests that these may in turn be associated with adult morbidity and early mortality.

A third candidate system focuses on a later developing system that includes aspects of perceived purpose, hope, meaning, and identity. This system is uniquely human, arising as a coevolution of culture and mind (Donald 2001). The primary focus here is the prefrontal cortex (PFC) of the brain, which is disproportionately larger (relative to body-size-corrected brain volume) in humans, both archaeologically and in comparison to contemporary nonhuman primates. The PFC achieves this differential size largely during the adolescent transition, and the enlargement is connected in developmental time with increased speed and quantity of connections to other brain systems (Keating 2004). The implication is that the achievement of the specifically human level of consciousness involves an increased role of PFC governance of brain and biologic systems. A second implication from the nature of growth (the proliferation of new synapses in early adolescence, and the subsequent pruning of those during later adolescence) is that it is sensitive to developmental experience, in much the same way that early experience shapes brain and biologic systems. The precise connections from these biodevelopmental acquisitions and outcomes in developmental health are more difficult to specify given the complexity of the system, but there is an established link between related aspects, such as hopelessness or lack of meaning, to a range of negative health outcomes (Everson-Rose and Lewis 2005; Everson et al. 2000; Everson et al. 1997; Everson et al. 1996).

Developmental Determinants

This final point raises an important issue about the pattern of developmental determinants. Contrary to caricatures of developmental determinism, experiences throughout the life course continue to influence health. Early adversity may be moderated by later resilience; early advantage may be hampered by later trauma. It is helpful therefore to briefly consider various patterns of developmental effects.

Drawing on work by Clyde Hertzman (1999) and Diana Kuh and Yoav Ben-Shlomo (2004), W. Thomas Boyce and Daniel Keating (2004) describe three ways in which childhood circumstances may affect health outcomes over the life course.

One pattern progresses through stability of socioeconomic circumstances from childhood to later life, with an accumulation of risk from a variety of sources. In other words, individuals who grow up in more stressful circumstances tend to experience those same circumstances throughout their development. The implication of this *cumulative pattern* is that broad societal differences in the quality of the social and physical environment play a major role in developmental health outcomes. This happens through the overall degree of social partitioning and the SES-related patterns that emerge in early life and continue into later life. A second set of childhood influences may be thought of as *pathway effects*, comprising chains of risk or protection. For example, educational attainment plays a substantial role in both subsequent health and social status. Beyond simple continuity, it is likely that the early acquisition of competencies, skills, and dispositions—or "capabilities," to use Amartya Sen's (1999, 18) term—has direct effects on the pathways leading toward future health, and these capabilities are contingent on core biodevelopmental acquisitions. Such associations are likely attributable to sequences of linked exposures, in which early risk factors increase the likelihood of subsequent exposures, which in turn augment the probability of encountering others. A third type of influence can be thought of as critical period, sensitive period, or *latent effects*. Even after removing the effects from other, later sources—adult SES, differential developmental pathways, and so on—there is often a nontrivial impact of childhood circumstances on life-course health outcomes. For example, the early instantiation of an overreactive stress-response system may affect developmental trajectories through success in selected environments (that is, pathway effects); in addition, it may create a health risk that will become manifest only at a later stage in the life course as stressors accumulate or grow more intense (Worthman and Kuzara 2005). Understanding the underlying mechanisms and the ways in which their effects are manifested improves the prospects for more precisely evaluating the impact of various policies, whether or not they are focused on health per se.

THE IMPACT OF HUMAN DEVELOPMENT POLICIES ON HEALTH

To examine the impact of human development policies on health, we consider two categories of policy interventions: early-childhood intervention programs as well as more general national-level policies. In this analysis, it is essential to consider both direct health effects as well as potential indirect effects on later health. These indirect effects operate through effects on significant pathways associated with attained SES including cognitive development, education, income, and social participation (employment and rate of incarceration).

EVALUATING THE EFFECTS OF EARLY-CHILDHOOD INTERVENTION PROGRAMS

Early-childhood intervention programs in the United States have been designed with the intent of helping low-income children overcome the developmental disadvantages of growing up in poverty, and have, with few exceptions, been targeted exclusively at low-income children or children who are otherwise perceived as being at high risk for adverse developmental outcomes. Such interventions would thus be expected to reduce the slope of socioeconomic gradients in developmental health outcomes by improving outcomes among children from low-SES family backgrounds. Drawing upon several excellent reviews of early-childhood education programs (Barnett 2002; Currie 2001; Karoly et al. 1998; Barnett 1995), we focus upon two general types of programs: model early-childhood demonstration programs and large-scale publicly funded programs. We distinguish between these two types of early-childhood programs because of substantial differences in their associated levels of funding and resources; intensity, duration and age of entry; teacher qualifications, training and pay; scale of implementation, and suitability of design for statistical inference.

Model early-childhood demonstration programs, many of which have used randomized assignment to define treatment and control groups for evaluation, have had higher levels of funding per child, lower child-teacher ratios, more highly qualified teachers, longer duration, earlier age of entry, and more intensive programming than large-scale publicly funded early-childhood programs such as Head Start and the Chicago Child-Parent Centers (CPC). For example, the full-day, fifty weeks per year, preschool component of the Carolina Abecedarian Project, which continued for five years from infancy through age four, cost approximately fifteen thousand dollars (in 1999 dollars) per child, per year (Ramey, Campbell, and Blair 1998; Currie 2001). This model program had a child-teacher ratio that ranged from three-to-one during infancy to six-to-one during preschool. In contrast, in 1998 it cost approximately five thousand dollars for a child to attend a part-day Head Start program for thirty-four weeks per year (Currie 2001).

The estimation of treatment effects for early-childhood intervention programs poses numerous practical and methodological challenges. We would ideally like to estimate the effect of an intervention on children's outcomes compared with what would have been observed for the same group of children had they not attended preschool, holding all else constant. However, we are unable to observe the same child simultaneously attending and not attending a given early-childhood program. Accounting for this inability to observe the counterfactual—the same child in the absence of intervention—is one of the primary challenges facing efforts to evaluate the effectiveness of early-childhood education programs. Two general types of approaches are used to address this challenge: experimental studies and quasi-experimental studies.

Experimental studies, or randomized controlled trials (RCTs), are generally regarded as the "gold standard" for the estimation of intervention effects. In this study design, each member of a study population is randomly assigned to participate in either a specified early-childhood program (this is called the *treatment group*) or to not participate in the early-childhood program (this called the *control* or *comparison group*). If the sample size is sufficiently large and the randomization mechanism is successful, the two groups will be comparable with respect to both observed and unobserved characteristics. The average effect of the intervention can then be estimated by the difference between the average outcomes observed for the treatment and control groups.

Quasi-experimental study designs based on observational data are typically used to estimate treatment effects in social-science contexts where RCTs would be impractical, unethical, or prohibitively expensive. In observational studies, children are not randomly assigned to early-childhood programs. Estimates for the effects of early-childhood programs on child outcomes may be biased if the study design fails to adequately control for observed and unobserved family characteristics that may be correlated with both selection into the preschool program and child developmental outcomes. Several commonly used approaches to address selection bias and potential confounding effects include multivariate statistical adjustment, fixed effects models, instrumental variables, and propensity-score methods (Currie 2005; Karoly and Bigelow 2005). Janet Currie provides an excellent review of the strengths and limitations of these study designs and statistical methods (Currie 2005).

We review findings from quasi-experimental studies of two large-scale publicly funded early-childhood programs: the Chicago Child-Parent Centers (CPC) and Head Start. Studies of the effects of the Chicago CPC program are based on data collected as part of the Chicago Longitudinal Study (CLS), which includes all children who enrolled in CPCs with preschool and kindergarten programs in 1983. There was significant natural variation in the duration of program participation: some children participated only in the preschool components, while others continued through third grade (a range of one to six years). The comparison group was composed of children who completed full-day kindergarten programs at randomly selected schools serving predominantly low-income families in neighborhoods where CPC services were not available. A school-age intervention was also offered during the first three years of elementary school at several of the included project centers. Thus, the CLS uses a four-way design to assess the effects of intensive preschool intervention with and without an enriched curriculum for school-aged children, as well as participation in only the school-age intervention, relative to a control group that did not receive either stage of intervention.

Studies of the effects of Head Start on child and adult outcomes have had to address a number of formidable challenges. First, the only randomized trial of Head Start began in 2002 (Administration for Children and Families 2005). The absence of an experimental design during the implementation of Head Start has greatly complicated the task of defining appropriate comparison groups for the estimation of treatment effects. Children who actually attend Head Start have been found to be especially disadvantaged, even relative to the full subpopulation of children defined as eligible to attend Head Start (Oden, Schweinhart, and Weikart 2000; Lee, Schnur, and Brooks-Gunn 1988). Noncomparability of the Head Start and comparison groups may result in a bias against finding positive effects of Head Start participation on child outcomes. Second, the nationwide heterogeneity of funding, of locally defined curriculum content, and of program services across both space and time entails that there is not a single, consistent "Head Start program" for evaluation.

The strongest individual-level studies of Head Start have used fixed effects models and data from nationally representative cohort studies to compare outcomes of Head Start participants with those of siblings who did not attend the program (Garces, Thomas, and Currie 2002; Currie and Thomas 1999; Currie and Thomas 1995). Fixed effects models are advantageous insofar as they enable researchers to control for observed and unobserved household and maternal characteristics that are assumed to be fixed through time and across siblings.

EVIDENCE FOR DIRECT EFFECTS OF EARLY-CHILDHOOD PROGRAMS ON HEALTH OUTCOMES

In this section we review evidence for the existence of direct effects of early-childhood intervention programs on developmental health outcomes. We have restricted our review to model early-childhood programs that have used randomized assignment of program-participation status and that have relatively large study samples with low levels of sample attrition. The three programs chosen which meet these criteria are the Carolina Abecedarian Project, the Infant Health and Development Program (IHDP), and the Perry Preschool Project. These three demonstration programs each had different enrollment criteria: the Carolina Abecedarian Project enrolled low-SES children, the Perry Preschool Project was targeted at low-SES children who had low IQ scores, and the IHDP, based on the design and curriculum of the Abecedarian Project, enrolled a socioeconomically heterogeneous sample of preterm, low-birthweight infants. Our review of outcomes for large-scale publicly funded programs is limited to those having large sample sizes and longer-term longitudinal follow-up across multiple sites: the Chicago CPC program and Head Start.[1]

Model Early-Childhood Intervention Programs

All three of the chosen model early-childhood programs have examined longer-term effects of childhood program participation on a limited set of adult health behaviors and outcomes. At age twenty-seven, Perry Preschool Project program participants were significantly less likely than controls to report smoking cigarettes (45 percent versus 56 percent) or drinking alcoholic beverages several times a week (16 percent versus 26 percent); they were more likely to report never drinking alcoholic beverages and always wearing seatbelts when driving (57 percent versus 34 percent) (Schweinhart, Barnes, and Weikart 1993). At age forty, significantly fewer Perry Preschool Project male participants (compared to control males) reported using sedatives, sleeping pills, or tranquilizers (17 percent versus 43 percent); marijuana or hashish (48 percent versus 71 percent); or heroin (0 percent versus 9 percent) (Schweinhart et al. 2005). Similar, although not statistically significant, findings for reduced rates of cigarette smoking among program participants were also observed for twenty-one-year-old adults who had participated in the Carolina Abecedarian Project (39 percent versus 55 percent) (Campbell et al. 2002). At age twenty-one, Carolina Abecedarian Project participants were less likely than controls to have smoked marijuana during the past thirty days (18 percent versus 39 percent). No significant differences were observed for binge drinking.

A longer-term evaluation of the IHDP examining the effects of program participation on risk behaviors including conduct problems, suicidal ideation and attempts, smoking, alcohol and marijuana use, and risky sexual behaviors found that risk-behavior scores for program participants at age eighteen did not differ from those observed for the control group (McCormick et al. 2006). No differences were found between caregiver-reported and youth self-reported health status for participants relative to the control group. Measures of health status included self-reported general health status, limitations in activities because of health problems, physical pain, level of vitality and fatigue, and general mental health. The authors did not examine the extent to which the heterogeneity of household SES in this sample may have moderated the effects of program participation on health outcomes.

Large-Scale Publicly-Funded Early-Childhood Programs

Evaluations of the effects of large-scale public programs have examined associations between program participation and several child health outcomes such as receipt of immunizations (Currie and Thomas 1995), height-for-age (Currie and Thomas 1995), substantiated reports of child maltreatment (Reynolds and Robertson 2003), and county-level child mortality among children aged five to nine from causes potentially addressed by Head Start health services and resources (Ludwig and Miller 2005).

Race-specific fixed effects models were used to examine the effects of Head Start participation on immunization rates for measles and height-for-age among black and white children (Currie and Thomas 1995). Children who participated in Head Start were compared with two control groups: siblings who did not attend preschool and siblings who attended programs other than Head Start. Black and white children who attended Head Start were more likely to have received a measles immunization than children who were not enrolled in any preschool program. Head Start program participation was not associated with nutrition and health status as measured by height-for-age.

A regression discontinuity design was used to assess the effects of Head Start health on county-level child mortality from outcomes that would plausibly be detected and addressed by the health care resources included as part of Head Start programming. These outcomes included tuberculosis, whooping cough, infections, polio, measles, diabetes, malnutrition, anemias, and respiratory problems such as asthma, bronchitis, and pneumonia (Ludwig and Miller 2005). This analysis exploited differential levels of early funding for Head Start to compare child mortality rates for the three hundred poorest counties in the United States—a group that received augmented funding during the early years of Head Start implementation from 1965 to 1979—with those observed for poor counties immediately above the cutoff for augmented funding and that received standard levels of Head Start funding. A 50 to 100 percent increase in Head Start funding was associated with a 33 to 75 percent decline in mortality rates from Head Start susceptible causes for children between five and nine years old. From 1973 to 1983, the mean and median county mortality rates from Head Start susceptible causes for American children five to nine years old were 2 and 1.8 per 100,000, respectively. The study's conclusions are supported by findings indicating no significant discontinuities for causes of death unrelated to Head Start health programming and no reductions for other age groups who were not eligible for enrollment in Head Start. These results may offer a conservative estimate for the effects of Head Start programming on relevant child mortality outcomes because the comparison group of counties also received Head Start funding and resources, albeit at lower levels of funding.

An examination of the effects of participation in the Chicago CPC program on substantiated reports of child maltreatment found that preschool intervention enrollment at ages three or four was associated with a 52 percent reduction in the cumulative rate of documented child abuse or neglect by age seventeen (5 percent of program participants versus 10.5 percent of the control group) (Reynolds and Robertson 2003). Participation in the school-age component of the CPC program was not in itself associated with lower rates of child maltreatment. However, a dose-response effect was evident for extended program participation; children enrolled for four to six years had lower rates of child maltreatment than those participating for one to four years. The effects of preschool program participation on child maltreatment were found to increase over time, with significant reductions in child abuse and neglect for the intervention group only evident after age nine. Parental involvement in school was found to be a significant mediator of intervention effects on child abuse and neglect.

EVIDENCE FOR INDIRECT EFFECTS OF EARLY-CHILDHOOD PROGRAMS ON HEALTH OUTCOMES

While few studies have examined direct associations between early-childhood programs and physical health outcomes, a number of studies have documented significant associations between such programs and developmental outcomes that, while important in their own right, are also likely contributors to subsequent physical health outcomes. These include cognitive function, academic achievement, high school completion, educational attainment, employment status, and income. We hypothesize that early-childhood programs may indirectly influence health outcomes through their longer-term effects on SES for those most at risk for future adverse health outcomes. Increasing academic achievement, educational attainment, and subsequent income among children from low-SES households may be a policy lever for flattening the socioeconomic gradients in developmental health outcomes.

Model Early-Childhood Intervention Programs

In this section we review findings related to model early-childhood intervention programs for four types of outcomes: cognitive development, educational outcomes, criminal involvement, and economic well-being.[2] These outcomes have been associated with subsequent health, and thus need to be considered for their potential indirect effects on health outcomes.

Cognitive Development   All of the included model early-childhood programs reported significantly higher IQ scores for program participants during and immediately after program participation. Significant effects on IQ were sustained longest for children enrolled in the Carolina Abecedarian Project (until age twelve) and the IHDP; both were intensive full-day, full-year programs which began during infancy (Campbell and Ramey 1995). The IHDP found that only low-birthweight infants at the upper end of the weight spectrum (2,001 to 2,500 grams) had significantly higher IQ scores than controls at age eight and at age eighteen (McCormick et al. 2006; McCarton et al. 1997). A significant cognitive advantage for children participating in the Perry Preschool Project relative to controls was sustained until age seven (Weikart, Bond, and McNeil 1978).

The Carolina Abecedarian Project, based upon a four-way treatment design, also examined the relative effects of preschool intervention with and without a parent-mediated school-age intervention offered during the first three years of elementary school, participation in only the school-age intervention component, and no participation in either stage of intervention. Preschool participation was associated with significantly higher child IQ scores through age twelve (Campbell and Ramey 1995). Scores for children who received the extended intervention were virtually identical to those for children who received only the preschool component. Participation in the school-age intervention alone was not associated with significant effects on child IQ scores.

These findings suggest that very early intensive interventions with relatively long periods of duration may have larger and longer-lasting effects on child cognitive development. The Carolina Abecedarian Project and the IHDP both provided intensive full-day, full-year, center-based care and preschool for disadvantaged children for the first three to five years of life. The small number and nature of model programs that have significantly enhanced long-term child cognitive development do not allow us to disentangle the independent effects of program timing, intensity, duration, and modality of treatment on child cognitive functioning.

Educational Outcomes In contrast to the findings for cognitive development, results for longer-term intervention effects on educational outcomes are consistently positive. Model-program participants have higher achievement test scores, lower rates of grade retention, lower use of special education services, lower rates of dropout, higher rates of high school graduation, higher rates of college enrollment, and higher overall educational attainment. Rates of high school completion among participants in the Perry Preschool Program were found to differ significantly by sex. While rates for high school completion did not differ for male preschool participants relative to controls, female participants were significantly more likely to have completed high school than women in the control group (84 percent versus 32 percent) (Schweinhart et al. 2005). An evaluation of educational outcomes among eighteen-year-old adults who had participated in the IHDP was unable to assess program effects on educational attainment and high school graduation due to the young age of the sample (McCormick et al. 2006). However, this study did find that IHDP participants who had been higher low-birthweight infants had significantly higher verbal and math achievement scores than controls on the Woodcock-Johnson Tests of Achievement-Revised (Woodcock and Johnson 1990).

While the Carolina Abecedarian Project did not find significant differences for high school graduation, preschool participants had higher reading and math scores and were more likely to have enrolled in college by age twenty-one (36 percent versus 14 percent) (Campbell et al. 2002). The authors note that the exceptionally high quality of the local school system subsequently attended by all program participants and controls may have closed some of the academic gaps between treatment and control groups (Campbell and Ramey 1995). Participation in the school-age component did not, in the absence of preschool participation, lead to significantly higher academic achievement. While those who participated in both the preschool and school-age components had higher reading scores, participation in the extended intervention did not lead to significant increases in math scores or IQ scores (Campbell and Ramey 1995). Participation in the preschool component conferred the largest and most sustained effects on cognitive and academic outcomes.

Criminal Involvement The two studies that have examined associations between early-childhood program participation and adult criminal involvement and incarceration present ostensibly contradictory findings. Former participants in the Perry Preschool Project had significantly lower rates of arrest and imprisonment from ages nineteen to forty (Berrueta-Clement et al. 1984; Schweinhart, Barnes, and Weikart 1993; Schweinhart et al. 2005). Treatment effects were especially marked for male program participants: 52 percent of the control group had been sentenced to jail at some point before age forty as compared with only 28 percent of program participants (Schweinhart et al. 2005). In contrast, the Carolina Abecedarian Project found no significant differences between preschool participants and controls at age twenty-one with respect to types of crimes committed, age of first arrest, or number of charges by type of offense (Clarke and Campbell 1998). These findings indicate that significant increases in cognitive functioning and educational outcomes, as noted among the Carolina Abecedarian project participants, did not necessarily lead to reductions in crime and delinquency.

The authors examined differences between the Perry Preschool Project and the Carolina Abecedarian Project in light of these divergent intervention effects and questioned whether parental program involvement during the preschool years, a notable difference between the two interventions, may have mediated the Perry Preschool Project's significant and enduring effects on subsequent criminal involvement. Indeed, early-childhood programs that have successfully led to future reductions in crime, delinquency, and school misbehavior have all combined early-childhood education with intensive family support including home visits and family counseling (Clarke and Campbell 1998; Yoshikawa 1995).

Economic Outcomes   The Perry Preschool Project is the only model program to have examined the effects of program participation on longer-term adult economic well-being. Program participants were more likely to be employed (76 percent versus 62 percent), to own a car (82 percent versus 60 percent), to own their own home (37 percent versus 28 percent), and to have higher median earnings at ages twenty-seven and forty than controls. Long-term follow-up analyses for participants at ages nineteen, twenty-seven, and forty indicate that significant economic advantages have persisted and, in some instances, increased through adulthood (Schweinhart et al. 2005; Schweinhart, Barnes, and Weikart 1993; Berrueta-Clement et al. 1984). For example, the difference between median annual earnings for program participants and controls increased from $2,000 at age twenty-seven to $5,500 at age forty. At age forty, 60 percent of the program participants had annual incomes over $20,000 as compared with 40 percent of the control group (Schweinhart et al. 2005). Program participants were also more likely to have a savings account at age 40 (76 percent versus 50 percent).

Large-Scale Publicly Funded Early-Childhood Programs

In this section, we review evidence for the effects of the Chicago CPC program and Head Start on educational outcomes, criminal involvement, and economic well-being. Measures of academic skills and achievement have typically been used as proxy measures of cognitive functioning. These findings on large-scale intervention programs paralleled those for the model intervention programs.

Educational Outcomes   Evaluations of the effects of the Chicago CPC program on educational outcomes have found that preschool participation was significantly associated with higher achievement test scores, a lower rate of high school dropout (46.7 percent versus 55 percent), a higher rate of high school completion by age twenty (55.9 percent versus 46.7 percent), and more years of completed education (Reynolds et al. 2001; Reynolds, Ou, and Topitzes 2004). The effects of preschool participation on rates of high school dropout were found to differ by sex. Adjusted rates of school dropout were significantly lower for male preschool participants relative to controls (51 percent versus 67.7 percent), but not for females (42.4 percent versus 41.7 percent). Program participation was also associated with higher rates of high school completion by age twenty for males (42.6 percent versus 29 percent), but not for females (56.5 percent versus 48 percent). These findings are notable in light of high rates of school failure and dropout among black males in the United States.

In contrast, participation in only the school-age CPC component was not associated with high school graduation, dropout, or educational attainment relative to the control group after controlling for preschool participation and other model covariates. However, participation in the school-age component for at least one year was associated with lower rates of special education and grade retention after controlling for preschool status (Reynolds et al. 2001). Those who participated in the extended intervention had the lowest rates of use of special education services and of grade retention. An analysis of the effects of CPC preschool participation and total duration of program participation indicated that both were associated with school achievement and rates of grade retention (Reynolds 2000). A dose-response effect was noted for the effects of extended intervention on achievement and dropout (Temple, Reynolds, and Miedel 2000).

Confirmatory program evaluations have been used to assess the roles of several hypothesized mechanisms and causal pathways in mediating the effects of CPC preschool participation on high school completion (Reynolds 2004; Reynolds, Ou, and Topitzes 2004; Miedel and Reynolds 1999; Reynolds et al. 1996). The school-support hypothesis postulates that the effects of early-childhood intervention are sustained to the extent that children subsequently attend schools of sufficient quality to maintain or enhance the effects of program participation. Measured by post-program magnet school attendance and school mobility, the school-support hypothesis explained the largest percentage (31 percent) of the indirect effects of CPC preschool participation on high school completion (Reynolds, Ou, and Topitzes 2004). The school-support hypothesis, especially magnet-school attendance, explained more of the association between CPC participation and high school completion than several other hypothesized pathways: family support (the extent to which program participation enhances parents' abilities to support child development) explained 28 percent, cognitive advantages (improvements in children's abilities) explained 23 percent, motivational advantages (changes in participants motivational development) explained 1.7 percent, and social adjustment (improved social adjustments and self-regulation) explained 0.8 percent (Reynolds 2004).

Examinations of the effects of Head Start on reading vocabulary and grade retention for Hispanic (Currie and Thomas 1999), Caucasian, and African American children (Currie and Thomas 1995) have used sibling fixed effects models to compare outcomes for Head Start participants with those of siblings who did not attend preschool or who attended a preschool program other than Head Start. Statistically significant and positive effects of Head Start on subsequent achievement test scores were initially found only for Caucasian (Currie and Thomas 1995) and Hispanic Head Start participants (Currie and Thomas 1999). However, the addition of a program-by-age interaction term to the model revealed that Head Start participation had significant and initially equal direct effects on test scores for black and white children (Currie and Thomas 1995). A significant program-by-age interaction for black children indicated that Head Start effects on achievement scores for black children "faded out" by age ten, while white children retained 71 percent of their initial gains. Measures for home and family environment did not moderate retention of Head Start effects among black children. Among white children, Head Start participation was also associated with reduced grade retention (Currie and Thomas 1995).

These findings parallel results from earlier studies of Head Start (Lee et al. 1990; Lee, Schnur, and Brooks-Gunn 1988). The effects of Head Start participation on measures of cognitive function were examined using control groups composed of children from the same neighborhoods who were eligible for Head Start but did not attend preschool or attended another preschool program. The Head Start participants, especially black children, had significantly larger increases for measures of cognitive function after controlling for substantial differences in initial cognitive and socioeconomic factors between the two groups (Lee, Schnur, and Brooks-Gunn 1988). Yet despite these substantial gains, Head Start participants still had absolute measures of cognitive function that were significantly lower than those found for either control group following program completion. A subsequent analysis based on the subsample of black children found that Head Start effects on cognitive ability were sustained but diminished following completion of first grade (Lee et al. 1990).

Two studies have examined potential explanations for the gradual fadeout of the effects of Head Start on cognitive and achievement outcomes among black children (Currie and Thomas 2000; Lee and Loeb 1995). First, Head Start participants were found to subsequently attend middle schools that had lower average student SES, lower average academic achievement, and lower overall academic quality and safety (Lee and Loeb 1995). The same data was later used to examine potential racial differences in the quality of middle schools subsequently attended by black and white Head Start participants (Currie and Thomas 2000). Black children who had participated in Head Start were, unlike white Head Start participants, systematically more likely to attend poorer quality middle schools than other black children. While black Head Start children attended middle schools with low average achievement test scores and low levels of variance across children, white Head Start children were found to attend average quality schools that did not differ from those attended by the average white student.

Two studies have examined associations between Head Start participation and high school graduation and college enrollment at the individual (Garces, Thomas, and Currie 2002) and county levels (Ludwig and Miller 2005). An analysis based on sibling fixed effect models found that while whites who attended Head Start as children were more likely to complete high school and to attend college than siblings who did not attend Head Start or who attended other preschools, there were no significant effects for black program participants. Differences by gender were also observed: both black and white males were more likely to complete high school than female participants (Garces, Thomas, and Currie 2002).

A regression discontinuity design was used to examine the effects of differential levels of Head Start funding on county-level measures of adult educational attainment (Ludwig and Miller 2005). Evidence of positive discontinuities for county-level rates of high school completion and college attendance was found at the federal cutoff for county eligibility for augmented Head Start funding during the earlier period. Increases in high school completion and college attendance were concentrated exclusively among cohorts born late enough to have been exposed to the Head Start program. No discontinuities were noted for college graduation. However, such a result is not unexpected given the relatively young age of the Head Start cohort in the time period of 1988 to 1990, the period of outcome ascertainment.

Criminal Involvement　Two studies have examined associations between participation in large-scale childhood interventions and future delinquency and crime involvement (Reynolds, Ou, and Topitzes 2004; Garces, Thomas, and Currie 2002; Reynolds et al. 2001). Participation in the preschool component of the CPC program was associated with significantly lower rates of juvenile arrests for both violent (9 percent versus 15.3 percent) and nonviolent crimes (14.4 percent versus 19.2 percent) by age eighteen (Reynolds et al. 2001). In contrast, participation in only the school-age component of the CPC program was not associated with reduced rates of arrest or with any other measure of delinquency or crime. Extended program participation through third grade did not confer additional benefits with respect to further reductions in risk for juvenile delinquency by age eighteen. A series of confirmatory analyses were later conducted to assess potential mediators of the effects of CPC preschool participation on juvenile arrest. The two strongest mediators of the effects of CPC preschool participation on court-reported juvenile arrest by age eighteen were subsequent enrollment in a magnet school and parental involvement in school (Reynolds, Ou, and Topitzes 2004).

Fixed effects models have been used to compare rates of criminal history (that is, ever having been booked for or charged with a crime) for Head Start participants with siblings who did not attend the program. Blacks who were enrolled in Head Start as children were significantly less likely to have been booked for or charged with a crime (Garces, Thomas, and Currie 2002). There were no significant effects on criminal involvement for white program participants relative to their siblings.

Economic Outcomes　Only one study has thus far examined the effects of a large-scale childhood intervention program on adult earnings (Garces, Thomas, and Currie 2002). Little evidence was found for significant effects of Head Start participation on earnings among employed adults ages twenty-three to twenty-five. However, the earnings advantages associated with higher rates of high school completion and college attendance may only emerge as program participants continue on in their work life and employment trajectory.

SUMMARY OF EVIDENCE ON EARLY-CHILDHOOD INTERVENTION PROGRAMS

While differences in the sample and program characteristics of the early-childhood programs reviewed here make it difficult to generalize with certainty, the evidence suggests that early-childhood programs have significant and sustained direct and indirect effects on health and well-being through childhood and into adulthood. Evidence for long-term intervention effects on academic achievement and educational attainment is especially consistent and robust across studies. Participation in early-childhood programs can lead to sustained increases in adult SES measured in a number of ways—more education, more and better employment, and lower levels of criminal behavior.

Several themes and questions for future research arise from this review of the literature. First, evidence suggests that earlier interventions may be more effective than those offered during the primary-school years. Second, comprehensive programs that address multiple risk factors by combining early-childhood education with family support services and health and nutrition resources may more effectively address multiple dimensions of child and adult well-being. Third, the quality of the school attended after the intervention program may mediate or moderate the effects of early-childhood programs on developmental health outcomes through childhood and into adulthood.

Earlier Interventions May Be Most Effective

The two projects that had the strongest and most enduring effects on child cognitive functioning—the Carolina Abecedarian Project and the IHDP—both enrolled participants during infancy and offered highly intensive, center-based preschool interventions that lasted between three and five years. The different sampling characteristics of these studies (study eligibility for the Carolina Abecedarian Project was defined by low SES; for the IHDP, it was defined by low birthweight and prematurity) limit our ability to compare intervention effects across samples. The Perry Preschool Project, which enrolled participants in intensive center-based preschool at three years of age, did not find statistically significant improvements in child cognitive performance for program participants after age seven.

However, evidence from the Carolina Abecedarian Project and the Perry Preschool Project indicates that preschool participation can have long-term effects on academic achievement and educational attainment, even in the absence of sustained significant effects on cognitive functioning. This may represent a classic pathway effect as described above: the improvement of general cognitive function places the child on a different trajectory, for which there are greater opportunities for building on educational input. Educational attainment is especially salient given its strong patterns of association with income, occupational status, and adult health behaviors and outcomes. Although effects were not always statistically significant, participants in all of the model preschool interventions and those in the Chicago CPC program had lower rates of grade retention, lower rates of use of special education, lower dropout rates, and higher rates of high school completion than their respective comparison groups. While evidence for the long-term effects of Head Start is still limited, program participation may be associated with higher rates of high school graduation and college attendance, especially among white participants. These findings collectively suggest that interventions that begin in preschool or infancy can effectively increase the educational achievement and attainment of socioeconomically disadvantaged and at-risk children.

Two of these studies—the Carolina Abecedarian Project and the Chicago CPC program—also examined the relative efficacy of preschool programs versus interventions offered only during the early grades of elementary school. Both found that interventions offered only during the early elementary school did not have significant effects on longer-term academic performance or educational attainment. While the school-age intervention did significantly reduce use of remedial services and grade retention among CPC program participants, it did not have significant effects on high school dropout, graduation rates, juvenile delinquency, or educational attainment (Reynolds et al. 2001). Preschool participation was found to have the largest and most persistent effects on child and adult outcomes (Campbell and Ramey 1995; Reynolds et al. 2001).

Comprehensive Programs that Address Multiple Dimensions of Child and Adult Well-Being

The most successful interventions have simultaneously addressed multiple dimensions of child well-being: cognitive and social development, health and nutrition, and familial relationships and parenting skills. The Perry Preschool Project, the Carolina Abecedarian Project, the IHDP, and the CPC program all included nutritional and health resources. The Perry Preschool Project and the CPC program also involved parents through home visits, counseling, and school involvement.

While few studies have evaluated the relative contributions of differing program components, evidence from the CPC program indicates that parental involvement in school activities and in encouraging child learning and development is an especially strong mediator of the effects of preschool participation on reading achievement, grade retention, special-education placement, substantiated cases of child abuse and neglect, high school completion, and juvenile arrest (Reynolds 2004; Reynolds, Ou, and Topitzes 2004; Reynolds and Robertson 2003; Miedel and Reynolds 1999). These findings underscore the importance of parenting support in mediating the effects of early-childhood programs and illustrate the importance of assessing potential pathways and mechanisms for intervention effects on child well-being.

Quality of Postprogram School May Mediate or Moderate the Effects of Early Intervention

Evidence from both of the large-scale, multisite public programs suggests that the quality of postprogram school may mediate or moderate the effects of early-child-hood interventions on subsequent child and adult outcomes. Subsequent postpro-gram magnet school attendance mediated the largest proportions of the indirect effects of CPC preschool participation on high school completion and court-reported juvenile arrest by age eighteen (Reynolds 2004; Reynolds, Ou, and Top-itzes 2004). Indeed, subsequent magnet-school attendance mediated more of the effects of the CPC intervention on these outcomes than measures of family support or measures of cognitive, motivational, and social adjustment gains arising from program participation.

Evidence from studies of the effects of Head Start suggests that postprogram school quality may moderate the persistence of program effects on subsequent ac-ademic achievement (Currie and Thomas 2000; Lee and Loeb 1995). While these studies were unable to explicitly test this hypothesis because of data limitations, racial differences in the quality of postprogram schools offer a potential explana-tion for the differential persistence of Head Start effects on academic achievement and performance outcomes among black and white children.

These findings highlight the importance of examining the effects of early-child-hood programs within the broader context of local, state, and national educational policy. The longer-term effects of early-childhood programs may depend upon the extent to which subsequent school experiences sustain and build upon the benefits of early intervention. Early-childhood programs cannot singlehandedly "inocu-late," or fully protect, children from the ongoing effects of socioeconomic disad-vantage. These findings reflect the effects of cumulative risk or protection: children tend to remain in similar environments across time. A policy implication is that, despite the demonstrated importance of early-childhood to subsequent develop-mental health, early-childhood programs alone are unlikely to be "magic bullets" that solve problems of population developmental health.

This review also underscores the need to consider the effects of model early-childhood programs within the context of their geographically and historically specific educational policies and resources. For example, all of the children partic-ipating in the Carolina Abecedarian Project (which was 98 percent black), con-ducted in a university town, subsequently attended schools in a district where 14 percent of the students were black and 80 percent were white. The investigators note that "efforts were made by all principals to obtain a fair and representative balance of ethnic and socioeconomic levels in all classrooms" (Campbell and Ramey 1995, 750). The racial and probable socioeconomic composition of the schools that the Carolina Abecedarian Project participants attended contrasts sharply with that of the schools attended by the average black students. During the 2002 to 2003 school year, the average black student attended a school that was 54 percent black and 30 percent white, and that had a 49 percent poverty rate (Orfield and Lee 2005). In the same school year, the average white student attended a school that was 78 percent white and 9 percent black, and that had a 23 percent poverty rate.

Future research may need to explicitly examine the extent to which local primary- and secondary-school composition, resources, and policies may mediate or moderate the effects of early-childhood interventions on child and adult developmental health outcomes. Early-childhood programs have thus far been structured and examined as independent entities without regard to the broader societal context within which they are embedded. Family, neighborhood, community, and school factors may all likely shape the short- and longer-term effects of early-childhood interventions on child, adolescent, and adult well-being.

NATIONAL EDUCATION AND HUMAN DEVELOPMENT POLICIES

The longer-term effects of early-childhood programs on socioeconomic attainment and developmental health outcomes may be conditional upon the national- and state-level policies that influence the financing, quality, and social composition of primary and secondary schools. One potentially salient feature of educational and human development policies in the United States is decentralized state and local funding of public services and goods such as education, public welfare, and police and corrections. Distributional systems that govern the funding and allocation of public goods are examples of human development policies that may have enduring effects on community resources and developmental health outcomes among children and adults. The United States is rare among industrialized nations in its heavy reliance upon local property taxes for the funding of public goods and services; this financing system that may lead to large disparities in levels of funding for education and resources across communities having different tax bases.

Theoretical models from the fields of economics and public finance contrasting the potential short- and long-term effects of decentralized (that is, local) and centralized (that is, state or national) funding of public education offer a framework for considering the effects of finance policies on educational outcomes and subsequent health outcomes (Benabou 2000; Benabou 1996a; Benabou 1996b; Durlauf 1996; Tiebout 1956). Decentralized funding based on property taxes may induce economic segregation and stratification as lower-income families are unable or unwilling to pay higher taxes to fund school and other public services. The resulting stratification may lead to persistent inequality in education and earnings across generations since the educational achievement and attainment of each successive generation is contingent upon local social and financial resources (Benabou 1996b).

Persistent inequality and "poverty traps" may arise when poor families become completely isolated from the rest of the economy, leaving poor children structurally unable to accrue sufficient human capital through either educational opportunities or through exposure to role models and mentors (Durlauf 1996). The absence of shared education or social interactions leads to separate and independent trajectories and equilibriums for poor and wealthy families segregated in different neighborhoods. Residential segregation effectively determines the material and social environment, educational and employment opportunities, and subsequent socioeconomic status for low-income and minority populations, and it functions as a central mechanism for creating and sustaining racial and socioeconomic health inequalities in the United States (Acevedo-Garcia and Lochner 2003; Williams and Collins 2001). The education finance system in the United States may play a substantial role in generating and sustaining the socioeconomic and racial segregation and the concentrated disadvantage that early-childhood education programs are designed to address.

Empirical evidence indicates that state and local investments in public goods are associated with child and adult well-being (Dunn, Burgess, and Ross 2005; Harknett et al. 2005). After adjustment for state variation in the cost of providing services, states having greater total per capita expenditures as well as greater per capita spending on education, environment, housing, public welfare, and police and corrections relative to the United States average had significantly lower mortality rates (Dunn, Burgess, and Ross 2005). Public expenditures on education were found to have the largest and most significant effects on state mortality rates.

While state-level expenditures for education vary, a number of studies have documented increasing equalization of school expenditures across districts within states in response to legal cases challenging the constitutionality of local funding of public schools (Corcoran et al. 2004; Murray, Evans, and Schwab 1998). However, these ostensible equalized district-level educational expenditures have not accounted for the differential costs of providing school inputs across districts or the differing needs of disabled students, children from low-income families, and children for whom English is a second language (Wilson, Lambright, and Smeeding 2004; Rubenstein 2002). While unadjusted educational expenditures and those adjusted for the differential costs of providing educational inputs were found to be largely equal across districts, adjustment for the additional costs of effectively addressing student needs revealed large racial inequalities across the entire income distribution, with African American and Hispanic students having lower levels of adjusted educational expenditures than white students of comparable income across all levels of family income (Wilson, Lambright, and Smeeding 2004). Differences in local revenue accounted for differential levels of adjusted educational expenditures across socioeconomic and racial-ethnic groups. Thus, equal educational expenditures do not adequately offset inequalities arising from residential segregation and a decentralized system of educational finance based upon revenue from local property taxes.

Economic segregation may have significant effects on educational achievement, educational attainment, and socioeconomic gradients in educational outcomes (OECD 2004; Willms 2004; Mayer 2002). An examination of the effects of changes in economic segregation in the United States between 1979 and 1990 (both between and within census tracts in the same state) on overall educational attainment and on educational attainment for students from low- and high-income households found that an increase in economic segregation between census tracts increased the gap in educational attainment between high- and low-income students by increasing educational attainment among high-income children and reducing educational attainment among low-income children. These effects were found to offset one another and lead to a net change of zero in overall levels of state educational attainment. Thus, policies which contribute to the emergence and persistence of increasingly segregated and economically homogeneous communities may lead to increased disparities in educational attainment across measures of parental SES. Given the robust evidence of associations between educational attainment and health, such policies would also be expected to maintain or increase the slope of socioeconomic gradients in health outcomes by reducing the intergenerational mobility and socioeconomic achievement of children from households having lower levels of SES.

This review has focused upon early-childhood programs, and to some extent on primary and secondary schools and on the finance system underlying the distribution of public goods in the United States, as examples of human development policies that influence individual health, socioeconomic gradients, and population health. It is essential to also consider the full range of policies that may have profound, albeit often unintended, effects on health across the life course. As one example, maternal and parental leave policies may have significant and enduring effects on health beginning in utero and extending through the life course (Tanaka 2005; Berger, Hill, and Waldfogel 2005; Ruhm 2000). The United States, with no national mandated job-protected paid leave, had the shortest period of leave (an average of twelve weeks of unpaid leave) among the eighteen OECD countries included in one cross country study based on data from 1969 to 2000 (Tanaka 2005). In contrast, the range of weeks of job-protected paid leave for all other countries included in the study ranged from fourteen weeks (in Germany, Ireland, and Japan) to sixty-eight weeks (in Sweden).

Weeks of job-protected paid leave were associated with significant reductions in rates of low birthweight, and infant, postneonatal, and child mortality (Tanaka 2005). Weeks of unpaid leave and non-job-protected leave, the only option available to many families in the United States, did not have significant effects on any of the child health outcomes considered. Additional evidence from the United States indicates that mother's return to work within the first twelve weeks of giving birth was associated with increases in externalizing behavior among children, reductions in child immunizations, and reductions in the initiation and duration of breast-feeding; effects were generally stronger for women who returned to work full-time (Berger, Hill, and Waldfogel 2005; Chatterji and Frick 2003). Similarly, a national-level longitudinal United States sample found significant (though small) negative effects on social behavior of early-beginning, high-quantity child care (NICHD Early Child Care Research Network 2006). While these studies do not examine potential interactions by race or socioeconomic position, studies of breast-feeding have noted that rates of initiation are lowest among black mothers, unmarried mothers, and among those having lower levels of income and educational attainment (Li et al. 2005). Breast-feeding is associated with significantly lower blood pressure (Martin, Gunnell, and Smith 2005), reduced risk for adult overweight (Harder et al. 2005), and increased cognitive ability (Evenhouse and Reilly 2005). These findings suggest that the enactment of a universally available policy of paid job-protected maternal leave in the United States could have potentially profound effects on a range of child health outcomes, racial and socioeconomic health disparities, socioeconomic gradients, and overall levels of population health in the United States.

Another example of a broad policy intervention is that of Programa de Educación, Salud y Alimentación (PROGRESA), a multifaceted program for the mothers of preschool and school-aged children in Mexico, begun in 1997. The core of this intervention was to provide cash transfers to mothers of poor children contingent upon their participation in the program. The program included regular health visits during preschool, which ensured the child's attendance at school, as well as attending regular meetings at which health and nutrition issues were discussed, receiving nutritional supplements for the child, and regular monitoring of child growth. In this sense, there are both health and human development components to this policy intervention. A number of program evaluations have shown direct health effects, including increased growth and reduced stunting (Behrman and Hoddinot 2005), and indirect effects, including decreased rates of grade retention and dropout as well as increased rates of returning to school after early leaving (Behrman, Sengupta, and Todd 2005). Whether comparable effects could be obtained in the United States or similarly economically advantaged jurisdictions is uncertain, given that core nutritional needs are less implicated (Fogel 2003) and that school attendance during the main impact years in PROGRESA may have ceiling effects. An adaptation of this approach—contingent cash transfers to mothers for investment in child health and development—is a policy experiment potentially worthy of investigation. Such a program could include the health education and monitoring components used by PROGRESA and could perhaps add participation in early-childhood development and education programs as a new component. Whether such a model is politically feasible in the United States or elsewhere, however, remains unclear.

A HUMAN DEVELOPMENT AGENDA FOR HEALTH

In this overview of the impact of human development policies on health, we have sought to describe a conceptual framework within which to view the impact of such policies on health, including direct and indirect effects, and to review an interdisciplinary range of evidence arising from such a framework. The evidence supports the view that these policies, individually and in the aggregate, are significant contributors to outcomes of developmental health. A coordinated research and policy agenda may be needed to begin to better understand relationships between human development policies and developmental health across the life course. On the research side, interdisciplinary investigations that identify the pathways from social disparities in circumstances to disparities in outcomes, including the underlying developmental mechanisms, represent an important scientific program. On the policy side, understanding the connections among human development and health policies would provide substantial leverage to improve childhood circumstances, and consequently, population health. The political will to enact such reforms may be strengthened by a deeper understanding in the public at large of the depth, strength, and health implications of prevailing policies and practices that affect human development.

NOTES

1. Supplemental tables summarizing the characteristics of included early-childhood programs and findings for the direct and indirect effects of early-childhood programs on developmental health outcomes are included in the working-paper version of this chapter and are available at the website for the National Poverty Center at the University of Michigan (http://www.npc.umich.edu/) or from the authors.
2. Criminal involvement and incarceration are included since incarceration is associated with many adverse health outcomes such as hepatitis C, tuberculosis, and infection with human immunodeficiency virus (HIV) (Johnson and Raphael 2005; MacNeil, Lobato, and Moore 2005; Hammett, Harmon, and Maruschak 1999). A criminal record has also been found to be associated with low wages, unemployment, and family instability (Pager 2003; Western, Kling, and Weiman 2001; Holzer 1996).

REFERENCES

Acevedo-Garcia, Dolores, and Kimberly A. Lochner. 2003 "Residential Segregation and Health." In *Neighborhoods and Health*, edited by Ichiro Kawachi and Lisa F. Berkman. New York: Oxford University Press.

Administration for Children and Families. 2005. *Head Start Impact Study: First Year Findings.* Washington: U.S. Department of Health and Human Services.

Antonovsky, Aaron. 1967. "Social Class, Life Expectancy and Overall Mortality." *The Milbank Memorial Fund Quarterly* 45(2): 31–73.

Barnett, W. Steven. 1995. "Long-Term Effects of Early Childhood Programs on Cognitive and School Outcomes." *The Future of Children* 5(3): 25–50.

———. 2002. "Early Childhood Education." In *School Reform Proposals: The Research Evidence*, edited by Alex Molnar. Greenwich, Conn.: Information Age Publishing.

Behrman, Jeve R., and John Hoddinot. 2005. "Programme Evalution with Unobserved Heterogeneity and Selective Implementation: The Mexican PROGRESA Impact on Child Nutrition." *Oxford Bulletin of Economics and Statistics* 67(4): 547–69.

Behrman, Jeve R., Piyali Sengupta, and Petra Todd. 2005. "Progressing Through PROGRESA." *Economic Development and Cultural Change* 54(1) 237–76.

Benabou, Roland. 1996a. "Equity and Efficiency in Human Capital Investment: The Local Connection." *Review of Economic Studies* 63(2): 237–64.

———. 1996b. "Heterogeneity, Stratification, and Growth: Macroeconomic Implications of Community Structure and School Finance." *American Economic Review* 86(3): 584–609.

————. 2000. "Unequal Societies: Income Distribution and the Social Contract." *American Economic Review* 90(1): 96–129.

Berger, Lawrence M., Jennifer Hill, and Jane Waldfogel. 2005. "Maternity Leave, Early Maternal Employment and Child Health and Development in the U.S." *Economic Journal* 115(February): F29–47.

Berrueta-Clement, John R., Lawrence J. Schweinhart, Steven W. Barnett, Ann S. Epstein, and David P. Weikart. 1984. *Changed Lives: The Effects of the Perry Preschool Program on Youths Through Age 19.* Ypsilanti, Mich.: High/Scope Press.

Boyce, W. Thomas, and Daniel Keating. 2004. "Should We Intervene to Improve Childhood Circumstances?" In *A Lifecourse Approach to Chronic Disease Epidemiology*, edited by Yoav Ben-Shlomo and Diana Kuh. Oxford: Oxford University Press.

Brooks-Gunn, Jeanne, Greg J. Duncan, and Pia Rebello Britto. 1999. "Are Socioeconomic Gradients for Children Similar to Those for Adults? Achievement and Health of Children in the United States." In *Developmental Health and the Wealth of Nations: Social, Biological, and Educational Dynamics*, edited by Daniel P. Keating and Clyde Hertzman. New York: Guilford Press.

Campbell, Frances A., and Craig T. Ramey. 1995. "Cognitive and School Outcomes for High-Risk African American Students at Middle Adolescence: Positive Effects of Early Intervention." *American Educational Research Journal* 32(4): 743–72.

Campbell, Frances A., Craig T. Ramey, Elizabeth Pungello, Joseph Sparling, and Shari Miller-Johnson. 2002. "Early Childhood Education: Young Adult Outcomes from the Abecedarian Project." *Applied Developmental Science* 6(1): 42–57.

Case, Anne, Darren Lubotsky, and Christina Paxson. 2002. "Economic Status and Health in Childhood: The Origins of the Gradient." *American Economic Review* 92(5): 1308–34.

Caspi, Avshalom, Karen Sugden, Terrie E. Moffitt, Alan Taylor, Ian W. Craig, HonaLee Harrington, Joseph McClay, Jonathan Mill, Judy Martin, Anthony Braithwaite, and Richie Poulton. 2003. "Influence of Life Stress on Depression: Moderation by a Polymorphism in the 5-HTT Gene." *Science* 301(5631): 386–89.

Cavelaars, Adrienne E., Anton E. Kunst, Jose J. Geurts, Roberta Crialesi, Liv Grotvedt, Uwe Helmert, Eero Lahelma, Olle Lundberg, Andreas Mielck, Niels K. Rasmussen, Enrique Regidor, Thomas Spuhler, and Johan P. Mackenbach. 2000. "Persistent Variations in Average Height Between Countries and Between Socio-economic Groups: An Overview of 10 European Countries." *Annals of Human Biology* 27(4): 407–21.

Cavelaars, Adrienne E., Anton E. Kunst, Jose J. Geurts, Roberta Crialesi, Liv Grotvedt, Uwe Helmert, Eero Lahelma, Olle Lundberg, Jil Matheson, Andreas Mielck, Andree Mizrahi, Niels K. Rasmussen, Enrique Regidor, Thomas Spuhler, and Johan P. Mackenbach. 1998. "Differences in Self Reported Morbidity by Educational Level: A Comparison of 11 Western European Countries." *Journal of Epidemiology and Community Health* 52(4): 219–27.

Chatterji, Pinka, and Kevin Frick. 2003. "Does Returning to Work After Childbirth Affect Breastfeeding Practices?" National Bureau of Economic Research Working Paper No. 9630. Cambridge, Mass.: National Bureau of Economic Research.

Chen, Edith, Karen A. Matthews, and W. Thomas Boyce. 2002. "Socioeconomic Differences in Children's Health: How and Why Do These Relationships Change with Age?" *Psychology Bulletin* 128(2): 295–329.

Clarke, Stevens H., and Frances A. Campbell. 1998. "Can Intervention Early Prevent Crime

Later? The Abecedarian Project Compared with Other Programs." *Early Childhood Research Quarterly* 13(2): 319–43.

Corcoran, Sean, William N. Evans, Jennifer Godwin, Sheila E. Murray, Robert M. Schwab, and Sheila Murray. 2004. "The Changing Distribution of Education Finance: 1972–1997." In *Social Equality*, edited by Kathryn M. Neckerman. New York: Russell Sage Foundation.

Currie, Janet. 2001. "Early Childhood Education Programs." *Journal of Economic Perspectives* 15(2): 213–38.

———. 2005. "When Do We Really Know What We Think We Know? Determining Causality." In *Work, Family, Health and Well-Being*, edited by Suzanne M. Bianchi and Lynne Casper. Mahwah, N.J.: Lawrence Earlbaum Associates.

Currie, Janet, and Duncan Thomas. 1995. "Does Head Start Make a Difference?" *American Economic Review* 85(3): 341–64.

———. 1999. "Does Head Start Help Hispanic Children?" *Journal of Public Economics* 74(2): 232–62.

———. 2000. "School Quality and the Longer-Term Effects of Head Start." *Journal of Human Resources* 35(4): 755–74.

Dickerson, Sally S., and Margaret E. Kemeny. 2004. "Acute Stressors and Cortisol Responses: A Theoretical Integration and Synthesis of Laboratory Research." *Psychological Bulletin* 130(3): 355–91.

Donald, Merlin. 2001. *A Mind So Rare: The Evolution of Human Consciousness*. New York: W. W. Norton and Company.

Dunn, James R., Bill Burgess, and Nancy A. Ross. 2005. "Income Distribution, Public Services Expenditures, and All Cause Mortality in the U.S. States." *Journal of Epidemiology and Community Health* 59(9): 768–74.

Durlauf, Steven N. 1996. "A Theory of Persistent Income Inequality." *Journal of Economic Growth* 1(1): 75–94.

———. 2001. "The Memberships Theory of Poverty: The Role of Group Affiliations in Determining Socioeconomic Outcomes." In *Understanding Poverty in America*, edited by Sheldon Danziger and Robert Haveman. Cambridge, Mass.: Harvard University Press.

Evenhouse, Eirik, and Siobhan Reilly. 2005. "Improved Estimates of the Benefits of Breastfeeding Using Sibling Comparisons to Reduce Selection Bias." *Health Services Research* 40(6): 1781–802.

Everson, Susan A., George A. Kaplan, Debbie E. Goldberg, and Jukka T. Salonen. 2000. "Hypertension Incidence Is Predicted by High Levels of Hopelessness in Finnish Men." *Hypertension* 35(2): 561–67.

Everson, Susan A., George A. Kaplan, Debbie E. Goldberg, Riitta Salonen, and Jukka T. Salonen. 1997. "Hopelessness and 4-year Progression of Carotid Atherosclerosis. The Kuopio Ischemic Heart Disease Risk Factor Study." *Arteriosclerosis, Thrombosis, and Vascular Biology* 17(8): 1490–5.

Everson, Susan A., Debbie E. Goldberg, George A. Kaplan, Richard D. Cohen, Eero Pukkala, Jaako Tuomilehto, and Jukka T. Salonen. 1996. "Hopelessness and Risk of Mortality and Incidence of Myocardial Infarction and Cancer." *Psychosomatic Medicine* 58(2): 113–21.

Everson-Rose, Susan A., and Tene T. Lewis. 2005. "Psychosocial Factors and Cardiovascular Diseases." *Annual Review of Public Health* 26: 469–500.

Fogel, Robert. 2003. "Secular Trends in Physiological Capital: Implications for Equity in

Health Care." National Bureau of Economic Research Working Paper No. 9771. Cambridge, Mass.: National Bureau of Economic Research.

Galobardes, Bruna, John W. Lynch, and George Davey Smith. 2004. "Childhood Socioeconomic Circumstances and Cause-Specific Mortality in Adulthood: Systematic Review and Interpretation." *Epidemiologic Review* 26: 7–21.

Galobardes, Bruna, George Davey Smith, and John W. Lynch. 2006. "Systematic Review of the Influence of Childhood Socioeconomic Circumstances on Risk for Cardiovascular Disease in Adulthood." *Annals of Epidemiology* 16(2): 91–104.

Garces, Eliana, Duncan Thomas, and Janet Currie. 2002. "Longer-Term Effects of Head Start." *American Economic Review* 92(4): 999–1012.

Graham, Hillary. 2004. "Social Determinants and Their Unequal Distribution: Clarifying Policy Understandings." *Milbank Quarterly* 82(1): 101–24.

Gunnar, Megan, and Bonny Donzella. 2002. "Social Regulation of the Cortisol Levels in Early Human Development." *Psychoneuroendocrinology* 27(1–2): 199–220.

Hammett, Theodore M., Patricia Harmon, and Laura M. Maruschak. 1999. "1996–1997 Update: HIV/AIDS, STDs and TB in Correctional Facilities. Issues and Practices." Publication NCJ 176344. Washington: U.S. Department of Justice.

Harder, Thomas, Renate Bergmann, Gerd Kallischnigg, and Andreas Plagemann. 2005. "Duration of Breastfeeding and Risk of Overweight: A Meta-analysis." *American Journal of Epidemiology* 162(5): 397–403.

Harknett, Kristin, Irwin Garfinkel, Jay Bainbridge, Timothy Smeeding, Nancy Folbre, and Sara McLanahan. 2005. "Are Public Expenditures Associated with Better Child Outcomes in the U.S.? A Comparison Across 50 States." *Analyses of Social Issues and Public Policy* 5(1): 103–25.

Harper, Sam, John W.Lynch, Wan Ling Hsu, Susan A. Everson, Marianne M. Hillemeier, Trivellore E. Raghunathan, Jukka T. Salonen, and George A. Kaplan. 2002. "Life Course Socioeconomic Conditions and Adult Psychosocial Functioning." *International Journal of Epidemiology* 31(2): 395–403.

Hayward, Mark D., and Bridget K. Gorman. 2004. "The Long Arm of Childhood: The Influence of Early-life Social Conditions on Men's Mortality." *Demography* 41(1): 87–107.

Hertzman, Clyde. 1999. "Population Health and Human Development." In *Developmental Health and the Wealth of Nations*, edited by Daniel Keating and Clyde Hertzman. New York: Guilford Press.

Holzer, Harry J. 1996. *What Employers Want: Job Prospects for Less-Educated Workers*. New York: Russell Sage Foundation.

Johnson, Rucker C., and Steven Raphael. 2005. "The Effects of Male Incarceration Dynamics on AIDS Infection Rates Among African American Women and Men." Unpublished manuscript. Goldman School of Public Policy, University of California, Berkeley.

Kaplan, George A., and Julian E. Keil. 1993. "Socioeconomic Factors and Cardiovascular Disease: A Review of the Literature." *Circulation* 88(4): 1973–98.

Kaplan, George A., Gavin Turrell, John W. Lynch, Susan A. Everson, Eeva Liisa Helkala, and Jukka T. Salonen. 2001. "Childhood Socioeconomic Position and Cognitive Function in Adulthood." *International Journal of Epidemiology* 30(2): 256–63.

Karoly, Lynne A., and James H. Bigelow. 2005. *The Economics of Investing in Universal Preschool Education in California*. Santa Monica, Calif.: RAND Corporation.

Karoly, Lynne A., Peter W. Greenwood, Susan S. Everingham, Jill Hoube, M. Rebecca Kilburn, C. Peter Rydell, Matthew R. Sanders, and James R. Chiesa. 1998. *Investing in Our Children: What We Know and Don't Know About the Costs and Benefits of Early Childhood Interventions.* Santa Monica, Calif.: RAND Corporation.

Keating, Daniel P. 2004. "Cognitive and Brain Development." In *Handbook of Adolescent Psychology,* edited by Richard Lerner and Laurence Steinberg. New York: John Wiley and Sons.

Keating, Daniel P., and Clyde Hertzman. 1999. *Developmental Health and the Wealth of Nations: Social, Biological and Educational Dynamics.* New York: Guilford Press.

Kuh, Diana, and Yoav Ben-Shlomo, editors. 2004. *A Life Course Approach to Chronic Disease Epidemiology.* Oxford: Oxford University Press.

Kunst, Anton E., and Johan P. Mackenbach. 1992. *An International Comparison of Socioeconomic Inequalities in Mortality.* Rotterdam: Erasmus University.

———. 1994. "The Size of Mortality Differences Associated with Educational Level in Nine Industrialized Countries." *American Journal of Public Health* 84(6): 932–7.

Lantz, Paula M., John W. Lynch, James S. House, James M. Lepkowski, Richard P. Mero, Marc A. Musick, and David R. Williams. 2001. "Socioeconomic Disparities in Health Change in a Longitudinal Study of U.S. Adults: The Role of Health-Risk Behaviors." *Social Science Medicine* 53(1): 29–40.

Lee, Valerie L., and Susanna Loeb. 1995. "Where Do Head Start Attendees End Up? One Reason Why Preschool Effects Fade Out." *Educational Evaluation and Policy Analysis* 17(1): 62–82.

Lee, Valerie L., Elizabeth Schnur, and Jeanne Brooks-Gunn. 1988. "Does Head Start Work? A 1-year Follow-up Comparison of Disadvantaged Children Attending Head Start, No Preschool and Other Preschool Programs." *Developmental Psychology* 24(2): 210–22.

Lee, Valerie L., Jeanne Brooks-Gunn, Elizabeth Schnur, and Fong-Ruey Liaw. 1990. "Are Head Start Effects Sustained? A Longitudinal Follow-up Comparison of Disadvantaged Children Attending Head Start, No Preschool, and Other Preschool Programs." *Child Development* 61(2): 495–507.

Li, Ruowei, Natalie Darling, Emmanuel Maurice, Lawrence Barker, and Lawrence M. Grummer-Strawn. 2005. "Breastfeeding Rates in the United States by Characteristics of the Child, Mother, or Family: The 2002 National Immunization Survey." *Pediatrics* 115(1): e31–e37.

Ludwig, Jens, and Douglas L. Miller. 2005. "Does Head Start Improve Children's Life Chances? Evidence From a Regression Discontinuity Design." National Bureau of Economic Research Working Paper No. 11702. Cambridge, Mass.: National Bureau of Economic Research.

Lynch, John W., George A. Kaplan, and Jukka T. Salonen. 1997. "Why Do Poor People Behave Poorly? Variation in Adult Health Behaviours and Psychosocial Characteristics by Stages of the Socioeconomic Lifecourse." *Social Science Medicine* 44(6): 809–19.

Mackenbach, Johan P., Adrienne E. Cavelaars, Anton E. Kunst, and Feikje Groenhof. 2000. "Socioeconomic Inequalities in Cardiovascular Disease Mortality: An International Study." *European Heart Journal* 21(14): 1141–51.

MacNeil, Jennifer R., Mark N. Lobato, and Marissa Moore. 2005. "An Unanswered Health Disparity: Tuberculosis Among Correctional Inmates, 1993 through 2003." *American Journal of Public Health* 95(10): 1800–5.

Marmot, Michael. 2004. *The Status Syndrome: How Social Standing Affects Our Health and Longevity*. New York: Henry Holt and Company.

Marmot, Michael, George Davey Smith, Steven Stansfield, Chandra Patel, Fiona North, Jenny Head, Ian White, Eric Brunner, and Amanda Feeney. 1991. "Health Inequalities Among British Civil Servants: The Whitehall II Study." *Lancet* 337(8754): 1387–93.

Martin, Richard M., David Gunnell, and George Davey Smith. 2005. "Breastfeeding in Infancy and Blood Pressure in Later Life: Systematic Review and Meta-analysis." *American Journal of Epidemiology* 161(1): 15–26.

Mayer, Susan E. 2002. "How Economic Segregation Affects Children's Educational Attainment." *Social Forces* 81(1): 153–76.

McCarton, Cecelia, Jeanne Brooks-Gunn, Ina Wallace, Charles Bauer, Forrest Bennet, Judy Bernbaum, Sue Broyles, Patrick Casey, Marie McCormick, David Scott, John Tyson, James Tonascia, and Curtis Meinert. 1997. "Results at 8 Years of Intervention for Low-Birth-Weight Premature Infants: The Infant Health and Development Program." *Journal of the American Medical Association* 277(2): 126–32.

McCormick, Marie C., Jeanne Brooks-Gunn, Stephen L. Buka, Julie Goldman, Jennifer Yu, Mikhail Salganik, David T. Scott, Forrest C. Bennett, Libby L. Kay, Judy C. Bernbaum, Charles R. Bauer, Camilia Martin, Elizabeth R. Woods, Anne Martin, and Patrick H. Casey. 2006. "Early Intervention in Low Birth Weight Premature Infants: Results at 18 Years of Age for the Infant Health and Development Program." *Pediatrics* 117(3): 771–80.

McEwan, Bruce S. 2005. "Stressed or Stressed Out: What Is the Difference?" *Journal of Psychiatry Neuroscience* 30(5): 315–8.

Miedel, Wendy T., and Arthur J. Reynolds. 1999. "Parent Involvement in Early Intervention for Disadvantaged Children: Does It Matter?" *Journal of School Psychology* 37(4): 379–402.

Muntaner, Carles, William W. Eaton, Richard Miech, and Patricia O'Campo. 2004. "Socioeconomic Position and Major Mental Disorders." *Epidemiologic Review* 26: 53–62.

Murray, Sheila, William N. Evans, and Robert M. Schwab. 1998. "Education-Finance Reform and the Distribution of Education Resources." *American Economic Review* 88(4): 789–812.

Navarro, Vicente, and Leiyu Shi. 2001. "The Political Context of Social Inequalities and Health." *Social Science and Medicine* 52: 481–91.

NICHD Early Child Care Research Network. 2006. "Child-care Effect Sizes for the NICHD Study of Early Child Care and Youth Development." *American Psychologist* 61(2): 99–116.

Oden, Sherri, Lawrence J. Schweinhart, and David P. Weikart. 2000. *Into Adulthood: A Study of the Effects of Head Start*. Ypsilanti, Mich.: High/Scope Press.

OECD. 2004. *Learning for Tomorrow's World-First Results from PISA 2003*. Paris: OECD.

Orfield, Gary, and Chungmei Lee. 2005. *Why Segregation Matters: Poverty and Educational Inequality*. Cambridge, Mass.: The Civil Rights Project at Harvard University.

Pager, Devah. 2003. "The Mark of a Criminal Record." *American Journal of Sociology* 108(5): 937–75.

Ramey, Craig T., Frances Campbell, and Clancy Blair. 1998. "Enhancing the Life Course for High Risk Children." In *Social Programs that Work*, edited by Jonathan Crane. New York: Russell Sage Foundation.

Reynolds, Arthur J. 2000. *Success in Early Intervention: The Chicago Child-Parent Centers*. Lincoln, Neb.: University of Nebraska Press.

————. 2004. "Research on Early Childhood Interventions in the Confirmatory Mode." *Children and Youth Services Review* 26(1): 15–38.

Reynolds, Arthur. J., and Dylan L. Robertson. 2003. "School-based Early Intervention and Later Child Maltreatment in the Chicago Longitudinal Study." *Child Development* 74(1): 3–26.

Reynolds, Arthur J., Suh-Ruu Ou, and James W. Topitzes. 2004. "Paths of Effects of Early Childhood Intervention on Educational Attainment and Delinquency: A Confirmatory Analysis of the Chicago Child-Parent Centers." *Child Development* 75(5): 1299–1328.

Reynolds, Arthur. J., Nancy A. Mavrogenes, Nikolaus Bezruczko, and Mavis Hagemann. 1996. "Cognitive and Family-Support Mediators of Preschool Effectiveness: A Confirmatory Analysis." *Child Development* 67(3): 1119–40.

Reynolds, Arthur J., Judy A. Temple, Dylan L. Robertson, and Emily A. Mann. 2001. "Long-Term Effects of an Early Childhood Intervention on Educational Achievement and Juvenile Arrest: A 15-year Follow-up of Low-Income Children in Public Schools." *Journal of the American Medical Association* 285(18): 2339–46.

Rubenstein, Ross. 2002. "Providing Adequate Educational Funding: A State-by-State Analysis of Expenditure Needs." *Public Budgeting and Finance* 22(4): 73–98.

Ruhm, Christopher J. 2000. "Parental Leave and Child Health." *Journal of Health Economics* 19(6): 931–60.

Sapolsky, Robert M. 2005. "The Influence of Social Hierarchy on Primate Health." *Science* 308(5722): 648–52.

Schweinhart, Lawrence J., Helen V. Barnes, and David P. Weikart. 1993. "Significant Benefits: The High/Scope Perry Preschool Study Through Age 27." *Monographs of the High/Scope Educational Research Foundation* No. 10. Ypsilanti, Mich.: High/Scope Press.

Schweinhart, Lawrence J., Jeanne Montie, Zongping Xiang, Steven W. Barnett, Clive R. Belfield, and Milagros Nores. 2005. "Lifetime Effects: The High/Scope Perry Preschool Study Through Age 40." *Monographs of the High/Scope Educational Research Foundation* No.14. Ypsilanti, Mich.: High/Scope Press.

Sen, Amartya. 1999. *Development as Freedom*. Oxford: Oxford University Press.

Smith, James P. 2004. "Unraveling the SES Health Connection." *Institute for Fiscal Studies* W04/02. London.

Suomi, Stephen J. 2000. "A Biobehavioral Perspective on Developmental Psychopathology." In *Handbook of Development Psychopathology*, edited by Arnold J. Sameroff, Michael Lewis, and Suzanne M. Miller. 2nd edition. New York: Kluwer Academic Publishers.

Tanaka, Sakiko. 2005. "Parental Leave and Child Health Across OECD Countries." *Economic Journal* 115(February): F7–F28.

Temple, Judy, Arthur J. Reynolds, and Wendy Miedel. 2000. "Can Early Intervention Prevent High School Dropout? Evidence from the Chicago Child-Parent Centers." *Urban Affairs* 35(1): 31–56.

Tiebout, Charles M. 1956. "A Pure Theory of Local Expenditures." *Journal of Political Economy* 64(5): 416–24.

Tremblay, Richard E. 1999. "When Children's Social Development Fails." In *Developmental Health and the Wealth of Nations: Social, Biological, and Educational Dynamics*, edited by Daniel P. Keating and Clyde Hertzman. New York: Guilford Press.

Vagero, Denny, and Robert Erikson. 1997. "Socioeconomic Inequalities in Morbidity and Mortality in Western Europe." *Lancet* 350(9076): 516–8.

Vagero, Denny, and Olle Lundberg. 1989. "Health Inequalities in Britain and Sweden." *Lancet* 2(8653): 35–36.

Weikart, David P., James T. Bond, and Judy T. McNeil. 1978. "The Ypsilanti Perry Preschool Project: Preschool Years and Longitudinal Results Through Fourth Grade." *Monographs of the High/Scope Educational Research Foundation* No. 3. Ypsilanti, Mich.: High/Scope Press.

Western, Bruce, Jeffrey R. Kling, and David F. Weiman. 2001. "The Labor Market Consequences of Incarceration." *Crime and Delinquency* 47(3): 410–27.

Williams, David R., and Chiquita Collins. 2001. "Racial Residential Segregation: A Fundamental Cause of Racial Disparities in Health." *Public Health Reports* 116(September–October): 404–16.

Willms, J. Douglas. 1999a. "Inequalities in Literacy Skills Among Youth in Canada and the United States." Catalogue #89-552-MIE, no. 6. Ottawa, Ontario: Statistics Canada.

———. 1999b. "Quality and Inequality in Children's Literacy." In *Developmental Health and the Wealth of Nations: Social, Biological, and Educational Dynamics*, edited by Daniel P. Keating and Clyde Hertzman. New York: Guilford Press.

———. 2003a. "Literacy Proficiency of Youth: Evidence of Converging Socioeconomic Gradients." *International Journal of Educational Research* 39(3): 247–52.

———. 2003b. "Ten Hypotheses About Socioeconomic Gradients and Community Differences in Children's Developmental Outcomes." Canada Working Paper SP-560-01-03E. Ottawa, Ontario: Applied Research Branch, Human Resources Development.

———. 2004. *Reading Achievement in Canada and the United States: Findings from the OECD Programme for International Student Assessment*. Quebec: Human Resources Skills and Development Canada.

Wilson, Kathryn, Kristina Lambright, and Timothy Smeeding. 2004. "School Finance, Equivalent Educational Expenditure and Income Distribution: Equal Dollars or Equal Chances for Success?" Working Paper No. 62. Syracuse, N.Y.: Maxwell School of Citizenship and Public Affairs, Center for Policy Research.

Woodcock, Richard W., and M. Bonner Johnson. 1990. *Manual for the Woodcock-Johnson Tests of Achievement-Revised*. Allen, Tx.: RCL Enterprises.

Worthman, Carol M., and Jennifer Kuzara. 2005. "Life History and the Early Origins of Health Differentials." *American Journal of Human Biology* 17(1): 95–112.

Yoshikawa, Hirokazu. 1995. "Long-Term Effects of Early Childhood Programs on Social Outcomes and Delinquency." *Future of Children* 5(3): 51–75.

Part III

Income Transfer Policy

Chapter 4

Income Support Policies and Health Among the Elderly

Pamela Herd, James S. House, and Robert F. Schoeni

There is increasing evidence that health care accounts for only a modest fraction of the variation in individual and population health (McGinnis,
Williams-Russo, and Knickman 2002). At the same time, there are strong and
well-documented associations between health and socioeconomic factors. This
suggests that "non-health" factors (that is, social and economic determinants) and
related policies deserve heightened attention, alongside biomedical factors, in determining individual and population health. Although researchers and policy
makers increasingly recognize the general importance of social and economic factors for health, the peer-review research literature includes very limited research
on or discussion of the health effects of public policy in these "non-health"
domains.

In particular, though there is a large and rapidly growing body of research that
documents a strong and robust association of income with health (Haan, Kaplan,
and Syme 1989; Lantz et al.1998; Duncan 1994; Mare 1990; McDonough et al. 1997;
Marmot et al. 1991; Menchik 1993; Pappas et al. 1993), there is little research examining the effects of income-support policies on health. Understanding the impact
on health of major government income-support or income-supplementation policies is important for understanding the role this major domain of social and economic policy may play in improving individual and population health.

This paper explores both the promise and the problems associated with research
on the relationship between government income-support policies and health. We
first briefly review the extensive empirical research supporting claims that income
affects health. We next consider recent work focused on the causal direction of the
relationship between income and health, and we suggest that this and the more
general literature on income and health indicate the utility for both science and
policy of better understanding how much, when, and why income-support policies affect health. Then, we describe why income-support policies targeted at the

elderly provide particularly fertile ground for studying the effects of income supports on health. Last, we review prior evidence and some new data on the health effects of income supports targeted at the elderly, and present some new analyses regarding the Supplemental Security Income (SSI) program, an income support targeted at the poorest elderly Americans.

WHY SHOULD WE STUDY HEALTH EFFECTS OF INCOME-SUPPORT POLICIES AND WHY DON'T WE?

The rationale for asking whether income-transfer policy causally affects health is the considerable evidence of a strong and predictive association between income and mortality and morbidity. Several decades of sociological and epidemiological research supporting the hypothesis that income affects health suggest that we may be able to significantly improve population health by supporting and supplementing incomes at the broad lower end of the income distribution and particularly among the poor. However, only direct study of the extent to which income supports affect health can evaluate this policy implication.

Empirical Evidence from Social Epidemiology and Sociology

Why do sociologists and epidemiologists believe that income affects health? First and foremost, people with low incomes die sooner than people with higher incomes (Duleep 1986; Haan, Kaplan, and Syme 1989; Menchik 1993; Duncan 1994; Fox, Goldblatt, and Jones 1985; Mare 1990; McDonough et al. 1997). This is reflected in data from the American Changing Lives Study, which began in 1986 and is a nationally representative sixteen-year longitudinal study of participants ages twenty-five and older. By 2000, over 40 percent of those with 1986 incomes below ten thousand dollars had died; meanwhile, less than 10 percent of those with 1986 incomes above thirty thousand dollars had died (House, Lantz, and Herd 2005). Table 4.1 shows mortality analyses for those ages forty-five and older using the Panel Study of Income Dynamics between 1972 and 1989. While 23 percent or more of those with incomes of less than $15,000 died, just 4 percent of those with incomes greater than $70,000 died (McDonough et al. 1997). As table 4.1 also demonstrates, however, income has diminishing returns: increases in income have the greatest impact on health for the poorest individuals, and they have still substantial but diminishing effects up to around the median income level (Backlund, Sorlie, and Johnson 1996; House et al. 1990; Mirowsky and Hu 1996; Sorlie, Backlund, and Keller 1995).

Second, low-income people have more chronic conditions and functional limitations, higher rates of mental health problems, and generally report lower health

TABLE 4.1 / Proportionate Mortality, By Age and Income, Panel Study of Income Dynamics, 1972 to 1989

Five-Year Average Annual Household Income, 1993	Ages Forty-Five and Older		Ages Forty-Five to Sixty-Four	
	Sample Proportion	Proportion of Deaths	Sample Proportion	Proportion of Deaths
Less than $15,000	0.17	0.23	0.07	0.11
$15,000 to 20,000	0.08	0.18	0.06	0.09
$20,001 to 30,000	0.15	0.14	0.06	0.06
$30,001 to 50,000	0.25	0.07	0.3	0.04
$50,001 to 70,000	0.17	0.06	0.24	0.04
Greater than $70,000	0.17	0.04	0.23	0.03

Source: McDonough et al. (1997).

status (House et al. 1994; Kington and Smith 1997; Mirowsky and Ross 2001; Mulatu and Schooler 2002). Table 4.2 shows the proportion of individuals, by poverty status, reporting an array of health problems in the 2003 National Health Interview Study (National Center for Health Statistics 2005). Compared to those living above 200 percent of the poverty level, those living below 100 percent of the poverty level were more likely to have asthma attacks, back and neck pain, a disabling chronic condition, vision and hearing problems, psychological problems,

TABLE 4.2 / Reported Health Problems in 2003 among Adults Eighteen Years and Over, By Poverty Level,[a] National Health Interview Survey

Health Problem	Poor	Near Poor	Nonpoor
Asthma attack	5.3	4.1	2.9
Severe headache or migraine	21.0	18.7	13.3
Low back pain	33.2	30.6	25.8
Neck pain	17.9	16.3	13.8
Disabling chronic condition[b]	23.1	17	9.2
Vision problems	13.7	11.6	7.3
Hearing problems	3.9	3.6	2.8
Fair or poor health[b]	20.4	14.4	6.1
Psychological distress	8.7	5.4	1.8
Hypertension[c]	23.3	23.0	18.0

Source: National Center for Health Statistics (2005).
[a] "Poor" is defined as below 100 percent of the poverty level, "near poor" is between 100 percent and 200 percent of poverty, and "nonpoor" is above 200 percent of poverty. Rates take account of family size. For example, in 2003, 100 percent of the poverty level for a family of four was $18,660.
[b] Measured for all ages.
[c] Measured for those twenty years and over.

and hypertension, and they were more than three times as likely to report their general health as fair or poor.

Finally, studies have also found that the duration of poverty matters for health: the longer the poverty spell, the worse one's health is (Lynch, Kaplan, and Shema 1997). In the 1984 Panel Study of Income Dynamics, those who reported transient poverty had self-reported health scores that were 17 percent lower and those who had persistent poverty had self-reported health scores that were 32 percent lower compared to those who reported no poverty spells over the prior sixteen years (McDonough and Berglund 2003).

But, what are the mechanisms that connect this relationship between income and health? Low incomes and the associated lack of health insurance adversely affect access to and quality of health care. Health insurance and health care, however, likely account for only 10 to 20 percent of this relationship (McGinnis, Williams-Russo, and Knickman 2002). Over two decades of epidemiological and sociological research has focused on how material deprivation, psychosocial factors, and work link income to health. Poor people have difficulty meeting basic needs such as good nutrition and safe and healthy home and work environments, which are imperative to good health (Adler et al. 1993; Stokols 1992). For example, poor children are more likely to report food insufficiencies and are more likely to be iron deficient (Alaimo et al. 2001). Furthermore, studies find that a substantial part of the relationship between low incomes and health can be explained by deprivation (that is, individuals reporting they could not afford basic amenities such as housing, food, and clothing) (Stronks, van de Mheen, and Mackenbach 1998).

Low incomes are also predictive of less tangible psychosocial risk factors, which, in turn, are predictive of health (House and Williams 2000). Low-income people face high levels of stress, which play a significant role in the onset of disease (Adler et al. 1993; Byrne and Whyte 1980; Cohen, Tyrell, and Smith 1993; Hayward, Pienta, and McLaughlin 1997). In addition, low-income individuals are more vulnerable to undesirable life events such as job loss, large financial losses, separation and divorce, widowhood, and deaths of loved ones, and they also experience more chronic stress at home and work (McLeod and Kessler 1990; Turner, Wheaton, and Lloyd 1995). Low-income individuals are more socially isolated, which is predictive of poor health (House, Landis, and Umberson 1988; Turner and Noh 1988; Turner and Marino 1994). Having a limited sense of control over one's life, increased levels of hostility, and increased levels of hopelessness are traits more common among poor people which are also predictive of poor health (Rodin 1986; Rowe and Kahn 1987; House and Williams 2000). Moreover, environmental hazards and physical demands at work and home, to which lower-income people are also more exposed, may negatively affect health over time (Borg and Kristensen 2000; Bosma et al. 1997; Lundberg 1991; Moore and Hayward 1990).

One of the most cited explanations for socioeconomic differences in health is based on behavioral factors. Individuals with low incomes are more likely to smoke, drink, and exercise less (Lantz et al. 1998). However, these factors account for only 10 to 20 percent of the association between socioeconomic status and mortality (Lantz et al. 1998). Moreover, these behaviors are more strongly associated with educational attainment than they are with income (Mirowsky and Ross 2003). Nonetheless, the association between poverty and risk behaviors clearly explains some of the relationship between income and health.

Recent Research on Causal Effects of Income on Health (and Vice Versa)

Despite this evidence, the research has not translated into income policies aimed at improving population health. This lack of policy development is partly related to an overemphasis on medical care and access to health insurance. But in the specific case of income supports, the limited policy action is also related to remaining questions about causality in the relationship between income and health.

Unlike sociologist and epidemiologists, some policy researchers and economists do not believe the evidence supports a causal effect of income on health status. Part of this doubt reflects the fact that their theory and research has historically focused on the opposite relationship: how health status affects earnings, income, and wealth. Basically, health is a human-capital variable (alongside education and training) that determines economic well-being, not the reverse (Grossman 1972). Health shocks lead to high out-of-pocket medical expenses, job loss, wage reductions, and changes in consumption behavior, all of which limit the accumulation of income and assets (Smith 1999; Palumbo 1999; Lillard and Weiss 1996).

But much of their criticism also focuses on methodological issues. They criticized early epidemiological and sociological work because it relied largely on cross-sectional data to show the relationship between income and health (House et al. 1990; Kessler and Neighbors 1986; Ross and Huber 1985). Thus, these data could provide support for the hypothesis that income was correlated with health, but could not provide strong causal evidence. Though longitudinal studies throughout the 1980s and 1990s became more common, allowing researchers to control for baseline health status and to examine how income levels and trajecto ries predicted subsequent changes in health (Fox, Goldblatt, and Jones 1985; Haan, Kaplan, and Syme 1989; House et al. 1994; Lantz et al. 1998; Lynch, Kaplan, and Shema 1997; Maddox and Clark 1992; McDonough et al. 1997; Moore and Hayward 1990), some researchers argued that studies like these could not rule out unobserved individual characteristics that determine both income and health (Adams et al. 2003).

Consequently, a small but growing body of research, largely in economics, has begun to estimate the extent to which the undisputedly sizable association between income and health is a product of the effect of income on health rather than vice versa. Recent studies using longitudinal data have implemented individual fixed effect models with panel data to control for time-invariant unobserved individual characteristics such as genetics (Adams et al. 2003; Frijters, Haisken-DeNew, and Shields 2005; Lindahl 2005). While this approach addresses unobserved individual characteristics, it cannot fully account for the temporal ordering of the health and income changes within individuals across time.

Some studies have focused on children or the elderly, as health shocks are less likely to have a direct causal effect on family income for these populations. Anne Case, Darren Lubotsky, and Christina Paxton (2002) found large impacts of parental income on childhood health (measured as self-reported health status, number of days spent in bed due to illness, number of days that health restricted normal activities, the number of hospital episodes, and number of school days missed due to illness) using both cross-sectional and longitudinal data. They were able to rule out health at birth, genetic factors, parental health, and health insurance as explanations for the income effects. Furthermore, the income disparities in health widened as children aged. These findings were particularly striking given the limited variation in childhood health.

Peter Adams and colleagues (2003) focused on those ages seventy and older and found mixed evidence. Linking individual measures of socioeconomic status to health showed that education was predictive of diabetes, arthritis, and cognitive impairment. Wealth was linked to lung disease. Income was linked to psychiatric problems, and poor housing conditions were linked to general self-rated health. But given the nonlinearity between wealth and income and health, an alternative approach that compared individuals of low and high SES produced more significant results.[1] Low SES was predictive of cancer, lung disease, arthritis, hip fractures, cognitive problems, psychiatric problems, depression, and self-rated health.

The mixed findings of Adams and colleagues may be due to their focus specifically on the older population. It has been shown that the simple correlation between SES or income and health becomes weaker in old age (Beckett 2000; Herd 2006; House et al. 1990). One common explanation is that mortality selection operates differentially by income and SES, leaving an increasingly healthier (at least relatively) population of lower-income and lower-SES individuals at older ages. Another explanation is that biological factors become even more powerful predictors of health in old age than social factors (Herd 2006; Robert and House 1994). Though individuals with high educational attainment and high income are able to stave off health decline longer than their peers with limited educational attainment and low incomes, even those who are well off cannot escape ill health and mortality in old age. Finally, Social Security provides substantial income for most older individuals, thus potentially reducing socioeconomic differences.

Other researchers have exploited quasi-experimental unanticipated increases in income. Jonathan Meer, Douglas Miller, and Harvey Rosen (2003) examined whether changes in wealth had effects on health. They found a small effect of wealth on health which was rendered statistically insignificant when wealth was instrumented using inheritances. There are a couple of concerns with using inheritances as an instrument. First, if inheritances involve the death of a parent, they could reflect adverse intergenerational influences on health and hence not be exogenous to health. Second, since inheritances occur mainly at the upper end of the income distribution, and the association between income and health is strongest at the bottom end of the income distribution, the study is biased against finding an effect of income on health. Furthermore, the authors used only a dummy variable for self-reported health status ("excellent, very good, or good health" versus "fair or poor health"), hence capturing limited variation in health and further biasing the effect downward.

In contrast, a study in Sweden found a strong effect of income on mortality, obesity, and mental health (Lindahl 2005). Around 20 percent of the survey sample had received lottery winnings and estimates of the effect of income on health were not altered when income was instrumented using lottery winnings.

Finally, Paul Frijters, John Haisken-DeNew, and Michael Shields (2005) examined how increases in income associated with East Germany's transition to a market-based economy (that is, increases which were exogenous to individuals) affected individuals' satisfaction with their health. Satisfaction was based on a scale from one to ten, ranging from "very satisfied" to "very unsatisfied." They found small but significant impacts. However, given the enormity of the change associated with a transition from a centralized economy to a market-based economy, along with the other profound social changes associated with the transition from being a Soviet bloc country to a Western European country, there may have been unobserved factors for which the researchers could not account that may have had an opposite effect on satisfaction with health.

In sum, findings from recent research that have attempted to address causality head-on have been mixed though largely consistent with an impact of income on health. Some studies have found small effects for specific health measures and other studies have found large effects. While these studies have better addressed selective individual characteristics and the confounding effects of employment, many had other limitations, including omitted-variable bias. In particular, prior research has emphasized the finding that it is poverty which is bad for health, but most of these studies test a linear relationship between income and health. A recent review by the Government Accountability Office (GAO) concluded that economic studies on the relationship between poverty and health clearly demonstrate the negative effects of poverty on health (Government Accountability Office 2007). Further, many of these studies capture short-term changes in health, while other evidence suggests that chronic poverty, as opposed to short-term poverty, has the largest association with health (McDonough and Berglund 2003).

The Need for Research on the Effects of Income-Support Policies on Health

All of the above suggests the need for increased attention to the potential health impacts of income-support policies. Unresolved questions regarding the causal relationship between income and health provide one powerful rationale for pursuing this line of research. Changes in income-transfer policies arguably represent sizable long-term exogenous shocks or natural experiments, providing an alternative way to estimate the causal impact of income on health. Thus, evaluation of the health impacts of planned and unplanned changes in income-support policies can advance basic scientific understanding of the extent of the impact of income on health.

But there are even more important policy-related rationales for pursuing this research. First, if income supports affect health, there is a powerful new rationale for maintaining and strengthening existing income-support policies as well as creating new ones: enhancing the quantity and quality of life and health in the United States. Presently, when policy analysts consider the ramifications of changes to income-support policies like Social Security, SSI (a means-tested income support for the elderly, blind, and disabled), and the Earned Income Tax Credit (EITC), they do not consider the potential health implications. This additional outcome could have a profound impact on cost-benefit analyses of policy formulation and reform.

Second, this evidence could fundamentally reframe how policy makers think about health policy. No longer would policy makers think about expanding access to health insurance and expanding funding for biomedical research as the only avenues for improving population health. Income-support policies could be among the most important non-health policies affecting health and consequently may help resolve America's paradoxical crisis of paying more for health care than other developed nations, but getting less in terms of levels of population health. The United States ranks at the bottom of comparably developed countries in regards to infant mortality and life expectancy (Starfield 2000).[2] At the same time, the United States also has the highest poverty rates (calculated as the percentage of individuals living below half of median income) in the industrialized world (Smeeding, Rainwater, and Burtless 2002). These high poverty rates are largely attributed to limited income-support policies in the United States compared to other countries (Smeeding, Rainwater, and Burtless 2002). Lagging population health in the United States may be a consequence of our high poverty rates.

Clearly, further research on the effects of income supports on health could advance both policy research as well as our basic scientific understanding of the relationship between income and health. But we also note that while our focus is on testing the effects of income supports on health, a greater focus is also needed on the effects of health policy on socioeconomic outcomes ranging from education and occupations to income and wealth. A considerable body of historical economic and demographic research suggests that improvements in health substantially improve people's educational attainment, employment, productivity, earnings, and general economic well-being (Fogel 2004).

Focusing on the Health Effects of Income Supports on the Elderly

In the United States, perhaps the most viable strategy for assessing the effect of income supports on health is to focus on the elderly. Although the gap in health status between the rich and poor decreases with age, it is still substantial for people in their sixties and seventies (Herd 2006; House et al. 1990; House et al. 1994). Furthermore, there is no other point in the life course when incomes are so affected by income-support policies. On average, for those aged sixty-five and older, Social Security composes 40 percent of annual incomes; for one-fifth of the elderly, it composes 80 percent of their income (Social Security Administration 2004). Furthermore, for those that fall below eligibility guidelines for Social Security or whose incomes fall well below the poverty threshold, SSI provides an additional safety net to offset extreme poverty, further subsidizing incomes for about 6 percent of elderly Americans.

Social Security and SSI have been remarkably effective at improving income security among the elderly. This is critical from a health perspective because almost all prior evidence shows that the largest reductions in health are associated with changes in income among those with the most limited incomes (Backlund, Sorlie, and Johnson 1996). Between 1960 and 2005, the elderly poverty rate dropped from almost 30 percent to 10 percent, which is largely attributable to rising Social Security benefits (Engelhardt and Gruber 2004). SSI further protects the very poor. Though eligibility criteria vary by state, almost all elderly persons qualify if their incomes fall below about 75 percent of the poverty level.

Another reason to focus on the older population is that income disparities in health widen from childhood through adulthood, but then diminish at older ages. Differences in both morbidity measures and mortality measures between those with low incomes and high incomes expand all the way across the life course until around when individuals reach the eligibility age for Social Security and the old-age component of SSI, at which point they begin to lessen. These patterns are consistent with the claim that Social Security and SSI have important beneficial effects on health (Herd 2006; House et al. 1994). Of course, most people become eligible for Medicare and Social Security at the same time, so the pattern of changes in health status may be due to Medicare as well as, or even instead of, Social Security. Although explanations for declining health disparities in old age remain largely speculative at this point, they do suggest interesting questions and hypotheses surrounding generous income supports in old age.

Another rationale for focusing on the elderly is that most significant and costly health transitions occur in old age. If income transfers benefit health at these ages, they could have large effects on population health and possibly on health care spending. While increasing life expectancy among the elderly will not "save" money, it is possible that if income supports help reduce the number of years the elderly spend in ill health (that is, if they lead to morbidity compression), there may be reductions in medical spending. Given the fact that the fastest increases in medical spending over the last forty years have occurred among the elderly, any reduction in medical spending on this group would help reduce rapidly rising health care costs (Meara, White, and Culter 2004).

EVIDENCE FOR EFFECTS OF INCOME-SUPPORT POLICY ON HEALTH AMONG THE ELDERLY

There have been only a handful of studies that directly estimate the causal effects of income-transfer policies on the health of the elderly. These studies have been done both outside of and within the United States, and we examine both here.

International Evidence

There have been a few studies on income-transfer policies in developing countries, though the extent of their applicability to the developed world is arguable. Under an income-support experiment titled PROGRESA the Mexican government has provided since 1997 approximately $800 million in aid to 2.6 million rural families (almost one-third of all rural families in Mexico). The program has certain conditions that families must meet to obtain aid. Families must seek preventative health care, children up to age five must have their growth monitored in clinic visits, and mothers must receive prenatal care and health education counseling. Additional income supplements were also available if school-age children attend school. The income was distributed directly to mothers, which is an important distinction in a patriarchal culture (Gertler 2000).

The results showed striking improvements in health for children, adults, and those over age fifty. Participants over age fifty, whose only requirement for participation was an annual preventative checkup, experienced significant reductions in activity limitations due to illness, fewer days bedridden due to sickness, and, more generally, an increase in energy levels as measured by their ability to walk distances without significant fatigue. Children and adults also showed improved outcomes. However, it could not be proven that income had an independent effect on the children's health due to the medical-care requirements linked to the receipt of income benefits. Because of its success, the program is now being generalized to urban Mexico and was adopted by Argentina, Colombia, Honduras, and Nicaragua.

Another study, though not an experimental one, looked at the expansion of pension income to black South Africans. The expansion offered recipients pension levels that were comparable to whites' pensions. Thus, recipients' families had more than twice the median per capita income of black South African families on the whole. Anne Case (2004) found that in households that pooled income into a common household fund, the receipt of pension income was positively connected to the self-reported health status of all household members and to height for children. In households that did not pool income, however, the relationship between receipt of pension and health status was only observed for the pensioner. The health improvements seemed to be a product of better nutrition, better living environments, and less stress, all of which resulted from higher incomes.

Evidence from the United States

Social Security   Social Security is the most obvious elderly income-support program to examine given the magnitude of the program's effect on incomes, especially on poverty among elderly Americans. However, it is also quite difficult to estimate whether Social Security affects health. Simply examining whether those with higher Social Security benefits have better health will not indicate whether

Social Security benefits improve health. This is because the benefits are based on individuals' prior earnings, which may have been negatively affected by prior health. Thus, Social Security benefits may have been determined by prior health status.

One approach to examining the effects of Social Security on health is to focus on the impact of Social Security on population health over time. Ongoing work by Peter Arno, Clyde Schecter, and James House has sought to detect a health impact of Social Security by examining the mortality experience of different adult age groups over the twentieth century. An advantage of this approach is that it takes into account the nonlinearity in the relationship between income and health. Changes to Social Security over this period led to a massive poverty reduction among the elderly. The hypothesis is that two large positive exogenous shocks from Social Security to the income of the elderly occurred over this period, first following its inception in the late 1930s and early 1940s, and secondly after it was de facto and then de jure indexed to inflation during the 1960s and early 1970s. These changes should have produced discontinuous acceleration of the decline of mortality rates in the elderly age groups (ages sixty-five to seventy-four and seventy-five to eighty-four)—but not in adult age groups below age sixty-five—in the ten to fifteen years following these changes.

Visual inspection of mortality trend lines in figure 4.1 is consistent with these expectations. There is a dramatic fall in mortality for those ages seventy-five to eighty-four; in comparison, there is basically no change for those ages fifty-five to sixty-four. This pattern is confirmed by statistical tests for the change in slopes for the fifteen years before and after 1940 and 1970. However, these differences are not as clear or significant if mortality is logged to adjust for the very different average rates of mortality across age groups. Even if the differences are clearly sustained by more refined analysis, the greater improvement in older-age mortality may also be due to the introduction of antibiotics in the period from 1935 to 1955 and the introduction of Medicare in the period from 1965 to 1985. Still, these aggregate data are consistent with a potential positive health impact of the poverty reduction and income expansion produced by Social Security for the older population. Moreover, it suggests the utility of further research which can yield clearer causal inferences.

Stephen Snyder and William Evan (2006) take a different approach to examine whether higher Social Security benefits affect health. This study was based on a quasi-experimental design which compared individuals born within six months of one another but who had differing Social Security benefits due to the "notch." Errant Social Security legislation led to individuals with the exact same work histories born before January 1, 1917 to receive higher Social Security benefits in old age than those born after this date. Thus, the study compared mortality rates between those born in the last three months of 1916 (the experimental group) and those born in the first three months of 1917 (the control group). They found that those in the experimental group, who had higher benefits despite similar work histories to the control group, also had higher mortality rates after age sixty-five than those in the control group who had lower benefits. To explain this finding, which contradicts almost all current evidence that having more income is good for your health, the authors concluded that the group with lower benefits had to work more, which

FIGURE 4.1 / Mortality Trends and the Implementation of Social Security

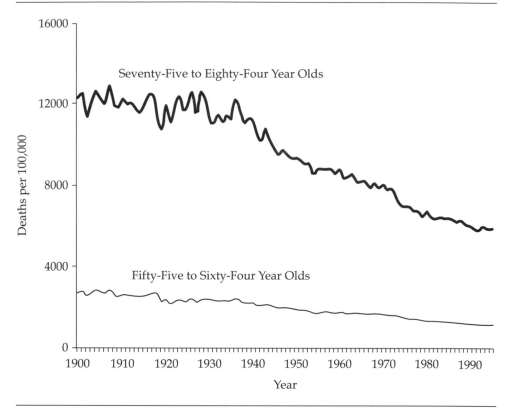

Source: Arno, Schecter, and House (n.d.).
Social Security Benefits Become Regular and Ongoing, January 1940.

lead to more social interaction and thus lower mortality rates despite their lower Social Security benefits.

While the use of the notch to help identify the effects of Social Security on health is novel, some features of this approach are noteworthy. Most importantly, the study looked at how minimally to modestly higher Social Security benefits affected the health of wealthier and healthier individuals. Previous research, however, has shown that the relationship between income and health is predominantly present at the bottom of the income distribution. A notch beneficiary retiring at age sixty-two without a high school degree had just a 1 percent higher benefit, or five dollars extra per month, compared to a similar individual born before the notch. Healthier beneficiaries received larger benefit increases because those retiring at age sixty-five received larger benefit increases than those retiring at age sixty-two, who tend to be much sicker than later retirees (Haveman et al. 2003). Those who retired around age sixty-two had a limited benefit increase—seven dollars per month on average—whereas those retiring at sixty-five had a one hundred and ten dollar average increase. The reason why those who retired later received higher benefits is simply because retiring before age sixty-five leads to a reduction in one's benefit. The later one retires, the higher is one's benefit. And those with higher Social Security benefits generally benefited more highly from the notch. Consequently, this study largely measured the effect of increases for those who are wealthier and healthier on average.

Supplemental Security Income Program (SSI)   While Social Security may have had an important impact on health, it is very difficult to design a study that can lead to unbiased estimates of Social Security's effect today, if ever, because of its universality and the way that an individual's health affects their choice to collect Social Security. SSI, though more limited in the population affected and its total effects on income, has some advantages for testing the effects of income supports on health. A key advantage is that SSI is targeted at the poorest elderly Americans (though the blind and disabled under age sixty-five are also eligible), and past research suggests that income supports which raise the incomes of the poorest individuals should have the largest health effects (Backlund, Sorlie, and Johnson 1996).

SSI was implemented in 1974, though it actually evolved out of the 1935 Social Security Act. In its original form it was called Old Age Assistance (OAA). From the late 1930s through the mid-1950s OAA was a much larger income support than was Social Security, at points providing income for upwards of 30 percent of elderly Americans. But OAA benefits varied across states, with some states providing very generous benefits, and others providing few, if any, benefits. Thus, Congress stepped in and established SSI, which has a federal minimum income guarantee.

The first study that examined the health effects of SSI looked at whether the implementation of the program had any effect on health. Paul Taubman and Robin Sickles (1983) used the Retirement History Survey to examine how the health of elderly recipients changed after they started receiving SSI. Individuals reported how their health compared to those of similar age. The researchers found that SSI had a positive impact on the health of elderly beneficiaries. The health of individuals eligible for SSI previous to implementation was statistically significantly worse than the health of those not eligible. In both 1975 and 1977—after SSI was implemented—the difference in heath was no longer significantly different between these two groups. There are some limitations with this study, however. First, declining differences in health may have been due to mortality selection: SSI recipients may have reflected a more robust group of survivors. Furthermore, SSI eligibility also guaranteed access to Medicaid as a supplement to Medicare. Thus, improved health may have been due to Medicaid instead of SSI.

Given both the promise and problems associated with this study, we have pursued an alternative empirical design to test whether SSI impacts health. Instead of testing whether the implementation of SSI has an effect on health, we tested whether variation in SSI benefits over time within states predicts changes in health. Numerous studies have exploited state variation in maximum state SSI benefits to examine the effects on trends in retirement, savings, and living arrangements among the elderly (Costa 1999; McGarry and Schoeni 2000; Neumark and Powers 1998, 2000, 2003). Our research extended these analyses to look at health, specifically disability. The basic assumption behind the design is that changes in state SSI benefits are exogenous to changes in old-age disability rates, conditional on the covariables.

Though there is a federal minimum, SSI maximum benefits vary between states at a point in time and within states over time. The federal minimum is set around three-quarters of the poverty line. As with Social Security benefits, the federal SSI minimum is adjusted to account for inflation. In 2000, the federal monthly income minimum was $532 for single individuals and $789 for married couples.[3] Some states supplement that benefit. In 1990 and 2000, twenty-five and twenty-seven states, respectively, supplemented the federal benefit. Table 4.3 shows the federal benefit levels and supplements (for singles) in each state, the percentage change in benefits between 1990 and 2000, the annual dollar benefit change between 1990 and 2000, and the maximum annual SSI benefit in each state in 2000.

While many of the percentage changes in monthly benefits appear small, they need to be considered on an annual basis and relative to the baseline income levels without supplementation. Column 4 shows the annual difference in benefits in dollar terms, and column 5 shows the maximum annual benefit in 2000. For example, in Michigan, the benefit change was a 3.9 percent reduction between 1990 and 2000, which may seem small. But this change totaled $258 when the maximum annual income of SSI recipients in Michigan was just $6312. Thus, it is important to keep two things in mind: First, even a small change in income for individuals living well below the poverty level can, for example, be the difference between having and not having enough to eat. Second, because studies of income and health show that small differences in income at the bottom end of the income distribution are correlated with large differences in health, it is possible that the differences in income displayed in table 4.3 could be proportionately more consequential for those with lower incomes and lead to meaningful changes in disability. Of course, there are also some states with very large overall changes in benefits. Connecticut's benefit between 1990 and 2000 dropped by 25 percent and California's dropped by 17 percent.

Using United States census data in 1990 and 2000, we examined the association between state variation in the change in SSI-benefit policy and the change in elderly health. Health was defined as whether or not an individual has mobility limitations, a standard measure in gerontology. The respondent indicated whether he or she had any physical or mental health condition that had lasted six or more months and which made it difficult or impossible to go outside the home alone. Its validity as a health measure is evidenced by the fact that it is highly predictive of Medicare expenditures and mortality (Ferraro and Farmer 1999).

The maximum state SSI benefit (adjusted for inflation) was merged to the 1990 and 2000 census microdata. Using the individual SSI benefit received by each individual, or even using the average of such benefits for a state, would produce endogeneity problems because SSI benefits are inversely related to labor-force participation and earnings, which are correlated with health. Other covariates included age, race, sex, ethnicity, immigrant status, and education. To control for

TABLE 4.3 / State Variation in Maximum SSI Benefit for Single Persons, 1990 and 2000 (in 2000 Dollars)

	Maximum Monthly Benefit[a]		Percent Change in Maximum Monthly Benefit: 1990 to 2000	Annual Dollar Benefit Change: 1990 to 2000	Maximum Annual Income SSI Receipts Can Have: 2000
	1990	2000			
Alaska	944	874	−7.4%	−841	10488
California	829	692	−16.6	1650	8304
Colorado	579	548	−5.4	−374	6576
Connecticut	990	747	−24.6	−2919	8964
D.C.	528	512	−3.0	−189	6144
Hawaii	515	517	0.5	29	6204
Iowa	508	534	5.1	312	6408
Idaho	604	565	−6.5	−470	6780
Maine	521	522	0.2	10	6264
Massachusetts	678	641	−5.5	−444	7692
Michigan	548	526	−3.9	−258	6312
Minnesota	607	593	−2.3	−166	7116
Nebraska	558	519	−7.0	−469	6228
Nevada	555	548	−1.3	−89	6576
New Hampshire	544	539	−0.8	−55	6468
New Jersey	549	543	−1.1	−70	6516
New York	621	599	−3.6	−268	7188
Oklahoma	592	565	−4.6	−328	6780
Oregon	511	514	0.7	40	6168
Pennsylvania	550	539	−2.0	−134	6468
Rhode Island	592	576	−2.8	−196	6912
South Dakota	528	527	−0.1	−9	6324
Utah	516	512	−0.8	−47	6144
Vermont	591	570	−3.6	−252	6840
Washington	545	539	−1.1	−71	6468
Wisconsin	644	596	−7.4	−572	7152
Wyoming	534	522	−2.3	−148	6264
Federal Maximum (Remaining States)[b]	508	512	0.8	48	6144
Average Across All States	558	544	−2.5	−166	6533

Source: Authors' compilation.
[a] These figures are rounded to the dollar, but annual benefit change reflects changes in monthly benefits to the cent.
[b] SSI benefits are automatically adjusted each year to account for inflation. The difference in the federal minimum benefit between 1990 and 2000 is because the CPI adjuster used for automatic cost-of-living increases (for both Social Security and SSI) is different than the CPI adjuster used in most studies to account for inflation.

within-state changes in economic conditions between 1990 and 2000, the state unemployment rate is included. Prior studies have shown a strong connection between unemployment rates and health, even for the elderly (Ruhm 2000). We include an institutional-status measure which captures whether an individual lives in an institution (that is, a formally authorized, supervised care or custody such as a nursing home, hospital, mental institution, or jail). Because SSI can be used to pay for institutional care, it is important to control for this factor. The last covariates include indicators for state of residence and census year (1990 or 2000). Reported results are based on OLS models, but probit models produced nearly identical findings. We report standard errors for all models that allow for an arbitrary correlation matrix within states (the so-called Huber-White sandwich estimator) because of the possibility of serially correlated errors within states.[4]

One significant issue is whether there are other factors correlated with within-state changes in the maximum SSI benefit over time that may lead to a spurious correlation between the maximum SSI benefit and disability. Of particular concern is the fact that Medicaid eligibility is linked to SSI eligibility. Changes in SSI benefits automatically lead to changes in Medicaid eligibility. Thus, there is the possibility the results could reflect Medicaid program effects as opposed to SSI policies. Those recipients potentially affected by this change have Medicare coverage but rely on Medicaid to supplement copayments, deductibles, and goods and services that Medicare does not cover. It is, however, important to consider that this will only be true for those individuals with incomes that fall between the SSI federal benefit and the maximum state benefit. Over 85 percent of SSI beneficiaries in states with supplements have incomes below the federal maximum, so the change potentially affects just 15 percent of recipients (Social Security Administration 2001). Thus, these individuals would remain eligible for Medicaid regardless of whether the state supplement changed. Further, almost half of the states with supplements provide Medicaid benefits to those falling below 100 percent of the poverty level (keep in mind that the state supplement almost never brings individuals above the 100 percent poverty level). Finally, every elderly American in every state can receive some supplemental insurance if they fall anywhere below 150 percent of the poverty line. All states are required to provide varying degrees of coverage up to the 150 percent poverty level through the Qualified Medicare Beneficiary (QMB) and Specified Low Income Beneficiary (SLMB) programs. While these benefits are not as generous as a full Medicaid supplement, this would substantially soften the effect. All of that said, we still use the Current Population Survey to examine whether changes in maximum state SSI benefits between 1992 and 2000 are correlated with changes in Medicaid participation.[5]

The results from these analyses provide support for the hypothesis that more generous SSI benefit levels lead to improvements in mobility limitations. Table 4.4 shows the results for single individuals ages sixty-five and older. The key variable of interest, the maximum state SSI benefit, was a significant and negative predictor of mobility limitations: the higher the SSI maximum benefit, the lower the rate of mobility limitations. For single individuals, every one hundred dollar increase in maximum benefits led to a 0.46 percentage point reduction in the probability of mobility limitation across all individuals. Since 30 percent of the elderly single population had a mobility limitation, this translates into roughly a 1.5 percent decline in disability. It is important to keep in mind that, in essence, we are measuring the average treatment effect rather than the effect of the treatment on the treated. The methodological rationale for this approach is due to concerns about selection. Narrowing the sample to only those receiving SSI benefits would produce endogeneity problems because SSI benefit eligibility is related to labor-force participation and earnings, which are correlated with health. Further, the 1990 census did not ask specifically whether individuals were receiving SSI. This compounds an already existing problem that individuals underreport SSI receipt in surveys.

Columns 2 and 3 of table 4.4 show subgroup analyses. The first subgroup analysis is limited to those in the bottom quarter of the income distribution. These are the individuals most likely to be receiving SSI and for whom a given change in the state-level benefits would be proportionately greater, and hence for whom the effects should be greater (which they are). A one hundred dollar increase in the maximum SSI benefit led to a 1.8 percentage point reduction in the probability of mobility limitations among the poorest 25 percent of the population, thus lowering disability rates among the poorest elderly from roughly 38 percent to 36.2 percent. The third column in table 4.4 shows the effect for those in the top quarter of income distribution. As would be expected, there is no effect for this group.

The following sensitivity analyses further supported the finding. First and foremost, maximum state SSI benefits were a strong predictor of actual SSI benefits. Thus, individuals living in states that had generous SSI benefit schemes on paper did, in fact, have higher SSI benefits reflecting that generosity. Second, an alternative health measure that captured whether individuals had difficulty with activities of daily living, such as toileting alone, produced similar results. Third, because SSI and Medicaid are linked in some cases, improvements in health may have been due to increases in receipt of Medicaid as opposed to increases in SSI benefits. Additional analyses, however, showed that within-state changes in the state SSI maximum did not predict within-state changes in Medicaid receipt. Further, other analyses that controlled for within-state changes in Medicaid spending and Medicaid benefit generosity had little impact on the findings. Finally, the results remained consistent when excluding Connecticut and California, which had the largest change in benefits over the 1990 to 2000 period.

CONCLUSION

Studying the effects of income-support policies on health, instead of the effects of income per se, holds both promise and problems. From a scientific perspective, studying the effects of income-support policies on health can help sort out an increasingly heated debate over the potential protective effects of income on health. All nonexperimental study designs make assumptions on the data to infer causality between variables. In the case of our SSI analyses, the key assumption is that

TABLE 4.4 / Mobility Limitation Regressed on Maximum State SSI Benefit Among
Single Individuals

	All	Less Than or Equal to 25th Income Percentile	Greater or Equal to 75th Income Percentile
Maximum monthly state SSI benefit (parameter estimates multiplied by 100)	−0.0046* (.0019)	−0.01836* (.0075)	0.00112 (.0023)
Female	0.0392** (.0010)	0.0460*** (.0024)	0.0440*** (.0016)
Age (reference = eighty-five or older)			
Sixty-five to seventy-four	−0.3061*** (.0028)	−0.2233*** (.0043)	−0.3795*** (.0044)
Seventy-five to eighty-four	−0.1982*** (.0019)	−0.1328*** (.0033)	−0.2564*** (.0031)
Marital status (reference = widow)			
Divorced	−0.0030** (.0012)	−0.0049* (.0022)	−0.0088*** (.0021)
Never married	−0.0020 (.0019)	0.0121*** (.0031)	−0.0255*** (.0020)
Race-ethnicity (reference = white)			
Black	0.0505*** (.0053)	0.0349*** (.0060)	0.0540*** (.0042)
Hispanic	0.0382*** (.0081)	0.0275*** (.0074)	0.0298*** (.0081)
Immigrant	0.0217*** (.0044)	0.0141** (.0045)	0.0264*** (.0049)
Years of education (reference = high school)			
Less than high school	0.1074*** (.0022)	0.0682*** (.0029)	0.1370*** (.0027)
College degree	0.0409*** (.0017)	0.0187*** (.0031)	0.0526*** (.0018)
State unemployment rate	0.0044** (.0017)	0.0068* (.0031)	0.0012*** (.0013)
Institutionalized	0.5002*** (.0060)	0.5136*** (.0054)	0.4213*** (.0120)
Year 2000	0.0434*** (.0013)	0.0226*** (.0026)	0.0437*** (.0017)
Mean of dependent variable	0.30	0.39	0.23
Number of observations	1563910	376616	413015

Source: Authors' compilation.
All models include state fixed effects.
Standard errors in parentheses.
*$p < 0.05$
**$p < 0.01$
***$p < 0.001$

changes to state SSI policies are exogenous to changes in state old-age disability rates, conditional on changes in sociodemographic and other factors in the state accounted for in the regression. While not innocuous, this assumption is very plausible and has been asserted in papers evaluating the effects of SSI on retirement, savings, and living arrangements. An added benefit of this approach is that from a policy perspective it answers the question facing policy makers: how will population health be affected if we modify the generosity of the program?

Our conclusion is that the current evidence tends to support the claim that expansions of income support, particularly for lower-income elderly, can have beneficial affects on old-age disability and perhaps on health more broadly, as the results of quasi-experimental designs are generally consistent with those based on nonexperimental research designs that require stronger assumptions to infer causality.

If income-support policies do influence health, the implications are enormous. Billions of dollars are spent on income transfers each year, and assessments of the efficacy of these programs should include the beneficial effects on health. Moreover, health policy and income policy should not be made independently. Health policy makers must realize that one of the central goals they are trying to achieve (that is, longer and healthier lives) can be affected by policies outside of their control. Further, to the extent that such policies improve health and hence reduce utilization of and spending on health care, they become more cost effective and contribute to resolving America's paradoxical crisis of high health care spending more on health care yet getting relatively less in terms of population health.

Yet, while our analyses to date imply that greater attention should be paid to the potential effects of income on health, there are also considerable challenges to this line of research and policy. First and foremost, until recently there has been limited data available to do these analyses. Few data sources include extensive information on both income and health, particularly in a longitudinal framework. And longitudinal surveys that track outcomes with the goal of estimating the effects of social and economic policy often fail to collect extensive information on health. For example, while some surveys were created as part of evaluations of negative income tax policies in the 1970s and welfare reform in the mid- to late 1990s, these studies largely focused on economic well-being and labor-force participation. An exception is the work by Marianne Bitler and Hilary Hoynes (chapter 9, this volume), who use the available measures collected in these evaluations to examine the effects of welfare reforms on health. Of course, part of the explanation for the lack of longitudinal studies, particularly of those with experimental designs, is both their cost and feasibility. Collecting extensive data, particularly over time, costs significant amounts of money and is challenging in terms of maintaining participation due to the survey length that is required to capture all of these dimensions of well-being.

That said, simply having good data may not always be enough to test the health effects of income supports. Income supports are generally linked to other factors which may confound their effects. Most income supports do more than just increase income. For example, Social Security and the negative income tax are linked to labor-force participation. Though these links make it more difficult to sort out *how* these policies affect health, we can still be clear about *whether* they affect health. If researchers want to provide useful information for policy makers, they must be willing and able to deal with the messiness associated with real policies and their multiple goals.

Better research on the health effects of income-support policies will require new studies that include very careful measures of both income and health. Certainly, many surveys, particularly longitudinal designs, that are intended to focus on income, employment, and family dynamics are starting to incorporate more health measures. For example, the Panel Study of Income Dynamics has, in recent years, added health measures to its core samples. Alternately, studies focused largely on health should incorporate more careful measures of employment and economic resources. For example, the National Health Interview Survey (NHIS) and the National Health and Nutrition Examination Study (NHANES) have the most comprehensive measure of health of almost any nationally representative study, but they contain limited measures of income, employment, and economic resources. Though it is a move in the right direction to add measures to already existing surveys, ideally they would be a part of survey designs from the start.

Moreover, the development of experimental designs that include both sets of measures is perhaps even more important. Imagine if many of the experimental demonstrations surrounding welfare reform had included measures of health that matched the breadth and depth of the income and employment measures. Further, a wider range of outcomes should be considered in both nonexperimental and experimental studies. The proposed causal pathways between income and health, which are based on considerable empirical work, include basic resources (for example, housing and food insecurity), psychosocial resources (for example, stress, social supports, and self-efficacy), and risky behaviors (for example, smoking, drinking, exercise, and obesity). Measures of these intervening mechanisms should be included. Ultimately, including measures of these intervening mechanisms can provide a greater awareness of the links between income and health.

While increased research on and attention to the health impacts of income supports is critical, United States research and policy on the relationship between income, income supports, and health should also be placed in an international perspective. The United States outspends, by two times, other comparable countries on health care, but it at best breaks even in terms of health outcomes, and at worst lags well behind. And though we devote enormous resources to health care, we devote relatively few resources, compared to other industrialized countries, toward policies that buffer people's economic security. Consequently, the United States has the highest relative poverty rates in the western world (Smeeding, Rainwater, and Burtless 2002). Does this explain the mediocre health outcomes in the United States? While this is by no means an easy question to answer, these are the kinds of questions that need to be asked and explored to gain a better understanding about the relationship between income and health as well as the best policy approaches to improving population health.

NOTES

1. High SES was defined as being in the top quartile in wealth and income, having a college education, and living in a good neighborhood and dwelling. Low SES was defined as being in the bottom quartile in wealth and income, having less than a high school education, and living in a poor neighborhood and dwelling.
2. There has been some concern that measurement issues play a role in the United States' relatively low world ranking on infant mortality (Congressional Budget Office 1992). But even with alternative measures, the United States only moves from twenty-second to nineteenth place. Accounting for the greater likelihood of physicians in the United States to resuscitate infants younger than twenty-eight weeks gestational age may further shrink this gap. But even if this were to entirely close the gap, which is very unlikely, the United States would still spend twice as much on medical care and at best get the same outcomes.
3. Some income can be disregarded to obtain eligibility for SSI. An individual is allowed a disregard of twenty dollars for any income and sixty-five dollars for income obtained through employment. Asset levels also determine eligibility. The maximum allowed asset levels are two thousand dollars for individuals and three thousand dollars for couples. Currently, a house of any value and a car worth a maximum of four thousand dollars can be excluded from these limits. About 6 percent of the elderly receive SSI benefits.
4. See Herd, Schoeni, and House, (forthcoming) for more detail.
5. The 1992 CPS was used because questions regarding type of health insurance did not appear in the 1990 or 1991 CPS.

REFERENCES

Adams, Peter, Michael Hurd, Daniel McFadden, Angela Merrill, and Tiago Ribeiro. 2003. "Healthy, Wealthy, and Wise?" *Journal of Econometrics* 112(1): 3–56.

Adler, Nancy, Thomas Boyce, Margaret Chesney, Susan Folkman, and S. Leonard Syme. 1993. "SES and Health." *Journal of the American Medical Association* 269(24): 3140–6.

Alaimo, Katherine, Christine M. Olson, Edward A. Frongillo, and Ronette R. Briefel. 2001. "Food Insufficiency, Family Income, and Health in U.S. Children." *American Journal of Public Health* 91(5): 781–6.

Backlund, Eric, Paul Sorlie, and Normal J. Johnson. 1996. "The Shape of the Relationship Between Income and Mortality in the United States." *Annals of Epidemiology* 6(1): 12–23.

Beckett, Megan. 2000. "Converging Health Inequalities in Later Life—An Artifact of Mortality Selection." *Journal of Health of Social Behavior* 41(2): 106–19.

Borg, Vilhelm, and Tage S. Kristensen. 2000. "Social Class and Self Rated Health." *Social Science and Medicine* 51(7): 1019–130.

Bosma, Hans, Michael G. Marmot, Harry Hemingway, Amanda C. Nicholson, Eric Brunner, and Stephen A. Stansfeld. 1997. "Low Job Control and Risk of Coronary Heart Disease in Whitehall II Study." *British Medical Journal* 314(7080): 558–65.

Byrne, D. G., and H. M. Whyte. 1980. "Life Events and Myocardial Infarction Revisited: The Role of Measures of Individual Impact." *Psychosomatic Medicine* 42(1): 1–10.

Case, Anne. 2004. "Does Money Protect Health Status? South African Pensions." In *Perspectives on the Economics of Aging*, edited by David Wise. Chicago, Ill.: University of Chicago Press.

Case, Anne, Darren Lubotsky, and Christina Paxton. 2002. "Economic Status and Health in Childhood: The Origins of the Gradient." *American Economic Review* 92(5): 1308–34.

Cohen, Sheldon, David Tyrell, and Andrew Smith. 1993. "Negative Life Events, Perceived Stress, and Susceptibility to the Common Cold." *Journal of Personality and Social Psychology* 64(1): 131–40.

Congressional Budget Office. 1992. *Factors Contributing to the Infant Mortality Ranking of the United States*. Washington: Government Printing Office.

Costa, Dora. 1999. "A House of Her Own: Old Age Assistance and the Living Arrangements of Older Nonmarried Women." *Journal of Public Economics* 72(1): 39–59.

Duleep, Harriet Orcutt. 1986. "Measuring the Effect of Income on Adult Mortality Using Longitudinal Administrative Data." *Journal of Human Resources* 21(2): 238–51.

Duncan, Thomas. 1994. "Like Father, Like Son; Like Mother, Like Daughter: Parental Resources and Child Height: Brazil, Ghana and United States." *Journal of Human Resources* 29(4): 950–88.

Engelhardt, Gary V., and Jonathan Gruber. 2004. "Social Security and the Evolution of Elderly Poverty."National Bureau of Economic Research Working Paper No. 10466. Cambridge, Mass.: National Bureau of Economic Research.

Ferraro, Kenneth and Melissa Farmer.1999. "Utility of Health Data from Social Surveys: Is There a Gold Standard for Measuring Morbidity?" *American Sociological Review* 64(2): 303–15.

Fogel, Robert William. 2004. *The Escape from Hunger and Premature Death, 1700-2100*. Cambridge: Cambridge University Press.

Fox, A. J., P. O. Goldblatt, and D. R. Jones. 1985. "Social Class Mortality Differentials: Artifact, Selection, or Life Circumstances." *Journal of Epidemiology and Community Health* 39(1): 1–8.

Frijters, Paul, John Haisken-DeNew, and Michael Shields. 2005. "The Causal Effect of Income on Health: Evidence from German Reunification." *Journal of Health Economics* 24(5): 997–1017.

Gertler, Paul. 2000. *Final Report: The Impact of Progresa on Health*. Washington: International Food Policy Research Institute.

Government Accountability Office (GAO). 2007. "Poverty in America." GAO-07-344. Washington: Government Accountability Office.

Grossman, Michael. 1972. "On the Concept of Health Capital and the Demand for Health." *Journal of Political Economy* 80(2): 223–55.

Haan, M. N., George Kaplan, S. Leonard Syme. 1989. "Socioeconomic Status and Health: Old Observations and New Thoughts." In *Pathways to Health: The Role of Social Factors*, edited by John P. Bunker, Deanna S. Gomby, and Barbara H. Kehrer. Menlo Park, Calif.: Henry J. Kaiser Family Foundation.

Haveman, Robert, Karen Holden, Kathryn Wilson, and Bobbie Wolfe. 2003. "Social Security, Age of Retirement, and Economic Well-Being." *Demography* 40(2): 369–94.

Hayward, Mark, Amy Pienta, and Diane McLaughlin. 1997. "Inequality in Men's Mortality." *Journal of Health Social Behavior* 38(4): 313–30.

Herd, Pamela. 2006. "Do Health Inequalities Decrease in Old Age? Educational Status and Functional Decline Among the 1931–1941 Birth Cohort." *Research on Aging* 28(3): 375–82.

Herd, Pamela, Robert Schoeni, and James House. Forthcoming. "Upstream Solutions: Does the Supplemental Security Income Program Reduce Disability Among the Elderly?" *Milbank Quarterly*.

House, James S., and David Williams. 2000. "Understanding and Reducing Socioeconomic and Racial/Ethnic Disparities in Health." In *Promoting Health: Intervention Strategies from Social and Behavioral Research*, edited by Brian D. Smedly and S. Leonard Syme. Washington: National Academy Press.

House, James, Karl Landis, and Debra Umberson. 1988. "Social Relationships and Health." *Science* 241(4865): 540–5.

House, James, Paula Lantz, and Pamela Herd. 2005. "Continuity and Change in the Social Stratification of Aging and Health over the Life Course." *Journals of Gerontology Series B* 60(2): S15–126.

House, James, Ronald Kessler, A. Regula Herzog, Richard Mero, Ann Kinney, and Martha Breslow. 1990. "Age, Socioeconomic Status, and Health." *Milbank Quarterly* 68(3): 383–411.

House, James, James Lepkowski, Ann Kinney, Richard Mero, Ronald Kessler, and A. Regula Herzog. 1994. "The Social Stratification of Aging and Health." *Journal of Health and Social Behavior* 35(3): 213–34.

Kessler, Ronald, and Harold Neighbors. 1986. "A New Perspective on the Relationships Among Race, Social Class, and Psychological Distress." *Journal of Health and Social Behavior* 27(2): 107–15.

Kington, Richard, and James Smith. 1997. "Socioeconomic Status and Racial and Ethnic Differences in Functional Status." *American Journal of Public Health* 87(5): 805–10.

Lantz, Paula, James House, James Lepkowski, David Williams, Richard Mero, and Jieming Chen. 1998. "Socioeconomic Factors, Health Behaviors, and Mortality." *Journal of the American Medical Association* 279(21): 1703–8.

Lillard, Lee, and Yoram Weiss. 1996. "Uncertain Health and Survival: Effect on End-of-Life Consumption." *Journal of Business and Economic Statistics* 15(2): 254–68.

Lindahl, Mikael. 2005. "Estimating the Effect of Income on Health and Mortality Using Lottery Prizes as an Exogenous Source of Variation in Income." *Journal of Human Resources* 40(1): 144–68.

Lundberg, Olle. 1991. "Causal Explanations for Class Inequality in Health—An Empirical Analysis." *Social Science and Medicine* 32(4): 385–93.

Lynch, John W., George Kaplan, and Sarah J. Shema. 1997. "Cumulative Impact of Sustained Economic Hardship on Physical, Cognitive, Psychological, and Social Functioning." *New England Journal of Medicine* 337(26): 1889–95.

Maddox, George, and Daniel Clark. 1992. "Trajectories of Functional Impairments in Later Life." *Journal of Health and Social Behavior* 33(2): 114–25.

Mare, Robert D. 1990. "Socioeconomic Status Careers and Differential Mortality Among Older Men in the United States." In *Measurement and Analysis of Mortality: New Approaches*, edited by Jacques Vallin, Stan D'Souza, and Alberto Palloni. Oxford: Clarendon Press.

Marmot, Michael, George D. Smith, Stephen Stansfeld, Chandra Patel, Fiona North, Jenny Head, Ian White, Eric Brunner, and Amanda Feeney. 1991. "Health Inequalities Among British Civil Servants." *Lancet* 333(8758): 58–59.

McDonough, Peggy, and Pat Berglund. 2003. "Histories of Poverty and Self-Rated Health Trajectories." *Journal of Health and Social Behavior* 44(2): 198–214.

McDonough, Peggy, Greg J. Duncan, David Williams, and James House. 1997. "Income Dynamics and Adult Mortality in the United States, 1972 through 1989." *American Journal of Public Health* 87(9): 1476–83.

McGarry, Kathleen, and Robert Schoeni. 2000. "Social Security, Economic Growth, and the Rise in Elderly Widows' Independence in the 20th Century." *Demography* 37(2): 221–36.

McGinnis, Michael J., Pamela Williams-Russo, and James Knickman. 2002. "The Case for More Active Policy Attention to Health Promotion." *Health Affairs* 21(2): 78–93.

McLeod, Jane, and Ronald Kessler. 1990. "Socioeconomic Status Differences in Vulnerability to Undesirable Life Events." *Journal of Health and Social Behavior* 31(2): 162–72.

Meara, Ellen, Chapin White, and David Culter. 2004. "Trends in Medical Spending by Age, 1963–2004."*Health Affairs* 23(4): 176–83.

Meer, Jonathan, Douglas L. Miller, and Harvey Rosen. 2003. "Exploring the Health-Wealth Nexus." *Journal of Health Economics* 22(5): 713–30.

Menchik, Paul L. 1993. "Economic Status as a Determinant of Mortality Among Black and White Older Men: Does Poverty Kill?" *Population Studies* 47(3): 427–36.

Mirowsky, John, and Paul Hu. 1996. "Physical Impairment and the Diminishing Effects of Income." *Social Forces* 74(3): 1073–96.

Mirowsky, John, and Catherine E. Ross. 2001. "Age and the Effect of Economic Hardship on Depression." *Journal of Health and Social Behavior* 42(2): 132–50.

———. 2003. *Education, Social Status, and Health*. New York: Aldine de Gruyter.

Moore, David E., and Mark Hayward. 1990. "Occupational Careers and Mortality of Elderly Men." *Demography* 27(1): 31–53.

Mulatu, Mesfin Samuel, and Carmi Schooler. 2002. "Causal Connections Between Socioeconomic Status and Health: Reciprocal Effects and Mediating Mechanisms." *Journal of Health and Social Behavior* 43(2): 22–41.

National Center for Health Statistics. 2005.*Health, United States, with Chartbook on Trends in the Health of Americans*. Hyattsville, Md.: National Center for Health Statistics.

Neumark, David, and Elizabeth Powers. 1998. "The Effect of Means-Tested Income Support for the Elderly on Pre-Retirement Saving." *Journal of Public Economics* 68(2): 181–205.

———. 2000. "Welfare for the Elderly: The Effects of SSI on Pre-Retirement Labor Supply." *Journal of Public Economics* 78(1–2): 51–80.

———. 2003. "The Effects of Changes in State SSI Supplements on Pre-Retirement Labor Supply." National Bureau of Economic Research Working Paper No. W9851. Cambridge, Mass.: National Bureau of Economic Research.

Palumbo, Michael. 1999. "Uncertain Medical Expenses and Precautionary Saving Near the End of the Life Cycle." *Review of Economic Studies* 66(227): 395–421.

Pappas, George, Susan Queen, Wilbur Hadden, and Gail Fisher. 1993. "The Increasing Disparity in Mortality Between Socioeconomic Groups in the United States, 1960 and 1986." *New England Journal of Medicine* 329(2): 103–9.

Robert, Stephanie A., and James S. House. 1994. "Socioeconomic Status and Health Over the

Life Course." In *Aging and Quality of Life*, edited by Ronald P. Abeles, Helen C. Gift, and Marcia G. Ory. New York: Springer Verlag.

Rodin, Judith. 1986. "Aging and Health: Effects of Sense of Control." *Science* 233(4770): 143–9.

Ross, Catherine, and Joan Huber. 1985. "Hardship and Depression." *Journal of Health and Social Behavior* 26(4): 312–27.

Rowe, John W., and Robert L. Kahn. 1987. "Human Aging: Usual and Successful." *Science* 237(4811): 143–9.

Ruhm, Christopher. 2000. "Are Recessions Good for Your Health?" *The Quarterly Journal of Economics* 115(2): 617–50.

Smeeding, Timothy M., Lee Rainwater, and Gary Burtless. 2002. "United States Poverty in a Cross-National Context" In *Understanding Poverty*, edited by Sheldon H. Danziger and Robert H. Haveman. New York: Russell Sage Foundation.

Smith, James P. 1999. "Healthy Bodies and Thick Wallets: The Dual Relation Between Health and Economic Status." *Journal of Economic Perspectives* 13(2): 145–66.

Snyder, Stephen, and William Evans. 2006. "The Effect of Income on Mortality." *Review of Economics and Statistics* 88(3): 482–95.

Social Security Administration. 2001. *Annual Statistical Supplement 2001*. Baltimore, Md.: Social Security Administration.

———. 2004. *Income of the Aged Chartbook, 2002*. Baltimore, Md.: Social Security Administration.

Sorlie, Paul D., Eric Backlund, and Jacob B. Keller. 1995. "U.S. Mortality by Economic, Demographic and Social Characteristics." *American Journal of Public Health* 85(7): 949–56.

Starfield, Barbara. 2000. "Is U.S. Health Really the Best in the World." *Journal of the American Medical Association* 284(4): 483–5.

Stokols, Daniel. 1992. "Establishing and Maintaining Healthy Environments: Toward a Social Ecology of Health Promotion." *American Psychologist* 47(1): 6–22.

Stronks, Karien, H. Dike van de Mheen, and Johan P. Mackenbach. 1998. "A Higher Prevalence of Health Problems in Low Income Groups: Does it Reflect Relative Deprivation?" *Journal of Epidemiology and Community Health* 52(9): 548–57.

Taubman, Paul J., and Robin C. Sickles. 1983. "Supplemental Social Insurance and the Health of the Poor." National Bureau of Economic Research Working Paper No. 1062. Cambridge, Mass.: National Bureau of Economic Research.

Turner, R. Jay, and Franco Marino. 1994. "Social Support and Social Structure: A Descriptive Social Epidemiology." *Journal of Health and Social Behavior* 35(3): 193–212.

Turner, R. Jay, and Samuel Noh. 1988. "Physical Disability and Depression." *Journal of Health and Social Behavior* 29(1): 23–37.

Turner, R. Jay, Blair Wheaton, and Donald A. Lloyd. 1995. "The Epidemiology of Social Stress." *American Sociological Review* 60(1): 104–25.

U.S. Congress, House and Ways Committee. 2004. House and Ways Committee Prints: 108–6, 2004 Green Book. Washington: Government Printing Office.

Chapter 5

Did the Introduction of Food Stamps Affect Birth Outcomes in California?

Janet Currie and Enrico Moretti

D o welfare programs that raise the income of poor mothers affect infant mortality? Over the 1960s, United States infant mortality fell dramatically. The rate for whites fell from twenty-three to seventeen per one thousand, while the African American rate fell from forty-three to thirty-two per one thousand. These declines are coincident with the introduction of federal transfer programs including Medicaid and the Food Stamp Program (FSP). But it is not clear whether there is an actual link between welfare programs and improvements in infant mortality.

While there is little doubt that improving maternal nutrition can lead to healthier babies, it is less clear that the introduction of a program like the FSP will have significant effects either on maternal nutrition or on infant health outcomes. To the extent that transfers made under the FSP are fungible, they may or may not lead to improvements in nutrition. It is possible, for example, that FSP transfers could lead to increases in smoking or alcohol consumption. Even if the FSP improves maternal nutrition, it is possible to have negative effects on average *measured* infant health. For example, if more unhealthy fetuses survive, or if fertility increases among those women who are most likely to have poor birth outcomes, average infant health could decline.

Hence, the effect of the FSP is theoretically ambiguous and must be examined empirically. Douglas Almond and Kenneth Chay (2005) find that the narrowing of the gap in infant mortality between blacks and whites was concentrated in the South and coincided with the introduction of Medicaid and the FSP. However, the hypothesis that declines in mortality were related to the introduction of specific programs has not been directly tested.

We use individual-level data from birth certificates in California to assess the impact of the introduction of the FSP on fertility, the probability of fetal survival, and the incidence of low birthweight. The FSP was introduced on a county-by-county basis in California, and we argue that in many cases the exact timing of its introduction was beyond the control of the local authorities. Hence, the phased-in introduction offers a useful research design for determining the effects of the program.

We find that the introduction of the FSP increased the number of births, particularly in Los Angeles. Some of this Los Angeles-specific effect may actually measure the migration of young women into Los Angeles in response to the city's relatively early adoption of the new benefit. However, among blacks in other counties, we also find increases in the number of births in response to the introduction of the FSP. This is also true among mothers with higher parity births who may be less likely to have migrated than new mothers.

We find some evidence that the FSP increased the probability of fetal survival among the lightest white infants, but the effect is very small and only detectable in Los Angeles. Notably, we find that the FSP *increased* (rather than decreased) the probability of low birthweight but the estimated effect is small and concentrated among teenagers giving birth for the first time. Thus, it appears that the FSP increased fertility, especially among black teenagers, but this increase in fertility was not strongly concentrated among the women most likely to bear low-birthweight infants.

CONCEPTUAL MODEL

Low birthweight has long been considered to be an important indicator of infant health and a predictor of future outcomes. Multiple studies (Currie and Hyson 1999; Black, Devereux, and Salvanes 2005) show that low birthweight is linked to lower educational attainment and probabilities of employment in adulthood. Janet Currie and Enrico Moretti (2007) show that low birthweight is also transmitted intergenerationally and that such transmission is more likely if the mother is also poor.

Although birthweight has a genetic component, it is strongly affected by maternal nutrition. Poor nutrition during pregnancy increases both the probability of miscarriage and the probability of low birthweight (defined as birthweight less than 2500 grams) in a pregnancy that results in a live birth.

The introduction of the FSP could have affected fertility and birth outcomes through several channels. First, by improving the quality of the diet available to people with a given level of resources, the program may have increased the probability of fetal survival. Infants born at less than 1500 grams were unlikely to survive in the 1960s. By pushing some infants over this survival threshold, the program could have increased the number of live births. We will call this the *survival effect*. But unless the program pushed infants from less than 1500 grams to more than 2500 grams, most of the infants "saved" by the program will still be low birthweight. Hence, the survival effect could lead to an increase in the number of low-birthweight live births.

Second, a variety of income effects are possible. As discussed above, increases in income could be spent on goods harmful to infant health such as cigarettes or alcohol. Alternatively, if children are treated as a normal consumer good, then we might expect to see an increase in the number of children born to the extent that the program increased people's income. We call this a *fertility effect*. The fertility effect may be larger among the people who were most likely to be constrained by lack of income prior to the introduction of the program. For example, Rajeev Dehejia and Adriana Lleras-Muney (2004) show that African Americans have fewer births during times of high unemployment, which may reflect credit constraints that are binding on women of childbearing age. If the persons who are most likely to be constrained in the absence of the program are also most likely to bear low-birthweight children, other things being equal, then the fertility effect will also increase the number of low-birthweight children.

Third, it is possible that the introduction of the FSP improved the fetal nutrition of infants who would have survived in any case. We call this a *nutrition effect*. To the extent that some infants who would have been in the 1500- to 2500-gram range are pushed above the 2500 gram threshold, the nutrition effect will reduce the probability of low birthweight.

Finally, migration in response to the FSP may also lead to increases in measured fertility and negative measured effects on birthweight, if those who migrate in response to the new benefits are more likely to have poor birth outcomes. There are two reasons why migration is a particular concern in this study: First, since the benefits were introduced county-by-county, it may have been relatively easy for women to cross county lines to take advantage of the new program. For instance, Los Angeles may have seen an influx from nearby counties in response to its relatively early adoption of the benefit. Second, California as a whole grew tremendously over the period under study as people migrated from other states. About one-third of net population increase in California over the 1960s was due to migration from other states. Many of these migrants were black. Between 1940 and 1970, the black population of Los Angeles climbed from 63,744 to almost 763,000 (Sides 2004). In the 1970s, American migrants lost their importance while immigrants accounted for about half of the net increase in population (McCarthy and Vernez 1997). Los Angeles, in particular, became the preeminent destination for immigrants to the United States in the 1970s: the share of all immigrants locating in Los Angeles rose from between 12 and 15 percent in the 1960s to over 20 percent by 1974 (Pitkin 2004).

While it is difficult to control for migration in our data, we do include county-specific time trends that control for trends in immigration. We will also consider the potential impact of migration and the fact that many of the new migrants relocated to Los Angeles in order to explore the sensitivity of our results.

In summary, the effect of the introduction of the FSP on birth outcomes is theoretically ambiguous: If the nutrition effect is large, then it may have a positive effect on balance. However, there are several reasons to expect negative measured effects, particularly if there are large impacts on survival probabilities, fertility, or migration.

BACKGROUND OF THE FOOD STAMP PROGRAM

The FSP was established in the fall of 1964 and was an outgrowth of a pilot program that began in 1961. As of December 1968, the program worked in the following way: Families paid a set amount (the purchase requirement) for coupons based on adjusted net income and the number of persons in the household. The purchase requirement varied with the household's income. For example, in 1974, a household with four people and monthly income of less than $100 per month would pay $22 for coupons worth $142, while a similar household with monthly income of less than $500 would pay $118 for the same coupons (Food Stamp Management Branch 1975). The coupons could be redeemed for most foods at local stores. Alcohol, tobacco, other nonfood items, and imported foods (except coffee, tea, cocoa, and bananas) were prohibited. Recertification was required every three months for households not on public assistance (Smith and Jensen 1968).

The FSP was introduced on a county-by-county basis, as shown in table 5.1. In California, the exact timing of its introduction was beyond the control of the local authorities. This is important because it offers a useful research design for determining the effects of the program.

The introduction began with a pilot in Humboldt County in 1963; all counties had joined the program by 1974 (by federal mandate). Note that Humboldt was the only county that participated in the pilot program. Larger counties tended to join earlier, but this was not always the case (Food Stamp Management Branch 1975).

In order to join, a county's Board of Supervisors needed to pass a resolution and develop a plan for operating a program. The names of counties that had developed a plan were forwarded to the U.S. Department of Agriculture (USDA) by the state and were placed on a pending list since the funds available to add counties were limited in each year. There were initially some glitches in this process: Three California counties had drafted plans by the beginning of 1965, but the state did not pass their plans on to USDA because it had not yet passed its own enabling legislation (Smith and Jensen 1968). The state finally passed the necessary legislation on June 30, 1965. Los Angeles and Contra Costa Counties were able to start operations in December 1965, with San Francisco County following in September 1966. At the other end of the spectrum, seventeen counties did not join until 1974, when they were compelled to do so by federal legislation. Hence, for early adopters, the exact timing of adoption was determined both by the state bureaucracy and by the availability of USDA funding; for late adopters, the timing was determined largely by federal mandate.

In some counties, the FSP replaced a free surplus commodity distribution program (counties could not operate both). To the extent that Food Stamps replicated an existing program, the estimated effects of its introduction may be biased downwards. However, USDA studies of eight pilot county programs suggested that even in households that had previously been receiving surplus commodities,

TABLE 5.1 / California Food Stamp Program Entry Date, By County (1969 County Population and Poverty Rate)

County	Entry Date	1969 Population	1969 Pov. Rate	County	Entry Date	1969 Population	1969 Pov. Rate
Humboldt	3/63	98,868	0.132	Riverside	11/69	450,477	0.135
Contra Costa	12/65	546,362	0.077	San Luis Obispo	11/69	102,648	0.145
Los Angeles	12/65	6,989,910	0.108	Yuba	12/69	44,660	0.171
San Francisco	9/66	726,294	0.134	Yolo	6/70	89,817	0.154
Santa Clara	3/67	1,033,442	0.077	Madera	7/70	41,079	0.213
Modoc	4/67	7,261	0.147	Tehama	9/70	29,044	0.133
San Mateo	4/67	552,230	0.056	Santa Barbara	11/70	261,991	0.112
Sonoma	6/67	200,920	0.132	Tulare	7/72	185,701	0.191
Solano	12/67	168,394	0.109	Kern	9/72	325,549	0.160
Lassen	4/68	16,611	0.083	Butte	11/72	101,057	0.168
Shasta	4/68	76,290	0.128	Santa Cruz	12/72	122,243	0.144
Alameda	8/68	1,060,099	0.112	Merced	9/73	101,255	0.170
Monterey	2/69	255,128	0.109	Inyo	4/74	15,417	0.099
Del Norte	3/69	14,224	0.123	San Joaquin	4/74	284,769	0.142
Sacramento	3/69	618,673	0.107	Amador	5/74	11,240	0.100
Marin	4/69	203,506	0.064	El Dorado	5/74	43,168	0.116
Stanislaus	4/69	191,271	0.148	Kings	5/74	65,647	0.184
San Benito	7/69	18,103	0.136	Tuolumne	5/74	21,286	0.114
Imperial	8/69	73,604	0.204	Colusa	6/74	12,334	0.126
Mariposa	8/69	5,868	0.132	Mendocino	6/74	49,733	0.141
Nevada	8/69	25,264	0.129	Ventura	6/74	369,811	0.092
Placer	8/69	75,693	0.116	Alpine	7/74	398	0.111
Siskiyou	8/69	33,022	0.120	Glenn	7/74	17,207	0.131
Calaveras	9/69	13,328	0.116	Lake	7/74	18,799	0.189
Sierra	9/69	2,387	0.144	Napa	7/74	76,688	0.094
Fresno	10/69	408,304	0.188	Plumas	7/74	11,637	0.114
Mono	10/69	3,780	0.144	San Bernardino	7/74	671,688	0.119
Orange	10/69	1,376,796	0.066	San Diego	7/74	1,340,989	0.101
Trinity	10/69	7,261	0.134	Sutter	7/74	41,775	0.111

Source: Authors' compilation.

receiving Food Stamps increased consumption levels. Moreover, 80 percent of increased consumption was of livestock products and fresh fruit and vegetables, products not generally included in the surplus commodities program. For example, families in Detroit consumed 50 percent more fresh fruits and vegetables and increased their intakes of both vitamins A and C when they went on the FSP. Changes in dietary quality, holding calories constant, have been linked to higher-birth-weight infants (Mannion, Gray-Donald, and Koski 2006). Retail sales of food also increased about 8 percent in the pilot areas, suggesting that many people may have been severely constrained in terms of their food purchases (Smith and Jensen 1968).

SOURCES OF DATA

We have several independent sources of information about the FSP. Starting dates for each county are from state reports (Food Stamp Management Branch 1975, 1976). Data on FSP expenditures are from the Bureau of Economic Analysis's Regional Economic Information System data on transfer programs (data prior to 1965 is available on microfiche). Data on FSP participation comes from annual state forecasts of participation by county which were sent to the U.S. Food and Nutrition Service. Figure 5.1 shows the sharp rise in both participation and expenditures in the state as a whole after the introduction of the program.

FIGURE 5.1 / California Food Stamp Participation and Expenditure Levels, 1963 to 1974

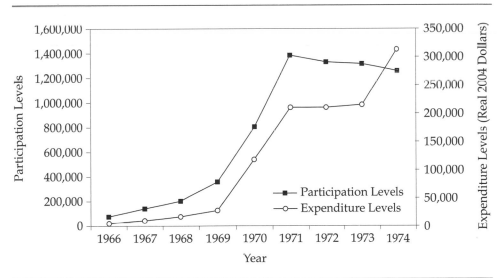

Source: Authors' calculations.

Figures 5.2 and 5.3 show however that Los Angeles County dominated FSP participation because its population was so much greater than that of any other county. That is, even though per capita participation was similar in the four largest counties, Los Angeles still had far and away the largest number of participants. Figure 5.4 shows that the same pattern holds for FSP expenditures.

Birth Records

Individual birth records are available in California from 1960 to the present, and we used data from 1960 to 1974. These files include maternal age, race, parity, birthweight, and county of residence. Figure 5.5 shows that median birthweights increased between 1960 and 1974 for both whites and blacks, though the increase is most noticeable after 1970. Rates of low birthweight start to fall earlier, trending downwards beginning in about 1967. However, large gaps remain between blacks and whites, and there is little sign of convergence in these data. It is important to note that Hispanics are not identified in these data, so that the increasing numbers of Hispanic immigrants who moved to California toward the end of our sample period are grouped with whites. Since Hispanic immigrants tend to have good birth outcomes, we do not believe that this biases our results.

Figures 5.6 and 5.7 show rates of low birthweight and median birthweight, respectively, for California's four largest counties. The data for blacks is noisy and

FIGURE 5.2 / Food Stamp Program Participation, 1963 to 1974 (Selected Large California Counties)

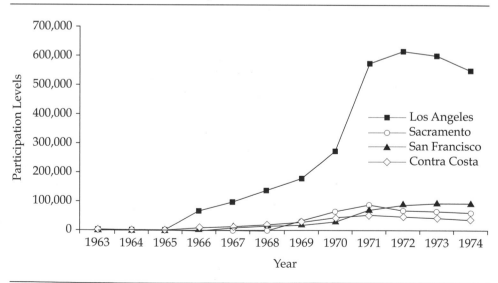

Source: Authors' calculations.

FIGURE 5.3 / Ratio of Food Stamp Program Participation Levels to County
Population, 1963 to 1974 (Selected Large California Counties)

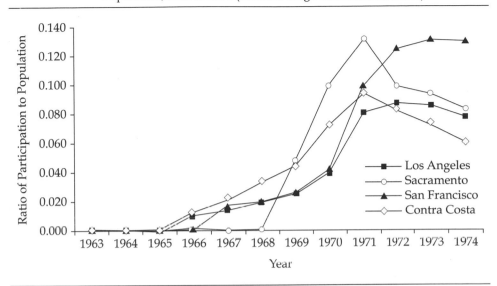

Source: Authors' calculations.

FIGURE 5.4 / Food Stamp Program Expenditures, 1963 to 1974 (Selected Large
California Counties)

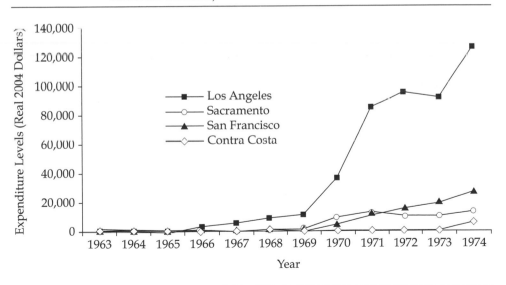

Source: Authors' calculations.

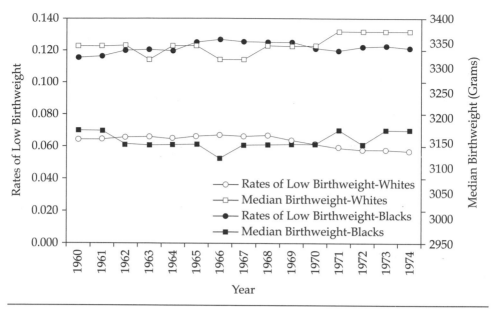

Source: Authors' calculations.

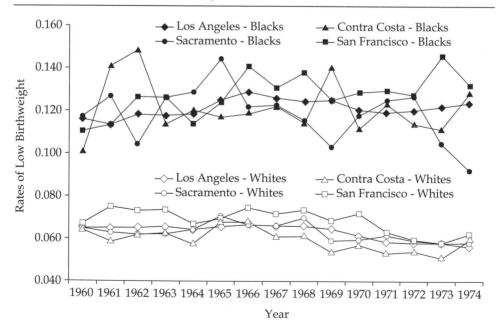

Source: Authors' calculations.

FIGURE 5.7 / Median Birthweight (in Grams), 1960 to 1974 (Selected Large California Counties)

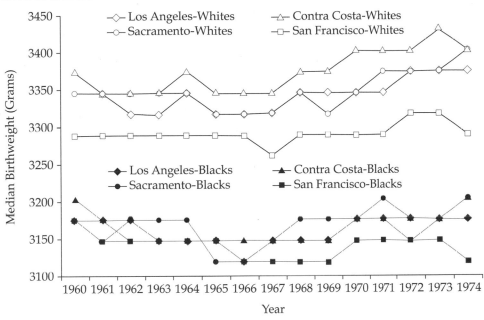

Source: Authors' calculations.

shows little clear trend. In contrast, the data for whites shows a clear, though modest, reduction in the incidence of low birthweight, and an increase in median birthweights. On the whole, the raw data suggest that events during the 1960s and early 1970s improved birth outcomes among whites but the effects among blacks are less clear.

Table 5.2 provides some additional summary statistics for all births, first births, teen births, and teen first births. The rationale for examining these subgroups is that they may be more likely to have low-birthweight births. Table 5.2 shows that this is certainly the case among teen mothers. Also, there are large racial differences in the probability of being exposed to the FSP: blacks were more likely to live in the large urban counties which were early adopters.

In order to study trends in the number of births, we aggregate the individual-level data into cells defined using county, race, year of birth, maternal age group, parity, and the third of the year. There are five maternal age groups ranging from ages fourteen to forty (births to women over forty are omitted as they are a small fraction of total births and including them results in small cell sizes). There are three parity groups (first births, second births, and third or higher parity births). If there are no births in a particular cell, then we assign zero births to that cell. There are 38,475 cells.

TABLE 5.2 / Sample Means

1960 to 1974 Individual Level Data	All Parities, White	All Parities, Black	1st Births, White	1st Births, Black	Teen, White	Teen, Black	Teen, 1st Birth, White	Teen, 1st Birth, Black
Proportion of low birthweight	0.062	0.121	0.061	0.121	0.072	0.134	0.066	0.126
Proportion of exposed to food stamps	0.339	0.458	0.39	0.543	0.329	0.507	0.345	0.539
Mean expenditure on food stamps in county if exposed (thousands of dollars)	10.7 [27.23]	18.05 [34.40]	12.38 [29.00]	22.17 [37.30]	10.39 [27.01]	20.27 [36.09]	10.82 [27.44]	21.9 [37.21]
Mean participation in food stamps in county if exposed (thousands of dollars)	70.43 [158.92]	118.41 [197.34]	80.92 [168.47]	142.85 [211.47]	68.58 [157.61]	132.06 [205.68]	71.42 [160.17]	141.59 [211.13]
Number of observations	4421791	442882	1579079	152907	681959	114630	526210	80181

Source: Authors' compilations.
Note: Standard deviations in brackets.

METHODS

In individual-level data we estimate models of the following form:

$$\text{low\_bw} = a_0 + a_1\text{FSP} + a_2\log(\text{Pop}) + a_3\text{Year}$$
$$+ a_4 \text{ County*Year} \, Q \, a_5 \text{ County*Age} + a_6\text{Parity} + a_7\text{Gender} + e, \qquad (5.1)$$

where low_bw = 1 if the individual was low birthweight. FSP is a measure of the food stamp program (either a dummy = 1 if the program had been introduced, log expenditures, or log participation). These three measures of the program capture somewhat different timing effects since participation grew rapidly but not instantaneously after the program was introduced. In all cases, the FSP indicator refers to nine months prior to the birth.

Pop is county population.[1] Year is a vector of year dummies that control for state-level trends (for example, Medi-Cal, the state Medicaid program, was introduced state-wide in 1965, replacing a previous state program available to categorically eligible persons). County*Year is a county-specific time trend that controls, for example, for differential migration trends in different counties, and differential trends in other forms of public assistance.[2] County*Age is a vector of fixed effects for each county and maternal age group which would pick up differences, for example, in county resources available to teen mothers. Parity is a vector of dummy variables indicating birth order (from first born to tenth born or higher), and Gender is a dummy = 1 if the child is male. These latter variables are included because they are known to affect birthweight.

In the data aggregated to cells we estimate:

$$N = a_0 + a_1\text{FSP} + a_2\log(\text{Pop}) + a_3\text{Year}$$
$$+ a_4 \text{ County*Year} + a_5 \text{ County*Age} + a_6\text{Parity} + e, \qquad (5.2)$$

where N is the number of births. These regressions are weighted by county population, given the large differences in cell sizes.

We estimate these models separately for blacks and whites given the large gap in the incidence of low birthweight between the groups. Given average differences in socioeconomic status between blacks and whites, it is also possible that blacks will be more affected by the FSP than whites. Unfortunately, few indicators of socioeconomic status are available in these data since income has never been reported in the Vital Statistics records and parents' education has not been reported until quite recently. However, we use teenage motherhood as a proxy for lower socioeconomic status and we examine teen mothers separately.

The preceding paragraphs describe a standard difference-in-difference analysis. We also conduct a pre-post analysis of Los Angeles County only, as well as analyses excluding Los Angeles County from our difference-in-difference specification. We look at Los Angeles separately because it is the only county large enough to bear this type of analysis. Also, there are many indications that Los Angeles was quite different than the other counties and it is also much larger. Hence, it is important to understand the extent to which difference-in-difference estimates based on the whole sample may be driven by the experience of this single large county.

ESTIMATION RESULTS

Table 5.3 shows models of the effect of the FSP on the number of births using the grouped data. While we do not see any statistically significant effects for whites as a whole, there are large, positive, statistically significant effects for the white subgroups of special interest (first births, teen mothers, and teen first births) and for all groups of black infants. Given that these are cell-level regressions and the cells for the different groups are of different sizes, it is somewhat difficult to directly compare coefficients. Hence, we also show the coefficient divided by the mean cell size. For example, the first panel of the table suggests that the introduction of the FSP was associated with approximately a 10 percent increase in the number of first births to white teens. The increase for first births to black teens is even larger at 24 percent. These effects are much larger than those for all blacks (though these are still substantial at 12 percent).

Panels 2 and 3 of table 5.3 show similar results for our two additional measures of FSP generosity: log expenditures and log participation. Here the coefficient divided by the mean cell size can be interpreted as the percent change in the number of births with a percent change in expenditures. Hence, for example, a 100 percent increase in expenditures would be associated with a 1.5 percent increase in the number of white teen first births and a 3.3 percent increase in the number of black teen first births. Similarly, a 100 percent change in participation would lead to a 1.1 percent increase in the number of white teen first births and a 2.6 percent increase in the number of black teen first births. These comparisons suggest that the implied effect of a 100 percent increase in program expenditures or participation is much smaller than the estimated effect of introducing the program. One interpretation is that the effects of the FSP on fertility are greatest for the poorest women.

The fourth panel of table 5.3 shows the effect of excluding Los Angeles from the calculations. Mean cell sizes are much reduced by this exclusion (from 940.77 to 229.0). What is more striking however is that outside of Los Angeles the FSP has no statistically significant effect on the number of births among whites. For blacks, the estimated effects of the FSP remain strongly statistically significant. For "all blacks" and for "black first births," the effects are of roughly similar magnitude to those shown in panel 1 (at least relative to the relevant cell mean). However, for black teens, the effects are much smaller outside of Los Angeles.

The contrast between the results with and without Los Angeles suggests that the effects for Los Angeles may be driven by city-specific factors. An obvious suspect is migration. If, for example, many young women migrated to Los Angeles at the time of the introduction of the FSP (perhaps because of the generosity of other welfare programs such as AFDC), then one might see that the FSP was associated with large increases in the number of births without any change in individual-level fer-

TABLE 5.3 / Effects of Food Stamps on Number of Births, 1960 to 1974

	White, All Parity	White, 1st Births	White, Teen Mom	White Teen, 1st Birth	Black, All Parity	Black, 1st Births	Black, Teen Mom	Black Teen, 1st Birth
1. Food stamp variable is food stamp variable	30.54	137.77	48.552	169.836	16.62	25.50	42.330	85.568
	[20.20]	[25.71]	[15.473]	[44.505]	[3.50]	[4.41]	[6.426]	[13.810]
Coeff. cell size	0.03	0.13	0.069	0.104	0.12	0.09	0.246	0.235
Number of observations	38475	12825	7695	2565	38475	12825	7695	2565
R-squared	0.744	0.984	0.673	0.9934	0.664	0.951	0.663	0.9903
2. Food stamp variable is Log food stamp expenditure	5.31	20.72	6.618	23.141	2.20	3.74	5.869	12.206
	[3.20]	[4.04]	[2.434]	[7.036]	[0.548]	[0.699]	[1.015]	[2.178]
Coeff. cell size	0.01	0.02	0.0095	0.014	0.02	0.01	0.034	0.033
Number of observations	35820	11940	7164	2388	35820	11940	7164	2388
R-squared	0.744	0.985	0.672	0.9938	0.664	0.956	0.664	0.9903
3. Food stamp variable is Log food stamp participation	3.70	15.47	5.133	17.961	1.70	2.81	4.532	9.350
	[2.37]	[2.94]	[1.793]	[5.173]	[0.398]	[0.505]	[0.731]	[1.584]
Coeff. cell size	0.00	0.02	0.007	0.011	0.01	0.01	0.026	0.026
Number of observations	36225	12075	7245	2415	36225	12075	7245	2415
R-squared	0.744	0.985	0.672	0.9938	0.664	0.956	0.664	0.9905
Cell size	940.77	1032.05	699.48	1628.5	134.29	280.68	171.5	362.98
4. LA not included. Food stamp variable is food stamp dummy	-2.79	1.94	-5.13	-12.877	1.500	2.74	2.04	6.05
	[2.53]	[3.56]	[2.51]	[6.73]	[.388]	[.794]	[1.14]	[2.89]
Coeff. cell size	0.012	0.008	0.03	0.032	0.081	0.136	0.082	0.114
Number of observations	37800	12600	7560	2520	37800	12600	7560	2520
R-squared	0.655	0.966	0.746	0.987	0.632	0.945	0.648	0.967
Cell size	229	255.51	172.33	407.93	18.59	20.14	24.97	53.06

Source: Authors' compilation.
Notes: Standard errors in brackets. Regressions are weighted by county population.
Dep. Var. is number of births in each county/year/race/maternal age/third of the year/parity cell. There are five maternal age categories: four-teen to nineteen, twenty to twenty-five, twenty-six to thirty, thirty-one to thirty-five, thirty-six to forty and three parity categories: 1, 2, and 3 or more. Regressions include log population, county time trends, county*mother age group effects, and parity. Standard errors are clustered at the county*year*third of the year level. Mean cell size is the same for panels 1 to 3.

tility. However, the relative stability of the coefficients for blacks suggests to us that there was a fertility effect for this group. Moreover, if we think that young women without children (and who are therefore at risk for a first birth) are more likely to migrate than older women who already have children, the fact that effects on fertility are found among blacks for all parities, as well as for first births, can be construed as additional evidence that the effect is real.

Table 5.4 uses the individual-level data for Los Angeles County to look for the survival and nutrition effects. The table presents a series of linear probability models for the probability that infants were less than 1500 grams, less than 2000 grams, less than 2500 grams, and less than 3000 grams. The data is restricted to conceptions that took place between one year before the implementation of the FSP and one year afterwards in order to abstract from any trends in the data. The regressions are similar to equation 5.1 and control for the child's gender, parity, and mother's age.

In our data, very few children who were born less than 1500 grams survived. If the FSP moved some infants who would not have survived above the 1500 threshold, then we should see an increase in the number of infants in the lowest low-birthweight category: 1500 to 2000 grams. Alternatively, if the FSP increases fertility *and* if the increases are concentrated among women who would be more likely to have low-birthweight infants in the absence of the program, then we should see a more general increase in the number of lower-birthweight infants, rather than an increase concentrated only in the lowest categories. Finally, if the FSP simply improved the outcomes of infants at risk of lower birthweight, then we should see a reduction in the number of infants in this category.

Table 5.4 suggests that the FSP had a statistically significant, but very small, effect on fetal survival. The estimated coefficients and standard errors are multiplied by one hundred, so column 1 implies that among whites, the FSP increased the probability that a surviving infant was in the 1500- to 2000-gram category by about 0.1 percent. Among white teen first births, there is also a somewhat larger positive effect on the probability that a surviving infant was in the less than 3000-gram category. This is what one would expect if the FSP encouraged fertility among a relatively negatively selected group of white Los Angeles teens. The coefficient suggests that in this group the probability of an infant being less than 3000 grams increased about 1 percent.

There is no evidence of a survival effect among blacks. But among black teens, the probability that a surviving baby was less than 3000 grams declines by 4 percent. The effect is slightly larger for teen first births at 5 percent. This pattern is consistent with improved nutrition reducing the fraction of low-birthweight births.

Table 5.5 extends the analysis of the microdata to all counties by estimating equation 5.1. The first five panels focus on the probability that a child is low birthweight, while the sixth and seventh panels examine the probabilities that they were less than 2000 grams and less than 3000 grams, respectively. In this table, results are also shown for models using log expenditures and log participation as the FSP variables.

The estimated effects are typically positive but very small (recall that coefficients

Table 5.4 / Change in Distribution of Birthweights in Los Angeles County From One Year Before Implementation of Food Stamps to One Year Afterwards.

	All White	All Black	1st Birth, White	1st Birth, Black	Teen, White	Teen, Black	Teen, 1st Birth, White	Teen, 1st Birth, Black
Effect of food stamps on:								
1. P(birthweight less than 2000 grams)	0.145	0.396	0.027	−0.355	0.274	0.592	0.328	−0.211
	[.064]	[.383]	[.119]	[.678]	[.110]	[.928]	[.102]	[.938]
2. P(birthweight less than 2500 grams)	0.217	0.366	−0.101	−0.01	0.296	0.254	0.22	0.254
	[.122]	[.420]	[.172]	[1.01]	[.239]	[1.47]	[.170]	[1.80]
3. P(birthweight less than 3000 grams)	0.402	−0.863	0.087	−2.93	0.852	−4.12	1.44	−4.95
	[.234]	[.649]	[.313]	[2.14]	[.705]	[1.69]	[.652]	[2.76]
Number of observations	204887	32716	74882	10840	31938	8379	25004	5696

Source: Authors' compilation.
Notes: Coefficients and standard errors multiplied by 100. Standard errors in brackets. Regressions are linear probability models estimated using L.A. births from one year before and one year after the introduction of Food Stamps. The reported coefficient is that of a dummy variable indicating that Food Stamps have been introduced nine months prior to the index child's birth. Regressions include controls for child's gender, parity, and mother's age.

and standard errors are multiplied by one hundred). The FSP coefficients are all statistically significant for whites in the model for teen births and in the models for teen first births (see panel 4). Among blacks however, the dummy for the introduction of the program is never statistically significant although increases in expenditures and participation are estimated to have significant effects on black teen first births.

A comparison of panels 4 and 5 shows that the results are very similar for the whole sample and for the sample of counties excluding Los Angeles. The point estimate in column 1 of table 5.4 suggests that, among whites, the introduction of the FSP increased the probability of low birthweight by 0.00285. Relative to the baseline probability of low birthweight among infants of white teen first-time mothers, this represents an increase of about 4 percent.

However, panels 6 and 7 show no impact of the FSP on the probability of birthweight less than 2000 grams, or of the probability of birthweight less than 3000 grams. This suggests that if the FSP did affect birthweights, it resulted in relatively marginal changes, perhaps due to an increase in births among the women who were most likely to have infants in the 2000- to 2500-gram range in any case.

EXTENSIONS OF THE RESEARCH

We have explored several possible extensions. First, we have examined the fetal-death records. In California, a fetal death is defined as a "product of conception" that does not show signs of life at the time of the birth. If fetal deaths were accurately reported, then we could use the fetal-death data to directly examine the hypothesis that the FSP improved fetal survival. However, it is clear from an examination of the data that fetal deaths are grossly underreported. For example, most fetal deaths are thought to occur in the first trimester, yet most reported fetal deaths occur in the last trimester of pregnancy (reporting of fetal deaths that occur earlier than twenty weeks is not even required). It is likely in fact that only fetal deaths requiring medical intervention are systematically reported.

We have also explored alternative lag structures. For example, it might be that it was necessary to improve nutrition before women became pregnant in order to have optimal effects on birth outcomes. Conversely, it might be nutrition in the last trimester (when the infant gains the most weight) has the largest effect on birth outcomes. However, given the very small effects that we find on outcomes other than fertility, we were not able to say anything convincing about optimal timing of nutrition support under the FSP.

We also asked whether effects of low birthweight in the mother's generation had effects on the distribution of birthweights in the child's generation. It would be of great interest if we could show that an intervention, such as the introduction of the FSP, helped to break the intergenerational cycle of low birthweight. Low birthweight is strongly heritable: mothers who are low birthweight are about 50 percent more likely to bear low-birthweight children than other mothers, even in models that compare sisters who are mothers (Currie and Moretti 2007). However,

TABLE 5.5 / Effects of Food Stamps on Incidence of Low Birthweight, 1960 to 1974

Food Stamp Variable and Race	Dummy, White	Dummy, Black	Log (Exp), White	Log (Exp), Black	Log (Part), White	Log (Part), Black
1. All						
Food stamp variable	−0.014	0.471	−0.005	0.055	-0.002	0.043
	[0.050]	[0.247]	[0.006]	[.034]	[0.005]	[.025]
Number of observations	4421132	442795	4415787	442769	4411467	442638
R-squared	0.002	0.004	0.002	0.004	0.002	0.004
2. 1st births						
Food stamp variable	0.062	0.261	0.003	0.065	0.002	0.049
	[.080]	[.365]	[0.010]	[.052]	[0.008]	[.037]
Number of observations	1579079	152907	1577419	152901	1575425	1532854
R-squared	0.002	0.005	0.002	0.005	0.002	0.005
3. Teen mothers						
Food stamp variable	0.268	0.175	0.028	0.034	0.023	0.032
	[.111]	[.467]	[.013]	[.051]	[.010]	[.040]
Number of observations	681891	114607	680928	114601	680207	114560
R-squared	0.002	0.005	0.002	0.005	0.002	0.005
4. Teen mothers, 1st births						
Food stamp variable	0.285	0.577	0.036	0.108	0.029	0.082
	[.116]	[.435]	[.014]	[.052]	[.011]	[.040]
Number of observations	527529	80185	526884	80181	526210	80154
R-squared	0.004	0.003	0.004	0.003	0.004	0.003
5. All counties except L.A.— Teen mothers, 1st births						
Food stamp variable	0.254	0.633	0.033	0.142	0.03	0.108
	[.153]	[.578]	[.018]	[.073]	[.015]	[.056]
Number of observations	356416	39712	355711	39708	355037	39681
R-squared	0.0004	0.004	0.0004	0.004	0.0004	0.004
6. All counties—teen mothers, 1st births, P(less than 2000 grams)						
Food stamp variable	0.102	−0.019	0.008	0.017	0.007	0.017
	[.072]	[.268]	[.009]	[.035]	[.007]	[.027]
Number of observations	527289	80185	526884	80191	526210	80154
R-squared	0.0003	0.0008	0.0003	0.0008	0.0003	0.0008
7. All counties—teen mothers, 1st births, P(less than 3000 grams)						
Food stamp variable	0.166	0.215	0.05	0.039	0.032	0.029
	[.238]	[.740]	[.029]	[.092]	[.022]	[.072]
Number of observations	527529	80185	526884	80181	526210	80154
R-squared	0.005	0.011	0.005	0.011	0.005	0.011

Source: Authors' compilation.
Notes: Coefficient and standard errors multiplied by 100. Standard errors in brackets. Standard errors are clustered at the county-year level. All regressions include dummy variables for parity, gender, county time trends, county* mother age group effects (county indicators multiplied by mother age group indicators), and the log of county population.

low birthweight is still a relatively rare condition. The estimated effect of the introduction of the FSP on birthweight in the first generation is very small. So it is not surprising that a very small increase in the prevalence of a condition that is rare to begin with does not appear to have any statistically significant effect in the second generation.

CONCLUSION

Lack of data places severe constraints on our ability to assess the effects of the introduction of many of the programs that were launched as part of the War on Poverty. Perhaps the greatest difficulty in the current study is our inability to measure migration. Current Vital Statistics data includes information about the mother's state of birth (or country of birth if she was born abroad). But even this limited information is not available in the early years of the data. It is also impossible to assess the effects on birth defects known to be affected by nutrition (such as neural tube defects) or pregnancy complications affected by maternal nutrition (such as gestational diabetes).

Despite these limitations, we conclude that the introduction of the FSP was associated with increases in the number of births among blacks overall and among whites in Los Angeles County. The increases in the number of births to teen first-time mothers were particularly pronounced. Among whites, there is evidence that the FSP was associated with small positive effects on the probability of fetal survival in Los Angeles, though no effect is found in the state as a whole. These increases in fetal survival probabilities are not large enough however to have much impact on the overall number of births. Among blacks in Los Angeles, the FSP was associated with a relatively large decline in the probability that a surviving infant was less than 3000 grams; however, again, we do not find this effect in the rest of the state.

When we focus on the 2500-gram cutoff, we find that although the FSP had little overall effect, it increased the probability of low birthweight slightly among infants born to teen first-time mothers. For blacks overall and for whites in Los Angeles, this is likely due to increases in the number of infants born to mothers likely to have negative birth outcomes. However, it is hard to say whether these increases are due to increased fertility among existing residents, or to increased migration into the county or state after the introduction of the FSP.

Among whites outside of Los Angeles, we see increases in low birthweight, even though there were no increases in the numbers of births. Taken at face value, this result suggests that the white women giving birth outside Los Angeles became more negatively selected after the introduction of the FSP. It is possible, for example, that better-educated women left smaller counties either for Los Angeles or for other states, and that the introduction of the FSP attracted other less well-off women to take their places.

The most striking finding of our study is negative in that the introduction of the FSP did not have any large, obvious positive effect on birth outcomes, as measured by the incidence of low birthweight. This does not preclude the possibility that the

FSP had more subtle positive effects or that it improved other health outcomes. Our simple analysis highlights the fact that programs like the FSP can have effects on many different margins, such that the overall effect may not be the one that was intended. In the case of the FSP, it is possible that the program did improve the outcomes of infants who would have been conceived in any case. For example, we do find a reduction in the probability that surviving black infants in Los Angeles were less than 3000 grams at birth. However, these positive effects may have been dominated by increases in fertility or migration among women with poorer average birth outcomes.

NOTES

1. The state of California constructs county-level estimates of population using data from a variety of sources including the census, birth records, and school records.
2. Expenditures for Aid to Families with Dependent Children (AFDC) increased dramatically over the time period of our study, particularly in Los Angeles County. The McCone commission of inquiry into the Los Angeles riots noted that "expenditures for the AFDC program have been increasing dramatically, far outrunning the population trends. Between 1960 and 1964, when county population increased 13 percent, expenditures for the AFDC program rose by 73 percent" (McCone 1965). It is important to control for differing trends in these variables.

REFERENCES

Almond, Douglas, and Kenneth Chay. 2005. "The Long-Run and Intergenerational Aspects of Poor Infant Health: Evidence from Cohorts Born During the Civil Rights Era." *Department of Economics* xerox. Columbia University.

Arno, Peter, Clyde Schechter, and James S. House. n. d. "Social Security and Mortality: The Role of Income Support Policies and the Public's Health." Unpublished paper.

Black, Sandra, Paul Devereux, and Kjell Salvanes. 2005. "The More, the Merrier: The Effect of Family Size and Birth Order on Children's Education." *Quarterly Journal of Economics* 120(2): 669–700.

Currie, Janet, and Rosemary Hyson. 1999. "Is the Impact of Health Shocks Cushioned by Socioeconomic Status?: The Case of Birth Weight." *American Economic Review* 89(2): 245–50.

Currie, Janet, and Enrico Moretti. 2007. "Biology as Destiny? Short and Long-Run Determinants of Intergenerational Transmission of Birth Weight." *Journal of Labor Economics* 25(2): 231–64.

Dehejia, Rajeev, and Adriana Lleras-Muney. 2004. "Booms, Busts, and Babies' Health." *Quarterly Journal of Economics* 119(3): 1091–1130.

Food Stamp Management Branch, Department of Benefit Payments. 1975. "The Food Stamp Program in California, Fiscal Year 1973–1974. Annual Report to the Legislature." Sacramento, Calif.: State of California.

————. 1976. "The Food Stamp Program in California, Fiscal Year 1974-1975. Annual Report to the Legislature." Sacramento, Calif.: State of California.

Mannion, Cynthia, Katherine Gray-Donald, and Kristine G Koski. 2006. "Association of Low Intake of Milk and Vitamin D During Pregnancy with Decreased Birth Weight." *Canadian Medical Association Journal* (April 25): 14882329.

McCarthy, Kevin, and Georges Vernez. 1997. *Immigration in a Changing Economy: California's Experience*. Santa Monica, Calif.: RAND Corporation.

McCone, John, chairman. 1965. "Violence in the City, an End or a Beginning?" *The Governor's Commission on the Los Angeles Riots*. Sacramento, Calif.

Pitkin, John. 2004. "Three Demographic Waves and the Transformation of the Los Angeles Region, 19702000." *Population Dynamics Research Group* working paper PDRG04-07. Los Angeles, Calif.: University of Southern California, School of Policy, Planning and Development.

Sides, Josh. 2004. *L.A. City Limits*. Berkeley, Calif.: University of California Press.

Smith, Russell, and Eileen Jensen. 1968. "Revised Summary of Information on the Food Stamp Program." Sacramento, Calif.: State of California, Department of Social Welfare.

U.S. Bureau of Economic Analysis, Regional Economic Information System. Accessed at http://www.bea.gov/regional/docs/reis2005dvd.cfm.

Part IV

Civil Rights

Chapter 6

Lifting Gates, Lengthening Lives: Did Civil Rights Policies Improve the Health of African American Women in the 1960s and 1970s?

George A. Kaplan, Nalini Ranjit, and Sarah A. Burgard

B ased on literally thousands of studies carried out over many decades, it is increasingly accepted that socioeconomic conditions act as important determinants of both individual health and the health of populations (Kaplan et al. 1987; Kaplan and Lynch 1997). Wages, income, wealth, the nature of work, investments in human capital, and the levels of resources and risks in communities are now recognized by many as arguably the most critical determinants of health (Kaplan 2001; Evans, Barer, and Marmor 1994). It seems possible that social and economic policies, in their ability to alter these determinants, might also impact health even if it is not their primary intent. Furthermore there is increasing recognition that historical and contemporary forces which differentially distribute these determinants to racial groups, within and across generations, may underlie many of the pernicious health gaps between racial groups that are found in the United States (Williams and Collins 1995).

While the evidence is compelling in its breadth and depth, for the most part it is based on observational studies of cohorts of individuals or aggregates, and as such it lacks some of the power that comes from experiments where randomization strengthens causal inference. When experiments are not possible, which is often the case, it becomes useful to focus on exogenous policy changes that have been demonstrated or are thought to lead to major changes in those factors which putatively influence the health of individuals and populations. We can then test whether or not health effects follow from these policy changes, as researchers are increasingly doing.

However, it is not a simple matter to find cases where social and economic policies have had a clear impact on possible determinants of health. Cases that come to mind in the last century or so are child labor laws, Social Security, the introduction of compulsory schooling, the elimination of restrictive covenants on land ownership, programs introduced by agencies such as the Federal Housing Administration that altered patterns of home ownership and housing development, the Earned Income Tax Credit and other measures designed to impact poverty levels, and mechanisms that altered support mechanisms for poor families such as Temporary Assistance for Needy Families (TANF). The list could be much longer, and these policies vary considerably in the extent of their success, the degree to which the changes might *ex ante* influence health, and the availability of health data to test whether or not they did have an impact on specific aspects of disease processes.

One compelling case that may have had an influence on important determinants of health was the Civil Rights Act of 1964. On July 2, 1964, Congress put in place "An Act to enforce the constitutional right to vote, to confer jurisdiction upon the district courts of the United States to provide injunctive relief against discrimination in public accommodations, to authorize the Attorney General to institute suits to protect constitutional rights in public facilities and public education, to extend the Commission on Civil Rights, to prevent discrimination in federally assisted programs, to establish a Commission on Equal Employment Opportunity, and for other purposes." (U.S. Congress, Senate 1964). In its guarantees of voting rights, equal access to public accommodations, public education, federally assisted programs, and work, and in its creation of the Equal Employment Opportunity Commission (EEOC), the Community Relations Service, and the extension of the Commission on Civil Rights, Congress laid the foundation for a potential and dramatic reshaping of the American fabric so heavily entwined in the "American Dilemma" of Myrdal and the racial divide of Du Bois.

The Civil Rights Act of 1964 and the Voting Rights Act of 1965 arguably represent the most important legislation regarding the nexus of race and society since Reconstruction. As political scientist and social psychologist Bernard Grofman (2000) puts it, the Civil Rights Act

> transformed the shape of American race relations. Supporters of the Civil Rights Act of 1964 sought, at a minimum, the elimination of segregation of the races in publicly supported schools, hospitals, public transportation, and other public spaces, and an end to open and blatant racial discrimination in employment practices. Judged in those terms, the act is a remarkable success story. If ever any piece of legislation showed the power of the central government to change deeply entrenched patterns of behavior, it is the Civil Rights Act of 1964. Together . . . [they] broke once and for all the Jim Crow legacy of post-Reconstruction South and largely ended the overt and legally sanctioned forms of discrimination against African Americans that had been found throughout the nation. In terms of the law, blacks were no longer second-class citizens. (1)

Thus through its potential impact on education, occupation, income, voting, and other aspects of civil society, as well as its impact on decreasing the marginalization of blacks, the Civil Rights Act (and the Voting Rights Act of 1965) could have had substantial health effects, even though that was not the primary intent. Indeed, other measures put in place at the same time which also attempted to create more of a level playing field seem to have improved infant health. Douglas Almond, Kenneth Y. Chay, and Michael Greenstone (2006) describe dramatic improvements in infant mortality in the years following 1964, which was the year that the Hill-Burton act was reformulated as a provision of the Public Health Service Act. Under the provisions of this act, a facility receiving funds was to be made available to all members of the community in which it was located, regardless of race, color, national origin, or creed. As these authors demonstrate, the effects of this improved access on postneonatal infant deaths due to diarrhea and pneumonia were pronounced.

Infants may not have been the only subpopulation to experience health gains in the wake of these legislative changes. African American women faced greatly broadened occupational opportunities which translated into economic and social gains in the late 1960s and through the 1970s, and which brought them closer to parity with white women. These relative socioeconomic gains map onto health improvements over that period. By contrast, black men did not experience the uniformly positive occupational and socioeconomic gains following civil-rights legislation to the same extent as their female counterparts. African American men experienced a mixed pattern of gains and setbacks, initiated by a large-scale move out of agricultural work into blue-collar operative jobs in the 1940s, but countered by rising unemployment relative to white men in the 1960s. This meant that gains in the 1970s resulting from the occupational changes catalyzed in the 1960s had differing effects on racial inequality for men and women. Black women's occupational distribution became more like that of their white counterparts, leading to a decline in income disparity. Income disparity increased among men because the average occupational status of white men rose and pulled away from the average status of black men, for whom a rising fraction had fallen out of the paid labor force (Alexis 1998). Thus, because we look to occupational and socioeconomic gains as the pathways by which civil-rights legislation could potentially improve health, we do not expect to see black men's health improving to the same extent as black women's health.

A review of existing studies on the social and economic changes that occurred during this period, as well as new analyses which show remarkable life-expectancy and mortality gains for black women compared to white women in this period, help us understand some of the potential mechanisms that could account for these gains. While we are confident about the existence of these relative improvements in the health of black women, we will call attention to the comment made by John Donohue and his Nobel Laureate colleague James Heckman (1991) when discussing their work on the reasons for economic gains for blacks during the era of improvements in civil rights. They note that their answers are more similar to the solution to a Sherlock Holmes puzzle than to the coefficients from an econometric model, and so shall ours be.

DATA AND METHODS

In these analyses, we examine socioeconomic trends by race and evaluate the extent to which changes in mortality rates track these socioeconomic trends. Socioeconomic data for blacks and whites of both sexes are evaluated using occupation data from the 1950 and 1960 U.S. Census and the Current Population Survey (CPS) March annual files 1963-1980, both obtained from the Integrated Public Use Microdata Series (IPUMS; Ruggles et al. 2004). We examine the main occupation for individuals thirty-five to sixty-four years of age who were currently in the paid labor force at the time of the respective survey. These data sets provide occupational data for the years 1950 and 1960 and a continuous (annual) data series for the period from 1963 to 1980. Data points for the periods 1951 to 1959 and 1961 to 1962 are obtained by linear interpolation. Slopes of trend lines reflecting the periods 1950 to 1964 and 1965 to 1980 are obtained by regressing percentages in a particular occupational category on calendar year for these two periods; we test for difference in the estimated slopes for the two periods for particular groups of interest and report relevant results of these tests below.

Mortality rates for the years following 1967 by region, race, sex, cause of death, and year are obtained from the Compressed Mortality files (1968 to 1978). For the period preceding 1968, we use tabulated data from annual volumes of the Vital Statistics data published by the National Center for Health Statistics (NCHS). We compare trends in mortality rates or ratios across two periods: 1955 to 1964 (the decade before passage of Civil Rights legislation), and 1965 to 1974 (the decade following passage of Civil Rights legislation). Because, for a variety of demographic, cultural, and political reasons, the Civil Rights Act of 1964 is considered to have had most of its impact in the South, we present some analyses disaggregated by region. A final set of analyses examines trends in age-adjusted cause-specific mortality rates, specifically for mortality due to heart disease, cerebrovascular disease, and neoplasms (primarily lung cancer). Most of the analyses presented are for females, with results for males described in the text. In general, analyses are limited to the working ages (thirty-five to sixty-four), the age group that is considered to have experienced the largest shift in occupational opportunity following Civil Rights legislation (Alexis 1998).

Life expectancy analyses are summarized as years of life expectancy remaining at age thirty-five (e35), and mortality rates (for persons ages thirty-five to sixty-four) are age-standardized to the corresponding region- and age-gender-specific population obtained from the 1968 Compressed Mortality files. Mortality rates by region, as well as those by region and cause, are presented primarily as changes or trends in black-white ratios in mortality. Standard linear regression analyses are used to estimate annual rates of change in e35, ten-year changes in black-white mortality ratios by region, and slopes of black-white mortality ratios by cause.

IMPROVED SOCIAL AND ECONOMIC POSITION FOR BLACK WOMEN IN THE POST-CIVIL-RIGHTS ERA

On the eve of the changes catalyzed by civil-rights legislation, there were large differences in the average economic status of blacks and whites. In 1960 the hourly wage ratio between black and white women was about 0.64. This wage variation was due in part to differences in average educational attainment and the concentration of blacks in the low-wage South (Cunningham and Zalokar 1992). However, another major factor was marked racial occupational segregation: black women were concentrated in low-skill and low-wage domestic service jobs and other service jobs, while the majority of working white women held white-collar jobs or did "pink-collar" clerical work (Blau and Beller 1992; King 1993; Zalokar 1990). Female workers have received less attention than male workers in studies of economic progress after civil-rights legislation; however, it was among women that economic status converged more completely between blacks and whites, and for whom occupational segregation and desegregation played the larger role (Cunningham and Zalokar 1992; Sundstrom 2000).

Indeed, the changes that occurred in the 1960s dramatically decreased racial differences in socioeconomic standing between black and white working-age women. Among the most notable changes, between 1950 and 1980 there was a major shift in the kinds of jobs typically held by black women (Conrad 2003; Cunningham and Zalokar 1992). Based on census data, figure 6.1 shows that the percentage of black women in the South reporting private household service work as their occupation declined from nearly 50 percent in 1950 to just over 11 percent in 1980; the percentage for black women in other regions fell from about 43 percent to under 5 percent. The dramatic exodus from private household service work occurred at a fairly consistent rate from 1950 to 1980 for black women outside the South, while among black southern women, the change was delayed until the 1960s. Fewer than 5 percent of white women did private household service work over this period, even in 1950, and the figure fell to about 1 percent nationwide by 1980.

What kind of work did African American women do if they were no longer doing private household service work? One of the notable changes of the 1960s was the increasing proportion of black women employed in white-collar work. Figure 6.2 shows that while there was an increase from 1950 to 1980 in the percentage of white women reporting a white-collar occupation (an increase from 54 percent in the South and 59 percent in the non-South in 1950, to approximately 63 percent in 1980), there was an even more impressive rise among black women, especially after 1964, with progress greatest in regions outside of the South. In 1950, between 10 and 12 percent of black women reported white-collar occupations, while by 1980 the percentage had increased almost four-fold for women outside of the South (difference in slopes outside the South: -1.23,

FIGURE 6.1 / Percentage of Women Thirty-Five to Sixty-Four Years Old Reporting Private-Household Service Work as Their Occupation, by Racial Group, Region, and Year[a]

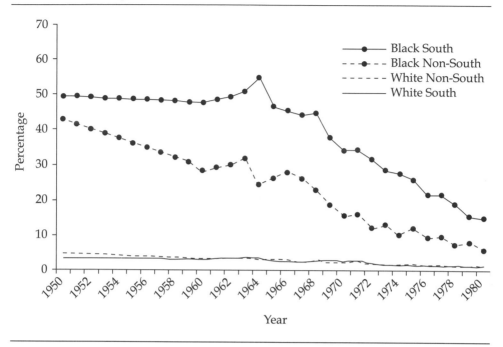

Source: Authors' calculations.
[a] IPUMS U.S. Census data using the OCC1950 recode variable for occupation, 1950–1980.

p < .001)and about three-fold for women in the South (difference in slopes: -0.996, p < .001).

Racial disparities among men did not change nearly as much during this period. Part of the reason for this was that gains for men had begun in the 1940s with a large-scale exodus from farming and farm labor into blue-collar positions including operative jobs, craft work, or other types of laborer positions (Allen and Farley 1986), and this source of rising occupational status had been largely exhausted by the mid-1960s. Figures 6.3 and 6.4 show the percentage of men ages thirty-five to sixty-four reporting "laborer" and white-collar occupations over the same period. Figure 6.3 shows that while menial work among black men fell in and outside the South, the exodus out of such work was not as dramatic as that seen among female private household service workers. Nonetheless, the percentage of black men in the South in laborer positions did not start to fall until the mid-1960s (difference in slopes: 0.797, p < .001), while a secular decline had started by 1950 for black men outside the South (difference in slopes: 0.065, p = 0.465). Similarly, figure 6.4 shows that there was a steady rise in the percentage of all male workers in white-collar jobs after the mid-1960s, with a consistent gap between whites, black men outside

FIGURE 6.2 / Percentage of Women Thirty-Five to Sixty-Four Years Old Reporting a White-Collar Occupation, by Racial Group, Region, and Year[a]

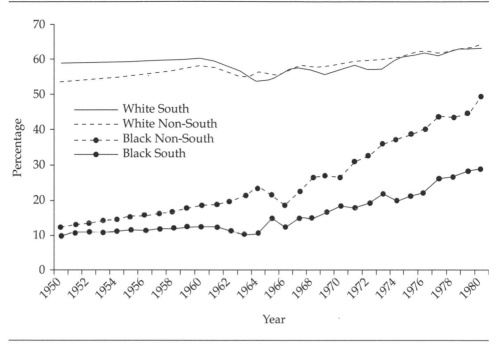

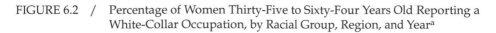

Source: Authors' calculations.

[a] IPUMS U.S. Census data using the OCC1950 recode variable for occupation, 1950–1980.

the South, and southern black men. These changes were important for male workers but were not as striking as the shifts in the work done by women, and they did not hold as much promise for reductions in overall racial disparities in socioeconomic standing. Black men made gains in white-collar positions in the 1960s, but the post-1964 period showed even more dramatic gains for black women (Smith 2003), particularly in the South.

During this period of major occupational gains for blacks, and especially for black women, there were also major gains in relative levels of wages and income for black women; for some age ranges, the trends were striking. For example, figure 6.5 (adapted from Allen and Farley 1986) shows the ratio of black to white median income for thirty-five- to forty-four-year-old males and females from 1949 to 1979, based on data from the U.S. Census 1950 to 1980. The figure demonstrates a complete closing of the income gap during this period for women and a far smaller narrowing for men.

Other analyses of decennial census data indicate that between 1960 and 1980 the black-white ratio in women's hourly wages increased from 0.64 to 0.99 (Cunningham and Zalokar 1992), even while wages for all workers were rising. The racial gap in men's wages also declined from the early 1960s to the mid-1970s; however,

FIGURE 6.3 / Percentage of Men Thirty-Five to Sixty-Four Years Old Reporting a "Laborer" Occupation, by Racial Group, Region, and Year[a]

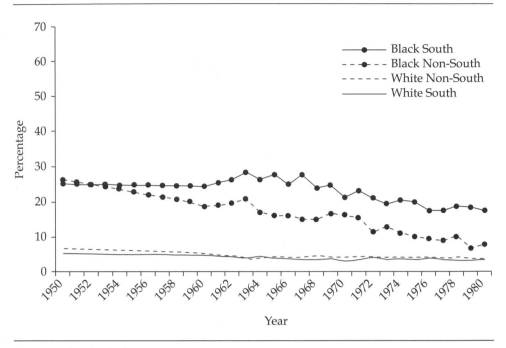

Source: Authors' calculations.
[a] IPUMS U.S. Census data using the OCC1950 recode variable for occupation, 1950–1980.

it then reversed and began to increase through the mid-1980s. The largest relative gains in the decade following civil-rights legislation were made by black women: from 1962 to 1973, real wages among white men increased by 17 percent, compared to 50 percent for black women (Smith 2003).

Not only did the types of occupations and income change, but the sectors in which work was being done also changed. There was a dramatic racial shift in the percentage of women employed in public-sector jobs in the immediate post-civil-rights period. Figure 6.6 shows that among thirty-five- to sixty-four-year-old black women, less than one in ten worked for a public employer in 1950. This number rose to about one in three in 1980, with the majority of the increase concentrated in the 1960s and 1970s. Over this same period, white women in the South hovered at just over 20 percent public employment, while whites outside the South rose from about 15 percent in 1950 to just over 20 percent in 1980. This meant that black women were less likely to have a public employer in 1950 and 1960, but they were equally or more likely than white women to be in public employment around 1970, and the gap widened thereafter. For men (not shown here), the changes were more muted, with a somewhat faster in-

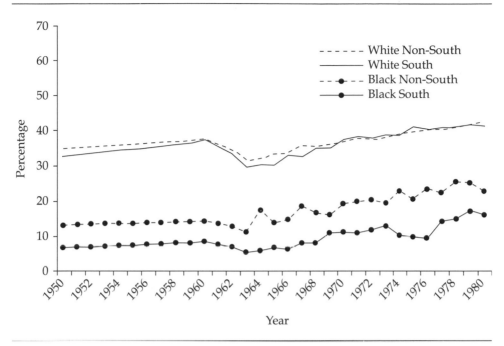

Source: Authors' calculations.
[a] IPUMS U.S. Census data using the OCC1950 recode variable for occupation, 1950–1980.

FIGURE 6.5   /   Ratio of Black-White Median Income (1983 Dollars) for Men and
Women, Age Thirty-Five to Forty-Four (1959 to 1979)

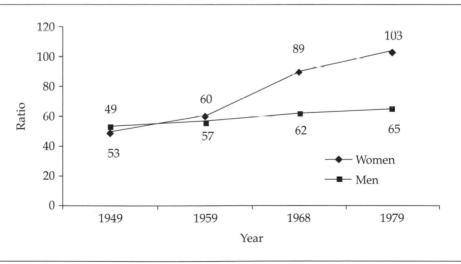

Source: Adapted from Allen & Farley (1986).

FIGURE 6.6 / Percentage of Women Thirty-Five to Sixty-Four Years Old Working for a Public Employer, by Racial Group and Region[a]

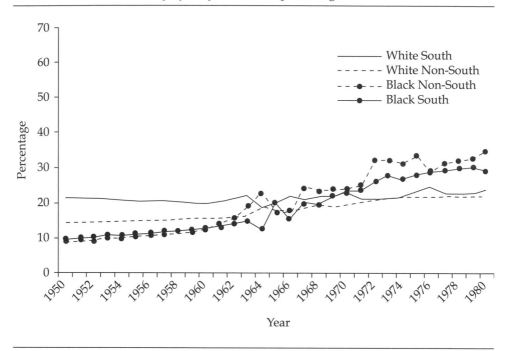

Source: Authors' calculations.
[a] IPUMS U.S. Census data, 1950 to 1980.

crease in public employment for black men and few regional differences. The implications of this rise in public-sector jobs for black women was not all positive: many of these jobs were of low quality relative to professional white-collar positions and were vulnerable to government funding fluctuation (Burbridge 1994). Nonetheless, relative to private household service work, these jobs probably represented a major advance in terms of prestige, wages, and other occupational features.

To summarize, black women experienced large occupational changes during the first decade or so of the civil-rights era, relative to white women and black men. They also experienced substantial increases in employment in the public sector and considerable improvement in economic fortunes consistent with all of these changes. Based on the considerable prior evidence that better socioeconomic position, increased economic security, and improved working conditions are associated with better health, these changes would be expected to translate into better health.

HEALTH TRAJECTORIES IN THE POST-CIVIL-RIGHTS ERA: WERE THERE BENEFITS OF RISING FORTUNES FOR BLACK WOMEN?

Table 6.1 shows the estimated annual rates of change in remaining life expectancy at age thirty-five (e35) by race and sex for the decade preceding the Civil Rights Act (1955 to 1964) and for the decade following passage (1965 to 1974). Rates are estimated from a regression of e35 against period, race, sex, and year, with all possible interactions allowed. We focus on e35 and e65 rather than the commonly used e0 (life expectancy at birth) to highlight improvements in mortality in the working-age population. Life-table measures are presented here as they use a comprehensive metric that summarizes the net effect of age-specific mortality rates.

In the decade prior to and including 1964, both black and white women experienced comparable annual gains in e35: life expectancy increased a little less than a month every year (a gain of between 0.07 and 0.08 years per year). During this period, mortality rates for males of both races were stagnant or declining (between -0.01 and -0.04). Following 1964, all groups experienced significant increases in e35 compared to the prior decade. Importantly, the gains in e35 for black women in this period outstripped the gains by other race and sex groups. In the decade following 1964, the annual increase in e35 among black women nearly tripled, from 0.07 years per year in the pre-civil-rights era to 0.26 years per year in the following decade. In contrast, during the same period, e35 for white women increased from 0.08 years per year to 0.15 years per year. Over a period of one decade, this translates to an additional year added to life expectancy at age thirty-five for black women compared to white women (2.6 years gain for black women versus 1.5 years gain for white women). Not surprisingly, the 0.19 years per year improvement in e35 for black women is significantly higher than the 0.07 years per year improvement for white women (difference = 0.12, p = 0.02).

TABLE 6.1 / Annual Rates of Change in Remaining Life Expectancy at Age Thirty-Five and Age Sixty-Five, By Sex, Race, and Era

		Black Women	White Women	Black Men	White Men
Annual rates of change in remaining	1956 to 1965	0.07	0.08	−0.04	-0.01
life expectancy at age thirty-five[a]	1966 to 1975	0.26	0.15	0.07	0.10
Annual rates of change in remaining	1956 to 1965	−0.06	0.07	−0.08	−0.02
life expectancy at age sixty-five	1966 to 1975	0.12	0.14	0.06	0.06

Source: Authors' calculations.
[a] Estimates are obtained from regressions of e(x) on year, period, and race-sex group, with all possible interactions between year, race-sex, and period, to estimate differences in slope.

The story is different when we examine remaining life expectancy at age sixty-five (e65). First, prior to 1964, black women ages sixty-five or older were at a significant disadvantage and experiencing a net annual decline in life expectancy (e65 = –0.06 years per year) compared to their white counterparts (e65 = 0.07 years per year). After 1964, however, this trend in e65 reversed and improved to the point where annual gains were comparable to those experienced by white women (0.12 years per year for black women, compared to 0.14 years per year for white women). Moreover, the numbers indicate that almost all the gains in e35 for white women were experienced by women ages sixty-five and older (0.14 out of 0.15). In contrast, for black women, more than half the gains in e35 (0.14 out of 0.26 years per year) were experienced by women ages thirty-five to sixty-five.

In general, the estimates for men suggest that both before and after 1964 gains for women exceeded those for men. Black males experienced much smaller improvements in life expectancy than black females. In general, however, this period saw black males reverse declining trends in life expectancy, and attainment of parity with white males in terms of annual rates of changes, though not in actual life expectancy. In summary, black women experienced larger relative gains in the rate of change of life expectancy following the passage of civil-rights legislation than any other race-sex group, and a substantial fraction of these relative gains were concentrated in the ages from thirty-five to sixty-five.

Figure 6.7 summarize these trends visually. The figure shows the estimated an-

Figure 6.7 / Change (Years per Decade) in Life Expectancy at Age Thirty-Five in the United States: 1955 to 1964 and 1965 to 1974

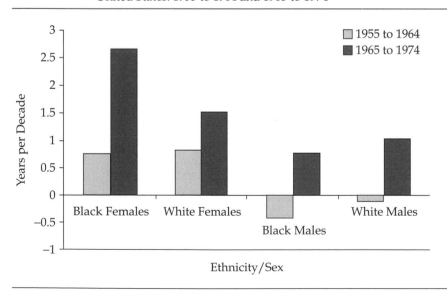

Source: Authors' calculations.

nual rates of change per decade in remaining life expectancy at age thirty-five (e35) by race and sex for the decade preceding the Civil Rights Act (1955 to 1964) and the decade following passage (1965 to 1974). It is evident that black women, alone among all race-sex groups, experienced a fairly pronounced upturn in e35 around 1964. Some evidence of upturn was evident in e65 as well, but the magnitude was much smaller, and it does not appear that this was unique to black women.

Analyses of Regional Differences in Mortality Trends

Because the impact of civil-rights legislation is widely believed to have been stronger in the southern states, an examination of region-specific trends in mortality is instructive. Figures 6.8 and 6.9 compare the rate of decline in black-white ratio for female mortality pre- and post-civil-rights legislation by region.[1] These estimates are of decadal changes in black-white mortality ratios based on age-adjusted mortality rates for women ages thirty-five to sixty-four, where rates were adjusted to the 1968 population.

While the black-white ratio for females was converging (negative estimates in figure 6.8 indicate black-white convergence) in three of the four regions even prior to civil-rights legislation, the relative advantage for black women accelerated dra-

FIGURE 6.8 / Change in Black-White Ratio of Female Mortality (Ages Thirty-Five to Sixty-Four): 1955 to 1964 and 1965 to 1974

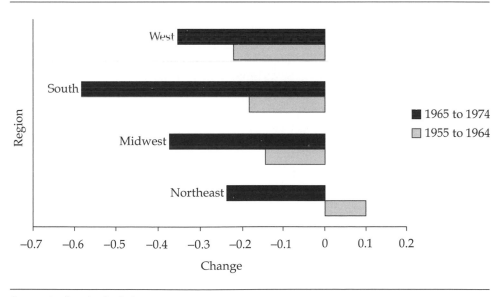

Source: Authors' calculations.

FIGURE 6.9   /   Change in Black-White Ratio of Male Mortality (Ages Thirty-Five to Sixty-Four): 1955 to 1964 and 1965 to 1974

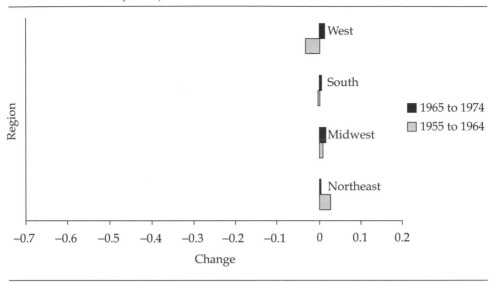

Source: Authors' calculations.

matically in the decade after 1964, with the greatest changes in the South. The pattern for males was very different. In the decade before 1964, mortality rates for blacks relative to whites were either unchanging or worsening in most regions (as indicated by small or positive estimates of change in the ratio), with particularly strong divergence in the Northeast. After 1964, there is some evidence that this diverging black-white trend slowed down in the Northeast, while the trends remained similar in the South and the Midwest. In contrast, patterns of change in mortality ratios over age sixty-five (estimates not shown) for males and females were similar. The black-white mortality ratio was increasing or stayed constant in all regions, both before and after 1964, except in the West, where both periods saw some racial convergence of rates for males and females.

Mortality Trends by Cause of Death

We also examined age-standardized mortality rates for ages thirty-five to sixty-four for black and white women in the South versus other regions, for three major cause-of-death categories: heart disease, stroke, and all neoplasms. These causes taken together accounted for nearly 70 percent of all mortality among women in this age group in 1965.[2]

For mortality from heart disease (figure 6.10), the black-white mortality ratio for females was declining in the South prior to 1964, while it was relatively flat in the

FIGURE 6.10   /   Trends in Ratios of Black-White Mortality from Heart Disease (Ages
Thirty-Five to Sixty-Four) for Females, By Region, 1955 to 1974

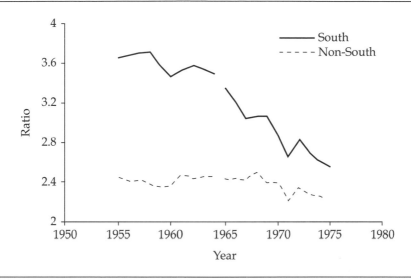

Source: Authors' calculations.

other regions. The rate of decline in the South accelerates post-1964. Between 1955
and 1964, the ratio declined by 8 percent (from 3.6 to 3.3), while in the decade after
1965, the ratio declined by 24 percent (from 3.3 to 2.5). In other regions, the black-
white mortality ratio from heart disease stagnated at about 2.3 for the entire period.

For cerebrovascular disease (see figure 6.11), black-white female mortality ratios
were increasing prior to 1964 in all regions. After 1964, there was a sharp acceleration in the rate of decline of the ratio in the South particularly, declining from 5.4
to 3.6 in the space of one decade. Declines in other regions were more muted, declining from 3.4 to 2.4.

In the case of deaths from neoplasms (see figure 6.12), the regional differences in
female black-white ratios are much smaller, with some indication of an accelerated
decline in the black-white mortality ratio although there is also considerable year-
to-year variability in the ratio.

These patterns are confirmed in table 6.2, which presents estimated slopes of the
trend in black-white ratios of cause-specific mortality. As is evident, trends of decline in heart-disease and stroke mortality ratios favored the South even before
1964, but following 1964 these differences widened remarkably in favor of the
South, particularly in the case of stroke mortality.

For men (not shown) there were few changes in trends in black-white mortality ratios in the post-civil-rights decade relative to trends in the prior decade. Regionally, in
the period preceding civil-rights legislation, trends in heart-disease and stroke mor-

Figure 6.11 / Trends in Ratios of Black-White Mortality from Stroke (Ages Thirty-Five to Sixty-Four) for Females, By Region, 1955 to 1974

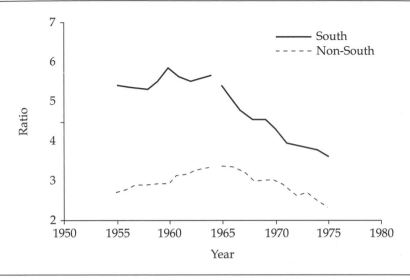

Source: Authors' calculations.

Figure 6.12 / Trends in Ratios of Black-White Mortality from Neoplasms (Ages Thirty-Five to Sixty-Four) for Females, By Region, 1955 to 1974

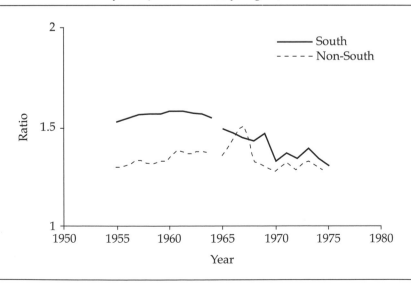

Source: Authors' calculations.

TABLE 6.2 / Slope of Trend in Ratios of Black-to-White Female Mortality, By Region, Era, and Cause of Death

	1955 to 1964			1965 to 1974		
	South	Non-South	South Non-South Difference	South	Non-South	South Non-South Difference
Heart disease[a]	-2.59 (0.73)	0.81 (0.73)	-3.4 (1.03)	-7.57 (0.62)	-2.36 (0.62)	-5.21 (0.88)
Stroke	-9.83 (1.07)	7.13 (1.25)	-3.33 (1.77)	-17.65 (1.07)	3.8 (1.25)	-7.82 (1.51)
Neoplasms	-0.46 (0.3)	0.85 (0.3)	-0.74 (0.42)	-1.65 (0.3)	0.1 (0.3)	-1.19 (0.43)

Source: Authors' calculations.
[a] Estimates based on regression of black-white mortality ratios against year, region, cause of death, and all two-way and three-way interactions.

tality ratios favored black males in the South more than those in the North. This is possibly reflecting the increased opportunities provided to black males by the expansion of the textile industry in the South after World War II. Male black-white mortality ratios from neoplasms were increasing both before and after 1964.

CONCLUSION

The results of our analyses indicate that there were important improvements in life expectancy and mortality from specific causes for black women in the decade after the enactment of the Civil Rights Act of 1964 compared to the previous decade. These improvements were concentrated in working-age black women, with black men showing smaller and qualitatively different patterns of improvement. Furthermore, the trends in increased life expectancy and decreased mortality rates were substantially stronger for black women than they were for white women, and during the decade after the enactment of the Civil Rights Act of 1964, the life-expectancy gains for black women were 73 percent greater than for white women. The health of black women improved most, in both relative and absolute terms, in the South compared to other regions. This reflects a strikingly different picture than that found for black and white females over the age of sixty-five or for men of all ages and races. Finally, comparing the trends in rates of death from heart disease and stroke in the decades pre- and post-1964, the most favorable trends are again seen for black women in the South.

For the most part, the improved trends in working-age life expectancy and mortality from vascular disease in black women compared to white women and both black and white men mirror the improved trends in socioeconomic and occupational status for black women compared to these other groups. The regional specificity of these patterns also mirrors these changes.

The similarity between these patterns, the specificity of the health effects, and the timing of the effects certainly add credence to the suggestion that the broad set of programs and other changes that were created or catalyzed by the Civil Rights Act of 1964 did, in fact, improve the health of black women. However, the consistency, specificity, and timing of these trends are not alone sufficient to make an entirely convincing causal story. We now examine a series of interpretive issues that bear upon our interpretation of these trends.

It is possible that the trends in labor markets as well as regional and cause-specific mortality represent independent secular changes or a continuation of independent existing trends. Turning to labor markets, then, we need to assess the extent to which the gains were triggered by civil-rights legislation as opposed to secular changes in labor markets. One study (Smith and Welch 1977, 1989) argues that evolving historical forces, especially improved education for blacks following desegregation and migration of blacks from the South to the North and from rural to urban areas, drove wage increase for blacks. However, a preponderance of other studies concluded that this increase in economic status was associated with civil-rights legislation. The big gains in relative median income of all blacks and of college-educated blacks of both sexes began in 1966, the year the initial impact of the Civil Rights Act of 1964 could be measured. The EEOC has been described as the single most important explanation for income convergence during this period, even after taking into account growth in gross national product and improvements in black education (Freeman 1976). This position is supported by a number of more recent studies. In a study of the South Carolina textile industry, the authors conclude that the EEOC was a major factor in increasing the demand even for less-educated black workers (Butler, Heckman, and Payner 1989). Most of the relative income gains that occurred during this period took place in the South, the region that was the target of early Title VII legislation (Donohue and Heckman 1991; Heckman 1990). Federal intervention also accounts for a large proportion of the gains in occupational attainment for minorities (DiPrete and Grusky 1990). One estimate is that improvements in school quality accounted for only one-quarter of the gains in relative income made by black men between 1960 and 1980, with the rest attributable to legislative changes (Card and Krueger 1992). Similarly, a sizable fraction of the gains made by black women relative to white men can be explained by a decline in wage discrimination (Carnoy 1996). While there is abundant evidence from these studies that federal legislation increased black incomes, these studies generally focus on black males rather than on black females, and a number of them focus on college-educated blacks. Thus, while they do not directly address the reasons for changes in the economic status of black women, particularly those who were not college-educated, they are certainly consistent with a similar argument for the role of civil-rights legislation in the occupational changes for women and their economic consequences.

What about mortality trends in the period preceding 1965? Between 1954 and 1963, some racial convergence among males was evident, but no such racial convergence was seen in the case of females. Among black women a steady slowing of the rate of decline of mortality was observed in all age groups below age sixty-five (Klebba 1966). Much of the slowing in decline observed during this period was due to an across-the-board increase in mortality from diseases of the heart (which constituted nearly 40 percent of all deaths to black women in 1963). Black women in particular experienced a large relative increase in mortality from heart disease (41 percent). Thus, it is apparent that in the decade preceding 1964, black women had significantly poorer trends in mortality improvements relative to all other race and sex groups. The reversal of these race- and sex-specific trends in 1964 is thus all the more remarkable.

This coincidence of relative gains in mortality for black women with marked changes in their occupational and income standing is thus not likely to be accidental. Further, although civil-rights legislation was not intended to be sex-specific, it is apparent from our results that the gains in labor-market conditions were stronger for women. Data presented here indicate that black men made weaker occupational and socioeconomic gains in the late 1960s and 1970s than did black women. One potential reason could be employers' weaker latent discriminatory feelings toward black women than toward black men; thus, when the law changed, black women were hired preferentially before black men. In addition, if nonunionization and the related negative sentiment toward blacks were more prevalent for "men's work" than for "women's work," women might advance more quickly after a legal shift. Given the near-complete restriction of black women to domestic service work in the early twentieth century, their move into new higher status occupations represented a dramatic shift in occupational and economic standing. Black women's occupational status gains were more substantial than those that black men experienced in this period. The pathway of black males was initially from agricultural labor into unskilled blue-collar work in the 1940s and 1950s, and then later into more skilled blue-collar positions (Collins 2003). Large shifts into white-collar work were not experienced even by white men over these decades.

Another potential alternative explanation for the gender differences in response to changes in the legislative landscape in 1965 lies in the authorization of Medicaid (Title XIX of the Social Security Act of 1965). Low-income families with dependent children and low-income elderly, blind, or disabled individuals were eligible for Medicaid benefits. These criteria for eligibility, as stipulated, consistently excluded nondisabled adult men. Low-income adult men generally could only become eligible for Medicaid coverage by becoming blind, disabled, or elderly (Satcher et al. 2005). In contrast, eligibility for low-income families with dependent children expanded the access for black women in particular. Health care access for black women probably also expanded as a result of increased public-sector employment. Such improved access may have played some role in reducing working-age mortality.

Next we consider whether the effects are biologically plausible and what the possible biological and behavioral pathways might be between the enactment of civil-rights legislation and improved health. We consider such a discussion to be an important component of evaluating the interpretation of the results of both observational and experimental studies. The finding that pre-1964 versus post-1964 improvements in mortality that favored black women were found for heart trouble and stroke but not for malignancies is instructive. Most malignancies develop over long periods, in some cases over many decades, before they are clinically evident, and they would not be expected to be responsive to short-term changes. Thus, the existence of noticeable short-term effects for malignancies would cause reason for concern. While it is true that the multiple clinical entities grouped under the categories of heart trouble and stroke represent chronic pathophysiologic processes that also develop over decades, mortality from these causes represents a combination of chronic degenerative, acute triggering, and secondary- and tertiary- care processes, with the latter two potentially responsive to changes over shorter periods. The clearest examples of this are increased rates of heart attacks post–natural disasters and after certain behavioral and psychosocial episodes (Katsouyanni, Kogevinas, and Trichopoulos 1986; Mittleman et al. 1995; Albert et al. 2000; Kaplan and Keil 1993). Unfortunately, while such acute triggers of vascular events are biologically plausible and have been empirically demonstrated, there are no data to our knowledge that would allow us to examine whether there was a decline in such triggers in the decade after 1964 and if such a decline was more prevalent for black women in the South. Speculatively, an extensive literature indicates that the prevalence of stressors is inversely associated with higher socioeconomic position (House 2002), and it is plausible that increased wages and income, better working conditions, and movement into a more supportive occupational sector may have reduced the prevalence of these stressors and their behavioral and physiologic sequelae.

A shared risk factor for mortality from most entities classified as "heart trouble" and "stroke" is cigarette smoking, and quitting smoking can have protective effects on cardiovascular mortality within five years or so. Is there any evidence that patterns of smoking and quitting changed, particularly for black women in the South, over the two decades under consideration? Again the data are sparse, particularly in the earlier period. For example, the National Health Interview Survey only collected national smoking data beginning in 1965. The data that are available post-1964 indicate lower rates of smoking for black women compared to white women, but not more favorable trends for black women. For example, among those ages forty-five and older in 1965, 44.4 percent of white women and 25.1 percent of black women were current smokers (McGinnis, Shopland, and Brown 1987). By 1976, the corresponding numbers were 35 percent and 26.7 percent. If anything, this indicates a worsening trend for black women compared to white women, which is not consistent with the differential mortality trends from heart trouble and stroke.

On the face of it, inspection of trends in hypertension control should be instructive both as an indicator of a disease process related to mortality from heart trouble and stroke as well as an indicator of access to medical care and to effective treatment. Again the data are not easily obtained. The data that do exist do not indicate, unlike the case for birth outcomes reported by Almond, Chay, and Greenstone, that improved medical care is likely to be responsible for what we have observed. A strong case is made that the federally mandated changes which increased access to facilities did improve health care, at least care which was hospital based, for blacks in the South. However the situation for hypertension is less clear. While there is a large emphasis on hypertension control currently, the state of both epidemiologic and clinical evidence for the importance of control of blood pressure was much less clear during the periods we are considering (Kannel 2000; Kannel, Gordon, and Schwartz 1971). Broad-scale federal efforts to control high blood pressure only began in the early 1970s, and effective therapies with low levels of side effects only became widely available in the mid-1970s (Moser 1986). Thus, it is unlikely that there were major events pre- and post-1964 that led to more effective control of hypertension among black women in the South. The data that do exist show consistently higher rates of hypertension among black women compared to white women. There are almost identical secular trends from the early 1960s to the mid-1970s for those women ages forty to fifty-nine and a substantial convergence of black-white difference in the prevalence of hypertension for women thirty to thirty-nine (Burt et al. 1995). However, as a small proportion of the deaths in the thirty-five- to sixty-four-year-old age group are contributed by those ages thirty to thirty-nine, the decreased prevalence of hypertension is not likely to explain the differential mortality trends. Data of sufficient quality are not available to make any regional comparisons.

What else might account for the relatively accelerated improvement in the health of black women, particularly in the South, in the decade following the passage of the Civil Rights Act of 1964? A number of possibilities suggest themselves, but data limitations and the lack of individual-level microdata do not permit us to examine them in any detail. One can imagine a cascade of material and psychosocial effects, and their interaction, in response to the changes in economic and occupational status. Certainly, the increases in income and wages for black women during this period may have translated into better living situations and more adequate nutrition, as well as less stress associated with housing problems, financial instability, family problems, under-resourced neighborhoods, or other demands. The accelerated movement into public-sector jobs may have led to positions with greater job security, enforcement of work rules, and health and other benefits. It is also possible that moving from domestic service jobs into clerical and professional-technical jobs led to increases in learning opportunities, formation of new peer groups, increased self-esteem, and lowered levels of depression. For those who moved into professional-technical jobs, such as teaching or management of small businesses, there may also have been increased job control. While there is some evidence that some of these factors are associated with better health outcomes (for example, job control), we have not been able to discover data that would allow us to determine if measures of these characteristics moved in a way consistent with the observed secular trends in health.

It is important to stress that these relative improvements in socioeconomic standing and mortality experienced by black women were transient. After the early 1980s, occupational gains stagnated (Fosu 1997) and earnings gains deteriorated (Conrad 2003). Perhaps not surprisingly, the decade of the 1980s was marked by relatively poorer mortality improvements for black women over age thirty-five. For example, between 1980 and 1988, the annual age-adjusted decline in ischemic-heart-disease mortality for the population ages thirty-five and older was as follows: 3.7 percent for white men, 3.1 percent for black men, 2.9 percent for white women, and 2.2 percent for black women. Remarkably, the rate of this annual decline was also slower in the South (2.9 percent) than in any other region (3.9 percent in the Northeast, 3.2 percent in the Midwest, and 3.1 percent in the West) (MMWR Weekly 1992). These reversals emphasize that the gains for black women, particularly in the South, seen in the period from 1964 to 1975 were episodic. This strengthens the case for their association with civil-rights legislation.

Here we return to Donohue and Heckman's (1991) comment that understanding the role of federal legislation in the employment and wage gains of blacks following the enactment of the Civil Rights Act of 1964 seems more reflective of a puzzle solved by Sherlock Holmes than an econometric paper. We concur, as the paucity of data makes it difficult to definitively assert a causal effect of the Civil Rights Act of 1964, and the similar lack of data on potential pathways that might have translated legislation into improved health makes it difficult to apply a closer interpretive lens to the changes we have observed. In addition, the Civil Rights Act of 1964 did not occur in a vacuum; it reflected many changes that had occurred post-Reconstruction (Filvaroff and Wolfinger 2000; Woodward 1968; Kousser 2000). Of course, this time period was also affected by the Economic Opportunity Act of 1965 that ushered in the War on Poverty and the dozens of programs that sprang from it (Clark 2002). Such a stew of history, politics, and race and class relations makes it difficult, despite the methodologic press, to construct any completely convincing connection between major legislation such as the Civil Rights Act of 1964 and putatively resultant socioeconomic and health changes. In addition, the historic position of black men, the small gains in occupational status that they had achieved earlier, and the continuing press of racism and discrimination against black men in particular may have provided a context that limited the potential impact of civil-rights legislation on the occupational and economic pathways that would lead to improved health. However, in a "Sherlock Holmesian" manner we propose that the patterns of health changes observed post-1964, their timing and consistency with what is known about social and economic determinants of health, and the gender- and region-based patterns of change strongly suggest that the Civil Rights Act of 1964 did have a salutary impact of the health of black women in the United States, especially in the South. These effects were not the focus or the intent of the legislation, but they provide some support for the proposition that social and economic policies are, indeed, health policies.

NOTES

1. Up until 1967, mortality statistics are only available for the race categories *white* and *non-white*; it was only after 1967 that separate tabulations for blacks are available. For national statistics, this is not expected to have much of an impact, as blacks constituted a large proportion of non-white races before this period. For regional statistics, however, this is no longer true. In western states, the non-white category included a signif-

icant non-black fraction. Race-specific statistics for western states prior to 1968 should accordingly be interpreted with caution.

2. For the most part, the pre-civil-rights era corresponds to ICD-7 (1958 to 1967 in the International Statistical Classification of Diseases and Related Health Problems), with some slight overlap with ICD-6 (1949 to 1957), while the post-civil-rights era corresponds to ICD-8 (1968 to 1978), with some overlap with ICD-7. Comparable codes for heart disease, stroke, and neoplasms were obtained across all three ICD code changes. ICD codes for the three cause of death categories were as follows: Heart disease was coded as 400 to 402 and 410 to 443 (ICD-6 and ICD-7), and 390 to 398, 402 to 404, 410 to 429 (ICD-8). Stroke was coded as 330 to 334 (ICD 6 and ICD-7), and 430 to 438 (ICD-8). Neoplasms were coded as 140 to 205 (ICD 6 and ICD 7), and 140 to 208 (ICD-8).

REFERENCES

Albert, Christine. M., Murray A. Mittleman, Claudia U. Chae, I.-Min Lee, Charles H. Hennekens, and Joann E. Manson. 2000. "Triggering of Sudden Death from Cardiac Causes by Vigorous Exertion." *New England Journal of Medicine* 343(19): 1355-61.

Alexis, Marcus. 1998. "Assessing 50 Years of African-American Economic Status, 1940–1990." *The American Economic Review* 88(2): 368–75.

Allen, Walter R., and Reynolds Farley. 1986. "The Shifting Social and Economic Tides of Black Americans, 1950–1980." *Annual Review of Sociology* 12: 297–306.

Almond, Douglas V., Kenneth Y. Chay, Michael Greenstone. 2006. "Civil Rights, the War on Poverty, and Black-White Convergence in Infant Mortality in the Rural South and Mississippi." MIT Department of Economics Working Paper No. 07-04. Massachusetts Institute of Technology, Cambridge, Mass.

Blau, Francine D., and Andrea H. Beller. 1992. "Black-White Earnings over the 1970s and 1980s: Gender Differences in Trends." *Review of Economics and Statistics* 74(2): 276–86.

Burbridge, Lynn C. 1994. "The Reliance of African-American Women on Government and Third-Sector Employment." *American Economic Review* 84(2): 103–7.

Burt, Vicki L., Jeffery A. Cutler, Millicent Higgins, Michael J. Horan, Darwin Labarthe, Paul Whelton, Clarice Brown, and Edward J. Roccella. 1995. "Trends in the Prevalence, Awareness, Treatment, and Control of Hypertension in the Adult U.S. Population: Data from the Health Examination Surveys, 1960–1991." *Hypertension* 26(1): 60–69.

Butler, Richard J., James J. Heckman, and Brook S. Payner. 1989. "The Impact of the Economy and the State on the Economic Status of Blacks: A Study of South Carolina." In *Markets in History: Economic Studies of the Past*, edited by David W. Galenson. New York: Cambridge University Press.

Card, David, and Alan Krueger. 1992. "Does School Quality Matter? Returns to Education and the Characteristics of Public Schools in the United States." *Journal of Political Economy* 100(1): 1–40.

Carnoy, Martin. 1996. *Faded Dreams: The Politics and Economics of Race in America.* New York: Cambridge University Press.

Clark, Robert F. 2002. *The War on Poverty: History, Selected Programs, and Ongoing Impact.* New Lanham, Md.: University Press of America.

Collins, William. 2003. "The Labor Market Impact of State-Level Anti-Discrimination Laws, 1940–1960." *Industrial and Labor Relations Review* 56(2): 244–72.

Conrad, Cecilia A. 2003. "Racial Trends in Labor Market Access and Wages: Women." In *America Becoming: Racial Trends and Their Consequences*, Volume 2, edited by Neil J. Smelser, William Julius Wilson, and Faith Mitchell. Washington: National Academy Press.

Cunningham, James S., and Nadja Zalokar. 1992. "The Economic Progress of Black Women, 1940–1980: Occupational Distribution and Relative Wages." *Industrial and Labor Relations Review* 45(3): 540–55.

DiPrete, Thomas A., and David B.Grusky. 1990. "Structure and Trend in the Process of Stratification for American Men and Women." *American Journal of Sociology* 96(1): 107–43.

Donohue, John J., III, and James Heckman. 1991. "Continuous Versus Episodic Change: The Impact of Civil Rights Policy on the Economic Status of Blacks." *Journal of Economic Literature* 29(4): 1603–43.

Evans, Robert G., Morris L. Barer, and Theodore E. Marmor, editors. 1994. *Why Are Some People Healthy and Others Not?* Hawthorne, N.Y.: Aldine De Gruyter.

Filvaroff, David B., and Raymond E. Wolfinger. 2000. "The Origin and Enactment of the Civil Rights Act of 1964." In *Legacies of the 1964 Civil Rights Act*, edited by Bernard Grofman. Charlottesville, Va.: University of Virginia Press.

Fosu, Augustin Kwasi. 1997. "Occupational Gains of Black Women Since the 1964 Civil Rights Act: Long-Term or Episodic?" *American Economic Review* 87(2): 311–14.

Freeman, Richard. 1976. *The Over-Educated American*. London: Academic Press.

Grofman, Bernard, editor. 2000. *Legacies of the 1964 Civil Rights Act*. Charlottesville, Va.: University of Virginia Press.

Heckman, James. 1990. "The Central Role of the South in Accounting for the Economic Progress of Black Americans." *American Economic Review* 80(2): 242–6.

House, James S. 2002. "Understanding Social Factors and Inequalities in Health: 20th Century Progress and 21st Century Prospects." *Journal of Health and Social Behavior* 43(2): 125–42.

Kannel, William B. 2000. "Fifty Years of Framingham Study Contributions to Understanding Hypertension." *Journal of Human Hypertension* 14(2): 83–90.

Kannel, William B., Tavia Gordon, and Melvin J. Schwartz. 1971. "Systolic Versus Diastolic Pressure and Risk of Coronary Heart Disease, the Framingham Study." *American Journal of Cardiology* 27(4): 335–46.

Kaplan, George A. 2001. "Economic Policy Is Healthy Policy: Findings from the Study of Income, Socioeconomic Status, and Health." In *Income, Socioeconomic Status and Health: Exploring the Relationships*, edited by James A. Auerbach and Barbara K. Krimgold. Washington: National Policy Association.

Kaplan, George A., and Julian E. Keil. 1993. "Socioeconomic Factors and Cardiovascular Disease: A Review of the Literature." *Circulation* 88(4): 1973–98.

Kaplan, George A., and John W. Lynch. 1997. "Whither Studies on the Socioeconomic Foundations of Population Health?" *American Journal of Public Health* 87(9): 1409–11.

Kaplan. George A., Mary N. Haan, S. Leonard Syme, Meredith Minkler, and Marilyn Winkleby. 1987. "Socioeconomic Status and Health." In *Closing the Gap: The Burden of Unnecessary Illness*, edited by Robert W. Amler and H. Bruce Dull. New York: Oxford University Press.

Katsouyanni, Klea, Manolis Kogevinas, and Mitrios Trichopoulos. 1986. "Earthquake-Related Stress and Cardiac Mortality." *International Journal of Epidemiology* 15(3): 326–30.

King, Mary C. 1993. "Black Women's Breakthrough into Clerical Work: An Occupational Tipping Model." *Journal of Economic Issues* 27(4): 1097–1125.

Klebba, A. Joan. 1966. "Mortality Trends in the United States 1954–1963." (PHS) 1000. NCHS Series 20(2) *Mortality Trends.* PB-281609. PC A04 MF A01. National Center for Health Statistics, Public Health Service Report.

Kousser, J. Morgan. 2000. "What Light Does the Civil Rights Act of 1875 Shed on the Civil Rights Act of 1964?" In *Legacies of the 1964 Civil Rights Act*, edited by Bernard Grofman. Charlottesville, Va.: University of Virginia Press.

McGinnis, J. Michael., Donald Shopland, and Clarice Brown. 1987. "Tobacco and Health: Trends in Smoking and Smokeless Tobacco Consumption in the United States 1987." *Annual Review of Public Health* 8: 441–67.

Mittleman, Murray A., Malcolm Maclure, Jane B. Sherwood, Richard Mulry, Geoffrey H. Tofler, Sue C. Jacobs, Richard Friedman, Herbert Benson, and James E. Muller. 1995. "Triggering of Acute Myocardial Infarction Onset by Episodes of Anger. Determinants of Myocardial Infarction Onset Study Investigators." *Circulation* 92(7): 1720–5.

MMWR Weekly. 1992. "Trends in Ischemic Heart Disease Mortality—United States, 1980 1988." *MMWR Weekly* 41(30): 548 9, 555 6.

Moser, Marvin. 1986. "Historical Perspective on the Management of Hypertension." *The American Journal of Medicine* 80(5, Supplement 2): 1–11.

Ruggles, Steven, Matthew Sobek, Trent Alexander, Catherine A. Fitch, Ronald Goeken, Patricia Kelly Hall, Miriam King, and Chad Ronnander. 2004. *Integrated Public Use Microdata Series: Version 3.0.* Minneapolis, Minn.: Minnesota Population Center.

Satcher, David, George E. Fryer Jr., Jessica McCann, Adewale Troutman, Steven H. Woolf, and George Rust. 2005. "What If We Were Equal? A Comparison of the Black-White Mortality Gap in 1960 and 2000." *Health Affairs* 24(2): 459–64.

Smith, James P. 2003. "Race and Ethnicity in the Labor Market. Trends over the Long and Short Term." In *America Becoming: Racial Trends and Their Consequences*, Volume 2, edited by Neil J. Smelser, William Julius Wilson, and Faith Mitchell. Washington: National Academy Press.

Smith, James P., and Finis R. Welch. 1977. "Black/White Male Earnings and Employment: 1960–1970." In *The Distribution of Economic Well-Being*, edited by F. Thomas Juster. Cambridge, Mass.: National Bureau of Economic Research.

———. 1989. "Black Economic Progress After Myrdal." *Journal of Economic Literature* 27(2): 519–64.

Sundstrom, William A. 2000 "From Servants to Secretaries: The Occupations of African-American women, 1940–1980." Unpublished paper, Santa Clara University.

U.S. Congress, Senate. 1964. *H. R. 7152 Civil Rights Act of 1964.* 88th Cong. PL 88–352.

Williams, David R., and Chiquita Collins. 1995. "U.S. Socioeconomic and Racial Differences in Health: Patterns and Explanations." *Annual Review of Sociology*, 21: 349–86.

Woodward, C. V. 1968. *The Burden of Southern History.* 2nd edition. Baton Rouge, La.: Louisiana State University.

Zalokar, Nadja. 1990. *The Economic Status of Black Women: An Exploratory Investigation.* Washington: U.S. Commission on Civil Rights.

Part V

Macroeconomic and Employment Policy

Chapter 7

Macroeconomic Conditions, Health, and Government Policy

Christopher J. Ruhm

Many government policies influence short- and medium-run economic performance. Some, such as the monetary and interest rate targets, are explicitly designed to stabilize the economy. Fiscal policy has the potential to play a similar role, although it is not aggressively used for this purpose in the United States. The unemployment insurance and federal income-tax systems act as "automatic stabilizers" because they make government spending more expansionary during economic downturns and less so during booms. Other programs, such as the Earned Income Tax Credit (EITC), increase incomes during expansions when work is easier to find, and so operate in the opposite direction (Edwards 2005).[1] Spending by local governments also tends to be procyclical, because most states are required to balance their budgets and receive greater tax revenue when the economy is doing well.

These policies have been widely examined. Even when their primary purpose is unrelated to macroeconomic performance, the effects on these economic outcomes are at least partially understood. For instance, extensive research examines how the EITC affects labor supply and consumption decisions (Meyer and Rosenbaum 2001; Eissa and Hoynes 2004; Edwards 2004). However, macroeconomic conditions, and the government policies that affect them, may have unexpected and less-studied consequences for population health.

Health is conventionally believed to improve during economic expansions and deteriorate during downturns. Yet the empirical evidence supporting this view is quite weak and comes from studies containing methodological shortcomings that are difficult to remedy. Recent research, using methods that better control for many sources of omitted-variable bias, suggests that mortality *decreases* and many aspects of physical (although not necessarily mental) health *improve* when the economy temporarily weakens. This partially reflects reductions in external sources of death, such as traffic fatalities and other accidents, as well as environmental factors like decreases in pollution. However, changes in lifestyles and health behaviors also play a role, and the mechanisms for these effects are less obvious.

Before proceeding, two points deserve mention. First, a large body of epidemiological research examines how changes in *individual* economic status are related to a person's health. Importantly, there is a great deal of evidence that the unemployed and job losers are relatively unhealthy (Morris, Cook, and Shaper 1994; Ettner 2000; Gerdtham and Johannesson 2003). Determining whether such correlations represent causal relationships is a challenge, however, since bad health reduces employment probabilities, and these potential selection biases are often not fully accounted for (Bartley 1996; Goldney 1997; Stewart 2001).[2] The line of study summarized in this chapter asks a different question: how macroeconomic (rather than individual) conditions affect health. This research is sometimes criticized as being subject to the "ecological fallacy," whereby individual relationships are difficult to ascertain using aggregate data (Catalano and Bellows 2005). Such concern is largely misplaced. In particular, while unemployment rates (or similar labor-market measures) are often used to *proxy* economic conditions, the effects of the latter need not be restricted to or concentrated among persons changing employment status. For instance, the stress of job loss could induce negative health effects that are more than offset by improvements for workers whose hours or job-related pressures are reduced. In addition, the impact of risk factors such as pollution, traffic congestion, and social isolation are not limited to working-age individuals. Many important consequences of macroeconomic fluctuations are therefore missed when considering only how individual labor-market status is correlated with health or mortality.

Second, the diverse dimensions of health may be affected by a variety of mechanisms that have heterogeneous impacts across segments of the population. Macroeconomic conditions therefore need not uniformly affect all aspects of health or sectors of the population. The results summarized in this chapter primarily focus on average population health (with some examination of subgroups) and should not be viewed to provide definitive or universal conclusions.

TIME-SERIES ANALYSES

Researchers examining how macroeconomic conditions affect health or mortality have commonly used time-series data. A series of investigations by M. Harvey Brenner (1971, 1973, 1975, 1979, 1987) have been particularly influential. He presents evidence that recessions and other sources of macroeconomic instability raise overall mortality and deaths from several specific sources, as well as increasing some health problems (such as alcoholism) and admissions to mental hospitals. These findings are controversial. A number of investigators (Kasl 1979; Gravelle, Hutchinson, and Stern 1981; Stern 1983; Gravelle 1984; Wagstaff 1985; Cook and Zarkin 1986) point out serious technical flaws in Brenner's methods, including the choice of lag lengths and covariates, hypothesized pattern of lag coefficients, use of inconsistent and poorly documented data, plausibility of results, and estimation of substantially different specifications across studies without justification or discussion of the robustness of the results.

Studies correcting these problems (Forbes and McGregor 1984; Cook and Zarkin 1986; McAvinchey 1988; Joyce and Mocan 1993) fail to replicate Brenner's findings. Instead, as detailed in table 7.1, the results are sensitive to the choice of countries, time periods, and proxies for health. Significantly, most evidence suggests that the contemporaneous effect of economic downturns is to reduce fatalities.

Such "counterintuitive" findings are not new. Research undertaken as early as the 1920s by William Ogburn and Dorothy Thomas (1922) and Thomas (1927)—using United States and United Kingdom data from the late nineteenth and early twentieth centuries—identifies a positive association between macroeconomic activity and total mortality or deaths from several specific causes (with suicides being the exception). Joseph Eyer (1977) obtains similar findings using United States data from 1870 to 1975. These correlations hint that fatalities are *procyclical*. While inconclusive because they control for few other determinants of health, they present a serious challenge to Brenner's hypothesis, and even he has noted that mortality tends to decline during periods of rising unemployment.[3]

Researchers have attempted to correct for many of the aforementioned problems. For instance, Ian McAvinchey (1988) employs statistical rather than ad hoc methods to choose the lag length and order of the polynomial lag. Theodore Joyce and H. Naci Mocan (1993) and Audrey Laporte (2004) correct for nonstationarity in the time-series data.[4] José Tapia Granados (2004) implements spectral analysis and local regression techniques. Ulf-G Gerdtham and Magnus Johannesson (2005) experiment with multiple business-cycle indicators using data on individual, rather than aggregate, mortality risk. Despite these innovations, the results remain ambiguous. Most research continues to suggest that mortality is procyclical (Laporte 2004; Tapia Granados 2004, 2005a), but some studies find countercyclical effects (Gerdtham and Johannesson 2005), no impact (Joyce and Mocan 1993), or results that vary across countries (McAvinchey 1988).

This lack of robustness should not be surprising since any lengthy time series may contain omitted variables that are spuriously correlated with economic conditions and have a causal effect on health.[5] Consider estimates of specifications taking the form:

$$H_t = \alpha + X_t\beta + E_t\gamma + \varepsilon_t, \qquad (7.1)$$

where H measures health or mortality at time t, E indicates macroeconomic conditions, X is a vector of covariates, and ε is an error term. The coefficient of key interest, $\hat{\gamma}$, will be biased if $\text{cov}(E_t, \varepsilon_t) \neq 0$, which occurs if there are uncontrolled confounding factors.[6]

A potential solution to this shortcoming of aggregate time-series data, proposed by Stanislav Kasl (1979, 787), is to conduct "a more refined ecological analysis . . . [by] taking advantage of local and regional variations in the business cycle as well as in disease rates." In a similar vein, J. Stern (1983, 69) suggests using differencing techniques with panel data to remove the bias associated with time-invariant area

(*Text continues on p. 180.*)

TABLE 7.1 / Estimated Effects of Economic Conditions on Mortality Using a Single Time Series of Macroeconomic Data

Study	Sample	Major Findings	Comments
Ogburn and Thomas (1922)	U.S., 1870 to 1920	Trend deviations in mortality, tuberculosis deaths and infant mortality are positively correlated with macroeconomic conditions (R = 0.57, 0.32, and 0.42). Suicides are countercyclical (R = −0.74). Similar estimates obtained in models with lags or nine-year moving averages.	Macroeconomic conditions proxied by nine series on prices, industrial production, railroad activity, employment, imports, and bank clearings.
Thomas (1927)	U.K., 1854 to 1913	Trend deviations in mortality, infant mortality, and deaths from excessive alcoholism are positively correlated with macroeconomic conditions (R = 0.30, 0.28, and 0.38). Suicides are countercyclical (R = −0.50). Similar estimates in models with lags. Results fairly stable across subperiods, reducing likelihood of omitted-variable bias.	Macroeconomic conditions proxied by nine series on prices, industrial production, railroad activity, unemployment, exports, and bank clearings. Total mortality excludes epidemic diseases.
Brenner (1971)	U.S., 1900 to 1967; New York, 1915 to 1967	Countercyclical variation in detrended heart-disease mortality and lagged macroeconomic conditions in New York data. Countercyclical variation also obtained for U.S. data using a different specification (current not lagged economic conditions).	Specifications apparently chosen to maximize strength of countercyclical variation. Little detail on results provided.
Brenner (1973)	New York, 1914 to 1960	Trend deviations in first admissions to mental hospitals negatively correlated with changes in manufacturing employment for entire period and subperiods.	Confounding factors not controlled for. Lead as well as lagged employment included.
Brenner (1975)	U.S., 1933 to 1973	Cirrhosis mortality positively related to lagged unemployment (with a maximum effect after two years) and possibly to long-run per capita income.	Specifications and sample time periods are not consistent across parts of analysis.

Study	Location, period	Findings	Notes
Eyer (1977)	U.S., 1870 to 1975	Procyclical variation in total mortality (with key role for motor vehicle and other accidents) and influenza deaths. Countercyclical variation in suicides. Possible causes are social stress and uprooting of communities due to migration, as well as increased work hours and overtime.	Same macroeconomic series as Ogburn and Thomas (1922). Analysis is descriptive and includes examining economic conditions during twenty-four separate death rate peaks and declines.
Brenner (1979)	England and Wales, 1936 to 1976	Polynomial distributed lag of unemployment (trend growth in per capita income) positively (negatively) correlated with total and age-specific mortality. Strongest unemployment effects at lags of one or two years but inconsistent lag pattern (such as stronger effect for five-year lag than in years three and four).	Models include highly correlated covariates (like annual and medium-term income changes), making interpretation difficult.
Gravelle et al. (1981)	U.K., 1922 to 1976	Replicates Brenner's (1979) results for 1936 to 1976 data but finds no significant unemployment effect for longer (1922 to 1976) period and subperiods. Model is not structurally stable across periods. Results are not consistent with Brenner's claim that the peak unemployment effect occurs after around two years; no consistent pattern of lagged unemployment coefficients in unconstrained models.	Similar specification to Brenner (1979) but uses more consistent unemployment series and controls for GDP rather than disposable income.
Forbes and McGregor (1984)	Scotland, 1956 to 1978	No consistent evidence of an unemployment effect on either total male mortality or deaths from ischemic heart disease. Positive impacts for some age groups and specifications, negative predicted effects for others. Similar inconsistency controlling for long-term unemployment. Income effects generally small and insignificant.	Models include five or ten-year unemployment lags and control for real per capita health service expenditure and three real per capita income variables (long-run trend, deviations from it, short-run change).

TABLE 7.1 / (continued)

Study	Sample	Major Findings	Comments
Brenner (1987)	Nine Industrialized Nations, 1951 to 1980	Heart disease mortality negatively related to per capita GDP and positively correlated with unemployment and business failure rates. Strongest effects typically observed with a lag of around two years.	Up to eighteen-year lags included, reducing degrees of freedom and making it very difficult to interpret plausibility of results.
McAvinchey (1988)	Five European Nations, 1959 to 1982	The effects of unemployment vary across countries, with reductions in overall mortality predicted in seven of ten cases. Optimal lag lengths vary substantially and are often much shorter than those used in previous studies. The data also generally do not support the previous use of a second degree polynomial for Almond lag specifications.	Econometric methods incorporate goodness-of-fit criteria using corrections for lost degrees of freedom and order of polynomial lag. Sample years vary slightly across countries.
Joyce and Mocan (1993)	Tennessee, 1970 to 1988	Using monthly data, cyclical and structural unemployment are either uncorrelated or negatively related to the frequency of low birthweight (LBW). The data pass two diagnostic tests for absence of omitted-variable bias: lagged LBW does not predict current unemployment; leads of unemployment do not predict current LBW.	Unemployment decomposed into permanent and transitory components, which proxy structural and cyclical unemployment. VAR methods used to estimate relationship between unemployment and health.
Laporte (2004)	U.S., 1948 to 1996	Increased unemployment associated with reductions in overall mortality; long-run effect is twice as large as short-run impact. Increases in GDP correlated with lower mortality in long-run but not short-run. Models estimated using Hendry error correction mechanism, with first differences in mortality regressed on first differences in regressors plus lag of the dependent and independent variables.	Variables are nonstationary and integrated of degree one, so commonly used trend/cycle decomposition is not appropriate.

Tapia Granados (2004)	Sweden, 1800 to 1998	From 1800 to 1880, bad harvests were associated with higher mortality. Since 1910, deaths have been procyclical (with a one to two-year lag), although of smaller magnitude after the 1950s.	Uses time-series methods including cross-correlations, spectral analysis, and local regressions.
Tapia Granados (2005a)	U.S., 1900 to 1996	Mortality is positively correlated to cyclical increases in real GDP, manufacturing production, and weekly work hours, and it is negatively related to unemployment. Results are generally similar across sex, age, and race-ethnicity groups. Procyclical variation is found for deaths from cardiovascular, liver and renal diseases, pneumonia and influenza, and traffic accidents, but not cancer. Suicides are countercyclical.	Time-series methods compare deviations from trend in dependent and independent variables. Effects tend to be stronger when proxying macroeconomic conditions by unemployment rates than other indicators.
Gerdtham and Johannesson (2005)	Swedish Microdata for 1980 to 1996	Significant countercyclical variation in male mortality is found for four macroeconomic indicators (notification rate, capacity utilization rate, confidence indicator, change in GDP). An insignificant procyclical (countercyclical) fluctuation is obtained for the unemployment rate (deviation of GDP from trend). Among women, an almost significant procyclical variation is found using the unemployment rate and deviation of GDP from trend; small and insignificant estimates were obtained for the other four macroeconomic indicators.	Almost all of the secular decline in male mortality occurs during first eight years of the period (most in the first four), raising concern that omitted variables are confounded with the macroeconomic effects.

Source: Author's compilation.
Note: R is the correlation coefficient.

effects. Research using such strategies has become increasingly common during the last decade.

POOLED DATA WITH LOCATION-SPECIFIC FIXED EFFECTS

Many confounding factors can be controlled for using panel-data methods on samples containing multiple geographic locations observed at several points in time. Some analyses, including most examining mortality, utilize geographically aggregated data. Others, particularly those focusing on morbidities or behaviors, typically employ individual-level information but with the macroeconomic variables measured over larger areas.

Analyses using aggregate data usually estimate some form of the following equation:

$$Y_{jt} = \alpha_j + X_{jt}\beta + E_{jt}\gamma + \lambda_t + \varepsilon_{jt}, \qquad (7.2)$$

where Y_{jt} is a health outcome or input at location j and time t, E measures macroeconomic conditions, X is a vector of covariates, α is a location-specific fixed-effect, λ a general time effect, and ε is the regression error term. The corresponding equation with microdata is as follows:

$$Y_{ijt} = \alpha_j + X_{ijt}\beta + E_{jt}\gamma + \lambda_t + \varepsilon_{ijt}, \qquad (7.3)$$

where i indexes the individual and X is a vector of person-specific covariates.

In these models, the year effects hold constant determinants that differ uniformly across locations over time (such as many changes in medical technologies) and the fixed-effect accounts for those that vary across areas but are time-invariant (like some lifestyle differences between residents of Nevada and Utah). Two potential drawbacks deserve mention: First, some factors fluctuating within locations over time may not be accounted for. This problem can often be minimized by including a vector of location-specific time trends. Second, the consequences of macroeconomic conditions are identified from variations *within* areas, relative to the changes occurring in other locations.[7] This is problematic if the impact of national business cycles (which are absorbed in the general time effects) differ from those of more localized fluctuations.[8] For instance, Olivier Blanchard and Lawrence Katz (1992) emphasize the role of migration flows in response to local macroeconomic conditions. These militate against finding a procyclical variation in mortality if movers are relatively healthy and relocate into areas with robust economies. However, such a pattern might be induced if population projections (the denominator of estimated mortality rates) do not completely account for this migration.

Unemployment rates are the most common proxy for macroeconomic conditions, but others—such as the employment-to-population ratio or growth in real GDP—are sometimes used. The supplementary regressors often include individual or location-specific measures of income, age, education and race-ethnicity. Calendar month effects (with monthly data) or location-specific time trends may be added, and some analyses incorporate lags of the macroeconomic variables or use other methods to capture dynamics of the adjustment process.

TOTAL MORTALITY

Death rates are the main proxy for health in most studies. The use of mortality has several advantages: it represents the most severe negative health outcome, it is objective and well measured, and diagnosis does not require access to the medical system (frequently in contrast to morbidity). However, some health conditions (such as arthritis) are generally not life-threatening and so are not strongly related to fatality rates. Also, relatively small negative health shocks could accelerate the death of frail individuals while having little effect on overall life expectancy or population health.

Table 7.2 summarizes the results of recent investigations using pooled data and controls for location-specific fixed effects to examine the relationship between macroeconomic conditions and mortality. Despite differences in samples and time periods, and some variation in model specifications, there is widespread evidence of a procyclical fluctuation in fatalities. A 1 percentage point increase in the unemployment rate is typically associated with a 0.3 to 0.5 percent reduction in total mortality, corresponding to an unemployment elasticity of –0.02 to –0.06 (Ruhm 2000, 2006; Tapia Granados 2005b; Johansson 2004; Lin 2005).[9] Eric Neumayer (2004) estimates an even larger 1.1 percent decrease for Germany, and Tom Buchmueller, Michel Grignon, and Florence Jusot (2006) estimate a 0.8 percent drop for France. One exceptional result is a study by Athina Economou, Agelike Nikolau, and Ioannis Theodossiou (2004); however, since the models estimated include covariates determined by economic conditions (smoking, drinking, and pollution), the unemployment coefficients do not indicate the full effect of macroeconomic changes.[10]

Limited evidence (Ruhm 2000, 2006; Neumayer 2004) suggests a more pronounced cyclical fluctuation for twenty to forty-four year olds than for forty-five to sixty-four year olds, possibly reflecting the younger group's greater involvement in market employment and increased vulnerability to adverse economic shocks. However, fatality rates also change for senior citizens (sixty-five and older), who rarely participate in the labor force, indicating that the effects are not restricted to working-age persons. Less is known about whether the fluctuation in mortality risk differs by gender, although the available research (Neumayer 2004; Tapia Granados 2005b) suggests that any such disparities are small.

MORBIDITY AND SPECIFIC CAUSES OF DEATH

One reason that total mortality falls when the economy deteriorates is because driving, and consequently motor-vehicle fatalities, decrease. Christopher Ruhm

(*Text continues on p. 186.*)

TABLE 7.2 / Estimates of Consequences of Macroeconomic Conditions on Mortality Using Longitudinal Data with Location-Specific Fixed Effects

Study	Sample	Major Findings	Comments
Ruhm (2000)	U.S., 1972 to 1991	_Significant Unemployment Effects_ ALL: −0.5% [−.04]; twenty to forty-four year olds: −2.0% [−.14]; sixty-five or older year olds: −0.3% [−.02]; CVD: −0.5% [−.03]; FLU: −0.7% [−.05]; vehicle: −3.0% [−.21]; EXTERNAL: −1.7% [−.11]; suicide: 1.3% [.09]; homicide: −1.9% [−.13]; INFANT: −0.6% [−.04]; NEONATAL: −0.6% [−.04]. _Insignificant Effects_ forty-five to sixty-four year olds: 0.0%; CANCER: 0.0%; LIVER: −0.4%. Dynamic models generally yield larger medium-run than short- or long-run impacts. Income effects are mixed and inconsistent.	All models control for percent of state population in specified age, race-ethnicity, education, and marital status groups. Similar results obtained using EP ratio or change in payroll employment as alternative macroeconomic proxies, or including state-specific time trends.
Dehejia and Lleras-Muney (2004)	U.S. Vital Statistics Records, 1975 to 1999, and other sources	_Significant Unemployment Effects_ INFANT: −0.5% [−.03]; NEONATAL: −0.3% [−.02]; POSTNEO: −0.9% [−.06]. Stronger effects for blacks (−0.9%, −0.6%, −1.2%) than whites (−0.3%, −0.1%, −0.7%). Decreased infant mortality for blacks primarily results from fertility selection; reductions in risky behaviors during pregnancy play a greater role for whites.	Weaker effects obtained in models without trends. Fertility selection proxied by parent's education, age, and marital status. Risky pregnancy behaviors include smoking, drinking, and lack of prenatal care.

Study	Sample	Results	Comments
Economou et al. (2004)	Thirteen EU countries, 1977 to 1996	*Significant Unemployment Effects* ALL: 0.3% [.02]; fifty-five to sixty-four year olds: 0.5% [.04]; 55-64 year olds: 0.5% [.05]; ISCHEMIC: 0.8% [.07]; CANCER: 0.2% [.02]; suicide: 0.9% [.08]; homicide: 1.5% [.14]. *Insignificant Effects* Males: 0.2%; females: 0.1%; twenty-five to thirty-four year olds: −0.4%; thirty-five to forty-four year olds: 0.3%; sixty-five to seventy-four year olds: 0.1%; seventy-five to eighty-four year olds: −0.1%; VEHICLE: 3.0%.	Results difficult to interpret because models control for covariates (smoking, drinking, caloric intake, hospitalization, and sometimes pollution levels) that are determined by macroeconomic conditions.
Johansson (2004)	Twenty-three OECD countries, 1960 to 1997	*Significant Unemployment Effects* ALL: −0.4%; −0.3% for observations with information on work hours. Total mortality is negatively associated with per capita incomes and work hours.	Same sample and specification as Gerdtham and Ruhm (2006), except for addition of work hours in some models.
Neumayer (2004)	Sixteen German states, 1980 to 2000	*Significant Unemployment Effects* ALL: −1.1%; females: −1.3%; males: −0.9%; twenty to forty-five year olds: −1.1%; sixty-five or older year olds: −12% CVD: −1.8%; FLU: −3.1%; VEHICLE: −1.3%; suicide: −1.4%. *Insignificant Effects* forty-five to sixty-four year olds: −0.5%; CANCER: −0.1%; LIVER: 0.4%; homicide: 0.3%; EXTERNAL: 1.7%; INFANT: 0.2%; NEONATAL: −1.9%. Dynamic models generally yield larger effects in long-run than initially. Income effects are mixed and inconsistent.	Most specifications correspond to Ruhm (2000). Standard errors corrected for heteroscedasticity and autocorrelation. Models control for personal income, age and percent foreign. Similar results using real GDP growth as macroeconomic proxy.
Tapia Granados (2005b)	Fifty Spanish provinces, 1980 to 1997	*Significant Unemployment Effects* ALL: −0.3% [−.06]; females: −0.3% [−.04]; males: −0.2% [−.06]; CANCER: −0.1% [−.02]; infectious disease: −0.7% [−.14]; VEHICLE: −2.0% [−.38]. *Insignificant Effects* CVD: −0.1%; suicide: 0.5%; homicide: −0.3%.	Models control for age structure and per capita GDP. Similar results obtained using EP ratio as macroeconomic proxy. Inclusion of state-specific trends attenuates effects.

TABLE 7.2 / (continued)

Study	Sample	Major Findings	Comments
Lin (2005)	Eight Asia-Pacific Countries, 1976 to 2001	*Significant Unemployment Effects* Total Mortality: −0.7% [−.03]; CVD: −2.0% [−.07]; VEHICLE: −10.5% [−.37]; infant: 2.1% [.08]; suicide: 6.7% [.24]; CANCER: 2.5% [.09]. Income effects are mixed.	Models control for population age structure, percent male and rural, number of physicians and hospital beds, public health expenditures and country-specific time trends. Weaker effects in recent years.
Buchmueller, et al. (2006)	Ninety-six French départements, 1982 to 2002	*Significant Unemployment Effects* All: −0.8% [−.08]; CVD: −1.0% [−.11]; CANCER: −1.1% [−.11]; VEHICLE: −2.0% [−.21]; non-vehicle accidents: −2.5% [−.26]. *Insignificant Effects* LIVER: 0.3%; suicide: −0.5%; homicide: −0.6%.	Models control for age structure. Stronger effects in smaller areas, later time periods (when labor markets became more flexible).
Ruhm (2006)	Twenty largest states, 1978 to 1997	*Significant Unemployment Effects on AMI* ALL: −1.3% [−.09]; twenty to forty-four year olds: −2.3% [−.15]; forty-five to sixty-four: −0.9% [−.06]; sixty-five or older year olds: −1.4% [−.09]. Larger long-run than short-run effects for twenty to forty-four year olds but not older individuals.	Macroeconomic effects similar across sex; possibly larger for whites than blacks. Mixed effects for income and work hours.

| Gerdtham and Ruhm (2006) | Twenty-three OECD countries, 1960 to 1997 | *Significant Unemployment Effects* ALL: −0.4% [−.02]; CVD: −0.4% [−.02]; LIVER: −1.8% [−0.10];VEHICLE: −2.1% [−.12]; EXTERNAL: −0.8% [−.04]. *Insignificant Effects* CANCER: 0.1%; FLU: −1.1% [−.05]; suicide: 0.4%; homicide: 1.1%; INFANT: −0.2%. Dynamic models yield larger (smaller) long-run than initial effects for total mortality, FLU and LIVER (CVD, VEHICLE). Stronger effects found for countries with weak social safety nets. Income effects are mixed. | Models control for age structure of population, percent male and include country-specific time trends. Weaker macroeconomic effects on total mortality obtained without trends; stronger effects for large countries and in more recent years. |

Source: Author's compilation.

Abbreviations: ALL – total mortality; CVD – cardiovascular disease; ISCHEMIC – ischemic heart disease; AMI – acute myocardial infarction; CANCER – malignant neoplasms; FLU – pneumonia and influenza; LIVER – chronic liver disease; VEHICLE – motor vehicle; EXTERNAL – external causes and accidents other than from motor vehicles; INFANT – infant deaths (in first year); NEONATAL – neonatal deaths (in first twenty-eight days) POSTNEO – post-neonatal deaths (twenty-nine days through end of first year); EP ratio – employment-to-population ratio.

Note: Unemployment effects refer to predicted impact of a 1 percentage point increase, with elasticities in brackets. Unless otherwise noted, all models control for location-specific fixed effects and general time effects. Significant effects refer to those where the null hypothesis of no effect is rejected at the 0.05 level.

(2000) estimates that a 1 percentage point increase in unemployment reduces United States traffic deaths by 3 percent (an unemployment elasticity of -0.21). The corresponding declines predicted for Germany, Spain, France, and OECD countries are 1.3, 2.0, 2.0, and 2.1 percent (Neumayer 2004; Tapia Granados 2005b; Buchmueller, Grignon, and Jusot 2006; Gerdtham and Ruhm 2006). Shin-Jong Lin (2005) obtains a strong (and probably implausible) 10.5 percent decrease for Asia-Pacific nations. Other sources of accidental deaths also appear to diminish during periods of increased unemployment.

Most studies (Ruhm 2000; Neumayer 2004; Lin 2005; Buchmueller, Grignon, and Jusot 2006; Gerdtham and Ruhm 2006) identify a procyclical variation in cardiovascular fatalities—the leading source of death—with effect sizes that are similar or larger in percentage terms than for total mortality. Ruhm (2006) indicates especially strong fluctuations for deaths from heart attacks, which is relevant since this risk is particularly responsive to short-term changes in modifiable health behaviors and environmental factors. Economic downturns are also generally predicted to reduce deaths from influenza or pneumonia. Other major sources of mortality are usually estimated to decline but with less consistency across studies. For instance, procyclical variations in fatalities from liver disease and homicide are obtained by Ruhm (2000) and Ulf-G Gerdtham and Ruhm (2006), which contrast with insignificant countercyclical fluctuations by Neumayer (2004) and Buchmueller, Grignon and Jusot (2006).

Infant deaths in the United States also decrease when the economy weakens. Ruhm (2000) estimates that a 1 percentage point rise in unemployment reduces infant and neonatal mortality by 0.6 percent. Rajeev Dehejia and Adriana Lleras-Muney (2004) predict 0.5, 0.3, and 0.9 percent declines in infant, neonatal, and postneonatal deaths, respectively (with larger 0.9, 0.6, and 1.2 percent decreases for blacks). Conversely, infant mortality appears to be unaffected by macroeconomic conditions in Germany (Neumayer 2004) or OECD countries (Gerdtham and Ruhm 2006), with evidence of a countercyclical pattern for Asia-Pacific nations (Lin, 2005).

The results for suicide and homicide also differ across countries. Ruhm (2000) uncovers a strong countercyclical variation in suicides. Weaker and mixed findings have been obtained by Tapia Granados (2005b), Gerdtham and Ruhm (2006), and Buchmueller, Grignon, and Jusot (2006), while the results of Neumayer (2004) and Shin-Jong Lin (2005) indicate substantial procyclical fluctuations. The point estimates suggest that homicides increase with the strength of the economy in the United States, Spain, and France (Ruhm 2000; Tapia Granados 2005b; Buchmueller, Grignon, and Jusot 2006), but decline for Germany and the OECD (Neumayer 2004; Gerdtham and Ruhm 2006). Taken together, these results raise the possibility that some health effects of macroeconomic changes differ across countries or institutional arrangements.

Severe data restrictions have limited research on morbidity outcomes. One exception is Ruhm (2003), who used information from the 1972–81 National Health Interview Survey (NHIS) to estimate that a 1 percentage point increase in unemployment reduces the fraction of adults (thirty years and older) with one or more medical conditions by 1.5 percent and those with restricted-activity or bed-days during the prior two weeks by 1.2 and 1.6 percent. A substantially larger decrease is predicted for acute compared to chronic conditions (3.9 percent versus 1.1 percent), which makes sense since the former will more rapidly respond to changes in behaviors or environmental conditions. The 4.3 percent and 8.7 percent decreases in the estimated prevalence of ischemic heart disease and intervertebral disk problems are also noteworthy, since these medical problems are linked to stressful or unsafe working conditions (Price and Kompier forthcoming). They also contrast with a 7.2 percent rise predicted for non-psychotic mental disorders, further emphasizing the distinction between physical and mental health.[11]

Finally, the evidence suggests relatively pronounced effects for males, employed persons, and those of prime working age. For example, Ruhm (2003) indicates that a 1 percentage point increase in unemployment is associated with 1.9, 1.3, 4.2, 1.5, and 2.8 percent reductions, respectively, in the probability that thirty to fifty-five year olds have medical conditions, chronic ailments, acute morbidities, restricted activity days and bed-days. Kerwin Charles and Philip DeCicca (2006) similarly find stronger fluctuations for persons whose employment is most likely to be affected by macroeconomic changes.[12]

INCOME EFFECTS AND DYNAMICS

Worse health during *transient* improvements in the economy does not imply deleterious consequences of *permanent* progress. An important distinction is that temporary growth combines more intensive use of labor and health inputs with existing technologies. Conversely, lasting gains require innovations or expansions in the capital stock that have the potential to ameliorate negative health effects. Health investments are also more likely to be deferred in response to temporary increases in work hours compared to long-term increases in work hours, and sustained growth permits purchases of consumption goods (such as safer cars) that benefit health.

There is strong evidence that increased permanent income improves health in developing countries (Pritchett and Summers 1996). The findings are more ambiguous for industrialized nations, however, where most studies indicate a positive effect, but some find that average income is not important. There is also conflicting evidence on the role of income *inequality* or macroeconomic conditions at birth.[13]

Several empirical analyses verify differences in the effects of temporary versus permanent changes in income. John Graham, Bei-Hung Chang, and John Evans (1992) show that growth in the latter (as proxied by real per capita consumption) is associated with reduced mortality in the United States, whereas increases in the former (measured by reductions in unemployment) raise deaths. Christian Dustmann and Frank Windmeijer (2004) indicate that higher wealth profiles (measured by average incomes over a twelve-year period) predict improved health in Germany, but that health status worsens when wages temporarily increase.

Perhaps because of these diverse effects, the parameter estimates are mixed when national or personal incomes are included as supplementary covariates in panel-data models. For example, Ruhm (2000) obtains positive and significant income coefficients for total mortality and traffic fatalities but negative and usually insignificant estimates for most other outcomes. Similarly, Neumayer (2004) uncovers a positive income effect for total mortality and deaths due to cardiovascular disease, cancer, and some external sources, but he finds a negative coefficient for influenza and pneumonia fatalities.

It may seem surprising that econometric specifications controlling only for contemporaneous economic conditions are able to detect changes in mortality or morbidity. One reason that they can is because the macroeconomic proxies (such as unemployment rates) are highly correlated over time, so that the estimates actually capture the effects of economic influences over a considerable period. A second reason is that some sources of death (such as traffic accidents and infant mortality) have short gestation and quickly respond to economic fluctuations.

For many outcomes, however, we expect the effects of sustained changes in the economy to accumulate over at least some period of time. For example, in models of health capital (Grossman 1972), changes in investment flows slowly affect the stock of health, leading to small initial effects that gradually accrue. The results of studies examining dynamics of the adjustment process, while not completely consistent, suggest that this is usually the case. Specifically, the impact of a lasting change in economic conditions grows for at least one or two years, with subsequent attenuation obtained in some studies (Ruhm 2000) but not in others (Neumayer 2004; Gerdtham and Ruhm 2006).

Moreover, strong and rapid effects are commonly obtained for causes of death or illness likely to be especially responsive to short-run changes in the economy. One example is the previously discussed sensitivity of motor vehicle fatalities to macroeconomic conditions. Cardiovascular deaths, particularly those due to heart attacks, also increase substantially during good times. This is consistent with changes in health behaviors and environmental factors during periods of economic growth. A larger macroeconomic fluctuation in acute conditions compared to chronic health problems is anticipated and observed, as is the small cyclical fluctuation usually (but not always) obtained for cancer fatalities, where behavioral responses seem unlikely to have a large short-term impact.

WHY DOES HEALTH IMPROVE WHEN THE ECONOMY DETERIORATES?

Lifestyle changes explain some of the health improvements occurring during economic downturns. Alcohol consumption has been most widely studied. Using data for the period from 1975 to 1988, Ruhm (1995) shows that alcohol consumption and alcohol-involved vehicle fatalities vary procyclically.[14] Supporting evidence has been provided by both earlier and later studies (O'Neill 1984; Evans and Graham 1988; Wagenaar and Streff 1989; Freeman 1999). Since moderate alcohol use is linked to health benefits (Gaziano et al. 1993; Thun et al. 1997), reductions in drinking might imply *less* healthy lifestyles. However, this does not appear to be the case. Ruhm and William Black (2002) analyze microdata from the Behavioral Risk Factor Surveillance System (BRFSS) and demonstrate that the variation in overall consumption results reflects movements between heavy and light alcohol use, rather than between recreational drinking and abstaining.[15]

Limited research suggests that other behaviors also become healthier in bad times. Ruhm's (2005) analysis of the BRFSS data from 1987 to 2000 indicates that severe obesity, smoking, and physical inactivity fall, with larger (percentage) decreases in multiple health risks.[16] Using the same data over a longer period (1984 to 2002), Jonathan Gruber and Michael Frakes (2006) verify the decline in smoking. As with drinking, these variations appear to be dominated by changes at the intensive rather than extensive margins (that is, fluctuations mainly occur among existing tobacco users, with smaller variations in the likelihood of smoking at all).[17]

The evidence is more ambiguous for population subgroups or countries other than the United States. Temporary wage reductions are associated with increased exercise in Germany (Dustmann and Windmeijer 2004), but some of Petri Böckerman and colleagues' (2007) specifications indicate a *countercyclical* pattern of body weight among Finnish adults (with no relationship in other models). Jeff DeSimone (2004) obtains a procyclical variation in obesity for high school boys (but not for girls) in the United States, partly due to changes in physical activity. Dehejia and Lleras-Muney (2004) find that pregnant women consume less alcohol in bad times, but they find mixed results for smoking (which decreases for blacks but not whites).

The improvements in health occur despite reductions in medical care. Routine medical checkups and screening tests (mammograms, pap smears, and digital rectal exams) are less often received during downturns (Ruhm 2000), and both doctor visits and hospital episodes decrease (Ruhm 2003). On the other hand, Germano Mwabu (1988) and Jessica Vistnes and Vivian Hamilton (1995) report a negative relationship between employment and the utilization of medical care. Another study shows that pregnant women obtain earlier and more extensive prenatal care in bad economic times (Dehejia and Lleras-Muney 2004).

One possibility is that health gets better because increases in nonmarket "leisure" time make it less costly for individuals to undertake health-producing activities such as exercise and cooking meals at home.[18] More generally, if health is time intensive, the demand for both health and the inputs producing it are likely to rise when the price of time falls (Grossman 1972). This may help to explain the decrease in smoking, an activity that is not time intensive but is harmful to health. Indirect evidence linking time prices to obesity has been provided for both adults (Chou, Grossman, and Saffer 2004) and children (Anderson, Butcher, and Levine 2003; Ruhm 2004).[19] However, direct evidence on how work hours affect health outcomes is mixed. Edvard Johansson's (2004) analysis of twenty-three OECD countries indicates that hours are negatively related to total mortality. Conversely, Ruhm (2005) finds that employment hours are positively related to smoking, excess body weight, and physical inactivity among American adults. However,

Ruhm (2006) fails to uncover a relationship between hours and heart-attack deaths.

Many researchers argue that recessions worsen health by raising the stress associated with economic insecurity (Brenner and Mooney 1983; Catalano and Dooley 1983; Fenwick and Tausig 1994). However, population-wide measures are unavailable and a complementary literature emphasizes job-related stress (Baker 1985; Karasek and Theorell 1990; Fenwick and Tausig 1994; Price and Kompier forthcoming), which may decline in bad times as hours and, possibly, the pace of work decrease.

As mentioned, health is likely to be an input into short-term increases in the production of goods and services. Most obviously, hazardous working conditions and the physical exertion of employment could have negative effects, particularly when job hours are extended during economic expansions (Sokejima and Kagamimori 1998; Kivimäki et al. 2002, Liu, Tanaka, and the Fukouka Heart Study Group 2002). The extra work hours also reduce sleep (Biddle and Hamermesh 1990), which is linked to increased stress, decreased alertness, higher injury risk, elevated rates of obesity, and increased rates of physiological or psychological symptoms (Maruyama, Kohno, and Morimoto 1995; Sparks and Cooper 1997; Gangwisch et al. 2005). The already high injury rates in the cyclically sensitive construction and manufacturing sectors may be exacerbated by increased hiring of inexperienced workers and production speedups (Catalano 1979; Robinson 1988; Brooker, Frank, and Tarasuk 1997). Finally, some joint products of economic activity, such as pollution and traffic congestion, may present particular health risks for vulnerable sectors of the population—such as infants or senior citizens—who do not work (Clancy et al. 2002; Chay and Greenstone 2003; Peters et al. 2004). These groups may also be especially adversely affected if the migration induced by economic expansion increases social isolation or loss of community support (Eyer 1977; Tapia Granados 2004).

FUTURE RESEARCH QUESTIONS AND DATA NEEDS

People become less happy when the economy temporarily weakens (Di Tella, MacCulloch, and Oswald 2003) and their mental health may deteriorate. However, contrary to popular belief, most aspects of physical health appear to improve and mortality decreases. Some of this can be easily explained. Health benefits are associated with declining pollution; in addition, driving, and the associated risk of traffic fatalities, is reduced. However, sources of the decreases in many other types of morbidity and mortality are less well understood and deserve further study.

Individuals adopt healthier lifestyles in bad times, but the reasons for this are not yet clear. Some risky behaviors (such as drinking alcohol) decline when incomes fall, but income generally has a protective effect on health. Although time-intensive health investments (such as exercise) are plausibly easier to undertake when working fewer hours, the empirical evidence is mixed. Subsequent research needs to confirm these patterns and better identify the mechanisms underlying them.

Future investigations need to document the extent to which the effects of macro-economic conditions differ across population groups and explain the sources of these disparities. Previous research (Ruhm 2000, 2003, 2006; Neumayer 2004; Tapia Granados 2005b) generally indicates that subpopulations with the greatest exposure to labor-market fluctuations (such as prime-age individuals, males, and blacks) are most affected by macroeconomic changes. However, the results are not entirely consistent (for example, senior citizens often exhibit larger responsiveness than those who are slightly younger), and many important questions remain. For instance, it would be interesting to identify groups whose health does not fluctuate or varies relatively little with economic conditions.

Most microdata samples are too small to provide good answers to these questions. Vital statistics on mortality cover the entire population but lack demographic detail beyond age at death, race-ethnicity, and geographic location. Some recent investigations illustrate the promise of other data sources. For instance, Ryan Edwards (2006) utilizes information from the National Longitudinal Mortality Study to examine death rates for subsamples stratified by sex, race, age, occupation, and socioeconomic status.[20] An in-depth investigation of health behaviors may be possible using the BRFSS, which has large samples and reasonable demographic information. Similarly, the NHIS supplies detailed information on morbidity and has been used in previous research (Ruhm 2003; Charles and DeCicca 2006). However, the public-use versions generally provide limited geographic information, and health problems are self-reported (clinical assessments would be more accurate).

Economic downturns appear to be accompanied by reductions in problem alcohol use, heavy smoking, and complete physical inactivity, rather than movements from recreational drinking or light smoking to abstinence and from irregular to regular exercise. We do not yet know why. One possibility is that individuals with the least healthy lifestyles respond most to changes in economic incentives (such as income and time prices). Most theoretical models, however, predict changes at the extensive as well as intensive margins (across as well as within individuals). It is also plausible that the behavioral changes occur as part of a deliberate effort to reduce the probability of job loss or to offset the negative health effects if it does occur. Careful investigation of these issues is likely to require longitudinal or quasi-experimental multilevel research combining macroeconomic data with information on individuals experiencing the direct sequela of changes in economic conditions on their jobs or incomes. Unfortunately, the samples in most otherwise appropriate panel-data sets (such as the National Longitudinal Surveys and Panel Study of Income Dynamics) are too small to undertake more than rudimentary analysis.

We poorly understand the role of job stress and work intensity in explaining macroeconomic fluctuations in health. Some research cited in this chapter (Johansson 2004; Ruhm 2005, 2006) controls for work hours as a proxy for time prices. One feasible extension would be to disentangle the impact of hours conditional on employment from variations in the employment-to-population ratio.[21] A more ambitious endeavor would investigate the role of changes in work intensity and job stress, controlling for hours and employment rates. The data requirements are daunting, however, since we currently lack representative information on either of these measures. This represents only a partial listing of important topics for future research.

We also need more complete answers to questions on which preliminary analysis has been conducted. For instance, how long (if ever) does it take for a persistent improvement in the economy to lead to better health? How important are changes in health-related behaviors (such as drinking, smoking, and exercise) relative to variations in environmental factors (such as pollution and traffic congestion) in explaining the macroeconomic relationships? Do mental and physical health move in the opposite direction, and, if so, why? As mentioned, existing investigations have been severely constrained by the information sources currently available. An ideal data set for this analysis would provide sufficient detail on demographic, geographic, and individual health characteristics to permit multilevel modeling that untangles the diverse and potentially opposing effects of economic conditions on assorted aspects of physical and mental health. It would cover a lengthy time period and, in the best case, provide longitudinal data on a large and representative panel of individuals and families. For the foreseeable future, researchers will need to make due with sources containing some but not all of these characteristics.

IMPLICATIONS FOR POLICY

Evidence that health worsens in boom times indicates that economic progress need not have uniformly beneficial effects; however, it does *not* justify contractionary macroeconomic policies. Recessions have overwhelmingly negative consequences, even if they do not harm physical health. Moreover, prior research has not examined whether economic expansions and contractions have asymmetric effects (for instance, whether downturns improve health by less than booms cause it to deteriorate). Unless they do, a mean-preserving change in the variance of macroeconomic performance will have no net effect on long-term health.

On the other hand, the findings indicate that some previous advocates (such as Brenner 1984) have overly enthusiastically cited an assumed procyclical variation in health in arguing for macroeconomic stabilization policies. Moreover, the most important overall lesson for policy makers may be that it is an error to assume that transient economic improvements have strongly favorable effects on mortality or morbidity. Instead, these periods are probably associated with worse health. The results, moreover, illustrate that the large epidemiological literature emphasizing negative consequences of individual unemployment provides, at most, a partial indication of the overall consequences of economic downturns.

Interventions designed to reduce the negative health effects of expansions are likely to be microeconomic, rather than macroeconomic, in nature and vary with the health problem addressed. Deleterious consequences resulting from negative by-products of higher output, such as increases in pollution or traffic congestion, might be addressed by raising the cost of these activities during good times.[22] Policies designed to automatically have these effects, without the need for specific government intervention, may be particularly useful. For instance, allocating traffic enforcement funds as a fixed percentage of government revenues implies that larger amounts would be available during expansions, when tax collections increase. Similarly, the use of market-based pollution permits would raise emission costs in good times, as the pollution demand curve shifts to the right.

Economic incentives and public health initiatives could reduce the frequency and negative consequences of unhealthy behaviors. It may be politically infeasible for law makers to enact increases in "sin taxes" (for example, taxes on alcohol and tobacco) during economic upturns, when finances are flush. However, one step in this direction might be to switch from unit taxes (specified in nominal terms per unit) to ad valorem taxation (set as a percentage of the price). This is useful because the real value of the former will fall during expansionary periods that are accompanied by inflation, whereas the latter are automatically indexed and will increase further if robust conditions raise relative demand for the taxed goods. This could be accompanied by public-health campaigns that emphasize the existence, nature, and methods of preventing health risks. Eligibility for government-funded health insurance programs (such as Medicaid) might be modified to reduce the likelihood that individuals lose coverage when obtaining jobs. The cost of such policies is made more affordable by increases in the government revenues received during peak periods.

Policies could also be implemented to promote healthier employment and reduce the stress or physical demands of work. For instance, additional economic incentives could encourage employer-sponsored health-promotion activities and employee-assistance programs. Restrictions on overtime or the enactment of mandatory (and longer) vacations might also be considered, although such initiatives generally receive only limited support in the United States.

Finally, broader patterns of government involvement in the economy may be important. Amartya Sen (2001) emphasizes the long-term health benefits of using extra income to support poverty alleviation, public expenditures on medical care, and "support-led" processes giving priority to social services such as basic education. There is interesting, but not yet fully conclusive, evidence of stronger macroeconomic effects in countries with relatively weak social safety nets. For example, Gerdtham and Ruhm (2006) find that the procyclical fluctuation in mortality is smallest in countries with high levels of public social expenditure (as a percentage of GDP). They, as well as Buchmueller, Grignon, and Jusot (2006) show larger variations in later periods, generally characterized by more flexible labor markets.[23] This result, if verified by future research, suggests several possible mechanisms and mitigating factors relating macroeconomic conditions to health. For example, workers may have greater motivation to engage in healthy lifestyles that reduce the risk of job loss during bad economic times (when new employment is particularly hard to obtain). Such incentives may be muted in countries with generous social welfare systems or strong job protections, since both the likelihood and consequences of involuntary layoffs will be reduced. Employment hours and the pace of work may exhibit smaller cyclical fluctuations in less flexible labor markets, possibly mitigating the negative health consequences of economic booms. A full articulation of the policy implications of such results is likely to be complex and multi-faceted, and it will certainly need to await substantial additional research.

NOTES

1. Many government policies also influence long-run macroeconomic performance.
2. Pekka Martikainen and Tapani Valkonen (1996) find that the positive association between unemployment and subsequent mortality weakens when macroeconomic conditions deteriorate, which is consistent with the stronger health selection during good times.
3. For example, he states "the zero-lag relationship between unemployment and mortality rates is actually inverse" (Brenner 1995, 232). Presumably for this reason, his later research postulates that the negative health effects begin two or three years after the economy declines and persist for a decade or more (Brenner 1995). However, the analyses rarely provide sufficient information to verify this lag structure, and other researchers (Gravelle, Hutchinson, and Stern 1981; McAvinchey 1988) find little support for it. More generally, since business cycles typically last around four years, a two- or three-year lag implies that the most negative health consequences roughly coincide with the economic peak. It is also hard to imagine a process where the effects of downturns continue for more than a decade (up to eighteen years in some of Brenner's models), given that several business cycles occur during the intervening years.
4. The commonly used decomposition of macroeconomic variables into trends and the deviations from them is not appropriate with nonstationary series.
5. For example, much of the variation in unemployment during the four decades (beginning in the 1930s) covered by Brenner's early research resulted from dramatic reductions in joblessness following the Great Depression. Over this same period, mortality declined due to improved nutrition and increased availability of antibiotics.
6. Efforts have been made to examine whether such omitted variables cause bias when using time-series data. Hugh Gravelle, G. Hutchinson, and J. Stern (1981) find that their model is not structurally stable across time periods, with confounding factors a likely source of the instability. Conversely, Tapia Granados (2005a) obtains similar results across periods. Joyce and Mocan (1993) show that lagged values of low birthweight (their health outcome) fail to predict present unemployment rates and that future unemployment does not predict current low birthweight. Violation of either condition would suggest omitted-variable bias.
7. There must be substantial independent economic fluctuations across locations over time for this strategy to improve on standard time-series analysis. This condition is generally met. For instance, Ruhm (2000) documents the relatively low R-squared between the unemployment rate in almost all states and the national rate.
8. *Cyclical variations* and *macroeconomic effects* therefore refer to changes within areas rather than at the national level; terms such as *recessions* are used loosely to indicate deterioration in local economic conditions rather than reflecting technical definitions based on changes in national GDP.
9. The unemployment elasticity of mortality is equal to the percentage change in mortality resulting from a 1 percent change in the unemployment rate.

10. Their control for hospitalizations is even more problematic, since these are an indicator of health status.

11. Using MSA-level data from the 1997-2001 NHIS, Charles and DeCicca (2006) provide further evidence of a procyclical variation in mental health (measured by a six-item psychological distress scale), in contrast to physical status. One innovative feature is that they stratify the sample by *ex ante* employment probabilities (as well as by race and education).

12. Although it may seem useful to directly examine how health status of the unemployed changes with macroeconomic conditions, such estimates are actually quite difficult to interpret, because cyclical changes in the composition of jobless persons are likely to swamp the (relatively small) changes in individual health.

13. James Smith (1999), Angus Deaton (2003), and Gerdtham and Johannesson (2004) provide useful reviews. See Ralph Catalano (2002) and Gerard van den Berg, Marrten Lindeboom, and Farnce Portrait (2006) for somewhat conflicting evidence on the impact of macroeconomic conditions at birth.

14. An increase of one standard deviation (2.1 percentage point) in unemployment reduces predicted drinking by 1.3 percent and traffic fatalities by almost 7 percent.

15. Two earlier studies examined these issues with microdata. Susan Ettner's (1997) analysis of the 1988 National Health Interview Survey concluded that alcohol consumption and dependence are procyclical. Thomas Dee (2001), using data from the 1984-95 BRFSS, obtained the contradictory result that economic downturns are associated with reductions in overall and heavy drinking but a higher likelihood of binge consumption.

16. Obesity declines due to the aforementioned reductions in physical inactivity and because diets become healthier (Ruhm 2000).

17. Charles and DeCicca (2006) also provide suggestive evidence of declining obesity during economic downturns, but there is little consistent indication of effects on other health behaviors (such as smoking, drinking, and physical activity). However, statistical power may be limited since the National Health Interview Survey data covers just five years (1997 to 2001).

18. Income reductions during cyclical downturns have mixed effects, being linked to decreases in obesity, alcohol use, and heavy drinking (Freeman 1999; Ruhm 2002; Ruhm 2005) as well as to growth in smoking and physical inactivity (Ruhm 2005; Gruber and Frakes 2006).

19. Shin-Yi Chou, Michael Grossman, and Henry Saffer (2004) indicate that obesity is negatively related to the time price of (calorie-rich) prepared food and positively correlated with that of cooking (lower-calorie) meals at home. Patricia Anderson, Kristin Butcher, and Phillip Levine (2003) and Ruhm (2004) show that child obesity is positively associated with maternal employment, particularly for high socioeconomic status families.

20. His results vary but provide some indication of larger procyclical fluctuations in mortality for vulnerable population groups.

21. I thank Michael Grossman for this suggestion.

22. My thinking on these issues has benefited greatly from the discussion in Edwards (2005).

23. However, Neumayer (2004) provides evidence of sizable macroeconomic effects for Germany, a country with strong social protections.

REFERENCES

Anderson, Patricia M., Kristin F. Butcher, and Phillip B. Levine. 2003. "Maternal Employment and Overweight Children." *Journal of Health Economics* 22(3): 477–504.

Baker, Dean B. 1985. "The Study of Stress at Work." *Annual Review of Public Health* 6: 367–381.

Bartley, Mel. 1996. "Unemployment and Health Selection." *The Lancet* 348(9032): 904.

Biddle, Jeff E., and Daniel S. Hamermesh. 1990. "Sleep and the Allocation of Time." *Journal of Political Economy* 95(5): 922–43.

Blanchard, Olivier J., and Lawrence F. Katz. 1992. "Regional Evolutions." *Brookings Papers on Economic Activity* 1992(1): 1–75.

Böckerman, Petri, Edvard Johansson, Sata Helakorpi, Ritva Prättälä, Erkki Vartiainen, and Antti Uutela. 2007. "Does a Slump Really Make You Thinner? Finnish Micro-Level Evidence 1978–2002." *Health Economics* 16(1): 103–7.

Brenner, M. Harvey. 1971. "Economic Changes and Heart Disease Mortality." *American Journal of Public Health* 61(3): 606–11.

———. 1973. *Mental Illness and the Economy*. Cambridge, Mass.: Harvard University Press.

———. 1975. "Trends in Alcohol Consumption and Associated Illnesses." *The American Journal of Public Health* 65(12): 1279–92.

———. 1979. "Mortality and the National Economy." *The Lancet* 314(8142): 568–73.

———. 1984. *Estimating the Effects of Economic Change on National Health and Social Well Being*. Washington: Joint Economic Committee, U.S. Congress, U.S. Government Printing Office.

———. 1987. "Economic Change, Alcohol Consumption and Heart Disease Mortality in Nine Industrialized Countries." *Social Science and Medicine* 25(2): 119–32.

———. 1995. "Political Economy and Health." In *Society and Health*, edited by Alvin R. Tarlov and Diana Chapman Walsh. New York: Oxford University Press.

Brenner, M. Harvey, and Anne Mooney. 1983. "Unemployment and Health in the Context of Economic Change." *Social Science Medicine* 17(16): 1125–38.

Brooker, Ann-Sylvia, John W. Frank, and Valerie S. Tarasuk. 1997. "Back Pain Claims and the Business Cycle." *Social Science and Medicine* 45(3): 429–39.

Buchmueller, Tom, Michel Grignon, and Florence Jusot. 2006. "Unemployment and Mortality in France, 1982–2002." Unpublished paper, University of California, Irvine.

Catalano, Ralph C. 1979. "Health Costs of Economic Expansion: The Case of Manufacturing Injuries." *American Journal of Public Health* 69(8): 789–94.

———. 2002. "Economic Antecedents of Mortality Among the Very Old." *Epidemiology* 13(2): 133–7.

Catalano, Ralph C., and Benjamin Bellows. 2005. "If Economic Expansion Threatens Public Health, Should Epidemiologists Recommend Recession?" *International Journal of Epidemiology* 34(6): 1212–3.

Catalano, Ralph C., and David Dooley. 1983. "Health Effects of Economic Instability: A Test of the Economic Stress Hypothesis." *Journal of Health and Social Behavior* 24(1): 46–60.

Charles, Kerwin, and Philip DeCicca. 2006. "Labor Market Fluctuations and Health: Is There a Connection and for Whom?" Unpublished paper, University of Chicago.

Chay, Kenneth, and Michael Greenstone. 2003. "The Impact of Air Pollution on Infant Mortality: Evidence from Geographic Variation in Pollution Shocks Induced by a Recession." *Quarterly Journal of Economics* 118(3): 1121–67.

Chou, Shin-Yi, Michael Grossman, and Henry Saffer. 2004. "An Economic Analysis of Adult Obesity: Results from the Behavioral Risk Factor Surveillance System." *Journal of Health Economics* 23(3): 565–87.

Clancy, Luke, Pat Goodman, Hamish Sinclair, and Douglas Dockery. 2002. "Effect of Air–Pollution on Death Rates in Dublin, Ireland: An Intervention Study." *The Lancet* 360(9341): 1210–4.

Cook, Philip J., and Gary A. Zarkin. 1986. "Homicide and Economic Conditions: A Replication and Critique of M. Harvey Brenner's New Report to the U.S. Congress." *Journal of Quantitative Criminology* 2(1): 69–80.

Deaton, Angus. 2003. "Health, Inequality, and Economic Development." *Journal of Economic Literature* 41(1): 113–58.

Dee, Thomas S. 2001. "Alcohol Abuse and Economic Conditions: Evidence from Repeated Cross-Sections of Individual-Level Data." *Health Economics* 10(3): 257–70.

Dehejia, Rajeev, and Adriana Lleras-Muney. 2004. "Booms, Busts, and Babies' Health." *Quarterly Journal of Economics* 119(3): 1091–130.

DeSimone, Jeff. 2004. "The Cyclicality of Economic and Bodyweight Fluctuations Among High School Students." Unpublished paper, University of South Florida, November 2004.

Di Tella, Rafael, Robert J. MacCulloch, and Andrew J. Oswald. 2003. "The Macroeconomics of Happiness." *Review of Economics and Statistics* 85(4): 809–27.

Dustmann, Christian, and Frank Windmeijer. 2004. "Wages and the Demand for Health—A Lifecycle Analysis." Unpublished paper, University College London.

Economou, Athina, Agelike Nikolau, and Ioannis Theodossiou. 2004. "Are Recessions Harmful to Health After All? Evidence from the European Union." Unpublished paper, University of Macedonia.

Edwards, Ryan D. 2004. "Macroeconomic Implications of the Earned Income Tax Credit." *National Tax Journal* 57(1): 45–65.

———. 2005. "Commentary: Work, Well-Being, and a New Calling for Countercyclical Policy." *International Journal of Epidemiology* 34(6): 1214–21.

———. 2006. "Who Is Hurt by Procyclical Mortality." Unpublished paper, RAND.

Eissa, Nada, and Hillary W. Hoynes. 2004. "Taxes and the Labor Market Participation of Married Couples." *Journal of Public Economics* 88(9–10): 1931–58.

Ettner, Susan L. 1997. "Measuring the Human Cost of a Weak Economy: Does Unemployment Lead to Alcohol Abuse?" *Social Science and Medicine* 44(2): 251–60.

———. 2000. "The Relationship Between Labor Market Outcomes and Physical and Mental Health: Exogenous Human Capital or Endogenous Health Production." In *Research in Human Capital and Development: The Economics of Disability*, Volume 13, edited by David S. Salkever and Alan Sorkin. Stamford, Conn.: JAI Press.

Evans, William, and John D. Graham. 1988. "Traffic Safety and the Business Cycle." *Alcohol, Drugs, and Driving* 4(1): 31–38.

Eyer, Joseph. 1977. "Prosperity as a Cause of Death." *International Journal of Health Services* 7(1): 125–50.

Fenwick, Rudy, and Mark Tausig. 1994. "The Macroeconomic Context of Job Stress." *Journal of Health and Social Behavior* 35(3): 266–82.

Forbes, John F., and Alan McGregor. 1984. "Unemployment and Mortality in Post-War Scotland." *Journal of Health Economics* 3(3): 239–57.

Freeman, Donald G. 1999. "A Note on 'Economic Conditions and Alcohol Problems'." *Journal of Health Economics* 18(5): 661–70.

Gangwisch, James E., Dolores Malaspoina, Bernadette Boden-Albala, and Steven B. Heymsfield. 2005. "Inadequate Sleep and a Risk Factor for Obesity: Analyses of NHANES 1." *Sleep* 28(10): 1289–96.

Gaziano, J. Michael, Julie E. Buring, Jan L. Breslow, Samuel Z. Goldhaber, Bernard Rosner, Martin VanDenburgh, Walter Willett, and Charles H. Hennekens. 1993. "Moderate Alcohol Intake, Increased Levels of High-Density Lipoprotein and Its Subfractions, and Decreased Risk of Myocardial Infarction." *New England Journal of Medicine* 329(25): 1829–34.

Gerdtham, Ulf-G, and Magnus Johannesson. 2003. "A Note on the Effect of Unemployment on Mortality." *Journal of Health Economics* 22(3): 505–18.

———. 2004. "Absolute Income, Relative Income, Income Inequality, and Mortality." *Journal of Human Resources* 29(1): 228–47.

———. 2005. "Business Cycles and Mortality: Results from Swedish Microdata." *Social Science and Medicine* 60(1): 205–18.

Gerdtham, Ulf-G, and Christopher J. Ruhm. 2006. "Deaths Rise in Good Economic Times: Evidence from the OECD." *Economics and Human Biology* 43(3): 298–316.

Goldney, Robert D. 1997. "Unemployment and Health: A Re-appraisal." *International Archives of Occupational and Environmental Health* 70(3): 145–7.

Graham, John D., Bei-Hung Chang, and John S. Evans. 1992. "Poorer is Riskier." *Risk Analysis* 12(3): 333–7.

Gravelle, Hugh S. E. 1984. "Time Series Analysis of Mortality and Unemployment." *Journal of Health Economics* 3(3): 297–305.

Gravelle, Hugh S. E., G. Hutchinson, and J. Stern. 1981. "Mortality and Unemployment: A Critique of Brenner's Time-Series Analysis." *The Lancet* 318(8248): 675–9.

Grossman, Michael. 1972. "On the Concept of Health Capital and the Demand for Health." *Journal of Political Economy* 80(2): 223–55.

Gruber, Jonathan, and Michael Frakes. 2006. "Does Falling Smoking Lead to Rising Obesity?" *Journal of Health Economics* 25(2): 183–97.

Johansson, Edvard. 2004. "A Note on the Impact of Hours Worked on Mortality in the OECD." *European Journal of Health Economics* 5(4): 335–40.

Joyce, Theodore J., and H. Naci Mocan. 1993. "Unemployment and Infant Health: Time-Series Evidence from the State of Tennessee." *Journal of Human Resources* 28(1): 185–203.

Karasek, Robert A., and Töres Theorell. 1990. *Healthy Work: Stress, Productivity, and the Reconstruction of Working Life.* New York: Basic Books.

Kasl, Stanislav V. 1979. "Mortality and the Business Cycle: Some Questions About Research Strategies When Utilizing Macro-Social and Ecological Data." *American Journal of Public Health* 69(8): 784–8.

Kivimäki Mika, Päivi Leino-Arjas, Ritva Luukkonen, Hilkka Riihimaki, Jussi Vahtera, and Juhani Kirjonen. 2002. "Work Stress and the Risk of Cardiovascular Mortality: Prospective Cohort Study of Industrial Employees." *British Medical Journal* 325(7369): 857–61.

Laporte, Audrey. 2004. "Do Economic Cycles Have a Permanent Effect on Population Health? Revisiting the Brenner Hypothesis." *Health Economics* 13(8): 767–79.

Lin, Shin-Jong. 2005. "The Effects of Economic Fluctuations on Health Outcome: Empirical Evidence from Asia-Pacific Countries." Unpublished paper, Ming Chuan University.

Liu, Y, H. Tanaka, and the Fukouka Heart Study Group. 2002. "Overtime Work, Insufficient Sleep, and the Risk of Non-Fatal Acute Myocardial Infarction in Japanese Men." *Occupational and Environmental Medicine* 59(7): 447–51.

Martikainen, Pekka T., and Tapani Valkonen. 1996. "Excess Mortality of Unemployed Men and Women During a Period of Rapidly Increasing Unemployment." *The Lancet* 348(9032): 909–12.

Maruyama, S., K. Kohno, and K. Morimoto. 1995. "A Study of Preventive Medicine in Relation to Mental Health Among Middle Management Employees (Part 2)—Effects of Long Working Hours on Lifestyles, Perceived Stress and Working Life Satisfaction Among White-Collar Middle Management Employees." *Nippon Eiseigaku Zasshi* 50(4): 849–60.

McAvinchey, Ian D. 1988. "A Comparison of Unemployment, Income and Mortality Interaction for Five European Countries." *Applied Economics* 20(4): 453–71.

Meyer, Bruce D., and Dan T. Rosenbaum. 2001. "Welfare, Earned Income Tax Credit, and the Labor Supply of Single Mothers." *Quarterly Journal of Economics* 116(3): 1063–114.

Morris, Joan K., Derek G. Cook, and A. Gerald Shaper. 1994. "Loss of Employment and Mortality." *British Medical Journal* 308(6937): 1135–39.

Mwabu, Germano M. 1988. "Seasonality, the Shadow Price of Time and Effectiveness of Tropical Disease Control Programs." In *Economics, Health, and Tropical Diseases*, edited by Alejando N. Herrin and Patricia L. Rosenfield. Manila: University of the Philippines Press.

Neumayer, Eric. 2004. "Recessions Lower (Some) Mortality Rates." *Social Science and Medicine* 58(6): 1037–47.

Ogburn, William F., and Dorothy S. Thomas. 1922. "The Influence of the Business Cycle on Certain Social Conditions." *Journal of the American Statistical Association* 18(139): 324–40.

O'Neill, Brian. 1984. "Recent Trends in Motor Vehicle Crash Deaths." *American Association for Automotive Medicine* 6: 29–32.

Peters, Annette, Stephanie von Klot, Margit Heier, Ines Trentinaglia, Allmut Hörmann, Erich Wichmann, and Hannelore Löwel, for the Cooperative Health Research in the Region of Augsburg Study Group. 2004. "Exposure to Traffic and the Onset of Acute Myocardial Infarction." *New England Journal of Medicine* 351(17): 1721–30.

Price, Richard H., and Michiel Kompier. Forthcoming "Work Stress and Unemployment: Risks, Mechanisms, and Prevention." In *Prevention of Mental Disorders: Evidence Based Programs and Policies*, edited by C. M. Hosman, E. Jane-Llopis, and S. Saxena. Oxford: Oxford University Press.

Pritchett, Lant, and Lawrence H. Summers. 1996. "Healthier is Wealthier" *Journal of Human Resources* 31(4): 841–68.

Robinson, James C. 1988. "The Rising Long-Term Trend in Occupational Injury Rates." *American Journal of Public Health* 78(3): 276–81.

Ruhm, Christopher J. 1995. "Economic Conditions and Alcohol Problems." *Journal of Health Economics* 14(5): 583–603.

———. 2000. "Are Recessions Good for Your Health?" *Quarterly Journal of Economics* 115(2): 617–50.

———. 2003. "Good Times Make You Sick." *Journal of Health Economics* 22(4): 637–58.

———. 2004. "Maternal Employment and Adolescent Development." National Bureau of

Economic Research Working Paper No. 10691. Cambridge, Mass.: National Bureau of Economic Research.

———. 2005. "Healthy Living in Hard Times." *Journal of Health Economics* 24(2): 341–63.

———. 2006. "A Healthy Economy Can Break Your Heart." National Bureau of Economic Research Working Paper No. 12102. Cambridge, Mass.: National Bureau of Economic Research.

Ruhm, Christopher J., and William E. Black. 2002. "Does Drinking Really Decrease in Bad Times?" *Journal of Health Economics* 21(4): 659–78.

Sen, Amartya. 2001. "Economic Progress and Health." In *Poverty, Inequality and Health: An International Perspective,* edited by David A. Leon and Gill Walt. New York: Oxford University Press.

Smith, James P. 1999. "Healthy Bodies and Thick Wallets: The Dual Relationship Between Health and Economic Status." *Journal of Economic Perspectives* 13(2): 145–66.

Sokejima, Shigeru, and Sadanobu Kagamimori. 1998. "Working Hours as a Risk Factor for Acute Myocardial Infarction in Japan: A Case-Control Study." *British Medical Journal* 317(7161): 775–80.

Sparks, Kate, and Cary Cooper. 1997. "The Effects of Work Hours on Health: A Meta-Analytic Review." *Journal of Occupational and Organizational Psychology* 70(4): 391–408.

Stern, J. 1983. "The Relationship Between Unemployment and Morbidity and Mortality in England." *Population Studies* 37(1): 61–74.

Stewart, Jennifer M. 2001. "The Impact of Health Status on the Duration of Unemployment Spells and the Implications for Studies of the Impact of Unemployment on Health Status." *Journal of Health Economics* 20(5): 781–96.

Tapia Granados, José. 2004. "Mortality and Economic Fluctuations in Sweden, 1800–1998." Unpublished paper, University of Michigan.

———. 2005a. "Increasing Mortality During the Expansions of the U.S. Economy, 1900–1996." *International Journal of Epidemiology* 34(6): 1194–202.

———. 2005b. "Recessions and Mortality in Spain, 1980–1997." *European Journal of Population* 21(4): 393–422.

Thomas, Dorothy Swaine. 1927. *Social Aspects of the Business Cycle.* New York: Alfred A. Knopf.

Thun, Michael J., Richard Peto, Alan D. Lopez, Jane H. Monaco, S. Jane Henley, Clark W. Heath Jr., and Richard Doll. 1997. "Alcohol Consumption and Mortality Among Middle-Aged and Elderly U.S. Adults." *New England Journal of Medicine* 337(24): 1705–14.

van den Berg, Gerard J., Marrten Lindeboom, and Farnce Portrait. 2006. "Economic Conditions Early in Life and Individual Mortality." *American Economic Review* 96(1): 290–302.

Vistnes, Jessica P., and Vivian Hamilton. 1995. "The Time and Monetary Costs of Outpatient Care for Children." *American Economic Review* 85(2): 117–21.

Wagenaar, Alexander C., and Frederick M. Streff. 1989. "Macroeconomic Conditions and Alcohol-Impaired Driving." *Journal of Studies on Alcohol* 50(3): 217–25.

Wagstaff, Adam. 1985. "Time Series Analysis of the Relationship Between Unemployment and Mortality: A Survey of Econometric Critiques and Replications of Brenner's Studies." *Social Science and Medicine* 21(9): 985–96.

Chapter 8

The New Employment Contract and Worker Health in the United States

Richard H. Price and Sarah A. Burgard

Historically there have been three arenas of policy debate in the United States relevant to the health effects of employment for workers and their families. First, the *physical environment* of the workplace and its health impact has been a major arena of policy debate. The pathways from the physical environment to health include exposure to chemical and biological hazards leading to disease, as well as physical risks to safety. Second, the *demanding nature of work activities* has also been the topic of policy debate. The pathway from work activity to health most often implicates work stressors involving too little task control and high levels of demand, and the biological consequences of stress in response to work demands. Most recently, the *contractual nature of jobs*—their insecurity and their lack of benefits—has become a third major arena of policy debate. Here the pathway to ill health involves the stressful anticipation of involuntary job loss, the stresses associated with economic hardship following job loss, and the health-compromising conditions associated with managing part-time or otherwise nonstandard jobs that lack predictability, adequate benefits, and adequate income.

The debate on conditions of work and health is complex and has involved many different stakeholders. The various stakeholders have included organized labor, business organizations, legislators, and advocates for particular macroeconomic policies aimed at controlling inflation or economic growth. Furthermore, the employment policies that emerge from these debates are not the simple result of a single piece of legislation. Instead, they often involve long-running debates involving Congress, the courts, regulatory agencies, and unions. Workplace policies adopted by employers in the absence of any regulatory or protective legislation can also influence worker health.

THE POLICY DEBATE

The debate on the physical environment of the workplace and its health impact has revolved around the Occupational Safety and Health Administration, created by Congress through the Occupational Safety and Health Act signed by President Nixon in 1970. OSHA is responsible for receiving complaints about work dangers, inspect industries, maintain records to assure employer compliance, and render fines on employers for violations of workplace safety and health regulations. Among the policies established by OSHA are standards for workplace safety and health; training of workplace inspectors; creation of state OSHA programs; and exposure standards for cotton dust, lead, blood pathogens, asbestos, and vinyl chloride. There is evidence that these policies have improved worker health and safety. Susan Fleming (2001) reports that even though the workforce has greatly expanded since 1971, occupational fatalities have been decreasing. However, these successes have not been won easily or without considerable partisan policy debate.

The protection of the physical health of American workers by OSHA regulation and standards has been the subject of sharply partisan debate, with shifts in policies swinging from one administration to the next. In its early stages, OSHA focused on physical safety, retrofitting industrial machines for safety despite objections to the costs involved. Later the Carter administration expanded the OSHA focus to include exposure to toxic chemicals and biohazards. A watershed change in policy occurred under the Reagan and Bush administrations, which oversaw the initiation of the Voluntary Protection Program. This program put regulation substantially in the hands of industry. The Clinton administration advocated "stakeholder satisfaction" aimed at compromise, but with the Republican congressional majority of 1994, legislation moved to support employer interests with the Small Business Regulatory Enforcement Fairness Act of 1996 and the Congressional Review Act. The George W. Bush administration has moved decisively to institute policies that shift mandatory guidelines to voluntary status and to increase budgetary support for earlier voluntary programs. The U.S. General Accounting Office (2004) has issued a report indicating that these programs are likely to reduce OSHA's enforcement budget and are of questionable effectiveness in regulating business practices.

Turning to the regulatory history around work activities themselves, there is a substantial body of evidence that their timing, speed, demands, and the way they structure relationships with coworkers can be stressful and threaten health through a number of biological, behavioral, and psychosocial pathways. For example, shift work can disrupt circadian rhythms and produce psychosomatic complaints (Frese and Zapf 1986). Lack of variety, complexity, or stimulation; demands for speed; and long hours all can produce stress and health problems (Kahn and Byosiere 1992; Karasek and Theorell 1990; Price and Kompier, forthcoming; Semmer 2003). In addition, ambiguous or conflicting work roles create stress and anxiety (Kahn 1981). Jobs with high levels of demand and low control are particularly likely to produce chronic stress and health problems (Karasek and Theorell 1990). The biological pathways by which stressful work conditions can "get under the skin" (Taylor and Repetti 1997) are increasingly well understood. Work that is low in control can produce catecholamine/cortisol imbalances (Frankenhaeuser 1991). Anger, anxiety, and depression can produce cardiac illness through the chronic stimulation of the sympathetic-adrenal-medullar system and the hypothalamic-pituitary-adrenocortical axis (Taylor and Repetti 1997). It has also been shown that high blood pressure in stressful work situations can be reduced by supervisor social support (House 1981; House and Kahn 1985), suggesting that it may be possible to buffer the negative effects of these conditions.

Despite the large volume of research on the links between work demands, stress, and health, only limited policy debate and regulation of work activities have resulted. However, one important exception has been the debate on ergonomics standards. Although work conditions leading to musculoskeletal injuries such as carpal tunnel syndrome (which is associated with repetitive motion) and back injuries account for one-third of serious work injuries, they have received little regulation and have been the subject of intense partisan policy debate. After extensive study, in 2000 OSHA issued an ergonomics standard to protect workers. The OSHA standard was promptly repealed on March 29, 2001, by Congress, and the repeal was one of the first pieces of legislation signed by President George W. Bush in his first term in office (Uchitelle 2006).

Furthermore, new health risks for American workers that are not covered by existing safeguards are now beginning to appear, and the policies have shaped the employment contract of American workers and their influence on health is less understood. Over the last forty years, there have been important changes in legislation and business practices that have reshaped the employment contract of American workers. The new employment contract imposes new working conditions on workers; for example, involuntary job loss, job insecurity, and the increased prevalence of part-time nonstandard work, all of which may have effects on health.

A CHANGED EMPLOYMENT CONTRACT

The last four decades have seen a dramatic series of changes in the nature of work (Cooper 2002; Price, 2006) which have shaped the employment contract for American workers. Improvements in the technology to support work promised to ease the burden of jobs, but at the same time it may have reduced job security (Rifkin 1995). A new wave of union management struggles in the 1970s and 1980s resulted in lower levels of union membership (Tausig et al. 2004) and in reduced benefits for American workers. The "enterprise culture" of the 1980s encouraged strong movement for deregulation of American business and privatization of government services. Economic downturns in the 1980s and 1990s produced a wave of downsizing in the manufacturing sector (Baumol, Blinder, and Wolff 2003), and at the turn of the century the influence of globalization on the American workplace has produced the "offshoring" of American jobs. Finally, women have entered the American workforce in rapidly increasing numbers (Tausig et al. 2004), and families have had to deal with the conflicting and stressful demands of combining family and household responsibilities and work (Geurts and Demerouti 2003; Hochschild 1997). The new employment contract and its consequences for health have not been shaped by a single legislative act or executive order. Instead, a complex political process has influenced industrial policy (Shapiro 2005). Legislation has been written jointly by labor and management, and it has combined with adjustment of macroeconomic policy. Other private interests such as the insurance industry, which is concerned with pension and health plans, have also become involved in shaping legislation affecting workers and their families. Together, policy developments over the last four decades help to explain the emergence of the new employment contract.

Faced with rising unemployment rates in 1975, Congress eventually enacted the Full Employment and Balanced Growth Act of 1978, popularly known as the Humphrey-Hawkins Act. The legislation directed the Federal Reserve Board to reduce the unemployment rate to 4 percent by 1983, but, over time, many of the crucial provisions were stripped from the original bill (Uchitelle 2006). In the same period, the Federal Reserve raised interest rates to combat inflation, which reduced the availability of new jobs. This was also a period of deregulation in a number of industries where jobs had previously been relatively secure. The Airline Deregulation Act of 1978 was followed by deregulation in banking, telephones, trucking, and utilities, all of which created layoffs and increased job insecurity.

Business strategy also began to change in the 1970s and 1980s in ways that transformed secure jobs into layoffs. Mergers and acquisitions as well as leveraged buyouts produced layoffs as firms consolidated their assets. International trade agreements enacted by Congress but resisted by labor—such as the North American Free Trade Agreement (NAFTA)—meant that factories in the United States closed and jobs moved to Mexico where they could be performed at much lower cost (Uchitelle 2006). In a detailed economic analysis, William Baumol, Alan Blinder, and Edward Wolff (2003) find evidence that downsizing has resulted in increased profits for American industry through reduced wages per unit of productivity. Ironically though, they note that even though downsizing appears to have been used as a strategy for holding down wage increases, it was not rewarded by increased stock values.

Accompanying a decline in union membership over this same period (Tausig et al. 2004), there has been a decline in bargaining power to protect worker health. In the past, unions helped in a number of ways (Mischel and Walters 2004), including formulating legislation to protect workers, informing members of their rights with regard to government programs, enforcing the standards of the Occupational Safety and Health Act, and helping members in disputes with employers (Weil 2003). Unions also helped workers receive benefits due them from workers' compensation and encouraged compliance with the Fair Labor Standards Act to provide a minimum wage for hourly wage earners (Trejo 1991). The nature of collective bargaining has changed dramatically in the last few decades as foreign and domestic nonunion competition has risen rapidly in many industries, increasing employer demands for concessions and compelling unions to give up demands for wage increases and benefits. In addition, strikes—once a powerful union tool for improving working conditions, benefits, and pay—have become a tactic of last resort (Tochan, Katz, and McKersie 1986).

These policy developments have changed the nature of the employment contract

(Cooper 2002; Rousseau 1995), the nature of jobs themselves, and the ways they may influence worker health. Rousseau (1995) observes that employer-employee relations have changed from long-term, more informal, and relationally oriented arrangements to shorter-term, contract-based arrangements. Standard jobs that promised the exchange of regular pay and benefits for full-time work are being replaced by lower-paying, part-time or other nonstandard jobs with fewer or no benefits, fewer health and safety protections, and less job security (Kalleberg 2000). In response to increased competitive pressures, employers have adopted a number of practices to restructure standard positions into part-time and contingent jobs (Houseman 1999). This "just in time" workforce strategy is an important contributor to the working conditions that nonstandard workers now face. The new employment contract is an important feature of American working life, and it has important implications for the health and well-being of workers and their families.

As a result of these shifts in the landscape of work in the United States, individuals' perceptions of job insecurity have persisted into a period of relatively low official unemployment and have even spread to a wider proportion of the workforce (Elman and O'Rand 2002; Schmidt 2000). Involuntary job loss is still a threat to many workers (Hamermesh 1989; Keltzer 1998), and employment contracts that do not offer benefits or stability are increasingly commonplace (Kalleberg, Reskin, and Hudson 2000).

EVIDENCE FOR LINKS BETWEEN EMPLOYMENT CONDITIONS AND HEALTH

We turn now to a review of the empirical evidence for negative relationships between health and unemployment, job insecurity, and nonstandard work, as well as discussing key mechanisms that may explain these relationships.

Unemployment and Health

Numerous studies over time and across societies have demonstrated that unemployment is a serious stressor with negative implications for health. These implications include mental health conditions such as increased depressive symptoms (Dooley, Catalano, and Wilson 1994), reduced self-reported well-being (Laheima 1989), self-reported physical illness (Kessler, House, and Turner 1987), and mortality from suicide (Platt 1984). In some studies, unemployment is also associated with increased use of tobacco and alcohol (Montgomery et al. 1998), which could impact physical health in the long term. Stronger evidence that unemployment causes health decline can be drawn from factory-closure studies (Kasl, Gore, and Cobb 1975). When an entire organization closes, it is unlikely that specific characteristics of a particular worker are responsible for the job loss, making it clearer that the job loss caused health to decline. Plant-closure studies have found an increased risk of mental distress as well as increased physician consultations, illness episodes, and hospital referrals and attendance (Hamilton et al. 1990; Keefe et al. 2002). Studies of longitudinal population-based samples, which sample individuals experiencing a variety of reasons for job loss, have shown that job loss is linked to a greater number of reported medical conditions, higher rates of medical-services use and pension-disability use (Ferrie et al. 1998a; Westin 1990), poorer physical functioning (Gallo et al. 2000), and poorer self-reported physical illness (Turner 1995). Such studies have also shown that job loss is associated with worsening of psychological symptoms such as depression, somatization, and anxiety (Burgard, Brand, and House 2006; Gallo et al. 2000; Turner 1995). Finally, involuntary job loss is associated with declines in the well-being of families as well as increased child abuse and marital conflict (Catalano et al. 1993a, 1993b; Price 1992; Price, Choi, and Vinokur 2002).

An involuntary job loss may be a precipitating factor and an acute blow for a worker, but it can also give rise to a more chronic stress process associated with the ongoing difficulties of unemployment or reemployment in a job of inferior quality (House 1987; Pearlin et al. 1981). Even job displacements—job losses that occur through no fault of the worker—typically entail a substantial period of nonemployment, resulting in a major loss of income and increased financial strain which has lasting effects on long-term earning potential (Farber 2003; Hamermesh 1989; Jacobson, LaLonde, and Sullivan 1993). Losing a job may also have consequences for both health-related and non-wage economic benefits derived from employment, such as health insurance coverage, pension, and other benefits (Brand 2006). This substantial economic strain accompanying job loss is associated with increases in depression (Kessler, Turner, and House 1987; Price, Choi, and Vinokur 2002) and produces a variety of secondary stressors (Price et al. 1998). Finally, an involuntary job loss could also entail the loss of psychosocial assets, including diminished goals and meaning in life, social support, sense of control, and time structure (Jahoda 1982; Pearlin et al. 1981). Furthermore, being unemployed is a stigmatized condition in American society and may create a sense of anxiety, insecurity, and shame (Newman 1988).

Job Insecurity and Health

While massive layoffs are less frequent now than they were several decades ago, the potent threat of economic and social turmoil associated with unemployment affects a wide range of contemporary workers. Changes in the implicit contract between employers and employees mean that many workers fear job loss, and some studies have suggested that prolonged exposure to the threat of job loss might be even more harmful than the experience of unemployment itself (Aronsson 1999; Heaney, Israel, and House 1994). A central proposition of stress research is that anticipation of a stressful event represents an equally important, or even greater, source of anxiety than the actual event itself (Lazarus and Folkman 1984). Workers who feel that their job is insecure are under stress because of the psychological strain associated with being in a powerless position, the anticipation of the problems of job loss, and the ambiguity about what the future holds and what responses would be most appropriate (Heaney, Israel, and House 1994). Furthermore, the effect of negative events is mediated by a person's perception of the predictability and control of such stimuli (Dohrenwend and Dohrenwend 1974), and perceived job insecurity is a condition defined by feelings of inability to control one's employment stability. Workers who experience prolonged and intense levels of job insecurity may experience negative health consequences because the stress response releases hormones that affect many organ systems (Gazzanizga and Heatherton 2003). The effects of constant stressors and intense stressful events also accumulate to impair the function of the immune system, increasing the likelihood and severity of illness (McEwen 2002).

There has been only limited empirical study of perceived job insecurity, but what exists provides suggestive evidence for negative health consequences. Several studies have shown that job insecurity negatively affects mental health and well-being (Burgard, Brand, and House 2006; De Witte 1999; Ferrie et al. 1998b). Fewer studies have examined physical health differences, but these studies suggest negative associations with overall self-rated health or morbidity (Burgard, Brand, and House 2006; Ferrie et al. 1995; Pelfrene et al. 2003), physical symptoms (Ferrie et al. 1998b; Heaney, Israel, and House 1994), and cardiovascular risk factors (Ferrie et al. 2001; Siegrist et al. 1988). Consensus on the negative health effects of job insecurity has not been reached, particularly for physical health outcomes (Kasl, Gore, and Cobb 1975; Mattiasson et al. 1990). Many of the existing studies have been conducted in Western Europe, which limits the applicability of their results to the United States context. Nonetheless, existing evidence suggests that contemporary threats to job security could have significant negative implications for the well-being of American workers. However, Christopher Ruhm (chapter 7, this volume) indicates that expanding economic cycles may also be associated with health-compromising behavior. Increased consumption of intoxicating substances, increased work hours, and other apparent "health risks of prosperity" have been found at the population level, and epidemiological research will be needed to determine their actual health impacts at the individual level.

Nonstandard Work and Health

In the past several decades, in response to economic and policy changes, firms have increasingly pursued more flexibility in their employment relationships. They increasingly separate employees into a core group with standard, continuous, and secure jobs, and a peripheral group employed in involuntary and at-will nonstandard jobs (Tilly 1996). A commonly used definition of *standard work* characterizes it as full-time, typically on a fixed schedule, with the expectation of continued employment, and at the employer's place of business under the employer's direction (Kalleberg 2000). *Nonstandard work* then encompasses alternate employment relationships that vary on these bases, including on-call work and day labor, temporary-help agency employment, employment with contract companies, independent contracting, other self-employment, and part-time employment in otherwise "conventional" jobs (Kalleberg, Reskin, and Hudson 2000). By one measure, these categories taken together made up almost 30 percent of the American workforce in 1995 (U.S. Bureau of Labor Statistics 1997).

Nonstandard employment arrangements were common until World War II, declined in the growth years of the 1950s through the mid-1970s, reemerged in the late 1970s, and appear to have been growing in importance since then (Blank 1998; Polivka and Nardone 1989).

Two explanations have been forwarded for the recent increase in nonstandard work. The first highlights employers' use of these kinds of arrangements in response to the requirements of lean production in a globalizing economy; nonstandard workers can be easily hired and cut in response to demand. An alternate explanation is that employers are accommodating worker preferences as the labor force becomes increasingly female and workers juggle other (often caretaking) responsibilities.

Both sides of the argument offer some evidence. On the one hand, high proportions of temporary-help agency employees would prefer a standard contract and are thus involuntary nonstandard workers (Kalleberg et al. 1997). Coupled with the relatively high growth in this form of nonstandard work, the evidence suggests that employers' preferences, not workers' preferences, are responsible for the increase in temporary-help agency work (Goldman and Appelbaum 1992; Kalleberg, Reskin, and Hudson 2000). Furthermore, in some studies businesses have cited the cost savings of not providing benefits as a reason for using nonstandard workers (Houseman 2001); this indicates that nonstandard work could be good for employers but bad for employees.

On the other hand, studies have shown that two types of nonstandard workers—self-employed people and independent contractors—are still less likely to have fringe benefits, but they earn more than workers in standard jobs and, on average, prefer their arrangements to a standard job (Kalleberg et al. 1997; Polivka 1996). Preferences for nonstandard work contracts may also be higher among young families, people nearing or past the legal retirement age (Christensen 1990; Wenger and Appelbaum 2004), and people with disabilities (Schur 2003), and these populations may be healthier under such arrangements (Isaksson and Bellagh 2002). Nonetheless, there is considerable debate about the extent of individual choice that nonstandard workers, and women in particular, exercise in accepting nonstandard work contracts versus the extent that they are channeled into these forms of work due to the constraints of a stratified labor force (Walsh 1999).

It is clear that there is considerable heterogeneity in the characteristics of nonstandard jobs and their incumbents. One study finds that while there are high- and low-wage jobs available to contract workers, the self-employed, temporary-help agency employment, on-call, day-labor, and part-time work tend to be associated with worse characteristics in terms of working conditions and available benefits compared to standard full-time jobs (Kalleberg, Reskin, and Hudson 2000). Furthermore, nonstandard work is concentrated among women (Amott and Matthaei 1991). Within the nonstandard work arena, women are particularly likely to be in part-time jobs (Kalleberg et al. 1997; Nollen 1996); minority women and those of low economic standing are overrepresented in the poorest nonstandard work arrangements (Nollen 1996). The diversity of nonstandard work arrangements and their uneven distribution across the working population suggest that the health-related consequences of nonstandard working arrangements are likely to be complex.

Despite the fact that nonstandard work accounts for an increasing fraction of the occupational opportunities in this country, we know relatively little about the potential consequences for health, and the existing evidence is equivocal. In some studies, nonstandard employees reported greater psychological distress and, to a lesser extent, poorer physical health than standard employees (Benach et al. 2004; Dooley and Prause 2004; Friedland and Price 2003; M. Virtanen et al. 2005). Nonstandard workers have also shown a higher risk of mortality than permanent employees, but a lower risk than the unemployed; meanwhile, those who moved from a temporary to permanent position had the lowest risk of mortality, even controlling for socioeconomic differences (Kivimaki et al. 2003). Nonstandard employees are at risk of deterioration in occupational health and safety in terms of injury rates, disease risk, and hazard exposures (Quinlan, Mayhew, and Bohle 2001). This remains true even after controlling for worker's personal characteristics, family status, occupation, and industry (Kalleberg, Reskin, and Hudson 2000). Nonetheless, there are important health variations across different types of nonstandard workers. For example, there are differences between on-call or substitute workers versus those on temporary but full-time contracts that otherwise resemble permanent jobs (P. Virtanen et al. 2003, 2005). Other studies find that individuals in nonstandard contracts are as physically healthy or healthier than their peers who work under standard arrangements (Bardasi and Francesconi 2004; M. Virtanen et al. 2003; P. Virtanen et al. 2002), though they may report greater job dissatisfaction, fatigue, backache, and muscular pains (Benavides et al. 2000). Part-time work has even appeared to be protective for women in some studies (Bardasi and Francesconi 2004; Nylen, Voss, and Floderus 2001).

The lack of clear consensus on the health effects of nonstandard work may result from the variety of circumstances under which people accept and perform nonstandard work. First, various forms of selection may influence the empirical results aside from the impact of the working arrangements themselves. Nonstandard workers, as well as those who experience job insecurity or unemployment, may have poorer subsequent health because they differ on a set of baseline characteristics and resources than predict health independently of working conditions (Benach et al. 2000, 2002). For example, women, racial-ethnic minority-group members, and people of low-socioeconomic position have traditionally been more likely to work under nonstandard arrangements (Hipple 2001), and these groups often report poorer health than white men and people of higher social status. In addition, people initially in poorer health may be more likely to be hired for a nonstandard position than for a standard job (Schur 2003), and their subsequent health outcomes will be poorer, at least in part, because of earlier health deficits. By contrast, some nonstandard workers are younger people who combine work with school or other responsibilities; they may be more resilient because of their age.

Second, some people are compelled to take nonstandard or insecure jobs for lack of other opportunities due to deficiencies in qualifications, such as education or relevant skills. For these individuals, we would expect the negative health consequences of nonstandard work to be greatest. Workers with few options in the labor market may be compelled to take nonstandard jobs characterized by irregular hours and split shifts, and which necessitate rapid rearrangement of family-life schedules (Zeytinogku et al. 2004). Some workers may also be compelled to combine two or more nonstandard jobs to increase earnings.

Third, the lack of available benefits can play a role in health outcomes. Nonstandard workers and their families have far lower rates of health insurance coverage than workers with standard jobs (Distler, Fisher, and Gordon 2005). Lack of health insurance can be risky when neglect of acute health problems can lead to chronic complications (Panel on Musculoskeletal Disorders and the Workplace 2001).

Finally, and in contrast to workers who would prefer standard work but are unable to obtain it, some workers may prefer nonstandard arrangements and suffer few health consequences. For example, some nonstandard workers may have access to protective resources, such as a partner with higher earnings and benefits, which could buffer the potential resource deficits associated with nonstandard jobs.

AN EMPIRICAL EXAMINATION OF NONSTANDARD WORKING ARRANGEMENTS AND HEALTH

We present a brief description and analysis using a nationally representative sample of American men and women to illustrate relationships between nonstandard work and health. We use the Americans' Changing Lives (ACL) study, a nationally representative cohort initiated in 1986 with follow-up interviews conducted in 1989, 1994, and 2001 to 2002 (House, Lantz, and Herd 2005). With this sample we observe workers in different nonstandard employment arrangements over long periods of follow-up, we distinguish workers who report that they prefer part-time employment from those who would rather work full-time, and we have information on several health outcomes as well as health "shocks" that occur between survey waves. These features of the data make our study unique, as careful assessment of the potential influence of health selection and stated preferences for nonstandard work typically are not included in existing studies.

We focus on employment type, distinguishing respondents who do standard work (thirty-five or more hours per week) from those doing nonstandard work. The latter category includes voluntary part-time workers who prefer to (and do) work less than thirty-five hours per week, involuntary part-time workers who work part-time but would prefer to work more hours, and respondents who report that they are self-employed (regardless of the number of hours worked per week).[1] At baseline in the ACL study, about 63 percent of working women hold a standard job, while about 16 percent are voluntary part-time workers, 7 percent are involuntarily working part-time, and about 13 percent are self-employed. Among working men, about three-quarters are working in standard jobs, while 18 percent are self-employed, 3 percent are voluntary part-time workers, and just over 3 percent are involuntarily working part-time. This gender difference reflects the much longer history and social acceptability of female part-time employment.[2] Basic characteristics of these workers are presented in table 8.1, separated by sex and by the type of employment reported by the respondent at baseline. Notably, voluntary part-time and self-employed workers are older than others, while black men and women are less likely than non-blacks to be self-employed. For women, the amount of child care provided is higher among part-time workers; among men, part-time and self-employed workers report less child care than those in standard work. Among women, average schooling is lowest among the involuntary part-time workers and highest among standard workers. Men who are voluntarily working part-time have the lowest average educational attainment in this sample, while self-employed men report the highest level of education. Regardless of sex, involuntary part-time workers report the lowest annual household incomes. Many women work in service industries, with voluntary part-time workers most likely to do so. Voluntary part-time male workers are also most likely to work in a service industry, while men in standard employment arrangements are least likely to do so. Job dissatisfaction is highest among involuntary part-time women and lowest among self-employed women; there is no significant difference among groups of male workers.

Baseline health differences are also a potentially important source of differences in the kind of employment that individuals obtain as well as in health over follow-up. For each self-reported measure used here, higher scores reflect worse health.[3] While average self-rated overall health does not vary across employment types among women in 1986, men voluntarily or involuntarily working part-time have significantly worse self-rated health than others. For both women and men, involuntary part-time and standard workers showed more depressive symptoms than voluntary part-time and self-employed workers in 1986. There are no significant differences in baseline body mass index (BMI) across employment types for men or women, but all groups fall into the "overweight" category or just below it. Finally, table 8.1 shows the proportion of respondents who reported in 1989 that they had experienced a negative health shock or an involuntary job loss since 1986.[4] There are no significant differences in the frequency of health shocks across employment types for this period, but involuntary job losses over follow up were significantly more common for men involuntarily working part-time in 1986.

For estimation of multivariate models we create a "stacked" data set with up to three person-spell observations per respondent. Breaking the information into multiple observations per individual allows us to take advantage of all the information on work and health that is available, even if a respondent leaves the sample at some point over follow-up. The first potential person-spell, for example, contains information about background characteristics and health in 1986 and employment type and health in 1989, as well as health shocks that occur in the in-

TABLE 8.1 / Means or Percentages for Independent Variables by Employment Type in 1986, Americans' Changing Lives Study Men and Women

	Women					Men				
	Standard	Voluntary Part-Time	Involuntary Part-Time	Self-Employed	P-Value for Diff.	Standard	Voluntary Part-Time	Involuntary Part-Time	Self-Employed	P-Value for Diff.
Age	39.7 (10.4)	45.7 (12.9)	40.4 (12.4)	45.3 (14.8)	<.001	39.2 (10.6)	59.3 (13.4)	38.7 (15.2)	45.4 (13.0)	<.001
Percentage black	14.2	7.28	16.4	5.36	<.001	11.0	23.0	10.1	5.62	<.001
Percentage married	60.7	78.9	67.3	75.4	<.001	76.6	73.0	49.5	79.0	0.005
Annual childcare hours (in hundreds)	8.17 (9.33)	10.4 (10.4)	10.2 (10.2)	7.67 (10.0)	0.005	6.08 (7.48)	0.403 (1.61)	3.29 (6.05)	3.83 (6.54)	<.001
Years of education	13.3 (2.38)	12.9 (2.15)	12.5 (2.49)	12.8 (2.44)	0.001	13.1 (3.00)	12.1 (4.15)	12.6 (2.95)	13.4 (2.87)	0.004
Total annual household income (in 2005 dollars)	58,367 (37,014)	71,002 (44,865)	43,346 (31,407)	78,185 (60,055)	<.001	68,015 (40,674)	31,118 (23,246)	27,192 (19,333)	74,915 (55,816)	<.001
Percentage blue collar job	27.5	27.2	41.5	41.1	0.005	51.7	54.0	71.5	35.5	<.001
Percentage manufacturing industry	18.3	2.87	3.77	4.11	<.001	33.9	0.00	13.0	8.01	<.001
Percentage service industry	40.5	70.2	47.7	49.1	<.001	18.4	53.7	27.2	37.4	<.001
Dissatisfaction with work (1 = low, 5 = high)	2.23 (1.01)	1.93 (0.836)	2.49 (1.15)	1.83 (0.820)	<.001	2.13 (0.911)	1.86 (0.907)	2.42 (0.710)	2.02 (0.963)	0.233
Self-rated health	2.05 (0.914)	2.01 (0.877)	2.20 (0.834)	2.01 (0.859)	0.442	1.96 (0.872)	2.58 (1.08)	2.21 (1.23)	2.00 (0.937)	<.001
Depressive symptoms score	0.087 (1.06)	-0.171 (0.940)	0.137 (0.867)	-0.109 (1.07)	0.002	-0.153 (0.879)	-0.197 (0.854)	-0.162 (0.734)	-0.235 (0.857)	0.026
Body mass index	24.6 (4.60)	24.6 (4.83)	25.7 (5.68)	24.8 (4.44)	0.678	26.0 (4.06)	28.2 (5.23)	26.1 (3.80)	26.8 (3.96)	0.360
Percentage with health shock (1986 to 1989)	20.1	21.1	27.7	23.9	0.578	19.3	28.9	30.5	15.1	0.429
Percentage with involuntary job loss (1986 to 1989)	6.26	5.53	7.63	4.02	0.260	10.1	3.73	31.3	6.93	0.013
N	609	160	72	130		673	29	31	161	

Source: Authors' compilation.

Notes: Standard errors associated with variable means presented in parentheses. Figures based on weighted data, except for column totals. Kruskal-Wallis or Chi-Square tests for difference between categories of employment type were conducted separately for men and women with significance levels at the * p < .05, ** p < .01, *** p < .001 levels and are presented in the final column for each sex.

terim. The second and third person-spells include the equivalent information for the periods from 1989 to 1994 and from 1994 to 2001 or 2002. Using this analytic sample of person-spells, we first estimate multinomial logistic regression models predicting employment type as a function of earlier sociodemographic, work, and health characteristics. We then estimate OLS regression models of self-rated overall health, depressive symptoms, and body mass index as a function of earlier employment status and health. Models are estimated using Stata 9.0SE, adjusted for the multiple observations per individual.[5] All models also include an indicator (not shown) for the number of years in the person-spell under observation.

We estimated multinomial logistic regression models predicting employment type in a given survey wave as a function of all of the characteristics from table 8.1, measured at the prior survey wave. The results from these models supported the findings shown in table 8.1, so we do not show these results, and we discuss only key findings. In particular, we do not find any significant effects of baseline health or health shocks over follow-up on subsequent employment type in models controlling for all predictors, though in simpler models, poorer baseline health increased the likelihood of working part-time at follow-up. Also, having lost a job involuntarily in the past three years is associated with a significantly greater likelihood of involuntary part-time work at follow-up among men. Taken together, the descriptive and multivariate evidence suggests that there are important differences in the characteristics of individuals who enter standard and nonstandard employment. Self-employed workers appear to be similar to standard workers in terms of their resources and well-being, while involuntary part-time workers are considerably worse off. Voluntary part-time work is a relatively common choice for women and is associated with higher baseline household incomes and greater satisfaction at work than among standard workers. However, voluntary part-time workers are older than standard workers and more likely to be married. Among men, voluntary part-time work appears to be the domain of those nearing retirement. These men are in worse overall health at baseline because of their age, but they report higher job satisfaction and lower depressive symptoms than standard workers.

We now turn to models that estimate the impact of employment type on subsequent health. Table 8.2 shows selected results from OLS regression models of overall self-rated health, depressive symptoms, and BMI, separately for women and men. Model 1 includes only age and employment type as predictors, while model 2 also includes indicators of race, marital status, child care hours, education, and household income. Model 3 adds characteristics of the job and employment status at the time that health was measured, and model 4 adds indicators of baseline health and health shocks. Here we focus on the impact of nonstandard employment type and changes in the estimates over this set of models.

We find that self-employed women have significantly better self-rated health than standard workers, while men who voluntarily work part-time have significantly worse self-rated health than their counterparts in standard employment arrangements. Controls in model 4 for sociodemographic characteristics and particularly for baseline health and health events over follow-up considerably weaken the health advantage of self-employed women, though it is still signifi-

TABLE 8.2 / Selected Unstandardized Coefficients from OLS Regression Models of Health Predicted by Employment Type (Standard Employment Omitted, Other Predictors Not Shown)

	Women				Men			
	Model 1	Model 2	Model 3	Model 4	Model 1	Model 2	Model 3	Model 4
Overall self-rated health								
Voluntary part-time	−0.096	−0.074	−0.095	−0.021	0.283*	0.250†	0.260†	0.189
	(0.069)	(0.070)	(0.072)	(0.054)	(0.131)	(0.130)	(0.135)	(0.136)
Involuntary part-time	0.170	0.058	0.034	0.034	0.139	0.14	0.131	0.092
	(0.126)	(0.126)	(0.128)	(0.095)	(0.172)	(0.155)	(0.158)	(0.147)
Self-employed	−0.248**	−0.214*	−0.230*	−0.127*	−0.092	−0.065	−0.035	−0.034
	(0.088)	(0.088)	(0.089)	(0.061)	(0.076)	(0.075)	(0.074)	(0.049)
Depressive Symptoms								
Voluntary part-time	−0.214**	−0.208**	−0.211**	−0.128*	0.041	−0.062	−0.049	−0.010
	(0.066)	(0.067)	(0.068)	(0.057)	(0.129)	(0.132)	(0.121)	(0.101)
Involuntary part-time	0.223	0.09	0.07	0.034	0.286†	0.142	0.107	0.117
	(0.150)	(0.149)	(0.154)	(0.136)	(0.166)	(0.160)	(0.151)	(0.109)
Self-employed	−0.084	−0.061	−0.036	0.026	−0.063	−0.030	0.003	0.019
	(0.098)	(0.094)	(0.096)	(0.073)	(0.070)	(0.068)	(0.068)	(0.052)
Body mass index								
Voluntary part-time	−1.36**	−1.14*	−1.18*	−0.498**	−0.713	−0.837	−0.833	0.087
	(0.467)	(0.483)	(0.490)	(0.147)	(0.694)	(0.732)	(0.755)	(0.298)
Involuntary part-time	0.023	−0.383	−0.401	−0.144	−0.129	0.016	0.079	−0.684
	(0.860)	(0.836)	(0.843)	(0.317)	(0.869)	(0.861)	(0.877)	(0.445)
Self-employed	−1.05*	−0.779	−0.746	−0.281	0.239	0.331	0.35	−0.133
	(0.491)	(0.506)	(0.533)	(0.197)	(0.473)	(0.469)	(0.475)	(0.122)

Source: Authors' compilation.
Note: Coefficients obtained from OLS linear regression models, with standard errors of estimates in parentheses, and significance levels denoted by † $p < .10$, * $p < .05$, ** $p < .01$. Models control for all predictors in table 1 except involuntary job loss, and include indicators for the number of years in the person-spell. Models are adjusted for repeated observations on the same individual.

cant. Meanwhile, these factors explain a substantial fraction of remaining differences across male employment groups.

Turning to depressive symptoms, we find that women voluntarily working part-time have significantly lower depressive symptoms than standard workers. Among men, involuntary part-time workers report more depressive symptoms than standard workers, though the difference is only marginally statistically significant because there are only a handful of such workers. Differences in sociodemographic characteristics account for much of the disadvantage of involuntary part-time men, while level of depression at the baseline of the person-spell and health shocks over follow-up account for a meaningful proportion of the advantage of voluntary part-time women.

Finally, we find a significant association between body mass index and nonstandard work for women: those voluntarily working part-time and those who are self-employed have significantly lower body mass index measures than standard workers. With adjustments for sociodemographic characteristics in model 2, the differences are reduced and self-employed women no longer significantly differ from standard workers. Among voluntary part-time women, a large fraction of the advantage is explained by baseline BMI and health shocks over follow-up, but they still show substantively and significantly lesser increase in body mass index over follow-up than standard workers.

All results in table 8.2 are robust to controls for the number of chronic health conditions reported by the respondent at the baseline of the person-spell, which is a more objective measure of underlying health status, as well as their neuroticism score in 1986, which is an indicator of an individual's overall negative reporting style. Our results are robust to the controls, suggesting that these results are not driven solely by health selection or a bias deriving from self-reports of health. We also explored an indicator of any functional limitations in daily life activities to capture a more objective indicator of health, but there were very few working-age individuals who reported such limitations.

We also tested a series of interactions (not shown) to further explore potential differences within categories of nonstandard workers. Most importantly, we found that the lower depressive symptoms shown by voluntary part-time women were restricted to those who reported child care responsibilities; the greater the number of annual child care hours, the more strongly part-time work was associated with better mental health. In addition, the interaction models revealed that women with child care responsibilities had better self-rated health if they worked part-time voluntarily rather than working a standard job—an effect which was obscured in the full model. These findings highlight the variation in circumstances that produce health-enhancing or health-damaging conditions, and they suggest the importance of family conditions as the context for women in nonstandard work.

Overall, our brief analysis has shown that nonstandard work arrangements can have effects on subsequent health, even when we take into account the differences across groups of workers at baseline. Self-employed women report better self-rated health than standard workers in our full models. It is also important to consider an individual's stated preference for work hours. Here, we find that women working fewer than thirty-five hours per week have lower depressive symptoms and lower body mass indexes than standard workers only if they prefer to work part-time. Relatively few men work in part-time arrangements, and the differences we observe in their subsequent health are fully explained by their baseline social and health disadvantages. This analysis also supports other work suggesting that are important differences even within groups of nonstandard workers (P. Virtanen et al. 2005). For example, we found that the health advantages observed for women voluntarily working part-time were restricted largely to those with child care responsibilities.

Finally, we explored some potential explanatory mechanisms for relationships between nonstandard work and subsequent health in models not shown here. One often-cited mechanism is the perceived job insecurity faced by many nonstandard workers. We found that self-reports of job insecurity were associated with subsequent health but did not explain the impact of nonstandard work. We also examined detailed job titles of workers in different types of employment to see whether there were large differences in the work done by voluntary part-time and self-employed women that set them apart from standard workers. In general, it does not appear that either standard workers or voluntary part-time workers have clearly superior jobs in terms of prestige or working conditions. However, self-employed women were more distinctive, with large fractions working as managers or administrators, private child care workers, hairdressers, and dressmakers. These job titles suggest a considerable amount of control over working conditions and possible ownership of a business. Considerable further work remains to explain different health outcomes across categories of employment type among American workers.

HEALTH CONSEQUENCES OF THE NEW EMPLOYMENT CONTRACT WITH AMERICAN WORKERS

Shifts in national policy over the last forty years have shaped worker safety, work activities, and the contractual agreements between employers and workers. This is not the consequence of a single piece of legislation. Instead, it is the result of a series of policy initiatives aimed at deregulation of industries, the systematic shift of power in union-management relations, and policy shifts in the approach to government regulation of worker health and safety. Indeed, the contract between employers and workers governing the nature and benefits of jobs themselves has shifted. Long-term, full-time, secure jobs with health and retirement benefits are being replaced by nonstandard work arrangements that lack the security, benefits, and pay of regular jobs.

The health consequences of these policy changes for workers and their families are just beginning to be documented by systematic research. Hard-won progress in workplace physical safety and hazard exposure is less certain under new, voluntary, employer-based initiatives. Stressful and demanding work activities that may threaten worker health have resisted policy regulation despite extensive research evidence of health risks. Economic and policy changes over the last four decades have also increased the risk of job loss and job insecurity. The research evidence is now quite strong that involuntary job loss increases the risk of illness episodes, visits to physicians, depression, somatic symptoms, anxiety, child abuse, and marital conflict. The perception of insecurity has its own health risks. The available research indicates that job insecurity is associated with increased psychological distress, feelings of helplessness, reports of physical symptoms, and poorer self-rated health and morbidity.

Finally, standard secure jobs with benefits are being replaced by nonstandard part-time jobs with few health protective benefits. Our empirical investigation of nonstandard work has produced results that illustrate the complexity of the relationship between new employment contracts and worker health. While many nonstandard employment contracts involve "bad" working conditions, existing research has shown that some nonstandard workers, such as self-employed or voluntary part-time workers, have relatively "good" jobs which they prefer and which involve high wages, control over working conditions, or the flexibility to combine work and other activities (Tilly 1996). These workers are not likely to suffer major health consequences, which is a potential explanation for some past findings of better health for nonstandard workers than their standard-work counterparts (Bardasi and Francesconi 2004; Nylen, Voss, and Floderus 2001; M. Virtanen et al. 2003; P. Virtanen et al. 2002). In our analyses we find that self-employed women show better overall self-rated health and voluntary part-time workers show more favorable changes in depressive symptoms and body mass index than those with standard working arrangements. Importantly, these findings for positive health associated with voluntary part-time work are restricted to women with child care responsibilities.

However, other less fortunate nonstandard workers are trapped in low-paying, tenuous employment without fringe benefits such as health insurance or pension coverage, and would prefer standard work. Our findings on these nonstandard workers contribute to the existing empirical evidence for greater psychological distress, poorer physical health, and increased risk of mortality found in other studies (Benach et al. 2004; Dooley and Prause 2004; Friedland and Price 2003; Kivimaki et al. 2003; M. Virtanen et al. 2005). The descriptive analysis revealed that involuntary part-time men and women were clearly disadvantaged in terms of health and socioeconomic position at baseline, and there is some suggestion of poorer self-rated health and greater depressive symptoms at follow-up. These suggestive differences were reduced with controls for baseline characteristics, which indicates that socially disadvantaged individuals are more likely to involuntarily end up in nonstandard employment contracts.

We should note that the present investigation and others on this topic are substantially limited by serious data constraints. In our sample there were only a small number of involuntary part-time workers, and we were unable to identify other forms of nonstandard employment, such as temporary-help agency employment. Hence, our ability to detect negative consequences from such "bad" jobs was limited. In general, existing data sources either provide excellent information on the health and socioeconomic characteristics of respondents, or the requisite details about their type of employment contract to create a detailed picture of standard and nonstandard jobs; but seldom do they provide both. More attention to both of these elements in longitudinal data collection is essential as nonstandard work contracts become more common. Taken together, however, findings from this and other analyses illustrate that a one-size-fits-all policy approach to new employment contracts is unlikely to successfully alleviate some potential negative health consequences.

POLICY AND PROGRAM GAPS THAT THREATEN WORKER HEALTH

The new world of job loss, unemployment, job insecurity, and nonstandard work is one with fewer benefits and protections for workers, and the health risks of these policy changes are only now becoming evident.

Gaps in Unemployment Insurance and Need for Reemployment Programs

A policy gap in unemployment insurance provisions provides a ready example of a policy gap that threatens worker health. Laid-off workers in many states must have held full-time work for a specified period of time and must have sufficient past earnings, in addition to being engaged in seeking full-time work, to obtain unemployment insurance. Half of the states in the country currently deny unemployment insurance to part-time, full-year workers earning the minimum wage (Economic Policy Institute 2004).

Workers experiencing job loss need programs to help them cope with the multiple stresses of unemployment and to conduct a job search leading to reemployment and a return to economic and family stability (Price, Choi, and Vinokur 2002). A program to aid unemployed workers in successful job search has been developed and evaluated in replicated randomized field trials (Caplan et al. 1989; Vinokur, Price, and Schul 1995). The program returns unemployed workers to higher paying new jobs more quickly (Vinokur et al. 1991), reduces mental health problems associated with prolonged unemployment (Vinokur, Price, and Schul 1995), prevents the occurrence of major depressive episodes up to two years later (Vinokur et al. 2000), and is particularly effective in preventing depression among those most vulnerable to mental health problems (Price, van Ryn, and Vinokur 1992; Vinokur, Price, and Schul 1995).

Lost Opportunities for Training and Lack of Health Insurance in Nonstandard Work

Irregular and part-time work also disadvantages workers in terms of eligibility for pensions and in training needed to obtain secure jobs in the future. Those who frequently change jobs will have greater difficulty qualifying for retirement plans created by employers. Opportunities for training are also curtailed by nonstandard work arrangements, and as technological changes continue to place greater demands on worker skills, training to upgrade skills becomes even more essential to secure high quality jobs (Houseman 1999).

Finally, having a job that offers health insurance as a benefit is one of the most important protections for the health of American workers. Uninsured workers are much less likely to seek needed health care, which often turns treatable acute conditions into chronic health conditions. Access to employer-provided health insurance is declining for both workers with standard and nonstandard working arrangements (Distler, Fisher, and Gordon 2005), but nonstandard workers already face a serious coverage disadvantage. In 2001, 74 percent of standard workers had health insurance through their jobs, but only 21 percent of nonstandard workers had such coverage. Furthermore, families are also affected: spouses and children of nonstandard workers covered at only one-third of the rate of families of workers with standard employment (Distler, Fisher, and Gordon 2005). Unemployed workers most often lose their health insurance along with their jobs. There is now evidence that people who are only intermittently insured are more likely to have a major decline in health (Baker et al. 2001).

Limited access to health insurance coverage, unemployment insurance, necessary on-the-job training, and adequate retirement planning are all major threats to workers as the American employment contract continues to transform. Four decades of change in workplace policies in the United States are already showing their influence on the health and vulnerability of workers and their families. We expect to see even more health impacts as the evidence continues to accumulate. Renewed emphasis on policies and programs to protect worker health is urgently needed.

NOTES

1. An analysis using Current Population Survey data has shown that classifying workers as "involuntary part-time" on the basis of their reported hours and reasons for not working at least thirty-five hours per week does reflect "involuntary" part-time work (Stratton 1996). In the present analysis, an employment type indicator was created for each survey wave using answers to questions about the number of hours the individual was currently working, whether she would prefer to work more hours, and the sector of employment (private, public, or self-employed).

2. We would prefer to include a more diverse array of nonstandard work types, some of which would include larger groups of men. Instead, we focus here on the key categories distinguishable in these data and on women, who dominate nonstandard work arrangements (P. Virtanen et al. 2005). We consider self-employment as well as the part-time employment categories for men in our analysis, but the small numbers in part-time work reduces our ability to ascertain statistically significant differences from standard workers.

3. Respondents were asked to rate their overall health at the time of the survey with the typical five-category item for self-rated health (values ranged from excellent, 1, to poor, 5). Depressive symptoms are measured using an eleven-item subset of the commonly used Epidemiological Studies Depression Scale or CES-D (Radloff 1977). Responses to each item scored on a four-item Likert scale, standardized scores of all present items averaged, and the score then standardized (with all standardization based on the mean

and standard deviation of the total 1986 ACL sample), with a final range from –1.2 (least depressed) to 4.7 (most depressed). Body mass index is calculated based on the respondent's self-report of his or her height and weight.

4. The definition of a "serious" or "life-threatening" life event was left to the respondent, so there may be some variation in the objective severity of the event; however, in the present analysis we assume that any self-reported serious or life-threatening event could potentially impact an individual's employment type or subsequent health.

5. We tested for potential effects of selection out of the analytic sample due to survey nonresponse or death by estimating a series of multinomial logistic regression models of health outcomes that included alternate categories for survey nonresponse and death. We found that employment type was not a statistically significant predictor of nonresponse or death when we included the covariates in the OLS models of health presented here.

REFERENCES

Amott, Teresa, and Julie Matthaei. 1991. *Race, Gender, and Work: A Multicultural Economic History of Women in the United States.* Boston, Mass.: South End Press.

Aronsson, Gunnar. 1999. "Influence of Worklife on Public Health." *Scandinavian Journal of Work and Environmental Health* 25(6): 597–604.

Baker, David W., Joseph J. Sudano, Jeffery M. Albert, Elaine A. Borawski, and Avi Dor. 2001. "Lack of Health Insurance and Decline in Overall Health in Late Middle Age." *New England Journal of Medicine* 345(15): 1106–13.

Bardasi, Elena, and Marco Francesconi. 2004. "The Impact of Atypical Employment on Individual Wellbeing: Evidence from a Panel of British Workers." *Social Science and Medicine* 58(9): 1671–88.

Baumol, William J., Alan S. Blinder, and Edward N. Wolff. 2003. *Downsizing in America: Reality, Causes and Consequences.* New York: Russell Sage Foundation.

Benach, Joan, M. Amable, Carles Muntaner, and Fernando G. Benavides. 2002. "The Consequences of Flexible Work for Health: Are We Looking in at the Right Place?" *Journal of Epidemiology and Community Health* 56(6): 405–6.

Benach, Joan, Fernando G. Benavides, Steven Platt, Ana Diez-Roux, and Carles Muntaner. 2000. "The Health-Damaging Potential of New Types of Flexible Employment: A Challenge for Public Health Researchers." *American Journal of Public Health* 90(8): 1316–7.

Benach, Joan, David Gimeno, Fernando G. Benavides, Jose Miguel Martinez, and Maria Del Mar Torne. 2004. "Types of Employment and Health in the European Union: Changes from 1995 to 2000." *European Journal of Public Health* 14(3): 314–21.

Benavides, Fernando G., Joan Benach, Ana V. Diez-Roux, and C. Roman. 2000. "How Do Types of Employment Relate to Health Indicators? Findings from the Second European Survey on Working Conditions." *Journal of Epidemiology and Community Health* 54(7): 494–501.

Blank, Rebecca M. 1998. "Contingent Work in a Changing Labor Market." In *Generating Jobs: How to Increase Demand for Less-Skilled Workers*, edited by Richard B. Freeman and Peter Gottschalk. New York: Russell Sage Foundation.

Brand, Jennie E. 2006. "The Effects of Job Displacement on Job Quality: Findings from the Wisconsin Longitudinal Study." *Research in Social Stratification and Mobility* 24(3): 275–98.

Burgard, Sarah A., Jennie E. Brand, and James S. House. 2006. "Job Insecurity and Health in the United States." PSC Working Papers report 06-595. Population Studies Center, University of Michigan, Ann Arbor.

Caplan, Robert D., Amiram D. Vinokur, Richard H. Price, and Michelle van Ryn. 1989. "Job Seeking, Reemployment, and Mental Health: A Randomized Field Experiment in Coping with Job Loss." *Journal of Applied Psychology* 74(5): 759–69.

Catalano, Ralph, David Dooley, Georjeanna Wilson, and Richard Hough. 1993a. "Job Loss and Alcohol Abuse: A Test Using Data from the Epidemiologic Catchment Area Project." *Journal of Health and Social Behavior* 34(3): 215–25.

Catalano, Ralph, David Dooley, Raymond W. Novaco, Georjeanna Wilson, and Richard Hough. 1993b. "Using ECA Survey Data to Examine the Effect of Job Layoffs on Violent Behavior." *Hospital and Community Psychiatry* 44(9): 874–9.

Christensen, Kathleen. 1990. "Bridges Over Troubled Water: How Older Workers View the Labor Market." In *Bridges to Retirement: Older Workers and a Changing Labor Market*, edited by Peter B. Doeringer. Ithaca, N.Y.: ILR Press.

Cooper, Cary. 2002. "The Changing Psychological Contract at Work." *The Journal of Occupational and Environmental Medicine* 59(6): 355.

De Witte, Hans. 1999. "Job Insecurity and Psychological Well-Being: Review of the Literature and Exploration of Some Unresolved Issues." *European Journal of Work and Organizational Psychology* 8(2): 155–77.

Distler, Elaine, Peter Fisher, and Colin Gordon. 2005. "On the Fringe: The Substandard Benefits of Workers in Part-time, Temporary, and Contract Jobs." *Commonwealth Fund Publication* 879.

Dohrenwend, Barbara S., and Bruce P. Dohrenwend. 1974. "Overview and Prospect for Research on Stressful Life Events." In *Stressful Life Events: Their Nature and Effects*, edited by Barbara S. Dohrenwend and Bruce P. Dohrenwend. New York: John Wiley and Sons.

Dooley, David, and JoAnn Prause. 2004. *The Social Costs of Underemployment: Inadequate Employment as Disguised Unemployment*. New York: Cambridge University Press.

Dooley, David, Ralph Catalano, and Georjeanna Wilson. 1994. "Depression and Unemployment: Panel Findings from the Epidemiologic Catchment Area Study." *American Journal of Community Psychology* 22(6): 745–65.

Economic Policy Institute. 2004. "EPI Issue Guide: Unemployment Insurance." Accessed at http://www.epinet.org/content.cfm/issueguides_unemployment_index.

Elman, Cheryl, and Angela M. O'Rand. 2002. "Perceived Job Insecurity and Entry into Work-Related Education and Training Among Adult Workers." *Social Science Research* 31(1): 49–76.

Farber, Henry S. 2003. "Job Loss in the United States, 1981–2001." National Bureau of Economic Research Working Paper No. 9707. Cambridge, Mass.: National Bureau of Economic Research.

Ferrie, Jane E., Martin John Shipley, Michael Gideon Marmot, Stephen Alfred Stansfeld, and George Davey Smith. 1995. "Health Effects of Anticipation of Job Change and Non-employment: Longitudinal Data from the Whitehall II Study." *British Medical Journal* 311(7015): 1264–9.

———. 1998a. "An Uncertain Future: The Health Effects of Threats in Employment Security in White-Collar Men and Women." *American Journal of Public Health* 88(7): 1030–6.

———. 1998b. "The Health Effects of Major Organizational Change and Job Insecurity." *Social Science and Medicine* 46(2): 243–54.

Ferrie, Jane E., Martin J. Shipley, Michael Gideon Marmot, Pekka Martikainen, Stephen Alfred Stansfeld, and George Davey Smith. 2001. "Job Insecurity in White-Collar Workers: Toward an Explanation of Associations with Health." *Journal of Occupational Health Psychology* 6(1): 26–42.

Fleming, Susan H. 2001. "OSHA at 30: Three Decades of Progress in Occupational Safety and Health." *Journal of Occupational Safety and Health* 12(3): 23–32.

Frankenhaeuser, Marie. 1991. "The Psychophysiology of Workload Stress, and Health: Comparison Between the Sexes." *Annals of Behavioral Medicine* 13(4): 197–204.

Frese, Michael, and David Zapf. 1986. "Shiftwork, Stress and Psychosomatic Complaints: A Comparison Between Workers in Different Shift Work Schedules." *Ergonomics* 29(1): 99–114.

Friedland, Daniel S., and Richard H. Price. 2003. "Underemployment: Consequences for the Health and Well-Being of Workers." *American Journal of Community Psychology* 32(1–2): 33–45.

Gallo, William T., Elizabeth H. Bradley, Michele Siegel, and Stanislav V. Kasl. 2000. "Health Effects of Involuntary Job Loss Among Older Workers: Findings From the Health and Retirement Study." *Journal of Gerontology: Social Sciences* 55B(3): S131–40.

Gazzanizga, Michael S., and Todd F. Heatherton. 2003. *Psychological Science: Mind, Brain, and Behavior.* New York: W. W. Norton and Company.

Geurts, Sabine A. E., and Evangelia Demerouti. 2003. "Work/Nonwork Interface: A Review of Theories and Findings." In *The Handbook of Work and Health Psychology*, edited by Marc J. Schabracq, Jacques A. M. Winnebust, and Cary L. Cooper. New York: John Wiley and Sons.

Goldman, Lonnie, and Eileen Appelbaum. 1992. "What Was Driving the 1982–88 Boom in Temporary Employment: Preference of Workers or Decisions and Power of Employers?" *American Journal of Economics and Sociology* 51(4): 473–91.

Hamermesh, Daniel. 1989. "What Do We Know About Worker Displacement in the United States?" *Industrial Relations* 28(1): 51–59.

Hamilton, V. Lee, Clifford L. Broman, William S. Hoffman, and David S. Renner. 1990. "Hard Times and Vulnerable People: Initial Effects of Plant Closings on Autoworkers' Mental Health." *Journal of Health and Social Behavior* 31(2): 123–40.

Heaney, Catherine A., Barbara A. Israel, and James S. House. 1994. "Chronic Job Insecurity Among Automobile Workers: Effects on Job Satisfaction and Health." *Social Science and Medicine* 38(10): 1431–7.

Hipple, Steven. 2001. "Contingent Work in the Late 1990s." *Monthly Labor Review* 124(3): 3–27.

Hochschild, Arlie. 1997. *The Time Bind: When Work Becomes Home and Home Becomes Work.* New York: Henry Holt and Company.

House, James S. 1981. *Work Stress and Social Support.* Reading, Mass.: Addison Wesley.

———. 1987. "Chronic Stress and Chronic Disease in Life and Work: Conceptual and Methodological Issues." *Work and Stress* 1(2): 129–34.

House, James S., and Robert L. Kahn. 1985. "Measures and Concepts of Social Support." In

Social Support and Health, edited by Sheldon Cohen and Sherman Leonard Syme. Orlando, Fla.: Academic Press.

House, James S., Paula M. Lantz, and Pamela Herd. 2005. "Continuity and Change in the Social Stratification of Aging and Health Over the Life Course: Evidence from a Nationally Representative Longitudinal Study from 1986 to 2001/2 (The Americans' Changing Lives Study)." *Journal of Gerontology: Series B* 60B(Special Issue 2): S15–26.

Houseman, Susan N. 1999. "The Policy Implications of Nonstandard Work Arrangements." In *Employment Research Fall 1999, W. E. Upjohn Institute for Employment Research*. Kalamazoo, Mich.: W. E. Upjohn Institute.

———. 2001. "Why Employers Use Flexible Staffing Arrangements: Evidence from an Establishment Survey." *Industrial and Labor Relations Review* 55(1): 149–70.

Isaksson, Kerstin S., and Katalin Bellagh. 2002. "Health Problems and Quitting Among Female 'Temps.'" *European Journal of Work and Organizational Psychology* 11(1): 27–45.

Jacobson, Louis S., Robert L. LaLonde, and Daniel G. Sullivan. 1993. "Earnings Losses of Displaced Workers." *American Economic Review* 83(4): 685–709.

Jahoda, Marie. 1982. *Employment and Unemployment. A Social-Psychological Analysis*. Cambridge: Cambridge University Press.

Kahn, Robert L. 1981. *Work and Health*. New York: John Wiley and Sons.

Kahn, Robert L., and Phillipe Byosiere. 1992. "Stress in Organizations." In *Handbook of Industrial and Organizational Psychology*, edited by Marvin D. Dunnette and Leatta M. Hough. Palo Alto, Calif.: Consulting Psychologists Press.

Kalleberg, Arne L. 2000. "Nonstandard Employment Relations: Part-time, Temporary and Contract Work." *Annual Review of Sociology* 26: 341–65.

Kalleberg, Arne L., Barbara F. Reskin, and Ken Hudson. 2000. "Bad Jobs in America: Standard and Nonstandard Employment Relations and Job Quality in the United States." *American Sociological Review* 65(2): 256–78.

Kalleberg, Arne L., Edith Rasell, Naomi Cassirer, Barbara F. Reskin, Ken Hudson, David Webster, Eileen Applebaum, and Roberta M. Spalter-Roth. 1997. *Nonstandard Work, Substandard Jobs: Flexible Work Arrangements in the U.S.* Washington: Economic Policy Institute.

Karasek, Robert, and Tor Theorell. 1990. *Healthy Work: Stress, Productivity, and the Reconstruction of Working Life*. New York: Basic Books.

Kasl, Stanley V., Susan Gore, and Sidney Cobb. 1975. "The Experience of Losing a Job: Reported Changes in Health, Symptoms and Illness Behavior." *Psychosomatic Medicine* 37(2): 106–22.

Keefe, Vera, Papaarangi Reid, Clint Ormsby, Bridget Robson, Gordon Purdie, Joanne Baxter, and Ngati Kahunguni Iwi. 2002. "Serious Health Events Following Involuntary Job Loss in New Zealand Meat Processing Workers." *International Journal of Epidemiology* 31(6): 1155–61.

Keltzer, Lori. 1998. "Job Displacement." *Journal of Economic Perspectives* 12(1): 115–36.

Kessler, Ronald C., James S. House, and J. Blake Turner. 1987. "Unemployment and Health in a Community Sample." *Journal of Health and Social Behavior* 28(1): 51–59.

Kessler, Ronald C., J. Blake Turner, and James S. House. 1987. "Intervening Processes in the Relationship Between Unemployment and Health." *Psychological Medicine* 17(4): 949–61.

Kivimaki, Mika, Jussi Vaherta, Marianna Virtanen, Marko Elovainio, Jaana Pentti, and Jane E. Ferrie. 2003. "Temporary Employment and the Risk of Overall and Cause-Specific Mortality." *American Journal of Epidemiology* 158(7): 663–8.

Lahelma, Eero. 1989. "Unemployment, Reemployment and Mental Well-Being. A Panel Survey of Industrial Job Seekers in Finland." *Scandinavian Journal of Social Medicine* 17(43): 1–170.

Lazarus, Richard S., and Susan Folkman. 1984. *Stress, Appraisal and Coping*. New York: Springer Verlag.

Mattiasson, Ingrid, Folke Lindgarde, Jessica A. Nilsson, and Tores Theorell. 1990. "Threat of Unemployment and Cardiovascular Risk Factors: Longitudinal Study of Quality of Sleep and Serum Cholesterol Concentrations in Men Threatened with Redundancy." *British Medical Journal* 301(6750): 461–6.

McEwen, Bruce S. 2002. "The Neurobiology and Neuroendocrinology of Stress: Implications for Post-Traumatic Stress Disorder from a Basic Science Perspective." *Psychiatric Clinics of North America* 25(2): 469–94.

Mischel, Lawrence, and Matthew Walters. 2004. "How Unions Help All Workers." Economic Policy Institute Briefing Paper 143. Washington: Economic Policy Institute.

Montgomery, Scott M., Derek G. Cook, Mel J. Bartley, and Michael E. J. Wadsworth. 1998. "Unemployment, Cigarette Smoking, Alcohol Consumption and Body Weight in Young British Men." *European Journal of Public Health* 8(1): 21–27.

Newman, Katherine S. 1988. *Falling From Grace: The Experience of Downward Mobility in the American Middle Class*. New York: Free Press.

Nollen, Stanley D. 1996. "Negative Aspects of Temporary Employment." *Journal of Labor Research* 17(4): 567–81.

Nylen, Lotta, Margaretha Voss, and Brigitta Floderus. 2001. "Mortality Among Women and Men Relative to Unemployment, Part Time Work, and Extra Work: A Study Based on Data from the Swedish Twin Registry." *Occupational and Environmental Medicine* 58(1): 52–57.

Panel on Musculoskeletal Disorders and the Workplace. 2001. "Musculoskeletal Disorders and the Workplace." Washington: National Academy of Science, Institute of Medicine.

Pearlin, Leonard I., Morton A. Lieberman, Elizabeth A. Menaghan, and Joseph T. Mullen. 1981. "The Stress Process." *Journal of Health and Social Behavior* 22(4): 337–56.

Pelfrene, Edwin, Peter Vlerick, Michel Moreau, Rudolf P. Mak, Marcel Kornitzer, and Guy De Backer. 2003. "Perceptions of Job Insecurity and the Impact of World Market Competition as Health Risks: Results from Belstress." *Journal of Occupational and Organizational Psychology* 76(4): 411–25.

Platt, Stephen. 1984. "Unemployment and Suicidal Behavior." *Social Science and Medicine* 19(2): 93–115.

Polivka, Anne E. 1996. "Into Contingent and Alternative Employment: By Choice?" *Monthly Labor Review* 119(10): 55–74.

Polivka, Anne E., and Thomas Nardone. 1989. "On the Definition of 'Contingent Work.'" *Monthly Labor Review* 112(12): 9–16.

Price, Richard H. 1992. "Psychosocial Impact of Job Loss on Individuals and Families." *Directions in Psychological Science* 1(1): 9–11.

———. 2006."The Transformation of Work in America: New Health Vulnerabilities for

American Workers." In *America at Work: Choices and Challenges*, edited by Edward E. Lawler III and James O' Toole. New York: Palgrave Macmillan.

Price, Richard H., and Michiel Kompier. Forthcoming. "Work Stress and Unemployment: Risks, Mechanisms, and Prevention." In *Prevention of Mental Disorders: Evidence Based Programs and Policies*, edited by Clemens M. Hosman, Eva Jane-Llopis, and Shekhar Saxena. Oxford: Oxford University Press.

Price, Richard H., Jin Nam Choi, and Amiram D. Vinokur. 2002. "Links in the Chain of Adversity Following Job Loss: How Financial Strain and Loss of Personal Control Lead to Depression, Impaired Functioning, and Poor Health." *Journal of Occupational Health Psychology* 7(4): 302–12.

Price, Richard H., Michelle van Ryn, and Amiram Vinokur. 1992. "Impact of a Preventive Job Search Intervention on the Likelihood of Depression Among the Unemployed." *Journal of Health and Social Behavior* 33(2): 158–67.

Price, Richard H., Daniel S. Friedland, Jin Nam Choi, and Robert D. Caplan. 1998. "Job Loss and Work: Transitions in a Time of Global Economic Change." In *Addressing Community Problems*, edited by Ximena B. Arriaga and Stuart Oskamp. Thousand Oaks, Calif.: Sage Publications.

Quinlan, Michael, Claire Mayhew, and Philip Bohle. 2001. "The Global Expansion of Precarious Employment, Work Disorganization, and Consequences for Occupational Health: A Review of Recent Research." *International Journal of Health Services* 31(2): 335–414.

Radloff, Lenore S. 1977. "The CES-D Scale: A Self-Report Depression Scale for Research in the General Population." *Applied Psychological Measurement* 1(3): 385–401.

Rifkin, Jeremy. 1995. *The End of Work: The Decline of the Global Labor Force at the Dawn of the Post Market Era*. New York: G. P. Putnam's Sons.

Rousseau, Denise M. 1995. *Psychological Contract in Organizations: Understanding Written and Unwritten Agreements*. Newbury Park, Calif.: Sage Publications.

Schmidt, Stefanie R. 2000. "Job Security Beliefs in the General Social Survey: Evidence on Long-Run Trends and Comparability with Other Surveys." In *On the Job: Is Long-Term Employment a Thing of the Past?* edited by David Neumark. New York: Russell Sage Foundation.

Schur, Lisa A. 2003. "Barriers or Opportunities? The Causes of Contingent and Part-Time Work Among People with Disabilities." *Industrial Relations* 42(4): 589–622.

Semmer, Norbert K. 2003. "Job Stress Interventions and Organization of Work." In *Handbook of Occupational Health Psychology*, edited by James Campbell Quick and Lois E. Tetrick. Washington: American Psychological Association.

Shapiro, Ian. 2005. *The Flight from Reality in the Human Sciences*. Princeton, N.J.: Princeton University Press.

Siegrist, Johanne, Herber Matschinger, Peter Cremer, and Dieter Seidel. 1988. "Atherogenic Risk in Men Suffering from Occupational Stress." *Atherosclerosis* 69(2–3): 211–8.

Stratton, Leslie S. 1996. "Are 'Involuntary' Part-Time Workers Indeed Involuntary?" *Industrial and Labor Relations Review* 49(3): 522–36.

Tausig, Mark, Rudy Fenwick, Steven L. Sauter, Lawrence R. Murphy, and Corina Graif. 2004. "The Changing Nature of Job Stress: Risk and Resources." In *Research in Occupational Stress and Well Being*, Volume 4, edited by Pamela L. Perrewé and Daniel C. Ganster. New York: JAI Press.

Taylor, Shelley E., and Rena L. Repetti. 1997. "Health Psychology: What Is an Unhealthy Environment and How Does it Get Under the Skin?" *Annual Review of Psychology* 48: 411–47.

Tilly, Chris. 1996. *Half a Job: Bad and Good Part-Time Jobs in a Changing Labor Market*. Philadelphia, Penn.: Temple University Press.

Tochan, Thomas A., Harry C. Katz, and Robert B. McKersie. 1986. *The Transformation of American Industrial Relations*. New York: Basic Books.

Trejo, Stephen J. 1991. "The Effects of Overtime Pay Regulation on Worker Compensation." *American Economic Review* 81(4): 719–40.

Turner, J. Blake. 1995. "Economic Context and the Health Effects of Unemployment." *Journal of Health and Social Behavior* 36(3): 213–29.

Uchitelle, Louis. 2006. *The Disposable American: Layoffs and Their Consequences*. New York: Alfred A. Knopf.

U.S. Bureau of Labor Statistics. 1997. "Contingent and Alternative Employment Relationships. USDL Report 97–422." Washington: U.S. Bureau of Labor Statistics.

U.S. General Accounting Office. 2004. "Workplace Safety and Health: OSHA's Voluntary Compliance Strategies Show Promising Results, but Should Be Fully Evaluated Before They Are Expanded." In *Report to the Chairman, Subcommittee on Workforce Protections, Committee on Education and the Workforce, House of Representatives*. Washington: Government Printing Office.

Vinokur, Amiram D., Richard H. Price, and Yacov Schul. 1995. "Impact of the JOBS Intervention on Unemployed Workers Varying in Risk for Depression." *American Journal of Community Psychology* 23(1): 39–74.

Vinokur, Amiram D., Michelle van Ryn, Edward M. Gramlich, and Richard H. Price. 1991. "Long-Term Follow-up and Benefit-Cost Analysis of the JOBS Program: A Preventive Intervention for the Unemployed." *Journal of Applied Psychology* 76(2): 213–9.

Vinokur, Amiram D., Jukka Vuori, Yakov Schul, and Richard H. Price. 2000. "Two Years After a Job Loss: Long-Term Impact of the JOBS Program on Reemployment and Mental Health." *Journal of Occupational Health Psychology* 5(7): 32–47.

Virtanen, Marianna, Mika Kivimaki, Marko Elovainio, Jussi Vaherta, and Jane E. Ferrie. 2003. "From Insecure to Secure Employment: Changes in Work, Health, Health Related Behaviours, and Sickness Absence." *Occupational and Environmental Medicine* 60(12): 948–53.

Virtanen, Marianna, Mika Kivimaki, Matti Joensuu, Pekka Virtanen, Marko Elovainio, and Jussi Vaherta. 2005. "Temporary Employment and Health: A Review." *International Journal of Epidemiology* 34(3): 610–22.

Virtanen, Pekka, Virpi Liukkonen, Jussi Vahtera, Mika Kivimaki, and Markku Koskenvuo. 2003. "Health Inequalities in the Workforce: The Labour Market Core-Periphery Structure." *International Journal of Epidemiology* 32(6): 1015–21.

Virtanen, Pekka, Jussi Vaherta, Mika Kivimaki, Virpi Liukkonen, Marianna Virtanen, and Jane E. Ferrie. 2005. "Labor Market Trajectories and Health: A Four-Year Follow-up Study of Initially Fixed-Term Employees." *American Journal of Epidemiology* 161(9): 840–6.

Virtanen, Pekka, Jussi Vaherta, Mika Kivimaki, Jaana Pentti, and Jane E. Ferrie. 2002. "Employment Security and Health." *Journal of Epidemiology and Community Health* 56(8): 569–74.

Walsh, Janet. 1999. "Myths and Counter-Myths: An Analysis of Part-Time Female Employees and Their Orientations to Work and Working Hours." *Work, Employment and Society* 13(2): 179–203.

Weil, David. 2003. "Individual Rights and Collective Agents: The Role of Old and New Workplace Institutions in the Regulation of Labor Markets." National Bureau of Economic Research Working Paper No. 9565. Cambridge, Mass.: National Bureau of Economic Research.

Wenger, Jeffrey B., and Eileen Appelbaum. 2004. "New Jobs, Old Story: Examining the Reasons Older Workers Accept Contingent and Nonstandard Employment." Working Paper, Center for Woman and Work, Rutgers University: 1–22.

Westin, Steinar. 1990. "The Structure of a Factory Closure: Individual Responses to Job-Loss and Unemployment in a 10-Year Controlled Follow-Up Study." *Social Science and Medicine* 31(12): 1301–11.

Zeytinogku, Isik U., Waheeda Lillevik, M. Bianca Seaton, and Josephina Moruz. 2004. "Part-Time and Casual Work in Retail Trade: Stress Factors Affecting the Workplace." *Relations Industrielles* 59(3): 516–43.

Part VI

Welfare Policy

Chapter 9

Welfare Reform and Indirect Impacts on Health

Marianne P. Bitler and Hilary W. Hoynes

B eginning in the early 1990s, many states used waivers to reform their Aid to Families with Dependent Children (AFDC) programs. This state experimentation resulted in landmark legislation that eliminated AFDC in 1996 and replaced it with Temporary Assistance for Needy Families (TANF). TANF—like the earlier AFDC program—provides cash grants to low-income families with children and is a key element of the nation's economic safety net. The roots of this reform lie in long-time concern that AFDC led to reductions in work, decreases in marriage, and increases in nonmarital births among low-income women.

These important policy changes, known collectively as *welfare reform*, were implemented with a desire to increase work among low-skilled single-parent families, reduce dependency on welfare, reduce births outside marriage, and increase the formation of two-parent families. In the wake of welfare reform, welfare caseloads declined by 50 percent between 1990 and 2000 (U.S. Department of Health and Human Services 2007), and the employment rate of low-skilled single parents with children increased by 13 percentage points, from 74 percent to 87 percent (Eissa and Hoynes 2006). An enormous literature has developed which evaluates the impact of welfare reform on caseloads and labor supply, as well as on income, poverty, fertility, marriage, and family and child well-being.[1]

Importantly, these goals of welfare reform had little to do with health or health insurance directly. Despite this lack of direct connection to health, however, we argue that welfare reform may have important indirect impacts on health. Understanding if and how welfare reform impacts health is extremely important given the preexisting inverse relationship between income and health. Welfare recipients are worse off than the general population. This both complicates the task of deciphering the effects of welfare reform and makes the possible negative health impacts of welfare a topic of extra concern. For example, Kaplan et al. (2005) show that current and former welfare recipients are more likely to smoke; be obese; have higher rates of hypertension, diabetes, and elevated glycosylated hemoglobin levels; and have worse self-reported health status compared to other women of the same age and race.

Key policy changes in welfare reform occurred over this period. The central changes in the TANF program include lifetime time limits for receiving cash assistance, work requirements, financial sanctions, and enhanced earnings disregards.[2] At the same time, there were concurrent changes in public health insurance for poor families through the expansions of Medicaid and introduction of the State Children's Health Insurance Program (SCHIP).

There are multiple pathways by which welfare reform may affect health-related outcomes. One pathway is through health insurance—reform leads to reductions in welfare participation, which is expected to reduce health insurance coverage (employer-provided coverage may increase but by less than Medicaid coverage declines). The other pathways are more indirect; for example, welfare reform may impact families' economic resources, time endowment, and levels of stress which may then affect health care utilization and health status.

The early studies on this issue documented very low rates of health insurance coverage following federal reform. For example, Bowen Garrett and John Holahan (2000) found that one year after leaving welfare, one-half of women and almost one-third of children are uninsured.[3] This "leaver" analysis provides an important profile of the well-being of families departing the welfare rolls. However, an analysis of welfare leavers is largely descriptive and not adequate for identifying the impact of welfare reform. There are many forces that can lead to transitions off welfare (for example, labor market opportunities, changes in living arrangements, and welfare reform). Leaver studies are not designed to separate out these forces and identify the impacts of welfare reform and, therefore, provide largely descriptive evidence.

The literature on the impacts of welfare reform on health includes nonexperimental estimates (typically state-panel models using variation in the timing and presence of reform across states) and experimental estimates (randomized experimental evaluations of state waiver programs). These two approaches have important and distinct advantages and disadvantages. Nonexperimental (or observational) studies have the advantage of measuring impacts on the overall population, but they are subject to concerns about identification due to sample selection and endogenous policies. Experimental studies have the advantage of randomization, but the results apply to the experimental context—typically one state, one set of policies, and one group of welfare recipients. Overall, a review of the literature shows that welfare reform led to reduction in health insurance coverage, with small and often insignificant impacts on health care utilization and health status. Some studies find evidence of a modest decrease in utilization and small changes in health behaviors. They suggest that welfare-to-work programs need not have large negative health effects.

We augment the literature review with an analysis of data from separate state welfare-reform experiments in Connecticut, Iowa, Florida, Minnesota, and Vermont. Each of these states represents reforms prior to TANF. However, all randomized experimental evaluation of welfare reform were of state waivers, while there were no evaluations of TANF. We present estimates of the impact of reform on health insurance, health utilization (child doctor or dentist visits and whether the child has a place to go for routine care), and health status (parent-rated child health status, whether the case head is at risk for depression, and whether the focal child scores poorly on a Behavioral Problem Index). These five states were chosen because their experimental evaluations provided the most comprehensive data on health and their welfare reform policies were the most similar to the eventual federal TANF policies. It is important to note, however, that our results reflect the specific policies that were implemented by these states and do not necessarily reflect "average" TANF policies. With that caveat, our analysis of these five states finds that reform led to small changes in health insurance coverage, mixed evidence on health care utilization, and suggestive evidence of improvements in child health status for children between two to nine years old at the beginning of the experiments.

An important drawback of this analysis and indeed much of the existing literature on welfare reform and health is that most of the available data is quite limited. The experimental literature, while able to avoid issues of selection bias that are common to observational studies, is restricted to looking at health outcomes about which information was collected during surveys administered to participants. These surveys tended to ask about health insurance coverage in some detail, and a number also collected information about some health outcomes. Yet the experimental surveys did not collect data on many other important health outcomes of interest, such as whether the children are suffering from developmental delays, asthma, or chronic ear conditions; whether the children or recipients are obese or overweight; whether recipients suffer from substance abuse or sexually transmitted diseases; whether the recipients have negative health behaviors such as smoking; and whether the recipients have chronic conditions such as asthma, hypertension, or diabetes. A number of health surveys (which could be used for nonexperimental analyses) do collect information on these outcomes and others of interest, but they either do not contain information allowing one to identify whether women are in a group likely to be affected by reform, do not contain information for a consistent panel of states and years spanning reform, or do not have large enough samples to plausibly identify the effects of reform. Consequently, we are left with the outcomes on which we and the previous literature have focused.

WELFARE REFORM IN THE 1990S

Beginning in the early 1990s, many states were granted waivers to make changes to their AFDC programs. About half of the states implemented some sort of welfare waiver between 1993 and 1995 (Office of the Assistant Secretary for Planning and Evaluation 2001). Following this period of state experimentation, the Personal Responsibility and Work Opportunity Reconciliation Act (PRWORA) was enacted in 1996, replacing AFDC with TANF. PRWORA originally indicated that all states had to have TANF programs in place by July 1, 1997, although subsequently this deadline was relaxed (Administration of Children and Families 2002). All states implemented PRWORA in a seventeen-month period between September 1996 and January 1998 (Crouse 1999; Administration for Children and Families 1997).

The main goals of welfare reform were to increase work, reduce dependency on welfare, reduce births outside marriage, and to increase the formation of two-parent families. While waiver and TANF policies varied considerably across states, the reforms were generally welfare tightening and pro-work. More specifically, the welfare-tightening elements of reform include work requirements, financial sanctions, time limits, family caps, and residency requirements.[4] The loosening aspects of reform include liberalized earnings disregards (which promote work by lowering the tax rate on earned income while on welfare), increased asset limits, increased transitional Medicaid coverage, and expanded welfare eligibility for two-parent families. Importantly, welfare reform—both the goals and resulting policies—had little directly to do with health or health insurance.

During this period of welfare reform, however, other policies expanded public health insurance for low-income families. Historically, eligibility for Medicaid for the nonelderly and nondisabled was tied directly to receipt of cash public assistance. In particular, the AFDC income-eligibility limits adopted by a state would also be used for Medicaid, and AFDC conferred automatic eligibility for Medicaid. Thus, a family that received AFDC benefits would also be eligible for health insurance through Medicaid. Conversely, if a family left AFDC, its members generally would lose Medicaid coverage.[5] However, in a series of federal legislative acts beginning in 1984, states were required to expand Medicaid coverage for infants, children, and pregnant women beyond the AFDC income limits, leading to large increases in eligibility (Gruber 1997). These are known as the poverty-related or Omnibus Reconciliation Act (OBRA) Medicaid expansions. By 2001, these expansions mandated that all children in families with income up to the federal poverty limit were eligible for Medicaid, provided that they met other requirements.

PRWORA further weakened the link between AFDC and Medicaid by requiring states to cover any family that meets the pre-PRWORA AFDC income, resource, and family composition eligibility guidelines (Haskins 2001). This so-called 1931 program (named after the relevant section of the Social Security Act, as amended by PRWORA) also allowed states to expand eligibility for parents beyond the 1996 AFDC and Medicaid limits. Anna Aizer and Jeffrey Grogger (2003) report that by 2001, about half of the states had taken advantage of this program and expanded Medicaid access for parents above the welfare income cutoffs.

In addition to the time limits, work requirements, and sanctions, PRWORA also contained language restricting immigrant access to means-tested transfer programs including Medicaid. Specifically, immigrants arriving after August 1996 (when the law was passed) are prohibited from receiving any means-tested transfers (including Medicaid) for five years. Initially the law also restricted access to immigrants arriving before 1996, but this was never enacted. In the wake of these policy changes and the likely confusion over the coverage of earlier arriving immigrants, Medicaid caseloads declined significantly for foreign-born individuals compared to natives (Borjas 2003; Kaushal and Kaestner 2005). As discussed by George Borjas (2003), many states responded by providing immigrant access to Medicaid using newly created, state-funded "fill-in" programs. These policy changes suggest that the impacts of welfare reform may be larger among foreign-born low-income families.

Lastly, in 1997, Congress established the State Children's Health Insurance program (SCHIP), which allows states to expand public health insurance to children beyond the then applicable income eligibility limits in TANF and Medicaid. The idea was to expand coverage for children in families whose family income was above the eligibility income limit for Medicaid but who were uninsured. States could choose to implement SCHIP by expanding Medicaid, by creating a separate SCHIP program, or by doing both. There were also SCHIP resources allocated for outreach to achieve higher take-up rates. The funding for the program came from state funds with matching funds from the federal government, although federal funds were limited to a fixed block grant. States were also allowed to charge premiums, with the amount capped as a share of income for the lowest income SCHIP recipients. This expansion ensured that the bulk of uninsured children in families with income up to 200 percent of the poverty level would be eligible for publicly funded health insurance; many states even expanded eligibility to income levels beyond 200 percent of poverty. The fact that the contraction of welfare programs took place during a time of expansion of public health insurance for children suggests a potential cushioning of any adverse impacts of welfare reform on children. For this reason, it is important to understand the impacts of SCHIP.

WELFARE REFORM AND EXPECTED IMPACTS ON HEALTH

Despite the lack of a direct connection between welfare reform and health, there are many indirect pathways through which welfare reform may affect health outcomes.

First, welfare reform reduces welfare caseloads, leading to a decline in Medicaid coverage. The AFDC caseload has declined more than 60 percent since its peak in 1994 (U.S. Department of Health and Human Services 2007).[6] During this time period, the number of nondisabled adults and children on Medicaid also fell. Between 1995 and 1997, the number of nondisabled adults on Medicaid fell by 10.6 percent, with larger reductions among cash welfare recipients (Ku and Bruen 1999). The non-cash-assistance Medicaid caseload (especially children), on the other hand, grew, reflecting the separation of AFDC eligibility from Medicaid eligibility.

This expected loss in public coverage may be offset by elevated rates of private coverage due to increases in mothers' employment or coverage from other family members (that is, a *crowd-in effect*). However, these low-skill workers are likely to be employed in industry-occupation cells with traditionally low rates of employer-provided health insurance (Currie and Yelowitz 2000). In sum, welfare reform is predicted to be associated with a decrease in Medicaid coverage, an increase in private insurance, and likely a decrease in overall insurance.

This pathway of decreased insurance coverage may lead to changes in health. For example, a decline in insurance may lead to less health service utilization; for example, it may lead to less preventive care and prenatal care (Nathan and Thompson 1999). This decline in health care utilization may subsequently impact health outcomes. Importantly, there is an ongoing debate about the magnitude of the causal effects of health insurance coverage on health. Most observational studies show a positive and significant association between health insurance and health. However, as summarized in the recent review by Helen Levy and David Meltzer (2004), these observational studies are limited due to issues with endogeneity and selection. Instead, these authors argue that the best evidence about a causal link between health insurance and health comes from the quasi-experimental analysis of government policy expansions and the RAND health insurance experiments.[7] These studies show a much weaker, but still a generally positive, link between health insurance and health compared to the observational studies. The positive link is stronger for more vulnerable or disadvantaged populations.[8]

Welfare reform may also impact families' economic resources. While the evidence is less clear on this topic, research suggests that welfare reform has led to an overall increase in the incomes of low-skill families.[9] However, Marianne Bitler, Jonah Gelbach, and Hilary Hoynes (2006) find that reform has heterogeneous impacts across the income distribution, and there is some evidence of reductions at the lowest income levels. These changes in a family's economic well-being could then have impacts on health care utilization and health status (as well as on health insurance coverage).

Furthermore, reform-induced increases in employment may lead to changes in a parents' time endowment, which in turn can affect choices about health care utilization, diet, and health (Haider, Jacknowitz, and Schoeni 2003). Welfare reform could also lead to increases (or decreases) in stress, which in turn can affect health.

Discussion of these pathways illustrates that the impacts of welfare reform on health insurance coverage and health care utilization are more direct than the impacts on health status. This interpretation is consistent with Michael Grossman's (2001) health production model. In particular, health is a durable capital stock that will change slowly with investment (that is, with time, nutrition, exercise, and health services). Health services, on the other hand, are investment goods consumed each period. Therefore they would be expected to change more quickly in response to changes in prices, income, and time constraints. This has important implications for how to interpret and what to expect from empirical analyses of welfare reform on health. We might expect a somewhat immediate impact of reform on health insurance, while it may take months or years for welfare reform to impact health status.

EMPIRICAL IDENTIFICATION OF THE EFFECTS OF WELFARE REFORM ON HEALTH

Three challenges to identifying the impact of TANF are often raised in the literature (Blank 2001). First, at the same time that welfare reform occurred, the American economy also boomed. As documented by James Hines, Hilary Hoynes, and Alan Krueger (2001), the economic expansion of the 1990s led to important gains for disadvantaged families, especially in the last years of the decade. For example, the unemployment rate for African Americans fell to the lowest level ever recorded, and low-skill groups experienced the first increase in real wages since the 1970s. These gains in the economic position of disadvantaged families may, of course, have independent impacts on health. Second, all states implemented TANF between September 1996 and January 1998. This relatively short implementation period leaves less scope for identifying impacts of TANF through differences in the timing of TANF implementation across states. Identifying the impacts of welfare waivers, however, is considerably more straightforward, as there is variation across states and over time in the implementation of waivers. Third, welfare reform is multidimensional and consists of many different policy changes. In the end, there is no single waiver program or TANF program; rather, there are fifty individual state TANF programs. This makes it difficult to learn about the importance of any specific policy change.

In the face of these challenges, there are several different methodologies used in the literature. The first and most common approach is nonexperimental or observational. A typical approach is to use state-panel models such as

$$y_{ist} = \alpha + \delta R_{st} + \beta X_{ist} + \gamma L_{st} + \theta_s + \nu_t + \varepsilon_{ist}. \tag{9.1}$$

Here the main data source is the outcome variable y which is measured by state s and time period t. These data might be state averages or data on individuals (denoted by i subscript) from a household survey. Welfare reform is captured by R_{st}, and the parameter of interest is the treatment effect δ. One might also include controls for state-level labor-market and other policy variables (L_{st}), individual covariates X_{ist} (if applicable), as well as state (θ_s) and time (ν_t) fixed effects. In one common version of this model, R_{st} is a dummy variable equal to one if waivers or TANF are implemented for this state-year observation. In this case, identification comes from variation in the presence and timing of reform across states.

Because of the lack of variation in the timing of TANF implementation across states, many studies extend the above model to a difference-in-difference model:

$$y_{ist} = \alpha + \delta_1 R_{st} + \delta_2 TREAT_{ist} * R_{st} + \delta_3 TREAT_{ist} + \beta X_{ist} + \gamma L_{st} + \theta_s + \nu_t + \varepsilon_{ist}. \tag{9.2}$$

The parameter of interest is here δ_2 and is identified using the difference in trends postreform between a treatment and control group. The treatment group identifies those likely to be impacted by welfare (for example, low-educated female heads of household and their children). Various control groups are used in the literature;

single women without children, higher-income single women with children, married women with children, single men. Other nonexperimental studies add variation in the waiver and TANF reform variables by using detailed characteristics across states such as the length of the time limit or the severity of the sanctions. One challenge for studies using these methods is correctly characterizing the many reforms that states implemented.

Another variation of the basic model above is to replace the reform variable R_{st} with a measure of the welfare caseload (or per capita caseload) in the state-year cell, C_{st}. This approach seeks to take advantage of the variation in the declines in welfare caseloads across states and over time. The literature has shown that welfare reform accounts for only part of the fall in caseloads; other important factors are labor-market opportunities and other policies such as the Earned Income Tax Credit (Council of Economic Advisers 1997, 1999; Wallace and Blank 1999; Ziliak et al. 2000; Klerman and Haider 2004). Thus, these studies also control for such factors. Studies that use welfare caseloads to summarize the effects of reform may miss effects of reform which do not result in caseload changes. Another possible problem with using caseloads to identify the causal impact of reform on other outcomes is that the caseload and the outcomes of interest may be affected by unobserved variables.

The second approach is experimental. By federal law, all states implementing welfare waivers were required to evaluate their waivers, mostly using experimental methods. In these experimental evaluations, individuals were randomly assigned into the treatment (welfare reform) and control (AFDC) groups. Using the data from these experiments, the treatment effect of reform can be simply calculated as the difference between mean outcomes in the treatment and control groups. Importantly, all experimental analyses relate to welfare waiver programs; there is no experimental evidence of the effects of state TANF programs.[10] Generally, welfare waivers were less punitive and less severe compared to the TANF policies. Time limits, for example, which are a central feature of TANF, were only used in a few state waiver programs (prominent examples include Connecticut and Florida). We would expect, therefore, that the impacts of state waivers would be smaller than the federal welfare reform which replaced AFDC with TANF.

There are also results from "leaver analyses," which consist of national or state-level studies that examine the characteristics of families leaving welfare. The leaver studies provide an accurate snapshot of the experiences of those families that have left welfare. However, there is no counterfactual in these studies (no control group, no before-period data, and no comparison to exits from welfare in the prereform period), and thus they cannot identify the impacts of welfare reform (Blank 2002). First, there is no way to identify why the families left welfare—was it due to welfare reform or to other factors? Second, a significant fraction of the decline in welfare caseloads is due to reductions in initial entry into welfare (Grogger, Haider, and Klerman 2003), and the leaver studies do not capture this group.

Overall, the experimental and nonexperimental approaches have advantages and disadvantages. Nonexperimental analyses have the advantage of being nationally representative, but the usual identification concerns exist. That is, underlying trends in the outcome variables of interest could lead to spurious estimates of policy effects. A further disadvantage of nonexperimental analyses, especially as it relates to health outcomes, is that one is limited by the available data at the state level. An observational analysis requires measuring the outcome variable y consistently across states and over time in a representative sample. Some household surveys such as the Current Population Survey (CPS) or the Survey of Income and Program Participation (SIPP) have the state and time coverage, but they offer very limited data beyond health insurance coverage (as is the case with CPS) or only ask about health outcomes intermittently (as is the case with SIPP, for which the health outcome data are collected in topical modules). A number of health surveys collect information on a much wider set of health outcomes; however, these either do not contain information allowing one to identify whether women are in a group likely to be affected by reform, do not contain information for a consistent panel of states and years spanning reform, limit public access to relevant geographic data, or do not have large enough samples to plausibly identify the effects of reform.

Experimental studies have the appeal of random assignment, but they have limitations such as the limited coverage of TANF policies (as opposed to waivers), the inability to obtain nationally representative estimates, and the inability to account for effects of changes in entry behavior that result from welfare reform. Further, as is often noted in discussions of experimental methods for evaluating the effects of programs, effects may differ when a small-scale program is ramped up to a larger scale. Evaluators may be better funded or have a strong incentive to ensure that program participants understand the rules of the treatment. This may not be the case when the program is implemented everywhere. An advantage of the experimental analyses in the context of this study is that many state welfare waiver experiments collected data that allow for a somewhat richer analysis of health outcomes than would be possible with the CPS, for example. However, the small sample sizes in these surveys are a limitation compared to the large sample sizes in typical nonexperimental analyses.

WHAT DO WE KNOW FROM THE EXISTING LITERATURE?

Our review summarizes evidence from both experimental and nonexperimental analyses.[11] We organize our summary into two sections: the first examines the impacts of welfare reform on health insurance, and the second examines the impacts of reform on health care utilization and health status.

The nonexperimental literature utilizes national survey data that allows for identification of state-year cells. Such national datasets include the Behavioral Risk Factor Surveillance System (BRFSS), CPS, National Health Insurance Survey (NHIS), SIPP, and Vital Statistics detailed natality files.[12] The main source of data for experimental evaluations of welfare waivers is state administrative data for women participating in the experiments. These data, for example, are used to calculate impacts of reform on employment, earnings, welfare use, public-assistance payments, and, in a few cases, Medicaid enrollment. Relevant for this project, however, these administrative data have (in some experiments) been augmented by surveys measuring additional family and child outcomes (including health insurance coverage, utilization, and health status). In addition to the state welfare experiments, we also draw on the experimental evaluation of the Canadian Self Sufficiency Project (SSP), which, like TANF, is an income-support program with a time limit. We discuss impacts of SSP here for two reasons: First, SSP was associated with larger cash increases during the treatment before time limits than were most American programs. Second, the SSP data cover a longer follow-up period than the American experimental data. Both of these features may make possible the detection of long-term health effects of SSP if they exist.

Health Insurance Coverage

Health insurance coverage is by far the most analyzed outcome in the welfare-reform and health literature. The studies analyze the impact of reform on public health insurance coverage (usually Medicaid, or, in some cases for children, Medicaid or SCHIP), private health insurance coverage (such as employer-provided coverage or individually purchased coverage), and any insurance coverage. Reform should be expected to lead to overall reductions in health insurance—through decreases in public coverage and increases in private coverage—as families move off welfare and into work.

Welfare Reform Led to Small Reductions in Health Insurance Coverage   The literature is generally consistent with the prediction that reform is associated with a reduction in health insurance coverage. Among the nonexperimental studies, Bitler, Gelbach, and Hoynes (2005) use the BRFSS and find that state waivers and TANF implementation led to reductions in any insurance coverage for single women, with the largest impacts for Hispanic single women. The study uses a state-pooled-panel model with dummies for waivers and TANF implementation; it estimates a difference-in-difference model (with married women as controls) to control for other contemporaneous impacts on health insurance. John Cawley, Mathis Schroeder, and Kosali Simon (2005, 2006) extend this work by examining effects of reform on monthly health insurance coverage using the SIPP. They find an increase in the propensity to be uninsured, with somewhat smaller effects for children compared to their mothers. Robert Kaestner and Neeraj Kaushal (2004) use the CPS to estimate a difference-in-difference model comparing single low-educated mothers and their children to low-educated single women without children and low-educated married women with children. They find that declines in the AFDC caseload are associated with reductions in Medicaid, increases in employer-provided health insurance, and overall increases in uninsurance for single mothers and their children. They measure welfare reform using the AFDC and TANF caseload (the idea being that reform leads to reductions in the caseload, which leads to changes in health insurance and other outcomes). These estimates may reflect factors other than reform that lead to changes in the caseload or may miss effects of reform not captured in caseload declines.

The results using household survey data are consistent with Medicaid caseload analyses. Leighton Ku and Bowen Garrett (2000) examine the impact of pre-PRWORA welfare waivers on Medicaid caseloads. They find that waivers led to (statistically insignificant) declines in the adult and child Medicaid caseload.

In contrast to the above studies, Thomas DeLeire, Judith Levine, and Helen Levy (2006) conclude that welfare reform leads to *increases* in health insurance coverage for low-educated women. They use the CPS to examine the impacts of waiver and TANF implementation. They argue that reform could lead to increases in insurance if there are spillover effects of reform on nonrecipients. Indeed, because of these possible spillovers, they consider the "treatment" group to be all women regardless of marriage or presence of children.[13]

Jeffrey Grogger, Lynn Karoly, and Jacob Klerman (2002) review the experimental literature and find small, typically insignificant, and somewhat mixed impacts of welfare reform on the health insurance coverage of adult recipients and their children. In these studies, surveys are used to measure health insurance coverage at some point after random assignment (typically three to four years, depending on the particular study). These results are not necessarily at odds with the nonexperimental literature. Recall that the welfare experiments evaluated state waiver programs that tended to be less severe (for example, few had time limits and sanctions were less severe) compared to the eventual TANF programs. This leads to smaller reductions in caseloads and, hence, smaller reductions in Medicaid.

Overall, the balance of evidence—especially when focusing on the impacts of TANF—is toward finding decreases in insurance following reform. It is difficult to compare specific estimates across the studies (due to different measurement of public coverage and differences in samples and control groups), but the measured impacts are consistently relatively small. For example, Bitler, Gelbach, and Hoynes (2005) find that TANF led to an insignificant 4 percentage point reduction in insurance coverage among low-educated single women with children. This is in stark contrast to the very large rates of uninsurance reported in the leaver studies (Garrett and Holahan 2000). However, leaver studies are not useful for estimating the impacts of the policy change that is the focus of this study.

Medicaid Expansions and SCHIP Introduction Mitigated Declines in Insurance Coverage
Recall that concurrent with welfare reform there was a widespread expansion of public health insurance for low-income children through expansions in Medicaid and the introduction of SCHIP. The Medicaid expansions, which took place between the mid-1980s and the mid-1990s, led to relatively large increases in health insurance coverage among children in low-income families (Gruber and Simon 2007). The evidence suggests, however, that expanding public health insurance leads to a significant "crowd-out" of private coverage leading to smaller reductions in the uninsured than might be expected. Further, these *crowd-out effects* are larger higher up the income distribution among those eligible. SCHIP also leads to

increases in insurance coverage, but the magnitude is somewhat lower than the Medicaid expansions (Bansak and Raphael 2007; Cunningham, Hadley, and Reschovsky 2002; Gruber and Simon 2007; Hudson, Selden, and Banthin 2005; Lo Sasso and Buchmueller 2004; Duderstadt at al. 2006; Wolfe et al. 2006).

While most of expansions targeted children, the Medicaid 1931 program allowed states to expand eligibility for parents beyond the pre-PRWORA AFDC income eligibility limits. Aizer and Grogger (2003), as well as Susan Busch and Noelia Duchovny (2005), use the CPS to examine parental Medicaid expansions through the 1931 program. Aizer and Grogger (2003) find that these Medicaid expansions led to increases in health insurance coverage of women (with some crowd-out of private-insurance coverage). They also find that expanding parental coverage leads to increases in the health insurance coverage of children; this possibly arises from an increase in benefits relative to costs associated with taking up coverage.

It seems clear that in the absence of these expansions to public health insurance programs, any possibly negative impacts of welfare reform on health insurance (along with any commensurate impacts on health outcomes) would be larger in magnitude. It is also important that any analysis of welfare reform include controls for these state-level expansions to health insurance (Bitler, Gelbach, and Hoynes 2005).

Welfare Reform Led to Larger Reductions in Health Insurance Among Immigrants PRWORA imposed a five-year waiting period for TANF and Medicaid for new immigrants (those arriving after 1996). It is widely believed that there was confusion about this provision; in particular, it was unclear whether it applied to all immigrants. This suggests that the impacts of reform would be larger among the foreign-born population. Bitler, Gelbach, and Hoynes (2005), Namratha Kandula and colleagues (2004), and Neeraj Kaushal and Robert Kaestner (2005, 2007) show that welfare reform led to larger reductions in health insurance among the foreign-born or Hispanic populations compared to the entire low-income population. Borjas (2003), on the other hand, finds that more restrictive Medicaid policies did not reduce health insurance coverage among immigrants, because the loss in public coverage was offset by increases in private-insurance coverage. Heather Royer (2005) finds some evidence that more restrictive policies have reduced public coverage, but her findings abour overall coverage are inconclusive.[14]

Health Utilization and Health Outcomes

Far fewer studies provide evidence on health care use and health outcomes. The BRFSS allows for measuring outcomes for adult women. It includes health care utilization (for example, it includes indicators for recent checkups, Pap smears, breast exams, and whether one needed care but found it unaffordable), health behaviors (for example, smoking, drinking, and exercise), and health status (for example, obesity, lost work days, and self-reported health status). Another source of nonexperimental data is the detailed natality files, which, as a census of birth certificates, includes data on prenatal care and birth outcomes (for example, birth weight and gestation). Many state waiver experiments include surveys designed to obtain richer family and child outcomes. The NHIS also collects detailed health information, but researchers must use restricted-use data to link these outcomes with state-level data on TANF or caseloads. Individual-level panel data sets such as the Fragile Families and Child Wellbeing Study collect detailed health data but follow a single cohort (in this example, the cohort is parents giving birth in hospitals with a large share of nonmarital births).

Welfare Reform Had Small, Mixed Impacts on Health Care Utilization and Outcomes
The nonexperimental literature finds small, mixed, and often insignificant impacts on health. Janet Currie and Jeffrey Grogger (2002), as well as Robert Kaestner and Won Chan Lee (2005), use the detailed natality data to show that declines in welfare caseloads during the waiver period (Currie and Grogger) and TANF period (Kaestner and Lee) are associated with declines in prenatal care and small increases in the incidence of low birth weight for low-education women.

Bitler, Gelbach, and Hoynes (2005) use the BRFSS to show significant but small reductions in health care utilization, such as the probability of having gotten a checkup, Pap smear, or breast exam in the last year. They also find (insignificant) increases in the likelihood of needing care but finding it unaffordable. Kaestner and Elizabeth Tarlov (2006) also use the BRFSS and find no association between reductions in welfare caseloads and health behaviors (smoking, drinking, diet, and exercise) or health status (weight, days in poor health, and general health status).

The experimental estimates of the impact of reform on health are summarized in several reviews (Grogger and Karoly 2005; Grogger, Karoly, and Klerman 2002; Morris et al. 2001; Gennetian et al. 2002). (Estimates are also available from the final reports for each state's experimental evaluation.) Much of the experimental evidence examines the impact on children ages five to twelve years.[15] Health-utilization measures include when the child last saw a dentist or doctor, whether any children have had emergency room visits since random assignment, whether the child has a place to go for routine care, and whether various types of medical care were unaffordable. Health outcomes include parent-rated child general health status as well as indexes of maternal depression and child behavior problems. The estimates from these child surveys are mixed, with an equal number of unfavorable and favorable impacts of reform on health (Grogger and Karoly 2005). The Canadian SSP study examines somewhat different outcomes, focusing on injuries, long-term health limitations, parents' emotional well-being, and general health. The impacts of SSP are quite consistently positive; however, few are statistically significant.

The Impacts Varied by Demographic Group and by Type of Welfare Reform   Bitler, Gelbach, and Hoynes (2005) find that TANF led to larger reductions in health care utilization (that is, recent checkups, Pap smears, and breast exams) among Hispanic women compared to similar black and white women. Much of the other evidence that varies by demographic group or type of reform compares immigrants to other women (Kaushal and Kaestner 2005, 2007). Jean Knab, Irv Garfinkel, and Sara McLanahan (chapter 10, this volume) study the effects of reform on unmarried mothers using the Fragile Families and Child Wellbeing study. They look at a range of maternal health and health behaviors, but their analysis is limited by the fact that the data follow a single cohort of mothers in eighteen cities over time.

The experimental studies of child well-being find that any improvements in behaviors tend to be concentrated among young children, while there are more likely to be negative impacts on behaviors for adolescent children (Morris et al. 2001; Gennetian et al. 2002). The experimental literature also finds that improvements are more likely to be present with welfare reforms that lead to increases in income (such as those with generous earnings disregards). Examples of more generous reforms include the state reforms in Connecticut and Minnesota, as well as the Canadian SSP program.

ILLUSTRATING IMPACTS OF REFORM FROM EXPERIMENTAL DATA

To get a better understanding of the results from the literature, here we present our own estimates on the impact of reform from five state welfare waiver evaluations. Each state waiver (but none of the TANF programs) was evaluated using randomized experiments. Further, state waivers varied significantly in terms of their policy scope, and many of the state waivers did not include time limits or enhanced earnings disregards (which were two of the key policies included in TANF).

Here, we analyze public-use data from state waiver experiments in five states: Connecticut (CT-JF), Florida (FL-FTP), Iowa (IA-FIP), Minnesota (MN-MFIP), and Vermont (VT-WRP). The primary reason for choosing these states was that they were among a relatively small number of states whose evaluations include data on health. Most state evaluations relied on administrative data on employment and welfare participation, while these five states (and a few others) supplemented this administrative data by fielding a survey to a subset of treatment and control participants. This is the main source of data used for the literature on family and child well-being (Gennetian et al. 2002; Morris et al. 2001). We chose to study Connecticut and Florida in particular because they included time limits as part of their waiver experiments. Overall, these five states provide a good range of welfare-reform policies: they range from more generous (CT-JF and MN-MFIP) to less generous (FL-FTP and VT-WRP), and they include states with time limits (CT-JF and FL-FTP) and without time limits (IA-FIP, MN-MFIP, and VT-WRP). This is useful for evaluating alternative sorts of welfare reforms. However, they are less useful purely as a TANF evaluation exercise.

The outcomes we explore include health insurance coverage, health care usage (that is, whether the child has seen a doctor in the past two years, whether the child has seen a dentist in the past two years, whether the child has a place to go for routine care, and whether the family is not able to afford the doctor or dentist), and health status (that is, parent-rating of the child overall health status, whether the mother is at risk for depression, and whether the focal child scores poorly according to a Behavioral Problem Index). Table 9.3 contains information on the outcomes by state of experiment. While some of the experimental surveys collected other health or health related outcomes (such as whether a child had been to the emergency room or clinic since randomization, whether a child had had any accidents since randomization, or whether the family was food insecure), we do not show results for these additional outcomes because these data are not available for all the experiments, the events varied little across the groups, or the events were very rare in the population.

Description of the Policies in the Five States

Table 9.1 presents the policies for AFDC and the welfare waivers in the five states (AFDC is the control group program in each case). We document three central policies that are required in TANF programs: time limits, work requirements, and financial sanctions. We also include earnings disregards, as quite commonly they were made more generous in TANF programs and they are very important for determining how reform affects family income.

Very few welfare waivers included time limits. In our set of states, CT-JF and FL-FTP have time limits. There are several other states that included time limits, one of which—Indiana—had public-use data available. However, we excluded Indiana's reform due to limited data on health outcomes. All of the state waivers had work requirements that were stricter than the preexisting AFDC program. The states varied in terms of who was exempt from work requirements (typically, this is based on the age of the youngest child in the family), as well as whether the program was focused on employment (having a "work first" policy) or instead aimed recipients toward education and training.

The earnings disregards determine the rate at which benefits are reduced as earnings increase. In the AFDC program, after three months of working and receiving welfare, all earnings over a basic deduction level were "taxed" at 100 percent. This high benefit reduction rate played a central role in the adverse work incentives in the prereform system. All of the states (except VT-WRP) offered more generous disregard policies than did AFDC. The most generous states in our sample are CT-JF (where all earnings below the poverty line were disregarded) and MN-MFIP. FL-FTP and IA-FIP had somewhat less generous reforms. Highlighting the earnings disregards is important because this liberalization leads not only to increases in benefits, but also to an increase in the break-even income point (which implies increases in welfare participation, at least before time limits hit). Thus, we have an opposite prediction for the effects of reform in the short run compared to our long-run prediction of reform causing a decrease in welfare participation.

Financial sanctions (which are triggered when a client does not comply with the

TABLE 9.1 / Policies in Welfare-Reform Experiments and Preexisting AFDC Program

	Connecticut Jobs First (JF)	Florida Family Transition Program (FTP)	Minnesota Family Investment Program (MFIP)	Iowa Family Investment Program (FIP)	Vermont Welfare Restructuring Project (WRP)
General	Two-tiered system based on job readiness	Two-tiered system based on job readiness	Two-tiered system for long-term and short-term recipients. Two treatments-incentives only and full treatment	Control group subject to TANF rules in 1997	Two treatments: incentives only and full (we only consider full treatment)
Time limit	Twenty-one months with six-month extensions	Twenty-four months (of every sixty) for job ready; thirty-six months (of every seventy-two) for others	None	None	None
Work requirements	Mandatory work first, exempt if child younger than one year	Mandatory job search and employment for job ready; education and training for others; exempt if child younger than six months	Mandatory employment and training for long-term; exempt if child younger than one year	Employment and training; exempt if child younger than six months (eliminated in 1997)	Half-time work required after thirty months on aid

Earnings disregards	All earnings disregarded up to poverty line	$200 + 50% of remaining earnings	38% of earnings disregarded up to 140% of poverty; maximum grant increased by 20% if working	40% of earnings disregarded (all earnings disregarded for first four months of work if "new worker" through 1997)	$150 + 25% of remaining earnings
Financial sanctions	Cut in grant for first and second offense; three month suspension for third	Adult portion of grant eliminated until compliant (until June 1997)	10% reduction in grant	Three months reduced benefits, six months no benefits	None
Selected other policies	Two years transitional Medicaid	One year transitional Medicaid	One year transitional Medicaid	One year transitional Medicaid	Three years transitional Medicaid
Benefit level, family of three at start of experiment	$636	$303	$532	$426	$640

Sources: Bloom et al. (2000, 2002); Fraker et al. (2002); Gennetian, Miller, and Smith (2005); Scrivener et al. (2002).

work requirements or other rules) also varied across the states, with the most stringent policy in FL-FTP. Finally, the pre-existing AFDC policy provided twelve months of transitional Medicaid assistance to families leaving welfare. This was expanded by CT-JF (to two years) and VT-WRP (to three years). The final row of the table shows how the states vary in terms of the level of the maximum welfare grant at the time of random assignment. FL-FTP and IA-FIP have less generous maximum grants while CT-JF's and VT-WRP's grants are quite generous.

The experiments in VT-WRP and MN-MFIP had two treatments: incentives only and full treatment. The incentives-only policies included the enhanced earnings disregards but not the work requirements. In our analysis below, we analyze both treatments in MN-MFIP, but for VT-WRP we present the full treatment only. (The VT-WRP incentives-only program was only mildly more generous than the preexisting AFDC program, and thus would not be expected to have significantly different impacts than AFDC.) It is also important to note that FL-FTP had a two-tiered policy that assigned one treatment "job ready" (which included a shorter time limit and a work-first employment program) and another "non–job ready" (which included a longer time limit and more emphasis on education and training). We evaluate the average treatment effect across both FL-FTP groups.

Overall, CT-JF and FL-FTP are the most "TANF-like" of our sample programs due to the presence of the time limit. CT-JF and MN-MFIP are the states whose waivers were most likely to lead to increases in income and welfare use (at least before time limits bind in CT-JF) due to the enhanced earnings disregards. VT-WRP was probably the most "gentle" of the reforms, with a weaker work requirement, no time limit, and the longest transitional Medicaid benefits. Again, there is an important caveat: these states provide a good range of possible welfare reform policies but are less useful as a pure TANF evaluation exercise.

Description of Evaluations and Our Samples in the Five States

Table 9.2 describes the details of each of the five experiments and the samples that we use in our analysis. We begin with the timing of the experiment (random assignment and follow-up period), the geographic range of the experiment (statewide or partial state), and the sample size for the single-parent component of the evaluation (used in the final reports in each state). Most of the state caseloads consist primarily of single-parent families, and this is reflected in the evaluations that also primarily focus on single-parent families.

All of the impacts on health come from the surveys which are given to a (random) subset of the full sample.[16] We indicate in table 9.2 the timing of the surveys, the cohorts that faced the surveys, and the response rate on the surveys. The surveys tend to be fielded to specific cohorts between three and four years after random assignment. For example, in CT-JF there is survey data on 2,424 single-parent recipients who entered the experiment between April 1996 and February 1997. This number is a bit more than half of the full sample size for the evaluation. The information on health comes from the adult survey and the focal-child survey (with the exception being VT-WRP, which does not have a focal-child survey). The focal child is a child in the family who is between the ages of five and twelve at the time of the survey. Only one child is chosen as the focal child (randomly if there is more than one child of the correct age), and no child-survey information exists if there is no child in that age range. This explains why the number of observations for the child survey is less than the number for the adult survey.[17]

It is important to note that the timing of the survey (at three to four years after random assignment) is rather medium term. First, we might not expect much to change until after the time limits, which in the case of FL-FTP (and to a lesser extent in the case of CT-JF) are first reached close to the survey dates. Further, to comprehensively understand the impact of welfare reform on health status, we need to use data that span a very long follow-up period (which these surveys do not). On the other hand, we may expect that health insurance (and probably health care utilization) will respond more immediately. However, the expansions in transitional Medicaid assistance in several of these states may dampen any negative impacts on health insurance.

We also indicate in the table the samples that we use in our analysis. We have focused on samples of parents who were single at the time of random assignment.[18] For some states, this is simply the full sample (CT-JF and FL-FTP), as the public-use data are only for single parents. In MN-MFIP, we present estimates for single parents who were long-term welfare recipients living in urban counties. This is the group that was highlighted in the state's final report.[19] Because we consider both incentives only as well as full treatment in MN-MFIP, we report sample sizes for both treatments. We chose our IA-FIP sample to include single females in early cohorts.[20] Finally, for VT-WRP, we include only those receiving the "full" treatment.

A list of the outcome variables and how they are defined in each sample is provided in table 9.3.

Results

We present our results in six figures. In each case, we present an unconditional "percent effect" estimator (this is simply one hundred times the treatment-group mean minus the control-group mean divided by the control-group mean). This is weighted to be representative of the full experimental population at that point in time where sampling probabilities varied (for CT-JF, IA-FIP, and MN-MFIP). An alternative estimator, used often in the evaluation literature, is the standardized "effect size" (this is the treatment-group mean minus the control-group mean divided by the standard deviation of the control group). For those who prefer that measure, we present companion tables for each of the figures that present the effect size (as well as the difference, standard error of the difference [calculated to be robust to heteroskedasticity], the control-group mean, and the number of observations). Note that in our experiment, there is no need to differentiate between intent to treat and average treatment effects. Everyone in the treatment group is treated:

(text continues on page 255)

TABLE 9.2 / Welfare-Reform Experiments and Samples

	Connecticut Jobs First (JF)	Florida Family Transition Program (FTP)	Minnesota Family Investment Program (MFIP)	Iowa Family Investment Program (FIP)	Vermont Welfare Restructuring Project (WRP)
Timing of experiment (RA: random assignment FO: follow-up)	RA: 1/1996 to 2/1997 FO: 4 years	RA: 5/1994 to 2/1995 FO: 4 years	RA: 4/1994 to 3/1996 (urban counties through Q3 1995) FO: 2 to 4 years (through 6/1998)	RA: 9/1993 to 3/1996 FO: 6 to 7 years	RA: 6/1994 to 12/1996 FO: 6 years
Geographic range	Statewide waiver Evaluation in two offices	Partial state waiver Evaluation in one county	Partial state waiver Evaluation in seven counties (three urban counties)	Statewide waiver Evaluation in nine counties	Statewide waiver Evaluation in six districts
Sample size for evaluation	4,803 single-parent cases	2,815 single-parent cases	9,217 single-parent cases, 2,615 long-term urban recipients	7,823 single-parent cases	5,469 single-parent cases, 4,381 single parents for full WRP
Timing of survey	Collected three years after RA to cohort entering experiment between 4/1996 and 2/1997	Collected four years after RA to cohort entering experiment between 8/1994 and 2/1995	Collected three years after RA to cohort entering experiment between 4/1994 and 10/1994	Five to six years after RA to cohorts entering before 4/1996 for recipients	Collected forty-two months after RA to cohortentering experiment between 10/1994 and 6/1995

	All single-parent cases	All single-parent cases	Long-term single-parent recipients in incentives-only urban group (on welfare at least twenty-four of past thirty-six months): N = 1,769; Long-term single-parent recipients in full urban group: N = 1,780	Single females eighteen and older or sixteen to eighteen at RA with a pre-school child: N = 1,996; (Note: survey sample as here completing survey between four years, ten months to five years, eleven months after RA)	Full-WRP single-parent: cases, N = 4,381
Survey Response rate	80%	80%	80%	72%	80%
Maximum number of observations when using adult survey data	2,424	1,729	718 (incentives only) 724 (full MFIP)	1,201	842
Maximum number of observations when using focal-child survey data	1,469	1,103	573 (incentives only) 587 (full MFIP)	683	NA (no focal-child survey)

Source: Bloom et al. (2000, 2002); Fraker et al. (2002); Gennetian, Miller, and Smith (2005); and Scrivener et al. (2002).

TABLE 9.3 / Construction of Health Outcomes

	Connecticut Jobs First (JF)	Florida Family Transition Program (FTP)	Minnesota Family Investment Program (MFIP)	Iowa Family Investment Program (FIP)	Vermont Welfare Restructuring Project (WRP)
1. Insurance coverage (Figure 9.3 for head and 9.4 for children)					
Public health insurance (month before survey)	Adult head covered by public insurance. Any child of head covered by public insurance	Same as CT-JF	Same as CT-JF	NA	Same as CT-JF
Other non-public health insurance (month before survey)	Adult head has no public coverage and has some other coverage	Same as CT-JF	Same as CT-JF	NA	Same as CT-JF
Any health insurance (month before survey)	Adult head has public or non-public coverage. Any child of head has some coverage	Same as CT-JF	Same as CT-JF	NA	Same as CT-JF
Ever no coverage (any period of no coverage since random assignment)	Adult head had at least one spell of no coverage. Any child had at least one spell of no coverage	Same as CT-JF	Same as CT-JF	NA	NA

2. Health care utilization for focal child sample (child aged five to twelve in household) (Figure 9.5)			
Dentist visit past two years	Focal child had a dental visit during two years preceding survey	Same as CT-JF	Same as CT-JF	NA
Doctor visit past two years	Focal child had a doctor visit during two years preceding survey	Same as CT-JF	Same as CT-JF	NA
Place for routine care	Focal child has place to go for routine care	Same as CT-JF	Same as CT-JF	NA
Family cannot afford dentist	For focal-child sample families, someone needed to see a dentist during past year but could not afford to do so	Same as CT-JF	Same as CT-JF	NA
Family cannot afford doctor	For focal-child sample families, someone needed to see a doctor during past year but could not afford to do so	Same as CT-JF	Same as CT-JF	NA

TABLE 9.3 / (continued)

	Connecticut Jobs First (JF)	Florida Family Transition Program (FTP)	Minnesota Family Investment Program (MFIP)	Iowa Family Investment Program (FIP)	Vermont Welfare Restructuring Project (WRP)
3. Child and mother health outcomes for focal child sample (child aged five to twelve in household) (Figure 9.6)					
Mother at risk for depression	Mother has score of 16 or higher on 20-item Center for Epidemiological Studies Depression Scale (worst score is 60)	Same as CT-JF	Same as CT-JF	Same as CT-JF	NA
Child behavioral problem index in top 25th	Focal child's Behavioral Problem Index was in the worst 25 percentile range	Same as CT-JF	Same as CT-JF	Same as CT-JF	NA
Focal child has excellent or very good health	Focal child health is excellent or very good (rather than good, fair, or poor)	Same as CT-JF	Same as CT-JF	Same as CT-JF	NA

Sources: Authors' compilation of reports and public use data documentation.

everyone faces the new welfare-reform program. This characteristic is in contrast to, for example, the Moving to Opportunity Program, where the treatment is voluntary (Kling, Liebman, and Katz 2007).[21]

To begin, figure 9.1 presents the impacts of welfare reform on quarterly employment, quarterly welfare participation, and quarterly income. These estimates are important "first-stage" outcomes. For example, we may expect states with smaller reductions in welfare participation to have smaller reductions in health insurance coverage. Treatment-group members in states whose reforms led to large increases in income may show fewer adverse or more beneficial health outcomes compared to treatment-group members in states whose reforms led to decreases in income.

Figure 9.1 (and the companion table, table 9.4) presents these first-stage outcomes measured at the quarter that the survey was fielded (outcomes are not available for IA-FIP).[22] Information about employment and welfare participation at the time of the survey may present an incomplete picture of these important first-stage outcomes. For example, it may be important to know about longer-term welfare and employment exposure to understand impacts on health measured at the time of the survey. Figure 9.2 and table 9.5 provide a more comprehensive characterization of these impacts by presenting differences (between the treatment and control groups) in the outcomes averaged over all quarters between random assignment and the time of the survey. While an argument could be made in support of either time frame, we focus on the entire period up to the survey to reflect the fact that the health care utilization data refer to some look-back period and the health status variables are stock measures that adjust over a longer time period.

Figures 9.1 and 9.2 consist of three panels, where each panel corresponds to a different outcome: quarterly employment, welfare participation, and income (which includes earnings, cash assistance, and food stamps, as well as for MN-MFIP only General Assistance). Within each panel, we present percent effects for each of the states for which the outcome is available. There are a maximum of six estimates—one each for CT-JF, FL-FTP, IA-FIP, and VT-WRP, and two for MN-MFIP (incentives-only treatment and full treatment). Each estimate is shown as a bar; at the end of the bar we provide the percent effect along with the significance of the treatment control differences. (* denotes significant at the 10 percent level, ** significant at the 5 percent level, and *** significant at the 1 percent level.) Later figures differ only in how many panels are presented. The sample for the estimates in figures 9.1 and 9.2 is persons completing the survey who also have administrative data for all three outcomes.[23]

The results for figure 9.1 show that at the time of the survey, employment is higher in all states, with significant increases in CT-JF, VT-WRP, and MN-MFIP-Full. Welfare participation is significantly lower in CT-JF and FL-FTP, reflecting the period after the time limit. MN-MFIP shows higher welfare participation and higher income, reflecting the generous reform without time limits.

The results for figure 9.2, reflecting the average impact during the period between random assignment and the survey, show that all of the programs led to statistically significant increases in quarterly employment relative to AFDC. Effects on employment seem to be larger in the states with more generous earnings disre-

FIGURE 9.1 / Impacts of Welfare Reform on Employment, Welfare, and Income from Experimental Studies, Outcomes Measured at the Quarter of Survey (Percent Effects)

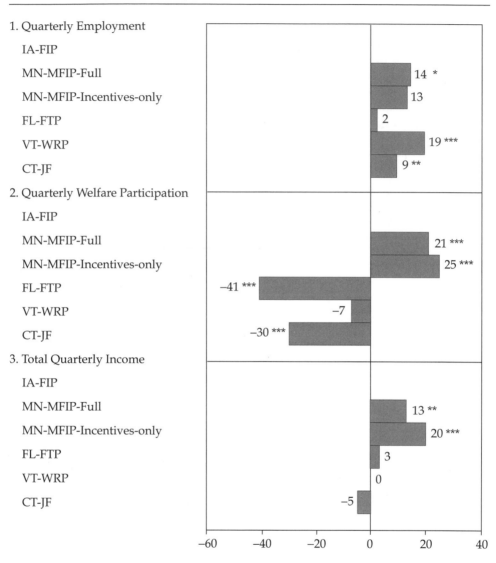

Source: Authors' compilation of public use data.
Note: The impacts are reported the outcomes at the quarter when the survey was conducted. For CT-JF, the survey was done thirty-six months after random assignment began; for VT-WRP, forty-two months; for FL-FTP, forty-eight months; for MN-MFIP, thirty-six months; and for IA-FIP, five to six years. Effect sizes reported are the treatment-control difference divided by the control mean. Significance levels (*** 1 percent, ** 5 percent, and * 10 percent) are for treatment-control differences.

TABLE 9.4 \ Impacts on Employment, Welfare, and Income, Quarter of Survey

	Difference	Std. Err., Difference	Mean (Controls)	Std. Dev. (Controls)	Percent Effect	Effect Size	N
1. Quarterly Employ- ment							
IA-FIP	NA						
MN-MFIP-Full	0.071*	0.040	0.50	0.50	14.13%	0.142	724
MN-MFIP-Incentives	0.064	0.041	0.50	0.50	12.72%	0.128	718
FL-FTP	0.009	0.024	0.54	0.50	1.69%	0.018	1,729
VT-WRP	0.102***	0.034	0.53	0.50	19.28%	0.204	842
CT-JF	0.050**	0.022	0.57	0.50	8.69%	0.100	2,414
2. Quarterly Welfare Receipt							
IA-FIP	NA						
MN-MFIP-Full	0.117***	0.040	0.56	0.50	20.97%	0.235	724
MN-MFIP-Incentives	0.137***	0.039	0.56	0.50	24.65%	0.276	718
FL-FTP	−0.082***	0.017	0.20	0.40	−40.77%	−0.204	1,729
VT-WRP	−0.029	0.034	0.42	0.49	−6.86%	−0.058	842
CT-JF	−0.121***	0.021	0.40	0.49	−30.26%	−0.248	2,414
3. Average Quarterly Income							
IA-FIP	NA						
MN-MFIP-Full	337.97**	146.04	2616.34	1829.27	12.92%	0.185	724
MN-MFIP-Incentives	512.71***	158.42	2616.34	1829.27	19.60%	0.280	718
FL-FTP	49.53	89.20	1799.48	1759.93	2.75%	0.028	1,729
VT-WRP	2.26	129.79	2527.20	1869.25	0.09%	0.001	842
CT-JF	−144.57	107.24	2974.01	2384.00	−4.86%	−0.061	2,414

Source: Authors' compilations of public use data.
Note: Shown are average quarterly employment rates, averages for any cash welfare receipt during quarter (to be comparable to the employment rates), and average quarterly income (cash welfare plus food stamps plus general assistance [MN only] plus earnings) for the quarter during which the survey was done (except for IA where we do not report values because no quarterly number is available). Statistics are for all observations completing the adult survey that also had data for all the outcomes. Numbers are weighted to be representative of survey design where relevant. Standard errors are robust to heteroskedasticity. Percent effect is one hundred times the treatment-control difference divided by control mean, effect size is treatment-control difference divided by control standard deviation. Significance levels (*** 1 percent, ** 5 percent, and * 10 percent) are for treatment-control differences.

gards (MN-MFIP and CT-JF). Welfare participation is significantly higher than under AFDC in MN-MFIP and somewhat higher in CT-JF, reflecting these states' more generous disregards; in the case of CT-JF, it also reflects the fact that more of the period was before the time limits. Welfare participation is significantly lower in FL-FTP.[24] Finally, panel 3 presents impacts on quarterly income from administrative sources. Total quarterly income was significantly higher for the treatment-group members in CT-JF and MN-MFIP, and it was approximately the same for the other states.

These findings may suggest various patterns for the impacts on health insurance coverage, health care utilization, and health status, depending on the importance of the various pathways for reform to affect these outcomes. For example, if the most important factor leading to public-insurance coverage is ongoing welfare participation, figures 9.1 and 9.2 suggest that we would find increases in coverage with reform for MN-MFIP and possibly for CT-JF. If, instead, employment is important, there are other implications. We should point out again that increases in welfare participation are not generally expected with TANF. This difference between welfare participation in the experiments compared with what we expect from TANF reflects the fact that only two of our states have time limits; furthermore, CT-JF (one of the two time-limit programs) is highly unusual in its generous earnings disregard and extension of the transitional Medicaid benefits. For those most interested in evaluating TANF, the results for FL-FTP are the most relevant.

Figure 9.3 and table 9.6 present the estimates of the effect of reform on the head of household's health insurance coverage. Reform led to increases in public-insurance coverage in MN-MFIP and CT-JF—this seems to be a direct result of longer stays on welfare (as shown in figure 9.2). Public-insurance coverage fell (though not significantly) in the other states. The bottom line is that reform leads to a significant increase in the head of household's overall insurance coverage in CT-JF, an insignificant increase for MN-MFIP, and negative, small, and insignificant effects for the other states. One interesting outcome available in some states is the presence of spells of uninsurance since the time of random assignment. This outcome shows large and significant decreases (a positive outcome) for MN-MFIP, perhaps reflecting increased welfare participation (as shown in figures 9.1 and 9.2).

The results for children's insurance coverage, presented in figure 9.4 and table 9.7, show small (1 to 2 percent) and insignificant impacts on any insurance coverage. Similar to the results for adults, any insurance and public-insurance coverage increase for CT-JF and MN-MFIP (as well as for IA-FIP) and decrease for the other states (VT-WRO and FL-FTP). However, the effects are smaller and fewer are significant compared to the adults. We would expect smaller impacts on child coverage given the other available public-insurance programs.[25] Again, the measure of any spells of uninsurance for any child shows positive effects for Minnesota (that is, negative estimates).

Figure 9.5 and table 9.8 present estimates for utilization, access, and affordability of care for the sample of focal children ages five to twelve (and for their families). Few of the estimates are significant, and for most variables there are an equal number of positive and negative estimates. For example, the variable "focal child has seen a doctor in the past two years" has one significant positive estimate; the rest are insignificant and very close to zero. There are some large negative estimates for the outcome "someone in the family could not afford to see a dentist or doctor." However, none of these are significant. Further, one might expect smaller decreases (or increases) in utilization in states with smaller decreases (or increases) in insurance. No such pattern emerges from this figure.

Finally, figure 9.6 and table 9.9 present the results for health outcomes for the focal-child sample, including the mother's risk for depression (a positive effect is

(*text continues on page 264*)

FIGURE 9.2 / Impacts of Welfare Reform on Employment, Welfare, and Income from Experimental Studies, Averages from Random Assignment to Quarter of Survey (Percent Effects)

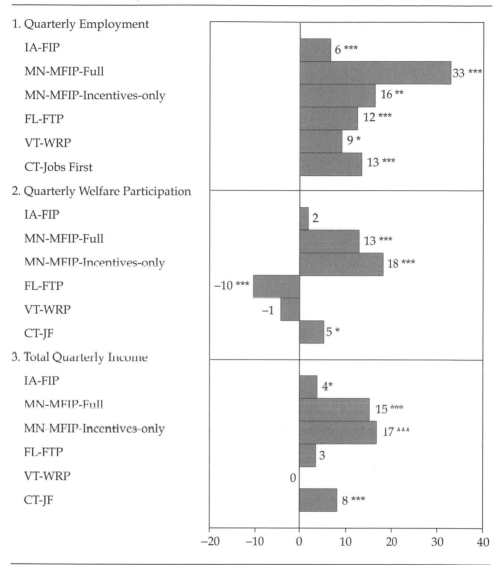

Source: Authors' compilation of public use data.
Note: The impacts are reported for quarterly averages from the time of random assignment through the quarter when the survey was conducted. For CT-JF, the survey was done thirty-six months after random assignment began; for VT-WRP, forty-two months; for FL-FTP, forty-eight months; for MN-MFIP, thirty-six months; and for IA-FIP, five to six years (we report the six-year average). Effect sizes reported are the treatment-control difference divided by the control mean. Significance levels (*** 1 percent ** 5 percent, and * 10 percent) are for treatment control differences.

TABLE 9.5 / Impacts on Employment, Welfare, and Income, Averaged over Period from
Random Assignment to Survey

	Difference	Std. Err., Difference	Mean (Controls)	Std. Dev. (Controls)	Percent Effect	Effect Size	N
1. Quarterly employment							
IA-FIP	0.033***	0.010	0.52	0.35	6.37%	0.095	7,823
MN-MFIP-Full	0.132***	0.029	0.40	0.36	32.92%	0.372	724
MN-MFIP-Incentives	0.065**	0.030	0.40	0.36	16.17%	0.183	718
FL-FTP	0.058***	0.016	0.47	0.34	12.36%	0.169	1,729
VT-WRP	0.043*	0.025	0.46	0.37	9.28%	0.116	842
CT-JF	0.067***	0.017	0.51	0.38	13.16%	0.174	2,397
2. Quarterly cash welfare receipt							
IA-FIP	0.008	0.009	0.47	0.34	1.68%	0.023	7,823
MN-MFIP-Full	0.091***	0.025	0.72	0.34	12.76%	0.270	724
MN-MFIP-Incentives	0.127***	0.024	0.72	0.34	17.77%	0.376	718
FL-FTP	−0.044***	0.015	0.43	0.33	−10.20%	−0.133	1,729
VT-WRP	−0.006	0.025	0.61	0.36	−0.98%	−0.017	842
CT-JF	0.029*	0.015	0.59	0.37	4.95%	0.079	2,397
3. Average quarterly income							
IA-FIP	83.23*	46.66	2215.24	1651.09	3.76%	0.050	7,823
MN-MFIP-Full	366.82***	88.79	2443.30	1133.39	15.01%	0.324	724
MN-MFIP-Incentives	404.10***	97.66	2443.30	1133.39	16.54%	0.357	718
FL-FTP	58.85	55.91	1750.35	1101.99	3.36%	0.053	1,729
VT-WRP	−2.84	72.42	2376.29	1030.16	−0.12%	−0.003	842
CT-JF	209.93***	71.43	2658.18	1517.52	7.90%	0.138	2,397

Source: Authors' compilations of public use data.
Note: Shown are average quarterly employment rates, averages for any cash welfare receipt during quarter
(to be comparable to the employment rates), and average quarterly income (cash welfare plus food stamps
plus general assistance [MN only] plus earnings) for the period from random assignment to the quarter during which the survey was done (except for IA, for which it is an average over the entire follow-up period).
Statistics are for all observations completing the adult survey that also had data for the full period, except
for Iowa, where they are for approximately the same cohorts as the survey data (the IA public-use data does
not contain the appropriate information to link the survey and administrative records). Numbers are
weighted to be representative of survey design where relevant. Standard errors are robust to heteroskedasticity. Percent effect is one hundred times the treatment-control difference divided by control mean (also
shown in figure 9.1), effect size is treatment-control difference divided by control standard deviation. Significance levels (*** 1 percent, ** 5 percent, and * 10 percent) are for treatment-control differences.

FIGURE 9.3 / Impacts of Welfare Reform on Head's Health Insurance from
Experimental Studies (Percent Effects)

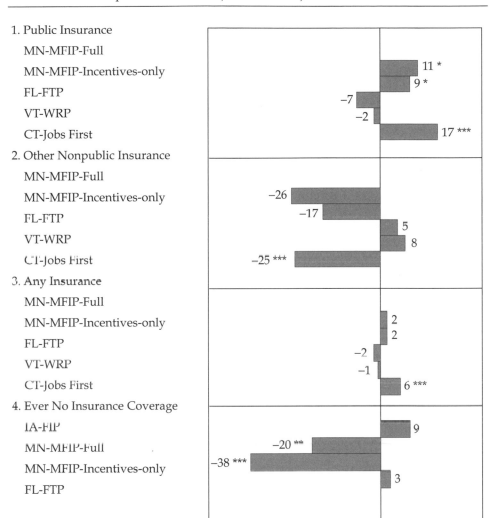

Source: Authors' compilation of public use data.
Note: The impacts are reported at the time of a follow-up survey administered to some recipients at some time after random assignment. For CT-JF, the survey was done thirty-six months after random assignment began; for VT-WRP, forty-two months; for FL-FTP, forty-eight months; for MN-MFIP, thirty-six months; and for IA-FIP, five to six years. Effect sizes reported are the treatment-control difference divided by the control mean. Significance levels (*** 1 percent, ** 5 percent, and * 10 percent) are for treatment-control differences.

TABLE 9.6 / Impacts on Head's Health Insurance, Survey Data

	Difference	Std. Err., Difference	Mean (Controls)	Std. Dev. (Controls)	Percent Effect	Effect Size	N
1. Public insurance							
IA-FIP	NA						
MN-MFIP-Full	0.072*	0.038	0.65	0.48	11.07%	0.152	712
MN-MFIP-Incentives	0.058	0.038	0.65	0.48	8.93%	0.122	709
FL-FTP	−0.025	0.023	0.37	0.48	−6.77%	−0.052	1,725
VT-WRP	−0.012	0.032	0.70	0.46	−1.71%	−0.026	840
CT-JF	0.099***	0.021	0.60	0.49	16.69%	0.203	2,418
2. Other nonpublic insurance							
IA-FIP	NA						
MN-MFIP-Full	−0.044	0.028	0.17	0.38	−25.77%	−0.117	707
MN-MFIP-Incentives	−0.029	0.028	0.17	0.38	−16.86%	−0.076	704
FL-FTP	0.013	0.021	0.25	0.43	5.24%	0.030	1,723
VT-WRP	0.011	0.024	0.14	0.35	7.84%	0.031	837
CT-JF	−0.055***	0.018	0.22	0.41	−25.23%	−0.133	2,402
3. Any insurance							
IA-FIP	NA						
MN-MFIP-Full	0.015	0.030	0.84	0.37	1.82%	0.042	708
MN-MFIP-Incentives	0.016	0.030	0.84	0.37	1.96%	0.045	705
FL-FTP	−0.011	0.023	0.62	0.49	−1.78%	−0.023	1,723
VT-WRP	−0.006	0.025	0.84	0.37	−0.71%	−0.016	837
CT-JF	0.046***	0.017	0.82	0.39	5.65%	0.119	2,403
4. Ever no insurance coverage							
IA-FIP	0.049	0.032	0.54	0.50	9.13%	0.098	1,190
MN-MFIP-Full	−0.079**	0.039	0.39	0.49	−20.15%	−0.161	723
MN-MFIP-Incentives	−0.149***	0.037	0.39	0.49	−38.15%	−0.305	717
FL-FTP	0.011	0.023	0.38	0.49	2.87%	0.023	1,729
VT-WRP	NA						
CT-JF	NA						

Source: Authors' compilations of public use data.
Note: Shown are survey estimates of insurance coverage for the recipient for month before survey, or of having had any spell of non-coverage since random assignment. Statistics are for all observations completing the adult survey that had data for the outcome. Numbers are weighted to be representative of survey design where relevant. Standard errors are robust to heteroskedasticity. Percent effect is one hundred times the treatment-control difference divided by control mean (also shown in figure 9.2), effect size is treatment-control difference divided by control standard deviation. Significance levels (*** 1 percent, ** 5 percent, and * 10 percent) are for treatment-control differences.

FIGURE 9.4 / Impacts of Welfare Reform on Child or Family Health Insurance from Experimental Studies (Percent Effects)

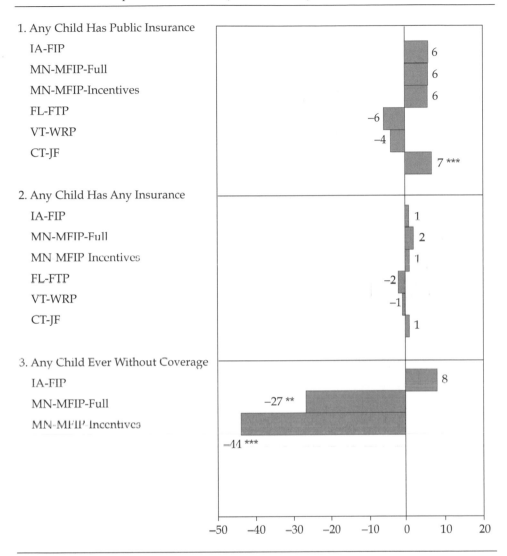

Source: Authors' compilation of public use data.

Note: The impacts are reported at the time of a follow-up survey administered to some recipients at some time after random assignment. For CT-JF, the survey was done thirty-six months after random assignment began; for VT-WRP, forty-two months; for FL-FTP, forty-eight months; for MN-MFIP, thirty-six months; and for IA-FIP, five to six years. Effect sizes reported are the treatment-control difference divided by the control mean. Significance levels (*** 1 percent and ** 5 percent) are for treatment-control differences. Values for IA are for any coverage within the family; those for other states are for any coverage for any child.

TABLE 9.7 / Impacts on Child or Family Health Insurance, Survey Data

	Difference	Std. Err., Difference	Mean (Controls)	Std. Dev. (Controls)	Percent Effect	Effect Size	N
1. Public insurance							
IA-FIP	0.031	0.033	0.49	0.50	6.32%	0.062	1,106
MN-MFIP-Full	0.045	0.036	0.72	0.45	6.34%	0.100	697
MN-MFIP-Incentives	0.044	0.036	0.72	0.45	6.14%	0.097	696
FL-FTP	−0.037	0.026	0.61	0.49	−6.06%	−0.076	1,471
VT-WRP	−0.029	0.029	0.82	0.39	−3.58%	−0.076	774
CT-JF	0.055***	0.019	0.78	0.42	7.14%	0.132	2,135
2. Any insurance							
IA-FIP	0.006	0.026	0.80	0.40	0.80%	0.016	1,105
MN-MFIP-Full	0.017	0.027	0.86	0.34	1.97%	0.049	698
MN-MFIP-Incentives	0.008	0.029	0.86	0.34	0.90%	0.022	697
FL-FTP	−0.017	0.020	0.82	0.38	−2.07%	−0.045	1,468
VT-WRP	−0.013	0.022	0.90	0.30	−1.45%	−0.044	772
CT-JF	0.005	0.010	0.95	0.22	0.57%	0.025	2,141
3. Any child ever **without coverage**							
IA-FIP	0.035	0.034	0.43	0.50	8.12%	0.071	1,004
MN-MFIP-Full	−0.094**	0.038	0.35	0.48	−27.08%	−0.197	698
MN-MFIP-Incentives	−0.154***	0.036	0.35	0.48	−44.32%	−0.323	697
FL-FTP	NA						
VT-WRP	NA						
CT-JF	NA						

Source: Authors' compilations of public use data.
Note: Shown are survey estimates of insurance coverage for any child of the recipient for the month before survey, or of any child having had any spell of non-coverage since random assignment. Statistics are for all observations completing the adult survey that had data for the outcome and had a child in their household at the time of the survey. Numbers are weighted to be representative of survey design where relevant. Standard errors are robust to heteroskedasticity. Percent effect is one hundred times the treatment-control difference divided by control mean (also shown in figure 9.3), effect size is treatment-control difference divided by control standard deviation. Significance levels (*** 1 percent and ** 5 percent) are for treatment-control differences.

an adverse impact in this case), the child having behavioral problems (a positive effect is an adverse impact in this case), and for the parent reporting that the child was in excellent or very good health (a positive effect is a good outcome in this case).[26] These estimates consistently indicate that welfare reform leads to improvements in health status, although few estimates are statistically significant. For example, four of five estimates indicate that the risk of maternal depression decreases (the exception is CT-JF); four of five estimates indicate that the child behavior index improves (the exception is FL-FTP); and three of five estimates indicate that child-health status improves (the exceptions are IA-FIP and MN-MFIP-Full). Again, the improvements tend to be most systematic for the most generous

(text continues on page 268)

FIGURE 9.5 / Impact of Welfare Reform on Child and Family Health-Care Utilization, Access and Affordability of Care from Experimental Studies (Percent Effects)

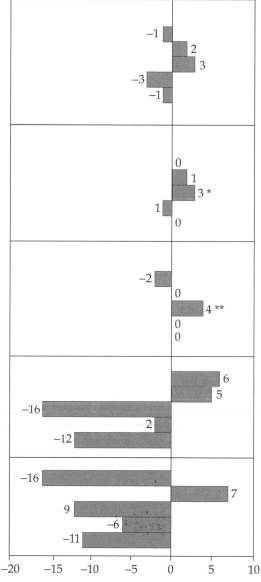

1. Focal Child Has Seen Dentist in Past Two Years
  IA-FIP
  MN-MFIP-Full
  MN-MFIP-Incentives-only, long-term recipients
  FL-FTP
  CT-JF

2. Focal Child Has Seen Doctor in Past Two Years
  IA-FIP
  MN-MFIP-Full
  MN-MFIP-Incentives
  FL-FTP
  CT-JF

3. Focal Child Has Place to Go For Routine Care
  IA-FIP
  MN-MFIP-Full
  MN-MFIP-Incentives
  FL-FTP
  CT-JF

4. Family Not Able to Afford Dentist
  IA-FIP
  MN-MFIP-Full
  MN-MFIP-Incentives
  FL-FTP
  CT-JF

5. Family Not Able to Afford Doctor
  IA-FIP
  MN-MFIP-Full
  MN-MFIP-Incentives
  FL-FTP
  CT-JF

Source: Authors' compilation of public use data.

Note: The impacts are reported at the time of a follow-up survey administered to some recipients at some time after random assignment. For CT-JF, the survey was done thirty-six months after random assignment began; for VT-WRP, forty-two months; for FL-FTP, forty-eight months; for MN-MFIP, thirty-six months; and for IA-FIP, five to six years. Effect sizes reported are the treatment-control difference divided by the control mean. Significance levels (** 5 percent and * 10 percent) are for treatment-control differences. Outcomes in panels 1, 2, and 3 are for focal child, those in panels 4 and 5 are for the family but for sample of focal children.

TABLE 9.8 \ Impacts on Child and Family Health-Care Utilization, Access, and Affordability of Care, Survey Data

	Difference	Std. Err., Difference	Mean (Controls)	Std. Dev. (Controls)	Percent Effect	Effect Size	N
1. Focal child has seen dentist in past two years							
IA-FIP	−0.005	0.021	0.93	0.25	−0.54%	−0.020	683
MN-MFIP-Full	0.022	0.025	0.89	0.31	2.47%	0.071	570
MN-MFIP-Incentives	0.029	0.024	0.89	0.31	3.25%	0.094	558
FL-FTP	−0.023	0.023	0.85	0.36	−2.68%	−0.064	1,063
VT-WRP	NA						
CT-JF	−0.013	0.012	0.96	0.21	−1.41%	−0.065	1,459
2. Focal child has seen doctor in past two years							
IA-FIP	0.004	0.014	0.97	0.17	0.40%	0.023	683
MN-MFIP-Full	0.008	0.018	0.95	0.22	0.79%	0.034	570
MN-MFIP-Incentives	0.027*	0.016	0.95	0.22	2.83%	0.121	559
FL-FTP	−0.012	0.011	0.97	0.16	−1.22%	−0.072	1,065
VT-WRP	NA						
CT-JF	0.002	0.004	0.99	0.07	0.16%	0.021	1,461
3. Focal child has place to go for routine care							
IA-FIP	−0.021	0.015	0.97	0.17	−2.14%	−0.123	682
MN-MFIP full	0.001	0.019	0.95	0.23	0.11%	0.005	570
MN-MFIP-Incentives-only	0.034*	0.016	0.95	0.23	3.59%	0.149	559
FL-FTP	0.004	0.018	0.90	0.30	0.41%	0.012	1,067
VT-WRP	NA						
CT-JF	−0.004	0.006	0.99	0.11	−0.37%	−0.035	1,460
4. Family not able to afford dentist							
IA-FIP	0.009	0.031	0.17	0.37	5.62%	0.025	682
MN-MFIP-Full	0.010	0.033	0.20	0.40	5.19%	0.026	587
MN-MFIP-Incentives	−0.031	0.032	0.20	0.40	−16.01%	−0.079	573
FL-FTP	−0.007	0.029	0.35	0.48	−2.14%	−0.016	1,107
VT-WRP	NA						
CT-JF	−0.019	0.019	0.17	0.37	−11.51%	−0.051	1,468
5. Family not able to afford doctor							
IA-FIP	−0.017	0.025	0.11	0.31	−15.68%	−0.055	682
MN-MFIP-Full	0.009	0.028	0.13	0.33	7.14%	0.027	587
MN-MFIP-Incentives	−0.012	0.027	0.13	0.33	−9.11%	−0.035	573
FL-FTP	−0.014	0.025	0.22	0.42	−6.43%	−0.035	1,107
VT-WRP	NA						
CT-JF	−0.014	0.017	0.12	0.33	−11.17%	−0.042	1,469

Source: Authors' compilations of public-use data.
Note: Shown are survey estimates for the focal child of the recipient of having seen a doctor or dentist during the two years before the survey, having a place to go for routine care, and, for the focal-child sample, whether the family had someone who could not see a doctor or dentist because they could not afford it during the last year. Statistics are for all observations completing the focal-child survey that had data for the outcome. Numbers are weighted to be representative of survey design where relevant. Standard errors are robust to heteroskedasticity. Percent effect is one hundred times the treatment-control difference divided by control mean (also shown in figure 9.4), effect size is treatment-control difference divided by control standard deviation. No focal-child survey was completed in Vermont. Focal-child sample is children 5 to 12. Significance levels (* 10 percent) are for treatment-control differences.

FIGURE 9.6 / Impacts of Welfare Reform on Child and Mother Health Outcomes from Experimental Studies (Percent Effects)

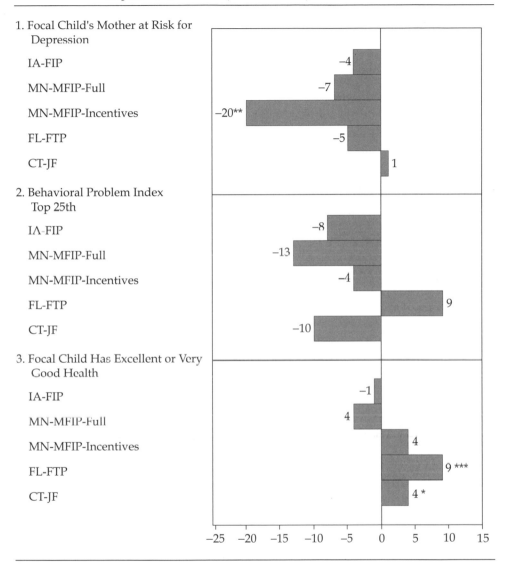

Source: Authors' compilation of public use data.
Note: The impacts are reported at the time of a follow-up survey administered to some recipients at some time after random assignment. For CT-JF, the survey was done thirty-six months after random assignment began; for VT-WRP, forty-two months; for FL-FTP, forty-eight months; for MN-MFIP, thirty-six months; and for IA-FIP, five to six years. Effect sizes reported are the treatment-control difference divided by the control mean. Significance levels (*** 1 percent, ** 5 percent, and * 10 percent) are for treatment-control differences.

TABLE 9.9 \ Impacts on Child and Mother Health Outcomes, Survey Data

	Difference	Std. Err., Difference	Mean (Controls)	Std. Dev. (Controls)	Percent Effect	Effect Size	N
1. Focal child's mother at risk for depression							
IA-FIP	−0.012	0.038	0.30	0.46	−3.88%	−0.025	676
MN-MFIP-Full	−0.036	0.044	0.55	0.50	−6.51%	−0.072	525
MN-MFIP-Incentives	−0.112**	0.044	0.55	0.50	−20.27%	−0.226	507
FL-FTP	−0.018	0.029	0.39	0.49	−4.70%	−0.038	1,091
VT-WRP	NA						
CT-JF	0.005	0.025	0.34	0.47	1.45%	0.010	1,436
2. Behavioral Problem Index in top 25th percentile							
IA-FIP	−0.023	0.037	0.28	0.45	−8.27%	−0.052	683
MN-MFIP-Full	−0.038	0.040	0.30	0.46	−12.73%	−0.083	510
MN-MFIP-Incentives	−0.012	0.041	0.30	0.46	−4.13%	−0.027	493
FL-FTP	0.023	0.027	0.26	0.44	8.70%	0.052	1,100
VT-WRP	NA						
CT-JF	−0.028	0.023	0.28	0.45	−9.92%	−0.063	1,450
3. Focal child has excellent or very good health							
IA-FIP	−0.012	0.029	0.85	0.36	−1.39%	−0.033	683
MN-MFIP-Full	−0.029	0.036	0.78	0.42	−3.74%	−0.070	570
MN-MFIP-Incentives	0.031	0.034	0.78	0.42	4.01%	0.075	559
FL-FTP	0.069***	0.026	0.73	0.45	9.43%	0.154	1,068
VT-WRP	NA						
CT-JF	0.033*	0.020	0.81	0.39	4.11%	0.086	1,466

Source: Authors' compilations of public use data.
Note: Shown are survey estimates for the focal child of the recipient of whether the mother was at risk for depression (score of sixteen or higher on twenty-item Center for Epidemiological Studies-Depression scale; worst score was 60), whether the focal child's Behavioral Problem Index score was in the worst twenty-fifth percentile range, and whether the mother reported the child's general health was "excellent" or "very good." Statistics are for all observations completing the focal-child survey that had data for the outcome. Numbers are weighted to be representative of survey design where relevant. Standard errors are robust to heteroskedasticity. Percent effect is one hundred times the treatment-control difference divided by control mean (also shown in figure 9.5), effect size is treatment-control difference divided by control standard deviation. No focal-child survey was completed in Vermont. Focal-child sample is children 5 to 12. Significance levels (*** 1 percent, ** 5 percent, and * 10 percent) are for treatment-control differences.

reforms: MN-MFIP has the largest improvements (perhaps related to their large increases in income) and CT-JF is close behind.

Given that we estimate effects for many outcomes, we need to be concerned about the possibility that the separate tests sometimes wrongly reject the null hypothesis of no impact. That is, we would expect some number of our many treatment-control comparisons to differ at a statistically significant level simply because of randomness. With the many comparisons we present, the probability of falsely rejecting at least one null hypothesis of no significant difference in means across the treatment and control group is much higher than each individual test would suggest. To address this concern about multiple inference, we also constructed summary measures for the types of outcomes within each table for each state. These allow us to test the effect of the treatment on each set of outcomes. For each set of outcomes (for example, quarterly employment, welfare receipt, and income since random assignment for figure 9.2), the summary measure is defined as the average of the standardized outcomes (after having converted all outcomes to be positive when they are good and normalizing them by the control-group standard deviation). So, for the outcomes in figure 9.2, the summary measure would be the average of the quarterly employment, quarterly income, and one minus quarterly welfare receipt (assuming, as per the intent of reform, that ongoing welfare receipt is a negative thing), each normalized by its control-group standard deviation. This new averaged variable is then regressed on treatment status for each state. Tests on this summary measure are then robust to over-testing (one is less likely to inappropriately reject a null hypothesis of no effect with the summary measure than if one looked independently at the significance levels of the constituent individual tests).

This does not entirely resolve the issue of multiple inference because there are still five such summary measures. It is important to consider hypotheses about each of these summary measures as members of families of hypotheses. This involves calculating cutoffs for test statistics such that the probability is less than a set amount (for example, 0.05) that at least one of the tests in the family would exceed the cutoff under a joint null hypothesis of no effects (the probability of falsely rejecting one null hypothesis). One such familiar but quite conservative test (if the test statistics are highly correlated) is the Bonferroni adjustment, in which the adjusted p-value is the observed p-value times the number of outcomes examined. Such a conservative test may result in not rejecting the null hypotheses of no effect even when there are some significant differences. More powerful tests remove hypotheses from the family of nulls if they are rejected and also produce adjusted p-values. An alternative method from the biostatistics literature used in recent papers (Kling and Liebman 2004; Kling, Liebman, and Katz 2007; Anderson 2005) involves calculating family-wise error-adjusted significance levels, using the Westfall and Young free step-down resampling method (Westfall and Young 1993).[27] We have also implemented this method to adjust our summary measure p-values for the multiple inference, using one thousand draws from the null distribution of no impact of each summary measure (for more details, see algorithm 2.8 in Westfall and Young 1993).

The results of our five summary measures for each of the states are reported in table 9.10. The table reports the treatment-control difference in summary measures for each state and figure, along with the standard error, the family-wise error adjusted p-values for each state, and the number of observations for each summary measure.[28] Each summary measure is for a single table and state; each averages all normalized reported outcomes for that treatment. The normalized outcomes are then all for positive outcomes (so the summary measure treatment-control difference is positive if the reform caused an improvement in the summary measure). For the employment, welfare, and income summary measure (figure 9.2), lack of welfare receipt is considered "good." For the adult health insurance coverage as well as the child and family health insurance coverage summary measures (figures 9.3 and 9.4), public coverage and the lack of any spells of coverage are considered "good." For the health care utilization summary measure (figure 9.5), being able to afford to see the doctor or dentist is considered "good." Finally, for the health status summary measure (figure 9.6), it is considered "good" if the child's mother is not at risk for depression and the child does not have a high Behavioral Problem Index measure.

Adjusting for the family-wise error rate definitely makes a difference in the overall interpretation of the results. For example, for the figure 9.2 summary measure (panel 1 of table 9.10), the treatment-control differences for IA-FIP, MN-MFIP-Full, FL-FTP, and CT-JF are all positive and significant at the 5 percent level if the p-value is unadjusted for the multiple testing (significance levels not shown in table). However, when multiple inference is controlled for, only FL-FTP and CT-JF have significant treatment-control differences in the summary measure, and only FL-FTP's is significant at the 5 percent level. For the adult health insurance measures in figure 9.3, the summary measure treatment-control difference is only statistically significant for CT-JF (and it is positive, suggesting an improvement in health insurance coverage for the head). None of the child and family health insurance summary measures (figure 9.4) are significant, although both the MN-MFIP-Incentives and CT-JF measures are both positive and come close to statistical significance (p = 0.107 and 0.103 respectively). Again, none of the figure 9.5 or figure 9.6 summary measure treatment-control differences are statistically significant, although all but one are positive. Thus, considering all the measures within each domain suggests a similar interpretation to the one derived from considering them one at a time. CT-JF had a positive and significant effect on income, employment, and leaving welfare, as well as on better adult insurance-coverage outcomes. Effects for child and family insurance, utilization, and health status are small and insignificant in general.

CONCLUSION

While there is a growing literature on the impacts of welfare reform on health insurance coverage, health care utilization, and health status, there are few clear findings. Most studies find that welfare reform leads to reductions in health insurance coverage, although some studies find the opposite. Results for utilization and health status are more mixed, but the balance is toward negative impacts which are small and rarely statistically significant.

To illustrate the findings in the literature review, we calculate estimates from five experimental evaluations of state welfare waivers (Connecticut, Florida, Iowa, Minnesota, and Vermont). We chose these five states because they had the best and

TABLE 9.10 / Summary Measure Impacts on Adult, Child, and Family Measures, Survey Data

	Difference	Std. Err, Difference	FWE Adjusted P-Value	N
1. Summary measure, employment, off welfare, and income, since RA				
IA-FIP	0.041	0.020	0.181	7,823
MN-MFIP-Full	0.113	0.051	0.115	724
MN-MFIP-Incentives	0.021	0.054	0.698	718
FL-FTP	0.110***	0.030	0.000	1,729
VT-WRP	0.046	0.048	0.671	842
CT-JF	0.078*	0.034	0.099	2,397
2. Summary measure: head's HI coverage				
IA-FIP	−0.049	0.032	0.409	1,190
MN-MFIP-Full	0.070	0.059	0.551	707
MN-MFIP-Incentives	0.118	0.059	0.125	704
FL-FTP	−0.021	0.051	0.900	1,723
VT-WRP	−0.007	0.038	0.849	837
CT-JF	0.060*	0.025	0.099	2,402
3. Summary measure: child/ family HI coverage				
IA-FIP	0.001	0.050	0.993	1,105
MN-MFIP-Full	0.114	0.062	0.235	697
MN-MFIP-Incentives	0.144	0.064	0.107	696
FL-FTP	−0.066	0.053	0.489	1,468
VT-WRP	−0.052	0.060	0.671	771
CT-JF	0.067	0.032	0.103	2,134
IA-FIP	−0.013	0.045	0.993	681
4. Summary measure: child/ family utilization, access, and affordability				
MN-MFIP-Full	0.015	0.058	0.857	570
MN-MFIP-Incentives	0.117	0.055	0.123	558
FL-FTP	−0.018	0.045	0.900	1,060
VT-WRP	NA			
CT-JF	0.006	0.024	0.801	1,453
5. Summary measure: child/ mother health outcomes				
IA-FIP	0.015	0.054	0.993	676
MN-MFIP-Full	0.030	0.062	0.857	509
MN-MFIP-Incentives	0.120	0.062	0.125	492
FL-FTP	0.065	0.044	0.435	1,048
VT-WRP	NA			
CT-JF	0.051	0.036	0.263	1,421

Source: Authors' compilations of public use data.
Note: Shown are survey estimates for summary measures for each state for each of the variables presented in figures 9.2 to 9.6. Each summary measure is the average of the outcomes on each figure (normalized by each outcome's control standard deviation), after converting each outcome to be positive when good (welfare participation is considered bad, but any kind of Health Insurance good). For the figure 9.2 summary measure, the sample is adults completing the survey with non-missing administrative data (for IA only, it is instead the same cohort as the survey). For the figure 9.3 summary measure, the sample is adults completing the survey with non-missing health insurance data. For the figure 9.4 summary measure, the sample is adults with a child in the household at the time of the survey completing the survey with non-missing child/family health insurance coverage data. For the figures 9.5 and 9.6 summary measures, the sample is survey recipients with a focal child completing the survey, with non-missing data on health care utilization, access, and affordability, or on health outcomes, respectively. Numbers are weighted to be representative of survey design where relevant. Standard errors are robust to heteroskedasticity. Difference is treatment-control difference in each summary measure. FWE adjusted p-value is p-value for comparison in row, adjusted for joint testing across all summary measures in the state. No focal-child survey was completed in Vermont. Focal child sample is children 5 to 12. Significance levels (*** 1 percent and * 10 percent) are for treatment-control differences, adjusted for family-wise errors.

most comprehensive data on health and they included the states with the most "TANF-like" welfare waiver policies. For example, Connecticut and Florida had time limits, which have proved to be very important feature of the TANF program. Overall, the results suggest that reform leads to small changes in health insurance and possible improvements in health. The results for health care utilization are less conclusive.

A major limitation of this chapter reflects a weakness in the literature: we know a lot about the impact of welfare reform on health insurance, but we know little about the impact of welfare reform on health. The major challenge limiting the existing literature is obtaining the data that is required for a more comprehensive analysis. The experimental literature is restricted to looking at health outcomes, about which information was collected during surveys administered to participants. These surveys asked about health insurance coverage in some detail, included a few questions on health care utilization, and had quite limited information on health status (which, like other outcomes, was self-reported). Ideally, these experimental surveys would have collected before and after data from objective evaluations of participants' health. Yet the experimental surveys did not collect data on many important health outcomes of interest, such as whether the children are suffering from developmental delays, asthma, or chronic ear conditions; whether the children or recipients are obese or overweight; whether recipients suffer from substance abuse or sexually transmitted diseases; whether they have negative health behaviors, such as smoking; whether they have encountered domestic violence; or whether they have chronic conditions, such as asthma, hypertension, or diabetes. A number of health surveys do collect information on these outcomes or others of interest, but they either do not contain information allowing one to identify whether women are in a group likely to be affected by reform, do not contain information for a consistent panel of states and years spanning reform, or do not have large enough samples to plausibly identify the effects of reform. These features are required to evaluate welfare reform using observational data where it is necessary to make comparisons across groups facing different policies in different states at different times.

An additional limitation is that many of these most important health outcomes are ones which do not change very quickly as other conditions change. Thus, despite having been collected approximately three or four years after reform, the experimental surveys may still have been collected too soon to capture reform-related changes in these outcomes. Further, these delays in the impacts of policies make it difficult to attribute changes to reform in observational data sets.

With these caveats, we have several important conclusions from our analysis of the experimental data and our reading of the broader literature. First, work-promoting reforms do not necessarily lead to bad outcomes. There is little evidence that reforms led to significant reductions in health care utilization or worse health. Second and more speculatively, the *type* of welfare reform likely matters. Reforms that encouraged work while increasing benefits (such as those in Minnesota or Connecticut)—even in the presence of work requirements and time limits—may lead to more consistent positive impacts on health. Finally, investments in data collection resulted in important improvements and increases in our knowledge. Our analysis (and many others' analyses) could not have been done without the randomized experimental data and the additional resources spent on surveys that provide a rich set of health, education, and well-being outcomes.

We have much to learn about the impacts of welfare reform on health. The study here is at best a short- to medium-term analysis, and thus it may be too early to inform us about the full impacts of reform. However, we need the appropriate data in order to complete this task. For example, one could field follow-up surveys to these experimental samples. There are other ways to improve access to data that facilitate both experimental and nonexperimental research. There are limited options for using household survey data to estimate the impacts of a state-varying policy such as welfare reform. The CPS is an option, but it only provides information on health insurance and, for some years, health status. The SIPP has richer outcomes but smaller samples, and no SIPP panel spanned all key reform periods. The NHIS is the obvious choice, but despite sample sizes comparable to the CPS, the public-use version of the NHIS data does not identify individual states; furthermore, the NHIS went through a redesign in the midst of TANF implementation. The BRFSS is another possibility, but the samples are smaller; also, there is no health information collected about children. Non-health surveys need to be expanded to include more information about health outcomes. Some health surveys might benefit from expanding the population surveyed; asking more about previous and concurrent use of programs; or including health outcomes that might respond to shorter-run changes in income, employment, or program participation. An example of the underlying demand for large-scale data with state identifiers and health outcomes is evidenced by the explosion of studies that use Vital Statistics natality data on births in the United States. The rich natality data permits analysis of birthweight, gestation, prenatal care, and other birth outcomes; these data also identify states and counties. Additionally, the natality data cover essentially the full population of births after 1985 and a large share before that year, enabling study of rare birth outcomes. Finally, it would be useful for experimental evaluators to provide researchers with links to administrative data on Medicaid claims. This would enable a richer characterization of health utilization and, possibly, health conditions.

The data used in this chapter are derived from data files made available to researchers by MDRC and Mathematica Policy Research (MPR). We thank MDRC and MPR for assistance with the public use data. The authors remain solely responsible for how the data are used or interpreted.

NOTES

1. Rebecca Blank (2002) and Jeffrey Grogger and Lynn Karoly (2005) provide recent and comprehensive reviews of the welfare-reform literature.

2. The new welfare programs include other changes as well. Especially relevant for health, many states expanded "transitional" Medicaid coverage which is received when leaving welfare.

3. Other leaver studies documented similar rates of coverage (Ellwood and Lewis 1999; Guyer 2000; Moffitt and Slade 1997; Pollack et al. 2003).

4. Family caps prevent welfare benefits from increasing when a woman gives birth while receiving aid. Residency-requirement policies mandate that unmarried teen parents who receive aid must live in the household of a parent or other guardian.

5. States could and did set up Medically Needy programs that allowed them to provide Medicaid benefits to families above the AFDC income cutoff if they had high medical expenses. States were also required to provide transitional Medicaid coverage for families who left AFDC due to an increase in earnings.

6. The literature on welfare reform includes an ongoing debate on what has contributed to this decrease in the welfare caseload. The leading candidate, besides welfare reform itself, is the booming economy of the late 1990s. Teen pregnancy rates also began to fall before TANF implementation.

7. The RAND Health Insurance Experiments, conducted in the 1970s, provide the only experimental evidence on the impact of the generosity of health insurance coverage on health care utilization and health outcomes.

8. For example, Currie and Jonathan Gruber (1996a, 1996b) found that expansions in Medicaid are associated with increased utilization and improved health outcomes among the poor. David Card, Carlos Dobkin, and Nicole Maestas (2006) found that the introduction of Medicare led to increases in insurance coverage and utilization, with larger impacts for more disadvantaged groups.

9. Several reviews offer recent summaries of the experimental and nonexperimental studies of welfare reform and family income (Blank 2002; Grogger and Karoly 2005; Moffitt 2002).

10. When federal law was passed, there were states that adopted their waiver programs as their TANF programs. Therefore some of the welfare waiver experimental studies do, then, estimate impacts of TANF.

11. The literature on the impacts of welfare reform is quite large. Here, we focus our review on what is known about the impacts of welfare reform on health. A related literature finds that prereform public assistance programs lead to improvements in health. Currie and Nancy Cole (1993) find that AFDC participation leads to improvements in birth outcomes (higher birth weight). Currie and Grogger (2002) find that higher pre-PRWORA welfare participation rates are associated with more prenatal care and improved birth outcomes. Price Fishback, Michael Haines, and Shawn Kantor (2007) find that increases in public assistance spending during the New Deal led to lower infant mortality, lower suicide rates, fewer deaths from diarrhea and infectious diseases, and higher birth rates.

12. The NHIS is less widely used in this area because the public-use data do not contain state identifiers. It is possible, through special arrangement, for researchers to access the file with state identifiers. Kaushal and Kaestner (2007) use the NHIS to examine impacts for immigrants using a difference-in-difference methodology and characterizing reform with caseloads.

13. Large spillover effects seem to be inconsistent with the small estimated impacts of welfare reform on marriage and fertility (Bitler et al. 2004; Grogger and Karoly 2005).

14. Royer (2005) also examines impacts on pregnant immigrants. She finds a temporary reduction in prenatal care but no effect on birth outcomes.

15. DHHS funded a number of state experimental evaluations to allow them to examine longer-term impacts of reform on various school and health outcomes for children who were two to nine years old at the time of random assignment (and thus approximately five to twelve years old at the time of the surveys).

16. In states conducting the focal-child evaluations, single parents with children of the appropriate age were oversampled for the adult survey as well. The data for these states include sample weights to make the survey data representative of the overall population in the survey. (These weights adjust for initial differences in sampling ratios for Connecticut, Iowa, and Minnesota.)

17. The table mentions the maximum number of available observations. Because of item nonresponse, the actual numbers of observations are lower than this for many outcomes. We chose to use a different number of observations for each outcome to maximize sample. Item nonresponse is generally low for most of our outcomes.

18. Some of the evaluations do not include data for two-parent families. We wanted a sample that was consistent across states to the extent possible.

19. It also has the advantage that there were no changes in the random-assignment ratios across the time period, mitigating the need for controls beyond the treatment indicator. Long-term recipients are those who were on welfare for at least twenty-four of the past thirty-six months.

20. To be precise, we include single females eighteen and older, or between sixteen and seventeen who had a preschool-aged child, and who were in a cohort randomly assigned at least fifty-seven months before the survey. The final report includes separate outcomes for ongoing recipients and applicants in three cohorts. We wanted the applicant sample to have been exposed to the new program or AFDC for as long as the ongoing recipients. Thus, we restricted the analysis to the earlier applicants. This was not an issue for the four other states, as the surveys in the other evaluations were only administered to narrow cohorts of participants. Also, in 1997, Iowa implemented TANF and applied the new TANF policies to the control group. Thus the treatment-control program differences are much smaller for later cohorts.

21. In the MTO study, persons were randomly assigned to a treatment group (which was offered a housing voucher to move to a low-poverty neighborhood) and a control group (which did not receive an offer). There is a need to examine the intent to treat for MTO because only a subset of persons in the treatment group accepted the offer. Here, everyone has applied to obtain—and been deemed eligible for—welfare, although a small share of each group does not take up welfare.

22. In this and all subsequent figures, there is a companion table that provides the supporting data and an alternative estimator.

23. The exception to this is Iowa, where it is impossible to merge the administrative and survey information with the public-use data. For Iowa, we have tried to match our survey sample as closely as possible.

24. The difference between CT-JF and FL-FTP reflects the fact that CT-JF had a much more

generous earnings disregard. Further, the CT-JF time limit was a short twenty-one months on paper; however, in practice extensions to the time limit were fairly common. Florida's time limit was also relatively short (for the "work ready," twenty-four months out of sixty), but it was more stringent than CT-JF's; meanwhile, the survey in Florida was administered four years out.

25. For example, many of these low-income children would be eligible for Medicaid via the poverty or OBRA expansions (children under age fifteen in families with income up to 100 percent of the poverty level).

26. The mother's risk for depression is determined if her score is at least sixteen (out of a possible sixty) on the twenty-item Center for Epidemiological Studies Depression scale. The child having behavioral problems is determined by whether the child's Behavioral Problem Index score was in the worst 25 percent. General health is reported on a five-point scale (excellent, very good, good, fair, or poor).

27. The Bonferroni adjustment is a one-step method. Broadly speaking, step-down methods involve ordering the p-values from smallest to largest, rejecting relevant null hypotheses, and removing the rejected nulls from the set of others being considered. Re-sampling is related to using the bootstrap to obtain distributions for p-values under the null hypothesis that no differences are significant.

28. The numbers of observations reported are less than the maximum possible numbers of observations because an observation will be missing if it is missing for any of the outcomes. A small share of observations is missing for each set of outcomes.

REFERENCES

Administration of Children and Families. 1997. *Temporary Assistance for Needy Families Program Instructions.* Transmittal No. TANF-ACF-PI-97-7. Washington: U.S. Department of Health and Human Services.

———. 2002. *Major Provisions of the Personal Responsibility and Work Opportunity Reconciliation Act of 1996.* P.L. 104-193. Washington: U.S. Department of Health and Human Services

Aizer, Anna, and Jeffrey Grogger. 2003. "Parental Medicaid Expansions and Health Insurance Coverage." National Bureau of Economic Research Working paper No. 9907. Cambridge, Mass.: National Bureau of Economic Research.

Anderson, Michael. 2005. "Uncovering Gender Differences in the Effects of Early Intervention: A Reevaluation of the Abecedarian, Perry Preschool, and Early Training Projects." Unpublished paper, Massachusetts Institute of Technology.

Bansak, Cynthia, and Steven Raphael. 2007. "The Effects of State Policy Design Features on Take-up and Crowd-Out Rates for the State Children's Health Insurance Program." *Journal of Policy Analysis and Management* 26(1): 149–175.

Bitler, Marianne P., Jonah Gelbach, and Hilary Hoynes. 2005. "Welfare Reform and Health." *Journal of Human Resources* 40(2): 309–34.

———. 2006. "What Mean Impacts Miss: Distributional Effects of Welfare Reform Experiments." *American Economic Review* 96(4): 988–1012.

Bitler, Marianne P., Jonah Gelbach, Hilary Hoynes, and Madeline Zavodny. 2004. "The Impact of Welfare Reform on Marriage and Divorce." *Demography* 41(2): 213–36.

Blank, Rebecca M. 2001. "Declining Caseloads / Increased Work: What Can We Conclude About the Effects of Welfare Reform?" *Federal Reserve Bank of New York Economic Policy Review* 7(2): 25–36.

———. 2002. "Evaluating Welfare Reform in the United States." *Journal of Economic Literature* 40(4): 1105–66.

Bloom, Dan, James J. Kemple, Pamela Morris, Susan Scrivener, Nandita Verma, and Richard Hendra. 2000. *The Family Transition Program: Final Report on Florida's Initial Time-Limited Welfare Program.* New York: Manpower Demonstration Research Corporation.

Bloom, Dan, Susan Scrivener, Charles Michalopoulos, Pamela Morris, Richard Hendra, Diana Adams-Ciardullo, and Johanna Walter. 2002. *Jobs First Final Report on Connecticut's Welfare Reform Initiative.* New York: Manpower Demonstration Research Corporation.

Borjas, George. 2003. "Welfare Reform, Labor Supply, and Health Insurance in the Immigrant Population." *Journal of Health Economics* 22(6): 933–58.

Busch, Susan H., and Noelia Duchovny. 2005. "Family Coverage Expansions: Impact on Insurance Coverage and Health Care Utilization of Parents." *Journal of Health Economics* 24(5): 876–90.

Card, David, Carlos Dobkin and Nicole Maestas. 2006. "The Impact of Nearly Universal Insurance Coverage on Health Care Utilization and Health: Evidence from Medicare." National Bureau of Economic Research Working paper No. 10365. Cambridge, Mass.: National Bureau of Economic Research.

Cawley, John, Mathis Schroeder, and Kosali Ilayperu Simon. 2005. "Welfare Reform and Health Insurance Coverage of Women and Children." *Frontiers in Health Policy Research* 8(1): Article 5.

———. 2006. "How Did Welfare Reform Affect the Health Insurance Coverage of Women and Children?" *Health Services Research* 41(2): 486–506.

Council of Economic Advisers. 1997. *Explaining the Decline in Welfare Receipt 1993–1996.* Washington: Executive Office of the President of the United States.

———. 1999. *Economic Expansion, Welfare Reform, and the Decline in Welfare Caseloads, an Update.* Washington: Executive Office of the President of the United States.

Crouse, Gil. 1999. *State Implementation of Major Changes to Welfare Policies, 1992–1998.* Accessed at http://aspe.hhs.gov/HSP/Waiver-Policies99/policy_CEA.htm.

Cunningham, Peter, Jack Hadley, and James Reschovsky. 2002. "Effects of SCHIP on Children's Health Insurance Coverage: Early Evidence from the Community Tracking Survey." *Medical Care Research and Review* 59(4): 359–83.

Currie, Janet, and Nancy Cole. 1993. "Welfare and Child Health: The Link Between AFDC Participation and Birth Weight." *American Economic Review* 83(4): 971–85.

Currie, Janet, and Jeffrey Grogger. 2002. "Medicaid Expansions and Welfare Contractions: Offsetting Effects on Maternal Behavior and Infant Health." *Journal of Health Economics* 21(2): 313–35.

Currie, Janet, and Jonathan Gruber. 1996a. "Health Insurance Eligibility, Utilization of Medical Care, and Child Health." *Quarterly Journal of Economics* 111(2): 431–66.

———. 1996b. "Saving Babies: The Efficacy and Cost of Recent Changes in the Medicaid Eligibility of Pregnant Women." *Journal of Political Economy* 104(6): 1263–96.

Currie, Janet, and Aaron Yelowitz. 2000. "Health Insurance and Less Skilled Workers." In *Finding Jobs: Work and Welfare Reform*, edited by David Card and Rebecca M. Blank. New York: Russell Sage Foundation.

DeLeire, Thomas, Judith A. Levine, and Helen Levy. 2006. "Is Welfare Reform Responsible for Low-Skilled Women's Declining Health Insurance Coverage in the 1990s?" *Journal of Human Resources* 41(3): 495–528.

Duderstadt, Karen G., Dana C. Hughes, Maj-J Soobader, and Paul W. Newacheck. 2006. "The Impact of Public Insurance Expansions on Children's Access and Use of Care." *Pediatrics* 118(4): 1676–82.

Eissa, Nada, and Hilary Hoynes. 2006. "Behavioral Responses to Taxes: Lessons from the EITC and Labor Supply." In *Tax Policy and the Economy*, Volume 20, edited by James Poterba. Cambridge, Mass.: MIT Press.

Ellwood, Marilyn R., and Kimball Lewis. 1999. "On and Off Medicaid: Enrollment Patterns for California and Florida in 1995." *Urban Institute* occasional paper No. 27. Washington: Urban Institute.

Fishback, Price V., Michael R. Haines, and Shawn Kantor. 2007. "Births, Deaths, and New Deal Relief During the Great Depression." *Review of Economics and Statistics* 89(1): 1–14.

Fraker, Thomas, Christine Ross, Rita Stapulonis, Robert Olsen, Martha Kovac, M. Robin Dion, and Anu Rangarajan. 2002. *The Evaluation of Welfare Reform in Iowa: Final Impact Report*. Final report 8217–125 and 530. Mathematica Policy Research, Washington, D.C.

Garrett, Bowen, and John Holahan. 2000. "Health Insurance Coverage After Welfare." *Health Affairs* 19(1): 175–84.

Gennetian, Lisa, Cynthia Miller, and Jared Smith. 2005. *Turning Welfare into a Work Support: Six-Year Impacts on Parents and Children from the Minnesota Family Investment Program*. New York: Manpower Demonstration Research Corporation.

Gennetian, Lisa, Greg Duncan, Virginia Knox, Wanda Vargas, Elizabeth Clark-Kauffman, and Andrew S. London. 2002. *How Welfare and Work Policies for Parents Affect Adolescents: A Synthesis of Research*. New York: Manpower Demonstration Research Corporation.

Grogger, Jeffrey, and Lynn Karoly. 2005. *Welfare Reform: Effects of a Decade of Change*. Cambridge, Mass.: Harvard University Press.

Grogger, Jeffrey, Steven J. Haider, and Jacob Klerman. 2003. "Why Did the Welfare Rolls Fall During the 1990s?" *American Economic Review Papers and Proceedings* 92(2): 288–292.

Grogger, Jeffrey, Lynn Karoly, and Jacob Klerman. 2002. "Consequences of Welfare Reform: A Research Synthesis." RAND working paper DRU-2676-DHHS. Santa Monica, Calif.: RAND Corporation.

Grossman, Michael. 2001. "The Human Capital Model of the Demand for Health." In *Handbook of Health Economics*, Volume 1A, edited by Joseph Newhouse and Anthony Culyer. Amsterdam: Elsevier.

Gruber, Jonathan. 1997. "Health Insurance for Poor Women and Children in the U.S.: Lessons from the Past Decade." In *Tax Policy and Economy*, Volume 11, edited by James Poterba. Cambridge, Mass.: MIT Press.

Gruber, Jonathan, and Kosali Simon. 2007. "Crowd-Out Ten Years Later: Have Recent Public Insurance Expansions Crowded Out Private Health Insurance?" National Bureau of Economic Research Working Paper No. 12858. Cambridge, Mass.: National Bureau of Economic Research.

Guyer, Jocelyn. 2000. "Health Care After Welfare: An Update of Findings from State Leaver Studies." Unpublished paper, Center for Budget and Policy Priorities.

Haider, Steven, Alison Jacknowitz, and Robert F. Schoeni. 2003. "Welfare Work Requirements and Child Well-Being: Evidence from the Effects on Breast-Feeding." *Demography* 40(3): 479–97.

Haskins, Ron. 2001. "Effects of Welfare Reform at Four Years." In *For Better and for Worse: Welfare Reform and the Well-Being of Children and Families*, edited by Greg Duncan and P. Lindsay Chase-Lansdale. New York: Russell Sage Foundation.

Hines, James R., Hilary Hoynes, and Alan Krueger. 2001. "Another Look at Whether a Rising Tide Lifts All Boats." In *The Roaring Nineties: Can Full Employment Be Sustained?*, edited by Alan Krueger and Robert Solow. New York: Russell Sage Foundation.

Hudson, Julie L., Thomas M. Selden, and Jessica S. Banthin. 2005. "The Impact of SCHIP on Insurance Coverage of Children." *Inquiry* 42(3): 232–54.

Kaestner, Robert, and Neeraj Kaushal. 2004. "The Effect of Welfare Reform on Health Insurance Coverage of Low Income Families." *Journal of Health Economics* 22(6): 959–81.

Kaestner, Robert, and Won Chan Lee. 2005. "The Effect of Welfare Reform on Prenatal Care and Birth Weight." *Health Economics* 15(5): 497–511.

Kaestner, Robert, and Elizabeth Tarlov. 2006. "Changes in the Welfare Caseload and the Health of Low-Educated Mothers." *Journal of Policy Analysis and Management* 25(3): 623–43.

Kandula, Namratha, Colleen Grogan, Paul Rathouz, and Diane Lauderdale. 2004. "The Unintended Impact of Welfare Reform on the Medicaid Enrollment of Eligible Immigrants." *Health Services Research* 39(5): 1509–26.

Kaplan, George A., Kristine Siefert, Nalini Ranjit, Trivellore Raghunathan, Elizabeth A. Young, Diem Tran, Sandra Danziger, Susan Hudson, John W. Lynch, and Richard Tolman. 2005. "The Health of Poor Women Under Welfare Reform." *American Journal of Public Health* 95(7): 1252–8.

Kaushal, Neeraj, and Robert Kaestner. 2005. "Welfare Reform and Health Insurance of Immigrants." *Health Services Research* 40(3): 697–722.

———. 2007. "Welfare Reform and the Health of Immigrant Women and Their Children." *Journal of Immigrant and Minority Health* 9(2): 61–74.

Klerman, Jacob, and Steven J. Haider. 2004. "A Stock-Flow Analysis of the Welfare Caseload." *Journal of Human Resources* 39(4): 865–86.

Kling, Jeffrey R., and Jeffrey B. Liebman. 2004. "Experimental Analysis of Neighborhood Effects on Youth." Unpublished paper, Harvard University.

Kling, Jeffrey R., Jeffrey B. Liebman, and Lawrence F. Katz. 2007. "Experimental Analysis of Neighborhood Effects." *Econometrica* 75(1): 83–119.

Ku, Leighton, and Brian Bruen. 1999. "The Continuing Decline in Medicaid Coverage." *Urban Institute* working paper A-37. Washington: Urban Institute.

Ku, Leighton, and Bowen Garrett. 2000. "How Welfare Reform and Economic Factors Affected Medicaid Participation: 1984–1996." Urban Institute Working Paper 00–01. Washington: Urban Institute.

Levy, Helen, and David Meltzer. 2004. "What Do We Really Know About Whether Health Insurance Affects Health?" In *Health Policy and the Uninsured*, edited by Catherine G. McLaughlin. Washington: Urban Institute.

Lo Sasso Anthony, and Thomas Buchmueller. 2004. "The Effect of the State Children's Health Insurance Program on Health Insurance Coverage." *Journal of Health Economics* 23(5): 1059–82.

Moffitt, Robert A., and Eric P. Slade. 1997. "Health Care Coverage for Children Who Are On and Off Welfare." *The Future of Children* 7(1): 87–98.

Morris, Pamela, Aletha Huston, Greg Duncan, Danielle Crosby, and Johannes Bos. 2001. *How Welfare and Work Policies Affect Children: A Synthesis of the Literature.* New York: Manpower Demonstration Research Corporation.

Nathan, Richard, and Frank Thompson. 1999. "The Relationship Between Welfare Reform and Medicaid: A Preliminary View." Typescript. Paper presented at the Health Policy Forum, February 26, 1999, Washington, D.C.

Office of the Assistant Secretary for Planning and Evaluation. 2001. *Setting the Baseline: A Report on State Welfare Waivers.* Washington: U.S. Department of Health and Human Services.

Pollack, Harold, Matthew Davis, Sheldon Danziger, and Sean Orzol. 2003. "Health Insurance Coverage and Access to Care Among Former Welfare Recipients." Unpublished paper, University of Michigan.

Royer, Heather. 2005. "The Response to a Loss of Medical Eligibility: Pregnant Immigrant Mothers in the Wake of Welfare Reform." Unpublished paper, Case Western Reserve University.

Scrivener, Susan, Richard Hendra, Cindy Redcross, Dan Bloom, Charles Michalopoulos, and Johanna Walter. 2002. *WRP: Final Report on Vermont's Welfare Restructuring Project.* New York: Manpower Demonstration Research Corporation.

Wallace, Geoffrey, and Rebecca M. Blank. 1999. "What Goes Up Must Come Down? Explaining Recent Changes in Public Assistance Caseloads." In *Economic Conditions and Welfare Reform*, edited by Sheldon H. Danziger. Kalamazoo, Mich.: W. E. Upjohn Institute.

Westfall, Peter H., and S. Stanley Young. 1993. *Resampling-Based Multiple Testing.* New York: John Wiley and Sons.

Wolfe, Barbara, Thomas Kaplan, Robert Haveman and Yoonyoung Cho. 2006. "SCHIP Expansion and Parental Coverage: An Evaluation of Wisconsin's BadgerCare." *Journal of Health Economics* 25(6): 1170–92.

Ziliak, James P., David N. Figlio, Elizabeth E. Davis, and Laura S. Connolly. 2000. "Accounting for the Decline in AFDC Caseloads: Welfare Reform or Economic Growth?" *Journal of Human Resources* 35(3): 570–86.

Chapter 10

The Effects of Welfare and Child Support Policies on Maternal Health and Well-Being

Jean Knab, Irv Garfinkel, and Sara McLanahan

In 1996 the U.S. Congress passed the Personal Responsibility and Work Opportunities Reconciliation Act (PRWORA), substantially reducing a family's rights to income support. PRWORA removed the entitlement to government-provided cash assistance and increased states' incentives to reduce welfare caseloads. At the same time it increased private responsibilities by encouraging greater work effort from mothers and more child support payments from nonresident fathers.

The PRWORA provisions raised concerns within the medical community and among other advocates interested in the health and well-being of at-risk families. The changes to cash welfare and child support policies had potential direct and indirect consequences for women's health. Most directly, by removing the entitlement to welfare, many feared that poor women would lose their health insurance coverage. While PRWORA included a provision to hold Medicaid eligibility constant, the administrative barriers to implementation for program staff and the confusing new rules suggested that many eligible women might lose coverage.

Less direct effects of welfare reform on maternal health were also of concern. Advocates feared that increased work requirements and stronger child support enforcement might increase maternal stress, leading to increases in mental health problems. They also expressed concern that stronger child support enforcement might expose mothers to more violence from fathers while stricter welfare requirements might make it harder for mothers to escape violent partners (Kaplan 1997). Finally, advocates feared that substance abusers and women with mental health problems would be disproportionately harmed by the new policies (American Psychological Association 2001; Metsch and Pollack 2005).

Research to date has generally focused on the impact of welfare reform on the health insurance coverage and health care utilization of low-income women. Some studies have found that more restrictive welfare policies are associated with small reductions in health insurance and, in some studies, indications of less health care utilization (Bitler, Gelbach, and Hoynes 2005; Holl, Slack, and Stevens 2005; Kaestner and Kaushal 2003). There is little evidence, however, that stricter welfare policies have had a negative impact on mothers' health. Indeed, one study found that reductions in welfare caseloads were associated with improvements in one health behavior: reductions in binge drinking (Kaestner and Tarlov 2006).

This chapter replicates and extends previous work on the impact of welfare policies on maternal health in several ways. First, we examine a broader range of outcomes than has been covered in previous studies. Second, we use data from the Fragile Families and Child Wellbeing Study (hereafter referred to as "Fragile Families"), which is a recent longitudinal study of unmarried parents and their children. To date, most of the research on the effects of welfare reform on maternal health has either used data from the Behavioral Risk Factor Surveillance System (BRFSS), which is a national data set, or data from one or a handful of states. Thus, trying to replicate some of the previous analyses using a different national data set is a useful exercise. A third extension is that no previous study has looked at the effects of child support enforcement on health outcomes. Since stronger child support enforcement was part of welfare reform, and since these two sets of policies may have complementary or offsetting effects on maternal health, it makes sense to examine them together. Finally, whereas prior studies looked at the effects of welfare *reform* on maternal health, we examine the effects of specific post-PRWORA policies to determine if policies that encourage high levels of welfare participation are associated with poorer maternal health and health behavior.

The Fragile Families study has a number of strengths that make these data attractive for studying the effects of welfare and child support policies on maternal health. The study, which oversamples nonmarital births and asks mothers a large array of questions about their health and health behaviors, provides extensive information on the population of women who are most likely to be affected by welfare and child support policies. Moreover, because the study is longitudinal, we are able to examine the association between changes in welfare use and child support receipt and changes in mothers' health. Finally, the cities in the Fragile Families sample were drawn via a stratified random sample that was designed to capture the extremes of welfare and child support policies and labor-market conditions.[1] Thus, differences in state policies that affect the likelihood that a mother is on welfare can be used to help determine the effects of welfare and child support policies on maternal health by using them as instruments to predict welfare and child support receipt.

The Fragile Families data also have limitations. Although the fixed effects models are an improvement over standard OLS models, they do not resolve all of the causality problems that arise from using observational data. In addition, the state policies that we use to identify the effects of welfare policies are measured only once, and therefore we cannot rule out the possibility that they are a proxy for some other variable that varies across states and affects maternal health.

THEORY AND EMPIRICAL EVIDENCE

An emerging body of research examines the link between the welfare reforms of the late 1990s and maternal and child health. Marianne Bitler, Jonah Gelbach, and Hilary Hoynes (2005), as well as Robert Kaestner and Elizabeth Tarlov (2006) provide thorough reviews of the empirical evidence on how welfare reform—primarily via transitions to employment—may impact maternal health. We take a broader perspective on the role of welfare and child support policies; specifically, we ask how the generosity and stringency of these policies may impact maternal health and well-being. In this regard, we view welfare reform as a set of policies that made public support less generous and private support more mandatory.

What does theory tell us about the potential effects of welfare and child support policies on maternal health and health behavior? With respect to welfare policies, theory is ambiguous and suggests two potential causal pathways through which welfare might affect health. First, Aid to Families with Dependent Children (AFDC), or "welfare," was designed to aid mothers in dire circumstances. For this reason, we would expect generous welfare policies to improve mothers' health, at least in the short run. Second, because welfare benefits are highly income tested, they discourage work; this may lead to economic dependence in the long run. Therefore, we might expect more generous welfare policies to reduce mothers' health and increase negative health behavior. Finally, estimating the correct effect of welfare policies on maternal health is difficult because of a serious selection problem. Since welfare is a last resort for most mothers, those who turn to it for support are likely to be in poorer health than those who do not. Thus we would expect to find a negative association between welfare use and health.

With respect to child support, theory suggests that stronger child support policies should improve maternal health by improving the overall bargaining positions of mothers and by improving total income in the long run. In contrast, the effect of child support enforcement on mothers who depend on welfare is likely to be negative because these mothers have little say in whether or not the father is ordered to pay child support. Furthermore, child support dollars may not increase their income in the short run, as money is often paid through the state and little money is passed through to the mother. Strong child support enforcement may actually reduce the income of mothers on welfare if they had previously been receiving informal transfers from the father. Formal child support payments often substitute for informal payments and typically go to the state rather than to the mother (Nepomnyaschy and Garfinkel 2006). Most importantly, strong child support enforcement may increase conflict between mothers and nonresident fathers, which is expected to have negative effects on maternal health and health behavior. As in the case of welfare, estimates of the effects of child support policies on maternal health are likely to be biased by selection into the child support system. For nonwelfare mothers, selection should be positive; that is, the most able and most healthy mothers should be the most likely to obtain a child support award. For mothers on welfare, however, selection should go in the opposite direction because welfare is selective of the least healthy mothers.

The empirical research on the impact of welfare and child support policies on maternal health and health behavior is very limited. Although a number of studies have examined the association between welfare participation and maternal health, much of this literature is descriptive. The most frequently studied health outcome is depression; here, the causal evidence is weak (Lennon, Blome, and English 2002), although some studies suggest a causal pathway (Ensminger 1995). A study by Janet Currie and Nancy Cole (1993), which focuses primarily on child outcomes, finds that selection into AFDC accounts for most of the association between welfare participation and maternal smoking or drinking during pregnancy. Research on the link between child support enforcement and maternal health is even more limited than research on the effects of welfare policies.

The welfare reform enacted in 1996 stimulated some research on the effects of more restrictive welfare policies on maternal health, but most of this research focused on health insurance coverage and, to a lesser degree, on health care utilization and health behaviors.[2] Evidence to date is mixed as to the effect of welfare reform on health insurance coverage. Many researchers find that tougher (that is, more restrictive) welfare policies are associated with a loss of health insurance (Cawley, Schroeder, and Simon 2006; Chavkin, Romero, and Wise 2000; Garrett and Holahan 2000; Holl, Slack, and Stevens 2005), while others find little to no effect (Bitler, Gelbach, and Hoynes 2005; Bitler and Hoynes, chapter 9, this volume; Kaestner and Kaushal 2003). While there is some debate as to the link between health insurance and health outcomes (Levy and Meltzer 2004), there is substantial evidence that having health insurance is associated with more preventative care (Institute of Medicine 2002). Therefore, it is not surprising that research suggests that stricter welfare policies are associated with less health care utilization (Bitler, Gelbach, and Hoynes 2005; Kaestner and Kaushal 2003; Kaestner and Lee 2005) and higher incidence of unmet health needs (Bitler, Gelbach, and Hoynes 2005; Polit, London, and Martinez 2001). A lack of health insurance coverage may contribute to future health problems if it inhibits mothers from seeking preventative care (Institute of Medicine 2002).

With respect to health behavior, the evidence is mixed. On the negative side, there is some evidence that tougher welfare policies and stricter work requirements reduce breast-feeding, which is positively associated with maternal and child health. According to one study, breast-feeding would have been 5.5 percent higher in the absence of welfare reform (Haider, Jacknowitz, and Schoeni 2003). There is also evidence that stronger child support enforcement is associated with increases in domestic violence, especially among mothers on welfare (Fertig, Garfinkel, and McLanahan 2007). On the positive side, researchers have found that reductions in welfare caseloads (resulting from more restrictive policies) are associated with a reduction in binge drinking (Kaestner and Tarlov 2006).

Despite the loss of health insurance, less use of preventative care, and some evidence of poorer health behaviors, there is little to no evidence that more restrictive welfare policies are associated with poorer health or mental health in the years following welfare reform. Researchers find no effects of welfare on mother's weight, days in poor mental or physical health, or overall health status (Kaestner and Tarlov 2006; Bitler, Gelbach, and Hoynes 2005). Although one study finds evidence that welfare recipients' health outcomes (that is, hypertension, obesity, and cholesterol) are worse after welfare reform, these results are based on a pre-post comparison of one state's welfare population compared with a national sample (Kaplan et al. 2005). It is also possible that the negative short-term impacts on health insurance coverage and health behaviors could have impacts on mothers' future health.[3]

DATA AND METHODS

In this chapter, we use data from the Fragile Families study to examine the effect of welfare and child support policies on maternal health outcomes. The Fragile Families study follows a cohort of approximately five thousand births in twenty large American cities between 1998 and 2000. Mothers were interviewed around the time of a child's birth, with follow-up interviews occurring around the child's first and third birthdays. At baseline, the Fragile Families sample included 1,186 married mothers and 3,712 unmarried mothers; the response rates were 82 percent and 87 percent respectively. Most of the health outcomes and behaviors are measured at the three-year follow-up. Therefore, we restrict the sample to mothers who responded to the three-year survey (N = 4,231, or 87 percent of mothers interviewed at baseline who remained eligible at the three-year follow-up). We exclude 1,051 mothers who were married at the time of their child's birth as they are not the target population of these policies. We also drop 378 immigrants from the sample because Fragile Families does not have data on the immigrants' legal status and welfare policies are applied differentially to legal immigrants depending on the date of their arrival. Finally, we drop 266 cases with missing data on one of our key measures or on the one-year follow-up interview (used in the fixed effects), resulting in a final sample of 2,536 mothers.

Maternal Health and Health Behaviors

Health outcomes and behaviors are measured at the three-year follow-up interview unless otherwise noted. For the fixed effects analyses, we present results for which we have repeated measures at the one- and three-year follow-up interviews. Unfortunately, we do not have comparable measures at baseline to allow us to include that wave in the fixed effects estimation.

We look at three measures of health inputs. Similar to the measures from the BRFSS, we look at indicator variables for whether the mother had any health insurance (private or Medicaid) and whether the mother reported anyone in the household did not go to doctor or hospital because he or she could not afford it. Because nutrition is an important health input that has been shown to impact women's health—for example, mental health (Heflin, Siefert, and Williams 2005; Siefert et al. 2004) and obesity (Olson 1999)—we also look at hunger. We do not have a full food-insecurity scale. Therefore, we include an indicator of whether or not the mother reports she or her child went hungry at the one-year follow-up.

We look at two measures of overall health and well-being. The first is a categorical indicator of overall health, which is measured by a question that asks mothers to describe their health on a five-point scale (with one representing "excellent health" and five representing "poor health"). The second is an indicator for whether the mother was depressed or anxious. This indicator is derived from the Composite International Diagnostic Interview Short Form or CIDI-SF (Walters et al. 2002). Respondents are classified as *depressed* if they report having feelings of dysphoria or anhedonia in the past year lasting for two weeks or more, if the symptoms lasted most of the day, and if they occurred everyday during the two-week period. Respondents are classified as *anxious* if they report feeling excessively worried or anxious about more than one thing, if the feeling occurred more days than not, and if they had difficulty controlling their worries.[4]

We examine five stress-related behaviors that may impact women's health outcomes and might be affected by welfare or child support policies; they include alcohol or drug dependence, binge drinking, smoking, parental conflict, and domestic violence. An indicator for alcohol or drug dependence is derived from the CIDI-SF (Walters et al. 2002). Respondents are classified as *alcohol dependent* if they had at least four drinks in one day and reported at least three out of the seven following dependence symptoms: role interference as a result of use, use in hazardous situations, emotional or psychological problems as a result of use, a strong desire or urge to drink, a great deal of time using or recovering, drinking more or longer than intended, or drinking more to get the same effect. Respondents are classified as *drug dependent* if they used at least one of the following drugs: sedatives, tranquilizers, amphetamines, analgesics, inhalants, marijuana, cocaine, LSD, and heroin. In addition, they must report three out of the seven dependence symptoms. We also include a less restrictive measure of alcohol abuse: binge drinking. *Binge drinking* is defined as having four or more drinks in one day.[5] We also have a measure of smoking, which is defined as any smoking in the month prior to the one-year follow-up.

Finally, we examine two measures of parental conflict: arguing and domestic violence. For the first measure, mothers were asked how often they argue with the child's father on a five-point scale (with one representing "always" and five representing "never"). We reverse-code this item so that higher numbers equal more arguing. For the second measure, mothers were asked if they were slapped or kicked or if they were hit with a fist or object that could hurt; they reported the frequency of such violence as occurring often, sometimes, or never. Mothers who said they experienced any of these forms of violence by the child's father or their current romantic partner often or sometimes are classified as having experienced domestic violence.

Table 10.1 shows the prevalence of health and stress-related outcomes and behaviors in the sample. Most of the mothers in the sample have health insurance (75

TABLE 10.1 / Means of Key Measures

	Unweighted Percent/Mean
Health inputs and outcomes	
Has health insurance (percent)	75.0
Didn't go to doctor or hospital because couldn't afford it (percent)	7.0
Mother or child went hungry[a] (percent)	4.9
Overall health (high = poor on scale of 1 to 5) (mean)	2.3
Depressed or anxious (percent)	24.5
Stress-related behaviors	
Alcohol or drug dependent (percent)	1.7
Binge drinking (percent)	11.8
Smoking[a] (percent)	34.7
Argues with child's father (high = more on scale of 1 to 5) (mean)	3.2
Domestic violence (any partner) (percent)	11.1

Source: Authors' calculations.
Notes: Fragile Families and Child Wellbeing Study.
Sample includes only mothers unmarried at the focal child's birth.
[a] Measured at the one-year follow-up.
N – 2,536

percent), although a substantial minority (25 percent) is not covered by health insurance at the three-year follow-up. Only 7 percent of mothers report that someone in their household did not go to a doctor or hospital when they needed to in the past year because they could not afford it. This is not surprising given that such a high percentage of mothers are covered by insurance. Note however that this finding means that nearly one-third of mothers without health insurance are not seeking medical treatment when they or their family need it. Five percent of mothers report that they or children went hungry compared to 3 percent nationally (Nord et al. 2002).

Mothers in the sample report somewhat less than very good health overall. On a five-point scale (on which one represents "excellent health" and five represents "poor health"), the average score is 2.31. Thirteen percent of our mothers report that they are in fair or poor health as compared to 5 percent of a national sample of women ages eighteen to thirty-four. Mothers in our sample also report high rates of depression and anxiety (23 percent). Rates of depression and anxiety can vary widely depending on how they are measured, but our estimates are in line with estimates of depression among mothers with young children (Heneghan et al. 1998; Jayakody and Stauffer 2000), and they are much lower than those found in some other studies (Mulvaney and Kendrick 2005).

Using strict definitions of dependence, rates of alcohol and drug dependence are low (2 percent) in our sample of unmarried mothers. However, rates of binge drinking are considerably higher (12 percent). Smoking rates are particularly high (35 percent) as compared with national estimates of 21 percent for females over eighteen years old in the period from 2000 to 2002 (National Center for Health Statistics 2004).

On average, mothers report arguing with the child's father between "sometimes" and "often." Eleven percent of mothers report that the child's father or a current partner has slapped, kicked, or hit them. These are rates of current and recent violence, as opposed to ever-experienced violence, so the prevalence is lower than it would have been if we had included all prior experience. Our estimates are in line with community samples of low-income women, falling on the lower side of these other estimates (Tolman and Raphael 2000).

Measuring the Effects of Welfare and Child Support Policies and Practices

As Marianne Bitler and Hilary Hoynes (chapter 9, this volume) discuss, it is difficult to study the effects of policies on health for several reasons. The first is that policies do not change very often. Changes in policies would help determine whether there were corresponding changes in behavior. Another is that when policies do change, the change often encompasses a package of changes, and therefore it is difficult to parse out which policy changes matter. Finally, one would ideally examine policy changes across varying contexts (for example, economic conditions) to be able to parse out the effects of policy changes in different environments.

Most of the research examining the effects of welfare policies on health outcomes is based on the welfare reforms of the late 1990s. Researchers used the fact that AFDC waivers essentially stretched out the welfare-reform period, providing more variation in time and context. While these studies are incredibly valuable and provide most of what we know about the effects of welfare policies on health, using welfare reform to study the effects of policies more broadly suffers from many drawbacks. First, welfare reform encompassed large-scale changes, with many policy changes occurring at the same time, making it difficult to determine which elements of policies might matter most. Welfare reform also occurred in a strong economy and in an era of public health insurance expansions (Blank 2002), and similar policy changes in an alternate environment may not have had the same effect.

Another approach to studying the effect of welfare policies is to use data from welfare-to-work evaluations. Experiments allow researchers to compare the effects of different program components, and they have the advantage of a control group. But experiments are also limited by context and, without a large number of experimental evaluations, suffer from an inability of parsing out the components of welfare policies that may impact health. Experimental evaluations also often miss the impact on those who never received welfare perhaps in response to the reforms themselves.

Using data from the Fragile Families study, we attempt to measure the post-reform effects of welfare policies on maternal health. We have longitudinal data from twenty cities in fifteen states; however, policies do not change very often, so we cannot examine state-level change using state fixed effects. Therefore, we rely on individual-level relationships to assess the relationship between welfare and child support policies on maternal health and well-being. We use a four-fold analysis strategy, triangulating results from ordinary least squares (OLS), fixed effects, reduced form, and instrumental variables analyses.

First, because welfare and child support policies have their most proximate effects via causing mothers to either be on welfare or to receive child support, we look at the relationships between welfare and child support receipt and maternal health behaviors and outcomes using OLS. We recognize that the associations between health and welfare and child support receipt are biased estimates of the effects of policies on health because poor health contributes positively to welfare receipt and, most likely, negatively to child support receipt. Thus the observed relationships provide upper-bound estimates of the effects of welfare and child support policies on health.

Next, for outcomes on which we have repeated measures at the one- and three-year follow-up interviews, we estimate individual fixed effects models in which the dependent variable is the change in health status and the key independent variables are the change in welfare and child support receipt. This more restrictive model looks at changes associated with moving into welfare and child support, net of observed and unobserved stable characteristics of the mother. However, the association between observed changes in welfare and child support receipt and health does not deal with the more serious bias of reverse causation; namely, it does not take into account that changes in health status or behavior may lead to changes in welfare receipt.

To try to get around the issues of selection bias and reverse causality, we employ instrumental variables. We use welfare and child support policies and practices as instruments to predict welfare and child support receipt. Specifically, we use welfare rules and the strength of child support enforcement as instrumental variables that determine welfare and child support receipt. Then we see if these predicted variables, which are purged of individual-level unobserved characteristics that may be correlated with welfare and child support receipt and with maternal health, are associated with maternal health. Essentially, one can interpret the instrumental welfare and child support variables like an index of the generosity of welfare policies and the stringency of child support enforcement policies. This is true because the more generous the welfare policies are in a city (in terms of higher benefits and more lenient sanctions), the more likely mothers are to receive welfare. Similarly, the more stringent the child support policies are in a city, the more likely mothers are to receive child support. There are two key assumptions required by the instrumental variables models. First, the policies must do a good job predicting welfare and child support receipt. The policies do appear to be good predictors of welfare and child support receipt and first-stage results are presented later in the methods section. Second, the policies should not be correlated with health outcomes except through their effects on welfare and child support receipt. While we think this is fairly plausible for most outcomes, there certainly could be unobserved city variables that are correlated with both policies and maternal health outcomes. To check this assumption, we compute a test of overidentifying restrictions using Hansen's J-statistic. Several of the models do fail this test (these are noted in the tables and text). Finally, we estimate reduced form models in which welfare and child support policies across cities and states are the key independent variables. The reduced form models test for the effects of welfare policies more generally, as opposed to welfare receipt specifically. Like the instrumental variables estimates, the reduced form models may be subject to omitted-variable bias.

For the individual-level analyses our measure of welfare receipt is an indicator for whether the mother reported receiving any income from TANF in the twelve months preceding the three-year follow-up.[6] Our measure of child support receipt is an indicator for whether the mother reported receiving any child support dollars from the focal child's father or the father of a different child. In all of the models, we control for individual-level characteristics that may be associated with welfare receipt and health, but which are exogenous to welfare and child support receipt (that is, mother's age, race-ethnicity, education, and whether it is her first birth). We also include two regional dummy variables (south and east), as different parts of the country may have different philosophies in terms of providing welfare support or enforcing child support; regions may also have other factors (such as culture or weather) that may be associated with the health behaviors or outcomes.

We use two indicators of welfare generosity in the instrumental variables and reduced form models: the maximum TANF plus Food Stamps benefit, and the harshness of sanctions for noncompliance. The maximum TANF plus Food Stamps benefit is calculated for a family of three with no other income in 1999 (obtained from the State Policy Documentation Project). This term is divided by one hundred dollars in the models. We also include a squared term to capture nonlinear effects of TANF benefits. To measure sanctioning policy, we use a variable that categorizes whether a state's sanctioning policies were lenient, moderate, or stringent (on a three-point scale, with one representing lenient and three representing stringent), as categorized by LaDonna Pavetti and Dan Bloom (2001). Stringent sanctions indicate that a state imposes immediate full-family sanctions or imposes gradual full-family sanctions with an immediate elimination of Food Stamps benefits or Medicaid. Moderate sanctions indicate that a state imposes gradual full-family sanctions with no sanction on Food Stamps benefits or Medicaid, or it imposes a partial sanction with a 100 percent sanction on Food Stamps benefits. Lenient sanctions indicate that a state imposes partial sanctions with less than a 100 percent sanction on Food Stamps benefits. We tried incorporating alternative measures of welfare generosity, including time limits, sanction amounts, work requirements, and earnings disregards. However, these variables were not significant in the presence of TANF, Food Stamps Benefits, and sanction policies, and thus we did not include them in the models.

To measure the strength of child support enforcement, we use an index that combines measures of the legal framework, state expenditures on enforcement, and a practice measure that captures states' actual performance in collecting child support. The index was constructed by Lenna Nepomnyaschy and Irwin Garfinkel (2006). The legal framework incorporates three groups of laws: a group of three laws pertaining to paternity establishment (allowing paternity to be established until the child is eighteen years old, mandating genetic testing, and making voluntary paternity conclusive); laws pertaining to universal wage withholding; and a group of the three most recent federally-mandated laws (the New Hires directory, license revocation for nonpayment, and automation). Paternity establishment is the prerequisite for enforcing support among the unmarried, and previous research has found universal withholding to be the single most important enforcement tool. Because all of these laws were mandated by the federal government during the 1980s and early 1990s, the index also includes the three most recently mandated laws. For each law, the year that the law became effective in the state is entered; it is then standardized to have a mean of zero and a standard deviation of one. Finally, it is inverted, so that the longer the laws have been on the books, the greater the value. Each index represents the average score for each state on that set of measures. Total state expenditures on child support enforcement in 1999 were divided by the state population and were also standardized. The final component is an adjusted payment-rate ratio from city-level census data from 2000. The ratio is constructed by regressing the probability that an unmarried mother received any child support on the mother's race-ethnicity, age, education, nativity, parity, presence of a child under age six, state-level median male wage, and maximum combined TANF plus Food Stamps benefit in the state. From this equation, an aggregate city-level probability of receiving support is predicted, and the raw aggregate probability of receiving support is divided by this adjusted measure. This measure is also standardized.

The welfare and child support policies for the states in the Fragile Families sample are displayed in table 10.2, along with the percent of mothers who received welfare in the past year and the percent of mothers who receive child support. Maximum TANF plus Food Stamps benefits ranged from $526 to $907. Nine states had stringent sanction policies, three had moderate sanction policies, and three had lenient sanction policies. The combined effect of the generosity of these welfare policies can be observed in the variation in mothers' rates of receiving welfare in the past year. Receipt rates generally rise with the generosity of TANF and Food Stamps benefits and with the leniency of sanctions. We also observe a strong relationship (particularly at the tails) between the strength of the state's child support enforcement (which is adjusted for the demographic composition of the state) and the percent of mothers' receiving child support. On the whole, an average of 30 percent of mothers received welfare in the past year and 28 percent received child support.

The results from the first stage of the instrumental variables models are presented in table 10.3. We used two-stage least squares regression, with standard errors clustered at the state level. The F-statistics for the test of the joint significance of the four instruments predicting welfare and child support receipt are large (12.0 and 27.3) and statistically significant (at the $p \leq 0.01$ level). This indicates that even

TABLE 10.2 / Welfare and Child Support Policies by State

State	Max TANF +FS /$100	Sanction Policies	Child Support Enforcement Index	Received Welfare Past Year	Receives Child Support
Texas	5.3	Moderate	−0.215	19%	30%
Tennessee	5.6	Strict	−0.602	30	28
Indiana	6.2	Lenient	−0.397	34	21
Virginia	6.2	Strict	0.657	27	33
Florida	6.3	Strict	−0.006	15	46
Illinois	6.8	Moderate	−0.826	31	15
Maryland	6.9	Strict	−0.297	25	26
Ohio	6.9	Strict	1.766	32	49
Pennsylvania	7.3	Moderate	0.021	37	26
New Jersey	7.4	Strict	0.741	35	26
Michigan	7.7	Strict	0.709	30	25
Massachusetts	8.5	Strict	0.187	44	34
New York	8.6	Lenient	−0.325	37	18
California	8.7	Lenient	0.162	37	21
Wisconsin	9.1	Strict	1.947	30	43
All States in Sample	7.0	Mod/Strict	0.248	30	28

Sources: Column 1, State Policy Documentation Project; column 2, Pavetti and Bloom (2001); column 3, Nepomnyaschy and Garfinkel (2006); columns 4 and 5, authors' calculations.

after controlling for individual-level characteristics, the instruments are significant predictors of welfare and child support receipt. Looking at the coefficients for the policies, we see that more lenient sanctions are associated with greater welfare receipt. The value of the cash benefits are not significantly related to the receipt of welfare, but the direction is as expected. The lack of statistical significance is likely due to the strong relationship between the region and value of welfare benefits. If we remove the regional dummies, the relationship between cash benefits and receipt is positive and significant. The three welfare policies are also jointly predictive of welfare receipt. The strength of child support enforcement is strongly related to the likelihood of receiving child support. Both measures of welfare generosity are associated with lower levels of child support receipt; considered jointly, they are significant at the $p \leq 0.01$ level. This result is not surprising if mothers view TANF as an alternative to child support. Meanwhile, it is surprising that, contrary to what has been found in other studies, strict child support enforcement is not associated with a reduced probability of receiving welfare in the past year. However, if we specify welfare as current receipt or total welfare dollars received, the sign on the child support enforcement coefficient is negative (though it is insignificant).

TABLE 10.3 / First-Stage Regression Equations

	Received Welfare	Received Child Support
Mother characteristics		
White	−0.154 **	0.006
	(.025)	(.020)
Hispanic	−0.128 **	−0.009
	(.021)	(.020)
Age	−0.004 ^	0.004 *
	(.002)	(.002)
Less than high school degree	0.145 **	−0.002
	(.023)	(.030)
Any college education	−0.098 **	0.068 **
	(.021)	(.020)
First birth	−0.022	−0.125 **
	(.019)	(.013)
City is in the south	0.009	0.046
	(.028)	(.046)
City is in the east	0.055 *	0.013
	(.019)	(.033)
Instruments		
(Max TANF+FS 1999)/$100	0.111	−0.233 ^
	(.088)	(.115)
((Max TANF+FS 1999)/$100)^2	−0.007	0.014
	(.007)	(.008)
Sanctions (higher = stricter)	−0.065 **	0.016
	(.021)	(.019)
Child support enforcement (higher = stronger)	0.021	0.087 *
	(.026)	(.030)
Constant	0.110	1.055 *
	(.294)	(.372)
F-statistic	12.0	27.3
p of F-statistic	0.000	0.000

Source: Authors' calculations.
Notes: Robust standard errors in parentheses. Standard errors clustered at state level.
** p < 0.01; * p < 0.05; ^ p < 0.10 two-tailed

Individual-level characteristics predict welfare and child support receipt in a manner consistent with previous research. Relative to African American mothers, Caucasian and Hispanic mothers receive less welfare. Mother's age and education are negatively associated with receiving welfare and positively associated with receiving child support. Mothers with first births are less likely to receive child support.

RESULTS

In the first part of the analysis, we examine the relationship between observed welfare and child support receipt and maternal health and health behaviors using OLS regression and controlling for a set of individual characteristics (table 10.4). In terms of the demographic characteristics of mothers, white mothers report lower rates of insurance coverage, higher rates of hardship (that is, they cannot afford a doctor or they go hungry), binge drinking, smoking, and domestic violence than black mothers. Hispanics report lower rates of health insurance coverage, better overall health, more domestic violence, and more binge drinking (but less dependence) than black mothers. Increasing age is associated with increased health insurance, but it is also associated with more smoking, alcohol and drug dependence, and worse overall health. Higher levels of education are associated with better health outcomes and behaviors (with the exception of medical hardships). Having only one child is associated with greater health insurance, less medical hardships, and less depression and smoking; however, it is also associated with more binge drinking and parental conflict. Residing in the South or the East, as opposed to the West or Midwest, is associated with less experienced hunger and less binge drinking. Southerners are less likely to have health insurance coverage, white Easterners are less likely to face medical hardships and be anxious or depressed.

In terms of our variables of interest, receiving welfare is associated with greater health insurance coverage. This is not surprising as the process for getting Medicaid is more straightforward for mothers on welfare than for mothers who are not on welfare (Gold 1999). Despite being associated with greater access to health insurance, welfare receipt is associated with a host of poor health outcomes and health behaviors. Mothers who received welfare in the last year report worse overall health, higher rates of depression and anxiety, and greater levels of food insecurity. For instance, mothers who received welfare had rates of depression and anxiety that were 8 percent higher than mothers who did not receive welfare in the previous year. Welfare receipt is also associated with higher rates of stress-related behaviors, including greater alcohol and drug dependence, smoking, parental arguing, and domestic violence. For example, mothers who received welfare were 4 percent more likely to report domestic violence by a partner than mothers who did not receive welfare. Again, we interpret the OLS model results as the upper bounds of the possible associations because of the selection on health into welfare receipt.

Child support receipt is not associated with as many maternal health behaviors and outcomes as welfare receipt. Receiving child support is associated with reductions in reporting having gone hungry and with higher rates of parental conflict and domestic violence. The latter two are consistent with previous findings on the effects of strong enforcement (Fertig, Garfinkel, and McLanahan 2007).

Table 10.5 repeats the results from the OLS models and adds the results from the fixed effects, instrumental variables, and reduced form regressions. We have reoriented table 10.5 so that the key independent variables (welfare receipt and policies, and child support receipt and policies) appear across the top and the outcome variables appear down the left-hand side column. Welfare results are presented in

Table 10.4 / OLS Models Predicting Effects of Welfare and Child-Support Receipt on Maternal Health and Health Behaviors

	Health Insurance	No Doctor	Hungry	Overall Health[a]	Depressed or Anxious	Alcohol or Drug Dependent	Binge	Smoke	Argues	Domestic Violence
Received welfare last year	0.207 **	-0.005	0.041 **	0.113 *	0.080 **	0.018 *	-0.017	0.063 **	0.091 ^	0.041 **
	(0.02)	(0.01)	(0.01)	(0.05)	(0.02)	(0.01)	(0.01)	(0.02)	(0.05)	(0.02)
Receives child support	0.013	-0.002	-0.021 *	0.028	0.005	-0.009	0.014	-0.034	0.253 **	0.028 ^
	(0.02)	(0.01)	(0.01)	(0.05)	(0.02)	(0.01)	(0.01)	(0.02)	(0.05)	(0.02)
White	-0.082 **	0.060 **	0.025 ^	0.090	0.030	0.007	0.102 **	0.269 **	-0.028	0.041 *
	(0.03)	(0.02)	(0.01)	(0.06)	(0.03)	(0.01)	(0.02)	(0.03)	(0.06)	(0.02)
Hispanic	-0.143 **	0.022	-0.008	0.092 ^	-0.030	-0.012 **	0.072 **	-0.025	-0.019	0.031 ^
	(0.02)	(0.01)	(0.01)	(0.06)	(0.02)	(0.01)	(0.02)	(0.02)	(0.05)	(0.02)
Age	0.003 *	0.001	0.000	0.028 **	-0.001	0.001 ^	-0.002	0.007 **	-0.005	-0.001
	(0.00)	(0.00)	(0.00)	(0.01)	(0.00)	(0.00)	(0.00)	(0.00)	(0.00)	(0.00)
Less than high school	-0.045 *	0.010	0.012	0.107 *	0.030	-0.005	-0.026 ^	0.131 **	0.042	0.022
	(0.02)	(0.01)	(0.01)	(0.05)	(0.02)	(0.01)	(0.02)	(0.02)	(0.05)	(0.02)
Any college	0.038 ^	0.024 ^	0.017	-0.099 ^	0.014	-0.002	0.004	-0.085 **	-0.012	-0.017
	(0.02)	(0.01)	(0.01)	(0.05)	(0.02)	(0.01)	(0.02)	(0.02)	(0.05)	(0.02)
First birth	0.058 **	-0.022 ^	-0.011	-0.059	-0.042 *	-0.003	0.032 *	-0.039 ^	0.083 ^	-0.017
	(0.02)	(0.01)	(0.01)	(0.05)	(0.02)	(0.01)	(0.02)	(0.02)	(0.05)	(0.01)
City is in south	-0.052 *	-0.003	-0.030 *	0.023	-0.010	0.006	-0.065 **	-0.005	-0.010	-0.019
	(0.03)	(0.02)	(0.01)	(0.06)	(0.03)	(0.01)	(0.02)	(0.03)	(0.06)	(0.02)
City is in east	0.022	-0.023 *	-0.039 **	-0.041	-0.037 ^	-0.005	-0.049 **	0.011	0.063	-0.019
	(0.02)	(0.01)	(0.01)	(0.05)	(0.02)	(0.01)	(0.01)	(0.02)	(0.05)	(0.01)

Source: Authors' calculations.

Notes: Robust standard errors in parentheses. Standard errors clustered at state level.

** p < 0.01; * p < 0.05; ^ p < 0.10 two tailed

[a] High = poor health

the top panel and child support results are presented in the bottom panel. Structuring the table in this way facilitates comparisons across the models. The results from the fixed effects models show the association between changes in welfare and child support receipt and changes in health outcomes between the one- and three-year follow-ups (roughly a two-year time span); they are not available for all of our health measures. For welfare, the fixed effects estimates indicate that receiving welfare is associated with greater access to health insurance, which is consistent with both theory and previous research. The rest of the coefficients are small in size and are not statistically significant. For child support, the estimates indicate that child support receipt is associated with greater maternal depression (significant at the $p \leq 0.10$ level).[7]

The fixed effects estimates are biased to the extent that causation runs from changes in health to changes in welfare and child support receipt. We also could not calculate fixed effects for all of the measures. Therefore, we employ both instrumental variables and reduced form models, which allow us to eliminate unobserved characteristics of mothers that do not change over time and which may be correlated with welfare and child support receipt and with maternal health. First, we use instrumental variables to predict mothers' welfare and child support receipt to see if the predicted receipt variables are associated with mothers' health and well-being. The interpretation of the instrumental welfare and child support variables is that they measure the generosity of welfare policies and the stringency of child support enforcement policies as they operate through welfare and child support receipt. The more generous the welfare policies are in a city—taking account of both benefit levels and sanctions—the more likely mothers are to receive welfare. Similarly, the more stringent the child support policies and practices are in a city, the more likely mothers are to receive child support. Note that as is conventional for instrumental variables models, the predicted levels of welfare and child support are estimated as linear functions. The same is true for the reduced form child support models. But, the reduced form models for welfare allow the effects of increased benefit levels to vary depending upon the level of benefits (using a squared term), and they allow the effects of benefits and sanctions to differ from one another.

Looking first at the top panel welfare results, the first thing to note about the instrumental variables estimates is that the magnitude of the coefficients is much larger than those obtained from the OLS and fixed effects models, and few of the welfare coefficients are significant.[8] This is not unusual for instrumental variables estimates, as both coefficients and standard errors frequently increase. By way of contrast, a large number of coefficients in the reduced form results are highly significant; and, most importantly, the linear and squared terms for benefit level have opposite signs. The latter provides a substantive explanation for why some of linear instrumental variables coefficients are insignificant (for instance, not affording a doctor and binge drinking). The relationship between increases in welfare generosity and health varies from negative at low levels of welfare benefits to positive at high levels of welfare benefits.

The way that the relationship between health and welfare benefits varies depending on the level of generosity can be seen in panels A, B, C, D, and E of figure 10.1, which displays the predicted health values at different levels of welfare benefits for each of the five health outcomes with significant coefficients in the reduced form models. Each benefit level is associated with three different levels of sanctions (lenient, moderate, and stringent), and therefore there are three curves for each outcome. Note, however, that only in the cases of alcohol and drug dependence and smoking are the sanction variables statistically significant.

Panel A indicates that when welfare benefits are very low, increases in generosity reduce the likelihood that mothers refrained from seeking needed medical care because they could not afford it. Once benefits reach a relatively high level, however, further increases in benefits actually have a negative effect. The initial decline in this measure of hardship makes sense. However, the increase in hardship that occurs when relatively high benefits increase is more difficult to explain. But, note that this pattern is consistent with the effects on depression and anxiety (panel C) and on binge drinking (panel D), and at least part of the curve is similar when looking at experienced hunger (panel B). Indeed the pattern of decreasing health benefits at the highest levels of welfare benefits holds for all of the significant measures of health except cigarette smoking (panel E).

Why increases in benefit levels should have positive effects at low benefit levels and negative effects at high benefit levels is a puzzle. One possible explanation is that at low levels of welfare benefits, increases in benefit levels have the intended effect of reducing maternal stress and thereby improving mental health. But once benefits reach a certain level, the negative effects of higher benefits outweigh the positive effects. High benefits could decrease work and increase isolation, and thereby increase depression, anxiety, and self-medication. These results are consistent with other research that examines the impacts of welfare receipt on mother's well-being (Casey et al. 2004; Ensminger 1995; Jayakody, Danziger, and Pollack 2000). While this explanation is plausible, it must remain only suggestive. The results are generated by a cross section of only twenty cities. In addition, the instrumental variables models predicting hunger and smoking failed the test of overidentifying restrictions, implying that these policies and outcomes may be related by other factors not measured here. This may also explain why the welfare effects on smoking follow a different curve than the other measures. However, it is useful to note that there are negative effects of welfare on depression and anxiety implied by nearly all of the models (for at least some benefit levels).

The child support results from the instrumental variables and reduced form models suggest that stronger child support enforcement is also associated with higher rates of maternal stress-related behaviors and outcomes. Stronger child support enforcement is associated with higher rates of depression, anxiety, and binge drinking, as well as with lower levels of subjective health. All of these outcomes could operate through higher rates of parental conflict. The coefficients of both the instrumental variables and reduced form coefficients are positive, although neither comes close to being significant. And, results also suggest reductions in the most extreme cases of parental conflict (that is, domestic violence).

TABLE 10.5 / OLS, Fixed Effects, Second-Stage IV, and Reduced Form Results for the Effects of Welfare and Child Support on Maternal Health and Health Behaviors

| | Received Welfare Last Year | | | Reduced Form | | | Receives Child Support | | | Reduced Form |
| | | | | | | Sanction (Higher = | | | | C.S. |
Outcome	OLS	FE	IV	TANF $	TANF²	Less Strict)	OLS	FE	IV	Index
Health inputs and outcomes										
Has health insurance	0.207 **	0.136 **	—	0.149	-0.005	-0.026	0.013	-0.015	—	-0.036
	(.017)	(.021)		(.153)	(.011)	(.026)	(.019)	(.024)		(.040)
No doctor or hospital because couldn't afford	-0.005	0.005	-0.242	-0.149 *	0.009 ^	-0.004	-0.002	0.006	-0.008	0.002
	(.012)	(.011)	(.151)	(.065)	(.005)	(.009)	(.011)	(.013)	(.080)	(.007)
Mother or child went hungry	0.063 **	N/A	—	-0.077 **	0.007 **	-0.005	-0.021	N/A	—	-0.014 *
	(.020)			(.025)	(.002)	(.004)	(.010)			(.005)
Overall health (high = poor)	0.113 *	-0.018	0.227	-0.208	0.014	-0.012	0.028	0.021	1.015 **	0.080 ^
	(.050)	(.048)	(.233)	(.127)	(.009)	(.026)	(.048)	(.052)	(.261)	(.039)
Depressed or anxious	0.080 **	0.013	0.388 **	-0.181 *	0.013 **	0.005	0.005	0.037 ^	0.324 ^	0.013
	(.020)	(.021)	(.148)	(.063)	(.004)	(.014)	(.019)	(.021)	(.179)	(.016)

Stress-Related Behaviors

Alcohol/drug dependent	0.018 *	N/A	0.138 **	–0.003	0.000	0.007 *	–0.009	N/A	0.018	0.002
	(.007)		(.052)	(.020)	(.001)	(.003)	(.006)		(.039)	(.005)
Binge drinking	–0.017	–0.013	–0.008	–0.175 *	0.011 *	0.006	0.014	0.015	0.249 *	0.028 ^
	(.014)	(.014)	(.162)	(.061)	(.004)	(.011)	(.014)	(.018)	(.116)	(.015)
Smoking	0.041 **	N/A	—	0.398 **	–0.029 **	0.043 **	–0.034	N/A	—	0.068 **
	(.010)			(.087)	(.006)	(.014)	(.024)			(.020)
Argues with father (high = more)	0.091 ^	N/A	–0.211	0.318	–0.023	–0.022	0.253 **	N/A	0.462	0.055
	(.048)		(.617)	(.206)	(.015)	(.039)	(.045)		(.443)	(.059)
Domestic violence (any partner)	0.041 **	0.004	–0.183	–0.011	0.001	–0.013	0.028 ^	0.017	–0.087 ^	–0.015 ^
	(.015)	(.016)	(.155)	(.038)	(.003)	(.009)	(.015)	(.017)	(.048)	(.008)

Source: Authors' calculations.

Notes: Robust standard errors in parentheses. Standard errors clustered at state level.

** p < 0.01; * p < 0.05; ^ p < 0.10 two-tailed

All models include controls for race-ethnicity, age, education, first birth, and region.

N/A means that model could not be estimated because do not have measures at two points in time.

"—" means the model fails test of overidentifying restrictions.

FIGURE 10.1 / Predicted Probabilities of Five Maternal Health Behaviors and Outcomes Derived from Reduced Form Results

Panel A

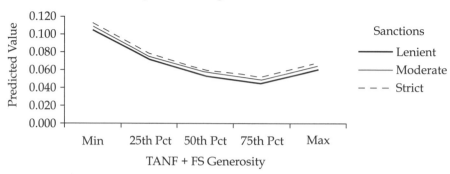

Panel B

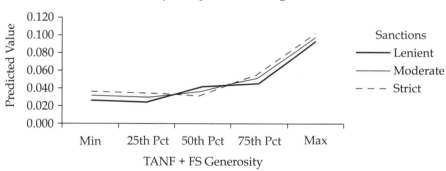

Panel C

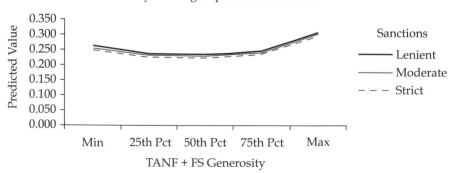

FIGURE 10.1 / (*Continued*)

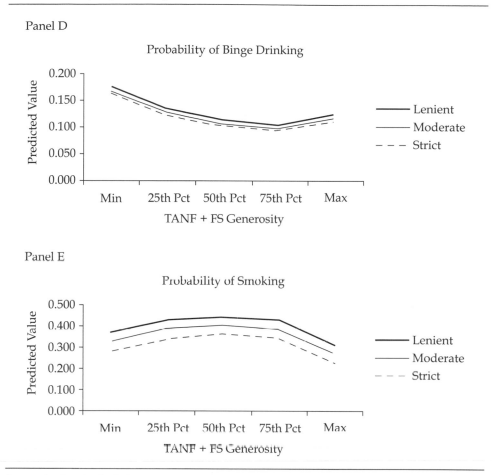

Panel D

Probability of Binge Drinking

Panel E

Probability of Smoking

Source: Authors' calculations.

CONCLUSION

This chapter examines the effects of welfare and child support policies on maternal health and health behaviors using data from the Fragile Families and Child Wellbeing Study. Theory is ambiguous with respect to how generous welfare policies, defined as policies that encourage welfare participation, might be expected to affect maternal health. On the one hand, welfare was designed to alleviate mothers' financial problems; in which case, policies that make it easy for a woman to obtain welfare should reduce stress and improve health. On the other hand, by encouraging economic dependence and lack of structure, welfare participation may actually increase stress and reduce maternal health. According to one set of the results presented here, both theories may be true: at low levels of welfare benefits, more generous benefits are associated with increases in health, while at high levels of welfare more generous benefits are associated with decreases in health.

We also argued that the effects of strong child support enforcement were ambiguous for unmarried mothers—especially for those at risk for being on welfare. Whereas strong child support enforcement might be expected to increase the incomes of mothers in the long run, it may actually reduce income in the short term by replacing informal support paid to the mother with formal child support paid to the state (Nepomnyaschy and Garfinkel 2006). Moreover, since low-income mothers are required to cooperate with the child support system in identifying nonresident fathers, stronger enforcement may lead to greater conflict between unmarried parents, thus further increasing stress. Our findings are consistent with a story in which stricter child support enforcement leads to increases in stress-related behaviors such as drinking, increases in depression, and ultimately to poorer overall health. The welfare and child support findings are consistent insofar as both imply that income-transfer policies have their greatest impact via mental health and mental health behavior.

Examining the health effects of welfare and child support enforcement is a difficult topic to study. At the macro-level, it is difficult to estimate the effects of policies because welfare and child support policies do not change often, and changes frequently co-occur with other policy changes. This makes it difficult to parse out the effects of the welfare policies and other factors. At the individual-level, policy effects may interact with individual characteristics, and it is difficult to parse out the effects of policies and program participation. Given these methodological complications, researchers would ideally rely on a large data set that included city-level data for all fifty states over time in order to be able to detect the effects of policy changes in different contexts, while employing city and state fixed effects to control for other city- and state-level factors that change. Ideally these data would also include a large sample of low-income women and detailed health data. However, few data sets meet these criteria. Experimental data are also useful, particularly as we accumulate more state-level studies over time.

Given the limitations of the Fragile Families data set for examining this topic, we attempted to triangulate results from four different types of individual-level analyses. However, our analysis has several limitations which should be kept in mind when interpreting the results. First, the OLS and fixed effects estimates are problematic because of selection, and many of the coefficients from the instrumental variables models are not measured precisely. Thus our results should be viewed as suggestive. Second, all of our health variables are measured by mothers' reports, which means that they are subjective and may be affected by response bias. The fact that the policies affect some of these measures and not others indicates to us that response bias is not a serious problem. Third, and perhaps most important, the policy instruments we use in this analysis are measured at only one point in time, and thus our estimates of their effect are based on between-city differences in policies rather than within-city changes in policies over time. We cannot rule out the possibility that the effects attributed to welfare and child support policies are due to some unmeasured characteristics of the city other than these two sets of policies.

Despite these caveats, we believe that our analysis makes a contribution to the literature by documenting both the positive and negative associations between welfare and child support policies and health outcomes and behaviors on a sample of low-income mothers of young children—the very mothers these policies are intended to help. Insofar as our results hold up in future analyses, they indicate that more attention should be given to the unanticipated consequences of income-transfer policies.

NOTES

1. Nancy Reichman and her colleagues (2001) provide more detail on the study design.
2. Marianne Bitler and Hilary Hoynes (chapter 9, this volume) provide a more detailed review of the welfare-reform literature.
3. Marianne Bitler and Hilary Hoynes (chapter 9, this volume) use evidence from welfare-to-work experiments which suggest that welfare reform may be associated with increases in maternal mental health and overall child health. While the results are consistently positive, few are statistically significant.
4. See the report from the Center for Research on Child Wellbeing (2006) for more information on how this measure is constructed.
5. At the one-year follow-up, *binge drinking* is classified as having five drinks or more in one day.
6. For the two outcomes measured at the one-year interview (hunger and smoking), the welfare and child support receipt measures refer to the year prior to the one-year interview.
7. This is robust to the inclusion of an indicator of relationship status at both waves, which would capture the effect of the relationship breakup on depression.
8. We could not estimate models for health insurance, hunger, or smoking, as they failed the test of overidentifying restrictions. Failing that test suggests that the instruments (policies in this case) are associated with factors other than welfare or child support receipt which influence maternal health outcomes and behaviors.

REFERENCES

American Psychological Association. 2001. *Mental Health Issues in TANF Reauthorization.* Memo to the U.S. Department of Health and Human Services. Washington: American Psychological Association.

Bitler, Marianne, Jonah Gelbach, and Hilary Hoynes. 2005. "Welfare Reform and Health." *Journal of Human Resources* 40(2): 309–34.

Blank, Rebecca. 2002. "Evaluating Welfare Reform in the United States." *Journal of Economic Literature* 40(4): 1105–66.

Casey, Patrick, Susan Goolsby, Carol Berkowitz, Deborah Frank, John Cook, Diana Cutts, Maureen M. Black, Nieves Zaldivar, Suzette Levenson, Tim Heeren, Alan Meyers, and the Children's Sentinel Nutritional Assessment Program Study Group. 2004. "Maternal Depression, Changing Public Assistance, Food Security, and Child Health Status." *Pediatrics* 113(2): 298–304.

Cawley, John, Mathis Schroeder, and Kosali Simon. 2006. "How Did Welfare Reform Affect the Health Insurance Coverage of Women and Children?" *Health Services Research* 41(2): 486–506.

Center for Research on Child Wellbeing. 2006. *Scales Documentation and Question Sources for the Fragile Families Three-Year Follow-up*. Princeton, N.J.: Princeton University.

Chavkin, Wendy, Diana Romero, and Paul Wise. 2000. "State Welfare Reform Policies and Declines in Health Insurance." *American Journal of Public Health* 90(6): 900–8.

Currie, Janet, and Nancy Cole. 1993. "Welfare and Child Health—The Link Between AFDC Participation and Birth-Weight." *American Economic Review* 83(4): 971–85.

Ensminger, Margaret E. 1995. "Welfare and Psychological Distress: A Longitudinal Study of African American Urban Mothers." *Journal of Health and Social Behavior* 36(4): 346–59.

Fertig, Angela, Irwin Garfinkel, and Sara S. McLanahan. 2007. "Child Support Enforcement and Domestic Violence Among Non-Cohabiting Couples." *Center for Research on Child Wellbeing* working paper No. 2002-17-FF. Princeton, N.J.: Princeton University.

Garrett, Bowen, and John Holahan. 2000. "Health Insurance Coverage After Welfare." *Health Affairs* 19(1): 175– 84.

Gold, Rachel Benson. 1999. "Implications for Family Planning of Post-Welfare Reform Insurance Trends." *Guttmacher Report on Public Policy* 2(6): 6–9.

Haider, Steven J., Alison Jacknowitz, and Robert F. Schoeni. 2003. "Welfare Work Requirements and Child Well-Being: Evidence from the Effects on Breast-Feeding." *Demography* 40(3): 479–97.

Heflin, Colleen M., Kristine Siefert, and David R. Williams. 2005. "Food Insufficiency and Women's Mental Health: Findings from a 3-Year Panel of Welfare Recipients." *Social Science and Medicine* 61(9): 1971–82.

Heneghan, Amy M., Ellen Johnson Silver, Laurie J. Bauman, Lauren E. Westbrook, and Ruth E. K. Stein. 1998. "Depressive Symptoms in Inner-City Mothers of Young Children: Who Is at Risk?" *Pediatrics* 102(6): 1394–1400.

Holl, Jane, Kristen Shook Slack, and Amy Bush Stevens. 2005. "Welfare Reform and Health Insurance: Consequences for Parents." *American Journal of Public Health* 95(2): 279–85.

Institute of Medicine. 2002. *Care Without Coverage: Too Little, Too Late*. Washington: National Academy Press.

Jayakody, Rukmalie, and Dawn Stauffer. 2000. "Mental Health Problems Among Single Mothers: Implications for Work and Welfare Reform." *Journal of Social Issues* 56(4): 617–34.

Jayakody, Rukmalie, Sheldon Danziger, and Harold Pollack. 2000. "Welfare Reform, Substance Use, and Mental Health." *Journal of Health Politics Policy and Law* 25(4): 623–51.

Kaestner, Robert, and Neeraj Kaushal. 2003. "Welfare Reform and Health Insurance Coverage of Low-Income Families." *Journal of Health Economics* 22(6): 959–81.

Kaestner, Robert, and Won Chan Lee. 2005. "The Effect of Welfare Reform on Prenatal Care and Birth Weight." *Health Economics* 14(5): 497–511.

Kaestner, Robert, and Elizabeth Tarlov. 2006. "Changes in the Welfare Caseload and the Health of Low-Educated Mothers." *Journal of Policy Analysis and Management* 25(3): 623–43.

Kaplan, April. 1997. "Domestic Violence and Welfare Reform." *Welfare Information Network Issue Notes* 1(8).

Kaplan, George A., Kristine Siefert, Nalini Ranjit, Trivellore E. Raghunathan, Elizabeth A. Young, Diem Tran, Sandra Danziger, Susan Hudson, John W. Lynch, and Richard Tolman. 2005. "The Health of Poor Women Under Welfare Reform." *American Journal of Public Health* 95(7): 1252–8.

Lennon, Mary Clare, Juliana Blome, and Kevin English. 2002. "Depression Among Women on Welfare: A Review of the Literature." *Journal of the American Medical Women's Association* 57(1): 27–32.

Levy, Helen, and David Meltzer. 2004. "What Do We Really Know About Whether Health Insurance Affects Health?" In *Health Policy and the Uninsured*, edited by Catherine G. McLaughlin. Washington: Urban Institute.

Metsch, Lisa R., and Harold Pollack. 2005. "Welfare Reform and Substance Abuse." *Milbank Quarterly* 83(1): 65–99.

Mulvaney, Caroline, and Denise Kendrick. 2005. "Depressive Symptoms in Mothers of Pre-School Children." *Social Psychiatry and Psychiatric Epidemiology* 40(3): 202–8.

National Center for Health Statistics. 2004. *Health, United States, 2004 with Chartbook on Trends in the Health of Americans*. Hyattsville, Md.: National Center for Health Statistics.

Nepomnyaschy, Lenna, and Irwin Garfinkel. 2006. "Fathers' Contributions to Their Non-marital Children." *Center for Research on Child Wellbeing*. Working paper No. 2006-09-FF. Princeton, N.J.: Princeton University.

Nord, Mark, Nader Kabbani, Laura Tiehen, Margaret Andrews, Gary Bickel, and Steven Carlson. 2002. *Household Food Security in the United States, 2000*. Research Report No. 21. Washington: Food and Rural Economics Division, Economic Research Service, U.S. Department of Agriculture, Food Assistance and Nutrition.

Olson, Christine M. 1999. "Nutrition and Health Outcomes Associated with Food Insecurity and Hunger." *Journal of Nutrition* 129(2): 521S–24S.

Pavetti, LaDonna, and Dan Bloom. 2001. "State Sanctions and Time Limits." In *The New World of Welfare*, edited by Rebecca M. Blank and Ron Haskins. Washington: Brookings Institution.

Polit, Denise F., Andrew S. London, and John M. Martinez. 2001. *The Health of Poor Urban Women: Findings from the Project on Devolution and Urban Change*. New York: MDRC.

Reichman, Nancy E., Julien O. Teitler, Irwin Garfinkel, and Sara S. McLanahan. 2001. "Fragile Families: Sample and Design." *Children and Youth Services Review* 23(4–5): 303–26.

Siefert, Kristine, Colleen M. Heflin, Mary E. Corcoran, and David R. Williams. 2004. "Food Insufficiency and Physical and Mental Health in a Longitudinal Survey of Welfare Recipients." *Journal of Health and Social Behavior* 45(2): 171–86.

State Policy Documentation Project. A joint project of the Center for Law and Social Policy and the Center on Budget and Policy Priorities. Accessed at http://www.spdp.org.

Tolman, Richard M., and Jody Raphael. 2000. "A Review of Research on Welfare and Domestic Violence." *Journal of Social Issues* 56(4): 655–81.

Walters, Ellen E., Ronald C. Kessler, Christopher B. Nelson, and Daniel Mroczek. 2002. *Scoring the World Health Organization's Composite International Diagnostic Interview Short Form (CIDI-SF)*. World Health Organization.

Part VII

Housing and Neighborhood Policy

Chapter 11

Residential Environments and Obesity: What Can We Learn About Policy Interventions from Observational Studies?

Jeffrey D. Morenoff, Ana V. Diez Roux, Ben B. Hansen, and Theresa L. Osypuk

D o policy initiatives that are aimed at changing physical or social features of the residential environment have measurable impacts on health?[1] It has become an increasingly popular view in the field of public health that physical and social features of the residential environment can affect health either directly (through contaminants in the air or water supply) or indirectly, by influencing behaviors related to health (such as physical activity, food intake, substance use, and utilization of medical care) or psychosocial factors (such as stress and social relationships that help cope with stress) that may be related to health through more complex causal chains (House 2002).

Although few studies have examined the health impacts of policies specifically directed at residential environments, an increasingly large body of associational studies, many of them from social epidemiologists and sociologists, demonstrates that there is considerable variation in mortality and other health outcomes across local geographic areas. They show that this variation is related to area socioeconomic status (that is, poverty rates and other measures of disadvantage and affluence), and the variation appears to be at least partly independent of personal measures of socioeconomic position (Diez Roux 2001; Morenoff and Lynch 2004). Living in impoverished neighborhoods appears to adversely affect health, independent of the negative health consequences of poverty per se (Robert 1998). However, there is less evidence on how impoverished neighborhoods produce these adverse effects or how they might be disrupted.

We examine the neighborhood variation in outcomes related to obesity using data from a recent study of adult health in Chicago neighborhoods. We also consider how interventions targeting residential environment might affect obesity. We focus on obesity because the rapid rise in obesity rates in the United States over the past two decades (Mokdad et al. 1999) cannot be explained solely in terms of biological and genetic factors (French, Story, and Jeffery 2001; Hill and Peters 1998). Furthermore, prior theory and research has identified specific features of residential environments that might be causally linked to physical activity and food intake, both of which are proximal determinants of obesity. Obesity and physical activity are also two of the few health outcomes for which there is experimental evidence from the Moving to Opportunities (MTO) study of a connection to residential environment (Orr et al. 2003). Still, systematic evidence is lacking on the extent to which obesity and behaviors related to obesity vary across residential contexts, making the current study an important contribution to this literature.

Our study is observational, as is much of the literature on which it builds. An important limitation of observational studies on residential environments and health is that people may self-select into neighborhoods on the basis of characteristics that are not measured or that are assessed with considerable measurement error. Neglecting these selection factors can lead to biased, and conceivably inflated, estimates of the causal effects of neighborhood residence on health (Kling, Liebman, and Katz 2007; Oakes 2004). Intervention studies yield stronger causal inferences but have limits. They are limited by costs and logistical challenges of implementing them; by ethical and political challenges inherent to imposing or selectively alleviating undesirable circumstances; and by the inherent difficulty of selectively intervening on factors of certain types, such as broadly shared attitudes and perceptions. Our empirical findings include some of this latter type, which are difficult to imagine emerging from a field experiment. Although it is important to bear in mind the limitations of observational studies, evidence relevant to residential-environment policies is too rare for observational evidence to be ignored.

RESIDENTIAL ENVIRONMENTS AND OBESITY

It is important to first consider the theoretical pathways through which residential environments are linked to obesity. One of the reasons we chose the case of obesity to illustrate the connections between health and residential environments is that it is easy to conceive of tangible ways in which neighborhoods might influence how physically active a person is and the quantity and type of food a person eats. If residential environments influence patterns of physical activity and eating, then we would expect these effects to manifest themselves rather quickly, even if a person has only lived in a particular neighborhood for a brief period of time, because behaviors can potentially be very responsive to changes in environmental conditions. However, we might not observe an immediate direct effect of neighborhood conditions on body mass because it may take prolonged exposure to a set of risky or protective environmental conditions before the cumulative effect of changed behavioral patterns becomes large enough to alter a person's body mass. Not surprisingly, most research on residential environments and health has focused on patterns of physical activity and travel behavior rather than on direct links to obesity per se. Although there is compelling evidence that many features of the social and built environment differ across neighborhoods, empirical evidence linking these features to obesity and health behaviors still remains scant.

Much of the recent scholarship on obesity and residential environments has focused on the role of the "built environment," which includes physical structures and other elements of human-made environments, such as stores, parks and recreational facilities, street grids, transportation structure, land use, and other features of urban design (Frank and Engelke 2005). It has also focused on conditions in the social environment that provoke stress and reduce physical activity outside the home, such as crime and disorder (Gomez et al. 2004; Molnar et al. 2004; Piro, Noss, and Claussen 2006; Wilson et al. 2004). In a recent overview of this literature, Lawrence Frank and Peter Engelke (2005) identify three key dimensions of the built environment that influence physical activity and travel behavior: proximity, connectivity, and design. Proximity refers to the availability of common destinations (such as places of work, stores, restaurants, and recreational facilities) within a short distance of one's residence; it is conceptually related to measures of population density, housing and building density, and the mixture of land uses (including residential, commercial, and industrial). Areas with higher density tend to offer a greater number of destinations within close proximity to a person's house, and areas where land uses are mixed tend to offer both a greater range and number of destinations. Connectivity refers to the availability of transportation linkages between destinations; it can be studied by counting the number of road intersections or transit stations in a given place, by calculating the travel distance between locations on a street grid, or by tracking the time it takes to travel between locations via public transit systems. Planners are also interested in how design features of streets and buildings influence behavioral proclivities and travel patterns. For example, some urban planners (Frank and Engelke 2005; Rapoport 1987) argue that areas with greater detail in their built environments—including multiple small buildings; architectural details on building facades; and elements of the streetscape and sidewalk, such as trees, mailboxes, benches, and lampposts—are more attractive places to walk, bike, and exercise.

There has also been much research on neighborhood safety and its association with physical activity. Many scholars have hypothesized that people will be less physically active in neighborhoods with higher crime rates or where residents perceive that it is not safe to walk, exercise, or utilize parks and recreational facilities in or near their neighborhoods. The results of this research have been mixed. Some studies find support for the idea that people who live in places with more crime, or those who perceive their neighborhoods to be less safe, are less physically active (Gomez et al. 2004; Gordon-Larsen, McMurray, and Popkin 2000; Molnar et al. 2004; Piro, Noss, and Claussen 2006). Meanwhile, other studies find no significant association between neighborhood safety and physical activity (Burdette and Whitaker 2005; Humpel, Owen, and Leslie 2002; Lee and Cubbin 2002), and one study shows that people who perceive their neighborhoods to be less safe are actually more physically active (Romero et al. 2001). It is difficult to compare findings across these studies because of differences in the nature of the samples (some study children and adolescents and others adults) and differences in how they measure neighborhood safety (some use the survey respondent's perceptions of safety; others use more objective measures of neighborhood safety, such as arrest rates or observations of disorder). A possible explanation for the finding that individuals' perceptions of unsafe neighborhoods are linked to higher levels of physical activity (Romero et al. 2001) is that people who are more physically active could be more aware of the conditions in their neighborhood, including crime. This suggests the need for a study that includes both subjective and objective crime measures for the same sample, which prior studies have not had.

A final stream of research on neighborhoods and obesity-related outcomes examines differences across neighborhoods in what has been termed "the local food environment"—that is, the availability and cost of healthy foods. Studies have documented differences across neighborhoods in the number and types of food stores available (Moore and Diez Roux 2006; Morland et al. 2002) as well as in the availability of healthy foods (Horowitz et al. 2004). We do not directly analyze the food environment in this chapter because good measures of this important dimension of residential environments are not yet available in the Chicago Community Adult Health Study.

ANALYTIC PLAN

Our analysis proceeds in two stages. First, we examine the extent to which obesity-related outcomes vary across neighborhood environments both before and after adjusting for potentially key confounders at the individual level. Second, we conduct a multilevel analysis of two behaviors that prior research suggests are substantially linked to obesity: exercise and walking. This analysis focuses on the mechanisms through which the social and built environments may be linked to physical activity. These mechanisms include violent crime and disorder (both subjective and objective assessments); the presence of parks, playgrounds, and other open spaces; the pervasiveness of mixed commercial-residential land use and detached single-family homes; the sociodemographic composition of the neighborhood; and population density.

We expect that people will exercise and walk less frequently in neighborhoods where crime and disorder are more prevalent and more frequently in neighborhoods with parks and playgrounds. Mixed land use has also been hypothesized to promote the frequency of walking because of the presence of more stores; it may also promote more exercise by providing greater access to health clubs and recreational facilities or by creating safer environments for exercising outside due to the greater number of "eyes on the street" in mixed residential and commercial areas (Jacobs 1961). For similar reasons, we predict that walking should be more frequent in neighborhoods with greater population density because the places people can walk to will be more closely situated and more people are likely to be seen on the street. We predict that walking should be less frequent in neighborhoods with more single-family detached homes because such housing usually increases the distances between different uses and it features more disconnected street networks.

We also expect that people who live in higher socioeconomic status neighborhoods will tend to be more physically active because affluent neighborhoods are likely to benefit residents in ways not captured by the measures we use here; for example, they offer greater access to private health clubs, more places to buy healthy foods (such as fresh produce), and more safe places to exercise. Affluent neighborhoods may also have design features that draw people outside to walk, such as architectural detail on buildings, more trees and decorative streetscapes, and higher quality sidewalks. For different reasons, we expect that living in a poor neighborhood may necessitate more walking (Ross 2000), especially if people living in these areas are less likely to own cars, rely more on walking for basic transport, or need to walk to nearby transportation hubs because they utilize public transportation more frequently.

DATA

We analyze data from a new study designed explicitly to investigate the role of residential environments, in conjunction with individual and household factors, in affecting adult health: the Chicago Community Adult Health Study (CCAHS). Between May 2001 and March 2003, the research team conducted face-to-face interviews and collected physical and biological measurements on a stratified, multistage, probability sample of 3,105 adults (ages eighteen and older), living in 343 neighborhood clusters (NCs) within the city of Chicago. One individual per household was interviewed, and the response rate was just under 72 percent. The NCs were defined for a previous study (Sampson, Raudenbush, and Earls 1997) as aggregations of census tracts (the typical NC consists of two census tracts) with meaningful physical and social identities and boundaries.[2] All data in the ensuing analysis are weighted to take account of the different rates of selection, household size, coverage, and nonresponse across NCs.[3]

Health Outcomes

In our analysis of neighborhood variation in health, we consider an array of outcomes related to obesity, including body mass index, waist size, blood pressure (systolic and diastolic), exercise, walking, fruit and vegetable intake, smoking, and drinking. Definitions of these measures are presented in table 11.1. Weight, height, waist size, and blood pressure were measured by the interviewers, while measures of exercise, walking, fruit and vegetable intake, smoking, and drinking are based on self-reports.

TABLE 11.1 / Definitions of Obesity-Related Outcome Variables

Variable	Definition
Body mass index (BMI)	BMI = (body weight in kilograms)/(height in meters)^2 - Height was measured using a tape measure while respondents stood in a doorway in stocking feet. - Weight was measured in stocking feet and street clothes (less sweaters or other heavy overgarments) using digital scales.
Waist size	Waist size was measured with a tape measure in inches.
Systolic and diastolic blood pressure	Three blood-pressure measures were collected, approximately one minute apart, using Omron oscillographic devices. We used the average of the final two measures of systolic and diastolic blood pressure, respectively. In cases where only two blood-pressure measurements were taken, we used the average of the two to define SBP and DBP, and in cases where blood pressure was measured only once, we used SBP and DBP values from that measurement.
Exercise	This scale was constructed from survey questions derived from the National Health Interview Survey that asked respondents whether they are currently confined to a bed or chair for most or all of the day because of their health; how many days a week do they do light or moderate leisure activities other than walking or working around the house for at least ten minutes that cause only light sweating or a slight to moderate increase in breathing or heart rate; when they do light-moderate leisure activities, do they generally do them for twenty minutes or more; how many days a week do they do vigorous activities for at least ten minutes that cause heavy sweating or large increases in breathing or heart rate; and each time they do vigorous activities, do they generally do them for twenty minutes or more. The scale was coded as follows: • 0 = *Never exercises*: Individuals who said they never engage in light-moderate leisure activities, never engage in vigorous activity, or were confined to a bed or chair. • 1 = *Light exercise*: Individuals who engage in light-moderate physical activity once a week or less regardless of duration, light-moderate physical activity two to three times per week for less than twenty minutes, or vigorous activity once per week or less for less than twenty minutes. • 2 = *Light-moderate exercise*: Individuals who engage in light-moderate activity two to three times per week for more than twenty minutes, light-moderate activity four or more times per week for less than twenty minutes, or vigorous activity once per week or less for more than twenty minutes.

TABLE 11.1 / (*Continued*)

Variable	Definition
	• 3 = *Moderate-heavy exercise*: Individuals who engage in light-moderate activity four or more times per week for more than twenty minutes, or vigorous activity two to three times per week regardless of duration.
	• 4 = *Heavy exercise*: Individuals who engage in vigorous activity four or more times per week regardless of duration.
Walking	This measure is based on the following survey question: "On the average over the past year, how many days a week do you walk continuously for 20 minutes or more, either to get somewhere or just for exercise or pleasure?" (1) Never, (2) Less than once a week, (3) Once a week, (4) Two to three times a week, (5) Four to five times a week, (6) Almost every day.
Fruit and Vegetable Intake	This measure is based on the following survey question: "How many servings of fruit or vegetables do you usually eat in a day? (A serving is a cup of fruit or vegetable juice or a half cup of raw or cooked vegetables or fruits. Include juices and all types of raw or cooked fruits and vegetables.)"
Cigarettes smoked per day	We measured cigarette smoking with two survey questions. First, respondents were asked whether they currently smoke any cigarettes. If they answered yes, they were then asked how many cigarettes they smoke in an average day. We used the latter response to measure cigarettes smoked per day. We created two versions of this measure: one with nonsmokers coded as zero and another with nonsmokers coded as missing.
Drinks per month	We measured intake of alcohol with three survey questions. First, respondents were asked whether they ever drink beer, wine, or liquor. If they answered yes, they were then asked how many days they drink beer, wine, or liquor in a typical month, and on days that they drink, how many drinks do they have. (A drink is specified as a can or bottle of beer, glass of wine, a shot of liquor, or a mixed drink.) For drinkers, we multiplied the number of days drinking per month by the number of drinks per day to estimate the number of drinks per month. We created two versions of this measure: one with nondrinkers coded as zero and another with nondrinkers coded as missing.

Source: Authors' compilation from Chicago Community Adult Health Study.

Measuring Residential Environments

In our multilevel analysis, we consider three general domains of residential environments: neighborhood sociodemographic structure, land use, and crime and public safety, in addition to a large set of individual-level control variables.

Sociodemographic Structure   We constructed twenty NC-level variables from the 2000 Census that include measures of neighborhood racial-ethnic mix, socioeconomic status, age composition, family structure, owner-occupied housing, and residential stability. We ran a principal factor analysis with an orthogonal varimax rotation of these census variables to analyze their dimensionality and to achieve variable reduction.[4] The results are displayed in table 11.2. The first four factors account for 96 percent of the shared variance in these variables, and the first three have eigenvalues greater than 1.0 (the conventional cutoff), while the fourth has an eigenvalue of 0.86.

The first factor, which we interpret as socioeconomic disadvantage, is characterized by strong positive loadings on the percentage of families with incomes of less than ten thousand dollars, the percentage of families in poverty, the percentage of families on public assistance, the percentage of unemployed adults in the civilian labor force, the percentage of families that are female headed, and the percentage of adults who have never been married. It is also characterized by negative loadings on percentage of families with incomes greater than fifty thousand dollars and the percentage of owner-occupied homes.

The second factor represents a mix of characteristics associated with neighborhood affluence (such as high education and a concentration in professional occupations) and gentrification (such as a residentially mobile population consisting of young adults and few kids under the age of eighteen). It is notably orthogonal to neighborhood socioeconomic disadvantage. It has strong positive loadings for the percentage of adults with sixteen or more years of education, the percentage of adults in professional or managerial occupations, the percentage of people ages eighteen to twenty-nine, and the percentage of people ages thirty to thirty-nine. It has negative loadings on the percentage of people who lived in the same residence in 1995 and the percentage of people under age eighteen.

The third factor represents racial-ethnic composition. It has strong positive loadings for the percentage of people who are Hispanic and the percentage of people who are foreign born. It has a negative loading for the percentage of people who are non-Hispanic black (we do not include the percentage of non-Hispanic whites in this analysis because it would be collinear with the other variables already in the model).

The final factor captures older age composition. This factor has positive loadings for the percentage of people over the age of seventy and the percent of people ages fifty to sixty-nine. There are negative loadings for the percentage of people ages eighteen to twenty-nine and the percentage of people who have never been married. We also use a measure of population density (people per square kilometer) in our analysis of walking and exercise, but we omitted this variable from the factor analysis after preliminary analysis showed that it did not load strongly onto any of the factors.

Land Use   Our measures of neighborhood land use were collected via systematic social observation (SSO) in which trained observers rated (by filling out a coding sheet) 1664 of the 1672 blocks in which potential survey respondents resided.[5] Each rater walked twice around the entire block, the first time walking along the "inside" block faces and the second along the "outside" block faces (a block face is one side of a street segment).[6] In this analysis, we use three measures of land use and built environment: the proportion of block faces in the NC where detached single-family homes occupy the most space of any housing type,[7] the proportion of block faces in the NC that have mixed commercial and residential land use, and an indicator of whether any block face within the NC has a park, playground, other recreational facilities, or waterfront.[8]

Crime and Public Safety   Our measures of neighborhood safety include both subjective assessments of survey respondents and official police reports of crime. The survey assessments include perceptions of violence and disorder in the neighborhood, reports of victimization, and perceptions of neighborhood safety. These survey assessments were used to characterize individual perceptions of crime and public safety. In addition, by aggregating the responses of all respondents within each NC, we also created measures for each NC.

We constructed scales of perceived violence and perceived disorder from the CCAHS survey at both the individual and neighborhood levels using empirical Bayes (EB) residuals from a multilevel measurement model, which adjusts for measurement error through a three-level model with separate variance components for scale items, persons, and neighborhoods (Raudenbush and Sampson 1999).[9] The perceived violence scale was constructed from questions that ask how frequently (often, sometimes, rarely, or never) the following types of violent events have occurred in the neighborhood during the past six months: fights in which a weapon was used, violent arguments between neighbors, gang fights, a sexual assault or rape, and a robbery or mugging. The perceived disorder scale was constructed from questions that ask how much (a lot, some, a little, or none) of the following the respondent sees in the neighborhood: litter, broken glass, or trash on the sidewalk or streets; graffiti on the buildings and walls; vacant and deserted houses or storefronts; people drinking in public places; people selling or using drugs; and unsupervised children hanging out on the street. Because the scales of perceived violence and perceived disorder were highly correlated at both the individual level (r = 0.62) and the neighborhood level (r = 0.72), we combined them by taking the average of the standardized scores.

Using the same multilevel methodology, we constructed individual- and neighborhood-level scales of victimization based on questions that ask respondents whether they or any member of their household were a victim of any of the following types of crimes while they were living in their current neighborhood: an act of violence (mugging, fight, or sexual assault), home burglary, property theft from their house, or damaged property (including damage to their vehicles).

We also constructed individual- and neighborhood-level scales of perceived neighborhood safety by taking the average standardized value to questions that asked whether there is any place within three blocks of their current home where they are afraid to walk alone at night and how safe it is to walk alone in the neighborhood after dark.

TABLE 11.2 / Factor Analysis of Neighborhood Cluster Sociodemographic Characteristics

| | Rotated Factor Loadings | | | | |
Variable	Disadvantage	Affluence or Gentrification[a]	Hispanic, Immigrant Non-Black[a]	Older Age Composition[a]	Uniqueness
Percent families with income less than $10K	0.91	-0.24	-0.21	0.00	0.06
Percent families with income $50K or higher	-0.83	0.45	-0.02	0.07	0.10
Percent families in poverty	0.86	-0.37	-0.19	-0.15	0.07
Percent families on public assistance	0.75	-0.40	-0.41	-0.09	0.10
Percent unemployed in civilian labor force	0.67	-0.41	-0.47	-0.07	0.16
Percent families female headed	0.71	-0.34	-0.57	-0.07	0.05
Percent never married	0.61	0.25	-0.39	-0.55	0.10
Percent less than twelve years of education	0.40	-0.73	0.38	-0.26	0.09
Percent sixteen or more years of education	-0.26	0.93	0.00	-0.10	0.06

Percent professional or managerial occupation	-0 23	0.92	-0.15	0.02	0.09
Percent non-Hispanic black	0 43	-0.26	-0.79	0.11	0.11
Percent Hispanic	-0 14	-0.34	0.77	-0.39	0.12
Percent foreign-born	-0 16	-0.04	0.91	-0.07	0.13
Percent homes owner occupied	-0 81	-0.21	-0.17	0.36	0.14
Percent in same residence in 1995	-0 20	-0.65	-0.41	0.41	0.20
Percent birth to seventeen years old	0 39	-0.85	-0.16	-0.18	0.07
Percent eighteen to twenty-nine years old	0.04	0.51	0.30	-0.71	0.15
Percent thirty to thirty-nine years old	-0.17	0.72	0.31	-0.38	0.22
Percent fifty to sixty-nine years old	-0.38	0.08	-0.38	0.70	0.22
Percent seventy or more years old	-0.15	0.20	-0.03	0.87	0.19
Eigenvalue	8.83	4.36	3.54	0.86	

Source: U.S. Census 2000.
a Factor loadings have been multiplied by -1 in order to facilitate interpretation.

In addition, we obtained data on arrests for violent crime from Chicago police records and constructed NC-level crime rates for homicide, robbery, and burglary by aggregating counts of each crime from 2000 to 2003, dividing by the total population in the NC from the 2000 Census, and multiplying by ten thousand.[10] We then constructed a single index of violent crime arrests by applying the arcsine transform to homicide, robbery, and burglary rates (in the interest of variable stabilization), and we extracted the first principal component from these transformed rates (the eigenvalue of the first component was 2.33; it accounted for 78 percent of the variance in these rates).

Individual-Level Covariates

In our multilevel models, we controlled for an extensive battery of individual-level variables including sex, age (eighteen to twenty-nine, thirty to thirty-nine, forty to forty-nine, fifty to fifty-nine, sixty to sixty-nine, and seventy and older), race-ethnicity (Hispanic, non-Hispanic white, non-Hispanic black, and non-Hispanic members of other races), immigrant status (first, second, and third or higher generations), education (less than twelve years, twelve to fifteen years, and sixteen or more years), income (less than $10,000; $10,000 to $29,999; $30,000 to $49,999; and $50,000 and over), marital status (married, separated, divorced, widowed, and never married), the presence of children in the household (no children, one child, two children, three children, four or more children), and car ownership (owns no cars, one car, two cars, and three or more cars). We also controlled for a scale of functional limitations that could impede walking and exercise by calculating the average standardized value of items measuring how much difficulty the person has performing the following activities: doing heavy housework; pulling or pushing a large object; stooping, crouching, or kneeling; lifting or carrying weights over ten pounds; reaching or extending the arms above the shoulders; getting up from a stooping, kneeling, or crouching position; standing up after sitting in a chair; walking up a flight of stairs; shopping; and walking one-quarter mile or two to three blocks.

NEIGHBORHOOD VARIATION IN OBESITY-RELATED OUTCOMES

An important first step in analyzing the mechanisms through which neighborhood interventions could potentially affect obesity is to examine how much neighborhood variance there is in health outcomes, behaviors, and psychosocial states related to obesity. In this descriptive analysis we assess the relative amount of neighborhood variation in physically measured health outcomes (body mass and waist size, systolic blood pressure, and diastolic blood pressure) and health behaviors related to obesity (exercise, walking, fruit and vegetable intake, smoking, and drinking). We also assess perceptions of neighborhood safety (scales of perceived violence and disorder, victimization, and perceived lack of neighborhood safety) because of their potential role in predicting physical activity.

To assess the extent to which these outcomes vary across neighborhoods, we rely on the intracluster correlation (ICC) coefficient, ρ, which is defined as the fraction of variance in an outcome that lies between neighborhoods. To estimate the ICCs, we ran an unconditional random effects model for each outcome, in which persons vary around a neighborhood mean and neighborhoods vary around a grand mean. This model is written as follows:

$$Y_{ij} = \gamma_{00} + u_{0j} + r_{ij}, \tag{11.1}$$

for person i in neighborhood j, with $r_{ij} \sim N(0, \sigma^2)$ and $u_{0j} \sim N(0, \tau_{00})$, and where $\rho = \tau_{00} / (\tau_{00} + \sigma^2)$.

If people were randomly sorted into neighborhoods, ρ would represent a causal effect of neighborhoods on health. However, since allocation of persons to neighborhoods is decidedly nonrandom—depending on household income, race-ethnicity, and a host of other personal characteristics that are also correlates of health outcomes—ρ unadjusted for these personal characteristics represents the combined contribution of the causal effects of interest plus the variation in the outcomes associated with variation in the personal characteristics that select persons into neighborhoods. A better indicator of neighborhood variance can be obtained by estimating a two-level model in which neighborhood random effects are adjusted for individual-level background characteristics.[11] The value of ρ defined on these adjusted random effects provides an unbiased estimate of the amount of within-neighborhood clustering under linear-model assumptions and under the strong assumption that all relevant covariates have been included in the model. Because both of these assumptions are potentially problematic, we interpret the adjusted ICCs as more refined descriptive indicators of neighborhood variance in obesity-related outcomes that persists after purging the effects of measured person-specific characteristics.[12]

Table 11.3 presents both the unadjusted and adjusted ICCs for each outcome. As a basis for comparison, unadjusted ICCs in educational and organizational research tend to range between 5 and 20 percent (Hox 2002; Snijders and Bosker 1999); but, for health outcomes, ICCs tend to be smaller (Morenoff 2003), rarely surpassing 10 percent. It is also important to keep in mind, as Greg Duncan and Stephen Raudenbush (1999) demonstrate, that small ICCs can still translate into moderate or large sizes for the main effects of specific neighborhood-level attributes. By these standards, the unadjusted ICCs are relatively high for all of the outcomes, indicating that there is substantial between-area variation.

The ICCs tend to be lower for the physically measured health outcomes than they are for most health behaviors and perceptions of neighborhood safety. This is especially true after adjusting for individual-level covariates. The adjustment makes the most difference for BMI and waist size, which suggests that some of the apparent neighborhood variation in body mass is accounted for by individual sociodemographic characteristics that sort people into neighborhoods. Between 6 and

TABLE 11.3 / Intra-Cluster Correlation (Percentage of Variance Between Neighborhoods) Before and After Adjusting for Individual-Level Covariates (CCAHS)

	Unadjusted	Adjusted[a]	n
Physical measurements			
Body mass index	10.06	6.32	3,105
Waist size	11.33	5.82	3,105
Systolic blood pressure	6.91	6.00	2,860
Diastolic blood pressure	6.84	6.76	2,860
Health behaviors			
Exercise	10.68	9.16	3,105
Walking	9.02	9.73	2,983
Fruit and vegetable servings per day	6.69	4.92	3,097
Cigarettes per day			
Full sample (non-smokers = 0)	5.41	4.44	3,105
Among smokers (non-smokers = missing)	15.99	19.44	812
Drinks per month			
Full sample (nondrinkers = 0)	11.37	10.13	3,105
Among drinkers (nondrinkers = missing)	13.99	13.58	1,864
Perceptions of Neighborhood Safety			
Perceived violence and disorder	39.18	43.94	3,105
Victimization	16.75	22.24	3,105
Perceived lack of safety	26.07	32.59	3,105

Source: Chicago Community Adult Health Study.
[a] The adjustment procedure, described in the text, controls for the within-neighborhood effects of sex, age, race-ethnicity, immigrant status, education, and income.

7 percent of the variance in systolic and diastolic blood pressure lies between neighborhoods, and these ICCs do not change very much after adjusting for individual-level covariates.

There is more neighborhood variation in health behaviors, and this variation appears to be less confounded by individual-level factors. More than 9 percent of the variation in exercise and walking is between neighborhoods, even after adjusting for individual-level factors. The adjustment actually increases the estimated variance between neighborhoods for walking. Further analysis (reported in table 11.5) revealed that people of lower socioeconomic status tend to walk more frequently, but they also tend to live in neighborhoods that discourage walking. Thus, the adjustment actually helps us see the neighborhood variation in walking that was suppressed by some of the individual-level covariates. Fruit and vegetable intake varies less across neighborhoods. This finding suggests that eating habits are more individualized than physical-activity patterns, but we also suspect that our relatively crude measure of fruit and vegetable intake contains more error than our other measures. We find relatively high amounts of neighborhood variation for the measures of smoking and drinking; this is especially true after we drop nonsmokers and nondrinkers from the analysis and measure the variance in frequency of smoking or drinking conditional on being a smoker or drinker.

The ICCs are very high for perceptions of neighborhood safety. This is not surprising given that these survey questions ask the respondent about conditions or experiences specific to the current neighborhood. It is more surprising though that these ICCs increase after adjusting for individual-level factors. This increase is the result of a somewhat complex and interesting pattern of relationships between individual-level factors and perceptions of crime and safety. Further analysis revealed that blacks and people of lower socioeconomic status report higher levels of violence and disorder and less neighborhood safety than whites and people of higher socioeconomic status; but, after adjusting for neighborhoods (via fixed effects), whites actually tend to perceive more crime and less safety than blacks, and socioeconomic status is no longer as strongly associated with perceptions. In other words, we initially found that blacks report more violence and disorder because they live in neighborhoods that are more beset by these problems. However, where whites and blacks share the same neighborhoods, whites tend to perceive more violence and disorder and less safety than blacks. Thus, when we adjust the ICCs for individual factors such as race and socioeconomic status, we actually find more neighborhood variation in perceptions of crime that was suppressed by the tendency of people who live in low-crime neighborhoods to perceive more crime.

In sum, although the neighborhood variance was relatively large in most of the outcomes we examined, it was higher for health behaviors than it was for health outcomes related to obesity. Perhaps contemporaneous neighborhoods are more salient for understanding behaviors than for health outcomes such as body mass and blood pressure because behaviors may be more responsive to environmental conditions over the short term, while the health outcomes may be more influenced by early-life factors or prolonged exposure to neighborhood conditions. This suggests that behavioral patterns, such as the frequency of exercise and walking, represent a potentially important set of mechanisms through which neighborhood environments come to affect outcomes such as body mass and blood pressure. We also found that perceptions of crime, disorder, and safety, which could be important determinants of physical activity, vary widely across neighborhoods. These neighborhood factors could represent key mechanisms through which the social environment is ultimately related to obesity.

MULTILEVEL ANALYSIS OF PHYSICAL ACTIVITY

In the second stage of our analysis, we conduct multilevel models of exercise and walking. We begin by estimating baseline models that contain only individual-level predictors of each behavior; we then sequentially add neighborhood-level measures of sociodemographic structural characteristics, land use, and neighborhood crime and public safety. We focus not only on the significance of regression coefficients in each of these domains, but also on the improvement of model fit when each block of variables is added (using the chi-square test of the difference between deviance statistics). In our final model, we add individual-level measures of perceived crime and safety to examine whether any apparent neighborhood effects related to crime are actually explained by these individual-level perceptions. Our estimates of the association between perceived crime, disorder, and safety and physical activity are somewhat problematic because a person's perceptions of crime and safety in the neighborhood are likely to be affected by how often he or she exercises and walks. Hence, we interpret these results with caution and are primarily interested in whether our neighborhood-level estimates are robust to these controls.

We present the results of the analysis of exercise in table 11.4. The results from model 1 show less exercise among females, older people, first-generation immigrants, those with less than twelve years of education (compared to sixteen or more), those with incomes under ten thousand dollars (compared to fifty thousand dollars or more), and those with more functional limitations. Meanwhile, Hispanics (compared to whites) and those who have never been married or are separated (compared to those who are married) exercise more frequently.

In model 2 we add measures of neighborhood sociodemographic structure and find that people who live in gentrified neighborhoods tend to exercise more frequently, net of individual-level characteristics. Also, after controlling for neighborhood sociodemographic characteristics, blacks (compared to whites) exercise more frequently. Model 3 shows that accounting for measures of land use (as a block of variables) significantly improves the fit of the model, and people who live in neighborhoods with recreational facilities or waterfront tend to exercise more frequently. We add measures of neighborhood crime and public safety in model 4; none of these measures are significantly related to exercise, nor does this block of variables explain significant additional variance in exercise.

In model 5 we control for individual-level perceptions of crime and safety and find that people who perceive more crime and disorder tend to exercise more regularly. This could reflect the reverse causal pathway: people who exercise more often could be more aware of the crime and disorder around them. Another finding from model 5 is that after controlling for individual-level perceptions of crime, the neighborhood-level measure of collectively perceived crime and disorder becomes significantly related to exercise in the negative direction. In other words, people who live in neighborhoods in which residents report, on average, that there is more crime and disorder exercise less frequently. Thus, the neighborhood-level findings are consistent with our expectation that neighborhoods with more crime and disorder discourage people from being physically active, even though the individual-level findings are not consistent with this hypothesis (possibly due to the problem of endogeneity).

In table 11.5 we present the same set of models to predict walking. Model 1 shows that blacks (compared to whites), people who live in households with two children (compared to no children), people who own three or more cars (compared to no cars), and people with more functional limitations walk less often. Meanwhile, people ages of fifty to fifty-nine (compared to people ages eighteen to twenty-nine), people with fifteen or fewer years of education (compared to sixteen or more), and people who are separated (compared to those who are married) walk more frequently. The finding that people with lower levels of education tend to walk more frequently suggests that people of lower socioeconomic status may rely more on walking as a basic means of transportation, although income was not significantly related to walking.

In model 2 we find that people who live in more disadvantaged neighborhoods and more densely populated neighborhoods tend to walk more frequently. This result is consistent with at least one previous study also conducted in Chicago (Ross 2000), which found a positive association between neighborhood disadvantage and frequency of walking. However, the association between neighborhood disadvantage and walking becomes statistically insignificant after controlling for measures of land use and neighborhood crime and safety in models 3 to 5. None of the land use measures introduced in model 3 are significantly related to walking, and, as a block of variables, they do not account for significant additional variation in walking.

The results from model 4 show that people walk less often in places where neighbors are collectively more fearful of walking alone or at night. Model 4 also suggests that people who live in places where neighbors report more crime and disorder tend to walk more frequently, but this association is reduced after controlling for individual-level perceptions of crime in model 5. Model 5 shows that people who perceive more crime and disorder are likely to walk more often, while people who have been victimized by crime tend to walk less often. Here again, we find a counterintuitive association at the individual level between perceiving more crime and disorder and being more physically active. This could be the result of reverse causality: people who walk more often are likely to be more aware of the crime and disorder in their neighborhood. At the same time, we also find that people who have been personally victimized by crime or who live with someone who has been victimized walk less frequently, and people who live in places where their neighbors are more fearful of crime also tend to walk less frequently. Thus there is some evidence to support the claim that neighborhood crime suppresses both walking and exercise, along with more limited evidence consistent either with an opposite relationship or, more plausibly, with walkers being more exposed to indications of crime and disorder.

In sum, our results suggest that residential environments are related to patterns of exercise and walking in distinct and somewhat complex ways. None of the neighborhood characteristics we included in our models significantly predicted both exercise and walking. We found that people tend to exercise more frequently when they live in neighborhoods that are more gentrified, that have recreational facilities or waterfront, and where reports of crime and disorder are lower. We also found that people tend to walk more often when they live in more densely populated areas and places where people are less fearful of their safety when walking alone or at night. Individuals who perceive more crime and disorder are likely to both exercise and walk more frequently, which leads us to believe that people who are more physically active are more aware of or sensitive to conditions in their neighborhood and thus report higher levels of crime in their neighborhoods (all

TABLE 11.4 / Hierarchical Linear Models of Exercise

	Model 1		Model 2		Model 3		Model 4		Model 5	
	Coef.	SE	Coef.	SE	Coef.	SE	Coef.	SE	Coef.	SE
Female	-0.27	(0.06)**	-0.27	(0.06)**	-0.27	(0.06)**	-0.27	(0.06)**	-0.25	(0.06)**
Age (ref = age eighteen to twenty-nine)										
Age thirty to thirty-nine	-0.11	(0.08)	-0.08	(0.08)	-0.09	(0.08)	-0.09	(0.08)	-0.08	(0.08)
Age forty to forty-nine	-0.24	(0.10)*	-0.22	(0.09)*	-0.22	(0.09)*	-0.23	(0.09)*	-0.21	(0.09)*
Age fifty to fifty-nine	-0.37	(0.10)**	-0.35	(0.10)**	-0.35	(0.10)**	-0.36	(0.10)**	-0.33	(0.10)**
Age sixty to sixty-nine	-0.42	(0.13)**	-0.39	(0.13)**	-0.40	(0.13)**	-0.41	(0.13)**	-0.37	(0.13)**
Age seventy or more	-0.80	(0.15)**	-0.77	(0.15)**	-0.77	(0.15)**	-0.78	(0.15)**	-0.73	(0.15)**
Race-Ethnicity (ref = Non-Hispanic White)										
Non-Hispanic black	0.03	(0.08)	0.24	(0.10)*	0.25	(0.10)*	0.23	(0.10)*	0.26	(0.10)*
Hispanic	0.21	(0.10)*	0.29	(0.10)**	0.29	(0.10)**	0.28	(0.10)**	0.30	(0.10)**
Non-Hispanic other	0.19	(0.18)	0.16	(0.18)	0.16	(0.18)	0.16	(0.18)	0.17	(0.18)
Immigrant status (ref = 3rd+ generation)										
1st generation immigrant	-0.29	(0.11)**	-0.29	(0.10)**	-0.28	(0.10)**	-0.29	(0.10)**	-0.24	(0.10)*
2nd generation immigrant	-0.13	(0.10)	-0.13	(0.10)	-0.12	(0.10)	-0.13	(0.10)	-0.13	(0.10)
Education (ref = sixteen or more years)										
Less than twelve years of education	-0.20	(0.10)*	-0.08	(0.10)	-0.08	(0.10)	-0.07	(0.10)	-0.05	(0.10)
Twelve to fifteen years of education	-0.10	(0.07)	0.00	(0.07)	0.01	(0.07)	0.01	(0.07)	0.01	(0.07)
Income (ref = $50,000+)										
Income less than $10,000	-0.40	(0.12)**	-0.37	(0.12)**	-0.37	(0.12)**	-0.37	(0.12)**	-0.36	(0.12)**
Income $10,000 to $29,999	-0.29	(0.09)**	-0.25	(0.09)**	-0.25	(0.09)**	-0.25	(0.09)**	-0.26	(0.09)**
Income $30,000 to $49,999	-0.14	(0.09)	-0.12	(0.09)	-0.12	(0.08)	-0.12	(0.08)	-0.12	(0.08)
Missing data on income	-0.40	(0.10)**	-0.32	(0.09)**	-0.32	(0.09)**	-0.33	(0.09)**	-0.31	(0.09)**

	(1)		(2)		(3)		(4)		(5)	
Marital status (ref = married)										
Separated	0.52	(0.13)**	0.54	(0.12)**	0.55	(0.12)**	0.55	(0.12)**	0.56	(0.12)**
Divorced	0.07	(0.10)	0.06	(0.10)	0.06	(0.10)	0.06	(0.10)	0.06	(0.10)
Widowed	0.15	(0.13)	0.16	(0.13)	0.17	(0.13)	0.17	(0.12)	0.18	(0.12)
Never married	0.26	(0.08)**	0.24	(0.08)**	0.24	(0.08)**	0.24	(0.08)**	0.23	(0.08)**
Presence of children (ref = no children)										
One child	-0.16	(0.09)	-0.10	(0.09)	-0.09	(0.08)	-0.09	(0.08)	-0.11	(0.08)
Two children	-0.13	(0.09)	-0.08	(0.09)	-0.07	(0.09)	-0.08	(0.09)	-0.09	(0.09)
Three children	-0.07	(0.13)	-0.01	(0.12)	-0.01	(0.12)	-0.02	(0.12)	-0.03	(0.12)
Four or more children	0.01	(0.15)	0.08	(0.15)	0.09	(0.15)	0.08	(0.15)	0.07	(0.15)
Car ownership (ref = no car)										
Owns one car	0.03	(0.08)	0.04	(0.07)	0.05	(0.07)	0.05	(0.07)	0.05	(0.07)
Owns two cars	-0.01	(0.09)	0.04	(0.09)	0.04	(0.09)	0.04	(0.09)	0.03	(0.08)
Owns three or more cars	-0.25	(0.16)	-0.16	(0.15)	-0.16	(0.15)	-0.17	(0.15)	-0.18	(0.15)
Functional limitations	-0.26	(0.03)**	-0.26	(0.03)**	-0.26	(0.03)**	-0.26	(0.03)**	-0.26	(0.03)**
Neighborhood sociodemographic (census)										
Disadvantage			-0.01	(0.04)	-0.01	(0.05)	0.00	(0.05)	0.00	(0.06)
Affluence, gentrification			0.23	(0.03)**	0.21	(0.04)**	0.20	(0.04)**	0.21	(0.04)**
Hispanic, immigrant, non–black			0.08	(0.05)	0.07	(0.05)	0.08	(0.05)	0.08	(0.05)
Older age composition			-0.04	(0.03)	-0.03	(0.03)	-0.03	(0.04)	-0.03	(0.04)
Population density[a]			-0.08	(0.07)	-0.08	(0.07)	-0.04	(0.07)	-0.04	(0.07)
Neighborhood land use (SSO)										
Prop BF detached single family homes					0.09	(0.17)	0.07	(0.17)	0.08	(0.17)
Prop BF mixed comm–resid land use					0.19	(0.18)	0.19	(0.18)	0.20	(0.18)
Recreat facilities or waterfront in NC					0.19	(0.06)**	0.20	(0.07)**	0.20	(0.07)**

TABLE 11.4 / (Continued)

	Model 1		Model 2		Model 3		Model 4		Model 5	
	Coef.	SE	Coef.	SE	Coef.	SE	Coef.	SE	Coef.	SE
Neighborhood crime and safety (police survey)										
NC violent arrest							0.06	(0.05)	0.06	(0.05)
NC perceived crime or disorder							−0.10	(0.06)	−0.17	(0.07)**
NC victimization							0.03	(0.03)	0.01	(0.04)
NC perceived lack of safety							0.01	(0.04)	0.02	(0.05)
Subject's perceptions of crime										
Perceived violence or disorder									0.13	(0.04)**
Victimization									0.06	(0.03)
Lack of safety									−0.03	(0.04)
Intercept	2.68	(0.15)**	2.37	(0.15)**	2.36	(0.15)**	2.37	(0.15)**	2.32	(0.15)**
Variance Components										
Level 1	1.32		1.31		1.31		1.31		1.30	
Percentage reduction from unconditional model	(41.45%)		(41.80%)		(41.81%)		(41.81%)		(42.27%)	
Level 2	0.10		0.07		0.06		0.06		0.06	
Percentage reduction from unconditional model	(55.94%)		(69.26%)		(72.31%)		(73.70%)		(74.14%)	
Deviance	9830.6		9773.2		9763.4		9758.9		9733.5	
Chi-Square (df)			57.3	(5)**	9.9	(3)*	4.5	(4)	25.4	(3)**

Source: Chicago Community Adult Health Study and U.S. Census 2000.
Note: Prop BF = Proportion of block faces; NC = neighborhood cluster
**p < .01; *p < .05
[a] Coefficients and standard errors have been multiplied by 10,000.

TABLE 11.5 / Hierarchical Linear Models of Walking

	Model 1		Model 2		Model 3		Model 4		Model 5	
	Coef.	SE	Coef.	SE	Coef.	SE	Coef.	SE	Coef.	SE
Female	0.00	(0.07)	0.01	(0.07)	0.01	(0.08)	0.02	(0.07)	0.04	(0.08)
Age (ref = age eighteen to twenty-nine)										
Age thirty to thirty-nine	0.07	(0.11)	0.08	(0.11)	0.08	(0.11)	0.08	(0.11)	0.08	(0.11)
Age forty to forty-nine	0.18	(0.12)	0.20	(0.12)	0.20	(0.12)	0.21	(0.12)	0.22	(0.12)
Age fifty to fifty-nine	0.28	(0.14)*	0.31	(0.14)*	0.31	(0.14)*	0.30	(0.14)*	0.35	(0.14)*
Age sixty to sixty-nine	0.04	(0.16)	0.08	(0.16)	0.07	(0.16)	0.09	(0.16)	0.15	(0.16)
Age seventy or older	-0.16	(0.20)	-0.11	(0.20)	-0.11	(0.20)	-0.10	(0.20)	-0.01	(0.20)
Race-ethnicity (ref = non-Hispanic White)										
Non-Hispanic black	-0.18	(0.11)	-0.34	(0.14)*	-0.34	(0.14)*	-0.31	(0.14)*	-0.32	(0.15)*
Hispanic	-0.07	(0.14)	-0.10	(0.14)	-0.11	(0.14)	-0.08	(0.14)	-0.07	(0.14)
Non-Hispanic other	-0.27	(0.26)	-0.32	(0.26)	-0.33	(0.25)	-0.31	(0.24)	-0.30	(0.25)
Immigrant status (ref = 3rd+ generation)										
1st generation immigrant	-0.04	(0.13)	0.00	(0.13)	0.00	(0.13)	0.03	(0.13)	0.07	(0.13)
2nd generation immigrant	0.15	(0.14)	0.19	(0.14)	0.19	(0.14)	0.20	(0.14)	0.21	(0.14)
Education (ref = sixteen or more years)										
Less than twelve years of education	0.27	(0.13)*	0.28	(0.13)*	0.28	(0.13)*	0.28	(0.13)*	0.26	(0.13)*
Twelve to fifteen years of education	0.18	(0.09)*	0.23	(0.09)*	0.23	(0.09)*	0.22	(0.09)*	0.21	(0.09)*
Income (ref = $50,000 or more)										
Income less than $10,000	0.03	(0.15)	-0.01	(0.15)	0.00	(0.15)	0.00	(0.15)	-0.02	(0.15)
Income $10,000 to $29,999	0.16	(0.11)	0.13	(0.12)	0.14	(0.12)	0.13	(0.12)	0.10	(0.12)
Income $30,000 to $49,999	0.16	(0.12)	0.15	(0.12)	0.16	(0.12)	0.15	(0.12)	0.14	(0.11)
Missing data on income	0.07	(0.11)	0.10	(0.12)	0.10	(0.12)	0.11	(0.12)	0.11	(0.12)
Marital status (ref = married)										
Separated	0.37	(0.16)*	0.35	(0.17)*	0.35	(0.17)*	0.35	(0.17)*	0.35	(0.16)*
Divorced	0.12	(0.12)	0.10	(0.12)	0.10	(0.12)	0.10	(0.12)	0.10	(0.12)
Widowed	0.10	(0.19)	0.10	(0.19)	0.10	(0.19)	0.11	(0.19)	0.11	(0.18)
Never married	0.08	(0.11)	0.06	(0.11)	0.06	(0.11)	0.06	(0.11)	0.05	(0.11)

TABLE 11.5 / (Continued)

	Model 1		Model 2		Model 3		Model 4		Model 5	
	Coef.	SE	Coef.	SE	Coef.	SE	Coef.	SE	Coef.	SE
Presence of children (ref = no children)										
One child	0.00	(0.11)	0.02	(0.11)	0.03	(0.11)	0.02	(0.11)	0.02	(0.11)
Two children	-0.28	(0.14)*	-0.24	(0.14)	-0.24	(0.14)	-0.25	(0.14)	-0.27	(0.14)
Three children	-0.03	(0.15)	-0.02	(0.15)	-0.02	(0.15)	-0.01	(0.15)	-0.02	(0.15)
Four or more children	0.21	(0.17)	0.20	(0.17)	0.21	(0.17)	0.18	(0.17)	0.16	(0.17)
Car ownership (ref = no car)										
Owns one car	-0.12	(0.10)	-0.09	(0.10)	-0.09	(0.10)	-0.08	(0.10)	-0.06	(0.10)
Owns two cars	-0.22	(0.12)	-0.15	(0.12)	-0.15	(0.12)	-0.14	(0.12)	-0.13	(0.12)
Owns three or more cars	-0.53	(0.20)**	-0.45	(0.20)*	-0.45	(0.20)*	-0.44	(0.20)*	-0.43	(0.20)*
Functional limitations	-0.35	(0.06)**	-0.35	(0.06)**	-0.35	(0.06)**	-0.35	(0.06)**	-0.35	(0.06)**
Neighborhood sociodemographic (census)										
Disadvantage			0.17	(0.05)**	0.15	(0.07)*	0.12	(0.08)	0.13	(0.08)
Affluence, gentrification			0.01	(0.05)	0.00	(0.05)	0.02	(0.06)	0.02	(0.06)
Hispanic, immigrant, non-black			-0.11	(0.07)	-0.11	(0.07)	-0.05	(0.08)	-0.06	(0.08)
Older age composition			-0.05	(0.04)	-0.04	(0.05)	-0.03	(0.05)	-0.03	(0.05)
Population density[a]			0.25	(0.10)*	0.24	(0.10)*	0.23	(0.10)*	0.24	(0.10)*
Neighborhood land use (SSO)										
Prop BF detached single family homes					-0.06	(0.24)	0.05	(0.25)	0.06	(0.25)
Prop BF mixed comm-resid land use					-0.03	(0.25)	-0.06	(0.25)	-0.05	(0.25)
Recreat facilities or waterfront in NC					0.10	(0.10)	0.11	(0.10)	0.11	(0.10)

	(1)	(2)	(3)	(4)	(5)
Neighborhood crime (police survey)					
NC violent arrest				0.04 (0.08)	0.04 (0.08)
Perceived violence or disorder				0.21 (0.09)*	0.10 (0.10)
NC victimization				−0.01 (0.05)	0.03 (0.06)
NC perceived lack of safety				−0.22 (0.06)**	−0.19 (0.07)**
Subject's perceptions of crime					
Perceived crime or disorder					0.18 (0.06)**
Victimization					−0.10 (0.04)*
Lack of safety					−0.05 (0.05)
Intercept	4.16 (0.18)**	4.17 (0.20)**	4.17 (0.20)**	4.14 (0.20)**	4.12 (0.20)**
Variance Components					
Level 1	2.17	2.17	2.17	2.16	2.15
Percentage reduction from unconditional model	(3.95%)	(4.07%)	(4.01%)	(4.13%)	(4.87%)
Level 2	0.20	0.16	0.16	0.14	0.14
Percentage reduction from unconditional model	(9.60%)	(28.84%)	(30.75%)	(39.39%)	(38.50%)
Deviance	10950.1	10916.4	10915.0	10896.9	10876.0
Chi-Square (df)		33.6 (5)**	1.4 (3)	14.7 (3)**	21.0 (3)**

Source: Chicago Community Adult Health Study and U.S. Census 2000.

Note: Prop = Proportion of block faces; NC = neighborhood cluster|

[a] Coefficients and standard errors have been multiplied by 10,000.

**p < .01; *p < .05

else being equal). Consistent with this interpretation, we found no significant associations between the crime measure constructed from police arrest data and either exercise or walking. In a supplemental analysis we found no association between a more objective measure of disorder constructed from data collected via systematic social observation (rather than survey respondents' perceptions) and either exercise or walking. At the same time, aggregated perceptions of crime and lack of safety among respondents' neighbors were distinctly predictive of reduced exercise and walking.

IMPLICATIONS FOR POLICY AND RESEARCH

The analysis we have presented in this chapter is an illustration of how collecting data on theoretically relevant features of the social and built environments can advance the current state of the literature on residential environments and health. It can also help pinpoint where to target future policy initiatives or interventions aimed at improving public health. Few studies have examined how community-targeted policies are associated with physical activity (Dannenberg et al. 2003) or obesity. Nonetheless, many scholars and public-policy advocates call for land-development practices that cultivate pedestrian-oriented communities in order to promote physical activity; such plans include locating goods and services as well as parks and recreation areas within walking distance of residences (Satariano and McAuley 2003) and changing zoning laws and land-use regulations that currently inhibit the development of mixed-use neighborhoods that have compact development and well-connected streets (Frank and Engelke 2005; Schilling and Linton 2005). Several programs have been launched in the past few years with the potential to influence obesity through modification of the built environment (Brisbon et al. 2005; Orleans et al. 2003; Sallis et al. 2004).[13] Analyzing the outcomes of these initiatives would certainly help inform future policy recommendations, as would observational studies that collect data on features of the built environment that such initiatives seek to alter and that link them to health outcomes.

Community-level interventions aimed at reducing crime and disorder—particularly those that simultaneously assuage fear of crime—may promote physical activity. A recent National Research Council report (Skogan and Frydl 2004) highlights the effectiveness of policing strategies that focus on addressing specific types of crime and proactively engaging with the community to change the conditions that foster these crimes. Such strategies depart from the standard policing model of random patrols; unfocused enforcement efforts; and reactive strategies, such as improving response time to service calls and improving follow-up investigations of crimes. One approach noted in the report for its effectiveness in reducing crime and disorder is problem-oriented policing, which involves systematic and empirical analysis of community problems and highly localized responses tailored to particular communities. A closely related strategy that has also proven successful is hotspots policing, in which police use crime-mapping computer software to analyze the geographic distribution of crime and then target their investigations and crackdown efforts on specific street corners, addresses, and blocks where there have been high concentrations of crime. Another approach is community policing, in which police directly engage community members and social-service agencies in helping to identify and solve priority problems. Although the evidence on the effectiveness of community policing programs (such as neighborhood watch, foot patrol, door-to-door visits, storefront police offices, and community meetings) at reducing crime and disorder is mixed, there is more consensus that these programs are effective at reducing the fear of crime and perceptions of disorder by making the police a more accessible and visible presence in the community. Much can be learned from the systematic evaluation of the health effects of policies like community policing, which are implemented for reasons totally unrelated to health but have many potential health consequences.

On a more methodological note, our findings also highlight the importance of moving beyond census-based measures of neighborhood demographic and socioeconomic composition and incorporating measures of mutable features of the built environment that are more theoretically linked to health and health behaviors. Systematic social observation is a reliable method for collecting data on the built environment. This could be fairly easily incorporated into the design of in-home surveys by asking interviewers to rate the block around each respondent's house. It is especially cost effective when the sample design is clustered within relatively small geographic areas—especially when multiple respondents live on the same block—which is often true of not only local studies such as this one in Chicago, but many nationally representative studies as well.

Another advantage of using systematic social observation is that it can support analysis of residential environments at multiple levels of geographic scale, including more micro levels of the residential environment such as the block face, street, or block on which a person lives. Although an exploration of geographic scale is beyond the scope of this chapter, it is important to note that some measures of the built environment are more theoretically relevant to health on a very small geographic scale, and others are more relevant on larger geographic scales. For example, whether a person lives on a street and block that is dominated by detached single-family homes may be more influential to determining how much that person walks than the neighborhood-based measure we use of the proportion of block faces in a neighborhood that have detached homes. The neighborhood level may be more suitable than the block level for analyzing the association between parks and recreational areas and physical activity, if having such a facility within walking distance from the home is more important than residing on the same block as the facility.

One limitation of the CCAHS design for conducting systematic social observation of neighborhoods is that it is based on a sample of blocks from each NC (the blocks on which sample members resided), and thus it does not provide complete geographic coverage of the built environment in any given neighborhood. However, there are secondary sources of data, which could be appended to survey data such as CCAHS, that provide complete geographic information on features of the built environment. These features include the location of businesses (food stores, restaurants, liquor stores, bars, health clubs, and health-care facilities), frequencies of parks and playgrounds, types of housing, land-use patterns, and street networks. Such data could be used to compute accessibility indices that measure the number of recreational facilities, food stores, or restaurants within a given band of geographical distance around a person's house as well as a variety of measures of the built environment related to land-use mix, street connectivity, and urban design.

The literature on residential environments and health is still in its early stages, as there have been relatively few attempts to date to design studies that collect data on both the health and behaviors of individuals and their residential context. Those that do collect data on health and neighborhood often give short shrift to the latter by relying solely on census-based measures or individual-level perceptions of the neighborhood. Thus, strategies for improving the measurement of residential environments represent one promising development in recent research, but improving measurement does not address all of the shortcomings of observational studies.

WHAT CAN WE LEARN ABOUT NEIGHBORHOOD EFFECTS ON HEALTH FROM OBSERVATIONAL STUDIES?

There are some clear limitations of observational studies, but such observational designs of neighborhood effects are still relevant to policy makers. To understand this stance, a deeper consideration of some of the criticisms of observational research on residential environments and health is necessary.

A major identification problem in neighborhood effects research is that "social stratification confounds comparisons" (Oakes 2004, 1938). The issue here is that when researchers introduce background attributes of individuals into multilevel models in an effort to control for the selection of people into neighborhoods, they run the risk of explaining away all or most of the true contextual variance in health. This is because these individual attributes also segregate people into distinctly different types of residential environments. Residential segregation does confound attempts to study certain types of neighborhood effects because adequate comparisons do not exist. For example, if the only neighborhoods in a city that have toxic-waste facilities are predominantly low-income neighborhoods, and if income groups were highly segregated within the city, then it would be very difficult (or impossible) to separate the effect of living near a toxic-waste facility from the effect of having a low income on health. To estimate such a contextual effect, there would need to be a substantial number of neighborhoods both near and far from toxic waste facilities in which people with high and low incomes live side by side.

Blanket dismissals of observational studies on neighborhood health effects due to the confounding effects of social stratification have two important limitations. First, the argument that the between-neighborhood variance component (τ_{00} in our notation) approaches zero when individual-level covariates are added to multilevel models (to control for selection factors) relies too heavily on the neighborhood variance component as an indicator of neighborhood effects. Studies that lack the power to detect between-neighborhood variance may still have sufficient power to detect fixed effects of specific neighborhood attributes (Diez Roux 2004; Snijders and Bosker 1999), so that reducing the neighborhood variance component to near zero does not necessarily imply that the study cannot detect neighborhood effects. Also, in some cases, the neighborhood variance component can be biased *downward* by the omission of confounding covariates from the model (Diez Roux 2004). The upshot is that the best way to test a hypothesis about a neighborhood effect is to test a hypothesis about a specific neighborhood attribute, as guided by prior theory, rather than testing a more diffuse hypothesis about the between-neighborhood variance component.

Second, the extent to which social stratification confounds comparisons can be examined empirically and may vary depending on the data set and the neighborhood attribute under investigation. Observational studies on neighborhood effects should not be rejected as lacking adequate comparisons, but instead they should be carefully scrutinized to determine whether the contexts they compare are sufficiently similar for causal interpretation of their differences to be persuasive (Harding 2003). As an illustration of the types of comparisons we have in mind, we present cross-tabulated frequencies of individual-level race-ethnicity, education, and income by quartiles of all four neighborhood-level factors in table 11.6. Despite substantial variance in the distribution of neighborhood characteristics across social groups, we find fairly sizable representations of all groups across the distribution of most neighborhood characteristics. Only in two cases does the cell count drop below fifty (there are only twenty-eight Hispanics in the lowest quartile of the Hispanic, Immigrant, Non-Black neighborhood factor; there are only forty-four people with incomes of less than ten thousand dollars in the lowest quartile of socioeconomic disadvantage). Not surprisingly, there is less overlap in the distribution of the Hispanic, Immigrant, Non-Black factor across racial-ethnic groups than there is with other factors. However, substantial numbers of blacks and whites can be found at all quartiles of neighborhood affluence and gentrification, older age composition, and, to a lesser extent, disadvantage. On the whole, the tabulations show substantial overlap in the distributions of neighborhood characteristics across the racial-ethnic and socioeconomic groups on which we focus.

To be sure, unaccounted-for differences in the characteristics of residents (the selection problem) are a major challenge in estimating neighborhood effects from observational data. But the magnitude of this problem can be examined empirically; for example, it can be examined by investigating the relationships between individual- and neighborhood-level variables similarly to what is presented in table 11.6. This approach allows researchers to judge the confidence they have in the effect measures reported from a particular dataset. Other approaches such as propensity scores, which can be used to explicitly match on selection-related factors and therefore ensure comparability on individual-level predictors, are also being increasingly used in studies of neighborhood effects. They are used in order to examine the robustness of measures estimated using traditional regression approaches.

Yet another approach is to actively search out exceptions to the rule—that is, "naturally" occurring situations where individual- and neighborhood-level factors

TABLE 11.6 / Unweighted Frequencies of Social Groups by Quartiles of Neighborhood Factors (N = 3,105)

Social Groups	Quartiles of Disadvantage				Quartiles of Affluence, Gentrification				Quartiles of Hispanic, Immigrant, Non-Black				Quartiles of Older Age Composition				Total
	1st	2nd	3rd	4th	1st	2nd	3rd	4th	1st	2nd	3rd	4th	1st	2nd	3rd	4th	
Race-ethnicity																	
Non-Hispanic white	373	315	225	70	121	138	307	417	57	202	461	263	256	212	207	308	983
Non-Hispanic black	243	196	303	498	322	480	286	152	663	416	100	61	188	380	386	286	1,240
Hispanic	136	279	284	103	407	136	159	100	28	70	191	513	403	210	96	93	802
Education																	
Less than twelve years	134	195	243	220	336	193	175	88	176	146	150	320	289	225	157	121	792
Twelve to fifteen years	412	399	395	370	441	457	418	260	445	365	365	401	363	428	387	398	1,576
Sixteen or more years	218	230	204	85	81	115	177	364	135	191	268	143	218	166	170	183	737
Income																	
Less than $10,000	44	76	102	143	112	101	88	64	116	108	57	84	100	107	76	82	365
$10,000 to $29,999	156	213	264	243	276	246	193	161	230	183	182	281	286	236	197	157	876
$30,000 to $49,999	137	176	147	121	157	127	145	152	119	133	165	164	179	153	131	118	581
$50,000 or more	242	213	159	84	116	140	195	247	152	169	227	150	168	167	170	193	698
Total	764	824	842	675	858	765	770	712	756	702	783	864	870	819	714	702	

Source: Chicago Community Adult Health Study and U.S. Census 2000.

are uncoupled or where there is variability in neighborhood-level attributes of interest even within neighborhoods of similar socioeconomic composition. Not all low-income neighborhoods are the same, and within large cities for example, it is often possible to find similarly low-income neighborhoods that differ in features of the built environment. This uncoupling of neighborhood socioeconomic composition and other neighborhood attributes has become more apparent as observational research on neighborhood effects has moved from initial investigation of the contextual effect of neighborhood socioeconomic status to much more specific investigations of the neighborhood attributes that are hypothesized to be related to health outcomes. Another promising avenue in observational studies of neighborhood effects is the evaluation of "natural" experiments—that is, the investigations of changes in health outcomes that occur as a result of a specific change in neighborhood environments, such as the opening of a new public space, the implementation of a new transportation policy, or the opening of a farmer's market. Neighborhoods change constantly, but these changes are rarely evaluated for their health effects. The documentation of the health impact of these changes would strengthen causal inferences regarding neighborhood effects and would also provide evidence of high relevance to policy makers. These types of evaluations will require the partnering of researchers with community groups, public agencies, and policy makers.

Skeptics may argue that, however hard we try, observational studies will never yield firm evidence of neighborhood effects or evidence that is directly relevant for policy. It has been argued, for example, that only randomized trials will solve the conundrum of neighborhood-effects research and will provide evidence that is relevant in the "real world" (Oakes 2004). But rather than calling generically for more experimental studies, it is important to critically consider whether randomized trials can be implemented in this area, what these trials would look like, and what we could actually learn from them. A first key requirement of experimental studies is that we have a clear specification of the intervention or treatment that we want to test. There is considerable debate on this topic among researchers. Would the ideal experiment be to move poor people to nonpoor neighborhoods (as the MTO study has done), or to intervene on neighborhoods themselves? And if the latter is preferable, what specific interventions should be considered as the highest priorities? Unfortunately, prior research on neighborhood effects cannot offer much guidance on this question, for it has not considered treatment conditions that are amenable to policy interventions. It is precisely in this context, when there is still considerable uncertainty on the treatment to be tested, that observational studies conducted in varying places and populations and with varying designs and measures are likely to be most useful, while controlled interventions offer less value relative to cost (Phillips 2001). We argue that this is exactly the current stage of research on neighborhood effects on health.[14] Although much work to date has established an association between neighborhood disadvantage and health, more observational studies are needed on mutable features of residential environments that could in the future be subjected for randomized community trials.

A second key consideration pertains to the logistics of implementing such a trial once the treatment has been defined. We believe the most appropriate design for assessing the effects of neighborhood characteristics on health is by randomly assigning neighborhoods to interventions, not via the random assignment of individuals to neighborhoods. When individuals are randomly assigned to neighborhoods (or allowed to select their own neighborhood within certain parameters, as was the case in the MTO study), researchers have no means of determining which features of the new neighborhoods brought about a given effect. But even assuming randomization of neighborhood interventions is feasible, there are major challenges in terms of the power of these designs. Studies that randomize changes to neighborhoods will typically have very little power unless many neighborhoods are randomized or additional assumptions are brought to bear. Suppose a trial with intervention was assigned to ten of twenty communities, each containing one thousand study participants. In classical randomization inference, the n of such a study is twenty, not twenty thousand (Gail et al. 1996). Other modes of inference increase the effective sample size, but they do so at the expense of adding assumptions about functional forms or even assumptions that key variables have not been omitted (Gail, Wieand, and Piantadosi 1984)—the same type of assumptions for which observational studies are often faulted. The analyst of a randomized-community trial thus confronts a dilemma between maintaining the purity of the approach at the cost of distinguishing only the strongest of effects from statistical noise, and seeking more power through the use of the same fallible, if potentially quite credible, assumptions that are characteristic of observational studies.

Another instance in which assumptions become necessary in experimental designs is when the treatment condition that is randomized covaries with other potential influences on health because of chance associations between the treatment condition and other features of neighborhoods. As an example, imagine an intervention that sought to create "active living" communities, perhaps by building mixed-use development projects in selected neighborhoods that were matched on socioeconomic status. Setting aside the practical concerns about how feasible such an undertaking would be and how many communities could be selected for the treatment group, there is the potential, even in a randomized design, for the realized assignment of treatments to covary with other neighborhood factors that could affect health. For example, even though the treatment and control groups in this hypothetical experiment were matched on socioeconomic status, the treatment neighborhoods could, by chance, be located next to areas with higher socioeconomic status than those surrounding control-group neighborhoods. This could encourage more walking in treatment areas because there are more stores and other common destinations within walking distance. Conversely, if the areas surrounding a treatment neighborhood were high in crime, this might discourage walking in the active living community. Thus, even in a randomized-community design, in which treatment and control communities were matched on socioeconomic status, there is still the potential that confounding influences could creep into the design—especially when the number of cases being randomized is small, as it often is in community trials—and the need to control such influences leads back to models that introduce parametric assumptions.[15]

In summary, neighborhood conditions may be important mechanisms linking broader social and economic policies to health outcomes. Identifying the specific features of neighborhoods or residential environments that are most important for health remains a major challenge. No single study—particularly, no single observational study—is likely to provide definitive evidence about how and why neighborhoods matter for physical activity and obesity. A combination of well-designed and rigorous observational studies, natural or quasi-experiments, and (when available) intervention studies can be expected to reveal which dimensions of neighborhood environments may be most relevant and which policies bear the most promise to address neighborhood conditions and to improve population health.

NOTES

1. In this chapter we use the terms *residential environment* and *neighborhood* interchangeably, but we prefer the former because the geographic boundaries used to demarcate residential environments usually do not attempt to represent neighborhoods as perceived by the residents.

2. The neighborhood data in CCAHS were collected in collaboration with the Project on Human Development in Chicago Neighborhoods (PHDCN) and included a second wave of the PHDCN Community Survey and Systematic Social Observation.

3. The weighted sample matches the 2000 Census population estimates for the city of Chicago in terms of age, race-ethnicity, and sex. The weights also take into account different rates of subsampling for final intensive interview completion efforts.

4. We took several steps to examine the robustness of this factor structure to alternative specifications. First, because factor analysis assumes multivariate normality, we applied arcsine transformations to all of the variables (in the interest of variance stabilization) and reran the factor analysis. Second, we tried multiple methods for conducting the analysis including principal factor, iterated principal factor, and principal component analysis. The factor structure displayed in table 11.3 was robust to all specifications of the model. We report the results of the factor analysis rather than the principal components because factor analysis is usually the preferred tool for exploring the dimensionality of a set of variables.

5. To ensure that interviewers can make reliable and valid observations, we conducted a pilot study during fall 2001 in which two raters made independent observations of the same block at the same time for eighty blocks, one in each of the focal NCs. In the second stage of the SSO, during fall 2002 and winter 2003, we collected observations from a single rater on almost every block in Chicago that contained a CCAHS survey sample address.

6. A total of 13,251 block faces were rated, and these were nested within 1,379 census block groups, 703 census tracts, and 343 NCs.

7. The SSO protocol asked raters to identify which types of residential housing are present on the block face and also which type of housing occupies the most space on the block face. We constructed the measure of detached single-family homes from the latter question because it carries more information about the prevalence of this form of housing.

8. The SSO protocol asked raters whether any "recreational facilities, parks or playgrounds" were present on the block face, but private health clubs were not enumerated as recreational facilities.

9. EB residuals are defined as the least-squares residuals regressed toward zero by a factor proportional to their unreliability (Raudenbush and Bryk 2002).

10. The Chicago police records data were geo-coded and made available to us by Richard Block at Loyola University, Chicago.

11. To the extent that the predictors of health at the neighborhood level are correlated with individual-level covariates, such an adjustment will produce a downward bias in the contribution of neighborhoods (Bingenheimer and Raudenbush 2004). This bias can be removed in a three-step procedure. First, we regress each outcome on a set of personal background characteristics, including sex, age, race-ethnicity, immigrant generation, education, and income, with neighborhood fixed effects. This provides within-neighborhood estimates of the effects of personal background characteristics that are purged of any correlation with neighborhood characteristics. Second, we adjust each outcome for individual background characteristics using the estimates of the coefficients from the fixed effects model, as follows: $j_{ij}^* = j_{ij} - \hat{\beta}'_w X_{ij}$, where $\hat{\beta}'_w$ are the within-neighborhood coefficients for the vector of covariates, X, as estimated from the fixed effects regression model described in the first step, and the results are the adjusted values of each outcome. Third, we decompose the variance in each adjusted outcome by estimating an unconditional random effects model and calculating an adjusted ρ as the fraction of variation in the adjusted outcome that lies between neighborhoods.

12. The linear model assumption is especially problematic for variables that are categorical in nature, such as the ordinal measures of exercise and walking, or that have truncated distributions, such as the smoking and drinking measures in which all nonsmokers and nondrinkers are coded as zero.

13. The initiatives include the Active Living by Design program funded by the Robert Wood Johnson Foundation (Brisbon et al. 2005; Orleans et al. 2003; Sallis et al. 2004), the Design for Active Living project sponsored by the American Society of Landscape Architects, the Smart Growth Network stimulated by the U.S. EPA and several nonprofit and government organizations, STEPS to a Healthier U.S. funding project sponsored by the U.S. Department of Health and Human Services (Brisbon et al. 2005), Active Community Environments Program (ACEs) sponsored by the CDC (Sallis et al. 2004).

14. For methods to identify the onset of the next stage of research, at which most observational studies diminish in value relative to randomized or natural experiments see Sander Greenland (2005).

15. Of course, there is the possibility of a nonparametric analysis that does not depend on a model for Y given X, but these will often have less power.

REFERENCES

Bingenheimer, Jeffrey B., and Stephen W. Raudenbush. 2004. "Statistical and Substantive Inferences in Public Health: Issues in the Application of Multilevel Models." *Annual Review of Public Health* 25: 53–77.

Brisbon, Nancy, James Plumb, Rickie Brawer, and Dalton Paxman. 2005. "The Asthma and Obesity Epidemics: The Role Played by the Built Environment—A Public Health Perspective." *Journal of Allergy and Clinical Immunology* 115(5): 1024–8.

Burdette, Hillary L., and Robert C. Whitaker. 2005. "A National Study of Neighborhood Safety, Outdoor Play, Television Viewing, and Obesity in Preschool Children." *Pediatrics* 116(3): 657–62.

Dannenberg, Andrew L., Richard J Jackson, Howard Frumkin, Richard A Schieber, Michael Pratt, Chris Kochtitzky, and Hugh H. Tilson. 2003. "The Impact of Community Design and Land-Use Choices on Public Health: A Scientific Research Agenda." *American Journal of Public Health* 93(9): 1500–8.

Diez Roux, Ana V. 2001. "Investigating Neighborhood and Area Effects on Health." *American Journal of Public Health* 91(11): 1783–9.

———. 2004. "Commentary: Estimating Neighborhood Health Effects: The Challenges of Causal Inference in a Complex World." *Social Science and Medicine* 58(10): 1953–60.

Duncan, Greg J., and Stephen W. Raudenbush. 1999. "Assessing the Effects of Context in Studies of Child and Youth Development." *Educational Psychologist* 34(1): 29–41.

Frank, Lawrence D., and Peter Engelke. 2005. "Multiple Impacts of the Built Environment on Public Health: Walkable Places and the Exposure to Air Pollution." *International Regional Science Review* 28(2): 193–216.

French, Simone A., Mary Story, and Robert W. Jeffery. 2001. "Environmental Influences on Eating and Physical Activity." *Annual Review of Public Health* 22: 309–35.

Gail, Mitchell H., S. Wieand, and S. Piantadosi. 1984. "Biased Estimates of Treatment Effect in Randomized Experiments with Nonlinear Regressions and Omitted Covariates." *Biometrika* 71(3): 431–44.

Gail, Mitchell H., Steven D. Mark, Raymond J. Carroll, Sylvan B. Green, and David Pee. 1996. "On Design Considerations and Randomization-Based Inference for Community Intervention Trials." *Statistics in Medicine* 15(11): 1069–92.

Gomez, Jorge E., Beth Ann Johnson, Martha Selva, and James F. Sallis. 2004. "Violent Crime and Outdoor Physical Activity Among Inner-City Youth." *Preventive Medicine* 39(5): 876–81.

Gordon-Larsen, Penny, Robert G. McMurray, and Barry M. Popkin. 2000. "Determinants of Adolescent Physical Activity and Inactivity Patterns." *Pediatrics* 105(6): e83–e91.

Greenland, Sander. 2005. "Multiple-Bias Modeling for Analysis of Observational Data." *Journal of the Royal Statistical Society, Series A: Statistics in Society* 168(2): 267–306.

Harding, David J. 2003. "Counterfactual Models of Neighborhood Effects: The Effect of Neighborhood Poverty on Dropping Out and Teenage Pregnancy." *American Journal of Sociology* 109(3): 676–720.

Hill, James O., and John C. Peters. 1998. "Environmental Contributions to the Obesity Epidemic." *Science* 280(5368): 1371–4.

Horowitz, Carol R., Kathryn A. Colson, Paul L. Hebert, and Kristie Lancaster. 2004. "Barriers for Buying Healthy Foods for People with Diabetes: Evidence of Environmental Disparities." *American Journal of Public Health* 94(912): 1549–54.

House, James S. 2002. "Understanding Social Factors and Inequalities in Health: 20th Century Progress and 21st Century Prospects." *Journal of Health and Social Behavior* 43(2): 125–43.

Hox, Joop. 2002. *Multilevel Analysis: Techniques and Applications*. Mahwah, N.J.: Lawrence Erlbaum Associates.

Humpel, Nancy, Neville Owen, and Eva Leslie. 2002. "Environmental Factors Associated with Adults' Participation in Physical Activity. A Review." *American Journal of Preventive Medicine* 22(3): 188–99.

Jacobs, Jane. 1961. *The Death and Life of Great American Cities*. New York: Random House.

Kling, Jeffrey R., Jeffrey B. Liebman, and Lawrence F. Katz. 2007. "Experimental Analysis of Neighborhood Effects." *Econometrica* 75(1): 83–119.

Lee, Rebecca E., and Catherine Cubbin. 2002. "Neighborhood Context and Youth Cardiovascular Health Behaviors." *American Journal of Public Health* 92(3): 428–36.

Mokdad, Ali H., Mary K. Serdula, William H. Dietz, Barbara A. Bowman, James S. Marks, and Jeffrey P. Koplan. 1999. "The Spread of the Obesity Epidemic in the United States." *Journal of the American Medical Association* 282(16): 1519–22.

Molnar, Beth E., Steven L. Gortmaker, Fiona C. Bull, and Stephen L. Buka. 2004. "Unsafe to Play? Neighborhood Disorder and Lack of Safety Predict Reduced Physical Activity Among Urban Children and Adolescents." *American Journal of Health Promotion* 18(5): 378–86.

Moore, Latetia V., and Ana V. Diez Roux. 2006. "Associations of Neighborhood Characteristics with the Location and Type of Food Stores." *American Journal of Public Health* 96(2): 325–31.

Morenoff, Jeffrey D. 2003. "Neighborhood Mechanisms and the Spatial Dynamics of Birthweight." *American Journal of Sociology* 108(5): 976–1017.

Morenoff, Jeffrey D., and John W. Lynch. 2004. "What Makes a Place Healthy? Neighborhood Influences on Racial/Ethnic Disparities in Health over the Life Course." In *Critical Perspectives on Racial and Ethnic Differences in Health in Late Life*, edited by Norman B. Anderson, Randy A. Bulatao, and Barney Cohen. Washington: National Academy Press.

Morland, Kimberly, Steve Wing, Ana Diez Roux, and Charles Poole. 2002. "Neighborhood Characteristics Associated with the Location of Food Stores and Food Service Places." *American Journal of Preventive Medicine* 22(1): 23–29.

Oakes, J. Michael. 2004. "The (Mis)estimation of Neighborhoods Effects: Causal Inference for a Practicable Social Epidemiology." *Social Science and Medicine* 58(10): 1929–52.

Orleans, C. Tracy, M. Katherine Kraft, Joseph F. Marx, and J. Michael McGinnis. 2003. "Why Are Some Neighborhoods Active and Others Not? Charting a New Course for Research on the Policy and Environmental Determinants of Physical Activity." *Annals of Behavioral Medicine* 25(2): 77–79.

Orr, L., J.D. Feins, R. Jacob, E. Beecroft, L. Sanbonmatsu, L.F. Katz, J.B. Liebman, and J.R. Kling. 2003. *Moving to Opportunity for Fair Housing Demonstration Program Interim Impacts Evaluation*. Washington: U.S. Department of Housing and Urban Development, Office of Policy Development and Research.

Phillips, Carl V. 2001. "The Economics of 'More Research Is Needed.'" *International Journal of Epidemiology* 30(4): 771–6.

Piro, Fredrik N., Øyvind Noss, and Bjørgulf Claussen. 2006. "Physical Activity Among Elderly People in a City Population: The Influence of Violence and Self Perceived Safety." *Journal of Epidemiology and Community Health* 60(7): 626–32.

Rapoport, Amos. 1987. "Pedestrian Street Use: Culture and Perception." In *Public Streets for Public Use*, edited by A. Moudon. New York: Columbia University Press.

Raudenbush, Stephen W., and Anthony S. Bryk. 2002. *Hierarchical Linear Models: Applications and Data Analysis Methods*. Thousand Oaks, Calif.: Sage Publications.

Raudenbush, Stephen W., and Robert J. Sampson. 1999. "Ecometrics: Toward a Science of Assessing Ecological Settings, with Application to the Systematic Social Observation of Neighborhoods." *Sociological Methodology* 29: 1–41.

Robert, Stephanie A. 1998. "Community-Level Socioeconomic Status Effects on Adult Health." *Journal of Health and Social Behavior* 39(1): 18–37.

Romero, Andrea J., Thomas N. Robinson, Helena C. Kraemer, Sarah J. Erickson, K. Farish Haydel, Fernando Mendoza, and Joel D. Killen. 2001. "Are Perceived Neighborhood Hazards a Barrier to Physical Activity in Children?" *Archives of Pediatric and Adolescent Medicine* 155(10): 1143–8.

Ross, Catherine E. 2000. "Walking, Exercising, and Smoking: Does Neighborhood Matter?" *Social Science and Medicine* 51(2): 265–74.

Sallis, James F., Lawrence D. Frank, Brian E. Saelens, and M. Katherine Kraft. 2004. "Active Transportation and Physical Activity: Opportunities for Collaboration on Transportation and Public Health Research." *Transportation Research Part A: Policy and Practice* 38(4): 249–68.

Sampson, Robert J., Stephen W. Raudenbush, and Felton Earls. 1997. "Neighborhoods and Violent Crime: A Multilevel Study of Collective Efficacy." *Science* 277(5328): 918–24.

Satariano, William A., and Edward McAuley. 2003. "Promoting Physical Activity Among Older Adults: From Ecology to the Individual." *American Journal of Preventive Medicine* 25(3, Supplement 2): 184–92.

Schilling, Joseph, and Leslie S. Linton. 2005. "The Public Health Roots of Zoning: In Search of Active Living's Legal Genealogy." *American Journal of Preventive Medicine* 28(2, Supplement 2): 96–104.

Skogan, Wesley, and Kathleen Frydl. 2004. *Fairness and Effectiveness in Policing: The Evidence*. Washington: National Academy Press.

Snijders, Tom A. B., and Roel Bosker. 1999. *Multilevel Analysis: An Introduction to Basic and Advanced Multilevel Modeling*. Thousand Oaks, Calif.: Sage Publications.

Wilson, Dawn K., Karen A. Kirtland, Barbara E. Ainsworth, and Cheryl L. Addy. 2004. "Socioeconomic Status and Perceptions of Access and Safety for Physical Activity." *Annals of Behavioral Medicine* 28(1): 20–28.

Chapter 12

Are Some Neighborhoods Better for Child Health than Others?

Rebecca C. Fauth and Jeanne Brooks-Gunn

I‌t is believed that the neighborhoods in which children and youth live are associated with their health and well-being. The underlying premise of this belief is that living in more affluent and safe neighborhoods results in better health (as well as increases the likelihood of doing well in school and obtaining better jobs and housing). While this assumption, on its face, seems obvious, it is incredibly difficult to substantiate from a social-science perspective. The primary reason is that families have some choice as to where they live. Consequently, when neighborhood influences are reported, individual-level variables may be accounting, wholly or in part, for the neighborhood-health links. The problem of selection bias in estimating effects of neighborhood residence on well-being is so unsettling (and difficult to solve in traditional regression analyses of cross-sectional and short-term longitudinal data) that social scientists are quite divided as to whether they accept this premise at all.

To better understand the source of this division, we examine literature on neighborhood-health links with a focus on children and youth. Our interest is informed by several policy-relevant situations. The first has to do with increases in neighborhoods of concentrated poverty in urban areas during the 1970s and 1980s, as documented by William Julius Wilson (1987) and Douglas Massey (1990). Although neighborhood poverty rates have dropped slightly in recent years, in 2000 more than 15 million people in the United States lived in extremely impoverished neighborhoods. These neighborhoods are characterized by poverty rates of at least 30 percent and high rates of female-headed households, low educational attainment, and high unemployment (O'Hare and Mather 2003). The vast majority of these individuals were African American or Latino. In part, these trends are influenced by conditions such as the relocation of nonpoor families from central cities to ring communities and the suburbs, the lower demand for unskilled laborers in the workforce, exclusionary housing and zoning policies, the construction of massive public housing projects in cities during the 1940s and 1950s, and the deteriorating condition of the housing stock in older cities (Massey 1990; Wilson 1987, 1996). Second, even though the increase in poverty concentration attenuated somewhat in the 1990s, the divide between more- and less-advantaged families is growing (Sawhill and McLanahan 2006), as evidenced by rising work and income differences between single- and two-parent families as well as between parents with postsecondary education and those without it. If these family-level differences remain or accelerate, it is likely that neighborhood poverty concentration, or at least the differences between affluent and other neighborhoods, will increase in the coming decades. Third, racial- and social-class gaps in school achievement and health are, for the most part, not closing (Jencks and Phillips 1998; Rouse, Brooks-Gunn, and McLanahan 2005). If neighborhood conditions are part of the underlying cause for the persistence of these gaps, then alteration of such conditions may be one strategy for reducing them.

There are multiple types of evidence for estimating neighborhood effects, and we focus on three research designs: neighborhood-cluster designs, "natural experiments" (which allow researchers to explore variation in neighborhood conditions due to exogenous changes), and relocation experiments. For historical purposes, we also consider cross-sectional and longitudinal designs without a cluster feature. These various types of studies offer evidence about associations between neighborhood conditions and physical health outcomes (such as respiratory problems, low birth weight, lead poisoning, obesity, and ratings of poor health) and emotional distress (depressive and anxious symptoms). In addition, prior studies also allow for the examination of the relationship between neighborhood and health compromising behaviors (such as juvenile delinquency and crime, substance use, and early sexual behavior). Throughout these literatures, one can connect specific characteristics of neighborhoods to health outcomes. These characteristics include exposure to violence, social processes and normative control, availability of resources and institutions, quality of housing stock, and presence of environmental pollutants.[1]

STANDARDS OF EVIDENCE FOR ESTIMATING NEIGHBORHOOD EFFECTS

The use of large-scale cross-sectional data sets to examine neighborhood effects on child and adolescent outcomes were the coin of the realm in earlier decades. Although these studies were not specifically designed to study neighborhood effects, they typically include a large range of neighborhood types—albeit with only a few children or families from each neighborhood—which allows for variation on measures of neighborhood dimensions (Duncan, Connell, and Klebanov 1997; Duncan and Raudenbush 1999). In most of the existing research, census tract–level data was appended to the cross-sectional data sets, and neighborhood effects were then estimated by regressing outcomes of interest on the census variables as well as individual- and family-level demographic control variables (for summaries, see Brooks-Gunn, Duncan, and Aber 1997; Leventhal and Brooks-Gunn 2000).

While innovative in their time, these studies are problematic for many reasons. First, because individuals were not sampled according to their neighborhood of residence, multilevel modeling cannot be done. Thus, variance in the outcome measure of interest cannot be parsed into within- and between-neighborhood components, as can be done in the neighborhood-cluster designs (Raudenbush and Sampson 1999). These models account for the fact that residents of the same neighborhood are likely to be more similar than residents of different neighborhoods. Second, while most of the studies in this genre include the standard battery of demographic-background variables as well as, in some cases, measures of maternal mental health, the possibility of selection bias still remains (Duncan, Connell, and Klebanov 1997; Tienda 1991). Typically, constructs such as motivation, self-efficacy, conscientiousness, determination, family routines, and parenting behavior are omitted from these studies even though they might be linked with where families choose to live (Dunifon, Duncan, and Brooks-Gunn 2001).

These studies also typically confound minority status, social class, and neighborhood residence. That is, since residence is so segregated, most studies have not included enough minorities living in the most affluent neighborhoods and not enough nonminorities living in the most disadvantaged neighborhoods in order to model links between neighborhoods and health for different ethnic or racial groups. However, many studies purport to be able to do so. For example, in Jeanne Brooks-Gunn, Greg Duncan, and J. Lawrence Aber's (1997) summary of six of these data sets, only one of the six data sets included any African American families living in affluent neighborhoods or white families living in disadvantaged neighborhoods. Even in the Panel Study of Income Dynamics (a nationally representative longitudinal data set), the distributions of African American and White families by neighborhood type were so disparate that we were unable to estimate comparable regression slopes along the entire distribution of neighborhoods for each racial group separately (Brooks-Gunn et al. 1993).

Studies with longitudinal data on family and neighborhood characteristics as well as outcomes provide a more rigorous approach for examining some health behaviors. For example, it is possible to examine neighborhood links to emotional distress or health compromising behavior by controlling for initial levels of such behaviors.[2] It is somewhat surprising that so few articles report such analyses (Leventhal and Brooks-Gunn 2000). Social scientists also have not modeled, to any great extent, changes in neighborhoods and changes in health compromising behaviors simultaneously. Longitudinal studies may also allow for sibling analyses. For example, siblings often live in different neighborhoods during their early-childhood years; this allows for within-family comparisons of neighborhood effects (Duncan et al. 1998). An intriguing design along the same lines is a twin design to estimate neighborhood effects (Caspi et al. 2000).

Neighborhood-Cluster Design

Recently, neighborhood-cluster studies have been designed specifically to study neighborhood effects by sampling children and families according to their neighborhoods and following them longitudinally (Leventhal and Brooks-Gunn 2003b). The two most well-known studies are the Project on Human Development in Chicago Neighborhoods (PHDCN) (Sampson, Raudenbush, and Earls 1997; Sampson 1997) and the Los Angeles Families and Neighborhood Study (LA FANS) (Sastry and Pebley 2003). In PHDCN, all 343 neighborhood clusters (which included two to three census tracts each) were classified in terms of neighborhood social class (by dividing the Chicago neighborhoods into socioeconomic status [SES] terciles, clusters were sorted into three groups) and neighborhood racial-ethnic makeup (clusters were sorted into seven groups based on proportions of African American, white, and Latino residents). The design resulted in twenty-one cells. For all but three cells, neighborhoods were identified. (No neighborhood was high SES and high proportion Latino, high SES and mixed African American and Latino, and low SES and high proportion white.) A random sample of eighty Chicago neighborhood clusters was selected by cell, resulting in a sample that is representative of neighborhoods and children in Chicago in the mid-1990s. Subsequently, a household survey was conducted within each of the neighborhood clusters (over thirty-five thousand households) to obtain a sample of about seven thousand children and youth in seven different age cohorts (birth, three, six, nine, twelve, fifteen, and eighteen years old). Enough children and youth were sampled in each neighborhood so that reliable estimates of within- and between-neighborhood variance in any particular outcome can be made. The children were seen three times over a seven-year period (Leventhal, Xue, and Brooks-Gunn 2006).

In addition, a Community Survey was also done by interviewing a separate sample of adults clustered by neighborhood. Residents answered questions about neighborhood processes, including social cohesion, norms, anomie, ties to neighborhood institutions, and existence of youth-serving organizations. The individuals' responses were summed to the neighborhood level, providing an estimation of how these processes differed between neighborhoods. This survey was conducted in the mid-1990s and again in the early years of the twenty-first century. Unlike other studies using interviews to obtain information about neighborhoods, the PHDCN took care to separate the community-level respondents from the family-level data collection. No other study has taken seriously the concern about shared-method variance when asking parents or adults about their own circumstances and mental health as well as the health of their offspring and, at the same time, asking about neighborhood processes (Sampson, Morenoff, and Earls 1999). The Community Survey and its sampling procedure have been used in cities in other countries, which allows for replication of links between neighborhood process and both structural characteristics and crime and violence (Sampson 2006).

Finally, observations were made of thousands of face blocks in the eighty neighborhood clusters. These were made via a slow-moving van, and the observations were videotaped. Data on physical disorder, loitering, vacant buildings, drug paraphernalia, and liquor stores were coded from these tapes (Raudenbush and Sampson 1999; Sampson and Raudenbush 1999).

LA FANS also stratified neighborhoods into three income groups. Then, sixty-five neighborhoods were randomly selected to yield a representative sample of very poor neighborhoods, poor neighborhoods, and nonpoor neighborhoods. Fifty households were randomly selected per neighborhood, oversampling for families with children. Thus, in both studies, individuals were sampled according to their neighborhood of residence. In order to estimate effects of migration, families who entered the target neighborhoods after the first wave of data collection were recruited into LA FANS.

These two studies allow for an estimation of between- and within-neighborhood variance on various outcomes. In general, to date, the between-neighborhood variance tends to range between about 4 and 14 percent. Are these estimates small or large? Given that family conditions are much more highly related with child outcomes than are neighborhood conditions, we consider 10 percent to be quite respectable (as between-family effects might be 30 percent or greater). Since hereditability plays a role in the expression of emotional distress, obesity, and health compromising behaviors, the amount of variance to be explained by environmental inputs (whether they be family, peer, school, or neighborhood) is certainly less than 100 percent. Estimates of hereditability for outcomes such as anxiety, depression, aggression, and obesity range from 0.4 to 0.6 (although these estimates typically include gene-by-environment interactions as well as genetic influences and perhaps an error term as well), or perhaps 20 to 35 percent of variance in outcomes. In light of the expected links for family, environmental, and genetic influences, finding that 10 percent of variance for a particular outcome is due to between-neighborhood differences seems large. As data from LA FANS and PHDCN are just beginning to be accessed through data archives, research on between-neighborhood effects is expected to increase substantially in the next few years.

Natural Experiments

In a natural experiment, some exogenous or external shift occurs that affects residents over time or differentially impacts neighborhoods. Although few of these studies focus on neighborhood or place, several have examined the impact of changes in environmental regulations such as the Clean Air Act of 1974 and its subsequent amendments on children's health—notably on infant mortality and morbidity (Chay and Greenstone 2003; Currie and Neidell 2005). Other studies have explored the impacts of sanitation interventions on infant mortality on Native American reservations (Watson 2006), how the closure of liquor stores in some communities in Los Angeles following the 1992 riots impacted gonorrhea rates (Cohen et al. 2006), and how declines in gasoline lead levels affected crime rates

(Reyes 2007). Still others have taken advantage of the fact that families in the military are expected to relocate often; these moves are for the most part random (Lleras-Muney 2005).

These econometric analyses use changes over time as well as area fixed effects and state-level data to model the possible influence of regulatory change, natural crises, or random relocations upon health outcomes. These designs are very strong, in that an extensive set of controls can be used to minimize the chances that some other event caused a change in health outcomes (difference-in-difference approach).

Relocation Experiments

Relocation experiments have been conducted where randomly selected families residing in public housing in impoverished neighborhoods are given the opportunity to relocate to less poor neighborhoods. Perhaps the most notable relocation program is the Moving to Opportunity Demonstration (MTO), which began in 1994 and targeted poor, African American and Latino families in Baltimore, Boston, Chicago, Los Angeles, and New York City. About one thousand families per city were assigned at random to one of three groups: relocation via special vouchers to neighborhoods where 10 percent or fewer residents were poor (with special assistance offered by the Housing Authority or nonprofit groups to identify rental units and to contact potential landlords), relocation with unrestricted Section 8 vouchers to private housing in any type of neighborhood (this is the current approach for moving poor families into private housing), or continued residence in public housing. This relocation demonstration involved a move from public to private housing, as well as from high-poverty to less-poor neighborhoods.

Another approach is demonstrated by the Yonkers Family and Community Program in Yonkers, New York (the fourth largest city in New York State, located just north of New York City). Like MTO, relocation in Yonkers was from public housing in high-poverty neighborhoods to less-poor neighborhoods. Unlike MTO, however, relocation in Yonkers was accomplished via scattered-site publicly funded townhouses constructed in middle-class white neighborhoods.

Moving to Opportunity (MTO) Demonstration   Following the reported success of the quasi-experimental Gautreaux Program in Chicago, the U.S. Department of Housing and Urban Development (HUD) initiated MTO (Goering and Feins 2003). Families with at least one child under the age of eighteen were recruited from housing projects located in neighborhoods where 40 percent or more of the population was living at or below the poverty line. MTO used a tenant-based approach, such that families who were selected to relocate were given Section 8 housing vouchers applicable for rent in program-approved private housing of their choice.

Participating families were randomly assigned to one of three conditions. For the two treatment groups, the voucher offer was valid for sixty days from the issue date, with deadline extensions provided at the discretion of the local housing authorities. Experimental families were required to stay in low-poverty neighborhoods for the tenure of their first-year lease. Their vouchers could be used in neighborhoods of their choice in subsequent years.

Baseline interviews with household heads were conducted between 1994 and 1999, prior to random assignment and relocation of those who moved, with follow-up studies conducted about two and a half and five years later.[3] The five-year follow-up had a 92 percent response rate and included interviews with the head of household (typically the mother, given that the vast majority of households had a single parent) and up to two children per household (including children as young as five years old).

Experimental program take-up was 47 percent. While nearly double the expectations of HUD, the take-up rate was low compared to other social demonstrations and programs with randomization, such as those conducted on welfare reform and early-childhood education. By 1997, 35 percent of the experimental families were residing in program-mandated neighborhoods with 10 percent or fewer poor residents. In contrast, 11 percent of regular Section 8 families and 3 percent of controls were living in similar low-poverty neighborhoods (Goering and Feins 2003). Moving did not alter the racial and ethnic mix of experimental families' neighborhoods quite as much: 44 percent of experimental families resided in neighborhoods where less than 40 percent of the residents were African American. In 2002, given the fact that many experimental families had moved from their original apartment in the low-poverty neighborhoods, only 25 percent were living in neighborhoods with 10 percent or fewer poor residents, and only 16 percent were living in neighborhoods where less than 40 percent of the residents were African American (Orr et al. 2003).

These results can be interpreted two ways. On the one hand, experimental families were significantly more likely to live in neighborhoods with relatively fewer poor families than were the control families or the families in the regular Section 8–voucher group. At the same time, the overall differences in neighborhoods between control and experimental families were quite small. As estimated by Christopher Jencks (2006), the average participant lived in a neighborhood with a 49 percent poverty rate at the time of the lottery; in 2002, the experimental group's average was 31 percent and the control group's average was 39 percent—only an 8 percentage point difference. The average percentage of minority-neighborhood residents was high at the time of randomization (91 percent). At the 2002 follow-up, the averages were 88 percent for the controls and 83 percent for the experimental group. Here, the difference between treatment and control groups was only 5 percentage points. The neighborhoods in which the experimental families in MTO ended up were much more similar to those in which the control families resided. In contrast, in its predecessor demonstration—the Gautreaux Program in Chicago—treatment families relocated to the suburbs rather than to the outlying neighborhoods of the city or to communities just outside of the city proper. In Gautreaux, families lived in primarily white, relatively affluent communities.

Of course, such experiments are limited in that not all families choose the offer to be placed in the lottery. And, they also focus on one group of poor families in poor neighborhoods: those living in public housing. The majority of families in poor neighborhoods do not live in public housing. In addition, not all experimental families initially took up the voucher offer. There is no doubt that these families differed in unmeasured ways from those who did not move. Also, it is not known whether more families (or a different subset of families) would have taken up the voucher if more supportive services had been offered. Such services might be important because families were required to move to neighborhoods different than those to which they typically would move if given a Section 8 voucher (indeed, the families in MTO who received the unrestricted Section 8 voucher moved to neighborhoods no different from those in which they had lived prior to moving). Further, not all families who actually moved stayed in their initial receiver neighborhoods, and some control families did move. Consequently, in the context of many policy experiments, the overall take-up of the treatment was not large; this limits the ability to detect treatment differences even with a relatively large sample size (and renders site-specific comparisons problematic).[4]

For these reasons, the MTO, while invaluable as an experiment, is unable to address questions about neighborhood residence in cases where neighborhood change was moderate or large. We interpret the MTO treatment itself as small to modest, in contradistinction to other demonstration programs and to the neighborhood-cluster designed studies, where residents lived in a much larger range of neighborhoods in terms of poverty and racial makeup. In general, the comparisons that can be made in MTO are between neighborhoods that might be characterized as poor and near-poor. And, the nonexperimental literature typically does not find effects when comparing such neighborhoods (that is, the effects are typically seen when looking at middle-class or affluent neighborhoods, as compared to poor and near-poor neighborhoods).

Yonkers Program In 1985, city-wide desegregation of public housing in Yonkers was mandated by the court-ruling in *United States v. City of Yonkers*. While much of the city was white and middle class, the southwest quarter, where the large public-housing projects were located, was disproportionately comprised of poor African American and Latino families (Briggs 1997; Briggs, Darden, and Aidala 1999). In the 1990s, following many years of negotiation and public unrest, two hundred two-story townhouse units were constructed as public housing in eight primarily white middle-class neighborhoods. The eight sites varied in townhouse density, ranging from fourteen to forty-eight units per site.

Residence in the new townhouses was determined by a lottery drawing. Families currently living in public housing (50 percent) or who were on the waiting list for public housing (50 percent) were eligible to enter the lottery. Eligibility criteria were based on families' residential history, household composition, income, past lease violations, and housekeeping. The two hundred families were randomly selected and 95 percent relocated to the scattered-site housing units between fall of 1992 and 1994 (double the rate of MTO). The plan to examine the impacts of this housing experiment was developed after families had relocated, and the Yonkers Housing Authority restricted access to information on the over one thousand families who had applied for the lottery, necessitating alternative recruitment methods for the control group.[5]

All families were interviewed in their home about two and seven years following relocation (about three hundred and fifty families in total). Children eight to eighteen years old in the household were also interviewed. At the seven-year follow-up, 78 percent of the households were reinterviewed.

The neighborhoods in which the families who had won the lottery resided were much more advantaged than the controls' neighborhoods. For example, only 5 percent of the residents were poor in the scattered-site housing neighborhoods, compared to 30 percent in southwest Yonkers. About 7 percent of the residents in the neighborhoods where the new townhouses were located were minorities, compared to 67 percent in southwest Yonkers. And, unlike MTO, almost all of the families who initially moved to the scattered-site housing were still there five to seven years later. However, the sample size was relatively small, which reduces the power to detect significant differences between those that moved and those that stayed in the high-poverty neighborhoods (especially when examining age or gender patterns).

What makes the Yonkers Program interesting is the fact that relocation was done not to private housing, as in MTO, but rather it was done to scattered-site low-income housing. The experimental families resided in enclaves of poor minority families surrounded by white middle-class residents. In one sense, the experimental families were living in neighborhoods more like those of the Gautreaux Program's experimental families in the suburbs of Chicago. However, the Yonkers movers were living in clearly recognizable public-housing units which were constructed after prolonged and bitter struggles (including having the New York state government intervene and a judge oversee the program) (Belkin 1999). These conditions probably explain the comments of many Yonkers movers, who felt quite disconnected from their middle-class neighbors and who kept close contact with friends from their old neighborhoods. Indeed, twelve to fourteen years after the lottery, the majority of the original movers had left their scattered-site units (Santos 2006).

ASSOCIATIONS BETWEEN NEIGHBORHOODS AND PHYSICAL HEALTH

The following section highlights links between neighborhoods and children's physical health using evidence from the relocation experiments, various natural experiments, and the neighborhood-cluster designs. We focus on health problems that are most prevalent in children's early years, notably asthma, low birth weight, and lead poisoning, as well as health outcomes that affect residents of all ages, including obesity and perceptions of overall health. Each of the outcomes examined is believed to be affected, in part, by neighborhood of residence.

Respiratory Problems in the Preschool Years

Asthma and upper-respiratory problems are quite common in childhood. About 11 to 12 percent of all children have had asthma at some point in their lives, and almost 6 percent have had an asthma attack in the last year. Asthma is more prevalent in children older than preschool-aged, in some racial minorities, in boys, and in poor children (Currie 2005). Asthma is believed to be associated with second-hand smoke (a smoker in the child's household), and allergens due to cockroaches, dust mites, and cats, the sources of which can all be contained in part by actions of parents. Mold, mildew, and pollen are other sources which may be controlled in part by parents (Bukowski et al. 2002; Liccardi et al. 2000). In addition, air pollution, which is associated with neighborhood residence, is linked to asthma.

Perhaps the best evidence for links between neighborhood residence and respiratory problems comes from natural experiments in which the outcomes are infant mortality, hospitalizations, and asthma. Kenneth Chay and Michael Greenstone (2003) examined links between shifts in particulate levels and infant mortality rates over a three-year period. The authors chose the years 1980 to 1982 because the country was in the midst of a recession at the time. Given that the recession resulted in the closure of pollution-inducing manufacturing plants, air-pollution levels were expected to shift dramatically in the areas hit hardest by the recession. A multitude of analyses were specified, with some including controls for weather, year effects, mothers' health endowment, family medical history, and others including groups of families from different areas who were matched in income. Findings revealed that declines in air pollution at the county level were associated with lower infant mortality rates (Chay and Greenstone 2003). Similarly, a time-series analysis in California examined links between air pollution (including carbon monoxide) and infant mortality following the 1990 Clear Air Act Amendment. Using individual-level and weekly zip code–level pollution data, findings revealed that the 1.1 unit decline in carbon monoxide over the course of the decade saved 991 infants' lives (Currie and Neidell 2005). Another analysis took advantage of the frequent moves made by children of military families; it also found links between air pollutants, particularly ozone, and hospitalizations (Lleras-Muney 2005).

With respect to the relocation experiments, the evidence on neighborhood residence and asthma is not as convincing. In the two-and-a-half-year follow-up of MTO children in Boston, those in the experimental group were less likely to experience asthma attacks that required medical attention than the controls according to maternal report (Katz, Kling, and Liebman 2001). However, these effects were not replicated in the five-year follow-up in all five cities. And no effects were found in the Yonkers Program either (Fauth, Leventhal, and Brooks-Gunn 2004). We suspect that no effects were seen since the likelihood of the receiver and sender neighborhoods differing in particulate matter in the air is unlikely (given that movers relocated, for the most part, within ten to twenty miles of their original locations). Also, the natural experiments examined respiratory problems in the infant or preschool years rather than across a larger age range. The relocation experiments had a relatively small number of infants and toddlers in their samples as compared to the natural experiments.

Of course, conditions within the apartment and building itself might be linked with respiratory problems in children (Evans 2004; Juhn et al. 2005). Several cross-sectional studies have reported links between asthma and neighborhood residence (Juhn et al. 2005; Saha, Riner, and Liu 2005). Whether these links are due to air pollution or to the presence of allergens in the home is unknown (assuming that the associations are not entirely due to selection bias). In terms of MTO, given that almost one-half of the experimental families moved to new apartments that they reported were in better physical condition than their previous apartments, it is somewhat surprising that reports of asthma were not reduced. Perhaps, when it comes to allergens within the household, families are replicating the environments that they had originally (that is, in terms of wall-to-wall carpets, bedding, cleanliness, pets, and pests). The fact that the few family-level interactions targeting allergens in the home have not proved successful is a case in point (Evans 2004; Sullivan et al. 2002).

Low Birthweight

Research on low birthweight has taken advantage of birth-record registries. While links are found between low-birthweight rates and neighborhood disadvantage (with higher rates of low birthweight in more disadvantaged neighborhoods), it is very difficult to tease apart neighborhood-level and individual-level influences given the level of data included in birth registries. Two analyses have used data on neighborhood-structure and neighborhood-process characteristics to examine variation in neighborhood rates of low birthweight (Buka et al. 2003; Morenoff 2003). Both use birth-registry data for their identification of rates of low birthweight, and both find evidence for links with neighborhood residence, but both studies are subject to the data limitations just mentioned. At this point in time, then, it is unclear to us whether neighborhood residence influences birthweight, over and above family-level and individual-level characteristics. One way to get a handle on this issue would be to estimate neighborhood effects on behaviors known to be linked to low birthweight (such as how smoking rates among young females of childbearing age are influenced by neighborhood residence).

Lead Poisoning

Research linking lead exposure and child health is quite strong. Exposure to lead, even at relatively low levels, is associated with childhood problems in cognition, attention, aggression, and impulse control (Bellinger 2004; Needleman 1979, 1990, 1996). These associations are due, in part, to the fact that children absorb much more lead than adults do (Bornschein et al. 1985). Although these data are not experimental, the consistency of findings is akin to that linking smoking to increased adult mortality and morbidity. The major sources of exposure to lead are gasoline emissions and house paint. Both sources are linked to neighborhood residence: densely populated, urban environments have high rates of car and truck emissions, and older housing stock is likely to have lead paint inside apartments and houses. From a health perspective, the links between even what used to be considered "safe" blood lead levels and poor health and academic outcomes suggest that lead poisoning is a major public-health issue for children. Interestingly, as more has been learned, the standards for blood lead levels have changed. For example, in 1975 a blood lead level of forty micrograms per deciliter or higher was deemed unsafe by the Centers for Disease Control and Prevention (CDC); in 1991, a blood lead level of ten micrograms per deciliter was set as the cutoff. It is now believed that even lower blood lead levels may be harmful (Canfield et al. 2003).

A rapid decline in concentrations of lead in gasoline followed changes in federal regulations. The Clean Air Act of 1973 stipulated that lead in gasoline be removed, with the Environmental Protection Agency (EPA) outlining a mandatory schedule for its removal. In fact, lead levels in gasoline declined 99 percent between 1973 and 1990 (U.S. Environmental Protection Agency 2000). As would be expected, given that lead emissions in gasoline was the largest contributor to lead exposure, blood lead levels declined during this period as well (Pirkle et al. 1994).[6]

Jessica Reyes (2007) has taken advantage of these declines over time to examine changes in crime rates. Her premise—that lowered lead levels in gasoline might have resulted in a lowered crime rate—builds on several key findings: lead exposure in childhood is associated with attention and cognitive problems, which are in turn associated with later delinquency and crime (Moffitt and Caspi 2001; Moffitt and Silva 1988); and lead levels are higher in youth who are delinquent relative to those who are not (Needleman et al. 2002). Looking at violent-crime rates for different birth cohorts as well as at lead exposure by state and time, Jessica Reyes finds that the two statistics tracked one another (even when using state fixed effects models and controlling for other state-level variables). An inquiry as to whether these declines are more pronounced in areas of the country which had the largest declines in lead emissions (such as urban areas versus rural areas) would be a further refinement of this hypothesis.

Obesity

Obesity during childhood and adolescence has increased at a dizzying rate during the past quarter of a century, leading some in public health to call it an epidemic (Brooks-Gunn, Fink, and Paxson 2006). The Robert Wood Johnson Foundation is committing $500 million of its funds to combating obesity in the next decade (Robert Wood Johnson Foundation Newsroom 2007). As many as one-third of children today may be overweight (above the eighty-fifth percentile for their weight taking height into account) and over 15 percent may be obese (above the ninety-fifth percentile) (Anderson and Butcher 2006; Paxson et al. 2006). Large numbers of children are overweight or obese as early as age three (Kimbro, Brooks-Gunn, and McLanahan 2007). Rates are higher for poor than for nonpoor children, and they are higher for African Americans and Hispanics than for Whites.

It is believed that neighborhood residence plays a role, although the evidence to date is not strong. Neighborhood-cluster designs are just beginning to look at within- and between-neighborhood differences in rates of childhood, adolescent, and adult obesity (Morenoff et al., chapter 11, this volume).

Relocation experiments have also looked at weight. In the MTO, at the five-year follow-up, the heads of households (typically mothers) who were in the experimental group were less likely to be obese than the in-place controls (36 percent versus 47 percent) (Orr et al. 2003). The size of this effect is larger than almost any individual treatment programs for obesity (Paxson et al. 2006). Somewhat surprisingly, then, no effects were found in MTO for obesity in children or adolescents. However, the teenage girls in the MTO experimental group did report that they exercised more than did those in the in-place control group. It is not known whether this increased exercise will translate into weight differences later in their lives.

With obesity rates on the rise, it is believed that access to healthy food and exercise facilities is important (Anderson and Butcher 2006). Indeed, findings from MTO revealed that the favorable program effect on adults' obesity rates was concomitant with the frequency of healthy eating and, to a lesser extent, exercising. Studies have linked neighborhood characteristics with the number and proximity of supermarkets, exercise facilities (including open public space), and fast-food restaurants. In high-poverty neighborhoods, supermarkets and exercise facilities are in low supply relative to fast-food restaurants; the availability of such resources, whether healthy or unhealthy, are directly linked with their usage (Blanchard et al. 2005; Hume, Salmon, and Ball 2005; Zenk et al. 2005). One study found that for every 5 percent decrease in median family income, there was a 10 percent increase in fast-food-restaurant density (Block, Scribner, and DeSalvo 2004). Related work on exercise indicates that perceptions of neighborhood safety are linearly associated with use of nearby exercise facilities and actual physical activity (Gomez et al. 2004; Romero 2005). Therefore, it is likely that the mere presence of parks and recreation institutions is unlikely to increase exercise if residents feel they must compromise their safety to get to them.

Ratings of Physical Health

In relocation experiments, positive effects on adults' perceived health were seen at the two-and-a-half-year follow-up in Boston MTO experimental movers (Katz, Kling, and Liebman 2003) and in the Yonkers Program movers (Fauth, Leventhal, and Brooks-Gunn 2004). However, the effects did not persist in MTO (Orr et al. 2003), but they did persist in Yonkers (Fauth, Leventhal, and Brooks-Gunn 2007). We are uncertain as what to make of these across-experiment differences.

Using data from Chicago (and attaching Community Survey data from PHDCN to it), Christopher Browning and colleagues have reported links between ratings of poor physical health and residence in less-affluent neighborhoods for individuals ages fifty-five and older (Cagney, Browning, and Wen 2005; Wen, Browning, and Cagney 2003). Many other studies have examined neighborhood-health links using nonexperimental data without a neighborhood-cluster design. In general, small, yet significant, associations in the expected direction are reported (Pickett and Pearl 2001).

It is not known why differences exist between findings from the MTO and nonexperimental studies on ratings of poor health in adults. One possibility is that the low rate of moving and the relocation of many original movers back to poorer neighborhoods meant that the neighborhoods of the MTO movers and in-place controls were too similar to one another for effects to appear. Indeed, the findings from several studies suggest that the associations between poor health and neighborhood residence were only seen when comparisons were made with affluent neighborhoods; none of the families in MTO lived in such neighborhoods. The fact that effects were seen in the Yonkers Program reinforces this possibility, since these movers were residing in middle-class, primarily white neighborhoods.

With respect to children, poor (maternal-reported) health and neighborhood residence do not seem to be associated in the relocation experiments. The neighborhood-cluster designed studies have not yet reported on maternal reports of child health. Since children as a group are quite healthy, we might not expect to find links with neighborhoods (that is, the percentage of children rated to be in poor health is usually less than 5 percent). In addition, the availability of Medicaid and the State Children's Health Insurance Program for most children up to 200 percent of the poverty threshold might contribute to the relatively favorable ratings of children's health in most studies.[7]

ASSOCIATIONS BETWEEN NEIGHBORHOODS AND EMOTIONAL DISTRESS

Emotional distress is thought to be a consequence of residing in poor or violent neighborhoods. The experimental evidence from MTO confirms this belief. At the two-and-a-half-year follow-up, adults in the experimental group in Boston reported feeling more calm and peaceful as well as less distressed and depressed than the in-place control-group adults (Katz, Kling, and Liebman 2001). A similar result was reported for the New York City two-and-a-half-year follow-up (Leventhal and Brooks-Gunn 2003a). These favorable program effects were sustained over time across all sites at the five-year follow-up; the follow-up effects were even larger in size than the initial effects (Orr et al. 2003).These effects are very large; indeed, they are larger than effects seen in experiments focused on reducing depressive symptoms in adults.[8]

Associations between adult emotional distress and residence have not yet been analyzed from the neighborhood-cluster designed studies. A series of cross-sectional studies do report more symptoms of depression in poorer neighborhoods, although these links are often attenuated by the addition of family-level characteristics (Henderson et al. 2005; Ross 2000).

With regard to children, the girls in the MTO experimental group had lower emotional distress scores than did the in-place controls. These effects were not seen for the boys. In the PHDCN, the Child Behavior Checklist was used to identify internalizing symptoms (anxiety, depression, and withdrawal symptoms) at two time points. Internalizing symptoms of children ages five to eleven were associated with neighborhood residence, with 11 percent of the variation accounted for by between-neighborhood differences (Xue et al. 2005). Residence in poor neighborhoods was associated with higher internalizing-symptoms scores, even after controlling for family-level characteristics and maternal depressive symptoms (which are almost always linked to reports of child behavior problems). In addition, not only were symptom scores associated with neighborhood residence, but cutoff scores identifying children at high risk for clinical diagnoses were also associated with neighborhood residence. These findings are particularly strong given that initial emotional-symptom scores were controlled. Unlike MTO, no gender differences were seen; that is, boys and girls showed the same pattern of associations. In addition, no age differences were found in associations between emotional distress and neighborhood residence.

The one jarring finding on children's emotional distress comes from the Yonkers Program. In the seven-year follow-up, children who relocated to low-poverty neighborhoods exhibited more anxious and depressed symptoms than children who remained in poor neighborhoods (Fauth, Leventhal, and Brooks-Gunn 2007). Interestingly, mediation analyses revealed that this finding was accounted for by lower levels of social contact in their new neighborhoods at the time of the two-year follow-up study. We suspect that these findings have to do with the stressful circumstances of moving into the scattered-site housing units where the Yonkers children were viewed with suspicion and perhaps hostility by their neighbors. While the mediator analyses are supportive, it is impossible to test this premise.

ASSOCIATIONS BETWEEN NEIGHBORHOODS AND HEALTH COMPROMISING BEHAVIORS

Although not health outcomes per se, delinquency and crime, substance use, and early sexual behavior are important constructs to examine for older children and adolescents. Participation in any of the three has the potential to compromise directly the health and well-being of youth. Delinquency and crime, in particular, has been one of the most commonly studied outcomes in the neighborhood research.

Delinquency and Crime

Delinquency and crime are the two health compromising behaviors that have been most frequently studied in the neighborhood literature; links are frequently reported (Sampson, Morenoff, and Gannon-Rowley 2002). Cross-sectional and longitudinal work is supportive of this link, as are results from the neighborhood-cluster designed studies. The links are less clear in the experimental relocation work given different gender patterns.

In MTO, the girls benefited from relocation out of impoverished neighborhoods, as they reported less delinquency than did their in-place control group counterparts at the five-year follow-up (Orr et al. 2003). Somewhat surprisingly, such effects were not seen for the MTO boys. Indeed, for the boys, property-crime arrests were higher in the experimental group than for the in-place control group; this finding that was seen at a three-and-a-half-year follow-up in Baltimore, which was the only site that had such data available in the earlier stages of the experiment (Ludwig, Duncan, and Hirschfield 2001).[9]

The picture from the Yonkers Program is more complex. At the two-year follow-up, the eight to twelve year olds in the experimental group had lower delinquency rates than did those in the control group. However, thirteen to eighteen year olds in the experimental group reported more problem behavior than those in the control group (Fauth, Leventhal, and Brooks-Gunn 2005). Whether these effects were more pronounced for boys, or whether they were seen for boys but not for girls, is difficult to test given limitations of sample sizes. By the seven-year follow-up, differences in delinquency were not seen (Fauth, Leventhal, and Brooks-Gunn 2007).

In an analysis of the PHDCN, delinquency behaviors were assessed at three time points using growth curve analyses and hierarchical linear modeling techniques (Xue et al. 2006). Between-neighborhood differences accounted for about 6 to 10 percent of the variance in outcomes, which is somewhat less than what was seen for emotional distress. Neighborhood disadvantage influenced the growth trajectories of delinquency for both boys and girls. (Although the rates of delinquency were higher for boys than girls, the age-related and neighborhood-related patterns were the same.)

In other studies, delinquency has been linked to neighborhood disadvantage (Loeber and Wikström 1993; Peeples and Loeber 1994). One longitudinal study suggested that neighborhood SES in early childhood was more strongly associated with adolescent externalizing behaviors than was neighborhood SES in adolescence (Wheaton and Clarke 2003). Typically, attention has not been paid to gender differences in this literature, or studies have focused on boys only.

The fact that MTO influenced girls more than boys, both in terms of reducing emotional distress and delinquency is, at first blush, surprising. The mediators available in the MTO data set have not yielded any insight into the lack of effects for boys. Boys might have not been influenced by the relocations for a variety of reasons, including more attachment to friends in the old neighborhood, more maternal latitude in terms of traveling back to the old neighborhood, less supervision by mothers, easier access to deviant peer groups in the new neighborhood, active recruiting of boys in deviant peer groups in the new neighborhood, less encouragement by teachers and staff in the new school to become engaged in the school, less commitment to school generally (which might make a move more disruptive), and so on. However, to date, we are unsure as to the reasons for the gender difference.

Substance Use

No effects on parents' substance use were found in MTO. In the Yonkers Project, however, the mothers in the relocation group were one-third less likely to report symptoms related to alcohol abuse than those in the in-place control group at the two-year follow-up (Fauth, Leventhal, and Brooks-Gunn 2004). Similar measures were not included at the seven-year follow-up, making it impossible to assess whether this program effect was sustained over time.

Nonexperimental studies have reported links between neighborhood disadvantage and smoking, drinking, and drug use, finding that substance use increases in more disadvantaged neighborhoods (Boardman et al. 2001; Goldsmith, Holzer, and Manderscheid 1998). Work from neighborhood-cluster designed studies has not reported on these adult outcomes yet.

The MTO results suggest that adolescent girls in the experimental group were less likely to smoke cigarettes or marijuana than girls in the control group (Orr et al. 2003). The former were also less likely to witness the sale of drugs. Again, boys' behavior was not influenced by neighborhood treatment. The youth in Yonkers in the experimental group reported less access to illegal substances at the two-year follow-up compared to the control group (Fauth, Leventhal, and Brooks-Gunn 2005). Yet, by the seven-year follow-up, the adolescents in the experimental group reported more cigarette, alcohol, and marijuana use than the control group (Fauth, Leventhal, and Brooks-Gunn 2007).

Sexual Behavior

Two studies using the PHDCN indicate that early onset of sexual behavior (intercourse by age sixteen) is associated with neighborhood residence (Browning, Leventhal, and Brooks-Gunn 2004, 2005). Two findings are highlighted: First, the racial differences in early onset are almost totally explained by neighborhood residence. Second, while boys and girls are both influenced by neighborhood residence, girls are also influenced by parental supervision. However, these studies are cross-sectional. It remains to be seen whether similar findings will be obtained from more stringent study designs.

Studies have also demonstrated an association between neighborhood residence and prevalence of teenage childbearing in the United States (Brooks-Gunn et al. 1993; Crane 1991; Hogan and Kitagawa 1985; South and Baumer 2000) as well as in Canada (Hardwick and Patychuk 1999). Using longitudinal data from the National Survey of Children, Scott South and Eric Baumer (2000) found that approximately one-third of the association between neighborhood socioeconomic disadvantage and teenage childbearing was due to teenagers' attitudes towards nonmarital childbearing. Differences among teenagers' educational aspirations did not explain variation in teenage childbearing by neighborhood (South and Baumer 2000).

Results from a natural experiment in Los Angeles provide some interesting findings with regards to sexually-transmitted diseases. Following the 1992 riots, many stores selling alcohol were destroyed, and zoning laws made it difficult for proprietors to renew their licenses or for new retailers to enter. Tracking gonorrhea rates from 1988 to 1996 in 1,481 census tracts, the authors found that tracts with high percentages of surrendered licenses in 1992 had lower gonorrhea rates over time than tracts with lower percentages of surrendered licenses and, hence, a higher density of liquor stores (Cohen et al. 2006).

SUMMARY OF RESEARCH ON NEIGHBORHOOD-HEALTH LINKS

Most of the neighborhood-health links that we consider in this chapter range from small to modest in size. In some cases, associations have not been conclusively demonstrated (or the results are mixed, as in the case of ratings of poor health, low birthweight, and obesity). The exceptions are the results for emotional distress, delinquency, respiratory problems, and, perhaps, early onset of intercourse and lead poisoning. We would interpret the findings for these health indicators as fairly robust and moderate in size. Even then, results are sometimes contingent on age. For example, respiratory problems and blood lead levels have typically been studied in preschool children; this is because it is believed that early exposure to lead and pollutants is more likely to affect an individual's health than later exposure. It is not known whether the links would be as strong for older children and youth. And, delinquency and sexual behavior are typically the province of adolescents (although both have precursors or predictors from earlier ages).

With respect to ratings of physical health, the experimental studies do not find consistent effects; this is perhaps because the neighborhoods into which MTO families moved were not that different from their original neighborhoods (and cross-sectional studies suggest that physical-health-neighborhood links appear when comparisons are made to affluent neighborhoods rather than to near-poor neighborhoods). In the Yonkers Program, in which the majority of families who initially relocated remained in their placement neighborhood over time, we saw health impacts on adults. Increased employment among relocated adults accounted for this program effect on physical health (no employment effects were seen in MTO) (Fauth, Leventhal, and Brooks-Gunn 2007, forthcoming).

With respect to children, the fact that they are quite healthy and they are eligible for health care might mitigate the possibility of neighborhood links. Further, given that schools are not necessarily tied to neighborhood of residence, school-age children may spend much of their lives outside of their actual neighborhoods.

The experimental effects on emotional distress (on mothers and daughters, at least) are very large. The associations found in the PHDCN are also large (more than 11 percent of the variance is between neighborhoods).[10] Whether emotional distress is lowered for females but not for males, as seen in MTO, is an area of potential interest. For example, are females more affected by neighborhood violence than boys? Are they more likely to fear for their safety, such that moving to a neighborhood with less crime is more advantageous for them?

Neighborhood effects for delinquency are found only for girls across longitudinal studies and in the experimental MTO. It is possible that a portion of this effect is due to the fact that experimental girls engaged in more structured activities during their after-school time than the control—group girls, while no group differences were seen for the boys. It is not known why mover boys were not more likely to participate in structured activities after school than their in-place peers (for ethnographic information on the MTO youth, see Clampet-Lundquist et al. 2006).[11]

Studies examining neighborhood variation on obesity and substance use are less common. At least for adults, recent findings suggest that residence in nonpoor neighborhoods may be beneficial. The findings for children are too inconsistent to make any conclusions at this stage. Across all of the outcomes, it is likely that neighborhood-structure variables, notably disadvantage, are not the neighborhood characteristics that might be influencing health. However, there are other related processes through which such neighborhood links might operate.

PATHWAYS THROUGH WHICH NEIGHBORHOODS MIGHT OPERATE

Neighborhood effects on children's health-related outcomes are likely a result of secondary factors that also vary by neighborhood characteristics. It is the interplay of these mediators that determines the strength and direction of neighborhood effects. Clearly the list of potential mediators or pathways is large, and this section only highlights four that are particularly relevant for health (we consider the research on environmental toxins to be quite strong as well). These include exposure to violence and neighborhood disorder, neighborhood social processes and normative control, access to resources and institutions including health care, supermarkets, and recreation programs, and finally, the quality of housing stock. A brief description of each of these potential pathways and related research follows.

Exposure to Violence

Violence is a concern of most parents. In fact, parents who participated in MTO and Yonkers cited their desire to reside in safer neighborhoods as their primary reason for signing up for the lottery. Their concerns are echoed by research demonstrating links between violence and health, most notably links to emotional distress. Several studies by Catherine Ross and colleagues (Hill, Ross, and Angel 2005; Ross, Reynolds, and Geis 2000; Ross and Mirowsky 2001) have demonstrated that perceptions of neighborhood disorder (including crime, unsafe streets, abandoned housing, and gangs) accounted for links between neighborhood disadvantage and adults' physical and mental health. Neighborhood danger may also be negatively associated with participation in exercise (Grzywacz and Marks 2001; Morenoff et al., chapter 11, this volume).

Links between neighborhood violence and poor children's mental health have also been reported in cross-sectional studies (Margolin and Gordis 2000; Osofsky 1999; Buka et al. 2001). Experimental studies corroborate these findings, given that the receiving neighborhoods were perceived as much safer than the original ones (Goering and Feins 2003; Fauth, Leventhal, and Brooks-Gunn 2004). In Yonkers, the high levels of disorder present in the in-place control neighborhoods partially accounted for the greater frequency of harsh discipline used by control parents (relative to experimental parents) at the time of the seven-year follow-up (Fauth, Leventhal, and Brooks-Gunn 2007). Although it is not a mental health outcome per se, reduction in harsh discipline among relocated parents might favorably affect their younger children's behavior (McLoyd 1998).

Social Processes and Normative Control

Neighborhood social processes include extant social networks as well as constructs, such as collective efficacy, normative control, and social cohesion. These constructs involve the willingness of neighbors to work together for the common good (Sampson, Raudenbush, and Earls 1997). Relocation efforts may disrupt preexisting social ties. On the other hand, low-poverty neighborhoods might offer access to informal social ties who serve as sources of information and opportunity for lower-income residents.

Evidence on neighborhood social processes as a mediator of neighborhood effects is meager. Reports from MTO and Yonkers mover families suggest initial difficulties socializing with their new neighbors (Fauth, Leventhal, and Brooks-Gunn 2004; Goering 2003). Interestingly, subsequent analyses of the Yonkers data revealed that the lack of frequent informal contact with neighbors during the first several years following relocation partially accounted for experimental children's elevated anxiety and depression relative to in-place controls (Fauth, Leventhal, and Brooks-Gunn 2005). No longer-term impacts on social ties or evidence of mediation were found in MTO; although, the mediator analyses to date have not taken into account the repeated moves of many of the original movers (the main impact analyses have done so) (Orr et al. 2003).

Turning to neighborhood-cluster designed studies, evidence to date suggests that neighborhood collective efficacy mediates, in large part, links between neighborhood-structure characteristics and health outcomes. Two studies using the Community Survey data from PHDCN and mortality information from Chicago's vital statistics reported associations between neighborhood collective efficacy and adults' premature mortality (Cohen, Farley, and Mason 2003) as well as asthma (Cagney and Browning 2004). The authors surmise that the collective nature of neighborhood social ties helped to promote health-related resources and prevent environmental hazards.

Using the longitudinal child data from PHDCN, links between neighborhood disadvantage and children's delinquency and emotional distress are accounted for by neighborhood-level collective efficacy (Sampson 1997; Xue et al. 2005, 2006). Studies that do not use neighborhood-clustered designs and do not have independent measures of neighborhood social processes also report links between family-level reports of neighborhood cohesion and youth outcomes (Elliott et al. 1996; Gorman-Smith, Tolan, and Henry 2000; Rankin and Quane 2002), although the size of these effects is probably overestimated given design limitations.

Availability of Resources and Institutions

Availability, accessibility, and quality of neighborhood resources are likely to be associated with neighborhood disadvantage. However, little has been found when examining neighborhood resources as mediating links between neighborhood disadvantage and child outcomes.

Using designs without the neighborhood-cluster feature, residents in disadvantaged neighborhoods are less likely to have a regular health care provider and are more likely to seek emergency-room care during times of illness compared to residents in low-poverty neighborhoods (Brooks-Gunn et al. 1998; Chow, Jaffee, and Snowden 2003; Halfon and Newacheck 1993). Yet in many cases, this is not due to a dearth of health care facilities in impoverished neighborhoods (Allard, Tolman, and Rosen 2003; Kirby and Kaneda 2005). Early research from the Yonkers Program revealed that relocated families reported more access to community resources, including medical care, compared to control-group families (Fauth, Leventhal, and Brooks-Gunn 2004).

Participation in organized social and recreational activities may foster children's and youth's health and well-being; however, the reverse may be true as well. Favorable associations between the availability of community resources for children and youth (including community centers, recreation programs, and mentoring programs) and positive behavior have been reported (Morrissey and Werner-Wilson 2005). The advantages of such programs are probably contingent on the degree to which they occupy children and youth in constructive, well-monitored activities and keep them safe. PHDCN youth's participation in community-based clubs was associated with increased anxiety and depression scores among youth who lived in violent neighborhoods (Fauth, Roth, and Brooks-Gunn 2007). Other research has shown that for poor youth, the proportion of after-school time spent in unsupervised activities with peers was significantly associated with externalizing of behaviors as well as with alcohol and drug use (Coley, Morris, and Hernandez 2004; Pettit et al. 1999). Evidence from MTO suggests that, for girls, moving to low-poverty neighborhoods may improve access to after-school activities (Orr et al. 2003). This favorable impact was not apparent for MTO boys or for Yonkers' youth, however.

Quality of Housing Stock

While the primary focus of neighborhood-mobility experiments is on neighborhood improvement, housing conditions may also be altered; mover families report significant improvements in housing conditions, including decreased rodent and pest infestation, plumbing or heating problems, and peeling paint (Fauth, Leventhal, and Brooks-Gunn 2004; Orr et al. 2003). Similar results are reported in the nonexperimental literature (Evans 2004; Evans and Kantrowitz 2002; Mayer 1997; Newman 2001). These nonexperimental studies have shown links between residential crowding and noise and the development and progression of a variety of illnesses influenced by stress such as hypertension, coronary disease, and psychological distress. Air quality is most commonly affiliated with illnesses that compromise breathing, including bronchitis, emphysema, and asthma. Exposure to environmental toxins, notably lead paint, is unfavorably associated with neurological problems, impulse control, and aggression, as discussed earlier.

CONCLUSION

The last decade has seen a surge in neighborhood research employing sophisticated designs. The current work allows for estimates of neighborhood effects that are less plagued by selection bias. At the same time, the relocation experiments have not been the panacea that many had hoped. In MTO, many families did not sign up for the lottery; for those who did and received the experimental treatment assignment, less than one-half actually moved. The neighborhoods to which they moved, while less disadvantaged then the original neighborhoods, were primarily minority and had low-quality schools; families did not move to the suburbs. And, many of these families moved again, ending up in poorer neighborhoods. A nonexperimental reanalysis of the five-year MTO data found that experimental adults' exposure to low-poverty *and* low-minority neighborhoods (that is, those similar to Yonkers neighborhoods) was favorably linked to their economic outcomes relative to control adults (Clampet-Lundquist and Massey, forthcoming). This indicates that both the socioeconomic *and* racial-ethnic composition of neighborhoods may be important.

Based on our review, policies to address neighborhood-health links should vary depending on the targeted outcome. Respiratory problems and cognitive deficits, which are often the result of airborne pollutants or lead exposure, are most likely affected by large-scale regulatory mechanisms aimed at improving the environment or housing stock. Although it is unclear if increased exercise accounted for the declines in obesity in MTO, access to walkways, parks, or recreational facilities—components of the built environment—might influence the likelihood that residents will exercise and subsequently maintain a healthier weight. Further, zoning limits on the density of fast-food restaurants, particularly in low-income communities, might influence children's and adults' weight. Feelings of fear and safety appear to be a mediating link between neighborhood residence and emotional distress. Crime reduction policies and community involvement tactics that make neighborhoods safer should support residents' emotional health. While favorable results from the neighborhood-relocation programs have been reported, small treatment effects and low take-up rates make them less viable from a large-scale policy perspective. It is likely that regulatory policies (for example, of air pollution, gasoline emissions, lead in house paint, pest control, and fast-food restaurants) are most likely to alter neighborhoods in ways that influence health. Access to institutional resources is also a likely policy lever (for example, youth-serving programs, after-school programs, parks and recreation, libraries, and health clinics). Policies should continue to target "place," as well as families, to improve health (Leventhal, Brooks-Gunn, and Kamerman 1997).

NOTES

1. However, since these constructs are often interrelated and frequently associated with high concentrations of poor neighbors, it is often not possible to separate out the independent contributions of each.
2. Several large national data sets have longitudinal measures of child health. The National Longitudinal Study of Youth-Child Supplement measures reading and math achievement and behavior problems every other year for the children born to the adolescent females first seen in 1979 as part of the NLSY (Chase-Lansdale, Michael, and Desai 1991). The longitudinal nature of these data has generally not been exploited for neighborhood analyses (for exceptions, see Chase-Lansdale et al. 1997; Klebanov et al. 1997). The Panel Study of Income Dynamics-Child Supplement has two time points and is about to collect a third, making it potentially useful as well (Brooks-Gunn et al. 2000). The National Longitudinal Study of Adolescent Health is another nationally representative school-clustered sample where outcomes are measured multiple times (Chantala and Tabor 1999). Given that schools are often neighborhood based, there is also some neighborhood clustering within the data. And, of course, the Panel Study of Income Dynamics is also a candidate data set.
3. For the two-and-a half-year follow-ups, specific evaluators in Baltimore, Boston, and New York City were commissioned by HUD to do local studies.
4. These treatment differences may be compared to those in the early-childhood-education literature, for which take-up rates are typically over 85 percent and relatively few families drop out of the treatment. In these evaluations, the treatment effect is usually about 80 percentage points, not 8 percentage points (Barnett 1995; Karoly et al. 1998; Love et al. 2005).
5. First, a network-sampling approach was used; the families who relocated named up to five families currently living in southwest Yonkers and who had expressed interest in relocating to the new townhouses. Second, families who recently moved into the old public housing in southwest Yonkers, following vacancies by the families who moved,

were also recruited via door-to-door canvassing. These two methods yielded nearly four hundred families who were then screened for eligibility to ensure that they were eligible for the housing lottery. All but three families agreed to participate in the study as the control group (n = 145). Of these, 46 percent had, in fact, entered the lottery and lost, while the remaining 54 percent had never applied to the housing lottery even though they were eligible. Analyses indicated that these groups were comparable to each other and to the experimental group on family-level characteristics (Fauth, Leventhal, and Brooks-Gunn 2004, 2005).

6. This was measured by blood lead levels in the National Health and Nutrition Examination Survey (NHANES).

7. However, one analysis of the PHDCN suggests that some (but not all) youth report poorer health if living in disadvantaged neighborhoods; such links were found for Latino young adolescents but not for African American or white young adolescents (Drukker et al. 2005).

8. Somewhat surprisingly, no comparable effects were seen in the Yonkers Project in either the two- or seven-year follow-up study (Fauth, Leventhal, and Brooks-Gunn 2004, 2007). The two studies did not employ comparable measures, which may account for the lack of consistency in the findings. Furthermore, the measures used in Yonkers were not standard measures of depressive and anxious symptoms.

9. The Baltimore three-and-a-half-year follow-up also found lower arrest rates for violent crimes in the experimental than in the control group; this finding did not replicate in the five-year follow-up (Ludwig, Duncan, and Hirschfield 2001).

10. The Yonkers experience is interesting: if anything, emotional distress was somewhat higher for the mover children, but it was not different for the mover parents. Perhaps the children had somewhat higher levels due to lack of acceptance and hostility of neighborhoods, although we cannot be sure of the reason especially since we would have expected to see similar trends in the mothers.

11. Youth who participated in the Yonkers Program had somewhat unfavorable outcomes in terms of delinquency and substance use. There are several possible reasons for this. First, the Yonkers youth moved to white middle-class neighborhoods, and these families reported a very low frequency of informal contact with their neighbors relative to the control group (Fauth, Leventhal, and Brooks-Gunn 2004). At the same time, parents who relocated reported lower levels of monitoring compared with families who did not relocate. Perhaps the parents who moved, given the relative levels of safety in the immediate neighborhood, felt that they did not need to monitor their youth as closely as those parents in more dangerous neighborhoods. Indeed, low monitoring among the experimental families accounted for, in part, the higher rates of cigarette, alcohol, and marijuana use among youth who relocated (Fauth, Leventhal, and Brooks-Gunn 2007). Finally, the Yonkers youth, for the most part, did not change schools when they moved (given widespread busing within Yonkers). Consequently, they were presumably exposed to similar levels of delinquency and substance use during the school day compared to the control students. Coupled with the decreased parental monitoring, the youth in scattered-site housing may have had more opportunities to engage in such behavior.

REFERENCES

Allard, Scott W., Richard M. Tolman, and Daniel Rosen. 2003. "Proximity to Service Providers and Service Utilization Among Welfare Recipients: The Interaction of Place and Race." *Journal of Policy Analysis and Management* 22(4): 599–613.

Anderson, Patricia M., and Kristin F. Butcher. 2006. "Childhood Obesity: Trends and Potential Causes." *Future of Children* 16(1): 19–45.

Barnett, W. Steven. 1995. "Long-Term Effects of Early Childhood Programs on Cognitive and School Outcomes." *Future of Children* 5(3): 25–50.

Belkin, Lisa. 1999. *Show Me a Hero: A Tale of Murder, Suicide, Race, and Redemption.* Boston, Mass.: Little, Brown, and Company.

Bellinger, David C. 2004. "Lead." Pediatrics 113 (4, Supplement): 1016–22

Blanchard, Chris M., Kerry R. McGannon, John C. Spence, Ryan E. Rhodes, Eric Nehl, Frank Baker, and J. Bostwick. 2005. "Social Ecological Correlates of Physical Activity in Normal Weight, Overweight, and Obese Individuals." *International Journal of Obesity* 29(6): 720–6.

Block, Jason P., Richard A. Scribner, and Karen B. DeSalvo. 2004. "Fast Food, Race/Ethnicity, and Income: A Geographic Analysis." *American Journal of Preventive Medicine* 27(3): 211–7.

Boardman, Jason D., Brian Karl Finch, Christopher G. Ellison, David R. Williams, and James S. Jackson. 2001. "Neighborhood Disadvantage, Stress, and Drug Use Among Adults." *Journal of Health and Social Behavior* 42(2): 151–65.

Bornschein Robert L., Paul Succop, Kim N. Dietrich, Scott C. Clark, Shane Q Hee, and Paul B. Hammond. 1985. "The Influence of Social and Environmental Factors on Dust Lead, Hand Lead, and Blood Lead Levels in Young Children." *Environmental Research* 38(1): 108–18.

Briggs, Xavier de Souza, editor. 1997. *Yonkers Revisited: The Early Impacts of Scattered-Site Public Housing on Families and Neighborhoods. A Report to the Ford Foundation.* New York: Teachers College, Columbia University.

Briggs, Xavier de Souza, Joe T. Darden, and Angela Aidala. 1999. "In the Wake of Desegregation: Early Impacts of Scattered-Site Public Housing on Neighborhoods in Yonkers, New York." *Journal of the American Planning Association* 65 (Winter): 27–49.

Brooks-Gunn, Jeanne, Greg J. Duncan, and J. Lawrence Aber, editors. 1997. *Context and Consequences for Children.* Volume 1 of *Neighborhood Poverty.* New York: Russell Sage Foundation.

Brooks-Gunn, Jeanne, Cassandra Fink, and Christina Paxson. 2006. "Obesity." In *Handbook of Adolescent Behavioral Problems: Evidence-Based Approaches to Prevention and Treatment,* edited by Thomas P. Gullotta and Gerald R. Adams. New York: Springer Verlag.

Brooks-Gunn, Jeanne, Lisa J. Berlin, Tama Leventhal, and Allison Sidle Fuligni. 2000. "Depending on the Kindness of Strangers: Current National Data Initiatives and Developmental Research." *Child Development* 71(1): 257–68.

Brooks-Gunn, Jeanne, Greg J. Duncan, Pamela K. Klebanov, and Naomi Sealand. 1993. "Do Neighborhoods Influence Child and Adolescent Development?" *American Journal of Sociology* 99(2): 353–95.

Brooks-Gunn, Jeanne, Marie C. McCormick, Pamela K. Klebanov, and Cecilia McCarton. 1998. "Health Care Use of 3-Year-Old Low Birthweight Premature Children: Effects of Family and Neighborhood Poverty." *Journal of Pediatrics* 132(6): 971–5.

Browning, Christopher R., Tama Leventhal, and Jeanne Brooks-Gunn. 2004. "Neighborhood Context and Racial Differences in Early Adolescent Sexual Activity." *Demography* 41(4): 697–720.

———. 2005. "Sexual Initiation in Early Adolescence." *American Sociological Review* 70(5): 758–78.

Buka, Stephen L., Theresa L. Stichick, Isolde Birdthistle, and Felton J. Earls. 2001. "Youth Exposure to Violence: Prevalence, Risks, and Consequences." *American Journal of Orthopsychiatry* 71(3): 298–310.

Buka, Stephen L., Robert T. Brennan , Janet W. Rich-Edwards, Stephen W. Raudenbush, and Felton Earls. 2003. "Neighborhood Support and the Birth Weight of Urban Infants." *American Journal of Epidemiology* 157(1): 1–8

Bukowski, John, R. Jeffrey Lewis, John F. Gamble, Nancy C. Wojcik, and Robert J. Laumbach. 2002. "Range-Finding Study of Risk Factors for Childhood Asthma Development and National Asthma Prevalence." Human and Ecological Risk Assessment 8(4): 735–65.

Cagney, Kathleen A., and Christopher R. Browning. 2004. "Exploring Neighborhood-Level Variation in Asthma and Other Respiratory Diseases: The Contribution of Neighborhood Social Context." *Journal of Internal Medicine* 19(3): 229–36.

Cagney, Kathleen A., Christopher R. Browning, and Ming Wen. 2005. "Racial Disparities in Self-Rated Health at Older Ages: What Difference Does the Neighborhood Make?" *Journals of Gerontology, Series B: Psychological and Social Sciences* 60B(4): S181–90.

Canfield, Richard L., Charles R. Henderson Jr., Deborah A. Cory-Slechta, Todd C. Cox, Todd A. Jusko, and Bruce P. Lanphear. 2003. "Intellectual Impairment in Children with Blood Lead Concentrations Below 10 µg per Deciliter." *New England Journal of Medicine* 348(16): 1517–26.

Caspi, Avshalom, Alan Taylor, Terrie E. Moffitt, and Robert Plomin. 2000. "Neighborhood Deprivation Affects Children's Mental Health: Environmental Risk Identified in a Genetic Design." *Psychological Science* 11(4): 338–42.

Chantala, Kim, and Joyce Tabor. 1999. "National Longitudinal Study of Adolescent Health: Strategies to Perform a Design-Based Analysis Using the Add Health Data." Unpublished paper. Carolina Population Health Center, University of North Carolina, Chapel Hill.

Chase-Lansdale, P. Lindsay, Robert T. Michael, and Sonalde Desai. 1991. "Maternal Employment During Infancy: An Analysis of Children of the National Longitudinal Survey of Youth (NLSY)." In *Employed Mothers and Their Children*, Volume 17 of *Reference Books on Family Issues*, edited by Jacqueline V. Lerner and Nancy L. Galambos. New York: Garland Publishing.

Chase-Lansdale, P. Lindsay, Rachel A. Gordon, Jeanne Brooks-Gunn, and Pamela K. Klebanov. 1997. "Neighborhood and Family Influences on the Intellectual and Behavioral Competence of Preschool and Early School-Age Children." In *Context and Consequences for Children*, Volume 1 of *Neighborhood Poverty*, edited by Jeanne Brooks-Gunn, Greg J. Duncan and J. Lawrence Aber. New York: Russell Sage Foundation.

Chay, Kenneth Y., and Michael Greenstone. 2003. "The Impact of Air Pollution on Infant

Mortality: Evidence from Geographic Variation in Pollution Shocks Induced by a Recession." *Quarterly Journal of Economics* 118(3): 1121–67.

Chow, Julian C., Kathleen Jaffee, and Lonnie Snowden. 2003. "Racial/Ethnic Disparities in the Use of Mental Health Services in Poverty Areas." *American Journal of Public Health* 93(5): 792–7.

Clampet-Lundquist, Susan, and Douglas S. Massey. Forthcoming. "Neighborhood Effects on Economic Self-Sufficiency: A Reconsideration of the Moving to Opportunity Experiment" *American Journal of Sociology*.

Clampet-Lundquist, Susan, Kathryn Edin, Jeffrey R. Kling, and Greg J. Duncan. 2006. "Moving At-Risk Teenagers out of High-Risk Neighborhoods: Why Girls Fare Better than Boys." *Princeton IRS* working paper No. 509. Princeton, N.J.: Princeton University.

Cohen, Deborah A., Thomas A. Farley, and Karen Mason. 2003. "Why Is Poverty Unhealthy? Social and Physical Mediators." *Social Science and Medicine* 57(9): 1631–41.

Cohen, Deborah A., Bonnie Ghosh-Dasidar, Richard Scribner, Angela Miu, Molly Scott, Paul Robinson, Thomas A. Farley, Ricky N. Bluthenthal, and Didra Brown-Taylor. 2006. "Alcohol Outlets, Gonorrhea, and the Los Angeles Civil Unrest: A Longitudinal Analysis." *Social Science and Medicine* 62(12): 3062–71.

Coley, Rebekah Levine, Jodi Eileen Morris, and Daphne Hernandez. 2004. "Out-of-School Care and Problem Behavior Trajectories Among Low-Income Adolescents: Individual, Family, and Neighborhood Characteristics as Added Risks." *Child Development* 75(3): 948–65.

Crane, Jonathan. 1991. "The Epidemic Theory of Ghettos and Neighborhood Effects on Dropping Out and Teenage Childbearing." *American Journal of Sociology* 96(5): 1226–59.

Currie, Janet. 2005. "Health Disparities and Gaps in School Readiness." *Future of Children* 15(1): 117–38.

Currie, Janet, and Matthew Neidell. 2005. "Air Pollution and Infant Health: What Can We Learn from California's Recent Experience." *Quarterly Journal of Economics* 120(3): 1003–30.

Drukker, Marjan, Stephen L. Buka, Charles Kaplan, Kwame McKenzie, and Jim Van Os. 2005. "Social Capital and Young Adolescents' Perceived Health in Different Sociocultural Settings." *Social Science and Medicine* 61(1): 185–98.

Duncan, Greg J., and Stephen W. Raudenbush. 1999. "Assessing the Effects of Context in Studies of Children and Youth Development." *Educational Psychologist* 34(1): 29–41.

Duncan, Greg J., James P. Connell, and Pamela K. Klebanov. 1997. "Conceptual and Methodological Issues in Estimating Causal Effects of Neighborhoods and Family Conditions on Individual Development." In *Context and Consequences for Children*, Volume 1 of *Neighborhood Poverty*, edited by Jeanne Brooks-Gunn, Greg J. Duncan, and J. Lawrence Aber. New York: Russell Sage Foundation.

Duncan, Greg J., W. Jean Yeung, Jeanne Brooks-Gunn, and Judith R. Smith. 1998. "How Much Does Childhood Poverty Affect the Life Chances of Children?" *American Sociological Review* 63(3): 406–23.

Dunifon, Rachel, Greg J. Duncan, and Jeanne Brooks-Gunn. 2001. "As Ye Sweep, So Shall Ye Reap." *American Economic Review* 91(2): 150–4.

Elliott, Delbert S., William Julius Wilson, David Huizinga, Robert J. Sampson, Amanda Elliott, and Bruce Rankin. 1996. "The Effects of Neighborhood Disadvantage on Adolescent Development." *Journal of Research in Crime and Delinquency* 33(4): 389–426.

Evans, Gary W. 2004. "The Environment of Childhood Poverty." *American Psychologist* 59(2): 77–92.

Evans, Gary W., and Elyse Kantrowitz. 2002. "Socioeconomic Status and Health: The Potential Role of Environmental Risk Exposure." *Annual Review of Public Health* 23: 303–31.

Fauth, Rebecca C., Tama Leventhal, and Jeanne Brooks-Gunn. 2004. "Short-Term Effects of Moving from Public Housing in Poor to Middle-Class Neighborhoods on Low-Income, Minority Adults' Outcomes." *Social Science and Medicine* 59(11): 2271–84.

———. 2005. "Early Impacts of Moving from Poor to Middle-Class Neighborhoods on Low-Income Youth." *Journal of Applied Developmental Psychology* 26(4): 415–39.

———. 2007. "Welcome to the Neighborhood? Long-Term Impacts of Moving to Low-Poverty Neighborhoods on Poor Children's and Adolescents' Outcomes." *Journal of Research on Adolescence* 17(2): 249–84.

———. Forthcoming. "Seven Years Later: Effects of a Neighborhood Mobility Program on Poor Black and Latino Adults' Well-Being."

Fauth, Rebecca C., Jodie L. Roth, and Jeanne Brooks-Gunn. 2007. "Does the Neighborhood Context Alter the Link Between Youth's After-School Time Activities and Developmental Outcomes? A Multilevel Analysis." *Developmental Psychology* 43(3): 760–77.

Goering, John. 2003. "Place-Based Poverty, Social Experimentation, and Child Outcomes: A Report of Mixed Effects." *Children, Youth, and Environments* 13(2) Accessed at http://www.colorado.edu/journal/cye/paymentrequest_current.htm#.

Goering, John, and Judith D. Feins, editors. 2003. *Choosing a Better Life? Evaluating the Moving to Opportunity Social Experiment*. Washington: Urban Institute.

Goldsmith, Harold F., Charles E. Holzer, and Ronald W. Manderscheid. 1998. "Neighborhood Characteristics and Mental Illness." *Evaluation and Program Planning* 21(2): 211–25.

Gomez, Jorge E., Beth Ann Johnson, Martha Selva, and James F. Sallis. 2004. "Violent Crime and Outdoor Physical Activity Among Inner-City Youth." *Preventive Medicine* 39(5): 876–81.

Gorman-Smith, Deborah, Patrick H. Tolan, and David B. Henry. 2000. "A Developmental-Ecological Model of the Relation of Family Functioning to Patterns of Delinquency." *Journal of Quantitative Criminology* 16(2): 169–98.

Grzywacz, Joseph G., and Nadine F. Marks. 2001. "Social Inequalities and Exercise in Adulthood: Toward an Ecological Perspective." *Journal of Health and Social Behavior* 42(2): 202–20.

Halfon, Neal, and Paul W. Newacheck. 1993. "Childhood Asthma and Poverty: Differential Impacts and Utilization of Health Services." *Pediatrics* 91(1): 56–61.

Hardwick, Deborah, and Dianne Patychuk. 1999. "Geographic Mapping Demonstrates the Association Between Social Inequality, Teen Births and STDs Among Youth." *Canadian Journal of Human Sexuality* 8(2): 77–90.

Henderson, Clair, Ana V. Diez Roux, David R. Jacobs, Catarina I. Kiefe, Delia West, and David R. Williams. 2005. "Neighbourhood Characteristics, Individual Level Socioeconomic Factors, and Depressive Symptoms in Young Adults: The CARDIA Study." *Journal of Epidemiology and Community Health* 59(4): 322–8.

Hill, Terrence D., Catherine E. Ross, and Ronald J. Angel. 2005. "Neighborhood Disorder,

Psychophysiological Distress, and Health." *Journal of Health and Social Behavior* 46(2): 170–86.

Hogan, Dennis, and Evelyn Kitagawa. 1985. "The Impact of Social Status, Family Structure, and Neighborhood on the Fertility of Black Adolescents." *American Journal of Sociology* 90(4): 825–52.

Hume, Clare, Jo Salmon, and Kylie Ball. 2005. "Children's Perceptions of Their Home and Neighborhood Environments, and Their Association with Objectively Measured Physical Activity: A Qualitative and Quantitative Study." *Health Education Research* 20(1): 1–13.

Jencks, Christopher. 2006. Comments. Paper read at Health Effects of Non-Health Policy, February 9, 2006, Bethesda, Md.

Jencks, Christopher, and Meredith Phillips, editors. 1998. *The Black-White Test Score Gap.* Washington: Brookings Institution.

Juhn, Young J., Jennifer S. Sauver, Slavica Katusic, Delfino Vargas, and A. Weaver. 2005. "The Influence of Neighborhood Environment on the Incidence of Childhood Asthma." *Social Science and Medicine* 60(11): 2453–64.

Karoly, Lynn A., Peter W. Greenwood, Susan S. Everingham, Jill Hoube, M. Rebecca Kilburn, C. Peter Rydell, Matthew Sanders, and James Chiesa. 1998. *Investing in Our Children: What We Know and Don't Know About the Cost and Benefit of Early Childhood Interventions.* Santa Monica, Calif.: RAND.

Katz, Lawrence F., Jeffrey R. Kling, and Jeffrey B. Liebman. 2001. "Moving to Opportunity in Boston: Early Results of a Randomized Mobility Experiment." *Quarterly Journal of Economics* 116(2): 607–54.

———. 2003. "Boston Site Findings: The Early Impacts of Moving to Opportunity." In *Choosing a Better Life? Evaluating the Moving to Opportunity Social Experiment*, edited by John Goering and Judith D. Feins. Washington: Urban Institute.

Kimbro, Rachel, Jeanne Brooks-Gunn, and Sara McLanahan. 2007. "Racial and Ethnic Differentials in Overweight and Obesity Among 3-Year-Old Children." *American Journal of Public Health* 97(2): 298–305.

Kirby, James B., and Toshiko Kaneda. 2005. "Neighborhood Socioeconomic Disadvantage and Access to Health Care." *Journal of Health and Social Behavior* 46(1): 15–31.

Klebanov, Pamela K., Jeanne Brooks-Gunn, P. Lindsay Chase-Lansdale, and Rachel A. Gordon. 1997. "Are Neighborhood Effects on Young Children Mediated by Features of the Home Environment?" In *Context and Consequences for Children*, Volume 1 of *Neighborhood Poverty*, edited by Jeanne Brooks-Gunn, Greg Duncan, and J. Lawrence Aber. New York: Russell Sage Foundation.

Leventhal, Tama, and Jeanne Brooks-Gunn. 2000. "The Neighborhoods They Live In: Effects of Neighborhood Residence Upon Child and Adolescent Outcomes." *Psychological Bulletin* 126(2): 309–37.

———. 2003a. "Moving to Opportunity: An Experimental Study of Neighborhood Effects on Mental Health." *American Journal of Public Health* 93(9): 1576–82.

———. 2003b. "Neighborhood-Based Initiatives." In *Early Child Development in the 21st Century: Profiles of Current Research Initiatives*, edited by Jeanne Brooks-Gunn, Allison Sidle Fuligni, and Lisa J. Berlin. New York: Teachers College Press.

Leventhal, Tama, Jeanne Brooks-Gunn, and Sheila B. Kamerman. 1997. "Communities as Place, Face, and Space: Provision of Services to Poor, Urban Children and Their Families."

In *Policy Implications in Studying Neighborhoods*, Volume 2 of *Neighborhood Poverty*, edited by Jeanne Brooks-Gunn, Greg J. Duncan, and J. Lawrence Aber. New York: Russell Sage Foundation.

Leventhal, Tama, Yange Xue, and Jeanne Brooks-Gunn. 2006. "Immigrant Differences in School-Age Children's Verbal Trajectories: A Look at Four Racial/Ethnic Groups." Child Development 77(5): 1359–74.

Liccardi Gennaro, Mario Cazzola, Maria D'Amato, and Gennaro D'Amato. 2000. "Pets and Cockroaches: Two Increasing Causes of Respiratory Allergy in Indoor Environments. Characteristics of Airways Sensitization and Prevention Strategies." *Respiratory Medicine* 94(11): 1109–18.

Lleras-Muney, Adriana. 2005. "The Needs of the Army: Using Compulsory Relocation in the Military to Estimate the Effect of Air Pollutants on Children's Health." Unpublished paper. Princeton University.

Loeber, Rolf, and Per-Olof H. Wikström. 1993. "Individual Pathways to Crime in Different Types of Neighborhoods." In *Integrating Individual and Ecological Aspects of Crime*, edited by David P. Farrington, Robert J. Sampson and Per-Olof H. Wikstrom. Stockholm, Sweden: National Council for Crime Prevention.

Love, John M., Ellen Eliason Kisker, Christine Ross, Helen Raikes, Jill Constantine, Kimberly Boller, Jeanne Brooks-Gunn, Rachel Chazan-Cohen, Louisa Banks Tarullo, Christy Brady-Smith, Allison Sidle Fuligni, Peter Z Schochet, Diane Paulsell, and Cheri Vogel. 2005. "The Effectiveness of Early Head Start for 3-Year-Old Children and Their Parents: Lessons for Policy and Programs." *Developmental Psychology* 41(6): 885–901.

Ludwig, Jens, Greg J. Duncan, and Paul Hirschfield. 2001. "Urban Poverty and Juvenile Crime: Evidence from a Randomized Housing-Mobility Experiment." *Quarterly Journal of Economics* 116(2): 665–79.

Margolin, Gayla, and Elana B. Gordis. 2000. "The Effects of Family and Community Violence on Children." *Annual Review of Psychology* 51: 445–79.

Massey, Douglas S. 1990. "American Apartheid: Segregation and the Making of the Underclass." *American Journal of Sociology* 96(2): 329–58.

Mayer, Susan E. 1997. "Trends in the Economic Well-Being and Life Chances of America's Children." In *Consequences of Growing Up Poor*, edited by Greg J. Duncan and Jeanne Brooks-Gunn. New York: Russell Sage Foundation.

McLoyd, Vonnie C. 1998. "Socioeconomic Disadvantage and Child Development." *American Psychologist* 53(2): 185–204.

Moffitt, Terrie E., and Avshalom Caspi. 2001. "Childhood Predictors Differentiate Life Course Persistent and Adolescence-Limited Antisocial Pathways Among Males and Females." *Development and Psychopathology* 13(2): 355–75.

Moffitt, Terrie E., and Phil A. Silva. 1988. "Self-Reported Delinquency, Neuropsychological Deficit, and History of Attention Deficit Disorder." *Journal of Abnormal Child Psychology* 16(5): 553–69.

Morenoff Jeffrey D. 2003. "Neighborhood Mechanisms and the Spatial Dynamics of Birth Weight." *American Journal of Sociology* 108(5): 976–1017.

Morrissey, Kathleen M., and Ronald Jay Werner-Wilson. 2005. "The Relationship Between Out-of-School Activities and Positive Youth Development: An Investigation of the Influences of Communities and Family." *Adolescence* 40(Spring): 67–85.

Needleman, Herbert L. 1979. "Lead Levels and Children's Psychologic Performance." *New England Journal of Medicine* 301(3): 163.

———. 1990. "The Long-term Effects of Exposure to Low Doses of Lead in Childhood: An 11-Year Follow-Up Report." *New England Journal of Medicine* 322(2): 83–88.

Needleman, Herbert L., Christine McFarland, Robert B. Ness, Stephen E. Fienberg, and Michael J. Tobin. 2002. "Bone Lead Levels in Adjudicated Delinquents: A Case Control Study." *Neurotoxicology and Teratology* 24(6): 711–7.

Needleman, Herbert L., Julie Riess, Michael Tobin, Gretchen Biesecker, and Joel Greenhouse. 1996. "Bone Lead Levels and Delinquent Behavior." *Journal of the American Medical Association* 275(5): 363–9.

Needleman, Herbert L., Charles Gunnoe, Alan Leviton, Robert Reed, Henry Presie, Cornelius Maher and Peter Barrett. 1979. "Deficits in Psychologic and Classroom Performance of Children with Elevated Dentine Lead Levels." *New England Journal of Medicine* 300(13): 689–95.

Newman, Sandra J. 2001. "Housing Attributes and Serious Mental Illness: Implications for Research and Practice." *Psychiatric Services* 52(10): 1309–17.

O'Hare, William, and Mark Mather. 2003. *The Growing Number of Kids in Severely Distressed Neighborhoods: Evidence from the 2000 Census.* Washington: Anne E. Casey Foundation.

Orr, Larry, Judith D. Feins, Robin Jacob, Erik Beecroft, Lisa Sanbonmatsu, Lawrence F. Katz, Jeffrey B. Liebman, and Jeffrey R. Kling. 2003. *Moving to Opportunity for Fair Housing Demonstration Interim Impacts Evaluation.* Washington: U.S. Department of Housing and Urban Development, Office of Policy Research and Development.

Osofsky, Joy D. 1999. "The Impact of Violence on Children." *Future of Children* 9(3): 33–49.

Paxson, Christina, Elisabeth Donahue, C. Tracy Orleans, and Jeanne Ann Grisso. 2006. "Introducing the Issue." *Future of Children* 16(1): 3–17.

Peeples, Faith, and Rolf Loeber. 1994. "Do Individual Factors and Neighborhood Context Explain Ethnic Differences in Juvenile Delinquency?" *Journal of Quantitative Criminology* 10(2): 141–57.

Pettit, Gregory S., John E. Bates, Kenneth A. Dodge, and Darrell W. Meece. 1999. "The Impact of After-School Peer Contact on Early Adolescent Externalizing Problems Is Moderated by Parental Monitoring, Perceived Neighborhood Safety, and Prior Adjustment." *Child Development* 70(3): 768–78.

Pickett, K. E., and M. Pearl. 2001. "Multilevel Analyses of Neighbourhood Socioeconomic Context and Health Outcomes: A Critical Review." *Journal of Epidemiology and Community Health* 55(2): 111–22.

Pirkle, James L., Debra J. Brody, Elaine W. Gunter, Rachel A. Kramer, Daniel C. Paschal, Katherine M. Flegal, and Thomas D. Matte. 1994. "The Decline in Blood Lead Levels in the United States: The National Health and Nutrition Examination Survey (NHANES)." *Journal of the American Medical Association* 272(4): 284–91

Rankin, Bruce H., and James M. Quane. 2002. "Social Contexts and Urban Adolescent Outcomes: The Interrelated Effects of Neighborhoods, Families, and Peers on African-American Youth." *Social Problems* 49(1): 79–100.

Raudenbush, Steve W., and Robert J. Sampson. 1999. "Ecometrics: Toward a Science of Assessing Ecological Settings, with Application to the Systematic Social Observations of Neighborhoods." *Sociological Methodology* 29: 1–41.

Reyes, Jessica. 2007. "Environmental Policy as Social Policy? The Impact of Childhood Lead Exposure on Crime." *National Bureau of Economic Research* working paper No. 13097. Washington: National Bureau of Economic Research.

Robert Wood Johnson Foundation Newsroom. 2007. "Robert Wood Johnson Foundation Announces $500-Million Commitment to Reverse Childhood Obesity in U.S." April 4, 2007. Accessed at http://www.rwjf.org/newsroom/newsreleasesdetail.jsp?id=10483.

Romero, Andrea J. 2005. "Low-Income Neighborhood Barriers and Resources for Adolescents' Physical Activity." *Journal of Adolescent Health* 36(3): 253–9.

Ross, Catherine E. 2000. "Neighborhood Disadvantage and Adult Depression." *Journal of Health and Social Behavior* 41(2): 177–87.

Ross, Catherine E., and John Mirowsky. 2001. "Neighborhood Disadvantage, Disorder, and Health." *Journal of Health and Social Behavior* 42(3): 258–76.

Ross, Catherine E., John R. Reynolds, and Karlyn J. Geis. 2000. "The Contingent Meaning of Neighborhood Stability for Residents' Psychological Well-Being." *American Sociological Review* 65(4): 581–97.

Rouse, Cecilia, Jeanne Brooks-Gunn, and Sara McLanahan. 2005. "School Readiness: Closing Racial and Ethnic Gaps. Introducing the Issue." *Future of Children* 15(1): 5–13.

Saha, Chandan, Mary E. Riner, and Gilbert Liu. 2005. "Individual- and Neighborhood-Level Factors in Predicting Asthma." *Archives of Pediatrics and Adolescent Medicine* 159(8): 759–63.

Sampson, Robert J. 1997. "Collective Regulation of Adolescent Misbehavior: Validation Results from Eighty Chicago Neighborhoods." *Journal of Adolescent Research* 12(2): 227–44.

———. 2006. "How Does Community Context Matter? Social Mechanisms and the Explanation of Crime Rates." In *The Explanation of Crime: Context, Mechanisms, and Development*, edited by Per-Olof H. Wikström and Robert J. Sampson. Cambridge: Cambridge University Press.

Sampson, Robert J., and Steve W. Raudenbush. 1999. "Systematic Social Observation of Public Spaces: A New Look at Disorder in Urban Neighborhoods." *American Journal of Sociology* 105(3): 603–51.

Sampson, Robert J., Jeffrey Morenoff, and Felton Earls. 1999. "Beyond Social Capital: Spatial Dynamics of Collective Efficacy for Children." *American Sociological Review* 64(5): 633–60.

Sampson, Robert J., Jeffrey Morenoff, and Thomas Gannon-Rowley. 2002. "Assessing 'Neighborhood Effects': Social Processes and New Directions in Research." *Annual Review of Sociology* 28: 443–78.

Sampson, Robert J., Stephen W. Raudenbush, and Felton Earls. 1997. "Neighborhoods and Violent Crime: A Multilevel Study of Collective Efficacy." *Science* 277(5328): 918–24.

Santos, Fernanda. 2006. "Mixed Success in Yonkers." *New York Times*, May 28, 2006.

Sastry, Naraya, and Anne R. Pebley. 2003. "Neighborhood and Family Effects on Children's Health in Los Angeles." RAND working paper DRU-240011-LAFANS. Santa Monica, Calif.: RAND.

Sawhill, Isabel, and Sara McLanahan. 2006. "Opportunity in America: Introducing the Issue." *The Future of Children* 16(2): 3–17.

South, Scott J., and Eric P. Baumer. 2000. "Deciphering Community Effects on Adolescent Premarital Childbearing." *Social Forces* 78(4): 1379–408.

Sullivan, Sean D., Kevin B. Weiss, Henry Lynn, Herman Mitchell, Meyer Kattan, Peter J.

Gergen, and Richard Evans. 2002. "The Cost-Effectiveness of an Inner-City Asthma Intervention for Children." *Journal of Allergy and Clinical Immunology* 110(4): 576–81.

Tienda, Marta. 1991. "Poor People and Poor Places: Deciphering Neighborhood Effects on Poverty Outcomes." In *Macro-Micro Linkages in Sociology*, edited by Joan Huber. Newbury Park, Calif.: Sage Publications.

U.S. Environmental Protection Agency. 2000. *National Air Pollutant Emissions Trends, 1900–1998*. Research Triangle Park, N.C.: Office of Air Quality Planning and Standards.

United States vs. City of Yonkers, et al. 1985. Civil Action #80CIV 6761 LBS: Southern District of New York.

Watson, Tara. 2006. "Public Health Investments and the Infant Mortality Gap: Evidence from Federal Sanitation Interventions on U.S. Indian Reservations." *Journal of Public Economics* 90(8/9): 1537–60.

Wen, Ming, Christopher R. Browning, and Kathleen A. Cagney. 2003. "Poverty, Affluence, and Income Inequality: Neighborhood Economic Structure and Its Implications for Health." *Social Science and Medicine* 57(5): 843–60.

Wheaton, Blair, and Philippa Clarke. 2003. "Space Meets Time: Integrating Temporal and Contextual Influences on Mental Health in Early Adulthood." *American Sociological Review* 68(5): 680–706.

Wilson, William Julius. 1987. *The Truly Disadvantaged: The Inner City, the Underclass, and Public Policy*. Chicago, Ill.: University of Chicago Press.

———. 1996. *When Work Disappears: The World of the New Urban Poor*. New York: Alfred A. Knopf.

Xue, Yange, Tama Leventhal, Jeanne Brooks-Gunn, and Felton J. Earls. 2005. "Neighborhood Residence and Mental Health Problems of 5- to 11-Year-Olds." *Archives of General Psychiatry* 62(5): 554–63.

———. 2006. "Neighborhood Effects on the Developmental Trajectories of Externalizing Problems." Unpublished paper. University of Michigan, School of Public Health.

Zenk, Sharon N., Amy J. Schultz, Barbara A. Israel, Sherman A. James, Shuming Bao, and Mark L. Wilson. 2005. "Neighborhood Racial Composition, Neighborhood Poverty, and the Spatial Accessibility of Supermarkets in Metropolitan Detroit." *American Journal of Public Health* 95(4): 660–7.

Part VIII

Conclusion

Chapter 13

Social and Economic Policies as Health Policy: Moving Toward a New Approach to Improving Health in America

Harold Pollack, George A. Kaplan, James S. House, and Robert F. Schoeni

T he evidence presented in the prior twelve chapters suggests that social and economic policies substantially influence individual and population health, and it begins to draw out the many policy domains in which this occurs. These chapters consider health effects of education, income-support, civil-rights, macroeconomics and employment, welfare, and housing and neighborhood policies. This not-so-thin volume justifiably could have been expanded to consider still other domains: environmental, law-enforcement, agriculture, and transportation policies, as well as others. Human health is too multifaceted, its determinants too varied, and the current state of our knowledge too limited, for any one volume to capture the full scope and complexity of the links between social and economic policies and health.

Future research and policy must grapple with these issues if we are to realize the full promise of social and economic policies as health policies in the same way that we already increasingly consider health policies to have major social and economic effects. First, we must establish the causal impact of social and economic policies for health. Where such causal effects can be established, we need secondly to better understand the pathways through which these effects occur; this is important for both scientific understanding as well as for developing more cost-effective social, economic, and health policies. Finally, better understanding of both causality and pathways requires that we generate better data and research designs for understanding the reciprocal relationships of social and economic policies to health policies.

PERVASIVE ISSUES OF CAUSALITY

Establishing causal links between particular policies and health outcomes is a pervasive issue for all policy research. Basic questions must be understood in this domain: What are the contributions and limitations of both planned and naturally occurring specialized experiments for understanding broader public policy? What are the corresponding merits and weaknesses of conceptually rich observational studies for the same purposes?

Such issues of causality and inference occasion deep disagreement among policy makers and researchers; this is particularly the case regarding both the necessity and the limitations of prospective randomized experiments in tracing links between economic and social policies and health. Contributing authors to this volume express diverse views on many of these points, but both within and across chapters they make a strong argument for multimethod approaches to complex problems; such approaches eschew fixation on any single approach, such as experimental methods.

This book reveals how few and far between true experiments really are, and probably can be, in many policy areas. This is particularly true in areas such as civil-rights and macroeconomic policy, in which randomly assigning individuals to different policies is infeasible or unethical. In domains such as income maintenance, housing, and education, in which policy experiments are possible, the logistical, financial, and often ethical obstacles are substantial (Heckman and Smith 1995). The most widely cited experiments—the RAND Health Insurance Experiment, Movement to Opportunity (MTO), and the income maintenance experiments of three decades ago—were large and complex, cost hundreds of millions of dollars, and sometimes required more than a decade to implement and to analyze the data (Burtless 1995; Heckman and Smith 1995).

By all accounts, these efforts contributed greatly to policy knowledge, and some of the resulting knowledge is chastening. For example, MTO results indicate that the benefits of neighborhood-mobility interventions, though real, are smaller and more complex than earlier, nonexperimental evaluations such as the Gautreaux intervention (Rubinowitz and Rosenbaum 2000) would lead us to expect.

Other experimental evaluations are more promising. As Daniel Keating and Sharon Simonton (chapter 3, this volume) relate, randomized evaluations of early-childhood education interventions demonstrate that high-quality interventions significantly improve educational and social outcomes for many children. The relationship between such best-practice and more typical interventions is complex. A burgeoning nonexperimental literature suggests that Head Start has important benefits, albeit smaller than those achieved by best-practice interventions (Currie 2002; Ludwig and Miller, forthcoming).

Policy experiments are often infeasible within domains of key interest for population health. For example, in the case of civil-rights policy, George Kaplan, Nalini Ranjit, and Sarah Burgard (chapter 6, this volume) examine racial health disparities before and after civil-rights legislation was passed. No experiment could credibly capture the health impact of the large policy changes that occurred in the mid-1960s. While some studies have been performed to examine the impact of such policies for particular health outcomes in particular states (Almond, Chay, and Greenstone 2003), we lack findings that apply more generally to the United States as a whole or to broader impacts on health. As George Kaplan, Nalini Ranjit, and Sarah Burgard point out, it is difficult to cleanly identify the impact of the 1964

Civil Rights Act, given nearly simultaneous enactment of Medicare and Medicaid, as well as major changes in food stamps, Aid to Families with Dependent Children (AFDC), and other related programs. However, the large health improvements, particularly for African American women in the South, that were coterminous with this period and largest where the policy changes were the greatest, strongly suggest that something significant happened.

In other policy domains, policy experiments can be performed, but their generalizability is open to question. Welfare reform in 1996 was preceded by many randomized evaluations of specific welfare-to-work interventions. The large research literature, both preceding and following this landmark legislation, underscores tradeoffs between experimental and nonexperimental evaluations in evaluating social policy.

In the realm of welfare policy, Marianne Bitler and Hilary Hoynes (chapter 9, this volume) examined five experimental evaluations of state waivers from traditional (pre-1996) welfare programs. Because of their experimental nature, these analyses achieve strong internal validity; they demonstrate that altering the traditional entitlement produced small changes in health insurance coverage and improvements in, albeit crude, measures of health status. Yet none of the examined waiver programs was as sweeping, as stringent, or as permanent as the actual 1996 legislation which enacted Temporary Assistance for Needy Families (TANF).

Other data sets provide different limitations. Jean Knab, Irv Garfinkel, and Sara McLanahan (chapter 10, this volume) examined nonexperimental data drawn from the Fragile Families study. One strength of the Fragile Families study was the explicit realization that health outcomes were crucially important to consider when evaluating the successes and failures of welfare policies. As a result, these authors are able to assess a relatively extensive set of health measures, including health behaviors, health insurance, and physical and mental health status for a large cohort of new mothers (some receiving and some not receiving aid through TANF). At the same time, the nonexperimental design makes it more challenging to estimate causal effects of TANF.

Even when prospective randomized experiments are performed, they often turn out to answer different questions from those one really wants to ask or what one might initially have expected the experiment to address. For example, existing research indicates that neighborhood characteristics influence some dimensions of health for certain subgroups. Policy makers who wish to understand the impact of neighborhoods on health have looked to residential-mobility experiments for guidance. Yet it is surprisingly difficult, through mobility-based interventions, to improve the neighborhoods in which individuals live. The improvements in the quality of neighborhoods are real. However, the changes are often modest and, not infrequently, fleeting, as individuals migrate back to former neighborhoods or to others more similar to them. Further, it is important to keep in mind the somewhat limited focus of the existing experimental studies. These studies have examined the effects of relatively short-term exposure to neighborhood factors—between three and five years—while it may be that such factors have their largest effect when individuals are exposed for decades or even generations. When it is completed, the ten-year follow-up evaluation to the MTO will provide some important evidence on this issue. Even then, mobility experiments cannot directly address the impact of policies which alter the specific neighborhoods in which families live. Policies that change the existing neighborhood, although not without their challenges, may have more consequential health benefits because families are not displaced from their social and economic networks.

In the absence of informative studies based on experimental designs, policy makers and researchers turn to other study designs to assess policy questions of interest. Cross-state differences in welfare policies, as well as changes in such policies within given states over time, provide alternative frequently used identification strategies. Such "policy experiments" can provide valuable insights, while at the same time they raise important questions for researchers and policy makers alike: Why do some states impose more stringent policies or implement policies more quickly than other states? To what extent do changes in simple indicators for "any policy change" meaningfully capture the wide array of policies that may have been adopted?

In many such cases, the clearest effects of public policies may be observed many years or even decades after the policy change, sometimes based on conditions extremely different from those applying to the current policy debate. David Cutler and Adriana Lleras-Muney (chapter 2, this volume) describe evidence that the enactment and timing of early- and mid-twentieth century compulsory attendance laws improved population health. George Kaplan, Nalini Ranjit, and Sarah Burgard (chapter 6, this volume) report large health gains for African American women associated with the classic period of civil-rights legislation of the 1960s and 1970s. Such studies are important for many reasons, not least because they establish basic links between examined policies and population health. Yet it is sometimes difficult to draw strong conclusions about current policies based upon results of interventions and policies implemented long ago under very different contexts.

Janet Currie and Enrico Moretti (chapter 5, this volume) illustrate the way that insights from interventions applied in one context can prove misleading in another. Many studies document the importance of maternal nutrition during pregnancy on subsequent infant health. Prior research within the United States found a strong impact of food-supplement programs for birth outcomes within extremely low-income populations (Currie 2002). Yet these authors' methodologically strong analysis finds much smaller impacts of expanded food assistance on infant birthweight in California during the 1960s. Apparently, marginal expansion in public aid had a small impact given the availability of other resources within the affected population.

THE PATHWAYS PROBLEM

Given that particular policies causally affect health, they almost always operate through multiple pathways. Untangling the relative size and direction of different pathways is often difficult. Yet such untangling is often important in guiding public policy and addressing issues such as those we label as *can we do it* and *cost-effectiveness*. These issues are well illustrated in the area of education, which appears in this volume and elsewhere to be perhaps the area of social and economic policy with the broadest potential effects on health.

David Cutler and Adriana Lleras-Muney (chapter 2, this volume) describe the well-documented and large educational gradients in health outcomes and in key health behaviors. *Why* less-educated people display greater behavioral risk is less clear. If such behaviors arise, or persist, because less-educated individuals are misinformed about key health risks, public information campaigns to impart pertinent knowledge might improve population health. If less-educated citizens are more likely to smoke to relieve job stress, or if their economic circumstances lead them to choose high-calorie, cheap food, public information campaigns will likely prove ineffective. If such behaviors are ultimately rooted in socioeconomic position—itself influenced by education—macroeconomic and redistributive policies might prove more successful in addressing behavioral risks.

Similarly, early-childhood education programs discussed by Daniel Keating and Sharon Simonton (chapter 3, this volume) might improve population health by raising cognitive performance. Or, these interventions might also provide a venue for nutrition and health services, by serving as an in-kind economic transfer to low-income families or by providing opportunities to improve parenting skills for low-income adults. Each of these pathways, and a number of other plausible candidates, offers distinct implications for the design and implementation of Head Start and related programs. Current research indicates that early-childhood education is valuable. This body of work does not yet clearly show which of these distinct pathways is most promising to improve child health.

The stakes are high because existing data raise the prospect that public educational investments bring large, usually neglected benefits for health. David Cutler and Adriana Lleras-Muney present back-of-the-envelope calculations in which they examine the health impact of grants to extend educational attainment of low-income children. Prior studies suggest that each one thousand dollar increase in grant aid is associated with an increase of 0.16 years in educational attainment. Combining these results with other analyses linking educational attainment to health, these authors estimate that such a schooling increase is associated with between 0.03 and 0.10 years of additional life.

To those outside the domain of health policy, these benefits might seem small. In fact, these estimated improvements in longevity are markedly larger than those obtained from widely accepted health interventions, such as screening mammography for women over age forty or colorectal-cancer screening (Frazier et al. 2000; Stout et al. 2006). Stated in another way, education grants appear highly cost-effective relative to standard thresholds used to evaluate medical and public-health interventions. David Cutler and Adriana Lleras-Muney's calculations imply that educational grants cost between $10,000 and $33,333 per year of life gained. By current policy analysis conventions, medical and public-health interventions are considered to be cost-effective when they cost less than $100,000 per "quality-adjusted life-year" (Hirth et al. 2000). Thus, ignoring all other benefits to the individual or to society that might arise from increased schooling, educational grants appear strikingly cost-effective when evaluated solely as investments in population health. But to maximize the cost-effectiveness of investments of education, we need to understand which aspects of education operating through which pathways have the strongest effects on health.

It is similarly important to understand the pathways through which income and civil-rights policies affect health. Do the effects operate via improved occupational opportunities and conditions, better housing, more accessible and higher-quality medical care, better nutrition, or other improvements in living conditions? Understanding whether some or perhaps all of these pathways are important will suggest whether the health benefits can be achieved through targeting specific pathways. For example, if the only way in which income transfers improve health is through improved nutrition, it will most likely be more cost-effective to target nutrition assistance than to expand income-transfer programs in general. On the other hand, if income transfers influence health through multiple pathways, and income transfers also lead to additional non-health benefits (such as reduced crime and improved childhood educational and cognitive outcomes), then expansion of income transfers may indeed be highly cost-effective.

Research on housing and the residential environment have identified different pathways to health that can inform policy. Neighborhoods influence the quality of public services that individuals receive. They alter children's peer networks and access to educational resources that influence health as well as adults' social networks. They influence residents' vulnerability to crime and other sources of traumatic injury. They share access to sidewalks, parks, and other opportunities for exercise. Geography influences market outlets for nutritious foods. Housing and geography influence individuals' exposure to lead paint and to other environmental health threats.

These multifaceted linkages suggest the possibility of tradeoffs when implementing large policy interventions. Relocating tenants from high-rise public housing may improve children's educational opportunities and safety from crime. Yet the same intervention could increase children's exposures to environmental health threats or reduce adults' access to social support.

Empirical research should examine the relative importance of these different pathways to maximize the benefits of policy interventions while minimizing accompanying harms. For example, residential-mobility programs (and thus the evaluation of these programs) have focused on improving educational, criminal-justice, and job-market outcomes of program participants. Such interventions have not emphasized the quality of housing or the social environment. If lead-paint exposure has a large impact on child health or if social isolation impedes development, policy makers can emphasize regulatory and investment policies to pursue lead-paint abatement and increase social connections within the context of these mobility programs.

Macroeconomic and employment policy provide an apt illustration of how specifying the pathways generated by a given policy can help us better understand its effects—even if they are seemingly paradoxical. Christopher Ruhm (chapter 7, this volume) provides surprising but compelling evidence from aggregate data of anticyclical effects on health: as macroeconomic conditions improve, population health worsens; as macroeconomic conditions worsen, population health improves. Richard Price and Sarah Burgard (chapter 8, this volume) review equally compelling evidence that those whose jobs are lost or adversely affected by economic contractions are more likely to become ill or die.

Discussion at the conference helped to resolve the apparent paradox between Christopher Ruhm's aggregate analysis suggesting increased health problems in times of economic expansion and Richard Price and Sarah Burgard's review of individual-level data indicating increased health problems among those experiencing job loss, insecurity, or adverse job change. It is plausible that in bad economic times, those directly affected via job loss, insecurity, or adverse job change suffer declines in health, while those seeking to avoid personal experience of these same things may modify their behavior, by choice or of necessity, in ways that promote both job retention and health (for example, by reducing substance use or abuse). Similarly, in good times those personally experiencing job loss and insecurity continue to be adversely affected, but those not affected are enabled to engage in more risky health behaviors. The aggregate results come out as they do because the number of people who are not directly experiencing job loss or insecurity greatly exceeds the number experiencing such loss or insecurity. What is ultimately needed to test this integrative hypothesis is longitudinal or quasi-experimental multilevel research that combines aggregate macroeconomic data with individual-level data. Such research has the potential to trace out health effects of broader economic conditions for both those directly affected by them, for better or worse, and those who remain relatively unaffected economically but may still experience effects on their health.

Finally, consideration of multiple pathways must extend to the biological level. As pointed out by George Kaplan, Nalini Ranjit, and Sarah Burgard (chapter 6, this volume), in addition to explicating behavioral, social, cognitive, economic, psychological, and other dimensions involved, one must identify plausible, and ideally demonstrable, links to the pathobiological processes that drive the health outcomes of interest. That is, the mix of external pathways must somehow get "under the skin." This places important mechanistic limits on the interpretation of health effects from social and economic policies. For example, we should have evidence that the policy changes have an impact on the known proximal determinants of these pathobiological processes and, ideally, evidence that modifications of these processes are consistent with increased disease risk.

Understanding the impact of social and economic policies on specific health outcomes also requires that one take into account what is known about the "natural history" of these health outcomes. Some diseases unfold over decades. It is thus hard to tease out, absent other evidence, short-term policy effects on these diseases. Others, such as coronary heart diseases, may have multiple stages. Some policy interventions may therefore be consistent with relatively short-term effects. For example, policies that lead to major increases in binge drinking, stress, or sleep problems might plausibly have an impact on triggering the acute clinical manifestations of previously subclinical disease. On the other hand, policies that lead to changes in dietary or physical-activity patterns might require a longer period for their health effects to be observed. This type of specificity poses additional challenges by creating the need to collect additional health and medical data. Yet such specificity also makes the evaluation task easier because it establishes clear criteria by which to assess the plausibility of observed effects.

THE NEED FOR BETTER HEALTH DATA IN OBSERVATIONAL AND EXPERIMENTAL RESEARCH ON SOCIAL AND ECONOMIC POLICY (AND VICE VERSA)

To better understand the causal impacts of social and economic policies on health, as well as the pathways through which such effects are produced, adequate health data must be collected during evaluations of social and economic policies. Much more will need to be collected than reports of self-rated health, which is commonly used, as the underlying pathobiological pathways for such an outcome are non-specific.

Fortunately, there is a rapidly growing body of experience to draw upon, and considerable sophistication has been developed in the collection of health data outside of clinical environments. Detailed health data are now routinely collected in different forms over time that might be linked to policy evaluations: specific local surveys, national epidemiological surveys, (such as the National Health and Nutrition Examination Survey, which collects considerable information on behavioral and biological pathways, the Behavioral Risk Factor Surveillance System, the Panel Study of Income Dynamics, and the National Health Interview Survey), and national panel surveys (such as the Health and Retirement Study and the National Longitudinal Study of Adolescent Health). Many clinical data systems also provide important data for epidemiology and policy. Ongoing high-quality data collection can facilitate empirical analysis in the wake of large policy changes. A good example of this is the use of information from national surveys on breast-feeding (Haider, Jacknowitz, and Schoeni 2003) to examine the impact of TANF work sanctions on a determinant of infant health.

In many cases, existing empirical efforts could be made more useful if data collection and dissemination were more carefully coordinated between data collectors and the research policy community using these data. Some practices, such as the routine masking of state identifiers in surveys such as the National Health Interview Survey, hinder the study of key policies that affect health. In other cases, elaborate data sets are narrowly prepared for one purpose or through the lens of one discipline, and, as a result, matters of physical or mental health are left unexplored. For example, large economic and social surveys like the March Current Population Survey, which is the source for official government estimates of poverty and contains high-quality income data, would increase its value to the policy community if it collected even a modest set of health status data.

Policy research would also benefit if health considerations were taken more seriously in the design and analysis of program evaluations. One modest step in this direction is the expansion of health measures in ongoing social and economic research and experiments, as has occurred to some extent within the MTO evaluation. Recent cohort studies of welfare recipients, and several evaluations of particular welfare-policy interventions, have pointed to the importance of including indicators of physical and mental health (Danziger et al. 2000). Additionally, George Kaplan and colleagues (2005) have demonstrated that explicit health data can be collected in studies of welfare recipients.

This book demonstrates the fruitful possibilities of linking researchers and policy makers in particular areas such as housing, income maintenance, or education with others who bring specific expertise in health. When large-scale evaluations are undertaken of welfare-to-work, criminal-justice, or housing interventions, modest additional investments could allow important health matters to be explored as well. Given the large economic and social burdens associated with poor health, policy evaluations would wisely include attention to health effects.

Attention to such effects is especially important given the paradox in the United States of high health expenditures and relatively poor health outcomes. Social policies not ostensibly aimed at medical care or even at public health provide a key venue through which public action will improve or erode population health. Yet in the absence of reliable evidence that is credible for policymaking, some of the most productive strategies for improving the health of the population will be neglected given increasing pressures on public budgets.

THE PARADOX AND PROMISE OF MORE CLOSELY LINKING SOCIAL AND ECONOMIC POLICIES WITH HEALTH POLICIES

Policy makers face great difficulties in striking the proper balance across different policy options that promote population health. Paradoxically, the very success and popularity of medical care threatens to undermine this balance. Although it is difficult to quantify the true economic and political effects of rising health care spending, rapid increases in Medicaid, Medicare, and other government health programs are generating increasing fiscal pressures on the funding of other public activities which affect population health. If new spending is financed by reduced (or more slowly growing) expenditures for housing, public safety, or education, unconstrained expenditure growth for medical services within current fiscal structures will have a decidedly mixed impact on overall population health.

Among states—whose capacity to run deficits and to raise revenue is constrained by financial and legal factors—some studies indicate that rising Medicaid expenditures "crowd out" other activities that assist low-income citizens (Baicker 2001). The federal government enjoys greater freedom to finance medical expenditures. The sheer size of health spending nonetheless affects available resources for alternative forms of expenditure. From a national perspective, the costs of economic and welfare policies that could sharply reduce poverty and the costs to massively increase spending for education pale in comparison to the projected increases in Medicare and Medicaid spending within the next decade (not to mention their total cost, which is predicted to exceed $750 billion annually by 2010).

To place this in perspective, a task force of the Center for American Progress recently proposed a set of policies designed to cut poverty in half within the United States (Greenberg, Dutta-Gupta, and Minoff 2007). The task force estimated that such policies would cost $90 billion annually. The expenditures required to implement such policies in the United States, though substantial, amount to less than 20 percent of current federal health care spending. The proposed increases in cash and in-kind transfers are comparable to those enacted in the United Kingdom (whose government has pledged to end child poverty by the year 2020 and has already markedly reduced child poverty through such measures during the Tony Blair years). Further evaluation of the impact of this reduction in child poverty on health could be revealing.

The federal budget outlook, as projected by the Congressional Budget Office in January 2005, further illustrates these dilemmas. In 2004, federal Medicare and Medicaid expenditures totaled $473 billion, with projections implying that spending would increase to $782 billion by 2010. Adjusting for inflation, this amounts to a real increase of $229 billion over the six-year period. Combined mandatory income-security expenditures—a category that includes such activities as Unemployment Compensation, Supplemental Security Income, the Earned Income Tax Credit, food stamps, TANF, child nutrition, and foster care—totaled $191 billion in 2004. Over the same period of rapid Medicare and Medicaid expenditure growth, income-security expenditures are projected to rise by less than 3 percent.

While many medical procedures and services have led to substantial improvements in population health, the accelerating dominance of medical expenditures exemplifies an unwise approach to reducing death and illness within the United States population (for a similar perspective from Canada, see Evans, Barer, and Marmor 1994). At the same time, survey data indicate that most Americans are substantially more willing to spend public funds to address unequal health outcomes and unequal access to medical care than they are willing to address unequal conditions of housing, education, and cash income (Schlesinger 2004). Such egalitarian aspirations, narrowly targeted at the arena of health, may prove self-defeating, or at least self-hindering. However, these attitudes may in fact be driven by a public misunderstanding of the factors that influence health. If the public knew that social and economic policies and programs could be equally or more effective in improving health than some medical-care interventions, they might be more willing to embrace such policies and programs.

If the argument of this book is right, economic and social policy *is* health policy. Improved population health requires attention to many domains outside the arenas of traditional public health and medical care. This book documents the necessity, and also the difficulty, of this large task.

REFERENCES

Almond, D., K. Chay, and M. Greenstone. 2003. "Civil Rights, the War on Poverty, and Black- White Convergence in Infant Mortality in Mississippi." Unpublished manuscript.

Baicker, Katherine. 2001. "Government Decision Making and the Incidence of Federal Mandates." *Journal of Public Economics* 82(2): 147–94.

Burtless, Gary. 1995. "The Case for Randomized Field Trials in Economic and Policy Research." *Journal of Economic Perspectives* 9(2): 63–84.

Currie, Janet. 2002. *Welfare and the Well-Being of Children: Harwood Fundamentals of Applied Economics.* Taylor and Francis.

Danziger, Sandra, Mary Corcoran, Sheldon Danziger, Colleen Heflin, Ariel Kalil, Judith Levine, Daniel Rosen, Kristin Seefeldt, Kristine Siefert, and Richard Tolman. 2000. "Barriers to the Employment of Welfare Recipients." In *Prosperity for All? The Economic Boom and African-Americans,* edited by Robert Cherry and William M. Rogers. New York: Russell Sage Foundation.

Evans, Robert G., Morris L. Barer, and Theodore R. Marmor. 1994. *Why Are Some People Healthy and Others Are Not? The Determinants of Health of Populations.* New York: Aldine de Gruyter.

Frazier, A. Lindsay, Graham A. Colditz, Charles S. Fuchs, and Karen M. Kuntz. 2000. "Cost-Effectiveness of Screening for Colorectal Cancer in the General Population." *Journal of the American Medical Association* 284(15): 1954–61.

Greenberg, M., I. Dutta-Gupta, and E. Minoff. 2007. *From Poverty to Prosperity: A National Strategy to Cut Poverty in Half.* Washington: Center for American Progress.

Haider, Stephen J., Alison Jacknowitz, and Robert F. Schoeni. 2003. "Welfare Work Requirements and Child Well-Being: Evidence from the Effects on Breast Feeding." *Demography* 40(3): 479–97.

Heckman, James J., and Jeffrey A. Smith. 1995. "Assessing the Case for Social Experiments." *Journal of Economic Perspectives* 9(2): 85–110.

Hirth, Richard A., Michael E. Chernew, Edward Miller, A. Mark Fendrick, and William G. Weissert. 2000. "Willingness to Pay for a Quality-Adjusted Life Year: In Search of a Standard." *Medical Decision Making* 20(3): 332–42.

IOM. 2006. *Preterm Births: Causes, Consequences, and Prevention.* Washington: National Academy Press.

Kaplan, George A., Kristine Siefert, Nalini Ranjit, Trivellore E. Raghunathan, Elizabeth A. Young, Diem Tran, Sandra Danziger, Susan Hudson, John W. Lynch, and Richard Tolman. 2005. "The Health of Poor Women Under Welfare Reform." *American Journal of Public Health* 95(7): 1252–8.

Ludwig, J., and D. Miller. Forthcoming. "Does Head Start Improve Children's Life Chances? Evidence from a Regression Discontinuity Approach." *Quarterly Journal of Economics.*

Newhouse, Joseph P. 1996. *Free For All? Lessons from the RAND Health Insurance Experiment.* Cambridge, Mass.: Harvard University Press.

Paneth, Nigel S. 1995. "The Problem of Low Birth Weight." *Future of Children* 5(1): 19–34.

Rubinowitz, Leonard S., and James E. Rosenbaum 2000. *Crossing the Class and Color Lines: From Public Housing to White Suburbia*. Chicago, Ill.: University of Chicago Press.

Schlesinger, Mark. 2004. "Reprivatizing the Public Household? Medical Care in the Context of American Values." *Journal of Health Politics, Policy, and Law* 29(4–5): 969–1004.

Stout, Natasha K., Marjorie A. Rosenberg, Amy Trentham-Dietz, Maureen A. Smith, Stephen M. Robinson, and Dennis G. Fryback. 2006. "Retrospective Cost-Effectiveness Analysis of Screening Mammography." *Journal of the National Cancer Institute* 98(11): 774–82.

Waldfogel, Jane. 2006. *What Children Need*. Cambridge, Mass.: Harvard University Press.

Index

access to health care: in five-state welfare reform study, 258, 265–6; for mothers on welfare, 297, 300; neighborhood effects on, 364; public willingness to fund, 388
access to information, education health gradients and, 47
accidental deaths, 186
ACEs (Active Community Environments Program), 340n13
ACL study. *See* Americans' Changing Lives study
Active Community Environments Program (ACEs), 340n13
Active Living by Design program, 340n13
Adbul Latif Jameel Poverty Action Lab (MIT), 15–16
Adults: income-transfer policies and health of, 106; multiple dimensions of well-being in, 81. *See also* Elderly
AFDC. *See* Aid to Families with Dependent Children
affordability of health care, 258, 265–6
age: association of income and, 99; and causal effect of income on health, 102; and effects of education on health/health behaviors, 39, 40, 42; and neighborhood effects on health, 358, 361; and nonstandard work, 208, 209, 211, 212; and total mortality, 181; *See also* adults; children
Aid to Families with Dependent Children (AFDC), 283; expenditures for, 141n2; Medicaid and decline in caseloads, 240; reform of, 231, 233–5; state policies for, 245
Airline Deregulation Act of 1978, 204
alcohol use/abuse, 7; and health during economic downturns, 188–9, 191; by mothers on welfare, 286–8, 295, 301; neighborhood effects on, 360, 362, 367n11; and unemployment, 205

Americans' Changing Lives (ACL) study, 98, 210
Anxiety: in mothers on welfare, 286, 287, 295, 300; neighborhood effects on, 358
asthma in preschool years, neighborhood effects on, 353–4
attention problems, lead exposure and, 355

Behavioral Risk Factor Surveillance System (BRFSS), 239, 243, 273, 282, 386
benefits, nonstandard work and, 210, 217–9
biomedical determinants of health: following civil-rights legislation, 163–4; other determinants vs., 8–10
biomedical science: as sole health perspective in earlier centuries, 5; translation into health policy and practice, 6, 15
birth outcomes, food stamps and. *See* food stamps and birth outcomes
birthweight: and Food Stamp Program, 123–4, 128, 130–1, 136–40; neighborhood effects on, 354; and unemployment, 194n6
Bonferroni adjustment, 276n27
Boyce, W. Thomas, 62
brain, prefrontal cortex of, 67
Brenner, M. Harvey, 174–79
BRFSS. *See* Behavioral Risk Factor Surveillance System
built environment, obesity and, 311. *See also* residential environments and obesity
business strategy, 204

California, food stamps and birth outcomes in, 122–41
Canadian Self Sufficiency Project (SSP), 240
candidate biodevelopmental systems, 66–67
Cannon, Walter, 5
Carolina Abecedarian Project, 69, 71, 72, 74–76, 80–82

causality, 11–12, 379–82; in associating education and health, 51, 52; in associating income and health, 101–3; and impact of social and economic policies on health, 14, 379; and lack of experimental studies, 380–1
CCAHS. *See* Chicago Community Adult Health Study
Center for American Progress, 388
Chicago Child-Parent Centers (CPC), 69, 70, 73; educational outcomes of, 76–77; effects of preschool participation in, 81; and later criminal involvement, 79; multiple dimensions of, 81; and postprogram school quality, 82
Chicago Community Adult Health Study (CCAHS), 313, 317, 333–4, 339n2
Chicago Longitudinal Study (CLS), 70
child abuse or neglect, early-childhood intervention programs and, 73
children: early development of. *See* early-childhood development policies and health; education level of, and health of parents, 44; income-transfer policies and health of, 106; maternal education and health of, 41, 43–45; multiple dimensions of well-being in, 81; neighborhoods and health of (*see* neighborhood effects on health); paid leave for care of, 85–86; welfare reform and well-being of, 243–4
child support policies: enforcement of, 282, 283 measuring effects of, 288–93; receipt of support and maternal health, 294, 298–9. *See also* maternal health, effect of welfare policy on
chronic diseases: modern "epidemics" of, 5–6; risk factors for, 6–7; and years of schooling, 32

cigarette smoking, 13–14
Civil Rights Act of 1964, 146–7, 162, 166
civil rights policies and health, 145–66; data and methods of studies, 148; experiments/studies on, 380–1; health trajectories in post-civil-rights era, 155–61; pathways for operation of policies, 384; results of analyses, 161–6; social and economic position improvements, 149–54
Clean Air Act of 1973, 355
Clean Air Act of 1974, 348
Clear Air Act Amendment of 1990, 353
CLS (Chicago Longitudinal Study), 70
cognitive functioning: and early-childhood intervention programs, 74, 78; and lead exposure, 355; and socioeconomic gradients, 64
colorectal screening, years of schooling and, 37–40
Congressional Review Act, 202
Connecticut, study of welfare reform policies in, 244–73
connectivity, environmental, 311
contraception, education health gradient and, 48
contractual nature of jobs, 201. See also new employment contract
contract workers, 208, 209. See also Nonstandard work
converging gradients, hypothesis of, 63–64
cost-benefit analysis, 11; for association of education and health, 52, 383–4; for health procedures/services, 388
cost-effectiveness of health care, 3, 4, 13, 14
CPC. See Chicago Child-Parent Centers
CPS. See Current Population Survey
crime rate: and lead levels in gasoline, 355; neighborhood effects on, 358–9; and physical activity, 311–12, 317–20, 324–33
criminal involvement: and health outcomes, 87n2; and large-scale, publicly-funded

early-childhood programs, 79; and model early-childhood intervention programs, 75–76
critical thinking skills, education health gradients and, 47
crowd-in effect, 236
crowd-out effects, 241–2
cumulative developmental effects, 68
Current Population Survey (CPS), 239, 273, 386

data on health, quality of, 386–7
day labor, 208. See also nonstandard work
delinquency: lead exposure and, 355; neighborhood effects on, 358–9, 362, 367n11
depression: and involuntary job loss, 206; in mothers on welfare, 286, 295, 300; neighborhood effects on, 357, 358; and new employment contract, 219–20n3; and years of schooling, 37–40
deregulation, economic, 204
desegregation of public housing, 351–2
Design for Active Living project, 340n13
design of residential environments, 311
developmental determinants of health, 62; in early childhood; patterns of effects, 67–68; See early-childhood development policies and health; early-childhood intervention programs
developmental health, 62; biodevelopmental origins and effects of, 66–67; national- and state-level policies affecting, 83–86; and socioeconomic gradients, 64
disabilities, preference for nonstandard work and, 208
discount rates, 48–49, 51
diseases: in current/former welfare recipients, 232; and early-childhood intervention programs, 73; education gradients for, 55n12; and housing conditions, 365; and macroeconomic conditions, 186, 188; natural histories of, 385–6; nonstandard work and increase in, 209; as post-

civil rights causes of deaths, 158–61, 163–5, 167n2; risk factors for, 7; and socioeconomic gradients, 64; sources of information on, 53n1; and years of schooling, 32
domestic violence, mothers on welfare and, 295
Donohue, John, 147
downsizing, 204
drug use/abuse: and level of education, 48; by mothers on welfare, 286–8, 295; neighborhood effects on, 360, 362, 367n11

early-childhood development policies and health, 61–87; candidate biodevelopmental systems in research, 66–67; and developmental determinants, 67–68; early-childhood intervention programs, 69–83; impact of policies, 68; at national/state/local levels, 83–86; pathways of policy operation in, 383; and socioeconomic gradients, 63–66
early-childhood intervention programs, 69–83; direct effects of, 71–73; earlier interventions as most effective, 80–81; indirect effects of, 73–79; large-scale publicly-funded programs, 72–73, 76–79; model programs, 71–72, 74–76; and multiple dimensions of well-being, 81; and quality of postprogram schools, 82–83
Earned Income Tax Credit (EITC), 173
eating habits, 7; neighborhood effects on, 356; and obesity, 315, 322
ecological fallacy, 174
economic determinants of health, 103, 149–54. See also employment conditions and health; macroeconomic conditions and health
economic outcomes: of large-scale, publicly-funded early-childhood programs, 79; of model early-childhood intervention programs, 76
economic segregation, 84–85
education: and comparisons in observational studies, 335,

336; financing of, 83–86; following civil rights legislation, 162; and nonstandard work, 210, 211

educational outcomes: of large-scale, publicly-funded early-childhood programs, 76–79; of model early-childhood intervention programs, 75, 80–81

education and health, 11, 29–53; and access to information/cognitive skills, 47–48; and age, 39, 40, 42; association between, 29–36; basic correlations between, 30; children's education and health of parents, 43; and college selectivity, 54n7; and disability, 41; in early childhood; and gender, 39, 41, 42; and income, 39, 42, 45–46; and labor market, 46–47; and life expectancy, 36, 37, 41; limitations of studies on, 29; maternal education and health of children, 41, 43; mechanisms for relationships between, 45–51; NHIS data on, 30–36; pathways of policy operation in, 383; policy implications of, 51–53; possible reasons for link between, 43–45; and preferences for educated individuals, 48–49; and relative position or rank in society, 49–50; returns from investment in, 383; and social networks, 50; of spouses, 43; and value of the future, 47; and variation in socioeconomic gradients, 63–64; and years of schooling, 37–39, 51. See also early-childhood development policies and health; early-childhood intervention programs

EITC (Earned Income Tax Credit), 173

elderly: causal effect of income on health in, 102; fatality rates for, 181; neighborhood effects on health of, 357

elderly, health effects of income supports on, 104–14; evidence from United States on, 106–14; international evidence on, 106; need for re-search on, 104–5; Social Security, 106–9; supplemental security income program, 109–14

emotional distress: neighborhood effects on, 346, 357–8, 361–2; in relocation studies, 367n10

employment: in five-state welfare reform study, 255–8; and health status, 174; welfare-reform-induced increases in, 236

employment conditions and health, 201–19; arenas of policy debate on, 201–3; during economic downturns, 190; during economic expansions, 193; job insecurity, 206–7; and new employment contract, 203–5, 216–7; with nonstandard work, 207–16; policy/program gaps that threaten health, 218–9; and socioeconomic gradients, 64; unemployment, 205–6

employment contract, new, 203–5, 216–7

employment outcomes, early-childhood intervention programs and, 76

environmental determinants of health, 8–10

epidemiology, 6–7, 12

ergonomics standards, 203

exercise: and health during economic downturns, 189, 191; neighborhood effects on, 356; and obesity related to residential environment, 323–32

experimental studies: of early-childhood intervention programs, 70; lack of, 380–1; need for better health data in, 386–7; of neighborhood effects, 337–8; of welfare reform and health, 232, 238, 243–73

Fair Labor Standards Act, 204

fast-food-restaurant density, income and, 356

feasibility of policies/interventions, 13, 14

fertility effect (FSP), 124

fetal death, 138

Florida, study of welfare reform policies in, 244–73

food insecurity, for mothers on welfare, 286, 287, 294, 295, 300

Food Stamp Program (FSP), 122, 290–3; background of program, 125–7; sources of data on, 127–32

food stamps and birth outcomes, 122–41; conceptual model for research, 123–4; estimation research results, 134–9; extensions of research, 138, 140; methods of study, 133–4; and migration, 124, 140; number of births, 123; sources of data on FSP, 127–32; studies of, 382

Fragile Families and Child Wellbeing Study, 243, 244, 282, 285, 381

FSP. See Food Stamp Program

Full Employment and Balanced Growth Act of 1978, 204

functional limitations, years of schooling and, 37–40

gasoline, lead levels in, 355

Gautreaux Program, 349, 350

gender: and early-childhood program educational outcomes, 75–79; and education gradients, 54n5; and effects of education on health/behaviors, 39, 41, 42; and health gains following civil rights legislation, 149, 163–5; and health related to macroeconomic conditions, 187; and neighborhood effects on delinquency/crime, 359, 362; and neighborhood effects on emotional health, 358, 361–2; and neighborhood effects on sexual behavior, 360; and nonstandard work, 208–16, 219n2; and occupation changes following civil rights legislation, 149–4, 163, 165; and post-civil rights health trajectories, 155–61. See also civil rights policies and health

gene-environment interactions, 67

germ theory of disease, 5

government involvement in economy, 193

Grofman, Bernard, 146

hazard exposures, nonstandard work and increase in, 209

Head Start, 69–73, 380; educational outcomes of, 77–79; effects of preschool participation in, 81; and later criminal involvement, 79; and postprogram school quality, 82

health: developmental, 62; interface between science and policy of, 14–16; major determinant of, 4–5; nonmedical determinants of, 5–8; risk factors for, 7; socioeconomic and race-ethnicity disparities in, 7–8; upstream vs. downstream approaches to understanding, 8–10

Health and Retirement Study, 386

health behaviors: educational gradients in, 383; effects of education on, 39–42, 52; in mothers on welfare, 294, 295; natural histories of, 385–6; neighborhood effects on, 322–3, 346, 358–61; and welfare reform, 285–8, 295, 297–301. See also education and health; residential environments and obesity

health care: affordability of, 258, 265–6; cost effectiveness of, 3, 4, 104; and quality of; population health, 4–5; spending on, 3–4, 387–8

health care utilization: in five-state welfare reform study, 253, 258, 265–6; and health outcomes, 242–4; by low-income women, 281–2; and welfare reform, 284

health data, quality of, 386–7

health inequalities, 29; education-related, 29; public expenditures to address, 388. See also education and health

health insurance coverage: decrease in, 236; in five-state welfare reform study, 252, 258, 261–4; and health care utilization, 274n7; and health outcomes, 274n7, 284; for immigrants, 242; of low-income women, 281–2; nonstandard work and, 210, 217–9; for welfare recipients, 232, 233; and welfare reform, 240–2, 272, 284, 294, 295

health outcomes: across geographic areas, 309; educational gradients in, 383; in five-state welfare reform study, 252, 258, 264, 267–69; and health care utilization, 242–44; and health insurance coverage, 284; and incarceration, 87n2; natural history of, 385–86; neighborhood variation in obesity, 313–15, 320–23; of pathobiological processes, 385; and socioeconomic gradients, 61–62; and welfare reform, 272–73, 285–88. See also education and health; maternal health, effect of welfare policy on

health policies, linking social and economic policies and, 387–8

health research and policy, 10–14

health risk factors: relation between education and, 32–36; in workplace, 203

Heckman, James, 147

homicide, macroeconomic conditions and, 186

housing conditions, health and, 365

HUD. See U.S. Department of Housing and Urban Development

human development policies, 61–62, 86–87; and developmental health, 62; national- and state-level, 83–86; range of, 61. See also early-childhood development policies and health; early-childhood intervention programs

Humphrey-Hawkins Act, 204

IHDP. See Infant Health and Development Program

immigrants: health insurance coverage for, 242, 275n14; Medicaid for, 234–5

incarceration, health outcomes and, 87n2

income: behavioral risk factors associated with, 100–101; and child support payments, 283; and comparisons in observational studies, 335, 336; and early-childhood intervention programs, 76, 79; and education/access to

health care, 45–46; and effects of education on health/behaviors, 39, 42, 52; of elderly, 104–5; in five-state welfare reform study, 255–8; following civil rights legislation, 147, 151–3, 162, 165; and funding of education, 84–85; government-supported; and health during economic downturns, 190, 195n18; and health related to macroeconomic conditions, 187–8; and investment in children's health and education, 44; and neighborhood fast-food-restaurant density, 356; pathways for health effects of, 384; strong association of health and, 97; welfare reform and increase in, 236. See income-support policies and health

income-support policies and health, 97–116; causal effects between, 101–3; for the elderly, 104–14; empirical evidence on relationship of, 98–101; need for research on, 103–4; total spending on programs, 388. See also food stamps and birth outcomes

independent contractors, 208

Infant Health and Development Program (IHDP), 71, 72, 74, 75, 80, 81

infant mortality, 4; and Food Stamp Program, 136; and macroeconomic conditions, 186; and socioeconomic gradients, 64; in United States, 104, 117n2, 122

injury rates, nonstandard work and increase in, 209

international trade agreements, 204

Iowa, study of welfare reform policies in, 244–73

job insecurity: and health, 206–7, 385; and new employment contract, 205, 216; in nonstandard workers, 216

job loss: and health status, 174, 205–6, 385; and likelihood of nonstandard work, 213; and new employment contract, 205, 216

just in time strategy, 205

Keating, Daniel P., 62

labor markets: and education health gradients, 46–47; and health during economic changes, 191; and health gains following civil rights legislation, 162; nonstandard jobs in, *See* nonstandard work
LA FANS. *See* Los Angeles Families and Neighborhood Study
land use, relationship of obesity and, 316–9, 332
large-scale publicly-funded early-childhood intervention programs, 72–73, 76–81
latent developmental effects, 68
lead poisoning, neighborhood effects on, 354–5
leave, child care, 85–86
leaver studies, 232, 238, 241
life expectancy, 4–6; and civil rights policies, 148, 155–7, 161, and effects of education on health/behaviors, 41; and level of education, 36, 37, 51, 383; and levels of stressors, 49–50; in United States, 104; *See also* mortality
lifestyle, health during economic downturns and, 188–91
linking social and economic policies with health policies, 387–8
literacy, socioeconomic gradients and, 64
location-specific effects, 180–1
Los Angeles Families and Neighborhood Study (LA FANS), 347, 348

macroeconomic conditions and health, 173–94; and changes in employment conditions, 203; future research questions and data needs, 190–2; and health improvement; during economic deterioration, 188–90; implications of research for policy, 192–4; income effects and dynamics, 187–8; morbidity and specific causes of death, 181, 186–7; mortality, 181–5; pathways for operation of policies, 384–5; pooled data with loca-

tion-specific fixed effects, 180–1; time-series analyses of, 174–80
magnet schools: early intervention effects mediated by, 82; educational outcomes of, 77
Manpower Demonstration Research Corporation (MDRC), 15–16
maternal education, health of children and, 41, 43–45
maternal health, effect of welfare policy on, 281–303; data and methods of research, 285–93; results of research, 294–301; theory and empirical evidence of, 283–5
MDRC. *See* Manpower Demonstration Research Corporation
Medicaid, 109, 112–13; caseload, 235; eligibility for, 234, 281; fiscal pressures from, 387; gender differences in eligibility, 163; for immigrants, 234–5; and immigrants' health insurance coverage, 242; and Medically Needy programs, 274n4; for mothers on welfare, 294; and neighborhood effects on health, 357' reductions in AFDC and caseload under, 240–1; and SCHIP, 241–2; spending on, 388; "transitional" coverage, 274n2; and utilization of health care/health outcomes, 274n8
medical care: and balance of policy options, 387; and health improvements during economic downturns, 189; and variation in population health, 6; *See also* health care
Medically Needy programs, 274n4
Medicare, 105; fiscal pressures from, 387; spending on, 388; and utilization of health care/insurance coverage, 274n8
mental health: income effects on, 103; and involuntary job loss, 206; and job insecurity, 207; and macroeconomic conditions, 187; neighborhood effects on, 357, 358; and neighborhood violence, 363; and unemployment, 195n11;

205; and welfare reform, 284, 285
Minnesota, study of welfare reform policies in, 244–73
model early-childhood demonstration programs, 71–72, 74–76, 80–81
morbidity: across life course, 105; and job insecurity, 207; and macroeconomic; conditions, 181, 186–8; sources of information on, 53n1
mortality: across geographic areas, 309; across life course, 105; and civil rights policies, 148, 157–63, 165–6; and early-childhood intervention programs, 72–73; during economic downturns, 173; and income, 98, 99, 103; and macroeconomic conditions, 175, 181–5, 188; and neighborhood collective efficacy, 363; nonstandard work and increase in, 209; and Social Security for elderly, 107–8; and socioeconomic gradients, 64; sources of information on, 53n1; statistics on, 166–7n1; and unemployment, 194n2, 194n3, 194n9; and years of schooling, 32, 37–40; *See also* life expectancy
motor-vehicle fatalities, 181, 186, 188
Moving to Opportunity (MTO) Program, 380–82; background of, 349–54; and neighborhood effects on health, 338; obesity and physical activity data from, 310; results of, 356–65; voluntary treatment in, 255, 275n21

National Death Index, 30
National education and human developmental policies, 83–86
National Health and Nutrition Examination Study (NHANES), 116, 386
National Health Interview Survey (NHIS), 30–36, 99, 116, 243, 273, 274n12, 386
National Longitudinal Mortality Study (NLMS), 51
National Longitudinal Study of Adolescent Health, 366n2, 386

National Longitudinal Study of Youth-Child Supplement, 366n2
National Poverty Center, University of Michigan, 87n1
National Survey of Children, 360
natural experiments: and causal effect of education on health, 45; on neighborhood effects on health, 337, 348–9; on neighborhood effects on sexual behavior, 361
neighborhood-cluster study designs, 347–8, 356, 363
neighborhood effects on health, 344–66; bias in studies of, 340n11; delinquency and crime, 358–9; emotional distress, 357–8; experiments/studies on, 381–2; and health compromising behaviors, 358–61; lead poisoning, 354–55; low birthweight, 354; natural experiments on, 348–9; neighborhood-cluster study design for, 347–48; obesity, 313–5, 320–3, 355–6; pathways for operation of policies, 362–5, 384; ratings of physical health, 356–7; relocation experiments on, 349–52; respiratory problems in the preschool years, 353–4; sexual behavior, 360–1; standards for estimating, 345–6; substance use, 360; See also residential environments and obesity
new employment contract, 203–5, 216–7
NHANES. See National Health and Nutrition Examination Study
NHIS. See National Health Interview Survey
1931 program, 234
NLMS (National Longitudinal Mortality Study), 51
nonexperimental studies: on health utilization and health outcomes, 242–3; on housing conditions and health, 365; on neighborhood effects on substance use, 360; on welfare reform health effects, 237–40
nonstandard work, 205, 207–16; defined, 207–8; health consequences of, 210–6; hetero-geneity in, 208–9; involuntary, 208; potential health consequences of, 209–10
nutrition effect (FSP), 124

OAA (Old Age Assistance), 109
obesity, 7; in current/former welfare recipients, 231; education effects on, 47; and health improvements during economic downturns, 189, 195n16, 195n17; income effects on, 103; and maternal employment, 195n19; neighborhood effects on, 355–6, 362; and prepared food vs. cooking meals at home, 195n19; and residential environment; See also residential environments and obesity
OBRA (Omnibus Reconciliation Act), 234
observational studies: of early-childhood intervention programs, 70; of health insurance—health association, 236; need for better health data in, 386–7; of residential environments and obesity, 334–9; of welfare reform health effects, 237, 239
Occupational Safety and Health Act, 204
Occupational Safety and Health Administration (OSHA), 201–3
Occupations: and education health gradients, 46–47; following civil rights legislation, 147, 149–54, 162, 163, 165
Old Age Assistance (OAA), 109
Omnibus Reconciliation Act (OBRA), 234
on-call work, 208, 209. See also nonstandard work
OSHA. See Occupational Safety and Health Administration

Panel Study of Income Dynamics, 98, 116, 346, 366n2
Panel Study of Income Dynamics-Child Supplement, 366n2
parental education: and health of children, 41, 43; and infant health, 44–45; and socioeconomic gradients, 64
part-time work, 208, 209, 219n1. See also nonstandard work

pathobiological processes, health outcome of, 385
pathway developmental effects, 68
pathways of health effects, 382–6; neighborhood effects, 362–5; residential environments and obesity, 310–2; welfare reform, 232
Perry Preschool Project, 71–72, 75, 76, 80, 81
Personal Responsibility and Work Opportunity Reconciliation Act (PRWORA), 233–5, 242, 281
PFC (prefrontal cortex), 67
PHDCN. See Project on Human Development in Chicago Neighborhoods
physical activity: and built environment, 311; and design of residential environments, 310, 312–3; and ergonomics standards, 203; and health during economic downturns, 189, 191; neighborhood effects on, 356; and obesity related to residential environment, 323–32
physical workplace environment, 201; under new employment contract, 216; OSHA regulation of, 202
plant-closure studies, 205–6
"policy experiments," 382
Pollution: and health during economic downturns, 190; and respiratory problems in preschool years, 353
population health: balance of policy options for, 387; cost-benefits of procedures/services for, 388; improving via social and economic policy, 4–8; in U.S. vs. other countries, 3–4
poverty: and health problems, 99–100; and informal social ties, 363; and neighborhood effects on health, 357; and neighborhood relocation experiments, 349–52; and obesity, 356; proposed policies for decreasing, 388; Social Security and reduction in, 107; in United States, 104; urban concentrations of, 344–5
poverty traps, 83–84
prefrontal cortex (PFC), 67
procyclical fatalities, 175, 186

Programa de Educación Salud y Alimentatión (PROGRESA), 86, 106
Project on Human Development in Chicago Neighborhoods (PHDCN), 347–8, 356, 358–61, 363, 364
proximity, environmental, 311
PRWORA. *See* Personal Responsibility and Work Opportunity Reconciliation Act
psychosocial determinants of health, 8–10; biodevelopmental origins and effects of, 66–67; and income level, 100; and involuntary job loss, 206; and socioeconomic gradients, 64
public health: focus of, 15; initiatives related to macroeconomic conditions, 193
Public Health Service Act, 147
Public housing, desegregation of, 351–2

Qualified Medicare Beneficiary (QMB) program, 112
quasi-experimental studies: on early-childhood intervention programs, 70–71; on health effects of changes in wealth, 102–3; on Social Security and health, 107–9
quasi-natural experiments, on education and health, 44–45

race/ethnicity: and birth effects of Food Stamp Program, 123, 134–8; and births during time of unemployment, 124; and comparisons in observational studies, 335, 336; and disparities in health, 7–8; and early-childhood intervention program success, 72, 77–79; and funding of education, 84; and health gains following civil rights legislation, 147; and impact of welfare reform on maternal health/child support receipt, 293, 294; and infant mortality rate, 122; mortality statistics based on, 166–67n1; and neighborhood effects on health, 318–9, 346; and neighborhood effects on sexual behavior, 360; and neighborhood relocation experiments, 349–52; and

nonstandard work, 208–9, 211; and obesity, 356; and post-intervention program school quality, 82–83; and poverty in urban neighborhoods, 344. *See also* civil rights policies and health
RAND Health Insurance Experiments, 274n7, 380
randomized clinical trials, 15–16
randomized experimental trials, 12; for demonstrating causality, 380, 381; of early-childhood intervention programs, 70–72, 380; of neighborhood effects, 338; in neighborhood relocation, 349–52; of welfare reform health effects, 233
reading skills, 48
relocation experiments (neighborhood effects on health), 349–52, 356, 357, 381–2, 384
residential environments and obesity, 309–39; crime and public safety, 317–20; data analysis, 313–20; land use, 316–9; multilevel analysis of physical activity, 323–32; neighborhood variation in outcomes, 320–3; observational studies of, 334–9; plan of study, 312–3; policy and research implications of, 332–4; sociodemographic structure, 316, 318–9; theoretical pathways of link between, 310–2; variation in neighborhoods, 313–5, 320–3
respiratory problems in preschool years, neighborhood effects on, 353–4
risk aversion, 49
Robert Wood Johnson Foundation, 355
rubric of stress, 6

safety: neighborhood effects on, 358–9, 362–3; and physical activity, 311–2, 317–20, 324–33, 356, 363
SCHIP. *See* State Children's Health Insurance program
school quality: and moderation/mediation of early intervention effects, 82–83; and school-support hypothesis, 77

seat belt use, education and, 37–40, 48, 54n10
sedentary lifestyle, 7
self-employment, 208. *See also* nonstandard work
self-reported health status (SRHS): variables in, 53–54n3; and years of schooling, 37–40
Self Sufficiency Project (SSP), 240
Selye, Hans, 5
SES. *See* socioeconomic status
sexual behavior, neighborhood effects on, 360–1
shocks, 12; and causal effect of income on health, 101, 102; and nonstandard work, 211
siblings, neighborhood effects on, 346
SIPP. *See* Survey of Income and Program Participation
SLMB (Specified Low Income Beneficiary) program, 112
Small Business Regulatory Enforcement Fairness Act of 1996, 202
Smart Growth Network, 340n13
Smoke detectors in home, years of schooling and, 37–40
smoking, 7, 13–14; by current/former welfare recipients, 231; education effects on, 47; and health during economic downturns, 189, 191; by mothers on welfare, 287–8, 295, 301; neighborhood effects on, 360, 362, 367n11; in post-civil-rights period, 164; and years of schooling, 37–40
social and economic policy: health effects of, 4–8; improving population health via, 10–14; linking health policies and, 387–8
social determinants of health, 62; biodevelopmental origins and effects of, 67; and civil rights policies, 149–54; and human development policies, 65–66
social epidemiologic perspective, 12
social epidemiology, 7
social networks, 50
social processes, neighborhood, 363–4

Index

social rank, health effects of, 49–50

Social Security, 104–9

social stratification, observational comparisons and, 334–5

socioeconomic determinants of health: across geographic areas, 309; interface between science and policy of, 14–16

socioeconomic gradients, 63–66; within and between countries, 63–64; defined, 61; and range of health outcomes, 61–62; and socioeconomic status, 61–64

socioeconomic status (SES), 8–10; and disparities in health, 7–8, 102; and early-childhood intervention programs, 74; following civil rights legislation, 149; high vs. low, 117n1; and income effects on health, 102; and neighborhood effects on delinquency/crime, 359; and neighborhood effects on sexual behavior, 360; physical activity and design of environments, 313; and socioeconomic gradients, 61–64

Specified Low Income Beneficiary (SLMB) program, 112

spending on health care, 3–4, 387–8

spouses, education level of, 43

SRHS. *See* self-reported health status

SSI. *See* Supplemental Security Income

SSP (Canadian Self Sufficiency Project), 240

standard work, 207

State Children's Health Insurance program (SCHIP), 232, 235, 241–2, 357

STEPS to a Healthier U.S., 340n13

Stress: and health during economic downturns, 190, 191; from involuntary job loss, 206; and job insecurity, 206–7; rubric of, 6; in unmarried mothers on welfare, 286–87; work-related, 202–3

substitute workers, 209

suicide, macroeconomic conditions and, 186

Supplemental Security Income (SSI), 105, 109–14; eligibility for, 117n3; federal vs. state benefits, 110–2; and Medicaid eligibility, 112–3; subgroup analyses, 113, 114

Surgeon General's Report on Smoking and Health, 7, 14

Survey of Income and Program Participation (SIPP), 239, 273

Survival effect (FSP), 123

TANF. *See* Temporary Assistance for Needy Families

taxes: as economic incentives, 193

teen births: FSP and, 131–38; and neighborhood effects on sexual behavior, 360

Temporary Assistance for Needy Families (TANF), 381; effects on maternal health, 290–3; empirical identification of effects of, 237–9; literature on, 239–44; state policies, 245; state waiver programs as, 274n10; and welfare reform, 231–5

temporary work, 208, 209. *See also* nonstandard work

tobacco use, 7, 205. *See also* smoking

traffic deaths, 181, 186, 188

unemployment: and accidental deaths, 186; births during time of, 124; and birthweight, 194n6; and health, 174, 205–6; and mortality, 194n2, 194n3, 194n9; and traffic deaths, 181, 186

unemployment insurance, policy gap in, 218

unemployment rates: and health, 112; legislative control of, 204; as proxy for macroeconomic conditions, 180, 188; and total mortality, 181

union membership, 203, 204

United States v. City of Yonkers, 351

U.S. Department of Housing and Urban Development (HUD), 349, 350

validity, internal vs. external, 12

Vermont, study of welfare reform policies in, 244–73

violence and health, neighborhood effects on, 362–63

Voluntary Protection Program, 202

Voting Rights Act of 1965, 146, 147

walking, 323–32

welfare reform and health, 231–73; empirical identification of effects, 237–9; expected health impacts of policies, 235–6; experiments/studies on, 244–73, 381; and goals of welfare reform, 231; health insurance coverage, 240–2; health utilization and health outcomes, 242–4; and income-support policies; literature on, 232, 233, 239–44; maternal health; and prereform public assistance programs, 274n11; and reform in the 1990s, 233–5. *See also* income-support policies and health; maternal health, effect of welfare policy on

well-being: after involuntary job loss, 206; and job insecurity, 207; multiple dimensions of, 81; and welfare reform, 243–4

Whitehall Study, 36

Women's Health Initiative, 16

work activities, 201; under new employment contract, 216; regulatory history around, 202–3

work hours, health and, 189–91

Yonkers Family and Community Program, 349, 351–3, 367nn8–11; and availability of resources/institutions, 364; and emotional distress, 357–8; and health-compromising behaviors, 358–61; and neighborhood social processes, 363; ratings of physical health in, 356–7